D1565830

JACKSON'S SWORD

JACKSON'S SWORD
THE ARMY OFFICER CORPS ON THE AMERICAN FRONTIER, 1810–1821

SAMUEL J. WATSON

UNIVERSITY PRESS OF KANSAS

© 2012 by the University Press of Kansas
All rights reserved

Published by the University Press of Kansas (Lawrence, Kansas 66045), which
was organized by the Kansas Board of Regents and is operated and funded by
Emporia State University, Fort Hays State University, Kansas State University,
Pittsburg State University, the University of Kansas, and Wichita State University

Library of Congress Cataloging-in-Publication Data

Watson, Samuel J.
Jackson's sword : the Army officer corps on the American frontier, 1810–1821 /
Samuel J. Watson.
p. cm. — (Modern war studies)
Includes bibliographical references and index.
ISBN 978-0-7006-1884-2 (cloth : alk. paper)
1. United States. Army—Officers—History—19th century. 2. Southern
States—History, Military—19th century. 3. United States—Territorial
expansion—History—19th century. 4. Civil-military relations—United States—
History—19th century. 5. Jackson, Andrew, 1767–1845—Military leadership.
I. Title.
UB413.W38 2012
355.00973'09034—dc23

2012027879

British Library Cataloguing in Publication Data is available.

Printed in the United States of America

10 9 8 7 6 5 4 3 2 1

The paper used in this publication is recycled and contains 30 percent
postconsumer waste. It is acid free and meets the minimum requirements of the
American National Standard for Permanence of Paper for Printed Library
Materials Z39.48-1992.

CONTENTS

PREFACE

During the last decade there has been considerable debate over the American experience in warfare and, by extension, the character of the American military experience more generally. The U.S. Army has been condemned as a Cold War dinosaur; celebrated for its rapid conventional victory in seizing Baghdad; condemned again as a blunt, outdated war-fighting instrument; and then celebrated for transforming itself in the midst of war into the adaptive force for counterinsurgency and nation building that many believe it should have become two decades ago. All these reactions were overblown, often driven more by political and institutional motives than by evidence or historical perspective. They have resulted in greater attention to the "small wars" of America's past, for which I have to be grateful. But the polemical ebb and flow have led to caricatures and straw men, an exaggerated dichotomy between conventional and unconventional, kinetic operations and counterinsurgency. There is and has historically been a wide spectrum of military missions and operations, often occurring simultaneously, that cannot be characterized simply as "small wars," "Indian wars," or "nation building."

This is the first of two volumes telling the tale of these "constabulary" roles and their effects in the years between the War of 1812 and the war with Mexico—years American historians have labeled the age of Jackson or, more recently, the age of Indian removal. The present volume examines the first big part of the story—the "problem" of institutional instability, multiple loyalties, and insubordination. The second volume explores the second part—the "solution," based on greater professional commitment, experience (as much political and diplomatic as military) developed during extended careers, and accountability to civilian authority, tempered in the forge of frustrating, politically complex constabulary operations along the nation's frontiers. If there was an American way of war (a debatable construct) during this period, *Jackson's Sword* shows that it was highly variable, adaptive, and contingent on specific situations and objectives rather than archetypal military developments (whether from Napoleonic example or technological change) or comprehensive American social phenomena (political ideologies of republicanism and Jacksonian democracy, the citizen-soldier ideal, or antagonism to standing armies). More important than any specific situation or skill set, the career officers of the national standing army developed greater professional commitment, practical experience, and subordination to civilian authority. Congress and the executive rewarded their effectiveness and accountability with insulation from partisan political attack and substantial autonomy in their implementation of national policy, a monopoly of strategic and operational command they have retained ever since.

The present volume focuses on the years when Andrew Jackson commanded the Division of the South and twice led it against the Spanish in Florida, contrary to orders from his civilian superiors. The minuscule national standing army tried to maintain order on the thinly settled frontier between Texas and Louisiana, first clashing and then collaborating with American citizens ("filibusters") who sought to undermine Spanish rule in Texas. The army also attempted to arrest the Baratarian corsairs (such as Jean Lafitte) and to prevent similar marauders and nonstate actors, particularly those sponsored by Latin American revolutionaries, from attacking Spanish Florida, even as up-and-coming young officers advised Jackson and the War Department to seize Cuba.

The core of this volume focuses on Jackson and his subordinates in their decade-long quasi-war with Spain and a variety of Creek, Mikasuki, and Seminole Indians along the northern border of Florida. Their pressure, combined with Britain's refusal to support Spain or the Indians in containing U.S. expansion, compelled Spain to cede Florida to the United States in 1821 (the Adams-Onís or Transcontinental Treaty), even as Jackson supported a junior subordinate in hindering another American filibuster against Texas. Chapter 6 of this volume anticipates the army's shift to the western frontier of white settlement and focuses on its most sustained campaign during this era—a series of expeditions to advance U.S. power up the Missouri River and drive British influence from the region of the Louisiana Purchase.

During these years the national Military Academy at West Point was reformed, and its graduates became more common within the officer corps, but most officers were veterans of the War of 1812 who had been commissioned because of their political connections in 1808 or 1812. Many of these men felt as much loyalty to a particular section (the South) or region (the frontier) as to the nation as a whole. Andrew Jackson set an example of repeated insubordination against civilian authority, and the officer corps remained as unstable as it had been since the end of the Revolution. These dysfunctional phenomena began to change during the 1820s, as the international situation calmed, War of 1812 veterans resigned their commissions to take advantage of the opportunities offered by the territorial expansion they had advanced, and the Military Academy gained a virtual monopoly on new officer commissions.

These developments, which ushered in the stability that enabled and encouraged the development of professional cohesion, responsibility, and expertise, are explored in chapter 7 and the conclusion to this first volume. These sections examine army missions, civil-military relations—particularly civilian demands on and reactions to the army—and officer socialization, commissioning, resignations, and assignments in the context of social, political, economic, technological, military, and cultural changes during the age of Jackson (the 1820s through the 1840s). Doing so establishes the background for the second volume, which begins by detailing the army's missions along the western frontier after 1825, when it withdrew from the Upper Missouri Valley at congressional behest. That volume explains the army's significance in western territorial expansion, as well as the defeat and effective pacification and removal of the Indians of Illinois, Wisconsin, Iowa, Missouri, Arkansas, and the Indian Territory (future Oklahoma)—ethnic cleansing that was accomplished with surprisingly limited loss of life among soldiers, white settlers, and Indians alike.

This coercive diplomacy (intimidation) and peacekeeping proved immensely frustrating for career army officers, who often found their fellow white citizens far more irritating and distasteful than Indians. This friction and its complex consequences for civil-military relations and the development of military accountability to civilian authority are explored in depth in volume 2 in a block of chapters on Indian removal. These range from the army's intervention to prevent the state of Georgia from conducting removal on its own in 1825 to its efforts to pressure the Cherokee to move west between 1836 and 1838, culminating in the "inglorious" war to drive the Seminoles from Florida between 1835 and 1842. Volume 2 then turns to the nation's Canadian border, where both British and American officials credited the national standing army with restraining filibusters and preventing war between Britain and the United States between 1838 and the diplomatic settlement of 1842 (the Webster-Ashburton Treaty). Volume 2 concludes with the army patrolling the Louisiana border and advancing American power, sometimes controversially, into the Southern Plains and Texas, ultimately going to war with Mexico, where U.S. victory, directed and led by career officers of the national standing army, paved the way for the Civil War, which these veterans would command.

Between 1810 and 1821 the officers of the national standing army were often motivated by highly subjective emotions of regionalism, sectionalism, and antagonism toward Indians, Spaniards, and Britons, born of their sympathy for frontiersmen and their experiences in the War of 1812. The resulting belligerence encouraged junior and field-grade officers to support Andrew Jackson in his usurpations of constitutional civilian authority, to repeatedly invade or threaten to invade Spanish Florida and Texas without authorization, pursuing primarily military solutions to complex intercultural and international dilemmas. After 1821 the officer corps became decisively more professional—more subordinate, responsive, and accountable to national civilian authority rather than local, regional, or sectional interests—in great part because of West Point socialization in nationalism and statism among junior officers, but even more so because of the frustrating experience of trying to keep the peace between white frontiersmen and Indians.

ACKNOWLEDGMENTS

Jackson's Sword has been more than twenty years in the making. It began as my dissertation, almost by default, but has become the focus of my life as a scholar. My debts extend far beyond those early, humid days in Houston, and I want to thank those in the other half of my life, who gave it balance. Such a long book deserves a long set of acknowledgments, and I have undoubtedly forgotten some of those who helped me over the years: to everyone not mentioned by name, thank you. I accept all responsibility for my interpretations and for any errors of fact.

I must first thank my history and English teachers at Herndon High School, Betty Swicord and Nancy Nyrop, and several professors from my undergraduate years at Indiana University: Robert Ferrell, George Wilson, George Brooks, James Riley, Larry Moses, Bernard Morris (a critical student of American foreign policy), and John Lovell (a student of the Military Academy and American national security policy). I was not a particularly focused or disciplined student back then, but they all helped.

My oldest friends are from northern Virginia and Indiana. My greatest thanks go to Ben and Kim Nguyen, whom I met walking back from the Fairfax County Public Library on Rolling Road in Kings Park in 1977 and to their families. In Herndon, thanks to Steve Ritsinias and Mike Rilee and especially to Bob Rilee—my best friend for twenty years; my comrade in politics, film, South Asian cuisine, and ASL; and my mom's best friend while I was settling in at West Point. At Indiana, thanks to John Bohdan and John Johnson, who introduced me to heavy metal, a great release when your mind becomes too dense with thoughts or frustrations grow too great—as so many students know. For a bookworm like me, the value of these friendships has been immeasurable.

I lived ten years as a graduate student and adjunct in Houston, far from the temperate suburbs of my northern Virginia youth, and I really grew up there. In seven years at Rice I amassed an indelible debt to my patient, faithful adviser and fellow scholar of military officers and professionalism, Ira Gruber; to my other professors, wise councilors, and friends, John Boles, Thomas Haskell, Marty Weiner, Ed Cox, Albert Van Helden, Atieno Odhiambo, Paula Sanders, and Patricia Seed; to the staffs at the *Journal of Southern History* and the *Papers of Jefferson Davis*, especially Evelyn Nolen, Patty Burgess, Linda Crist, Mary Dix, and Ken Williams; and to the department administrative coordinators and secretaries, Nancy Parker, Paula Platt, and Sandy Perez.

My fellow grad students were my sustenance during those long, usually delightful years: thanks to Tom Little, Maggie Kukis, Jeff Hooten (who introduced me to surf music), Barbara and Ken Rozek (who hosted me for three straight Thanksgivings), Li Jing, Jonathan Singer, Gunther Breaux, Carlos Blanton, Osaak Ollumwullah, Navanita Sharma, Leslie Lovett, Dawn Hayes, AJ Hood, Scott Dewey, Melissa Kean, Lynn Lyerly, Dave Dillard, Randall Hall, Patti Bixel, Angie Boswell, Anja Jabour, Tom Ndolo, Steve Wilson (who generously hosted me for a lecture I have since published), Scott Marler, Charles Israel, Matt Taylor, John Daly, and Brian Dirck (who first welcomed me to Houston). Above all, I thank Alioune Deme, who introduced me to the Senegalese community, *haleem*, and dancing at 4:00 A.M.

At the University of St. Thomas, where I taught as an adjunct for six years, I had some of the best days of my life. I would like to thank Ginger Bernhard, Irving and Janice Kelter, Father Richard Schieffen, Joseph McFadden, Father J. Michael Miller, Father Robert Lamb, Janet Lowery, my lunchtime basketball buddies, and the entire staff at that wonderful community. Maybe I should have been turning my dissertation into a book back then, but the combination of teaching, reading, and interacting with the students there made this grad student into a professional. If this were 2000, I would have dedicated *Jackson's Sword* to the hardworking students of St. Thomas, the working mothers who earned their degrees by taking classes in the evenings, the immigrants from around the world, the Vietnamese guys I played basketball with every day, and their sisters, who convinced them to take my classes. Many of my students at West Point eventually return to the Military Academy to teach, but my first students to earn their doctorates took their first history classes with me at UST. The St. Thomas community is exemplified by Ly Uyen Phan, a phenomenal woman who has returned to teach and mentor students there.

St. Thomas was a wonderful place and a unique experience, but all idylls must come to an end. In the spring of 1999, as I worried about the job market and considered leaving academia to get out of debt, my friend and Military Academy colleague Rob McDonald told me about the position I now hold. West Point has been my home since then. First, I have to thank the deans, department heads, deputy heads, and division chiefs who extended my one-year contracts and retained me in a permanent position. These men helped make employment at the Academy far more secure than our lack of tenure suggests: Colonel (Brigadier General, retired) Bob Doughty, Colonel (Brigadier General, retired) Lance Betros, Brigadier General Fletcher Lampkin, Brigadier General Daniel Kaufman, Brigadier General Timothy Trainor, Colonel Barney Forsythe, Colonel Gary Tocchet, Colonel Mat Moten (an old Rice colleague, in my cohort coming and going), and Colonel Cole Kingseed, my first division chief and still a role model for me. Other colonels have been friends and colleagues as much as administrative allies and authorities: Ty Seidule, Gian Gentile, Greg Daddis, Dana Mangham (another old Rice friend), especially Gail Yoshitani (a paragon of patience and moderation), and Brian DeToy (my comrade in tailgates, staff rides, and historical commemorations).

My fellow civilian professors have been the bedrock during my career at West Point, as Congress intended them to be when it mandated our introduction on a significant scale two decades ago. Cliff Rogers has been a role model in every way, Steve Waddell has always been there for me and for everyone else, and I have shared more good lunches with Rob McDonald than with anyone outside my immediate family. Thanks also to good buddies Chuck Steele, Paul Springer, and especially my neighbor and ally John Stapleton, my companions in war-gaming and fun, and to Antonio Thompson, who introduced me to the wonders of iTunes.

The Military Academy is unique, even among the service academies, in the essential role played by its junior faculty. These men and women, captains and majors with a decade in the army and at least a decade to go, earn their master's degrees to teach for two or three years. Much of officership is teaching, and our "rotaters" are remarkable teachers. Teaching common core courses in military and American history, working together on administrative matters and public service every day, makes us a tight community. I can thank only a few by name, but cheers especially to "shipmate" Scott Granger, the navy's greatest contribution to the Military Academy, my tailgate and poker buddy, and to Tom Rider, "real American hero" (sung as off-key as you like), my staff ride comrade and a true soldier-scholar.

In the International History Division, thanks to my cohort mates from 1999, Steve Olejasz, Tony Bennett, Charlie Brown, Diana Holland, and David Beougher; John Stark for the parties; Kevin Murphy, Mike McDermott, Dave Klingman, and Joe Alessi for keeping the tradition alive; Franz Rademacher, Bill Mengel, Steve Cole, Tori Campbell, Kevin Scott, and Beth Behn (also a fine American historian); Bob Heffington for upholding the standard; Buzz Phillips for making lunch bunch a more intellectually diverse place; John

Ringquist for his amazing scholarly curiosity and zeal; and the aforementioned Scotty G: well-played, sirs!

In the Military History Division, my first home at West Point, thanks to my teachers in the ways of the army and the Academy, the cohorts of 1997 and 1998, especially the wise Tom Goss, my officemate and comedian Dave Shugart and his wife Dudley, dedicated Dave Toczek (Let's Go!), and Jamie Fischer. Thanks to my cohort, the Dragoons, and to those who followed, especially Jeff French and his wife Cathy, Kevin Clark, CJ Horn, Matt Morton, Mike Runey, Tom Hanson, the wise and incisive Jason Musteen, fellow nineteenth-century American military historian John Hall and his wife Heidi, Jim Powell, Dutch Palmer, John Hawkins, Jim Doty, Pete Knight, Tony Burgess, two-fisted Christian Teutsch, JP Clark, Dave Gray, Brit Erslev, the ever-inquisitive Bob Mihara, Jon Due, smiling Keith Walters, Tom Spahr, and laughing Jeff Lucas.

From among my many friends in the American History Division (my second home at West Point), special thanks to George Sarabia, Dan Koprowski, Jon Scott Logel, Brian Hankinson, Dave Siry, Nate Haas, Joel Miller, Pat Schantz, Matt Hardman (All the Way!), gravel-voiced John Mini, Texan Jeremy James, Sean Sculley (who is Irish), Paul Belmont, and Brian Dunn (who is also Irish) and his wife Jenny—the hardest workers in showbiz.

West Point has provided many opportunities to work with colleagues outside the History Department. Thanks especially to these compatriots, civilian and military, present and past, for their collegiality and professional example: in English and Philosophy, Jeff Wilson, Bob Tully, Les Knotts, and Ted Westhusing; in Foreign Languages, Larry Mansoor and Geri Smith; in Geography and Environmental Engineering, Gene Palka and Mark Smith; in Law, Tim Bakken; in Civil and Mechanical Engineering, Kip Nygren, Fred Meyer, and Fred Hampton; in Math, Alex Heidenberg and Fred Rickey; and in Physics, ASL buddy Jeff Musk and Ray Nelson.

I owe a debt to the many dedicated civil servants, most of whom I know only by e-mail, in AAD, ARD, PRD, ORD, and DRM in Taylor Hall, particularly those who arrange research funding for me and the cadets. Lesley Beckstrom, Vicky Kiernan, and AnnMarie Riva, with whom I worked for six years arranging cadet internships, stand as exemplars of their service. In the History Department, Anne Lamb and Deb Moncks have not only kept the ship afloat but actually enabled it to move forward, no matter the current. Among the dedicated secretaries, I'd like to single out Melissa Mills and Yvette O'Neal, particularly for their work on the West Point Summer Seminar in Military History and on many staff rides. American Division secretaries Bea Villa,

Jennifer Thompson, and Patricia Higgins have written a decade of orders for my conference and research travel and AIADs: thank you.

The library is my third home at West Point: it's a testament to the History Department that I don't rank it second, because libraries have normally been my home away from home. Thanks to all the librarians in my life, from the Fairfax County Public Library system, Kings Park Elementary School, Washington Irving Junior High School, and Marshall and Herndon High School libraries, where history and historical fiction inspired me, to the libraries of Indiana (especially Lilly Library), Rice, and St. Thomas (truly amazing for its size). Special thanks to all those who have worked on interlibrary loans over the years at Rice, at St. Thomas, and at West Point, especially Sharon Gillespie, Heather Goyette, Jill Bickers, and Faith Coslett.

I go to Special Collections only occasionally now, but it was one of my principal archives when I began the dissertation that has become *Jackson's Sword* back in 1992. Thanks to Judith Sibley, Suzanne Christoff, Alicia Mauldin-Ware, and Casey Madrick; to veterans Susan Lintelmann and Debby McKeon-Pogue; and especially to Elaine McConnell and my old friend Alan Aimone. At the reference desk I thank friends Dan Pritchard, Ed Dacey, Laura Mosher, Paul Nergelovic, Debbie Jarrett, Celeste Evans, Mike Arden, and Wendy Swik, who have all done yeoman's work on interlibrary loans as well; at the circulation desk I thank Donna Chestnut, Jacey Pungello, Latisha Taylor, Linda Conley, Mona Fisher, Ed Pelkey, and Jim McEnery.

Donna Selvaggio, Amy Kennedy, David Stockton, and Rose Robischon always bought the books, serials, databases, and even microfilm I asked for: I don't forget them, even down in their amber room. Mark Colvson figured out how to make my wireless work in the library—no small matter when it means I can buy books on Amazon while watching baseball and pretending to work on the fifth floor, overlooking the Plain, Battle Monument, and the Hudson with the finest view I'll ever have.

The cadets are the reason I'm at the Military Academy. In the core courses we often complain that the cadets don't do enough to prepare, but in 3,000 class hours I have never had a truly dead discussion. Cadets are always coming up with insights—I can't imagine getting a thoughtful discussion a hundred times a semester anywhere else. From more than a thousand cadets I can single out only a few, even among those who wrote their senior theses with me: Matt Rasmussen and Jim Morin, Chris Thomas and Chris Sanchez (for the One Big Union), Mark Reid and Wes Moerbe (for Zachary Taylor), Phil Mix (especially for *Napoleonic Wars*), Nate Browning for the good cheer, Matt Rosebaugh (for Youngstown) and Christina Fenstermaker, David Banas (for the Union), and Max Lujan (for the Union and Texas). Others stand out because they have returned to teach with me: CJ Kirkpatrick, Bill Nance, Adrienne Harrison, Rocky Rhodes, Casey Baker, and Greg Hope. The HI 154 class of spring 2007 and the HI 397 class of fall 2010 deserve special praise for their wonderfully researched papers and thoughtful discussions.

Military service is why cadets are at the Military Academy. These cadets, momentarily my students, died in the service of our nation in Iraq and Afghanistan: Leif Nott, Todd Bryant, Len Cowherd, Robert Seidel, Torre Mallard, and Robert Collins.

I have lived a bit outside the scholarly mainstream at West Point, but many friends have helped me stay connected, and many have read and commented on my papers, chapters, and essays. Among the American historians, those I know from the Society for Historians of the Early American Republic (SHEAR) stand out. I first participated in SHEAR in 1994; no other organization of American historians means so much to me, and no other conference inspires me so much. Gene Allen Smith has been a great friend, host, conference roommate, and ally for fifteen years, as well as one of the key worker bees keeping SHEAR in the black. Gene has invited me to conferences and published my work; he and Bill Skelton read the original manuscript for *Jackson's Sword*, and his wife Tracy created the maps; I owe few men more. Gentleman Jim Broussard—who founded SHEAR when I was in junior high and still runs the poker game—smooth John Belohlavek, and sturdy Ed Townes stand out as friends, hosts, and conference roommates.

Friends from SHEAR, including Sam Haynes (who, with Chris Morris, published my breakthrough borderlands essay), Bob May, Richard John, Ted Crackel, Mary-Jo Kline, Dane Hartgrove, James Lewis, John Morris (who lent me his microfilm of the Jacob Brown Papers), Don Hickey, David Narrett, Ken Stevens, Dan Preston, David Nichols, Dan Howe, Peter Onuf, Alan Taylor, Craig Friend, and Mike Fitzgerald, have helped or encouraged me in my work. John Ifkovic, John Van Atta, Albrecht Koschnik, Doron Ben-Atar, Howard Rock, Mike Birkner, and John Quist have been good friends and sometime poker buddies. Mike Morrison, along with John Larson, the longtime coeditor of the superb *Journal of the Early Republic*, twice published my work and wrote a generous letter recommending my promotion to associate professor. Along with Gene Smith and Ed Townes, Joe Knetsch and Steve Belko have made the Gulf South History and Humanities conference a highlight every autumn: Joe helped me in my Florida research; Steve sought me out to contribute to an edited collection and takes me out on the town every time I visit.

The Society for Military History (SMH) provides the same extraordinary friendship and intellectual connectivity in military history. Bruce Vandervort, editor of the *Journal of Military History* and a military historian of nineteenth-century America, has welcomed my reviews and suggestions. My colleagues in nineteenth-century American military scholarship, all gentlemen and scholars, have also been good friends and supporters: Dave Fitzpatrick, Chip Dawson and Brian Holden Reid (who published one of my essays), Tim Johnson, Randy Mullis, Durwood Ball, Bob Wettemann, Mark Grimsley, Greg Urwin, Don Connelly, Greg Hospodor, Rick Herrera, David Fitz-Enz, Robert Wooster, Harry Laver, Irving Levinson, Rich Grippaldi, and Wayne Hsieh. Ethan Rafuse and I became fast friends when he arrived at West Point. Though he says I made a great sponsor, he already had all the zeal to succeed, and he has set an example of consistent writing that I only wish I could emulate. He read a large part of this manuscript and most of my other work at some point. Few historians have equal range, no one makes me think harder, and no one makes a better companion on a staff ride or anywhere else.

West Point has hosted a series of premier military historians as visiting professors or lecturers, including Don Higginbotham, Carole Reardon, Dennis Showalter (who published some of my work as the editor of *War in History*), Linda and Marsha Frey, Mac Coffman (who wrote for my promotion packet), Joe Glatthaar, Jeremy Black (who signed me up to edit a compilation), Mike Neiberg, Joe Guilmartin, Rob Citino, George Gawrych, and Roger Spiller. Brian Linn (another of my "promoters") has been especially good company; drinking beer and talking rock and roll with Brian are highlights every time we meet. The West Point Summer Seminar in Military History brings some of these friends back each year and creates many new ones to meet again at the SMH. The New York Military Affairs Symposium has been a joy to visit each year, thanks especially to Bob Rowen, Kathy Williams, Kay Larson, Frank Radford, and Gene Feit.

Many archivists have helped me over the years; I will doubtlessly leave some out and ask their forgiveness. In my dissertation research, Fred Bauman of the Library of Congress, Judy Sibley and Alan Aimone at West Point, and Michael Musick and Michael Meier at the National Archives provided enormous assistance. I have worked in many more archives since then, but it has never seemed like work: I think of it as an opportunity to travel, eat out and shop in bookstores in new towns, visit historic sites, and read all day in quiet, sunlit rooms. What could be more relaxing? Archives I downtown has been my most frequent research home since then; I thank the many archivists and the workers in the reading room for those twelve-hour days of wonder.

During 2003 I spent a delightful couple of weeks at the William L. Clements Library at Ann Arbor, where I really picked up on Korean pancakes. My thanks to Jack Dann, who let me stay late and then treated me to dinner; Brian Leigh Dunnigan; Barbara DeWolfe; Janet Bloom; Valerie Proehl; and John Harriman. The United States invaded Iraq during that trip, an unforgettable moment in recent history. During the spring of 2004 I spent a week at the William L. Perkins Library at Duke University and thank Naomi Nelson and Elizabeth Dunn. That summer I spent six weeks in Florida, where I was assisted by Burt Altman at Florida State; R. Boyd Murphee, Miriam Gan-Spaulding, and Jody Norman at the Florida State Archives; and especially Jim Cusick, Mil Willis, and their staff at the P. K. Yonge Library of Florida History at the University of Florida in Gainesville, a town named after one of the principal characters in *Jackson's Sword*. I found Florida and Michigan open places full of opportunity and freedom, used-book stores, and Asian food, not unlike Texas. In 2006 I spent three weeks at the New York State Library, where Fred Bassett, Paul Mercer, Vincent Bostick, and Victor DesRosiers were most helpful. Since 2005 I have spent nearly two months at the Historical Society of Pennsylvania. Among the many staffers there, Sarah Heim, Matthew Lyons, Ronald Medford, and Steve Smith stand out for their assistance.

I would also like to thank the following and their staffs: James Lewis, Brenna King, and Anna Lubieniecka at the New Jersey Historical Society; Elisabeth Proffen at the Maryland Historical Society; Angela O'Neal at the Ohio Historical Society; David Poremba at the Burton Historical Collection of the Detroit Public Library; James Cotham at the East Tennessee Historical Society; Paul Levengood (an old Rice colleague) and Gregory Stoner at the Virginia Historical Society; Jewell Anderson at the Georgia Historical Society; and Margaret Cook at the Earl J. Swem Library at the College of William and Mary. In addition, thanks to the staffs of the Southern Historical Collection at the University of North Carolina at Chapel Hill, the New York Public Library, the State Historical Society of Wisconsin, the Firestone Library at Princeton University, and the Sterling and Beinecke Libraries at Yale University. Thanks also to the Reverend Robert Alves, and to Chris Stowe for copies of the George Meade Papers from the Historical Society of Pennsylvania.

In Florida, Virginia, North Carolina, Michigan, Pennsylvania, and upstate New York, I took vacations from my research to visit battlefields and historic sites—something West Point turned me on to, and something all Americans should be grateful for. Thanks to the thousands of federal and state workers who hold down the fort so we can reflect on history where it happened.

Since 2002 West Point has provided annual funding for my research through its Faculty Development and Research Fund. However, the views expressed herein are my own and do not represent those of the Military Academy, the U.S. Army, the Department of Defense, or any other agency. I gratefully acknowledge permission to use portions of my past articles and essays from the *Southwestern Historical Quarterly*, the *Journal of the Early Republic*, *American Nineteenth-Century History*, Texas A&M University Press, Mercer University Press, the University Press of Virginia, Ashgate Publishing, and the University Press of Florida (these works are listed in the bibliography). Thanks also to Peter Stearns, who published my second article in the *Journal of Social History* more than fifteen years ago; to Jim DeFronzo, who published my essay on armed forces and revolution in his *Revolutionary Movements in World History*; and to Gordon Martel, who published my essays in his *Encyclopedia of War*. Above all, thanks to all the editors, editorial assistants, and production staffs who have labored on my work over the years; I couldn't do any of this without you.

Patience is the greatest virtue in research and teaching, and my editor, Mike Briggs, has been most patient of all. I have been a perfectionist when it comes to my writing. I sent him the original manuscript of *Jackson's Sword* in 2001, and we imagined publication in 2002 or 2003. Then I blew it up with material from the period 1784–1814 but ended up cutting that out; then I blew it up again, and now it's two volumes after all. I've given Mike a hard time, and I apologize for it here, as I have in so many e-mails. But most of all, I thank him for his faith in my work.

Before turning to my family, I would like to thank the same two men I thanked most in my dissertation: Bill Skelton and Jim Bradford. Another scholar recently wrote that "Skelton's intellectual legacy lives on" in my work, and I consider that a tribute to me and, I hope, to Bill. Skelton's *An American Profession of Arms* was the first full book on the army officer corps between the Revolution and the Civil War; though I have my quibbles with some of his conclusions, *Jackson's Sword* follows in Bill's footsteps, showing how officers' professional commitment and cohesion played out in the army's operations in the field. Bill has been a generous reader since I sent him a rather callow letter in 1994; he has read this bulky manuscript at least twice and most of my articles and essays before and after submission. His patience and faith in my work have been equaled only by those of my dissertation adviser Ira Gruber and by Mike Briggs.

Jim Bradford has been the staunchest of patrons and friends since 1994; he is my oldest academic friend outside of Rice. Back then, as the southwestern regional coordinator for the SMH, he got me on conference programs;

during the past decade he has published several of my essays; and in 2009 and 2010 he took me to Europe to teach with him—three of the best months of my life. Jim has been a perpetual font of stories, humor, advice, and wisdom. Listening to him, I hear generations, in Texas, in SHEAR (where he served many years as executive director), and in his work as an editor and administrator for so many organizations. Jim personifies the ideal of academic service; he is one of my greatest friends and role models.

Last, my family: to my dad, still setting an example working to build an effective, democratic government in Iraq forty years after he finished his second tour in Vietnam; to my fellow scholar Wendy and to Peter (an engineer and now a soldier) and to Wendy's parents, Ted and Liz Fibison; to my sister Jen, who has built her own life out West, and my niece Mary Elaine ("Focus!"); to the memories of my grandmothers and grandfathers; to my aunts and uncles, especially Jan and Gene and the boys in wonderful Texas; and to my brother Ed and his wife Sharon, my niece Allie, and my nephew James Eric, a soldier and a rockin' drummer: a true family to me. I dedicate *Jackson's Sword* to my mom, Mary Ann Ross Watson, who passed away in 2008. I am thankful that I had a sabbatical and could spend some time with her; I wish I had asked her more as she grew ill. I wish I had finished this book in time for her to see it, but that really doesn't matter; she knew I'd get it done eventually. Happy dreams, Mom.

INTRODUCTION

THE SOLDIER AND THE NINETEENTH-CENTURY AMERICAN STATE

Insulation, Autonomy, and Agency

Throughout the nineteenth century, the career officers of the U.S. Army served as federal, international, and interethnic mediators, national law enforcers, and de facto intercultural and international peacekeepers. They effectively advanced national objectives and power with remarkably little overt violence by extending and enhancing the authority and cohesion of the American nation-state along its borders and frontiers. Nineteenth-century military professionalism did not develop independent of civilian society, nor was it simply a matter of growing expertise in the art of warfare. By examining army officers' efforts to extend and maintain national sovereignty in the borderlands of the United States, *Jackson's Sword* explores their professional development; the strength, trajectory, and impact of the nineteenth-century American army and nation-state; and the everyday realities of civil-military relations.

The national standing army was almost continually challenged by nonstate actors, American or foreign, while being constrained by republican and liberal ideology, representative but racialist (white supremacist) democracy, adherence to due process and the constitutional separation of powers, and federalism and decentralization in sectional, regional, and localist forms. The officer corps' claim to professional status and to the right to participate in its definition depended on civilian acceptance of its claim to authority over a distinct role in society's division of labor, especially the power to select, promote, and exclude aspirants to that role. This claim was challenged by the anti–standing army and militia ideals, private and volunteer military units, and frontier constituencies that acclaimed those ideals and created such units when they believed that the regular army was acting contrary to their interests, as often seemed to be the case in the confused welter of borderlands diplomacy and settler expansion. Yet despite widespread criticism as aristocrats, martinets, dandies, and Indian sympathizers, the officers of the regular army secured a fundamental acceptance of their professional role in the federal government and among the middle classes and elites who served in and identified with it.[1]

This acceptance permitted extraordinarily secure employment, making possible careers that lasted an average of more than two decades, and it meant that the regulars ordinarily exercised senior-level command over volunteer and militia forces during wartime. The officer corps gained this acceptance through fiscally accountable administration; genteel interaction with local and national civilian elites; the exercise, through military command, of an authority most civilian elites could only dream about; and the politically reliable performance of their duties negotiating, mediating, intimidating, and coercing along the borders and frontiers. Officers also made cogent arguments for the value of experience and specialization in military tasks. These arguments were accepted by most nationalist Republicans, National Republicans, and Whigs, and the officers clearly proved their capability by advancing U.S. territorial expansion during the war with Mexico. Most previous accounts have suggested that the army was subordinated to partisan politics—essentially patronage, regardless of education or experience—when it came to officers' commissioning and promotion or that it was physically isolated and mentally alienated from civilian society. These assertions are inaccurate, individually and collectively. Crucially, unlike most other institutions of Jacksonian government, the army secured substantial insulation, even autonomy, from partisan politics and sectional or civilian economic interests in its internal administration and field operations. Yet the army officer corps became increasingly accountable to civilian authority in its internal institutional processes; in representative, constitutional, and federalist civil-military relations; and in the execution of foreign policy. Indeed, it struck a more diplomatic—a more just and less violent—balance among various social, political, and interest groups than most civilian frontiersmen or its European counterparts. The latter were thoroughly linked to civilian politics through commissioning and civilian officeholding, serving elite class power at home while launching imperial and colonial adventures abroad.[2]

Army operations in the Jacksonian borderlands restrained entropy, enhanced national security, and advanced orderly national territorial expansion. The efforts of the army's frontier diplomats, including their exercise of restraint, discipline, or command over citizens and citizen-soldiers, helped prevent the establishment of competing polities (nations, states, or other political entities) that might have constrained U.S. growth; limited settler and citizen-soldier atrocities against Native Americans; and played a crucial—perhaps decisive—role in averting a devastating war with Britain circa 1840. Their logistical expertise proved equally crucial to projecting U.S. national power, first to drive Indians from land sought by white citizens, then to do so against Mexico, and finally to reunite the nation during the Civil War. The army officer corps was certainly authoritarian in its internal discipline and in officers' attitudes toward Indians and frontier civilians, and it was certainly more oriented toward national government, centralized authority, and social and political hierarchy than the decentralization acclaimed by the majority of Americans. However, its growing and, in Jacksonian America, unique professional autonomy did not come at the expense of political accountability. Autonomy, and the insulation that sustained it, enhanced accountability and subordination to civilian authority, to due process and the rule of law, and to the processes of representative constitutional government, however frustrating officers sometimes found them. If one is looking for themes and keywords, mine are *responsibility, accountability,* and *subordination; institutional insulation* and *operational autonomy* rather than *isolation* or *alienation.*

The length of this work demands an extended introduction to set out my themes, assumptions, and exclusions in advance. Here, I briefly outline my views on larger theoretical and comparative questions of state formation, civilmilitary relations, and civil and military professionalism, and I discuss where my work fits in the study of early American politics and international relations. Because most theoretical attention in these areas has been directed toward the late nineteenth century—and is often rooted in twentieth-century experience rather than nineteenth-century realities—I address and critique the leading interpretations of the relationship between the nineteenth-century army and the national state, particularly those involving the timing and meaning of military professionalization.

Jackson's Sword is an exploration of diplomacy and civil-military relations on the frontier from the army's side—local rather than national civil-military relations. It examines what army officers thought, wrote, and did in frontier and border regions; their attitudes and reactions toward white citizens, Indians, foreign nations and their nationals, and nonstate actors; and the impact they had on interethnic, intranational, and international relations. It is not a study of military strategy or national security policy directed against "conventional" (interstate) threats; it does not address American coastal defenses, plans for the defense of the northern border or the western frontier, or limited planning for an offensive against Canada in case of war. Nor is it a detailed examination of officers' attitudes toward interstate war, Indian warfare, national security policy, or U.S. foreign relations and policy, although several chapters touch on the last topic. *Jackson's Sword* is intended to supply an analytic narrative that, though comprehensive in its treatment of significant army operations (which at that time meant almost anything above the squad or patrol level), is attuned to nonmilitary contexts and addresses larger questions in U.S. history. Although I emphasize officers' agency, I hope I do so within the material and ideational, physical and conceptual structures of continental and Atlantic politics and economics, Euro-American culture, Indian relations, American society, and government institutions.[3]

Jackson's Sword is not a study of civilian reactions to army operations or of civil-military relations from the civilian side. I hope to locate the officer corps in its American social, political, economic, and cultural contexts, as well as those of international relations and the development of western military institutions and professionalism. In particular, I hope to relate officers' attitudes to those of their society and culture, to connect motives, attitudes, and institutional developments and explore the links among the state, the elite and middle classes, and professional formation. But the narrative core of *Jackson's Sword* concerns the army officer's work as an agent of the national state. Between the end of 1814 and the outbreak of the war with Mexico, that work most often consisted of coercive diplomacy, whether expansionist intimidation or peace-keeping in support of stability. In other words, the army's most common mission was diplomacy backed by the threat of force, conducted as much by military commanders on the scene as by civilian diplomats in national capitals.

Jackson's Sword is not about enlisted soldiers. Much of the republican critique of standing armies was based on assumptions about the character of enlisted men, who were thought to be mercenary, dependent hirelings not much above slaves. American social and political leaders, and indeed officers themselves, shared this assumption, which was reasonable in terms of republican ideology, given the impoverished social origins of most enlisted men and the harsh discipline to which they submitted. Consequently, modern historical sensibilities notwithstanding, these subordinates appeared on elite radar screens (civilian or military) only when they resisted demands for obedience. Indeed, the hierarchical officer-enlisted relationship, whether seen as paternalistic or outrightly coercive, could serve as something of a model for class relationships among the increasingly conservative middle class in the decades of working-class formation after 1840. Ideology aside, civilian leaders thought of the army in terms of the genteel officer corps they dealt with on a day-to-day basis to handle practical military issues. Officers and civilian leaders were concretely linked by the process of nomination to West Point and often by personal friendship and informal influence over officers' assignments, as shown by the papers of any senior military leader and most junior officers and national politicians.[4]

Although it is a study of governance and administration in the broader sense, *Jackson's Sword* is not a study of organizational behavior or bureaucracy per se. It is not primarily a study of the educational or administrative institutions in the army and its officer corps, which William Skelton and others have effectively addressed. Skelton has ably explored the sources and manifestations of professional socialization, commitment, cohesion, and expertise in his path-breaking work *An American Profession of Arms*; here, I address them at length only in chapter 7 and the conclusion of this volume. I am not writing an internal, organizational, or institutional history of the officer corps; I am concerned primarily with its relations to the "outside" civilian world, particularly on the nation's borders and frontiers. One must be familiar with the former in order to understand the latter, however—a problem that plagues studies of the army by scholars who focus on partisan politics or ideology. By exploring the juncture between military operations, particularly "operations other than war," and civil-military relations, *Jackson's Sword* helps fill the current gap in the study of American civil-military relations between the Jeffersonian and Civil War eras. In doing so, it explains the hiatus that actually occurred in major civil-military tension between 1820 and 1860, notwithstanding some superficially vehement Jacksonian critiques of the army.[5]

It is hoped that this work will help historians better understand the complexities of territorial expansion and international relations, of relations between center and periphery, state and society, political rhetoric and ideology, and governance and political reality in the early American republic. Likewise, it should help scholars from a variety of disciplines refine their understandings of professionalism and professionalization and of state formation and consolidation. Military operations, civil-military relations, and intercultural and international relations all came together in upholding and extending U.S. sovereignty through peacekeeping and coercive diplomacy. Given the officer corps' role (tacit or overt) in mediating among local, national, international, and interethnic (or intercultural) forces, *Jackson's Sword* is a study of the negotiated and contested construction of local, sectional, national, and international interests and identities.

The history and historiography of the nineteenth-century army, and of nineteenth-century American military history and professionalism, revolve around two fundamental issues: civil-military relations, which are ultimately evaluated by the degree of military accountability to civilian control, and the military's ability to accomplish the missions assigned to it. Indeed, these are the two most crucial issues in the study of military professionalism, and they are critical to evaluating the utility of force as an instrument of national policy. Historically, these concerns were inextricably entwined: the degree of policy-maker emphasis on one or the other shaped contemporary force structures, and scholarly emphases on one or the other have strongly influenced interpretation and evaluation. This complex but crucial relationship is particularly evident in five major areas of scholarship: (1) military efficacy in general and (2) in the nineteenth-century army's conduct of the Indian Wars in particular; (3) the relations between regulars and citizen-soldiers (volunteers and the militia); (4) the desirability, development, character, and extent of military professionalism; and (5) civil-military relations more generally. *Jackson's Sword* provides an in-depth exploration of military attitudes and operations across the spectrum of coercion—from diplomatic communication to war—in the borderlands and frontier areas where the army conducted most of its operations prior to the Civil War.[6]

Exploring how the career commissioned officer corps of the national standing army reacted to these missions and the challenges and dilemmas they presented should allow a better understanding of five significant historical and theoretical questions posed by recent historians and political scientists. First, how strong and how influential was the early American state, particularly on the nation's frontiers, and did it grow stronger or weaker between 1800 and 1860? Second, how insulated or autonomous were the army and its officer corps? Were they able to concentrate on accomplishing their missions without bias or distortion from contested social, political, and cultural influences, particularly from the partisan pressures that dominated American political life following the rise of the Second Party System in the 1830s? This question is central to an assessment of professionalism and professionalization because some insulation from nonspecialist, nonexpert pressure is presumed to be necessary for specialists to impartially exercise their expertise and judgment in the performance of complex missions. My answer suggests that significant dimensions of nation-state autonomy—if only those justified by national security and centered in the executive branch—endured even in that increasingly destabilizing era of populist partisan democracy.[7]

Third, how isolated, or even alienated, were career officers from civil society, from the political system, and from American culture as a whole? This question is ultimately one of civil-military relations: even if officers were accountable in the formal sense of being subordinate to the constitutional, democratic civilian authority of the nation-state, were they responsive to its social, political, and cultural norms? Did they shirk the missions assigned to them by elected representatives? Was their professional group ethic a threat to civil society?

Fourth, what was the timing and trajectory of professional development in the officer corps of the national standing army? Did mental or physical isolation help officers focus on developing their professional capability, as several scholars, mostly of the late nineteenth century, have argued?[8] More important, what was the focus and *content* of American military professionalism during the early and mid-nineteenth century? Are the criteria employed by previous scholars relevant to that period, or would other criteria be more useful for a historical understanding and assessment?

Finally, what was the character of the nation's frontiers and borderlands during the early and mid-nineteenth century? What was the impact of American federalism? (This subject has rarely been explicitly addressed in studies of intercultural and international relations along borders and internal frontiers.) To what degree and at what point in time did the United States, or its white citizens, come to dominate these regions? Did it or they achieve hegemony, and if so, in what sense? How much freedom of action did indigenous peoples, the American nation-state, and its citizens have in pursuing their objectives in these contested zones? What role did the national standing army play in U.S. territorial expansion and the dispossession of the Native Americans?[9]

NINETEENTH-CENTURY AMERICAN GOVERNMENT: A "WEAK STATE" OF COURTS AND PARTIES?

Historical sociologist Michael Mann suggests that "professionalizing and bureaucratizing state militarism," or the nationalization and rationalization of armed force, was one of the four principal tracks of Euro-American societal development during the nineteenth century (the other three were the moves toward mature capitalism, greater political representation, and political centralization and nationalism). As Mann observes, encapsulating the conclusions of historical sociologists since Max Weber, "Bureaucracy entered states mainly through their armed forces, substantially bureaucratized well before civilian administrations." This was largely true in the United States as well, particularly after the decline of Federalist statism after 1800. Yet as historian Mark Wilson recently observed, scholars "have tended to search for the roots of American bureaucracy in virtually every field except the military." Many American historians and political scientists still write as if citizens need to pay income taxes or receive transfer payments to have meaningful interactions with the state. All too often, eminent scholars skim over or minimize the role and significance of the nineteenth-century American state, assuring us that most of the population never encountered the federal government except at the post office and that American government was dominated by parties and their patronage at every level.[10]

During the 1980s political scientists Martin Shefter and Stephen Skowronek drew on historian Morton Keller's portrayal of the post-Reconstruction period as an era of "organizational politics" to reinforce this interpretation, projecting it, without substantial archival evidence, backward throughout the century. This was epitomized in Skowronek's widely cited dictum that nineteenth-century American government was a "state of courts and parties." Skowronek was actually writing about executive branch agencies, so ultimately, the point was that partisan concerns (patronage more than ideology or policy) dominated the functioning of these agencies: inputs external to the policy questions at issue mattered far more than policy objectives or outputs. Whether the state was weak or strong, it was not autonomous. Taking this conclusion to its logical extreme, Daniel Carpenter, another political scientist writing about the Progressive Era, dismissed the early national state as "clerical."[11]

Arguments against a strong nineteenth-century state commonly stem from anachronistic comparisons with the twentieth century; from assumptions that republican ideological antagonism toward centralized power dominated American politics throughout the nineteenth century; from the focus on electoral politics rather than policy, characteristic of the "party period" and the ethno-cultural schools that dominated the historiography of nineteenth-century American politics between the 1970s and the turn of the century; or from apples and oranges comparisons with European states facing very different ideological and security environments. Social, cultural, and ethnohistorical perspectives—the linguistic and cultural turns in the social sciences and humanities since the 1970s—have privileged rhetoric and individual agency at the expense of policy and institutions. This has contributed to "a sense of statelessness" that probably characterizes modern scholars much more than the historical actors. None of these perspectives does much to examine the nineteenth-century American state on its own historical terms. Nor have the political scientists who compare the nineteenth-century state with the twentieth-century state relied on the papers of early- and mid-nineteenth-century executive branch officials or on an understanding of what their state—particularly the army—actually did in practice. These scholars study rhetoric, values, and political culture much more than governance or government.[12]

Historians cannot simply blame ignorance of the nineteenth-century state on political scientists. These assumptions, rooted in repetition rather than investigation, are among the most common anachronisms espoused by American historians. For many historians, including those of the nineteenth century, the belief in a weak or minimalist state depends on a belief in the continuing pervasiveness of classical republicanism, which was deeply suspicious of concentrated power. This belief was advanced to the point of scholarly orthodoxy by historians of colonial and Revolutionary America in the 1960s and 1970s who took contemporary partisan rhetoric, particularly that of republicanism, at full face value. Among historians specializing in American politics, the legislative focus of Richard L. McCormick—a variant of the "state of courts and parties" thesis—shaped similar views. McCormick recognized the impact and significance of the pre–Civil War nation-state as a distributive agent, but he saw policy making as almost solely the province of parties acting through legislatures, paying little attention to courts, much less to executive agencies, both of which seemingly did exactly what Congress told them to do, every time. The promotional or distributive politics of legislation that created direct and indirect subsidies (such as the import tariff, the employment of army officers to survey railroads and canals, or land grants to railroads, homesteaders, and veterans) thus became a large-scale version of Morton Keller's patronage politics.[13]

Historians who do not specialize in the early republic commonly accept glosses by political scientists like Skowronek and Shefter. They, in turn, draw from McCormick, from Keller, and from Louis Hartz's review of American liberalism to make huge generalizations about the dominance of Jacksonian ideas over their Whig competitors, with almost no archival evidence. Yet as William Skelton points out in "Samuel P. Huntington and the American Military Tradition," the historiographical foundation for this interpretation was shallow and highly overgeneralized to begin with and has been steadily undermined by the tremendous mass of archivally detailed work done by historians since 1960. Historians now recognize that, as a whole, early-nineteenth-century America was much less egalitarian, much less antagonistic to institutions and privilege, and, by the 1830s, much more receptive to specialization. The shorthand for this recognition can be expressed in two words: the Whigs. The Jacksonian Democrats maintained a slim, closely contested majority in American politics, a far cry from the overwhelming predominance Samuel Huntington found in the Jackson- and Jacksonian-centered historiography of the 1950s. Yet this recognition has not penetrated most historians' understanding of the state or its army.[14]

Scholarly inattention to the army of the Jacksonian era both in the historiography of the frontier and the West and in studies of American political development and the state proceeds from and reinforces this errant perspective. Skowronek recognizes that the state's "organization of coercive power was no less indispensable for its unobtrusive character. The early American state maintained an integrated legal order on a continental scale. . . . [D]espite the absence of a sense of the state, the state was essential to social order and social development in nineteenth-century America." Nevertheless, Skowronek blithely asserts that Americans "relegated . . . the [apparently insignificant] tasks of securing the frontier and aiding economic development" to the army. Keller opines that "before 1861 the army was a neglected arm of the government"; historian William Nelson contends that there was no "significant federal bureaucracy" before the Civil War and does not mention the army at all.[15] Yet even Joel H. Silbey, dean of the "party school" of interpreting nineteenth-century American political development, recognizes that "the purpose of all this partisan combat [or pluralist agency] was [to develop] particular public policies," whether distributing benefits through direct or indirect subsidy or attempting to control personal behavior. Indeed, Silbey recently suggested that "the lineaments of a nascent American state were becoming . . . more visible" during the Jacksonian period than they had been since the Federal era of the 1790s. Building on a wide range of detailed studies by a new generation of historians beginning with Richard John and William Novak, political scientist Ira Katznelson recently labeled the early republic "an assertive, expansive, and permeable liberal state." He recognizes that liberalism depends on power as much as any other public system, especially when constructing and maintaining coercive property relations—such as slavery and the expropriation of the Indians.[16]

I am not arguing that the origins of the welfare state lie in the 1830s or that partisan patronage did not undermine the efficiency, impartiality, and effectiveness of government during the Jacksonian era. On the whole, following Richard John, Ronald Formisano is right to label that period one of "state regression." Yet while government may have been a withered limb of nineteenth-century American society, the military was not neglected within it. Katznelson observes that between 1808 and 1848 the military absorbed at least 72 percent of the national budget every year; the army took about half the budget, with the navy and the civil service taking 20 to 30 percent each. Consequently, Katznelson concludes that "the military provides a privileged vantage point from which to probe the character, ambitions, and limits of the United States as a liberal state. . . . Both the American military and the state . . . have been underestimated badly. . . . It was the military that . . . defined the key contours of America's regime in space and in ambition." However inadequate by twentieth-century (or contemporary European) standards, the early- and mid-nineteenth-century American state proved sufficient to create and maintain a national military force capable of projecting power from Florida to Wisconsin to Texas, from California and Oregon to Mexico City.

In fact, Keller's statement that the Civil War army was "an organization whose size, power, and administrative complexity were unmatched in nineteenth-century American . . . history" is equally true for the antebellum army and antebellum American organizations, private as well as public. The experience of that army, the subject of this book, provided the basis for effective civil-military relations, logistics, and power projection in the army of the Civil War. Whatever the validity of the "state of courts and parties" and the "weak state" theses as generalizations, for comparison with European states or the twentieth-century American one, the national standing army was a critically—indeed, decisively—significant exception in its own time.[17]

CONTEXT IS (ALMOST) EVERYTHING: *JACKSON'S SWORD* AS A STUDY IN MILITARY PROFESSIONALISM

Examining the interests, values, and perspectives of American officers operating in the borderlands has important implications for the study of nineteenth-century American military professionalism, particularly officers' sense of professional mission and responsibility. Officers' actions and attitudes toward international relations, frontier diplomacy, and national security policy demonstrate a range of individual efforts to meld distinctly American beliefs and circumstances with the socially functional yet self-interested quest for preparedness expected of any military body. Examining this fusion between abstract model and social reality casts much-needed light on the influence of American belief in exceptionalism on a profession—and a historiography—founded on the example of European institutions and ideas. The American officers who gave conscious thought to wider policy issues often demonstrated a remarkable ability to recognize and accept the interdependence of military, political, economic, and even cultural resources and objectives, and they exhibited a socially responsible and politically accountable willingness to direct military policy and subordinate military goals to the service of objectives valued by the civilian polity. These patterns of thought and behavior also suggest significant limits on the mental isolation and alienation produced by military missions and socialization in the midst of an increasingly liberal society—an important issue in assessing the evolution of socially responsible and politically accountable civil-military relations.[18]

Notions of professionalism were unevenly developed and widely contested in Jacksonian America. This should not surprise us: like most complex human phenomena, professionalism is a shifting, relative, constructed phenomenon, not an unconditional or permanent one. It is asserted and defined both through the efforts of aspiring professionals and through the external social and political relationships—the demands of those the profession claims to serve—specific to particular historical contexts. Consequently, professionalization is always an ongoing process of jurisdictional definition and defense, as well as the development of commitment, expertise, and responsibility. The cultures of society, state, and profession (or of the occupations and organizations claiming professional authority) play an important part in establishing the aspiring profession's role in this process. The aspirants' expertise and the demand for their services are ultimately constituted—conceived, perceived, understood, recognized, and reconceived—by the society they serve, based on its values and priorities as well as on the threat environment. Although we may agree that all states share a desire for security, threat determination is a political process. Would-be professionals secure recognition as privileged claimants to mission and authority only when they convince society that they deserve it.

Doing so requires that aspiring professionals accommodate their expertise to society's needs. There can be no permanent, unquestionable professional status or skill set (beyond some of the most fundamental cognitive skills, such as critical thinking and the ability to focus one's study and analysis); there can be no single ideal-typical professionalism to which every military force or every claimant to professional status (civil or military) can aspire. Like civil-military relations or any other socially constituted relationship, professionalism can never be perfected for all eternity; it can only be improved to serve the society in which it is identified or asserted. When professionals, particularly those dealing with the political issues of conflict and war, advise their clients or constituents, they must do so critically, without imposing a preconceived solution. They must recognize that the clients possess the right to define their own interests, objectives, and priorities and thus the missions they will assign and (more indirectly) the skill sets they require.

Political scientist Samuel P. Huntington's enormously influential *The Soldier and the State* (1957) was the first American work to explicitly lay out a taxonomy of military professionalism. According to Huntington, the content of civil-military relations and the opportunity for developing professional capability revolved primarily around the degree of military autonomy from civilian control, which was presumed to be essential for the development of expertise for national defense. Huntington's advocacy of an idealized "objective civilian control," which he privileged as "objective civil-military relations" ultimately meant that civilians should leave the military alone to develop its expertise and to conduct warfare as effectively as possible. The onus was on politicians—the policy makers—and the political system to give the military the tools it needed (or said it needed) and to accept the military's definition of the problem at hand. International security—the primacy of foreign relations—trumped all social, economic, ideological, and even constitutional considerations. Any problems in civil-military relations came primarily from civilian refusal to recognize the priority of military expertise. If the civilians stayed out of military affairs, the military would focus on fighting foreign armies and leave the civilians alone. No coup, no problem.

In addition to being deficient as a measure of military subordination to civilian policies, this definition of the problem presumed that autonomy from civilian oversight (assumed to be destabilizing because of the unpredictable operation of politics—particularly democratic politics and politicians' inability to devote themselves to military matters) was necessary for aspiring professionals to develop expertise and provide expert advice. This expertise would emerge both through experience, which would require career stability free from politically motivated intervention in promotions and rewards, and through formal training and education, which should therefore be run by the increasingly expert military, including substantial control over the conditions of entry into the profession. This autonomy would enable the military to define threats (problems) and desired skill sets (solutions) without distraction or intervention by those lacking experience, training, and education. In return, the military would remain subordinate to the civil power by staying out of any policy questions that did not involve national security.

A rigid binary distinction between liberal civil society (with diverse interests represented by legislatures) and conservative military professionals (shielded from liberalism by the national executive) is the essence of Huntington's "objective" civilian control; it does much to account for his praise of the Prusso-German army of the Second Reich as a model for civil-military relations, which would have shocked most Anglo-Americans prior to the Cold War. If interaction with civilian society threatened military professionalism, professionalism could develop only in isolation; conversely, successful professional development would probably produce isolation as officers concentrated on their distinct, perhaps unique, mission while civilians went their own way. This process was essentially circular: left to itself, this closed loop was ahistorical both in evidence and in potential for change. The profession would define the problems it existed to combat; it would then claim superior expertise, and thus a superior ability to define the problem, on the basis of the training and education it developed to combat the problems it had initially defined. If it succeeded it defining which problems it would address—which missions it would accept—then its members would develop experience primarily in those missions and skill sets and would feel more strongly that they had identified the right ones.[19]

The officer's ideal of leadership and war: "Lundy's Lane," 1814, from Richardson, *Messages and Papers of the Presidents* (1903).

Nineteenth-century military professionalism did not develop independent of state or society, nor was it simply a matter of growing expertise in the art of conventional warfare. Government control meant government prodding, a pressure that officers frequently resisted, while their own proposals for reform were always subject to cost-conscious civilian review. The criteria of professionalism were the subject of constant if often tacit dispute between the advocates of socially elite "character" and leadership—inherently ascriptive and subjective—and the advocates of specialized and implicitly middle-class education and expertise—achievements that were at least theoretically measurable by standards applied to all aspirants. Sometimes governments pushed for the primacy of one or the other, but the mass of officers, especially those serving in regiments and central headquarters, saw character and esprit de corps as the indispensable moral underpinnings of internal cohesion, battlefield effectiveness, and political accountability. Since the development of distributed maneuver—maneuver by autonomous but coordinated formations to set up and exploit battles—during the Napoleonic era, analysts of military affairs have privileged "operational maneuver" and the operational art it is said to embody as the essence of conventional war fighting. By the 1980s, the crucial role of operations in linking tactical engagements and strategic intent led military officers to idealize the operational level, which is often viewed as the most intellectually challenging of the three levels of war (tactical, operational, and strategic) because it combines the specificity of tactics and the abstraction of strategy. Such complex coordination requires a great deal of the specialized expertise and extended abstract study (rather than on-the-job training) associated with professionalism, and the planning and conduct of large-scale operational maneuver was the forte of the Prussian and German general staff, the prototype for modern military coordination.

Nevertheless, however important Prussian developments were for the future of interstate war after midcentury, fears of Bonapartism in western European nations, and of social and political revolution in central Europe and Russia, conditioned debate about the character of European military establishments throughout the nineteenth century. The consensus among European elites in favor of the rigidly hierarchical status quo meant that systemic wars posing a major threat to national existence or the continental balance of power were unlikely to recur. Therefore, most debates about military reform turned more on internal considerations of political reliability than external ones of military efficiency. Loyalty to the standing order was ultimately far more important to social and political elites, including military officers themselves, than the development of military expertise per se; they feared that the triumph of technical specialists—implicit, in the most important example, in the era of Prussian reform between 1807 and 1819—might mean the disestablishment of privileged social classes and the derangement of the social and political order. The Prussian system of higher military education has long been held up for praise and emulation, and recent historians have emphasized the vitality of military reform movements in France and Britain. Yet the criteria of European military professionalism remained fundamentally social and subjective, elitist and ascriptive, rather than achievement based throughout the decades between Waterloo and the Crimean War. All officer corps, even that of bourgeois France, espoused a heroic or agonistic conception of warfare where honor— consisting of intangibles like chivalry, gallantry, and courage—was the most important value. To these men, professional success or failure seemed immeasurable save by the post facto judgment of combat itself. In the interim, the association between these subjective values and the landed classes and the aristocracy constrained officer selection, sustaining officer corps whose social composition and political values reinforced class hierarchy, even as the growing industrial working classes protested its injustice.[20]

Within armies, as Edward Spiers observes of the British, "preserving the esprit de corps of the regimental system was deemed the essence of military efficiency." Discipline and its supporting values of hierarchy, order, and cohesion seemed indispensable, given the physical and psychological chaos of the battlefield; the prevailing middle- and upper-class attitudes toward the working classes, which provided the bulk of enlisted men; and the possibility—

indeed, the probability, outside of Britain—that these troops would be deployed to coerce or kill their erstwhile fellows. After a quarter century of egalitarian revolution, middle- and upper-class European officers did not trust their men's initiative in battle or riot any more than they had during the era of Frederick the Great half a century before. Critical thinking seemed to lead to uncertainty and unrest, and the antidotes to military and political chaos remained subjective, class-derived character and morale, not matters of independent individual intellect or the quasi-objective efficiency of purely "military" expertise. Nineteenth-century officers were gradually compelled to address the evolving distinction between mind (character) and matter (technique) and the related phenomenon of remote, apparently unwilled causation. Yet it seemed difficult to adapt to these challenges without losing the institutional-occupational autonomy and sociopolitical accountability to elite rule that underlay the authority of command; European officers largely succeeded in ignoring that dilemma, ultimately to their detriment and that of the empires they defended.[21]

The officer corps of these European armies—to which American officers looked for examples of war-fighting expertise—presented widely varying pictures of expertise and cohesion, including the standardization of administrative procedures, but all of them save the French remained fundamentally subordinate to the political institutions of their social classes (the aristocracy and other elites). (The French army became an antidemocratic force after the 1830s, in large part due to its demoralization in Algeria.) Since these regimes were substantially undemocratic, and since the maintenance of elite class dominance and empire was a prominent factor boxing Europe into systemic war and catastrophe in 1914, this sense of responsibility and the resulting political accountability should concern us as much as any of the more specifically military developments in Europe. Yet the damaging role of the Prusso-German military in Wilhelmine-Hohenzollern constitutionalism and civil-military relations writ large was virtually invisible in Huntington's theory of "objective civil-military relations." It is highly debatable whether Prusso-German civilian control—to the degree civilians actually controlled the military—*was* objective: the rationale for executive (monarchical) control was as much to maintain social order—the order in which the army held so much prestige and authority—as to ensure national defense. Nowhere is Huntington's failure as a historian more clear than in his praise for the Prussian example (though supposedly in contrast to the Nazi one) as the epitome of successful civil-military relations. Whether the crisis was in 1848, 1914, or 1918, Huntington should not have needed to read Gordon Craig's *Politics of the Prussian Army* to recognize that something was not right with German military professionalism, long before the indisputably subjective civil-military relations of the Nazi era.

Nor did that professionalism suffice when Germany faced the international coalition its civil and military leaders feared. The First World War demonstrated the limits of the narrowly specialized expertise developed by professional military leaders, particularly the Germans that Huntington acclaims as his exemplars of objective civil-military relations. Attention to technical details and effectiveness in military tactics and operations—war fighting—trumped consideration of alternative national strategies or diplomacy in prewar plans for mobilization, deployment, and operations. Confidence in war-fighting prowess obscured strategic constraints and indeed the very objectives of warfare. Trying to avoid a stalemate and a long war they knew they could not sustain, senior European military commanders effectively tied the hands of their civilian rulers by presenting their plans for mobilization, deployment, and initial operations as faits accomplis that could not be altered without dooming the nation to catastrophic defeat. Nor did the autonomy to develop professional expertise actually produce tactical or operational asymmetries sufficiently decisive to overcome the constraints of scale and defensive technology when nineteenth-century military professionalism faced its supreme test in 1914. (However, we should acknowledge that the tactical dilemmas presented by growing scale and defensive firepower were to some degree intractable, given the technological limits of communications and mobility.)

Huntington's theory encouraged and appeared to intellectually validate a very present-minded, often very inflexible definition of military missions and expertise. Huntington and, more importantly, the Cold War and post–Cold War military officers and historians who found his work so congenial identified their principal mission as what is often called *war fighting*—primarily, defense against high-intensity conventional (or nuclear) attack by large-scale, essentially symmetrical forces serving other nation-states, akin to the recent world wars. Doing so was not at all unreasonable in 1960, given the devastating experience of world war and the intense ideological antagonisms between states possessing immense military forces with the power to subjugate or destroy entire nations. Yet Huntington's followers often attempted to define the threat in perpetuity, to resist acknowledging that historical circumstances change. They tended to depict any non-war-fighting missions, and often unconventional war-fighting ones like counterinsurgency, as "subjective"— that is, partisan, ideological, and unpredictable—civilian interference that would distract the profession from preparing to fight and win the nation's wars. They not infrequently implied that military leaders were right to resist developing new skill sets. The result was a wave of cognitive dissonance and uncertainty when the Soviet Union collapsed.

The argument widely expressed during the last generation—that the U.S. Army's core mission is to fight and win the nation's wars—appears innocuous enough. Yet choosing to specialize in that mission while making *war fighting* a moral buzzword, to the de facto and sometimes explicit exclusion of other missions and skill sets, ultimately amounts to an appropriation of the political decision to provide the army with mission taskings—"shirking," in the words of political scientist Peter Feaver, echoing Huntington's contemporary Samuel Finer. The assumptions (which are internally logical) are that society needs the military to fight large-scale wars to protect vital national interests and ensure national survival, and that multitasking degrades the efficiency encouraged by specialization in a single core function. Army officers have been making this argument for 200 years, not infrequently confusing past and present, history and personal preference, in their efforts—which all claimants to professional status make—to find a usable past.[22]

The predispositions of many officers and military historians notwithstanding, war-fighting expertise, particularly of the conventional sort, is not the most valid criterion for evaluating military professionalism in all historical or contemporary circumstances. Nor, of course, should we privilege counterinsurgency, irregular or unconventional warfare, operations other than war, or "stability and support" operations as "complex operations" that are somehow more challenging than large-scale conventional maneuver, as too many officers and civilian analysts are wont to do today. In either case, too many students and military practitioners misuse sociologist Andrew Abbott's innovative work on professional "jurisdiction" over missions and skill sets to attempt to shape current military professionalism in a predetermined manner, not as a tool for analysis or to respond effectively to the strategic concerns of civilian authorities. Indeed, these officers and scholars embody Abbott's arguments about professional self-aggrandizement through self- and problem definition. Technique supplants politics, means displace ends. Yet the question of professional mission and utility ultimately depends on the audience or constituency a profession claims to serve. Different varieties of expertise may be most relevant to the missions demanded by society and its political representatives at a particular point in time. At some early points in professional development, commitment and the consequent cohesion may be most important to professionalization, as William Skelton's work suggests; alternatively, responsibility to society's demands may be most significant, which is my own take for the period covered by this book. Thus, although much of *Jackson's Sword* demonstrates the remarkable autonomy of military professionals and the state in nineteenth-century America, the historically specific content and development of American military professionalism depended on the contingent, historically specific social context of that era: what did society want from those who claimed professional status? This was and is an inherently and inescapably *political* question, though it does not have to be a partisan one.[23]

As historian Michael Geyer observes of the Prussians, "it was the fragmentary condition of army reform rather than the complete remaking of the army, the simultaneous and [often] incoherent presence of multiple directions within the army and in the relations between army and society, that characterized the condition of the [Prusso-German] military in the first half of the nineteenth century. It took nearly half a century . . . to put the various elements of partial change together" to form a professionally capable—but hardly a professionally responsible—army. To observe that the U.S. Army lagged behind its European counterparts in preparations for large-scale or high-intensity conventional operations or that its bureaucracy was rigid does not mean that it was incapable of performing the missions it was actually assigned. In fact, the army proved an extremely successful agent of American power projection in the nation's decisive international conflicts—the war with Mexico and the Civil War—prior to 1898; to judge it based on its preparation for intervention in Europe or Asia—the only missions that would justify comparisons with Prusso-German developments—is highly anachronistic. Late nineteen-century army officers sought Prussian-style reform, but we can certainly question, as many contemporaries did, whether their initiatives suited American geostrategic realities.[24]

Yet the ahistorical presumption that the essence of military professionalism is expertise in conventional war fighting continues to drive the analyses and determine the conclusions of very capable historians, who are often looking forward to the Civil War or the United States' world role in the twentieth century rather than analyzing the antebellum era on its own terms. Most arguments that the army did not professionalize until after the Civil War ultimately depend on a narrow and, indeed, anachronistic definition of military professionalism as preparation for major conventional wars. Yet the scholarship of the past generation suggests otherwise: the commitment, persistence, and cohesion William Skelton demonstrates; the administrative and logistic skill, autonomy, and accountability historian Mark Wilson explores; and the actual evidence of expertise and capability in a variety of missions provided by these and other recent scholars like Durwood Ball, Wayne Hsieh, Mark Smith, and Robert Wooster. Scholars may search for evidence of preparation for a conventional civil war, but that was not the mission the American political nation gave the army. Overawing whites and Indians on the frontier was the regular army officer's primary purpose before 1861—that was the political and historical reality. Officers may have wanted to fight the British, but that was not the mission for which the government paid them tax dollars. It is fundamentally ahistorical to judge their actions, priorities, expertise, or performance as if their duty was to prepare for the Civil War or World War II.[25]

In the nineteenth-century U.S. Army, as in most armies, there were multiple professionalisms: expertise in conventional war fighting, which most officers preferred to develop because of its apparent political simplicity and potential for earning civilian applause, and expertise in constabulary or stability operations—peacekeeping and law enforcement—to name the most basic categories. (*Constabulary* operations is a vague term, but it may be less likely to mislead than the terms *peacekeeping* and *stability* operations, which imply an ethnocentric, sometimes morally objectionable American perspective. See appendix D for an outline of these types of operations on the nineteenth-century frontier.) Superficially, the distinction in expertise was embodied by the contrast between Winfield Scott, who built on a European inheritance to "conquer a peace" in Mexico, and Edmund Pendleton Gaines, Jackson's protégé and Scott's rival, who presented himself as an Indian fighter (until he came to disagree with Jackson's removal policy) and a practical man of the frontier. Yet in reality, Scott and Gaines both fought against the British in 1814, while Scott spent most of his "operational time" handling border crises as a diplomat—perhaps a third form of American military expertise in the nineteenth century, if it could be distinguished from constabulary, stability, or peacekeeping operations. As fondly as officers liked to imagine themselves gallantly outmaneuvering British opponents in a rematch of the War of 1812, the European threat proved much less urgent than frontier peacekeeping and law enforcement missions, where diplomacy and shows of force, rather than combat operations, were the principal instruments of national policy.[26]

Although they lacked a permanent strategic and operational planning staff after the Prusso-German model, nineteenth-century American civil and military policy makers did possess strategic visions and a military strategy for peace enforcement on the Indian frontier: the full range of coercive diplomacy, followed, if necessary, by violent power projection through punitive expeditions, material destruction, and battle. One might even argue that they inherited an operational tradition, or a sense of operational art, to guide and provide alternatives for operations against Native American groups. But—and this is a key *but*—that strategy, that operational tradition, required diplomatic, logistical, and tactical skills (roughly in that order of chronology and significance) much more than proficiency in large-scale distributed maneuver à la Moltke or Napoleon. Given these missions and their demands, my bibliography contains far more books on the British and Russian armies and empires, whose missions were roughly similar to those of the U.S. Army, than on the Prusso-German or even the French ones (despite their influence on nineteenth-century American military education).

Before assessing expertise and capability, which can vary so greatly by circumstances, we should recognize that every society wants its professionals to have some sense of responsibility and reliability; society needs some reason to trust them with the power of their expertise and the autonomy to employ it. This is particularly true of the military—the "armed services"—which are funded by governments to serve as their instruments. Governments create armies because they believe they need a *reliable* as well as a capable coercive instrument. The need for expertise—or, more specifically, effectiveness—in performance may be the reason professionalism comes into being, but that does not make it the *defining* criterion of professionalism, regardless of historical context. Since the seventeenth century, few governments have been willing to entrust control over an armed force to armies they have not created themselves. Thus, officers supply themselves in response to a demand not just for a certain set of services requiring a certain expertise but also for subordination, accountability, and responsibility in the performance of those services. Mercenaries were expert but not necessarily reliable. Noblemen and knights may have been expert, at least in individual combat, but they were often unreliable; many considered their individual interests as important as those of their sovereigns and were loath to accept subordination or incorporation into larger units. Indeed, most of the world's military history suggests that such subordination has been a necessary prelude to effective "national defense" (whatever the actual size of the political community in question) against foreign enemies, while its absence has often proved a threat to domestic tranquility and social peace. It is no accident that federal employees swear oaths to uphold the Constitution "against all enemies, foreign and domestic."

My interest in *Jackson's Sword* is not primarily in the supposed objectivity or subjectivity of civilian control over the military: my concern is with the objectivity (emotional detachment or, perhaps in some instances, impartiality) or subjectivity of the military in its relations to society, its sense of mission, subordination, and responsibility to those it is supposed to serve.

The militia—a caricature that regular officers could appreciate, by Edward Williams Clay, 1829. (Courtesy Library of Congress, LC-USZC4-11864)

Emphasizing professional responsibility—the primacy of context and mission, the necessity of conforming means to ends, expertise to mission, and supply to demand—may not suit those who believe that the "management of violence" means combat, particularly the conduct of large-scale distributed maneuver. But, as historians William Skelton and Mark Grandstaff have intimated, it provides a much more historically accurate explanation of how the regular army officer corps' claim to professional status and a degree of autonomy in the performance of its missions became accepted by American society and its representative constitutional authorities during the supposedly rampant egalitarianism of the Jacksonian era. Emphasizing responsibility also provides a more accurate understanding of the army's historical missions and skill sets and the complex, multivariate, and multilinear trajectory of American military professionalism in the nineteenth century and the twenty-first. The army officer corps of the Jacksonian and antebellum eras was professional in its socialization, commitment, and cohesion as an occupational group; in its autonomy, expertise, and effectiveness in the missions it was assigned; and in its responsibility, subordination, and accountability to constitutional civilian government and most civilian political norms. As such, the officer corps met all of Huntington's criteria for military professionalism, without the sociopolitical isolation he thought necessary for professional development.

THE LIMITS OF THE CITIZEN-SOLDIER IN MILITARY
OPERATIONS SHORT OF WAR: *JACKSON'S SWORD*
AS A STUDY IN PROFESSIONAL MONOPOLY

Ironically, Jacksonian Democrats and other decentralist politicians, who often
condemned the national standing army, compelled it to remain focused on
continental expansion and domestic constabulary or pacification missions,
such as armed diplomacy and peacekeeping along the Native American frontier, rather than preparing for interstate war. The army did so with remarkable success and no small degree of autonomy. The form and content of the
officer corps' professionalism varied widely, depending on the circumstances
and issues; its greatest success lay in the development of accountability to civilian political control, centralized in the nation-state. In turn, employment by
the nation-state was indispensable to the regular officer corps and its professionalization project because this sponsorship enabled the army to carve out a
legal position that was unavailable to other occupations aspiring to professional status in the face of Jacksonian antagonism toward monopoly.

Thomas Jefferson's first inaugural address is often employed as an epigram
demonstrating American adherence to the citizen-soldier ideal. The president
applauded "a well-disciplined militia"—which he knew from experience it was
not—as "our best reliance in peace and for the first moments of war," but
only "till regulars may relieve them." Thus, in practice, Jefferson relied on the
national standing army for the occupation of Louisiana and its defense during the Sabine River confrontation with Spain and the Burr crisis in 1806. He
tripled the size of the national standing army he had reduced in 1802 in order
to enforce his embargo and prepare for conflict with Britain. Madison followed suit during the War of 1812, while using the prewar standing force to
occupy western Florida; afterward, Monroe employed that army to intimidate
Spain to give up the rest of that peninsula. Monroe also relied on the standing
force to occupy critical posts in the Upper Mississippi and Missouri Valleys,
and his successors did so to protect the trade of the Santa Fe Trail. As president, Jackson relied primarily on national forces during Indian removal and
the consequent wars, augmenting the army by nearly 20 percent.[27]

Following Huntington's lead, Stephen Skowronek envisioned the army's
missions almost entirely in terms of large-scale conventional conflict against
symmetrical interstate adversaries, leading him to assert that "the backbone
of the American army was a locally based militia system," the only system available or feasible for raising such a force in nineteenth-century America. Yet in
practice, this was true only during the Civil War; it was not even remotely true

of western territorial expansion either before or after the Civil War or of offensive operations during the War of 1812 and the war with Mexico. To take the most important example, contrary to popular belief, apart from Buena Vista (a single defensive battle) and the small-scale campaign in Chihuahua, the war with Mexico was fought primarily by preexisting regular army units. (The First Dragoon Regiment shared the conquest of New Mexico and California, small-scale campaigns, with volunteers and the navy.) Only three of the twenty-five American regiments in the decisive Mexico City campaign were state volunteer units; fourteen were units of the antebellum standing army—virtually its entire force—and another was composed of federal marines led by Lieutenant Colonel Samuel Watson (no relation to the author). Seven were regular army regiments raised for the war; their officers, largely Democrats, were raised through state patronage machines, but they were commissioned by the federal government, subject to federal military law, and under the command of one of the most self-consciously professional American soldiers, Winfield Scott.[28]

By the 1830s, Secretary of War Lewis Cass, an experienced frontiersman and populist Democratic politician, openly admitted to Congress that citizen-soldiers were not "our most important means" of defense in any conflict short of large-scale war (meaning with Britain). President Martin Van Buren relied on national troops in the Second Seminole War and as peacekeepers during the Canadian border crises, for which Congress created a new regiment; James K. Polk did so to protect the Oregon Trail (creating another new regiment) and in the war with Mexico. Franklin Pierce did the same amid the violence in Bleeding Kansas and on the Texas Indian frontier, increasing the army more than 25 percent, and James Buchanan continued the pattern in Kansas and the expedition to assert U.S. sovereignty over the Mormons in Utah. Most slave unrest and localized maroonage (armed resistance to slavery, usually after flight) was repressed by militias or vigilantes, but two army officers, one a thirty-year veteran and the other a recent West Point graduate, led a contingent of marines to seize John Brown at Harpers Ferry.[29]

Often confusing regulars with the militia and volunteers, whose officers were usually appointed through political patronage, many authors depict the regular officer corps as politicized in terms of commissioning and promotion, with limited commitment or career persistence. Skelton's *An American Profession of Arms* refutes this with indisputable documentation, but his findings have not overcome this received wisdom. Most authors, including some students of the antebellum army who should know better, still write as if seniority did not dominate promotions, as if the majority (rather than a quarter) of the officer corps was commissioned directly from civilian life on partisan grounds, or as if the statistics Skelton painstakingly developed on career persistence and the rarity of resignation do not exist. Politics did influence the selection of officers for command, but not nearly as comprehensively as many think. Arthur P. Wade has argued that prior to 1900, most general officers were commissioned as generals directly from civil life without prior military training, education, or socialization. This was certainly true in the Revolutionary War (of course), the War of 1812 and the mobilization that preceded it, and even (by a slight majority) the war with Mexico and the Civil War. Yet Wade himself points out that the command of the peacetime army, constrained in size and rank by Congress, was almost entirely the province of long-serving regular officers, usually colonels with brevet (honorary) rank as brigadier generals. (Brevet rank was employed so that officers could command forces larger than their permanent ranks would normally allow, sometimes in order to deploy an officer who would outrank militia or volunteer competitors. The president and secretary of war normally supported this stratagem, precisely because they valued professional efficiency and reliability.) And as Skelton has made clear in his analysis of "High Army Leadership in the Era of the War of 1812," the men promoted to general rank in 1813 and 1814 were overwhelmingly officers of the prewar army who had risen to prominence through their meritorious wartime service.[30]

We should also remember that presidents usually relied on recommendations from other politicians for patronage appointments, which became a source of factional conflict and division as well as reward. In the worst case, a commander appointed via patronage or from the militia would pursue state, regional, or sectional interests contrary to national policy—as Andrew Jackson did during several of the operations explored in this book. Thus, career army officers, increasingly and ultimately predominantly graduates of the national Military Academy at West Point, held most strategic and operational commands throughout the nineteenth century. This was the case in the Second Seminole War, when the territorial governor of Florida, a War of 1812 veteran, was replaced as theater commander by regular army Quartermaster General Thomas Sidney Jesup, a veteran of that war who had remained in national military service. President Polk pressed a more open challenge to the professional direction of the war with Mexico, but he was unable to secure sufficient congressional support to replace Winfield Scott with senator and political ally Thomas Hart Benton. Indeed, all the theater commanders—Scott, Zachary Taylor, and Stephen W. Kearny—were regulars, and Taylor and Scott usually assigned the most difficult and important tactical missions to their regular subordinates.

Varying missions and skill sets aside, the acid test of any issue in nineteenth-

The reality of military frontier diplomacy: Stephen H. Long negotiates with the Oto and Pawnee Indians, 1819, by H. Charles McBarron. (Courtesy Army Art Collection)

century American military history remains its outcome or influence in the Civil War. Even in 1861, no one believed that mobilization would be as limited as it had been in 1812 and 1846; the enthusiasm of citizens on both sides led to mass volunteering, with larger forces mobilized and trained in 1861 than in the three wars with Britain and Mexico put together. Although regular army commanders like Scott attempted to preserve the cohesion and integrity of the peacetime army (fearing partisan politicization), junior officers (lieutenants, captains, and a few majors) seized the opportunity to gain rapid promotion by transferring to the volunteer regiments organized in the states. There were certainly plenty of "political generals" commissioned directly from civil life, and they usually had substantial leadership experience in inspiring and coordinating supporters. Yet Military Academy graduates, who made up 75 percent of the army's officers in 1860—probably the highest proportion in history—commanded most theaters, districts, departments, armies, and corps and eventually the majority of divisions throughout the conflict, and they almost completely supplanted political generals in the command of theater- and army-level formations by its end. Although the direct commission of civilian politicians or other civilians with political influence would continue until World War I, long-serving professional officers developed military strategy and directed the operational employment of national military force throughout the nineteenth century.[31]

Nor was the national standing army in any way subordinate to citizen-soldier forces, which its officers consistently commanded when citizen-soldiers were mobilized. Citizen-soldiers may have proved adequate to maintain white supremacy in the South, but they failed to advance the frontier of white territorial expansion, which was essential to the Jeffersonian and Jacksonian social visions. Consequently, the army's Jacksonian critics produced a lot of smoke but very little fire. The army was reduced in force in 1815 and 1821—essentially after the end of the undeclared war with Spain examined in *Jackson's Sword*—and after the war with Mexico, the Civil War, the world wars, the Korean War, the Vietnam War, and the end of the Cold War, but prior to Vietnam, the army virtually always came out larger than before it went to war. The 1821 reduction, essentially returning the army to its enlisted strength from a decade before, was the only exception, but even then, a disproportionately large number of officers were retained. Apart from these postwar reductions in force, careers in the regular army, particularly those of commissioned officers, have been virtually tenured, given good behavior: no more than a handful of officers have been discharged for reasons other than malfeasance during peacetime since 1821. The permanent army was augmented in 1832, 1836, 1838, 1846, and 1855, a growth of more than 70 percent in its number of regiments (and even more in the officer corps, because the staff was increased substantially in 1838), half occurring prior to the war with Mexico. In every case except for 1838, these augmentations were for western missions; in every single case, they were undertaken by Jacksonian Democrats who professed to fear or resent the national standing army. Scholars who see nothing but the retreat of state authority during the Jacksonian era are ignoring a significant area of state autonomy and power; they do not and cannot explain the central role played by professional military officers in the mobilization, supply, and strategic and operational direction of American military forces during the nineteenth century as well as the twentieth. Nor can they explain the actual process of U.S. territorial expansion and the expropriation of Native America.[32]

AUTONOMY, ACCOUNTABILITY, AND LONG-TERM IMPACT: *JACKSON'S SWORD* AS A STUDY IN BORDERLANDS AND DIPLOMATIC HISTORY

Nor have American foreign relations, whether diplomatic or military, been exempt from "weak state" interpretations privileging private and nonstate actors. The role of interstate competition and war is a commonplace in studies of European state formation, but with few exceptions outside military and diplomatic history, it has been insignificant or absent in the study of early- and mid-nineteenth-century American history. Yet the early American state was especially active in the realm of international relations, continental as well as transatlantic. The common public interest and elite leadership embodied in classical republicanism came together with the security concerns, liberal self-interest, and ethnocultural democracy (democracy for white men) expressed in territorial expansion to the south and west. The specialized division of labor characteristic of liberal capitalism meant that the democratic majority was no more capable of routine attention to the allocation and distribution of power and resources in the international arena than in the domestic one. Much as the majority turned to the new political and communications professionals—partisan politicians and newspaper editors—to represent their interests in the domestic political economy, they were compelled to rely heavily on another developing profession—the officer corps of the national standing army—to mediate and advance their interests in the international political economy of the North American continent. The navy performed much the same role outside the continent, although its deployments far from the oversight of American law and politics made its dynamics more akin to the imperial operations of European armies.[33]

Yet growing scholarly attention to the concepts of borderlands and "middle grounds" has aggravated rather than remedied the interpretive lacunae of "weak state" arguments. The original middle ground, as conceived by historian Richard White, was created by diverse white-Indian interactions sheltered by a balance of military power in the Upper Great Lakes region; it ended with the coming of American dominance, embodied in British retreat after the War of 1812 and the arrival of the U.S. Army, followed by massive civilian settlement. As Howard Lamar and Leonard Thompson point out in a comparison of North America and South Africa, "it took the united national power of the United States to defeat the Indians." Private, nonstate actors—settlers and railroads—motivated by individual or corporate profit were not a "united national power"; the national power united against Native America was state mobilized, state funded, state directed, and quintessentially military. Yet the destruction of successive middle grounds, the dominance of successive borderlands, and the conquest reemphasized by "new western historians" like Patricia Nelson Limerick have not led to a greater examination of the role of national military forces by historians in general, who prefer to examine the agency, diversity, and fluidity of middle grounds rather than the processes that brought them under American hegemony.[34]

The concept of borderlands presents similar dilemmas: most historians contrast borderlands with borders per se, using local and multicultural forces and influences as focal points, whereas those of nation-states and empires are refracted and diffused, if not deplored outright as hierarchical and oppressive. Yet borderlands are not synonymous with multicultural middle grounds; they are regions where nation-states and empires meet and compete, as in the Gulf of Mexico and its shores or the Canadian borderlands. Nor are borderlands the same as ethnocultural frontiers within the boundaries claimed by states and empires. Students of state formation and borderlands recognize that margins and peripheries can be just as significant to a nation and state as its center or core. Borders, which are internationally recognized as defensible with lethal force, are as significant an expression or measure of state power as can be found, particularly in preindustrial, prebureaucratic, prewelfare states. Borders define the limits of frontiers, not as zones but as boundaries of legal orders and action, of sovereignty and the putative state monopoly over legitimate violence. As historical sociologist Anthony Giddens observes, true borders "are only found with the emergence of nation-states." Without established borders, the sovereignty of the nation-state is open to competition and challenge not just from other nations and states but also from its own populace, which may seek to establish alternative political organizations and centers and ultimately alternative polities through migration or secession. Whether advancing or restraining settlers' interests, the frontier diplomats of the national standing army diminished the autonomy of nonstate actors and helped preclude secessionist challenges during the Jacksonian era.[35]

A more specific, power-centered concept of borderlands would be to see them as zones of imperial contact and competition, centered around territorial claims. An example would be the "Gulf South" borderlands during the 1780s and 1790s, where Spain claimed most of modern Mississippi and Alabama and much of Georgia and Tennessee, while the United States sought direct access to the Gulf of Mexico, whether by means of a right of transit through New Orleans or territorial control along the coast. Borderlands of this sort shifted with diplomatic agreements and the military balance of power: when the United States secured control of New Orleans, the Gulf borderlands became western Louisiana, still claimed by Spain; eastern Texas, invaded by American citizens and threatened by the army; and western Florida, claimed (however disingenuously) by the United States. After 1803 all the parties in Louisiana and Texas—the United States, Spain, and Mexico—had a sense of a border; they recognized the existence of different sovereignties, however weak in practice, on either side, and they adjusted their activities to take advantage of or reduce the effects of that border. The border shaped their options, decisions, and actions; it structured their opportunities and their agency.

The Gulf became even more of a borderland with the rebellions against Spanish rule after 1808. It ceased to be a borderland, at least between the United States and Spain, only when Spain gave up Florida and the United States recognized the Spanish claim to Texas in 1821. Yet the region remained unsettled, with the American South from Louisiana to Georgia constituting a frontier, or a set of distinct but connected frontiers, in the Turnerian sense of ethnocultural contact and friction. Texas extended that frontier zone for Anglo-Americans immigrating at Mexican invitation, but the areas along the Red and Sabine River borders remained borderlands in the sense of incomplete pacification by the nation-states on either side. Meanwhile, the Indians and maroons of Florida maintained contacts with Indians, maroons, and Spaniards in Cuba and the Bahamas. Since the first decade of the nineteenth century, a borderland had started to develop in what is now Oklahoma, manifested most concretely in the Santa Fe Trail after Spanish trade regulations ended in 1821. This borderland involved something much more akin to a middle ground with the Osage, the Pawnee, a wide range of Texan Indians, and above all the Comanche, who raided Mexico while trading with American citizens.

Under the federal territorial system, the process of geographic expansion was one of nation-state formation and societal integration, as well as extending the existing pattern of local self-government and regional or sectional political cultures. Territorial growth contained the potential both for social reproduction in the decentralized agrarian mode envisioned by the Jeffersonians and Jacksonians and for the institutional elaboration and political consolidation of a more powerful, authoritative nation-state as envisioned by the Federalists, National Republicans, and Whigs. Throughout the course of this process, the central government and its agents were constantly forced to reckon with the expansive—and potentially explosive—demands and actions of a mushrooming frontier population that could not be regulated and was capable of withholding its sanction from national policies or reshaping them in pursuit of local objectives. Yet despite the supposed weakness of American state power, and despite American individualism, libertarianism, and federalism—or perhaps, some would argue, partly because of that federalism—no substantial competitor states appeared in the interstices of the North American borderlands. With the exception of Texas (for less than a decade in duration), no sustained alternatives to the United States appeared among its millions of settler-citizens as they moved across the continent. Indeed, if we compare the thirty-year periods before and after 1815, we see a general shift from borderlands and middle grounds—regions or zones populated by a medley of native, nonstate, and civilian actors in which no one group was dominant—to frontiers shaped and often dominated by white, state, and military actors.

An examination of the officer corps in the borderlands can serve as a valuable exercise in the study of diplomatic history, American foreign policy and international relations, and nineteenth-century imperialism. During the last twenty years, American diplomatic historians have called for renewed attention to the foreign relations of the early republic and for the extension of our historical vision to include groups and individuals not usually examined in traditional studies of interstate diplomacy. The borderlands were a site of intersection between domestic and international, state and society, public and private, political and civil, a site of contestation not only between nation-states but also between racial-ethnic formations and sub- or nonstate and sub- or nonnational polities and societies. Though not formal policy makers, military officers served as "men on spot," exercising substantial and sometimes decisive discretionary influence over the implementation and final shape of national policy; they were mediators between local and national as well as international interests—the center *in* the periphery. Examining the national army officer corps in the borderlands therefore provides a study of governance—the practice of government and the execution of policy—in a middle ground or field of action between the reified, overly cohesive abstractions of traditional political and diplomatic history and the extreme diversity of social history. Focusing on the officer corps enables an analysis of policy execution closer to actual outcomes than would be possible with a focus on ideas, public opinion, or legislation. By exploring officers' language, we can exploit linguistic as well as material approaches to causation. But attention to policy implementation is necessary to close the circle of cause, effect, and response between the large structures of international relations, national politics, and ideology and the diverse agencies of borderlands inhabitants. As mediators between national policy and these diverse inhabitants, the officer corps was a significant contingent force.[36]

Military officers also played a more abstract sociocultural role as representatives of the national center; they represented gentility, education, science, and cosmopolitanism, as well as extralocal resources obtainable through political influence rather than the exchange of scarce economic assets. Indeed, they served not only as agents of the national government in international relations but also as agents of cultural as well as national stabilization, pacification, consolidation, and rationalization in the largest sense. As Giddens has remarked, the national professional standing army is the "correlate," if not necessarily the precondition, "of [an] internally pacified state-class relationship," or of sustained internal sociocultural pacification in the form adumbrated by Norbert Elias. Or, as Max Weber once asserted, "[modern] military discipline is the ideal model for the modern capitalist factory, as [ancient military discipline] was for ancient plantation." William Skelton has suggested that "social control [in the larger sense] was the *raison d'être* of the early army." Though overt social control was no longer the army's raison d'être after 1815, it certainly remained one of its most significant roles and often one of its missions, whether implicit or explicit, in the borderlands.[37]

The army's constabulary duties in the borderlands call attention to the roles of nonstate actors, especially the nation's own citizens, who challenged U.S. sovereignty far more often than nation-state competitors. Attention to the officer corps' work in the borderlands thus underscores divisions within as well as between nations and nation-states: the United States was not a fully unified actor in international relations on the continental or Atlantic stage. In particular, a borderlands approach highlights the role of racial-ethnic factors and American federalism, the pressure of white man's or herrenvolk democracy, and the projection of tensions (particularly class tensions) from within white society onto racial-ethnic "others."[38] Yet in comparison to the aggressively expansionist, sometimes strategically irresponsible or insubordinate behavior of British, French, and Russian officers stationed in India, Africa, and Asia, the U.S. Army exhibited a far greater degree of subordination and accountability to civilian control. In the process, by both aid and restraint, "the army helped to cement [the] loyalties of frontiersmen on the far-flung borderlands" to the nation, resulting in a larger, more abstract scale of allegiance and a more centralized entity than autonomous settlement would have produced.[39] Viewed from the centralist and often openly authoritarian perspective of officers charged with enforcing federal sovereignty, the most immediate product of territorial expansion usually seemed to be social entropy and disorder. As the most visible and potent agents of national power, army officers repeatedly had to confront and constrain aggressive private initiatives along the borders, often in the face of criticism from politicians from frontier regions. As armed mediators among so many interests, these frontier diplomats engaged in all the varieties of diplomacy recently conceptualized by political scientists and historians: armed and coercive diplomacy, "local" diplomacy, federal diplomacy, and the diplomacy of union.[40]

In a federal system, which issues are national, which are international, which are regional, and which are local? Who decides? To quote a leading historian of an earlier European empire, the result of American expansion was "a ramshackle empire, maybe, as most empires are." Yet the United States was an empire, with sufficient military power to expand without dissolving for more than half a century and then reunite by force—under the command of the career professional officers of the national standing army—after the secession of the slaveholding states. John Quincy Adams captured the paradox of the American federal empire, for better or worse, days after the defense of Fort McHenry in 1814: "I cannot imagine a possible state of [the] world for futurity in which the United States shall not be a great naval and military power. Between that and the dissolution of the Union there is no alternative."[41]

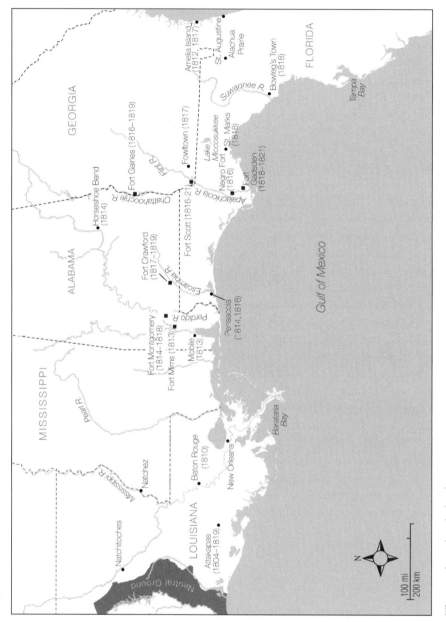

The southern borderlands

1

CONFIDENCE, BELLIGERENCE, AND INSUBORDINATION

Army Operations along the Texan and Maritime Frontiers of Louisiana, 1810–1814

For the United States, one of the most urgent problems posed by the breakup of Spain's American empire was the proliferation of armed nonstate actors and the potential that small but autonomous polities would appear along the nation's southern rim. These actors and polities might provide opportunities and pretexts for the intervention of stronger European powers—most dangerously, Britain—and the establishment of European military positions, constraining U.S. expansion and threatening incursions in time of war. In the Gulf South, such bases would attract fugitive slaves, and they could be used to encourage slave uprisings and maroonage during war. Even without European intervention, new polities might draw off American settlers, as Spain had attempted to do during the 1780s and 1790s with Kentucky, weakening the southern frontier economy and southern frontier defense. Even without the establishment of autonomous polities, the pervasive presence of armed nonstate actors—commonly U.S. citizens—meant privateering, smuggling, filibustering (armed incursions across international boundaries without state sanction), freebooting, and piracy. Filibustering, banditry, and marauding threatened the United States' legitimacy in the eyes of cautious citizens as well as European powers and neighbors.[1]

Maintaining control over international borders, and of U.S. citizens along those borders, was crucial to upholding U.S. sovereignty and preventing the development of rivals to U.S. authority in the Gulf borderlands. The challenges to American sovereignty and power are well known: the West Florida rebellion in 1810; the West Florida filibusters against Spanish-held territory, particularly around Mobile, in 1810–1811; the Gutiérrez-Magee expedition against Texas in 1812–1813; plots against Pensacola in 1816; and a slew of filibusters against Texas between 1815 and 1820. Scholars have addressed U.S. diplomatic policy toward Spain and the rebel "Patriots" (as, like the American revolutionaries of the 1770s, they commonly called themselves), but the active physical operations—that is, the uses of military force—in support of this policy are less well known. Historians tend to depict the role of the U.S. Army either as passive—and not very significant—or simply as an agent of expansion.

By 1810, the standing army already had a quarter century of experience policing the nation's borderlands and frontiers. The army's first mission after the Revolutionary War was to expel whites intruding on Indian land in what is now southern Ohio; during the 1790s this changed to conquering the Ohio Indians, but national military commanders continued to try to prevent expeditions, unauthorized by the federal government and in fact illegal, by white Kentuckians, Tennesseans, and Georgians against Native Americans. In the absence of substantial federal civil authorities on the frontiers, officers of the standing army served as the primary agents of the national civil government in far-flung outposts like Vincennes during the 1780s and Detroit when it first came under U.S. control in 1796 and 1797. They did so again after occupying former Spanish posts in Mississippi in 1798 and in Missouri and Louisiana (outside New Orleans) between 1804 and 1807. Whether through occupation, conquest, civil government, or expeditions of exploration, national military officers showed the flag; negotiated formally and informally with British and Spanish officials and with local inhabitants of many cultures, ethnicities, and political loyalties; and intimidated and coerced when doing so was necessary and feasible. As the most powerful agents of American national sovereignty in the borderlands, they generally attempted to restrain nonstate actors, particularly filibusters against Spanish Florida, Louisiana, and Texas, whose forays threatened to disrupt international peace and the advance of U.S. sovereignty and white settlement. Nevertheless, filibustering usually failed more because of lack of resources than effective law enforcement by the army.[2]

Such enforcement was complicated by the uncertainty pervasive in a young, barely established nation under pressure from the great European powers during the French Revolution and the Napoleonic wars. Indeed, many senior army officers, including the commanding general himself, James Wilkinson, were closely linked to leading intriguers and filibusters like Aaron Burr, although Wilkinson broke with Burr at the last moment. (Edmund Gaines, one of the principal players in *Jackson's Sword*, detained Burr and escorted him to Washington for trial.) The instability and contentiousness of American politics and the immaturity of American society (its lack of occupational specialization and institutional density) fostered instability in the commitment and careers of the officer corps, which encouraged political irresponsibility, insubordination, and disloyalty. Though the Federalists had sought something approximating military professionalism during the 1790s, the first tumultuous decade of the nineteenth century set the stage for Andrew Jackson's usurpations of civilian authority during the period explored in *Jackson's Sword.*

The army's greatest success before 1810 came in defeating the Ohio and other northwestern Indians and in providing the beginnings of a federal government presence in the newly acquired territories it occupied. By 1810, the rising tide of Jeffersonian nationalism, a blend of confidence in American virtue and grievance against Britain and Spain, encouraged military officers (now mostly Jeffersonian rather than Federalist appointees) to express more overtly belligerent expansionist attitudes and objectives. Local military support for George Mathews's invasion of East Florida in 1812, James Madison's use of the army in East and West Florida, Jackson's repeated seizures of Pensacola, and widespread military support for seizing St. Augustine between 1818 and 1820 demonstrate that the army served U.S. territorial expansion, whether at the president's initiative or that of impatient military commanders. Elements of the army provided some covert aid to the Gutiérrez-Magee expedition, named in part for a captain who resigned his commission to command the invasion. Commanders along the Texas border launched reconnaissance missions into the province between 1816 and 1818, ultimately occupying positions within the supposedly demilitarized Neutral Ground along the Sabine, established by U.S. and Spanish military commanders in 1806.

Though the rhetorical flourishes of the 1840s were absent, the phrase "Jeffersonian Manifest Destiny" effectively expresses the general Republican consensus, and much of its underlying rationale, in favor of territorial expansion in the years surrounding the War of 1812. That aggrandizement took different forms and moved at different speeds, depending on opportunities and European reaction. In West Florida, American expansionism proceeded through Anglo settlers (invited and otherwise) and army deserters, whose rebellion against Spanish authority, encouraged by President Madison, provided a pretext for U.S. intervention and occupation in 1810.[3] In East Florida two years later, federal agents ultimately exceeded their authority from the president when they encouraged rebellion and filibustering among American borderers, first assisted and then virtually supplanted by the national standing army, which engaged in intermittent small-scale combat with Spanish troops outside St. Augustine for an entire year. These actions gave the Federalists the ammunition they needed to deny the administration the authority for annexation, leading to the withdrawal of U.S. forces in 1813.[4]

James Madison, by Gilbert Stuart. (Courtesy Library of Congress, LC-DIG-ppmsca-19166)

However innocent they imagined themselves, American farmers, usually armed, who crossed international boundaries without passports were committing an act tantamount to invasion, illegal under national law and international custom. Native Americans saw intrusion on their lands the same way, and federal law actually sided with the Indians, however inadequately it was enforced. This migration, and its often violent manifestation in overt filibustering expeditions and declarations of local autonomy or independence from Spanish sovereignty, was a constant throughout the southern borderlands from 1774 onward, culminating in the conflicts in West Florida just before the War of 1812. Afterward, during the years of tension and skirmishing between 1815 and 1818, these American farmers flowed into the new territories of Mississippi and Alabama, which were being expropriated from the Indians by Jackson's army, rather than across the international border into Middle Florida, held more strongly than ever by the Seminoles, Mikasukis, and Red Stick Creeks fleeing Jackson. Thus, between 1810 and 1819, the population of Mississippi Territory and state increased fivefold, from 40,000 to 200,000, most of it during the first four years after the war. On the third frontier with Spain, between the Sabine River and the Arroyo Hondo in what is today western Louisiana, there was no overt pressure for aggrandizement against Texas from national civilian policy makers. This enabled federal military officers to remain faithful to the spirit of Wilkinson's informal 1806 agreement with Spanish military commander Simón de Herrera to create a demilitarized Neutral Ground, even when their civilian counterparts (federal, state, and local officials in Louisiana) did not. The willingness of many officers to consider joining Aaron Burr that year was not equaled in filibuster forays against Texas throughout the 1810s; nor did military commanders—mostly southerners, westerners, and advocates of American national growth and power—seek or take advantage of pretexts to push their soldiers across the Neutral Ground in support of filibusters.

For half a decade after the 1806 agreement, the primary issues confronting army officers at Natchitoches, the army's principal post along the Sabine frontier, involved law enforcement, which depended on the actions of civil authorities, and preparation to meet Spanish aggression, which became increasingly improbable after Napoleon's invasion of Spain. These dynamics changed with the beginning of the first Mexican Revolution—the Hidalgo Rebellion of 1810—combined with covert or tacit support for a new wave of filibustering from Secretary of State James Monroe in 1812. They changed again amid the more urgent U.S. concerns of fighting the war with Britain. The clarity of dealing with individuals according to the dictates of national sovereignty and international law or custom gave way to seven years of relative passivity toward unsanctioned aggression by U.S. citizens against Spain. After that, the army returned to international peacekeeping, acting against a final filibuster assault during the conclusion of the Adams-Onís Treaty, which ceded Florida but not Texas. Yet military ambiguity toward Texas was a matter of inattention, not a lack of confidence or assertiveness. Apart from the burning of Washington, which career officers blamed on the deficiencies of the militia, 1814 was a year of American military victory, however limited or defensive in character. American military commanders finished the War of 1812 flush with a new confidence born of increasingly successful combat experience, eager to turn from defensive operations against the British to offensive ones against more vulnerable opponents. Their personal and institutional quests for fame were united under the banner of national expansion, fostering a new sense of the potential for professional reputation—winning honor through duty (though often self-defined duty) to country.

Given the weakness of civilian administrative controls between 1814 and the end of 1817, as a series of executives—several no more than senior clerks acting as secretary—passed through the War Department, the result easily could have been a wave of military adventurism aimed at Texas, as was the case in Florida. Nevertheless, this newfound self-assurance did not produce universal military belligerence toward Spain. The army did, however, act to repress nonstate actors both within the United States—the Baratarian smugglers in Louisiana between 1812 and 1814—and along its borders—in the Neutral Ground in 1810 and 1812, in West Florida in 1810–1811, against privateers and pirates at Amelia and Galveston islands in 1817, and along the Sabine in 1819. U.S. commanders cooperated with their Spanish counterparts to disperse bandits and maintain international borders in 1810, 1812, and 1819, using force against filibusters and other nonstate actors as frequently as they did against Spain. Spanish weakness offered expansionist opportunities at both ends of the Gulf, but Florida posed a far greater threat than Texas to American security. Florida was home to strong red and black resistance to white expansion, threatening the growth of the slave plantation economy and the ability to sustain white democracy through expansion in Georgia and Alabama. Indeed, Andrew Jackson's victory over the Red Stick Creek resistance in 1814 actually increased the threat from Florida, as those Indians who refused subjection and expropriation fled southward. Thus, following the Treaty of Ghent and the end of hostilities with Britain, the Florida frontier again became the principal scene of army operations, until those operations compelled Spain to cede the colony to the United States at the end of the decade.

Senior civilian policy makers were restrained by concern over British inter-

James Wilkinson, from Erna Risch, *Supplying Washington's Army*. (U.S. Army Center of Military History, 1991).

vention and a renewal of war. "The object of the last war must perhaps, and not improbably, be fought for again," John Quincy Adams, then minister (ambassador) to Britain, observed, and "we must always take it for granted that British feeling and policy will be against us" in support of Spain. Yet they also counseled patience in the expectation that Britain might become overextended economically: "Let us not give them the chance of war, and they will soon be obliged to discard their system [of threats and intimidation] for one of real peace, or it will sink them." Senior military commanders in the army's Northern Division shared civilian concerns about British forces and influence along the Canadian border and the northwestern frontier, but their counterparts in the Southern Division showed little fear of British or Spanish action and were eager to punish Native Americans for their resistance to U.S. domination. For whatever reason—whether Jackson's short, triumphal New Orleans campaign versus the hard-won experience of officers who had fought British troops for three years in the North, southern commanders' belief that the strength of Spanish resistance required force, or their failure to recognize or understand alternative methods—the attitude in the Southern Division was sanguine and self-assured.[5]

Despite the broad objectives they shared with civilian policy makers— national expansion to enhance national security and to facilitate peace and prosperity—uncompromisingly self-assured military officers continually threatened to overstep the bounds of constitutional subordination to civilian control along the disordered southern frontier, endangering the separation of powers between the executive and Congress (to say nothing of civilian authority), regardless of the potential enemy. This pattern of usurpation did not culminate until 1818, with Jackson's destruction of native and maroon communities throughout West Florida, his seizure of the Spanish posts at Pensacola and St. Marks, and his hanging of British merchants trading with the Seminoles. Yet the thrust of his resolve was evident from 1814 forward. The army's return to the Florida frontier signaled a growing confidence, certainty, and assertiveness in motive and means among the officers of the nation's standing army, from Jackson down to his most junior lieutenants.

FROM INTERNATIONAL POLICING TO SUBVERTING SPANISH RULE: ARMY OFFICERS AND TEXAS, 1810–1812

Many westerners would have been happy to add Texas to the federal union. Nevertheless, despite some support from Secretary of State Monroe for a filibustering expedition against Texas in 1812, the Spanish province remained a secondary attraction for the national government, a sideshow or target of opportunity; it was occasionally claimed and bargained for or threatened with subversion, but it was not a military objective for the U.S. Army. Faced with overextension elsewhere, the Madison and Monroe administrations departed from Jefferson's example and focused most of their energies on other frontiers, leaving the Sabine River and Texas under an international peace that was intermittently disturbed by extralegal incursions by private individuals, mostly U.S. citizens. When these filibustering expeditions appeared in 1812–1813, repeatedly between 1814 and 1818, and in 1819 and 1820, federal civil officials (district attorneys, marshals, customs collectors) were charged with enforcing the neutrality laws of 1794 and 1818. Constrained by American constitutionalism and the national culture of individual mobility, these laws only forbade "any military expedition or enterprise" crossing international borders. As long as they maintained a veneer of deniability—however implausible to anyone but sympathetic local magistrates and juries of their peers, who would decide their innocence—filibusters were usually free to cross the border individually, if armed, or in groups if not.[6]

There was no standing civilian police force at the federal, state, or local level; the Customs Service was a small organization focused on regulating trade through the seaports; and federal marshals were individual officials who had to call for assistance to execute writs. Constrained by popular libertarianism, localism, and expansionism, the national government lacked much legal authority or popular sanction when it came to mobilizing civilian posses for law enforcement against citizens. Consequently, federal military officers were often called on to provide the armed force necessary to execute the laws and uphold national sovereignty. Yet the denationalized, demilitarized Neutral Ground complicated the enforcement of neutrality laws even more than usual. There was no agreement between the United States and Spain for the use of soldiers from either nation to disarm or arrest invaders there. Adventurers could enter the Neutral Ground in small groups, claiming that they carried weapons for hunting or for personal self-defense, before assembling to invade Texas. Once they were across the "border," neither U.S. nor Spanish officials could act against them without violating the Neutral Ground agreement, which had withdrawn the military forces of both nations from a twenty-mile-wide strip between the Sabine and the Arroyo Hondo. The agreement succeeded in reducing international tensions but opened the door for private citizens to seize the initiative. Smugglers, bandits, and filibusters quickly recognized and took advantage of this opportunity. Indeed, Colonel Thomas Cushing, General Wilkinson's principal aide during the Sabine crisis in 1806, later observed that "intruders have taken their present position [inside the Neutral Ground] in full confidence that neither nation can remove them without a breach of the Agreement."[7]

Nevertheless, the Sabine frontier became quiet for several years after the Neutral Ground agreement was negotiated, and the turmoil of the first Mexican Revolution, beginning in 1810, never spilled over into or directly threatened the United States. Knowing that Spanish officials had their hands full trying to hold Texas against the rebels while cut off from reinforcements from Europe, few American military officers saw any threat there. When they thought of taking advantage of Napoleon's war to seize Spanish possessions, their focus was overwhelmingly on Florida. Indeed, the army officer who commented most about Mexico was Zebulon Montgomery Pike, leader of James Wilkinson's reconnaissance into Spanish territory in 1806. Pike's usual aggressiveness gave way to a precocious Pan-Americanism, cultural as well as commercial, toward the future southern republic.[8] Yet drifters, deserters, and bandits—difficult to distinguish from ordinary farmers unless caught red-handed—were gathering in the ungoverned Neutral Ground and at Pecan Point on the northern boundary of Texas along the upper Red River, forming a volatile population easily recruited by adventurers trying to take advantage of the turmoil to the south. Enforcing the neutrality laws and keeping international peace without violating the due process rights of innocent agricultural settlers required the active cooperation of local civil officials or of federal civil officials, who were commonly appointed from within the locality in question or had developed business interests there. Such cooperation rarely proved forthcoming during the era of popular expansionism examined in this book; indeed, it appears that some of the trespassers were encouraged by federal Indian agent John Sibley, whom the military commander at Natchitoches accused of surveying and selling land in the Neutral Ground.[9]

National military officers from Spain and the United States made several attempts to forcibly disarm intruders in the demilitarized zone, but they found it difficult to coordinate joint action without violating diplomatic sensitivities. Expelling the trespassers required repeated efforts, and each initiative was suspect in the eyes of the side receiving the proposal. In September 1808 General Wilkinson asked President Jefferson to authorize the commander at Natchitoches to act against "armed bodies" masquerading "under the flag and uniform of our Government" in the Neutral Ground. Jefferson's response is unknown, but two months later, Texas governor Manuel Antonio Cordero reported that American troops had forced a Spanish merchant caravan to return from the Neutral Ground to Natchitoches, apparently on Sibley's initiative. This incident supposedly sprang from differences between the Spanish Indian agent at Nacogdoches and his partner in Natchitoches, but Sibley may have been trying to deny trade goods to the Spanish to undermine their diplomacy with the Indians, or he may have been retaliating for Spanish arrests of American merchants for trading in Texas without licenses. Worst of all, rumors that Americans might attack Nacogdoches to release those merchants sparked a flurry of correspondence among Spanish officials, halted only when Nemecio Salcedo, the military commander at Chihuahua, reassured his skittish subordinates.[10]

In July 1809 Salcedo helped pave the way for future cooperation by barring U.S. Army deserters from Texas. In April 1810 Texas governor Manuel Salcedo proposed a joint operation to eject a substantial group of squatters from the demilitarized zone around the former Spanish outpost at Los Adais; Colonel Cushing agreed that the intruders would form "a numerous & lawless banditti" if they were permitted to remain. In accordance with Wilkinson's standing order to maintain international demilitarization, Captain Charles Wollstonecraft, the U.S. commander at Natchitoches (and brother of British feminist author Mary Wollstonecraft), initially protested against Governor Salcedo's intention to cross the Sabine, but he forwarded the Spanish official's proposal up the American military chain of command. The Madison administration decided to cooperate with Salcedo, and in June, Wollstonecraft sent Lieutenant Augustus Magee to warn the squatters of the joint operation, lest they make good on their threat to attack the Spanish troops. The pejorative language national military officers used to characterize the trespassers was similar to that of their counterparts on the Louisiana-Florida border prior to the West Florida rebellion in 1810. Wollstonecraft shared Cushing's concern about these "desperate characters accustomed to plunder . . . who finding it prudent to quit orderly society, are only in safety where neither law [n]or justice prevails," and he warned that "the country will always be infested with these people" unless the army was authorized to burn their homes and crops. On July 29 the captain dispatched Magee with eighteen soldiers to meet the Spanish and "purge the country of those persons who are inimical to the public tranquility," language he drew from Governor Salcedo. During a two-week foray extending as far north as Bayou Pierre, the combined force worked "in perfect harmony" to destroy a dozen buildings and compel thirty-four people to move. Yet there was likely some tension between these national representatives over ends and means; the expedition left cattle and cornfields undisturbed, citing feelings of "humanity towards the Settlers," language the Spanish probably rejected.[11]

The joint operation to remove the intruders was hardly an example of "local diplomacy," as historian Peter Kastor has argued, unless that term is stretched to encompass every actor, local or national, outside national capitals. The initiative for the expedition came from a Spanish imperial official, not from American territorial officials or private interests, and it was transmitted to Washington and back primarily through the army chain of command. Cushing and Wollstonecraft did not refer to pressure from local interests in their requests for permission to act, nor was the operation conducted by local forces (militia or volunteers). Instead, it was an example of frontier or border diplomacy by nation-state actors who saw the Neutral Ground as a temporary but de facto international border, as a frontier in the military sense current at the time (as a potential "front" in interstate conflict), rather than a borderland or "middle ground" open to contestation by nonstate actors, in the sense common among historians today. That Washington did not recognize the government of Spain hardly made the expedition local, as Kastor asserts, either in initiative (Spanish) or in authorization (from Washington).

Nor was the Neutral Ground agreement routine, "a product of established diplomatic practice rather than of particular individuals." Although President Jefferson had suggested something very similar to the Neutral Ground, the negotiations were conducted on the spot by James Wilkinson, who had to restrain belligerent civilian territorial governor William C. C. Claiborne, who was also the senior State Department representative on the scene. There was certainly no "established practice," whether in procedure or in precedent, for U.S. military commanders to negotiate demilitarized zones along uncertain, disputed boundaries between nations; one wonders at the contradiction between Jeffersonian principle and practice. The Neutral Ground agreement, the operations to remove intruders from the area, and the return of deserters from Texas to Louisiana were examples of actions by "men on the spot" rather than high officials in national capitals. However, these men were either national or imperial officers, and the removal operations were sanctioned through national chains of command. Local opinion surely had some sway over these men, but that influence varied with the circumstances and was not necessarily dominant, particularly among officers commissioned by the American nation-state and socialized far from the borderlands they were called on to police.[12]

Recognizing the influence of local and nonstate actors should not obscure that of national ones. Strangely, Kastor interprets the Neutral Ground agreement as an example of agency from everyone involved *except* Wilkinson, the commander of the American forces along the Sabine. (No primary source refers to Claiborne as a significant participant in the negotiations; indeed, Claiborne was more belligerent than Wilkinson.) Claiborne and Wilkinson clearly failed to achieve their policy preferences, although ending the Sabine confrontation permitted Wilkinson to turn against Aaron Burr. Thus Kastor's discussion accurately portrays the Neutral Ground agreement as an American defeat, but it does not adequately explain why the Americans made such a concession. Although American officials sought Caddo support and certainly did not want the Caddo allied with the Spanish, their correspondence contains no evidence of fear of the Caddo—whose military force amounted to no more than several hundred warriors—that can explain why such aggressive expansionists as Wilkinson and Claiborne backed down. Following his argument for a substantial, perhaps decisive, Caddo role in the Neutral Ground agreement, Kastor asserts that "representatives" from the Caddo "agreed" to the joint removal operation in 1810 but again provides no evidence. Surely the Caddo applauded the efforts to remove lawless whites from their neighborhood, but the terms "representatives" and "approval" exaggerate Caddo agency. The army's actions with regard to the Neutral Ground, whether in 1806, 1810, or 1812 and beyond, can be better characterized (per Kastor) as dimensions in the "bifurcated diplomatic system in which the [armed forces] suppressed illegal commerce" and upheld national sovereignty, "while civil officials [like Claiborne] promoted domestic loyalty," often by supporting popular expansionism.[13]

Whatever its origin, the 1810 operation had little long-term effect on the

William C. C. Claiborne, governor of Louisiana.
(Courtesy Library of Congress, LC-USZ6-682)

excesses of frontier individualism and democracy, much like operations to drive
white squatters (who were also citizens) from Indian or public lands within
the boundaries of the United States. In August 1811 Spanish troops entered
the Neutral Ground to break up an armed encampment and reportedly pursued rebel leaders Bernardo Gutiérrez de Lara and José Menchaca (spelled
Manchac in some sources, a Spanish army officer who had joined the rebels)
into U.S. territory. Federal officers remained quiescent during this incursion,
although Gutiérrez met with military commanders at Natchitoches after escap-
ing Spanish pursuit. Menchaca returned to the Neutral Ground and was
involved when 300 Americans advanced (or were rumored to have advanced)
from Natchitoches to the Sabine in October 1811; they apparently turned
back before any fighting occurred, perhaps because Menchaca deserted back
to the Spanish.[14] Neither vigilantes nor filibusters threatened Natchitoches, so
U.S. officials were more concerned by the disruption of commerce than by
questions of sovereignty. Territorial judge John C. Carr declared that he would
arrest the filibusters "if they moved," but Governor Claiborne merely
observed that "it would seem that there have been some movements which

our Laws do not sanction." Indeed, expansionists like Claiborne attempted to use concern for the protection of commerce and property to advance American sovereignty to the Sabine, but they were rebuffed by army officers who favored maintaining the international equilibrium embodied in the Neutral Ground agreement. In January 1812 a group of Natchitoches merchants sent Claiborne a memorial suggesting that the United States establish a post on the Sabine and one or two more on the road across the Neutral Ground, on the pretext that the statute authorizing Louisiana statehood reasserted American claims to the area. Claiborne agreed, observing that "the efforts of the civil authority are wholly inadequate to the suppression of this Banditti," but the usually sympathetic General Wilkinson was still back east recovering from his court-martial for dereliction of duty the preceding fall.[15]

Brigadier General Wade Hampton, who had clashed with Claiborne over the army's role in West Florida a year before, refused the governor's request, intimating that Claiborne's objective was primarily offensive. Citing a conversation with President Madison, the brigadier played up the importance of military subordination to the national civil authority, while emphasizing the need to avoid unnecessary hostilities. "Every measure calculated to excite the jealousy of our Western neighbours ought . . . to be avoided," he noted, and "it is unquestionably more proper for the president of the U.S. to determine a point of so much political delicacy, than that a Military commander should take upon himself that authority," even at a governor's behest. "No such violent remedy" was required, "nor is it necessary for your militia to cross our borders," Hampton cautioned the governor. Yet seven months of complaints from Spanish and American merchants who were being harassed by brigands, combined with rumors that the marauders, perhaps filibusters from Natchitoches, threatened to seize Spanish Nacogdoches, could not be ignored. In February Hampton dispatched Lieutenant Colonel Zebulon Montgomery Pike to cooperate with Spanish troops to clear bandits and other potential predators from the Neutral Ground. Given the growing tension with Britain, the general had no desire to open another front against Spain, advising Pike that the Louisiana statehood legislation enacted by Congress was "merely conditional" and presumably less binding than the "military understanding" Wilkinson had made with his Spanish counterparts during the military confrontation in 1806.[16]

Like the subordinate officers in the region, Hampton apparently considered the Neutral Ground agreement much like an international treaty; he was certainly correct in assuming that the congressional declaration was less serious, having been intended primarily for political consumption, without provisions for implementation. Hampton told Pike to propose a joint effort with

Spanish officials to clear the Neutral Ground; if they refused, the colonel was authorized to launch an operation on his own authority, "justified . . . [by] necessity . . . and a regard to self-preservation"—almost exactly the same language Andrew Jackson would later employ to justify his invasions of Florida, but without Jackson's expansionist intent. Toward the end of the month, after bandits attacked an armed party of forty Spanish merchants, Pike dispatched Lieutenant William King to Nacogdoches with his proposal, but the Spanish commander, Bernardo Montero, declared that he was not authorized to undertake such an effort. Pike then instructed Lieutenants Augustus Magee and Elijah Montgomery to enter the area with forty soldiers, destroy the houses and crops of suspected "banditti," and arrest those unable to account for themselves. The paradoxes of official action in the Neutral Ground remained inescapable: however conditional Hampton considered U.S. claims to a Sabine boundary, Pike felt obligated to appeal to American legal sensibilities and public opinion to defend his actions, asserting that the orders were legally justified under federal statutes for ejecting citizen trespassers from public lands. The colonel appears to have shared Claiborne's expansionist sentiments toward the region, advising Hampton on the distribution of U.S. troops should the United States take possession of the Neutral Ground, but Pike also advocated negotiating commercial privileges with an independent Mexico.[17]

Hoping to demonstrate due process to American juries, the colonel tried to find a civil officer to accompany the foray and legitimize arrests. After creeping through thickets and exchanging fire with squatters, the lieutenants took fourteen prisoners, whom Pike hoped the courts would sentence to execution for the crimes of robbery and murder, as "a sacrifice to the insulted dignity of the laws." Since the Natchitoches jail was unprepared for so many prisoners, the colonel ordered Captain Walter Overton to hold them at Fort Claiborne until the civil authorities called for them, an incarceration that lasted two months. Pike was careful to observe that "this is not intended to form a *precedent*," although there was already a good deal of precedent—at Vincennes in the 1780s, at Cincinnati and Detroit in the 1790s, and at small outposts throughout Orleans Territory and West Florida. Either way, Pike reminded Overton, "it is our duty to assist the civil magistrates in the support of their authority." He then placed the burden of decision on Overton: "Situated as you are on an important frontier, and at a place where the civil authority has been and is daily openly put at defiance, many [such] occasions may transpire which may make it necessary for you to afford aid and support to the due execution of the laws: on those subjects you must act as circumstances direct." These circumstances included demands from local merchants, whether Amer-

Wade Hampton.
(Courtesy Library of
Congress, LC-USZ62-
56699)

ican or Spanish: Overton was to furnish escorts to groups of fifteen or more, of whichever nationality, so long as the applicants agreed to provide horses for the escort. The captain wrote to Montero proposing an "arrangement" to conduct joint operations; Montero asked Overton to contribute troops, and Spain dispatched twenty soldiers east of the Sabine in April, although the two nations' forces did not actually work side by side as they had in 1810.[18]

Official support for ensuring international peace and military accountability to statutory authority did not extend to enforcing the neutrality laws against the Mexican rebels. The most serious of the filibusters against Texas was the Gutiérrez-Magee expedition of 1812–1813. This insurgency combined Mexican revolutionaries, led by Bernardo Gutiérrez de Lara and José Alvarez de Toledo, with American adventurers and Texan Indians. After his escape from Texas in the fall of 1811, Gutiérrez was received at Fort Claiborne by Captain Overton, who wrote to General Wilkinson praising those American citizens "joining the cause of liberty and giving a vital stab to the old government" by filibustering into Mexico.[19] Gutiérrez then went from Natchitoches to Tennessee, where he met John Overton (a close friend of Andrew Jackson and a relative of the Natchitoches commander), before holding extended discussions with Secretary of State Monroe and Secretary of War William Eustis in Washington. Some of his expenses and those of his confederate Toledo were later reimbursed by the Treasury. Gutiérrez returned to Natchitoches in the spring of 1812 with a State Department agent, William Shaler (who later accompanied the Gutiérrez-Magee expedition into Texas as a senior adviser), and was feted by the officers at Fort Claiborne. American civil and military officials knew about filibuster recruiting efforts almost as soon as they began; they informed Eustis but did nothing to halt or discourage the plotting. Indeed, Captain Overton later reported to Wilkinson that "the business has never been a secret," asserting his belief that the administration supported Gutiérrez.[20]

The captain probably had excellent reasons for his opinion. Wilkinson deployed an artillery company to Natchitoches for a couple of weeks that summer, but its mission remains unclear: the artillerymen certainly did nothing to impede the foray, and some sources suggest that they may have transferred arms—perhaps cannon, presumably needed for the defense of New Orleans—to the filibusters. Cannon were shipped from New Orleans to the filibusters in Natchitoches that summer, but the sources do not make it clear from whom. Wollstonecraft's company may have conveyed these guns to the filibusters or their intermediaries (perhaps in the militia), or the guns (whether military or civilian in origin) may have been left unguarded to be taken by the filibusters. On the one hand, one must wonder why Wilkinson would send cannon to the Texas border when war with Britain was imminent. Although the Spanish junta was allied with Britain, there was no intelligence about Spanish belligerence or capable forces stationed in East Texas, and New Orleans was a far more important point than anything to its west. On the other hand, there were plenty of cannon available in New Orleans, from merchant ships and privateers, so it seems unlikely that Wilkinson stole army cannon. On July 10 Captain Wollstonecraft, the artillery company commander, reported to the general that he had met more than a hundred men traveling to join the filibuster expedition, but he professed to be more concerned by rumors that Spanish royalists would dispatch troops into the Neutral Ground to guard a caravan to Natchitoches. Wollstonecraft said nothing about the American convoy escorts that spring. The will to break up "banditti" in the Neutral Ground seems to have evaporated when the opportunistic expansionist Wilkinson replaced Hampton, and neither Wollstonecraft nor Overton attempted to stop the marauders, who apparently crossed into the Neutral Ground in small groups. Indeed, their willingness to speak to an officer in uniform implies that they neither expected nor feared prosecution, which ultimately depended on the action of some civil authority—under a strict Republican reading of the laws, perhaps that of the president himself.[21]

At the beginning of August, Wollstonecraft reported that the Natchitoches militia had joined the filibusters "to a man," that a former territorial legislator was recruiting among the militia in Rapides Parish, and that more men were coming from Natchez. Claiming that he feared the filibusters would seize arms and ammunition from Fort Claiborne, the captain left two small cannon with Overton but returned with his company to Baton Rouge. The lead elements of the Gutiérrez-Magee expedition crossed the Sabine into Texas on August 7, but Governor Claiborne did not ask for military aid until two days later and did not issue a proclamation against the plot until August 11, the day before the filibusters occupied Spanish Nacogdoches. Indeed, the governor's August 10 report to Secretary Monroe exuded expansion, alleging that a Spanish magistrate had taken up residence at Bayou Pierre, so that Claiborne "must necessarily extend . . . the authority of the State of Louisiana . . . within what has heretofore been called the neutral ground." On the same day, Wilkinson advised Secretary Eustis that he planned to order Overton "to put an end to the troubles" by arresting Magee and other filibuster leaders but would consult with Claiborne first. The brigadier added that "Gerard," one of his agents from 1806 and 1807, had brought "full and unreserved" messages from Gutiérrez, who sought arms and ammunition. Wilkinson stated that he had refused to provide these supplies and had instructed Gerard to warn Gutiérrez that the foray was an "illegal assembly," unauthorized by the U.S. government, that could not be "tolerated or justified" by federal officers. Yet the general never issued an order for the filibusters' arrest, although Claiborne advised Judge Carr he could call on the military for aid to enforce the neutrality laws.[22]

Scholars have debated how actively the Madison administration supported Gutiérrez. The U.S. government did not stir up the revolution that began in Mexico in 1810, but its failure to do much to stop extralegal recruiting provided tacit support for filibustering throughout most of the decade. Few officers other than Pike commented on Mexican affairs, although Wilkinson's negotiations in Cuba and West Florida seem to have spurred his thoughts along the path of Pike's enthusiasm for the Mexican revolutionaries. That autumn the general intimated that the president should "authorize me to speak to the poor native Mexicans," lest "some European mal-direction" lead them astray. In June Pike advised Monroe to employ John H. Robinson, Pike's civilian surgeon during his 1807 expedition across the Plains, to solicit

Zebulon Montgomery Pike. (Courtesy Library of
Congress, LC-DIG-ppmsca-03211)

an accommodation with Nemecio Salcedo, the commander of Spanish
defenses in northern Mexico. Robinson made the trip but was unable to persuade Salcedo; he then joined the Gutiérrez-Magee expedition and continued to organize filibusters against Texas throughout the decade.[23]

U.S. agents on the scene showed little enthusiasm for pursuing prosecutions that would almost certainly come to naught in the deliberations of American juries, particularly when the prospect of war with Britain would soon
require citizen-soldier volunteers. That probability, combined with Creek militancy and a rumor of slave rebellion that led Wilkinson to supply arms and
ammunition to the governor of Mississippi, may explain why the general
ordered the artillery company deployed to Natchitoches withdrawn back to
Baton Rouge. Commanders may well have feared that more soldiers would
desert and join the filibusters, who offered land, $40 a month (versus $5 in

the army), and the prospect of loot. Whatever the case, Wollstonecraft's company was no longer needed, whether to stop the expedition from crossing the border or to convoy supplies to assist it. Reporting to Secretary of War Eustis, Wilkinson opined that the incursion was illegal, was unlikely to succeed, and would cause war with Spain, and he suggested that Magee be arrested. (Once Magee resigned from the army, this required civil sanction, although in principle, Magee was still in the army until his resignation was accepted, so Wilkinson could have arrested him if he truly wanted to.) Yet the brigadier was hardly averse to bending the law or threatening Spain when he thought it would suit his interests and those of the United States. Characteristically, he made one last proposal that the federal troops under his command seize Texas rather than allowing an outlaw band to do so. Whether his expansionism was tempered by elitist gentility or he was concealing support for the filibusters, by November, Wilkinson referred to the adventurers as "the most worthless & desperate of our countrymen."[24]

The invasion became known as the Gutiérrez-Magee expedition because Augustus Magee resigned from the army on June 22, claiming that it offered too little chance for reputation and glory, and assumed command of filibuster military operations. War with England seemed a growing certainty, but Magee may have feared being stuck in a backwater during the war. There is no further evidence of his intentions, but he had clearly forged connections that he found more opportune. From one perspective, Magee was the exception that proved the rule: he was the *only* serving officer of the national army who actually resigned to join the expedition or any of the other filibusters of the early national era. The Burr expedition never got off the ground, of course; in East and West Florida national military officers could support American expansion without giving up their commissions; and the post-1815 cases involved men who had left the army at the end of the War of 1812. Yet eight men with prior experience as army officers joined the invasion of Texas, so national military involvement in the Gutiérrez-Magee expedition requires further assessment. (See appendix A for a list of these and other officers and former officers involved in filibusters between 1812 and 1821.) Like the officers implicated in the Burr conspiracy, these men had little army experience—a total of less than fifteen years' army service among them, with an average of two years apiece. Only two had served more than three years, and three had served a year or less. Much like the young junior officers, captains and lieutenants, linked to Burr in 1806, most (six) of the eight had been commissioned by the Jefferson administration, and only two by Federalist John Adams. Unlike the officers connected to Burr and the "Mexican Association," who came largely from the southern states and territories, these eight were equally divided between northerners and southerners. Most significantly, only two, Magee and Samuel Noah, the other West Point graduate among the eight, had seen service after the 1808 buildup aimed at Britain. Six of the eight had been out of the army for at least four years before they joined the Gutiérrez-Magee foray.

While we have no record of their individual decision-making processes, this composite portrait suggests that army service had little effect on participation in the expedition, except in drawing these men to the Southwest, where they made the connections that later led them to filibustering. Yet several filibusters were kin to important military commanders. Joseph B. Wilkinson, the general's third son (not to be confused with his brother James, who served in the army throughout these years and often engaged in diplomatic missions—however shady, given his father's intrigues—along the western frontier), had been a surgeon's mate in the army between 1800 and 1802; he acted as aide-de-camp to Toledo and helped transmit messages between the revolutionaries and his father. James Gaines (who also participated in the James Long filibuster against Texas seven years later) was a brother of longtime officer and future general Edmund Pendleton Gaines, although he never held an army commission. Former lieutenant Reuben Smith's brother was Thomas A. Smith, Wilkinson's emissary to Jefferson in 1806 and commander of U.S. forces in East Florida in 1812. Their actions were probably rooted more in immersion in the expansionist frontier milieu than in their experiences, attitudes, or values as former army officers, but their family links to leading expansionist officers suggest the pervasive influence of that frontier milieu among Americans of all stripes in the southern borderlands.[25]

Overton and Wilkinson continued to report on the expedition's progress that fall, but army operations along this frontier turned to the more specific delineation of borders and the affirmation of U.S. sovereignty against the threat of turmoil spilling over from Texas. In October Captain Overton took a detachment up the Red River from Natchitoches into the Neutral Ground to Bayou Pierre, where filibusters or Mexican revolutionaries had demanded that the inhabitants join them. The army wanted to assure the populace that their settlement had been incorporated into the United States by the statute authorizing Louisiana statehood. The captain's foray apparently did not stir any repercussions. Wilkinson probably agreed with Claiborne's interpretation of the statehood legislation, and Spanish authority did not return to the Sabine frontier for several years after the attackers seized Nacogdoches. Nevertheless, although the outbreak of war with Britain might have provided a flimsy pretext for overt U.S. action to preempt British use of Texas as a base for operations against Louisiana, the absence of port facilities and the distance from major slaveholding areas made it difficult for Madison to justify another addition to his bulging portfolio of military adventures.[26]

In late August 1812 Secretary Eustis tried to prevent Wilkinson from providing overt support for the expedition by ordering him to avoid hostilities with Spain and to limit his operations to the defense of New Orleans; Wilkinson was to cooperate with the civil authorities (at their request) to suppress illegal expeditions into Texas. Like Claiborne's proclamation or the orders issued to Andrew Jackson and Edmund Gaines against attacking Spanish posts in Florida between 1814 and 1818, the secretary's instructions came too late, even if we assume that Eustis, Wilkinson, and the local civil officials on whom military law enforcement depended seriously intended that those instructions be executed. A year later Claiborne lamented to Madison that he had "never understood how far the Executive . . . felt an interest in the Revolutionary Movements in Texas." Whether the president was Jefferson, Madison, or Monroe, the executive could point to its instructions to subordinates as evidence of good faith toward Spain, even though the orders had little real effect restraining American aggression. Yet, as in East Florida, the absence of sustained federal military support for aggression against Texas denied the invaders the one resource most likely to bring them success, and all their incursions came to naught, apart from devastating and depopulating the principal Spanish settlements. Note, however, the second-order effect of the U.S. government's failure to stop the filibusters: the destruction of Spanish settlements increased the Mexican government's desire for colonists during the 1820s, most of whom were Anglos from the United States, many of whom would rebel against Mexican rule a decade later.[27]

The army's experience along the Texas frontier demonstrated that military accountability to national and international law depended to a significant degree on the national and international situation, administration policy, and the strength of the international opposition faced by federal military commanders. The inattention of national civilian policy makers who were busy with Florida and preparing for war with Britain encouraged officers' adherence to the Neutral Ground agreement until mid-1812, while the onset of the War of 1812 restrained any official American military action during the Gutiérrez-Magee foray that autumn. After the final defeat of that expedition, along with indigenous Mexican rebels, by royal forces at San Antonio in August 1813, Overton requested reinforcements in case Spanish troops pursued fleeing filibusters across the Sabine, and he sought arms for former filibusters that he expected to recruit into the U.S. Army. Brigadier General Thomas Flournoy, commander of U.S. forces in East Florida during the incursions there in 1812 and 1813, seems to have learned something from that unhappy venture; he reprimanded Overton for thinking about fighting the Spanish and ordered him to take no action if Spanish units entered the Neutral Ground. Flournoy warned Overton not to aid "what you call the Republican army," but he did send arms in case the national army gained additional recruits.[28]

Yet the critical factor was strategic priority. Incursions into East Florida and Texas had proved to be unsustainable overextensions of the limited American forces available as war began with Britain. Had the United States not gone to war with that more powerful enemy, one wonders whether U.S. troops would have entered Texas in support of Gutiérrez and Magee or entered East Florida in larger numbers. (Of course, one also wonders whether Britain would have intervened, with or without a declaration of war, in defense of its Spanish ally.) In February 1813 the Senate rejected a bill to annex East Florida, and U.S. troops quickly withdrew. By mid-1813 the emphasis was clearly on the defense of New Orleans and the southern frontier, first from the Red Stick Creek uprising and then from British amphibious forces. These priorities could also lead to aggression, however, as American commanders linked Creek resistance to Spanish aid. After explaining his orders restraining Overton, Flournoy asked President Madison if he would be "justified in carrying our arms to the gates of Pensacola . . . to prevent the Spaniards from supplying the Indians with arms, & ammunition." Indeed, the brigadier went on to prefigure Andrew Jackson, inquiring whether he would be "justified in pursuing the flying Creeks into the town of Pensacola, & punishing them & the Spaniards together." Anticipating the next decade of events in West Florida with a ferocity equal to Old Hickory's, Flournoy concluded by positing whether he should then "destroy the town" or "endeavor to hold possession for the United States."[29]

The breakdown of Spanish sovereignty in Texas during the civil strife that began in 1812 reduced military officers' concern about aggressively enforcing the neutrality laws. Spanish debility reduced the need for American forces to prevent incursions that might ensnare the United States in war. At the end of the decade, American recognition of Spanish sovereignty over Texas in the Adams-Onís Treaty encouraged a temporary return to stricter enforcement of the neutrality laws and the restraint of American filibusters (the Long expeditions of 1819–1820) to maintain international peace in order to ease the transfer of Florida to U.S. rule. The sectional crisis over Missouri's admission to the Union as a slave state, combined with the difficulty of asserting anticolonial motives for incursions against independent Mexico, discouraged federal support for expansion into Texas during the 1820s and ultimately deferred annexation and military occupation for a decade after the successful Anglo-Texan rebellion against Mexico.

ASSERTING SOVEREIGNTY AND ENFORCING LAW
ALONG THE GULF LITTORAL: THE U.S. GOVERNMENT
AGAINST THE BARATARIAN CORSAIRS, 1812–1814

Following its initial success and growing internal dissension between Anglos and Spaniards, the Gutiérrez-Magee expedition was defeated at the Battle of Medina outside San Antonio in August 1813. Magee had died of disease that February, but several of the leading actors and several of the former officers mentioned earlier escaped and continued to plot incursions from the United States (see chapter 3). Yet the demands of war with Britain and the severity of the filibusters' defeat at Medina dissuaded the federal government from further sympathy of the sort Gutiérrez had received in 1812. Indeed, during the war, U.S. officials grew concerned about the increasing power of autonomous nonstate actors along the nation's southern periphery and began to clamp down on smugglers and freebooters. This process would continue, despite inaction toward privateers who preyed on Spanish shipping, after the Treaty of Ghent. Prior to the War of 1812, the largest concentration of these free agents along the American Gulf coast was at Grand Isle on the edge of Barataria Bay in Louisiana, under the leadership of Jean and Pierre Laffite. These men had begun congregating in Louisiana in 1805, and French privateers shifted their base of operations to Barataria after Britain captured Guadeloupe and Martinique in 1810. Many of the privateers were able to secure letters of marque from the rebel government at Cartagena, in modern Colombia, but they did not seek authorization from the United States; nor did they take their prizes to legitimate admiralty courts for valuation. When the War of 1812 began, they refused to seek American letters of marque allowing them to attack British shipping as privateers legitimately commissioned by their sovereign host; they continued to focus their depredations against Spanish shipping, violating the neutrality acts and the 1807 piracy law. Yet local public opinion supported them, due to the goods they sold, especially slaves.[30]

Lured by prize money and angered by such blatant defiance of national sovereignty, American naval commanders initially took the lead against the Laffites. In the spring of 1810, frustrated by the inaction of federal district attorney Philip Grymes, Captain David Porter took a contingent of gunboats and compelled three privateer vessels to surrender; two were soon released, with one paying a small fine. Frustrated by corruption in the legal process, Porter secured a transfer north that summer. By 1811, as many as 5,000 men were employed on the Baratarian ships—effectively an independent navy based in U.S. territory. Navy Commodore John Shaw had little success curbing them. Embarrassed by the challenge to his otherwise successful consolidation of American rule, Governor Claiborne blamed the freebooters for smuggling the African slaves thought to be responsible for the German Coast uprising that January, but New Orleans business interests defeated his request for funding to drive them from Louisiana.[31] The army was slow to get involved without aggressive civilian leadership to provide legal and political cover. In February 1812 Wade Hampton consulted with the New Orleans customs collector and deployed two "confidential officers" to Barataria at the collector's request, without much effect. Returning to command the Gulf theater that fall, James Wilkinson began more aggressive action, dispatching Captain Joseph Ballinger through the swamps against Grand Terre. Though historians have depicted the captain's mission as a reconnaissance, he clearly considered it more. Meeting several boats of "Pirates," Ballinger "exercised the men [in line of battle] . . . expecting that the appearance of United States troops might induce them to hoist colours, which would justify my going on board" to seize their vessels. The captain seemed to believe that he could do nothing unless the freebooters identified themselves, and he moved cautiously to avoid landing "within point blank shot," taking advantage of higher ground "to prevent their cannon raking me." Ballinger advised that infantry could not shut the entrance to the bay and suggested a gunboat and artillery battery to drive the corsairs from their anchorage.[32]

Unwilling to divert these resources from the defense of New Orleans and West Florida, Wilkinson next deployed Captain Andrew Hunter Holmes with forty dragoons to patrol the swamps "and preserve the honor of the country." During October Holmes seized some smuggled goods but lost them to a pirate counterattack the same night. He captured the Laffites without resistance the following month, killing one man who tried to escape, but the localism and corruption of Louisiana politics remained an insuperable obstacle to prosecution.[33] District attorney John Randolph Grymes (the former district attorney's brother) failed—in effect, refused—to take action for six months afterward, while federal marshal Pierre Duplessis failed three times to secure the brothers' appearance in court after their release on bond. In March 1813 Claiborne pressed Wilkinson to mount an assault on Barataria, and the federal customs collector formally requested military aid to enforce the laws against smuggling. Senior military commanders had been put off by the inaction of civil officials the previous autumn and were slow to respond. In May the federal marshal for New Orleans demanded that civilians move at least forty miles inland from the coast, and the following month Claiborne asked Brigadier General Thomas Flournoy, Wilkinson's successor in command, to declare martial law against smuggling and piracy. Unsure how to enforce martial law against a limited set of criminal offenses, Flournoy was unwilling to go that far, although he ordered that vessels entering the Mississippi estuary be searched more thoroughly. His subordinates demonstrated a similar range of views. That August, Henry Peire, newly commissioned major of the Forty-fourth Infantry and a future filibuster himself, undertook a reconnaissance west of Barataria Bay and reported that the freebooters had departed for Cartagena; redeployed closer to New Orleans, Peire soon found plenty of smuggled goods to suggest otherwise. Less intimately connected to Louisiana men of affairs, Charles Wollstonecraft was more easily irritated and criticized the federal customs collector for failing to show up after he had called for the captain's assistance.[34]

The Laffites grew bolder that autumn, threatening Flournoy and responding to Claiborne's offer of a reward by proclaiming their own reward for the governor. That October, they attacked and wounded a customs officer transporting confiscated goods and opened fire on a boatload of soldiers, wounding three; in January 1814 the pirates assaulted a group of revenue officers, killing several. Unwilling to give up profitable business, the state legislature still refused to authorize the use of the militia for law enforcement against the freebooters, but the federal executive branch began to bring a new level of pressure against the corsairs. Busy with the war and faced with new plans for filibusters against Texas and Mexico, President Madison issued a proclamation of neutrality toward Spain that June, reinforcing the strictures against attacking Spanish shipping. In July the Laffites were finally indicted for piracy, and the secretary of the navy ordered Commodore Daniel Patterson to attack and destroy the Baratarian complex. Yet local leaders continued to downplay the challenge to national sovereignty: the United States faced plenty of problems with Britain and the Creeks, and many prominent Louisianans counseled ignoring these affronts. Grymes actually resigned his post as district attorney to act as Pierre Laffite's lawyer. But more forceful federal officials—Daniel Patterson, Colonel George Ross (a former sheriff now commanding the Forty-fourth Infantry Regiment, created to defend New Orleans and the Louisiana coast), and Pierre Dubourg, customs collector for the Port of New Orleans—dominated the council Claiborne created to determine a course of action. In September a naval force of six gunboats and the brig *Argus*, much of Patterson's command, and seventy of Ross's infantry descended on Barataria Bay, taking eighty prisoners and confiscating twenty-six vessels.[35]

The pirates had already dispersed much of their loot to safer locales, and they did not resist Ross's raid. Although Andrew Jackson initially labeled them "hellish Banditti" and criticized Claiborne for allowing the "wretches" who had escaped the raid to wander New Orleans unrestrained, most of the Baratarians preferred the sympathetic juries, decentralization, and expansionist possibilities of American rule to the piracy prosecutions and executions they would face from imperial Britain. After extended parleys, they defied British threats and overtures and joined Jackson's defense of New Orleans. Yet federal officials were beginning to press for greater law and order in the region, so the pardons the freebooters received for their help in defending the city did not preclude prosecution for future violations of the neutrality laws, and the political climate in Louisiana became distinctly less favorable after the end of the war. Nevertheless, the departure of the British flotillas that had dominated the Gulf coast opened the way for new filibuster ventures, usually under the sanction, or cover, of the rebel governments of Mexico, Colombia, and Venezuela (forays examined in chapter 3).[36]

A romantically young Andrew Jackson, by Thomas Sully.
(Courtesy Library of Congress, LC-USZ62-435)

2

THE ARMY ASSERTS AMERICAN HEGEMONY ON THE FLORIDA FRONTIER

From the Creek War to the Destruction of the Negro Fort, 1813–1816

The army's principal theater of operations in the half decade immediately after the War of 1812 was Florida, where Spanish authority never recovered from the chaos fostered by American incursions between 1810 and 1814. Growing white intrusion on Indian lands, combined with the power vacuum created by the weakness of Spanish authority, provided greater motive and opportunity for native resistance along the Florida frontier. This endemic warfare, combined with Spain's inability to control the Indians or prevent the United States from attempting to do so, encouraged American military commanders to take an increasingly adamant stance. The most powerful of these hard-bitten veterans was Andrew Jackson, major general in command of the Southern Division throughout the period. Sharp Knife, as the Indians called him, escalated intermittent skirmishes with the Creeks and Seminoles into a full-scale invasion and occupation of Florida without authority from Congress or the executive. In doing so, the general provides one of the best illustrations of the tensions between officers' sense of substantive responsibility—usually to the nation's general interest in enhancing its security and power through expansion, but also to the interests of particular classes and sections, especially southern planters and settlers—and their formal procedural accountability to the Constitution and laws, which reflected republican ideals by demanding military subordination to civilian control without regard to material objectives or outcome.[1]

Jackson biographer Robert Remini argues that since "no one of like determination and military skill had command on the northern frontier, the course of American expansion . . . was directed southward."[2] This view fails to consider the strength of the resistance mounted by the British and Canadians and the difficulties of supplying large forces along the northern border as reasons for the failure of U.S. expansion there, but it does highlight the decisive role of individual leaders in the military operations and territorial expansion of the early republic. More important for this study, the offensive against Spanish Florida suggests the decisive role of national military power in the early republic's expansion. Although Jackson was not a career officer, the decisive phase in his lifelong career of expansionism occurred during his years as one of the army's two top-ranking generals between 1814 and 1821. With half the army at his command, Jackson would not repeat the stalemate that had kept East Florida in Spanish hands in 1812. Old Hickory was determined to secure the southern borderlands for American landholders, of whom he was characteristic, by whatever means he considered necessary, and his iron will drove this bellicose approach to the defense and aggrandizement of American interests in the southern borderlands from the War of 1812 until his death. As division commander he pursued a belligerent path throughout his tenure on the Florida frontier, one he self-righteously justified in a rhetorically rigid but flexibly pragmatic language of national sovereignty, self-defense, and honor that fellow officers easily identified with. Jackson summed up his willingness to disregard Spanish sovereignty and the inviolability of international borders for putatively defensive purposes when he prepared to invade Florida in 1817:

> The protection of our citizens will require that the Wolf be struck in his den, for . . . if ever the Indians find out that the territorial boundary of Spain is to be a sanctuary, their murders will be multiplied to a degree that our citizens on the southern frontier cannot bear. Spain is bound by treaties to keep the Indians within her territory at peace with us. Having failed to do this, necessity will justify the measure, after giving her due notice, to follow the marauders and punish them in their retreat.[3]

Once this was done, Jackson wanted the United States to replace ineffectual Spain with a truly sovereign power that would directly protect and project American interests.

The onset of war with Britain changed the international equation in West Florida, providing a much more viable rationale for preemptive occupation, since Britain was likely to exploit its naval power to make incursions along the Gulf coast. These incursions would threaten American slavery and empower the militant Creeks (known to white frontiersmen as "Red Sticks") in their resistance to accommodation and U.S. expansion. James Wilkinson feared "calamitous consequences" from the "menacing" Creeks, who still numbered in the thousands. Back in command at New Orleans in July 1812 following his exoneration by court-martial, Wilkinson immediately began planning to seize Mobile and Pensacola should the pretext arise, a move he thought "due the Interests & Honor of the nation, and to the character . . . of the executive." It mattered little to Wilkinson that Pensacola was outside the boundaries claimed by Madison's proclamation of sovereignty in 1810. Using language much like that he employed during the 1806 crisis along the Sabine, Wilkinson's stream-of-consciousness letters exemplify the national and statist orientation of senior military commanders, as well as the fusion of confidence, belligerence, and self-justification that was standard among American officials in the southern borderlands. Citing his restrictive instructions, the brigadier asked for authority to seize Pensacola, declaring that he would "most cautiously avoid wanton provocation" yet test Spanish "determination, in such a way as must make him [Spain] the aggressor & put him in the wrong." He intended to do so by advancing to the Mobile River and "inoffensively" asserting the right of navigation the United States had claimed since 1798. Wilkinson hoped Spain would respond militarily; this was unlikely, given the balance of power in the area, but if the opportunity arose, the general vowed he would "not hesitate a moment to offend with all my force, & to the utmost extent [meaning Pensacola] . . . within my reach."[4]

Wilkinson's letters suggest that his perpetual balancing act was growing more precarious in the aftermath of so many investigations, along with a remarkable willingness to lay things out in the open for his civilian superiors. "Dare I exercise my discretion for the public good, after all my grievous sufferings [his 1811 court-martial] for having saved the nation from a civil war [presumably by turning on Aaron Burr]? I will think of it, because I am ready to sacrifice myself in the cause of my country, or in the defense of innocent unoffending fellow Citizens." In other words, "I may decide to attack Mobile and Pensacola without instructions to do so, Mr. Secretary of War. But, if that bothers you, I was just rambling." Yet however deceitful his language and means, Wilkinson was much more in accord with the widespread spirit of militant expansionism among civilian politicians than most historians give him credit for. Congress authorized the seizure of Mobile in February 1813; two months later Wilkinson besieged the Spanish fort, which surrendered without bloodshed.[5]

Pensacola remained in Spanish hands until Jackson, a state militia general commissioned as a brigadier in the national army in April 1814, after his victories over the Creeks, compelled its surrender that November. He did so despite explicit orders not to do anything that would cause conflict with Spain.

Yet those orders were issued late and arrived even later, and they may have been nothing more than a gesture at plausible deniability. Nor was Jackson flying solo into Pensacola. Future Missouri senator Thomas Hart Benton, a colonel commanding the Thirty-ninth Infantry Regiment and an old rival of Jackson's from Tennessee, reported to Brigadier General Thomas Flournoy—who had sought authority to seize Pensacola a year earlier—that he had advanced against the Indians along the Escambia River in July, almost certainly into Spanish territory. Benton also dispatched a captain to Pensacola to gather intelligence on Spain's relations with the Red Sticks, which he used to justify aggression to Flournoy. Using morally freighted language much like Jackson's, Benton "deem[ed] it my duty to disperse" the Creeks, demanding to know whether "the law of nations, or the policy of the republic," could possibly "forbid us to go there and bayonet these villains." Though he was Jackson's personal enemy, Benton agreed with his fellow Tennessean that "the *occupation* of Pensacola" was "indispensable" to protect the frontier, and he offered a plan for a surprise march from the Escambia to crush the Red Sticks around Pensacola. When Benton became sick, militia lieutenant colonel George Nixon advanced to the banks of Pensacola Bay before returning to American soil.[6]

Sharp Knife began to set the table for a more sustained meal by demanding that Spanish governor Mateo González Manrique arrest the Red Sticks for conveyance to the United States, reporting intelligence that the British had landed supplies for them in West Florida, violating Spanish neutrality. The governor, who lacked the force to do so, whatever his intent, refused, citing the lack of American action against the Gutiérrez-Magee expedition and the Baratarian corsairs in Louisiana. Manrique further aggravated the belligerent Tennessean by referring Jackson to Spanish treaties that guaranteed the Creeks' right to "hospitality" in Florida. Indeed, the governor appeared determined to push all Jackson's buttons, declaring that the Apalachicola, the principal site of British activity in West Florida, was not Spanish territory, based on a 1765 treaty in which the Creeks had ceded part of West Florida to the British. Language barriers notwithstanding, Manrique appeared disingenuous. Whether Indian, Spanish, or American, wise men did not offer Andrew Jackson a choice of interpretations.[7]

Jackson was happy to take up the gauntlet, throwing it back with the sort of language only he would employ, threatening to execute three Spanish sailors should the Indians kill an overseer and two slaves they had captured. Meanwhile, he sent the War Department his initial demand, along with the report of the officer he had dispatched to Pensacola, and repeated his request for orders to take the town. On July 18 Secretary of War John Armstrong answered Jackson's first query with tacit approval: "If all the circumstances stated by you unite, the conclusion is inevitable. It becomes our duty to carry our arms where we find our enemies." Though he cautioned the general to check the facts, the secretary concluded that "the result of this enquiry must govern. If they admit . . . and cooperate with the British and hostile Indians, we must strike on the broad principle of self-preservation."[8] Nor was Jackson's belligerence exceptional: four days after the Tennessean wrote to Armstrong a second time, Adjutant and Inspector General Daniel Parker advised James Monroe, who had just replaced Armstrong as secretary of war, to seize Pensacola. Amazingly, Jackson did not receive Armstrong's message for six months. In the meantime, even though William C. C. Claiborne wished "to God, you had orders to take Pensacola," Jackson knew he lacked that authority and remonstrated that "it is alone by a manly dignified course of conduct that we ensure respect from other nations and peace to our own. Temporising will not do. . . . I can but regret that permission [has] not been given by the government . . . had this been done the American Eagle would now have soared above the fangs of the British Lyon."[9]

Sharp Knife did not rest, however. Hearing rumors of 35,000 British and Spanish troops in the Gulf of Mexico and that the governor of Pensacola had declared Jackson's treaty with the Creeks a violation of Spanish sovereignty, Old Hickory welcomed reports that Secretary of War Monroe supported belligerent measures. On October 10 the general repeated his request for authority to seize Pensacola, and he soon determined to go ahead unless he was positively forbidden to do so. On October 20 he advised his friend John Coffee, "I have been making every exertion to destroy the Hotbed of the war, and the asylum of our enemies . . . as soon as [I am] reinforced, a moment is not to be lost to make the blow . . . say nothing about the intended attack on P———a." Monroe finally responded the following day, stating that the president forbade an assault, but this letter arrived too late to alter Jackson's decision. On October 26 he wrote to Monroe that he would take Pensacola; he did so on November 7, after threatening to give no quarter during the assault. Meanwhile, an expedition led by Major Uriah Blue scoured Spanish territory along the Escambia for Red Sticks. Jackson had good strategic and operational reasons for seizing Pensacola—especially to deny its use to the British, who respected Spanish neutrality no more than the Americans did. Indeed, fire from a British naval squadron offshore caused Jackson to reorient his advance against the town. Nor had the general actually been prohibited from making the assault, since Monroe did not send the letter doing so until he had been in office for an entire month. Given the Virginian's record of support for Mathews, Gutiérrez, and the West Florida rebels and his later convenient lapses of

The Barrancas, Pensacola: the Spanish looked in the wrong direction. (Photograph by Jack E. Boucher, courtesy Library of Congress, HABS FLA, 17-PENSA, 3–1)

attention as president and commander in chief during Jackson's second invasion of Florida in 1818, one has to be suspicious: the assault on Pensacola was not simply "Jackson being Jackson." Nor did Monroe's failure to rebuke his chief southern general bode well for efforts to restrain Jackson during the later invasion, when the Tennessee tornado offered to seize Florida "without implicating the Government."[10]

Jackson's incursions into Florida grew out of British efforts to take advantage of the "Creek War" of 1813–1814. This conflict began as a civil war between Creek nativists and traditionalists—the conservative Red Sticks, who were roused to militant resistance to white expansion—and accommodationists, who hoped to preserve Creek autonomy by accepting some white ways and otherwise stalling for time. The general's long-term strategy for subjugating the Creeks was founded on his understanding of the dynamics of native resistance to American expansion. He first intended to cut the Creek territory in half by building a military road from Tennessee to Mobile, providing an avenue for accelerated American settlement and the gradual dispossession of the Indians. The intensified pressure of white settlement and the lure of white commerce would further divide the Creeks, socially and politically as well as geographically, aggravating the split between nativists and accommodation-ists. Jackson would then seize Pensacola to expel the Spanish and isolate the southern Indians by preventing British aid. Short-term security and long-range expansionism were intimately connected in the general's plans. In the words of his leading biographer, "There was no question in Jackson's mind that the removal of [European] influence . . . was essential to the final solution of the Indian problem. . . . He intended to eliminate all foreigners along the south-ern frontier as a necessary prelude to the systematic destruction of the Indian menace and the territorial expansion of the American nation."[11]

Jackson's victory over the Creeks at Horseshoe Bend in March 1814 forced thousands from Georgia and Alabama into Florida. The Treaty of Fort Jack-son, which he coerced from the friendly and accommodationist Creeks and some of the Red Stick leaders he had defeated, gave up 23 million acres of land to white settlement, connecting Georgia and Tennessee and isolating the Creeks from direct territorial contact with Florida. Nevertheless, the interna-tional boundary between Spain and the United States remained in place, a barrier to complete American hegemony over the southeastern Indians. Yet only British military power (or the military might of a combination of Euro-pean states permitted to cross the Atlantic by Britain) or divisions among U.S. policy makers could have checked American expansion. Thus, early in 1815, Spanish minister Luis de Onís proposed that Britain be given control of Florida in return for British military guarantees of Spanish rule over Cuba and Louisiana. The British and Spanish governments both rejected his plan as a prescription for continued war, which neither could afford. On the American side, Albert Gallatin, one of the peace commissioners at Ghent, was confident that the United States could seize Spanish Florida at any time, and he advised Monroe to keep the issue out of the negotiations with Britain to preserve American freedom of action.[12]

The Treaty of Ghent was supposed to restore the prewar status quo. Thus, Article 9 of the treaty required that the United States restore all lands taken from the Indians since 1811 (i.e., beginning with William Henry Harrison's assault on Tecumseh's northwestern confederacy). The treaty clearly man-dated that there would be no boundary changes due to the war unless explic-itly specified therein; the provisions of Article 9 applied to "all the tribes . . . with whom [the United States] may be at war at the time of [the treaty's] rat-ification." Yet the words of the treaty ran entirely counter to Jeffersonian views about Indian sovereignty, particularly those held by Andrew Jackson and the westerners he represented. Although the United States made treaties with Indian polities as if they were distinct nations, it did not recognize boundaries between whites and Indians as international borders like those with Spain and

Britain, and it considered the Native Americans subjects rather than citizens. Article 9 exemplified the British desire to employ the Indians as barriers to U.S. expansion, hearkening back to the prewar situation in which the United States had great influence but no real dominion over the Creeks, much less over tribes close to British supply and distant from U.S. power in Michigan, Illinois, or farther west. The war had changed that, certainly in the Southeast, and Jackson had no intention of giving up the opportunity to establish dominion over the Creeks.[13]

Indeed, implementing Article 9 would have been a clear step toward the development of the Indian buffer states sought by the British but rejected by U.S. negotiators at Ghent. Under the circumstances, one has to wonder how seriously either set of negotiators intended the provision. On the scene in Alabama, Jackson maintained that the Treaty of Fort Jackson had concluded hostilities and removed the Creeks from the jurisdiction of the treaty later ratified with Britain. Though it can be argued that American bullying still constituted a de facto state of war—in August 1814 Jackson warned Creek chiefs that "the war is not yet over"—active hostilities had receded to the point of occasional raids by a few Indians and white frontiersmen, fed by interethnic friction and competition for land. Diplomatically, the Creeks with whom Sharp Knife had made the treaty were not representative of the divided Creek nation, but this was true of virtually every agreement the United States had made with Native Americans. It was up to the British to decide whether they believed that Article 9 had been violated, and far more British pressure would have been necessary to enforce it.[14]

Gallatin's advice proved sound. With the Napoleonic Wars at an end, the British ministry sought improved relations with the United States, in large part to secure Britain's Atlantic strategic flank while it tried to preserve a European balance of power against the conservative monarchies of Russia, France, Austria, and Prussia. Doing so precluded the sustained commitment of resources to forceful diplomacy in North America: apart from a single warning by Foreign Minister Castlereagh to Ambassador John Quincy Adams in February 1816, there is little evidence that British policy makers ever seriously intended to resist U.S. pressure against Florida or to employ it as a pretext for containment or the renewal of war. Indeed, the occasion for Castlereagh's warning was his disavowal of any British interest in a rumored offer of Florida from Spain. Instead, the European and American theaters of British strategy came together in Britain's desire to penetrate Latin American markets, which required allowing the Latin American revolutions to run their course to independence or autonomy from Spanish regulation. Doing so depended on preventing the Continental monarchies from uniting to support Spanish efforts to reconquer the colonies. In effect, the end of the Napoleonic Wars fostered a rapid shift in Britain's efforts to preserve a balance of power, and to enhance its own power, that favored the United States. (Whether this underlying congruence of interests was present throughout the Napoleonic Wars is one of the great questions in the history of American foreign relations; the speed of the rapprochement after 1814 suggests that it was.) This shift made it very unlikely that Britain would intervene to save Spanish Florida from the United States; time and power were on the American side.[15]

It took some time before this dynamic became clear to American civilian policy makers, who worried that precipitate aggression would draw Britain to Spain's defense. Despite the mutual benefits of renewed access to each other's markets, tensions ingrained by two generations of conflict would take time to dissipate, and diplomatic historians have observed that civilian leaders "displayed deep concern and great insecurity" over the future of Anglo-American relations for several years after 1815. Indeed, British arrogance and hostility seemed to mount steadily throughout 1814; the British commanders dispatched against New Orleans were instructed that the Louisiana Purchase was illegitimate and that Louisiana might be restored to Spain should the offensive succeed. Yet British military planning and operations within the Gulf and American theaters were subordinate to national strategic policy and diplomacy, and the negotiations, signature, and ratification of the treaty went forward without regard for the campaign in the Gulf. British negotiating demands changed in the late summer along with the fortunes of war—most importantly, their defeat on Lake Champlain. Further stymied at Fort McHenry, operational commanders continued to pursue amphibious campaigns along the American coast, but it seems unlikely that victory at New Orleans would have led the British to repudiate the treaty, which they ratified and sent to the United States before the battle was fought. Nevertheless, the Treaty of Ghent was widely regarded as "a truce rather than a peace," to quote negotiator John Quincy Adams. The possibility of continued hostilities was suggested by an incident between an American gunboat and a British rocket vessel in mid-March, as well as persistent rumors that Britain might attempt to hold outposts along the Gulf.[16]

Under these circumstances, even policy makers previously identified as War Hawks or expansionists—most importantly Madison, Monroe, and Henry Clay—worried about the danger of renewed warfare with Britain, particularly in light of the divisions that had appeared within the United States during the War of 1812. As historian James Lewis has observed, civilian Republican leaders recognized what a close call the war had been and "generally lacked the public's sense of achievement and self-confidence" derived from victory at

"Jim Boy," a Red Stick Creek leader. (Courtesy Library of
Congress, LC-USZC4-12426)

New Orleans. Indeed, Lewis makes it clear that the major Republican factions
were unable to agree on the nature of the principal dangers the nation faced—
internal or external, too much power over citizens or too little against enemies. Hence, the administration initially took a much less sanguine, and much
less aggressive, view of the situation in the southern borderlands than the
army's generals, directing Jackson to secure the nation's Gulf and South
Atlantic coasts against the possibility of British attack before turning against
Indian threats.[17]

Secretary of War William Crawford reiterated this priority in March 1816,
yet Crawford's sense of priorities and possibilities was as far off as his timing.
There was little Jackson could do to strengthen the nation's coastal defenses,

which depended on appropriations for construction, repair, cannon, and garrison troops that Congress still hesitated to provide, but the general had a much more valuable goal in mind. The acquisition of Florida had been the leading territorial objective in American foreign policy since the Louisiana Purchase. Facing little effective resistance from President Madison or Congress, then bolstered by the tacit sanction of the Monroe administration and the overt support of most leaders in Georgia and Alabama, Sharp Knife and his subordinates enjoyed a virtual blank check for belligerence along the southern frontier. Writing from the perspective of national civilian policy makers, Lewis has characterized U.S. international policy during the immediate postwar era as a "quest for security."[18] Yet "security" has many sources and meanings. Senior military commanders—indeed, most senior civilian policy makers—had understood security preclusively since the days of Jefferson and Wilkinson. From Jefferson to Monroe, security continued to serve as justification for almost any course of action policy makers chose. Freebooters and filibusters aside, American officials were the most energetically aggressive actors in the Gulf borderlands, and military commanders were the most powerful, energetic, and aggressive U.S. officials on the scene. Junior or senior, these officers apparently felt little of the concern for British intervention that Lewis attributes to civilian policy makers; instead, they repeatedly employed exaggerated estimates of Spanish belligerence as pretexts for plans to invade Florida. Despite intermittent War Department instructions, it does not appear that Madison had a consistent policy toward Spain, Florida, or the Gulf borderlands, a policy-making vacuum the generals were happy to exploit.

The Tennessee generals took advantage of the disjunctures between popular politics and public policy, between public policy and rumored intent, incrementally developing a new level of autonomy from constitutional civilian control that would flower into undeclared war against Spain in 1818. Indeed, historians David and Jeanne Heidler have observed that the army's commanders often acted "as if it were an independent branch of government," taking advantage of opportunities for expansion on the nation's southern frontier. Although historians have increasingly argued that Monroe was a strong executive with a clear foreign policy vision, the real executive branch along the southern border, the most active and effective agency of the U.S. government, was the army.[19]

Broader institutional and technological factors also account for some of the ease with which the generals were able to act independently. Letters from Washington commonly took two to three weeks to reach the Georgia frontier and as much as a month to reach New Orleans; then they had to catch up with the movements of the intended recipients. Indeed, letters were supposed to be routed through the chain of command, so it could easily take at least six weeks for Crawford to write to Jackson in Nashville and for Jackson to write to Edmund Gaines (now a brigadier general) on the Florida frontier. To take advantage of or react to changing operational circumstances demanded a degree of flexibility and thus autonomy, leading to the issuance of very general instructions that gave military commanders plenty of discretion, commonly using that exact word.[20] The confidence of experienced veterans—eager to avoid any repetition of the 1815 reduction in force by demonstrating the army's value as an instrument of U.S. policy—also contributed to the army's operational autonomy, especially in light of the frequent turnover at the head of the War Department. Three different men—James Monroe, Alexander Dallas, and William H. Crawford—served as secretary of war during 1815. Former Georgia senator Crawford held the post for about a year in 1815 and 1816 before moving to the Treasury, after which the chief clerk of the War Department served as acting secretary during much of 1816 and virtually all of 1817. Without consistent civilian oversight, army leaders took executive authority into their own hands.

Congress met for no more than a couple of months a year during this era, and the specific goals and limitations of military operations were rarely delineated through a series of precise written orders or rules of engagement passed down the official chain of command from president to secretary to commanders in the field. Nor were political advisers or diplomatic emissaries from the State Department any more common than they had been before the War of 1812. If anything, they would have been less so—and less influential—since state governors had replaced federal territorial governors like Claiborne as the principal civil executives in the southern borderlands; because they were outside the federal executive branch, they had no claim to formal authority over federal military officers. Apart from the governors, Indian agents were the only federal civil officials in the region with significant institutional influence over Indian relations, international diplomacy, or security policy. But these agents were increasingly young men, often former army officers, who held little sway over the willful Jackson or the veteran Gaines, their former commanders. Benjamin Hawkins, longtime agent to the Creeks, died in 1816; Return Meigs, longtime agent to the Cherokee, died in 1823. The Choctaw and Chickasaw agents dealt with smaller tribes distant from the theater of army operations, and they were easily overawed by Jackson's ferocity. Indeed, after 1815 the generals resumed the leading role James Wilkinson had played in southern Indian diplomacy between 1800 and 1803. By the time John C. Calhoun took over the War Department as Monroe's third or fourth choice in December 1817, Jackson's subordinates had instigated the Seminole War, and the new secretary had to try to control independent-minded generals while dispatching their leader, the most independent of them all, to take command of the invasion of Florida. Lack of oversight combined with civilian recognition of the need for operational discretion made a mockery of military accountability to constitutional civilian control. Jackson could go as far as he wanted to, and he was not one to worry about consequences.[21]

Under these circumstances, the whole executive chain of command was covered by what later generations would call "plausible deniability." It proved impossible to hold an officer of Jackson's political stature—a virtual North American caudillo—accountable for his actions in the borderlands. The Madison and Monroe administrations should have recognized that they needed to exercise more direct control over a man of Jackson's demonstrated willfulness, yet no special diplomatic emissaries or civilian agents of the executive branch were ever dispatched to advise or constrain him. However, given Old Hickory's prestige in the borderlands and his political influence, it might have been difficult to change his course of action regardless of the mechanisms employed. Indeed, although the general deserved censure for his unconstitutional actions, his aggressive policy was essentially in accord with the wishes of the frontier citizenry and their elected representatives, to whom Jackson frequently referred when justifying his actions to his civilian superiors. No other career officer—with the occasional exception of Edmund Gaines, a longtime resident in the southern borderlands himself—would venture to make such political statements to his constitutional superiors, but Jackson's outspokenness reflected his rank and political influence rather than attitudes that were distinct from those of the majority of his subordinates or from southern citizens in general. Jackson's real power came from his personal qualities and the people whose interests he represented as much as from his commission from the president and its confirmation by the Senate. Representing the interests of the plantation South and the southern and western frontier more than those of the United States as a whole, Jackson and many of his officers (regardless of their place of birth) were fundamentally sectional agents rather than truly national ones: national security meant southern security, first and foremost.

Although British Foreign Minister Castlereagh quickly ordered an end to official contacts with the Indians and the withdrawal of British troops from posts on American soil, some British military officers persisted in unauthorized efforts to contain American expansion by providing aid to the Florida Indians and maroons (armed fugitives from slavery, particularly from Georgia). In 1814 British commanders had armed and trained as many as 4,000 Indians and 1,000 African American maroons in Florida. Early in 1815 Admiral Alexander Cochrane left Major Edward Nicholls (sometimes spelled

William Harris Crawford, by Daniel Huntington. (Courtesy Army Art Collection)

Nicolls) and Lieutenant George Woodbine with a contingent of black soldiers (both maroons and West Indian colonial troops) at a fort at Prospect Bluffs near the mouth of the Apalachicola River, about 130 miles east of Pensacola. Nicholls's initial orders were to protect the Creek refugees until their lost territory was restored, per Article 9 of the Treaty of Ghent. The British had left the fort's heavy cannon in place, and the major was given discretion to leave substantial amounts of small arms and other supplies for the Indians upon his departure.[22] Unaware of the signing of the Treaty of Ghent, the British armada left the New Orleans area on February 6 and moved to Mobile, where it took Fort Bowyer by siege on February 12. News of the treaty arrived the following day, but the British waited until they received news of the treaty's final ratification before returning the fort and departing on March 15. Two days before, unsure if or when the British would leave, Monroe had ordered Jackson to expel any British forces that did not evacuate the portion of West Florida (west of the Perdido River) claimed by the United States. On March 29 Nicholls was ordered to withdraw from Prospect Bluffs, a clear sign that the British had no intention of fighting to enforce Article 9, but slow communication and logistical difficulties delayed his departure until June. By that time, Brigadier General Gaines, Jackson's chief subordinate in the Southern Division of the U.S. Army, was advocating an attack on the fort, more than sixty miles south of the international border—a resumption of war with Britain.[23]

Gaines, a Tennessean who had almost assaulted Spanish Mobile as a captain in 1811, was the principal military commander—indeed, the most powerful and influential American official of any kind—on the frontier between the end of the War of 1812 and Jackson's resumption of field command nearly three years later. During the 1820s Gaines developed a more complex approach to dealing with Native Americans, but his faith in U.S. expansion was never shaken or blurred by ambiguity. Nor did concern about the great European powers dismay him as it did civilian policy makers like Madison, Adams, and Monroe. Pondering potential duty assignments in June 1815, the brigadier informed Jackson that "I like the South bordering upon the Floridas . . . because it seems probable that amid the throes and convulsions of Europe something may turn up from which the U. States may feel at liberty to take possession." Like many veterans of the War of 1812, Gaines's personal and professional motives were closely allied. The war had whetted his already considerable appetite for professional experience, excitement, and reputation, and he knew that "this [opportunity] may gain us some active service." Gaines wanted to know if Jackson was going to assign him to the Florida frontier (the Seventh Military Department) or the Mississippi (the Eighth). Sharp Knife saw a man after his own heart: the brigadier was just as aggressive as the elder Tennessean. Gaines's words and deeds provide the most powerful evidence that Jackson was not an anomaly among the hard-bitten veterans of the Southern Division. Nor, given the brigadier's outstanding wartime record and decade of experience along the Florida frontiers before the War of 1812, can it reasonably be said that he was just taking orders from Old Hickory. Instead, we find Jackson spending most of his time at Nashville and the Hermitage, while Gaines conducted American foreign policy along the Florida border, sometimes writing even more belligerently than his ferocious superior.[24]

Nor were the generals alone in their anger at the junior British officers encouraging red and black resistance. Benjamin Hawkins, the U.S. agent to the Creeks, initially opposed the harsh terms of Jackson's treaty and requested that the general be barred from further negotiations. Yet Hawkins felt no sympathy for British adventurers and soon vowed that the United States should "apply a military correction" to "crush" Nicholls if British officials did not recall him and the Spanish did not drive him from their territory. Responding to Nicholls's claims, Hawkins told the Creeks that the Treaty of Ghent did not invalidate the Treaty of Fort Jackson, and he threatened to "compel every Indian South of Ohio to obey the voice of our Chiefs." At the level of Atlantic diplomacy, Monroe, now secretary of state, protested against Nicholls's actions to the British chargé d'affaires in Washington.[25] Bolstered by Jackson's belligerence, Gaines began planning military operations against the opponents of American expansion as soon as he returned to the southern frontier. Intermittent violence, however small scale, demonstrated that Creek resistance had not ceased, and in May 1815 Gaines advised the War Department that "the Indians are under the impression that the land ceded to the United States by the treaty with General Jackson must be restored . . . and that their friends the British will reestablish them." Should the U.S. government uphold the Treaty of Fort Jackson, the brigadier thought there was "little doubt that these deluded savages [would] meditate a renewal of the war upon our frontier inhabitants." Gaines's proposed solution tied native and maroon resistance together. Though it would require advancing deeper into Spanish Florida than ever before, Gaines wrote, "I persuade myself [that] the Government may be at liberty to sanction . . . a decisive stroke upon the depots at Apalachicola" (the maroon fort established by Woodbine and Nicholls at Prospect Bluffs). Like Jackson, the brigadier argued that Spain had a responsibility to prevent native attacks originating from its soil. Disingenuously, he gave the Spanish just enough credit to urge that "if [Spain] does not restrain them we may conclude that she endeavored to do so but is unable; can she blame us . . . for restraining them ourselves?"[26]

Gaines did not really believe the Spanish were sincere; nor, in all probability, did he care. The brigadier added some telling lines to the "duplicate" letter he sent to Jackson: "The laws of nature as admitted by civilized nations sanction such a measure of self-preservation, and we are too well acquainted with the policy and principles of a Spanish provincial Governor to place any reliance upon his friendship or good offices on these occasions." Nor did Gaines trust his civilian superiors in Washington: while he asked the division commander to authorize an incursion into Florida, he merely advised the War Department that he was "unable to obtain satisfactory information as to the hostile intentions" of the Creeks. It thus remains unclear whether the brigadier promised Jackson "as much secrecy as possible" in order to deceive the Creeks, maroons, and Spaniards; to conceal his intentions from the secretary

A young Edmund Gaines, Jackson's protégé, engraving after John Wesley Jarvis, in Frank E. Stevens, *Black Hawk War* (1903).

of war; or both. Gaines's civilian superiors had to be content with assurances that he had instructed Major Reuben Chamberlin, dispatched to Pensacola as a spy, "to avoid giving offence to the Spanish authorities, or exciting their suspicions."[27]

The Senate ratified the Treaty of Ghent on February 15, 1815; the senators unanimously ratified the Treaty of Fort Jackson the following day, indicating that they saw no conflict between the two. Whether the Senate's action was due to confusion, inattention, an intention to secure the gains Jackson had won, or a desire to avoid controversy, it encouraged expansionist generals to choose the path they preferred, with little fear of effective rebuke from their civilian superiors in the executive branch. Announcing the Treaty of Fort Jackson the preceding August, Sharp Knife had warned the Creeks, "*We will run a line between our friends and our enemies.*" A year later, when acting secretary of war Alexander Dallas instructed Jackson to cooperate with federal commissioners appointed to treat with the southern Indians to clarify the prewar boundaries per Article 9, the general ignored him. Instead, he dispatched Gaines with the Seventh Infantry Regiment to guard a different group of federal commissioners, who were surveying the boundaries of the Fort Jackson cession as a prelude to selling the land to whites. Southern and western political pressure had led to a dual—indeed, two-faced—policy, which military commanders exploited to the hilt.[28]

The generals continually spoke and acted as if the struggle for the borderlands was occurring in a diplomatic vacuum, in willful contrast to civilian concerns about British intervention. Meanwhile, civilian control of the military was sorely tried by a vacuum in civilian leadership, the product of Republican factionalism and a remarkable inattention from presidents Madison and Monroe in the midst of war and postwar uncertainty. For three crucial years, from August 1814 to December 1817, the position of secretary of war was held by a series of temporary appointees: Monroe during the last third of 1814 and the final crisis of the War of 1812, while doing double duty as secretary of state; Dallas for the first half of 1815, while doing double duty as secretary of the treasury; Crawford in 1815 and 1816; and the chief clerk of the War Department, George Graham, in 1816 and 1817. Not coincidentally, the only sustained effort to exert strong civilian leadership came from Crawford. In contrast, Gaines had been serving on the Florida border since 1802; Jackson had served as U.S. senator a full decade before Crawford, representing a more populous state that had substantially resolved its "Indian problem" by defeating the Cherokee, which Crawford's Georgia had proved unable to do with the Creeks. Like James Wilkinson dealing with Louisiana territorial governor Claiborne before the War of 1812, Jackson and Gaines had little reason to regard the inexperienced secretaries as better informed about borderlands issues. Indeed, Jackson considered such men his superiors only in the most formal sense. In only one year out of the three was the secretary a powerful politician clearly sanctioned by senatorial confirmation, but Jackson felt little respect for Crawford, and the Georgian ultimately quit the War Department for the Treasury, a clear sign of his defeat by the general.

Moreover, despite the War Department's caution, the generals sometimes received intimations of approval from the highest civil authorities, a tacit sympathy that undermined their more restrictive instructions. Eight days after he instructed Jackson to cooperate with the Article 9 boundary survey commission, acting secretary of war Dallas conveyed Madison's views about Red Stick, Seminole, and maroon resistance to U.S. expansion to General Gaines: "The incompetency of the Spanish authorities . . . would certainly justify any use of our arms for self-defense." Madison may have had a different concept of "self-defense" than Gaines and Jackson, and Dallas may have been pandering to the generals or making what he considered a generic observation. But Dallas's statement, which virtually mirrored Gaines's arguments for attacking Florida and came just after Jackson's letters to that effect, must have seemed like an endorsement to the belligerent brigadier. The Tennesseans saw Spanish "incompetency" as fact and opportunity; they intended to use any latitude or discretion the president appeared to grant them.[29]

The generals received further confirmation of their views when the territorial governor of Mississippi, the highest federal civil official in the region, organized the Fort Jackson cession as Monroe County that month. Gaines's principal assignment during the remainder of 1815 was to run the boundary survey. Jackson had laid out the strategic rationale for the survey in his address to Creek leaders during the treaty's "negotiation" the preceding August, when he began to think about striking Pensacola:

> We know the war is not over. . . . *We will destroy our enemies* . . . enemies must be separated from Friends . . . our friends will sign the treaty. . . . Our enemies must depart. . . . We wish them to join their friends that all may be destroyed together. . . . [Your] signatures to this, will show your father the President of the United States *his friends*—our soldiers will *know them & their towns* by this paper. . . . Those who do not sign it shall have provisions to go to Pensacola.[30]

Either way, Jackson was happy: if the Creeks took advantage of his offer, he would surely use their presence in Pensacola as a cudgel to beat the Spanish.

Gaines was characteristically bellicose about this mission, instructing brevet Colonel James McDonald that, "Should you discover a spirit of hostility to prevail among [the Creeks], you will endeavour by a prompt movement, and decisive attack upon any force that may present itself, to check any attempt to oppose the running of the line." A month later, as Creek opposition increased, Gaines ordered the Fourth Infantry Regiment to join the Seventh in guarding the boundary survey; Jackson dispatched another warning to the Creeks, telling them, the "line must and will be run, and the least opposition brings down instant destruction on the heads of the opposers." In October, Gaines asked the War Department for authority to call on the governors of Georgia, South Carolina, and Tennessee for 5,000 militiamen to supplement his regulars. This would have created an army larger than any of those employed on the Canadian border against the British during the War of 1812, enabling the brigadier "to give the Seminola Indians that wholesome correction, by which alone, as long experience proves, savage enemies can ever be made friendly or harmless." Unwilling to wait for Washington's reply, Gaines seized the initiative and requested militia from the governor of Georgia five days later. Newly appointed Secretary of War Crawford, who would soon try to restrain the generals, rapidly approved Gaines's request, despite his deviation from procedure. (They did not mobilize 5,000 militiamen, however.)[31]

Six days after his request for militia, Gaines volunteered to replace fellow Tennessee Indian fighter John Sevier, who had just died, among the commissioners surveying the boundary. The other principal commissioner, longtime Creek agent Benjamin Hawkins, was also ailing and was replaced by Jackson confidant John Coffee, making a very forceful group. Indeed, it appears that Gaines expected to meet Creek resistance and pursue the Indians into Florida, where he hoped to snap the link with "their *British* establishments." Angry Creeks congregated at the junction of the Flint and Chattahoochee Rivers in opposition to the survey, but the intimidating presence of 800 regulars prevented violent resistance. Ironically, the strength of Gaines's force denied him the opportunity to launch the "decisive attack" he had advocated from a distance. A tense peace was preserved, and the brigadier engaged in some premature self-congratulation, dismissing the strength of native opposition to white expansion by asserting that only British or Spanish meddling could stir up more trouble.[32]

Continually sending mixed signals, neither Congress nor the executive provided sufficient guidance to restrain the generals, who had made up their minds years before. The appointment of two competing boundary survey commissions suggests that U.S. policy makers were guessing that Britain would not fight to enforce Article 9 and thus took the more politically popular route, allowing Old Hickory to insist on his treaty at the Creeks' expense. Doing so was easier because most of the Red Sticks who refused to accept the Treaty of Fort Jackson had retreated into Florida, enabling the U.S. government to allege that they were Seminoles, rather than true Creeks who might claim Georgia or Alabama land under Article 9. Nicholls responded on his own initiative, attempting to organize a government for the Florida Indians and asserting the existence of a military alliance between Britain and the Indians. Senior British officials quickly disavowed his actions and delayed for more than a year before granting a brief meeting to Red Stick leader Hillis Hadjo (aka Josiah Francis, the Creek Prophet) in London. Indeed, in September 1815 Lord Bathhurst, the colonial secretary, told Ambassador John Quincy Adams that "this government would make no such treaty" with the Indians. Bathurst had "advise[d] them to make their terms with the United States as well as they can." The British chargé d'affaires in Washington communicated all this to Secretary of State Monroe in December. Bathhurst noted that although Josiah Francis had received presents during his visit to London, these should not be taken as evidence of active support, merely as routine diplomatic practice. Francis had secured a British officer's jacket, but this probably came from Nicholls, who continued to aid and advocate for the Indians. Nor did the American generals show any fear of British aid to the Indians. If anything, that threat was simply another reason to attack and crush native resistance as soon as possible.[33]

Gaines also followed Jackson's lead by exploiting the deep divisions among the Creeks. He employed those who had accepted accommodation as allied auxiliaries or proxy forces, which could be used while maintaining deniability for the army and the executive branch. Gaines also acted to reinforce the dependence and subordination of those who had submitted to American dominance after Horseshoe Bend. In June 1815 the brigadier ordered a month's rations delivered to Fort Jackson to feed the "friendly" Creeks, whose planting and hunting had been disrupted by the war and their uncertainty over the future. Gaines warned the starving Indians that the rations would cease if the Creeks renewed the war, "that the Nation will be held responsible for the conduct of individual Indians or parties, in all cases."[34] This policy of collective responsibility served primarily as a pretext for further coercion and U.S. expansion rather than pacifying the Creeks, who had already accepted U.S. domination. The brigadier knew that it would be unwise to apply so severe a standard strictly or universally, and he was happy to divide and conquer, accepting Creek aid in capturing "outlaw" Red Sticks for punishment by white civil authorities. This intensified divisions among the Creeks, opening even deeper wedges for American influence and intervention. Yet the decentralization of the Creeks and Seminoles, limited cultural awareness among military leaders, and officers' efforts to facilitate expansion by emphasizing Indian resistance caused confusion among even the most self-assured commanders. Gaines would spend nearly three years figuring out which Indians he had sufficient pretext to strike.

The fate of the Fort Jackson cession spurred a tug-of-war between Jackson and his civilian superiors throughout 1815 and much of 1816. Jackson demanded that the new lands be opened for white settlement as quickly as possible, but this was not Madison's first priority. In December 1815, concerned by the unrestrained flood of settlement into native lands since the end of the war, the president issued a proclamation requiring the removal, forcibly if necessary, of "all persons who have unlawfully taken possession of or made any settlement on the public lands." Interagency inertia and the difficulty of finding or catching squatters limited the order's execution. Meanwhile, Jackson encouraged federal boundary commissioners, like his friend John Coffee, to run the lines as favorably as possible, using the claims of one tribe against another and threatening "immediate punishment" and "destruction" at any hint of native opposition to American policy.[35] The Creeks lacked the unity for effective diplomatic resistance, but the Cherokee were able to bypass Jackson's smothering influence and turn the tables by traveling to Washington, where they negotiated a treaty to regain land the Creek chiefs had ceded at Fort Jackson. Sharp Knife promptly complained to Secretary of State Monroe and blamed Secretary of War Crawford, Jackson's superior and Monroe's rival, for "wantonly surrender[ing]" the fruits of the general's victories by delaying the sale of public lands. To ensure that the presidential aspirant got the message, Old Hickory hinted that the southern public "believed that the President has been badly advised," that the "hasty convention" with the Cherokee was "much regretted & deprecated in this quarter." Recurring to his plans for the Creek War, Jackson protested that the "Territory ceded was of incalculable Value to the U States, as it opened a free communication to the lower country [the Gulf coast] through our own soil . . . cut off all communication & intercourse between the southern and northwestern Indians, gave us roads unshackled by Indian claims, & supplies for our army on these roads from the certain industry of our own citizens."[36]

Jackson's criticism of the new treaty accurately reflected the weight of opinion among southern whites. The general remained willing, even eager, to assert federal authority where he believed it was justified. That summer he obediently prepared an entire battalion—at least a third of the Eighth Infantry Regiment (a very substantial force, under the circumstances)—to eject white squatters from other Cherokee lands in East Tennessee, an operation that lasted six months. His adjutant general, Robert Butler, instructed Lieutenant Robert Houston, commander of the single company that was actually deployed, to "promptly put down all opposition or resistance with the best means in your power regardless of consequences," which implied authorization for the use of lethal force against American citizens. (Indeed, such company-scale operations were more frequent against white squatters than Indians until about 1834.) Yet Jackson also asked Tennessee senator George Washington Campbell to press for more detailed—and probably more lenient—instructions about removing trespassers from public land. Most important,

Old Hickory was able to win back the disputed Alabama lands by securing appointment as one of the commissioners dispatched to negotiate new boundaries—seeking a new land cession—from the Cherokee and Chickasaw that summer.[37]

The general's appointment meant that Madison and Monroe were more concerned with placating the Tennessee tornado, hoping to restrain him from action independent of cabinet control, than with sustaining Crawford or the Cherokee. Much like Jackson's counseling of Monroe, the commissioners took special care to emphasize their political influence, reporting to Crawford that the cession they had negotiated with the Chickasaw "secured the affections of the Population of the south & west to the present administration & restored that confidence that formerly existed between the Rulers & the People"—whose breach Jackson blamed on Crawford. In October, Sharp Knife notified Monroe that he had secured the retrocession of the Cherokee and Chickasaw claims that conflicted with the Creek treaty, rejoicing that "we will now have good roads, kept up and supplied by the industry of our own citizens, and our frontier defended by a strong population." (It seems that Jackson did not seek or realize much personal profit from the process, but he did offer extensive services related to purchasing and valuing land from the Fort Jackson cession for "any gentleman or company" willing to invest at least $10,000.) It seems reasonable to assume that the man about to be elected president learned a lesson in the politics of southern expansion and recognized the powerful influence his senior southern general could bring to bear.[38]

Overt military aggression was constrained by civil authorities hesitant to provoke British reaction, so the generals took things one step at a time. Having surveyed the boundaries of the Fort Jackson cession, Sharp Knife seized on the murder of several whites and ordered Gaines to prevent Creeks from entering the area until the killers were caught. In the meantime, any Creeks found in the cession were to "be treated as enemies," regardless of their actions or legal status. Old Hickory was known to issue off-the-cuff orders during bursts of fury, but given the millions of acres in the cession, it is hard to see how this instruction could have been anything other than a pretext for renewing war in order to sweep the Creeks—"friendly" and accommodationist as well as Red Stick militants—from the region. A southerner himself, Secretary Crawford recognized this and countermanded the division commander's orders that May, admonishing the Tennessee tornado on the locus of the constitutional authority to declare war and advising him to focus his energies on restraining white intrusions on Indian lands, per the president's December proclamation. Although Jackson questioned and, in effect, rejected Crawford's order against expelling the Creeks, he did not follow through on his removal order, and peace was temporarily preserved.[39]

This was only the first major challenge of the year to civilian authority over policy in the southern borderlands, for the generals' attitudes were immune to fundamental change. Two days after Crawford issued his restraining order, but long before it reached the frontier, Gaines instructed Lieutenant Colonel Duncan Clinch that the army had to establish a fort at the junction of the Flint and Chattahoochee Rivers, "even if we have to fight our way through the ranks of the whole [Creek] nation." The determined brigadier lectured the War Department that "To reason with *savage* man . . . is to effect nothing and leave him still a savage. Force, guided by justice [Gaines's justice] *may possibly* transform him into a civilized being, but nothing else will. . . . The savage must be taught and compelled to do that which is right, and to abstain from doing that which is wrong. . . . The strong mandate of justice must be resorted to and enforced."[40]

This was hardly the subordinate tone the Constitution envisioned from military commanders. Indeed, the emotional climate of Jackson's Southern Division was such that company-grade officers—captains and lieutenants— casually gossiped with the adjutant general about "fighting for the Floridas." One such captain, dispatched to Pensacola to demand Spanish cooperation in late May 1816, returned and assured Jackson that the town was "entirely defenseless," gleefully asserting "the dissatisfaction of the inhabitants . . . and the desire of a majority to see a change [American rule] effected." We cannot truly know what the Pensacolans wanted, other than security and prosperity, but Spanish power posed no threat to the United States. Absent British intervention, the struggle for Florida was only peripherally one between the United States and its declining neighbor: American policy makers preferred to blame Indian resistance on malign European influences rather than native choices, which would admit U.S. aggression.[41]

Jackson best described the opposition to American expansion when he labeled his second invasion of Florida a "Savage and Negroe War." Spanish sovereignty provided a sanctuary for maroon as well as Indian resistance to white expansion, and fugitive slaves posed a more insidious threat than any Indian to the American system of plantation slavery. Claiming that native hostility could be motivated only by outside interference (a common trope among southern whites for the next 150 years), the general was eager to take the harshest measures possible against maroons and British agents, whom he invariably identified as abolitionists. In September 1815 Jackson warned Gaines that British influence would be behind any native resistance to the boundary survey; anticipating Confederate orders to execute white officers commanding U.S. Colored Troops during the Civil War, the division commander directed that "every whiteman or negroe found in arms with the enemy must be put to the sword." There was no middle ground in Sharp Knife's world; there would be none in Florida.[42]

Indian resistance to American expansion was an everyday affair for the generals. Black people free of white control posed a threat on a different order of magnitude, a specter that brought together all the varied elements of the generals' fears as planters and slaveholders. Indeed, the free black threat to white supremacy and the advance of plantation agriculture, rather than Indian depredations or "savagery," led to the first significant American incursion into Florida after the War of 1812—an offensive to destroy the maroon community that had developed at Prospect Bluffs on the Apalachicola. Edward Nicholls claimed to have trained at least 500 free blacks, Afro-Seminoles, and maroons during the war, and after his departure in July 1815, they retained control over the fort, from which they could hinder the flow of American supplies to Fort Scott upriver. Gaines could anticipate Jackson's views long before he received the division commander's orders. In March 1816 the brigadier hinted to Jackson, "The Negroe Establishment is (I think justly) considered as likely to produce much evil among the blacks of Georgia and the Eastern part of the Mississippi Territory. Will you permit me to break it up?" Indeed, Gaines had first sought permission to destroy the fort in May 1815, a full year before his commander discussed that option. Then he had argued that if "Spain permits our enemy to assemble forces and make military depots for our annoyance within her territory, surely she cannot make no reasonable objection to our visiting these depots." (Spanish officials had discussed attacking the fort themselves that April, but worried that doing so would inflame the Indians.) Jackson may stand out for the ferocity of his language, but his views were representative of those of his subordinates; Gaines demonstrated just as much belligerence as his commander.[43]

It is not clear at what point these ideas made their way to the War Department or whether the generals actually intended to ask Secretary Crawford's permission before invading Spanish territory, but the logic of the situation made it easy for the secretary to anticipate the generals' plans. In March 1816, four days before Gaines's request to Jackson, Crawford warned the division commander that the Spanish must be permitted to deal with the fort, located 130 miles east of Pensacola and at least 60 miles south of the border; if they did not, the president would decide what to do. It is not clear when Jackson received the secretary's restraining order, nor is it clear that this would have made any difference. Indeed, Crawford erred by advising the general that the president would undertake prompt measures to attack the fort if Spain refused and Madison decided that congressional authorization was unnecessary. Since Jackson had no confidence in the Spanish, he probably took the secretary's caution as the dillydallying of a Washington bureaucrat and no real obstacle to his discretion as the commander on the spot. His instructions to Gaines early in April further illustrate the aggressiveness and self-assurance with which senior officers enlarged on their autonomy along the border. Whatever caution Jackson's words appeared to offer was overshadowed by his belligerent rhetoric and thinly veiled hints. Heedless of his civilian superiors, the army's most powerful general proclaimed that "half peace half war is a state of things which must not exist." Although no major Indian raids had occurred, Sharp Knife seized the initiative, directing that "the growing hostile dispositions of the Indians must be checked by prompt and energetic movements. . . . No retreat must provide an asylum for them. Any town or village" refusing to surrender native fugitives "must be destroyed." Jackson concluded by offering Gaines enough autonomy to start a war: "I . . . can only repeat that you possess the power of acting on your Discretion, which I hope you will exercise." The generals' policy would be national policy.[44]

ADVANCING SLAVERY BY CRUSHING "LAWLESS BANDITTI": INVADING FLORIDA TO DESTROY THE "NEGRO FORT," 1816

Jackson's tone suggested that his primary targets were Indians, but his immediate focus was the center of maroon resistance at Prospect Bluffs. Turning to this objective, the division commander laid out a series of vague prerequisites for action against the "Negroe Fort," each of which was sure to be met when viewed from the perspective of an ardent American expansionist and southern slaveholder like General Gaines. "If the conduct of these people is such as to encourage the Indian war—if the fort harbours the Negroes of our citizens . . . or hold[s] out inducements to the Slaves of our Citizens to desert from their owners' service—this fort must be destroyed." Justifying military aggression, but never making it clear whether he had obtained the civilian approval required by the Constitution, Sharp Knife labeled the maroons a "lawless banditti" devoid of nationality and the protection of international law. American policy makers had long employed such language toward those they planned to dispossess, such as the Indians in the Northwest Territory during the 1780s and 1790s. Growing more self-assured with every word, the division commander then framed the issue as a matter of law enforcement transcending Spanish sovereignty and the normal constraints of civil authority. Jackson vilified the maroons as "a band of outlaws": "This fort," the largest concentration of refugees from chattel slavery in the South between the end of the Revolution and the Civil War, "has been established . . . for the purpose of Murder rapine and plunder . . . it ought to be blown up regardless of the ground it stands on." The general took it for granted that his subordinate "should have formed the same conclusion," and he directed Gaines to "destroy [the fort] and return the stolen negroes and property to their rightful owners."[45]

Jackson instructed the brigadier to notify the Spanish governor of his entry into Spanish territory, but the generals were unwilling to wait for the results of diplomatic action, which they assumed would be ineffectual, given Spain's inability to control the maroons and its incentive to encourage their resistance to American encroachment. Two weeks later, in mid-April 1816, Jackson dispatched a staff officer to Pensacola to demand that the governor take action against the maroon refuge, but the following day he advised Crawford that he had given Gaines discretion to assault the fort. This was not exactly true—Jackson had actually *instructed* the brigadier to destroy the fort, and instructions from a division commander, particularly from Jackson, usually had the force of orders. But Sharp Knife had no intention of shifting responsibility or blame onto Gaines—giving him discretion simply meant that Gaines was the commander on the spot and that Jackson trusted his fellow Tennessean to do what he thought was right. (Always laudably conscious of logistical constraints, Jackson understood that organizing and supplying an expedition could take time.) He certainly felt no need to restrain his belligerence for the secretary's sake or from any concern about potential congressional inquiry, vowing that he hoped Gaines had already attacked the maroons. Indeed, two months later, Old Hickory lectured Crawford that "there can be no fear of disturbing the good understanding that exists between us and Spain, by destroying the negro fort." Neither Spanish sovereignty nor Spanish permission meant anything to Jackson; the governor's refusal to grant immediate sanction for U.S. intervention only increased the general's self-righteous determination. When Jackson wrote to Crawford that he would await orders, he merely expected confirmation. Truly the tail wagged the dog.[46]

Lacking Jackson's political stature, and sensing that civilian and international leaders might not share the generals' certainty, Gaines hoped to strike the fort without implicating the United States directly. The brigadier worked with Creek agent Benjamin Hawkins on an agreement to supply a group of allied Creeks with scarce corn if they would capture the fort and turn its occupants over to the army for a bounty of $50 per head. Mistrusting the United States and fearful of undermining the tenuous balance of power that kept the Americans from taking *their* land, the "allied Creeks" could not arrive at a consensus on Gaines's proposal. Meanwhile, at Fort Scott, Lieutenant Colonel Duncan Clinch (another slaveholder who would soon settle close to the Florida border in southeastern Georgia) planned to execute Jackson's instructions to remove the Creeks from the Fort Jackson cession, an operation that would be greatly facilitated by resupply via the Apalachicola. Recognizing that the maroons shared the Indians' opposition to white expansion, Gaines hoped to use the two groups' tacit alliance as an excuse for U.S. troops to mount an assault on the fort if the maroons obstructed American movement along that river. Clinch would move farther south, three to six days' march into Spanish territory, to "strike a blow in another quarter"—against the Negro Fort, lest the maroons disrupt army preparations for further operations against the Red Sticks and Seminoles. For the expansionist commanders in the Southern Division, each enemy, each operation, became prelude and justification for another campaign. Gaines would hang Indians and maroons alike, together or separately.[47]

Jackson was not completely oblivious to politics and the Constitution and continued to look for political cover for the incursion, writing to Crawford on May 12 (the same day he wrote to Monroe to blast Crawford's Cherokee policy) that he hoped the secretary would understand the situation and permit the army to attack the fort. By this point, the executive showed signs of wavering. Near the end of that month and again on July 1, Crawford instructed Gaines to seek Spanish permission to undertake the resupply effort on the Apalachicola, which had been withheld pending approval from the captain-general in Cuba. Much more significant, the secretary focused his instructions entirely on the resupply effort rather than the growing likelihood of operations against the fort, even though he received Jackson's May 12 letter, as well as his April 24 "discretionary" authorization for Gaines, during June. The strict orders Crawford had sent in March had not been rescinded, but they were never reinforced either. Even though the prerequisite for Spanish permission might appear to preclude an attack—and might have been intended to do so—Crawford surely knew the Tennessee generals too well to make such a cavalier assumption. Indeed, if Spain authorized the use of the Apalachicola, the maroons and their Indian allies would still resist, and the generals would surely attack the fort: it would have been disingenuous for the secretary to imagine otherwise.[48]

Ultimately, the generals moved much faster than the mail, particularly because respect for the military chain of command led Crawford to write to Jackson before he dispatched instructions to Gaines. In other words, the civilian secretary accepted Jackson's military authority as the legitimate conduit

for orders to Gaines, while Gaines was able to consult with his military superior before dealing with Crawford. Whether intentional or not, this situation
allowed Jackson to shield Gaines, and the generals could deny that they had
defied the secretary's orders, which would never arrive in time to halt operations that the generals portrayed as urgent responses to local emergencies.
Indeed, memories of the generals' machinations may have led acting secretary of war George Graham to issue orders to several staff officers in 1817,
spurring a series of Jacksonian tirades and presidential efforts to fine-tune the
proper distinction between civil and military command authority.

Crawford's orders, dispatched on May 27 and repeated in a more permis-
sive tone on July 1, arrived much too late to halt Clinch's offensive. Indeed,
James Lewis suggests that by June, the secretary and the president had given
up trying to restrain the assault on the fort, noting that Madison had decided
that the army's operations along the Apalachicola "may become essential to
public safety" and could not be "prescribed by the Executive." The president
cloaked his choice by referring to "military discretion guided by imperious
emergencies," but the only thing that made operations more urgent was Jackson's growing ferocity. The generals achieved their objective on July 26, probably before Jackson received Crawford's later order or was able to forward it
to Gaines, who would then have to forward it to Clinch. The fort was taken
after a week's siege, when cannon firing from American gunboats blew up the
fort's powder magazine, killing 270 refugees from slavery. The remaining
defenders were quickly massacred by Gaines's Creek allies.[49]

Clinch's official report proudly asserted that "the great Ruler of the Uni-
verse must have used us as an instrument in chastising the blood-thirsty and
murderous wretches" who held the fort. Presumably concerned about foreign
reactions, the Madison administration kept silent rather than rebutting critical
newspaper reports, leading Clinch to threaten to speak out and explain why
he thought his actions had been officially sanctioned. Jackson's adjutant
responded that "public acts, if not publicly censured, are tacitly approved,"
and the generals placated Clinch with assurances that he had acted under their
orders. Indeed, Sharp Knife was fully prepared to expand the colonel's "resupply" expedition into a war against the Seminoles. The division commander
suggested that Clinch "demand . . . an immediate surrender of the Negroes
protected by [the Seminoles] and belonging to U.S. citizens," while holding
his infantry "in readiness to chastise them" if they refused, as Jackson no
doubt expected. Clinch had already tried to engage a Seminole force supposedly moving to the fort's rescue, but the Indians had dispersed before he could
confront them.[50]

By the summer of 1816, it should have been clear to every unbiased

A young Duncan Clinch, commander of the assault on the
Negro Fort. (Courtesy Florida Historical Society)

observer that the leaders of the southern army were bent on war against the
Seminoles and confidently looked forward to an American Florida. The concern over filibusters, frontier chaos, and international stability that had
restrained some of the officer corps (albeit a minority) before the War of 1812
was no longer evident; the generals were eager to seize the initiative, and the
dilemmas of expansion seemed limited to the potential for European intervention, which worried military officers much less than their civilian superiors. No uncertainty, no ambiguity, no tensions between ends and means
clouded the officer corps' vision of national expansion on the southern frontier. The civilian leaders of the War Department often tried to restrain them,

but the winds favored the tornadoes from Tennessee. Jackson's self-assurance and determination reinforced that of Gaines and their subordinates: it is virtually impossible to find examples of strategic uncertainty, hesitation, or dissent among the officers of the Southern Division in these years. Yet the generals were not changing or challenging the goals of U.S. foreign policy. Their hopes for expelling Spain from Florida were shared throughout the nation's civilian leadership and by most citizens; antipathy for Indians, maroons, and British agents and adventurers was just as universal. If "where you sit is where you stand," Jackson and Gaines differed from Madison and Monroe primarily in their narrower perspective on the threats to U.S. national security and the means to defeat them. That perspective contributed to a remarkable self-assurance: the generals preferred preemption to deterrence, destruction to aversion, and they used the problems of long-distance communication to create a fait accompli on their own terms.

That self-confidence was also due to recent wartime experience. Gaines and Jackson recognized British power, but they had defeated the British army in battle, even when Napoleon's abdication allowed Britain to dispatch large veteran forces against the United States, while Madison and Monroe had been compelled to flee Washington. Whether the generals had truly defeated Britain in *war* was another question; they seem to have seen no distinction between battlefield victory and victory in the war as a whole. Like British veterans in India made confident by victory over France in the Peninsular War, they implicitly identified themselves as agents of national prowess and power by taking advantage of the chaos in the Gulf borderlands to initiate territorial expansion, heedless of civilian attempts at constraint.[51] One could argue that Jackson and Gaines lacked a sense of the wider strategic level of interstate competition, that they were theater and operational commanders narrowly focused on military campaigns within their area of responsibility. More likely, Jackson and Gaines felt confident that Britain was unlikely to defeat the United States decisively, that the British had not and could not translate coastal incursions into conquest and occupation. This implicitly assumed that British incursions would have no effect on American politics and national will. Perhaps Jackson's political experience, his service exclusively in the South, and the battlefield successes both men had experienced on the frontiers fostered a parochialism that led them to dismiss the potential for cracks in national cohesion, such as the Hartford Convention and the creation of state armies solely for local self-defense in 1814. Or perhaps they believed that Jackson's victory at New Orleans had so discredited the Hartford Convention that similar efforts would not recur.

Historian James Lewis has argued that there was a significant distance between civilian and military approaches to southern frontier policy until the late spring of 1816, when continuing tension and incidents with Spain, the threat of war with Britain, and rumors of Indian war combined to close the gap.[52] Yet the administration's Indian policy was only temporarily and contingently "conciliatory," and only in comparison to Jackson's impatient belligerence. Civilian policy makers feared that Indian war might lead to renewed war with Britain or make the United States more vulnerable in case of war. Jackson easily becomes a historical straw man, because few policy makers were more aggressive, but it is more accurate to see him as the most overt agent of an underlying dynamic that was almost universal in early American Indian policy. Most important for the course of events between 1816 and 1818, civil officials did little to effectively restrain the generals, which suggests a good deal of uncertainty and ambiguity among civilian leaders: they wanted to have their cake and eat it too, to get Indian lands without the entropy Jackson temporarily fostered (and, for Crawford, the general's growing popularity). Nor was the civil-military stress in the spring of 1816 especially profound or new: Madison's willingness to allow Gaines discretion reflects an underlying ambiguity and an immediate uncertainty, approaching paralysis, rather than a lasting or decided shift in policy. The military man on the spot might endanger international peace, might threaten or be perceived to threaten constitutional military subordination to civilian authority, but neither he nor a measure of the discretion delegated to him could be dispensed with.

Whether they considered expansion part of the nation's destiny or a necessity for enhancing its security, the officers of the national army operated amid a widespread consensus in its favor, and they felt none of the hesitance, or patience, of their civilian superiors. The question was when and how to achieve the objectives most American policy makers shared: what were the costs and benefits of different courses of action leading to the same goal? Given American demands for expansion, war was a near certainty, but when, and with whom? Constitutionally, these were choices for elected civilian officials: Congress and the president. Would the generals seize that power?

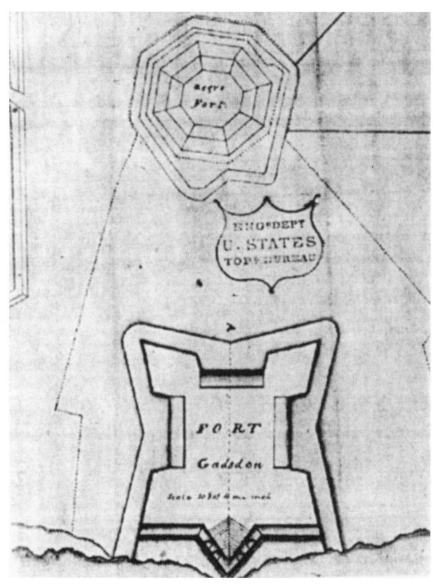

The extension of American empire: the Negro Fort and Fort Gadsden, map drawn
by an officer, c. 1818.

3

THE TENSIONS OF AGGRESSION AND ACCOUNTABILITY

Military Expansionism in the Gulf Borderlands, 1815–1817

Loosely governed by a declining metropole preoccupied with the French Revolutionary Wars and domestic political order, Spain's North American colonies were subjected to invasion by U.S. citizens from the first days of American independence. At no other point in the history of U.S. continental expansion was "flux on the peripheries"—in the borderlands between crumbling Spanish and growing American empires—so great, encouraging British, French, and U.S. citizens and policy makers to try to enhance their dominions.[1] The autonomy of individual citizens and local majorities frequently clashed with national sovereignty and the representative processes embedded in the Constitution, to say nothing of the customary norms of interstate conduct, thus threatening international war and endangering the cohesion of the national union. Nevertheless, despite the near-constant tensions and dilemmas fostered by so many interrelated problems, American leaders were confident that the nation would grow with time, and the United States never formally declared war against Spain. Instead, historian James Lewis observes that the Madison and Monroe administrations pursued "a careful balancing of risks and opportunities," "a carefully defined neutrality" that permitted Spanish American revolutionaries to divert Spanish attention from U.S. pressure against Florida, while enabling American policy makers to deny responsibility for aggressions against Spain, however implausibly.[2]

To avoid British intervention, however improbable, and to minimize sectional conflict as growth pushed or pulled the distinct interests of the nation's geographic regions onto increasingly different and even divergent paths, national policy makers gradually began to worry more about restraining adventurism by American citizens than about Spanish opposition. Despite widespread ideological resistance to more centralized or executive government, the national standing army was frequently policy makers' instrument of choice, and it was sometimes the only instrument they thought capable. Thus, the power vacuum to the south proved to be a mixed blessing for federal military officers. They found themselves in complex, often ambiguous situations as they attempted to uphold national sovereignty over U.S. foreign relations and mediate among the demands of American politicians, frontiersmen and filibusters (who were sometimes one and the same and were often tacitly supported by local, state, and even national politicians), and Spanish officials.

These dilemmas were aggravated when the Spanish colonies erupted in rebellion after 1809. Though historians have long recognized the limits of American sympathy for these revolutions during the 1820s, Lawrence Kaplan recently reminded us that "the appeal of the . . . revolutions was not confined to paranoids or romantics" during the preceding decade. Only Americans and other foreign adventurers could provide the reckless manpower for significant filibusters against Florida or Texas; the Mexican rebels and royalists were both drawn from small elites, while the majority of the population consisted of Indian or mestizo peasants who were untrained, unused to traveling far from home, and unwilling to risk their lives for elite interests. (They rebelled for their own reasons, particularly in central and southern Mexico, where civil war had a more social and class meaning than an anticolonial one.) In contrast, the British provided immensely more material aid—officially, unofficially, and semiofficially—to the South American "Patriots" than did the United States or its citizens, including the largest proportions of naval crews and entire field forces of discharged troops and officers. Like most American citizens, army officers were convinced of their nation's exceptional qualities and saw great opportunity for its political and economic growth in the turmoil to the south. Tried and blooded in the second war of independence against Great Britain, veteran military leaders were more eager than ever for excitement and glory: personal, institutional, and nationalist motives blended in the quest for professional experience and advancement in the southern borderlands. Confident American soldiers felt little patience for "delicate forbearance toward the insolent & aggressing Dons."[3]

Support for territorial expansion did not make the officer corps a monolith. Although soldiers generally favored the anticolonial revolutions as a diminution of European power, their official position and the nation's legal neutrality made it inappropriate, if not constitutionally insubordinate, to speak out or commit themselves to aiding the rebels. Filibustering spurred military suspicion of Latin insurgents and the private civilian advocates of American expansion from an early date, and national military officers anticipated the gradual disillusionment many Americans felt toward the South American republics by the early 1820s. Even if the revolutions led to territorial expansion by the United States, nationally minded soldiers worried that the freedom of American citizens and the weakness of federal laws might lead to international anarchy and war, threatening the nation's cohesion and endangering the union. Individual circumstances and contingency also made a difference, however. Officers of different backgrounds and rank, facing different missions and circumstances, responded in distinct if not fundamentally different ways to the complex and varied situations they confronted. We have significantly more evidence of how officers stationed in the South viewed those borderlands compared with those in the Northern Division who were focused on the Canadian border, and this chapter, like those that precede and follow it, is primarily the story of the army's Southern Division.[4]

The postwar officer corps was small enough that much of the Southern Division's aggressiveness during these years can be traced to the influence of Andrew Jackson, the major general in command of that division, whose unique willfulness and determination to expel Indians and "foreigners" from the borderlands of the United States are well known to historians. (Indeed, the turbulent Tennessean pondered leading a march on Mexico City as early as 1802.[5]) Although Jackson was not a career officer, he spent seven years as one of the top two commanders in the army and played that role with the deadly seriousness that characterized all his endeavors. No other officer had as much influence over the course of events in the South, or in the nation as a whole, during the crucial decade of the 1810s.

Yet Jackson was not alone. Numerous officers of all ranks shared his confident, belligerent expansionism. As chapter 2 shows, Edmund Gaines was just as aggressive as his commander, and we cannot reduce the story of the officer corps to that of Jackson or even that of the Tennesseans together. Diplomatic considerations, institutional rank, and the local balance of forces often posed complications, restraining potential aggression by less senior military leaders. Despite the substantial opportunities presented by the turmoil in Spanish Texas, captains commanding single companies on that border had to be more cautious than the hero of New Orleans and his favorite subordinate, with their multiregiment concentrations backed by thousands of state militia and volunteers on the Florida frontier. The complexity of expansionism and the difficulty of turning sentiment into action are evident in individuals like Brigadier General Eleazar Wheelock Ripley, a politically well-connected New Englander and the senior commander in Louisiana and West Florida between 1817 and 1819. In 1817 the brigadier reacted to proposals to cooperate with filibusters against Pensacola with a mixture of republican rhetoric and practical caution, but he also proposed invading Cuba and resigned three years later, helping to launch a second wave of filibusters against Texas. National security, international republicanism (essentially antagonism toward monarchy and hereditary aristocracy), and self-interest were all factors in the brigadier's calculations; his actions on the southern frontier would ultimately combine every dimension of the officer corps' response to the collapse of the Spanish empire in America, including intrigue, inaction, and exaggerated calls for reinforcement and military preparation. Indeed, many officers like Ripley, northern as well as southern, who were discharged between 1815 and 1821 settled in the Lower South as planters and politicians, profiting from the cotton kingdom they helped make possible.

Physical distance also made a great deal of difference (sometimes as a restraint) in military perspectives about the extent and timing of expansion. Tangled up in the political controversies occasioned by his invasion of Florida and eager to have his labors affirmed by its cession in the Transcontinental Treaty, Jackson supported peacekeeping efforts by the captain commanding on the Sabine River frontier with Texas in 1819, trying to mediate between American intruders and the Spanish troops sent to expel them. Although he provided rhetorical support for the most expansive military proposals to seize Cuba, none of these adventures took flight, defeated by the need for naval cooperation and civilian concerns about the diplomatic and racial disruption—British intervention and slave uprisings in Cuba—that an American invasion would probably foster. Troubled by piracy and the presence of free blacks and fugitive slaves, army officers were satisfied with the acquisition of Florida. Apart from Ripley, they did not invade or resign from the army with intentions to invade Texas or Cuba. They used American military power to restrain filibusters and other nonstate actors, including U.S. citizens; to disperse multiethnic and maroon communities; and to forestall attempts to create competing polities along the shores claimed by the United States. Like the National Republicans in the civilian political sphere, with whom they had so much in common, army officers used public power to maintain and reinforce the cords of union, enlarging the area of white freedom and the plantation empire and tightening the bonds of white supremacy embedded in American majoritarianism.

OPPORTUNITIES, SUSPENSE, AND AMBIVALENCE:
PIRACY AND FILIBUSTERING FROM TEXAS TO FLORIDA

Following the Battle of New Orleans, the most popular American heroes were the hunters of Kentucky, not the gray-clad regulars who had won the battles of Chippewa and Lundy's Lane in more difficult circumstances on the Niagara frontier. Frustrated by continuing popular acclaim for the militia, these veteran professionals saw new opportunities to gain distinction through expansion against Spain, a much weaker opponent than Great Britain. Nor did the destruction of the "British Negro Fort," as one influential former staff officer called it, transform the dynamics of slave flight and maroonage in Florida or secure the supply route up the Apalachicola to support offensive operations against Indian resistance to American expansion. Whites from Georgia and Alabama continued to pursue fugitive slaves into Florida, and the center of maroon life shifted east to the Suwannee River region until Andrew Jackson destroyed those villages during his second invasion two years later. Not surprisingly, the intervening period was full of tension between the United States and Spain. By 1815, the Latin American rebellions against Spain had spread throughout the Gulf of Mexico, aggravating the crisis of authority throughout the region. Whether they came from Latin America or the United States, filibusters and adventurers acting outside of recognized national sovereignty were a secondary concern for military commanders focused on Indian threats and the pretexts and obstacles they presented for U.S. expansion. Yet these nonstate actors posed a significant threat to peace between the United States and Spain, and to U.S. sovereignty and the future of national union, during the years around the First Seminole War. American citizens routinely committed acts of war against Spain; Henry Clay observed that American actions "exhibit the spectacle of a people at war and a government at peace."[6]

Army officers ruminating on the Latin American revolutions were motivated by both national chauvinism and fear of European monarchies' antagonism toward America's republican experiment. Officers up to the highest ranks claimed to support the Latin American independence movements based on idealistic republican motives, or what we might label republican internationalism. Traveling to observe the European armies occupying France late in 1815, Brigadier General Winfield Scott wrote to Secretary of State James Monroe expressing his hope that Congress would recognize the insurgents. A letter he dispatched from London the following March predicted their success: "The best friends of freedom in this country [Britain] . . . regard the present moment as peculiarly favorable to the independence of our hemisphere." Unlike many civilian policy makers, the future commanding general

did not seem worried about British intervention: "If the contest is to be sin-
gle-handed [probably meaning by Spain alone] against us the odds are entirely
on our side. Indeed I believe that our navy alone, would be fully adequate to
ensure the independence of Spanish America and to indemnify us in our just
demands." The brigadier did not elaborate on these demands, but annexing
Florida was surely foremost among them.[7]

Scott went on to relate news of his secret discussions with liberal Spanish
general Espoz y Mina concerning American material support for the rebels,
but these talks did not extend beyond rhetoric. Scott carefully noted his reservation that American provisions could be supplied by purchase alone, and only
if the United States itself were at war with Spain. The brigadier's reservations
did not convince Thomas Jefferson, however; the ex-president interpreted
Scott's letter as a proposal for war with Spain, a reading indicative of the officer corps' bellicose reputation. (Jefferson did not clearly express his own stance
toward Mina, although he had shown sympathy for Latin revolutionaries as
president.) Whether the brigadier's caution was intended more to protect himself or the government is not clear, but he felt confident enough of the propriety of his actions that he gave Mina letters of introduction to American civil
officials and met with him in New York later that year, before Mina's brother
led an expedition from that city against Texas.[8]

That meeting was the last of Scott's contacts with the revolutionaries and
adventurers who plagued the Gulf frontier during the second half of the
decade, but many southwestern businessmen and civil officials remained eager
to take advantage of opportunities in Texas and Mexico, whether they were
independent or under U.S. rule. By the end of 1813, the defeat of the Gutiérrez-Magee expedition had left several hundred filibusters loitering in East
Texas and the Neutral Ground, divided into two groups led by José Alvarez
de Toledo and John Hamilton Robinson. They or men like them remained
there throughout the decade, posing a constant threat to shift from farming
to marauding or filibustering. Nor did their leaders and former leaders remain
quiet. Indeed, Robinson's plans, hatched by the "Friends of Mexican Emancipation" headquartered in Natchez, attracted a new level of support among
local federal civil officials. In addition to Robinson (a doctor with Zebulon
Pike's reconnaissance into Spanish territory in 1806 and Secretary of State
Monroe's emissary to Spanish commandant Nemecio Salcedo in December
1812), the "Friends" included federal judge John Carr and federal Indian
agent John Sibley, both of Natchitoches. Sibley, who had been accused by an
army officer of selling land in the Neutral Ground several years before, was
supposed to become governor of the "emancipated" region. At least four former army officers were involved, although only one had seen recent or lengthy

service; three of these men were apparently involved in the Gutiérrez-Magee expedition, and the fourth went on to join filibusters with the "New Orleans Associates" and Francisco Xavier Mina (see appendix A).[9]

These later threats came from farther east along the Gulf frontier. By the spring of 1814 the Baratarian corsairs linked to the Laffite brothers had forged a connection with Mexican rebels near Tampico, leading to the formation of the New Orleans Associates to smuggle and sell arms to the insurgents, contrary to the neutrality laws. Like the "Mexican Association" in 1806, participants in the new venture underlined the persistent and growing gap between federal proclamations and popular expansionism in the Southwest. Prominent leaders included businessman Abner Duncan, former territorial attorney general of Mississippi and a militia commander during the expedition to occupy New Orleans in 1803; Edward Livingston, the wealthiest merchant in New Orleans; former federal district attorney John Randolph Grymes; and federal marshal Pierre Duplessis. Daniel Patterson, commander of the U.S. naval flotilla at New Orleans, also worked with the group, and there were rumors that Governor Claiborne had indicated sympathy. Prominent freebooters and filibusters linked to the New Orleans Associates included Bernardo Gutiérrez, Henry Perry, and Pierre Laffite.[10]

The political climate in Louisiana became less favorable to these extralegal ventures as federal law enforcement began to clamp down on challenges to U.S. sovereignty from nonstate actors amid the uncertainty of the war and its aftermath. After declaring martial law in December 1814, Andrew Jackson ordered the Louisiana militia to compel all civilians from Barataria and the coastline to move inland, and he halted most ships attempting to leave New Orleans during the first two months of 1815. These were emergency measures, unlikely to be repeated once the crisis was past, but the pardons the Baratarians received for defending New Orleans did not preclude their prosecution for new violations of the neutrality laws. Nevertheless, the departure of the British squadrons that had dominated the Gulf of Mexico in 1814 and early 1815 reopened opportunities for filibustering and privateering, usually under the umbrella of the revolutionary governments of Mexico, Venezuela, or Colombia. In New Orleans, Pierre Laffite published a call for a thousand men to invade Texas. By the summer, Governor Claiborne was reporting 400 to 500 freebooters, including former U.S. officers and soldiers, at the mouth of the Atchafalaya Bayou in western Louisiana, aimed at Matagorda, La Bahia, and San Antonio; it was rumored that a thousand more were lurking around Natchitoches. Claiborne, normally a fervent expansionist, maintained somewhat disingenuously that "the civil authority of Louisiana is not competent to the suppression of these expeditions," warning that "if the Government wish them put down Force must be applied." The governor admitted that the civil authority had never been able to halt filibustering, advising that without "sure corrective force," many of the adventurers would continue to believe that their plots "are secretly countenanced by the administration." Whether he was trying to shift blame or excuse inaction, Claiborne was only hinting at what most Louisianans, and probably most national policy makers, already knew: despite his clashes with the Laffites, the governor had never done much to prevent filibustering. But neither had Madison or Monroe.[11]

Enforcing national and international law carried domestic political costs, but the calculus was slowly shifting in Washington if not Louisiana. Responding to the new plots, or at least to the diplomatic irritation they created, President Madison issued a formal proclamation against filibustering in September 1815. This was the first direct, formal, public declaration of presidential opposition to such expeditions since Jefferson's proclamation against Aaron Burr—who had been seen as a secessionist as much as an expansionist (perhaps the ultimate distinction between Burr's policy and Jefferson's)—nine years before.[12] A number of reasons can be suggested for Madison's action: the lackluster performance of the East Florida incursion and the defeat of the Gutiérrez-Magee expedition in 1812 and 1813, fear of British or other European intervention on Spain's behalf, and concern about the appearance of new polities that might threaten the national union all made passivity seem a risk. Perhaps most important for a cautious expansionist like Madison was the long-standing assumption that Spain would gradually give ground before U.S. demands, a process that might be endangered if marauding adventurers gave European powers a pretext for intervention and war with the United States. In any case, it is clear that the Madison administration stopped actively supporting filibusters after the War of 1812, in contrast to its use of confidential agents to coordinate with rebels in Florida and Texas between 1810 and 1813.

Yet Madison recognized the strength of public opinion supporting territorial expansion and Latin American independence, as well as the pressure privateers and adventurers could exert on Spain. The administration tried to have things both ways, crafting an essentially duplicitous definition of neutrality, based on the strict letter of the 1794 neutrality law, which claimed to deny Americans' active participation in privateering but refused to exclude rebel ships from American ports. Given the connivance of local federal officials, particularly customs officers, and juries drawn from a population that profited from privateering, the practice continued virtually unabated from Baltimore, Charleston, and New Orleans. Secretaries of state Monroe and Adams continually dismissed and essentially ignored Spanish complaints, effectively recognizing the South American rebels as legitimate belligerents—a stance that would come back to haunt the United States during its own civil war. Indeed, as ambassador to Britain, Adams told the Spanish ambassador that the United States had "no army or corps of gendarmerie to support and give efficacy to measures of peace." Yet gunboats accompanying Duncan Clinch's incursion into Spanish Florida destroyed the Negro Fort two months later, probably before Monroe received Adams's dispatch.[13]

Many military officers had become confirmed expansionists, and Madison's proclamations did little to resolve their uncertainty (sometimes deliberately obtuse) about their specific legal responsibilities or authority to act against filibusters. Nor did the success of the navy's expedition against the Algerine corsairs portend equal or immediate decisiveness toward the freebooters of the Gulf. Indeed, Commodore Patterson dispatched the USS *Firebrand* (a prize taken from privateers) on at least three voyages, unauthorized by the Navy Department, to escort vessels conveying arms—apparently stolen from the federal arsenal, though presumably without the commodore's knowledge— and emissaries from the New Orleans Associates to Mexican rebels near Tampico and Veracruz between the autumn of 1815 and the following summer. Patterson even permitted the *Firebrand* to transport José Manuel de Herrera, a representative from the Mexican revolutionaries, an unauthorized act that implied diplomatic recognition. The commodore became more cautious after Spanish vessels detained the *Firebrand* for a day in August 1816, precipitating a war scare before the United States disavowed navy support for the rebels, but Patterson was soon transferred elsewhere. Madison personally drafted new rules to restrain naval commanders in the Gulf of Mexico, and Patterson's successors turned their zeal against the smugglers, privateers, and pirates who challenged American sovereignty and international order.[14]

As for Texas, the New Orleans Associates planned to dispatch Louisianan Henry Perry from the Sabine, where he was encamped with 150 recruits, to Matagorda Bay, where the Baratarians had established their base after being driven from Louisiana. Meanwhile, Gutiérrez would lead another expedition across the Sabine, and the two groups would rendezvous at La Bahia before advancing on San Antonio. The army's commander at Natchitoches announced that he would observe "strict neutrality"—not toward Spain, by enforcing the neutrality laws, but toward the marauders in the Neutral Ground along the Sabine—unless civil officials requested his assistance. Doing so adhered to the formal principle of strict civilian control over law enforcement and to the residual authority of the Neutral Ground agreement to keep national military forces out of the area between the Sabine and the Arroyo Hondo. But this was not the real neutrality supposedly embodied in Madison's proclamation or the 1794 law or recognized by international custom, whereby the United States would preserve the peace by respecting other nations' sovereignty and enforcing its own. Filibuster dissension and Spanish military action, always more energetic in Texas than in Florida, eventually put an end to these schemes. Looking for safer ways to profit from the turmoil, the Laffites secretly began taking Spanish pay in November 1815; Toledo began doing so the following summer, and the filibuster projects against Texas gradually fell into disarray. The exception was the expedition led by Francisco Xavier Mina, an authentic liberal revolutionary whose operations were rooted on the Atlantic seaboard rather than in Louisiana. Mina met privately with federal civil officials and recruited openly in eastern ports before landing on barren Galveston Island, where the Laffites and Louis Aury were headquartered in the spring of 1817.[15]

Mina's expedition attracted several former officers discharged after the War of 1812, but its historian has exaggerated their number. Like the former officers who joined the Gutiérrez-Magee expedition, these men, only three of whom have been identified by name, were short-timers, averaging two to three years' national military service. Indeed, only one, ex-Major Ross Bird, served more than two years, and then only during peacetime. A Louisianan, Henry D. Peire, was a volunteer aide-de-camp to James Wilkinson in 1812 and 1813, leading to his commission as a major in the Forty-fourth Regiment, which retook Grande Terre from the Baratarians. Peire commanded the Seventh Infantry in the battles around New Orleans, winning a brevet promotion for gallantry in combat, but like most officers commissioned during the war, he was discharged in 1815.[16] Henry Perry, one of the leading freebooters, seems to have been confused with Peire in a number of accounts; Perry was appointed deputy quartermaster general by Andrew Jackson during the defense of New Orleans and probably never received a formal commission. Perry joined Mina but then broke with him and advanced against La Bahia in June 1817; he either was killed in battle by the Spanish or killed himself after being wounded to avoid capture and execution (depending on the account). Mina was compelled to flee his base that month and joined the Mexican rebels, ceasing independent operations.

Former officers thus played significant roles commanding filibuster expeditions. Beyond their numbers or operational impact, their participation suggests the ambiguity of loyalties and the fluidity of careers, military and otherwise, in the early national borderlands. Indeed, several other filibuster leaders have been labeled army officers but were actually New Orleans businessmen and community leaders. Like "Kentucky colonels" throughout the nation, these civilians exaggerated their status and sought political influence through identification with the masculinity of military service and the national connections implied by a federal commission. Ironically, these men were demonstrating the popular acceptance of the national standing army during the continual war and rumors of war prevalent in the latter half of the Jeffersonian era, but scholars have exaggerated the expansionism of postwar army officers by lumping them in the army's ranks. Like Perry, Reuben Ross (whom scholars may have confused with Ross Bird), a leader in the Gutiérrez-Magee expedition, and Abner Duncan, leader of the New Orleans Associates, never received a rank in the army of the United States; some secondary sources refer to these men as "army quartermasters," but they did not hold that position by military commission from the president and confirmation by the Senate. They were civilians who sold supplies to the army; Duncan and John Randolph Grymes were also employed by Jackson as volunteer aides-de-camp during the defense of New Orleans. Whatever their actions say about southwestern expansionism and the political value of claiming military rank, they tell us little about career army officers.[17]

The British invasion and the U.S. mobilization were the culmination of a decade of effort by federal officials to incorporate Louisiana into the American union. Though it was not the French or Spanish renaissance sought by some Creoles, the British invasion posed the greatest threat to U.S. power, perhaps opening alternative diplomatic and political possibilities in Louisiana. To minimize the possibility that a fifth column might support the invasion, Jackson included many prominent community leaders, including known filibusters like José Alvarez de Toledo, in his "military family," hoping to strengthen their attachment to the United States in exchange for the prestige of associating with the general and participating in the national struggle. Under such desperate circumstances, the politician and former militiaman commanding the southern army easily appealed to the aspiring gentility and potential nationalism of borderlands leaders—men who, not unlike himself, sought a semblance of respectability but had little regard for formal procedure. These measures assisted the defense of New Orleans and may have reduced the outcry against the general's declaration of martial law. Yet few career officers would have undertaken such extensive outreach, and Jackson's temporary selection of civilian aides tells us nothing about expansionism in the standing army.[18]

Meanwhile, serving officers continued to report on Spanish movements in Texas and advised civilian policy makers on the likelihood and feasibility of military operations, whether by Spain or the United States. The year 1816 was crucial for U.S. policy toward Texas because the cabinet decided to exchange the American claim to that province for Florida. So limited was the administration's interest in Texas that the cabinet chose to demand cash, rather than territory, in case Spain offered a boundary farther west than the Sabine. Washington's disinterest was not shared in the southern borderlands: a month later, Jackson and Louisiana governor Claiborne combined to propose an American advance into the Neutral Ground, to the Sabine. Worried by Jackson's aggressiveness, Madison and Secretary of War Crawford refused, and Indian affairs quickly pushed the general's interest in Texas to the back burner. Yet his subordinates, the commanders of the Eighth Military Department headquartered in New Orleans, continued to raise the issue and dispatched troops to establish posts in the Neutral Ground until the Sabine boundary was embodied in the Transcontinental Treaty several years later. The first of these commanders, Major Thomas Sidney Jesup, was a Virginia-born Kentuckian and future plantation owner who shared Jackson's tendency to project American attitudes of belligerence and expansionism onto other nations. Jesup asserted that "altho' war with Spain may be distant, I think it certain," professing concern about possible Spanish threats to New Orleans and Mobile from Pensacola and Havana. Yet Jesup gave little attention to Texas, preferring to plot an invasion of Cuba. The ardent young major got along poorly with his immediate superior, Brigadier General Eleazar Ripley, due to Jesup's criticism of the general's cautious performance in the 1814 Niagara campaign, where the major earned his laurels. (He was a colonel by brevet, for gallantry at both Chippewa and Lundy's Lane. In both battles he led his regiment to turn the British flank.) Jesup was soon called away to staff duties with his patron (and Ripley's nemesis) Jacob Brown, the major general commanding the army's Northern Division.[19]

Kentucky-born Lieutenant Colonel William Trimble, Jesup's successor, was often stationed (or chose to station himself) at Fort Claiborne, the American post at Natchitoches, rather than at New Orleans, and he gave a great deal of thought to possible operations in Texas during 1817 and 1818. Trimble repeatedly sought intelligence on the Texan Indians (with whom Americans were actively trading, whatever the international boundaries) and on Spanish forces, and he offered to explore the region for the United States. This implied an American military expedition across the Neutral Ground created by U.S. and Spanish military commanders to resolve the Sabine frontier crisis in 1806—an armed intrusion on land the Spanish considered their own, in violation of an agreement adhered to by federal military officers for over a decade. Yet Trimble agreed with Jesup that war with Spain would be justified, claiming that Spanish officials were stirring up the Indians and trying to foment revolt among the French in western Louisiana. Sounding a lot like the Kentucky major plotting against Cuba, the colonel boasted to his brother that he could raise enough volunteers at Natchitoches "to march to the Rio del Norte."[20]

Indeed, Trimble sent a company of the Eighth Infantry, under brevet Major David Riddle, into the Neutral Ground in April 1817, after the federal agent for the Caddo Indians requested that the army enforce the Trade and Intercourse Acts of 1802 by expelling white liquor dealers from Caddo villages. Yet Trimble clearly had more in mind than enforcing a law of debatable jurisdiction. He ordered Riddle to gather any "geographical or topographical information" available, "to assure the different Indian tribes, of the friendly disposition of the United States; and the determination of the Government, to protect them against . . . evil disposed persons" and provide "a fair & honorable trade." When Trimble heard a rumor that Riddle had been attacked by Indians, he ordered Captain Joseph Selden to prepare two companies of reinforcements, but Selden convinced his superior that the rumor was false. Trimble's assessment of Spanish strength and intentions became more realistic during the course of 1817, and in December he advised Jackson (who was about to invade Florida) that San Antonio had become the eastern limit of Spanish power, which was hardly adequate for defense against the Comanche and other Indians. Trimble did not lose interest in the province, however, drafting a report asserting that, "Were it not for a doubt that the [U.S.] government might abandon their claims to that country, there would in a few years be a sufficient American population to defend the country."[21]

Whatever U.S. officials' intentions toward Texas, they had no desire to see ineffectual Spanish rule replaced by Indian war, illegal slave trading (to which Trimble alerted President Monroe in a letter dispatched outside the military chain of command), or freebooters preying on American commerce. Hence, they sought to clear Galveston Island of corsairs and privateers, advancing much the same arguments for American occupation as Gaines and Jackson used for Florida. During the autumn of 1817 the administration planned to occupy Galveston Island, ordering Jackson to prepare a contingent of regulars to cooperate with the navy, but the operation was repeatedly postponed. Meanwhile, the military was also employed to maintain order against international freebooters within American boundaries by preventing Jean Laffite's return to Louisiana: in February 1817 two companies moved from New Iberia in pursuit of 150 buccaneers said to be at Attakapas, though none were caught.[22]

Another threat to potential U.S. expansion in Texas came from a group of French Napoleonic exiles, mostly former officers, led by General Charles Lallemand (whose brother Henri authored a text on artillery that was used at West Point). These *grognards* were associated by experience and nationality with General Jean Joseph Amable Humbert, a veteran of French expeditions to Haiti and Ireland. Humbert had been sent to the United States by Napoleon in 1812, and he developed links to Toledo and the self-proclaimed "Patri-

William Allen Trimble, by Matthew Jouett. (Courtesy Ohio
Historical Society)

ots"—multinational adventurers against Spanish rule who congregated at New
Orleans. Despite warnings by Secretary of State Adams and former U.S. consul to Spain William Lee during the autumn of 1817, approximately a hundred Napoleonic veterans sailed from Philadelphia toward Mobile the
following January, in anticipation of an attack on Pensacola. Debarking at
Galveston instead, the Frenchmen settled on the Trinity River in Texas, some
said in preparation for an advance on the silver mines at San Luis Potosi far
to the south.[23] Trimble warned the War Department that if the exiles were
allowed to remain along the Trinity, they might interfere with American control over the Indian trade and provide a pretext for French intervention. If
nothing else, additional Napoleonic veterans might be attracted to the settlement, possibly presenting a significant obstacle to U.S. expansion—as Lalle-

Eleazar Wheelock Ripley, troubled commander. (Courtesy Hood Museum of Art, Dartmouth College)

mand had proposed to Spanish ambassador Luis de Onís the previous autumn. Trimble recommended American settlers be introduced into the region to preclude this possibility and advocated a military "tour of discovery" into Spanish territory that autumn, but he made no comment on the legality of such a move. (The United States still claimed Texas as part of the Louisiana Purchase.[24])

In response to all these intrusions on land still claimed by the United States, the cabinet initially decided to send the naval captain occupying Amelia Island on to Galveston. Jackson provided 150 soldiers for the expedition, but the cabinet soon reconsidered, perhaps fearing war with Spain or the consequences of overstretching limited American forces. Instead, the cabinet dispatched former acting secretary of war George Graham as an emissary "to ascertain the object of the recent lodgment" and warn the *grognards* "that they are upon the territory of the United States." For some unknown reason, Graham traveled overland and took three months to reach Galveston, where the French had retreated after receiving word of a Spanish expedition against them.[25] The Spanish force arrived in September but lacked the naval support to attack Galveston; a hurricane dispersed the French instead. Graham was later accused of plotting to allow the French to stay as a pretext for American occupation, but the evidence lies entirely in the correspondence of Spanish officials. Graham did advise Laffite to secure letters of marque from the Argentine revolutionaries and gave him a letter of introduction to their agent in New York, behavior that implied American recognition of the Argentines, which Secretary of State Adams labeled "altogether unauthorized." American military expansion against Texas lost an advocate the following year when Trimble resigned to serve as senator from Ohio; he died in 1821 from wounds suffered seven years earlier at the sortie from Fort Erie on the Niagara. Eleazar Ripley, wounded in the same battle, would soon follow him out of the army, entering civilian politics as the president of James Long's filibuster against Texas. The U.S. Navy finally compelled Laffite to evacuate Galveston Island in 1820; three companies of U.S. troops were used to guard convicted pirates awaiting execution in New Orleans that spring, but otherwise, piracy and privateering became naval concerns.[26]

The Patriot adventurers and corsairs also turned east toward Florida: Gutiérrez, Toledo, and Humbert all plotted to attack Pensacola during the winter of 1816–1817. Indeed, Humbert approached Ripley, now in command of the Eighth Department, who responded that, "in a State of Peace . . . I think it my duty to apprise you, that no act will be done on my part, or allowed of by any forces under my command, which will in any manner compromit the neutrality of the United States." Yet the brigadier's language shows he was torn between patriotisms, between the values of republican liberty and accountability to civilian political authority:

> I consider myself as a soldier bound to support the Government & Laws of my Country. . . . I view with the liveliest sympathy the struggles of the American Spaniards for their Independence. All the feelings of a man attached to free institutions prompt me to wish them unlimited success, while my duty as a Soldier requires me to refrain from assisting them without the orders of my Government. Such orders you may rest assured

will not be given unless the Congress of the Nation assume openly and avowedly a belligerent attitude [toward Spain].

Ripley advised the War Department that the Frenchman "has very little weight." As 1817 began, the department commander seemed committed to the constitutional separation of powers, civilian control of the military, and accountability to national and international law. Ripley hoped his inner tensions would be resolved through decisive American policy, proclaiming to Humbert:

> It is one of our principles of national policy to do nothing insidiously. While we remain apparently at peace with Spain, every duty which such a state requires will be enforced and practiced on the part of the government. Should aggressions finally arise to such a point as no longer bear toleration, the remedy would be found not simply in secret assistance to the Patriots, but . . . in again developing those moral and physical qualities which render the people of this Country invincible in Arms.

A state of war would provide moral, ethical, and legal clarity and satisfy the brigadier's sense of national pride and honor. Yet Ripley did not wholly disavow his connection with the filibuster: though he declared he would "not trouble" himself about the plotters, he asked the secretary of war to "keep Humbert's name a secret. I shall make the old man useful." Doing so might be valuable for keeping tabs on the filibusters, preventing violations of American neutrality, and avoiding crises that could escalate into war with Spain and even Britain, but the brigadier was entering a shadowy world of lures and snares, a fateful choice for his future.[27]

Ripley was usually a cautious, responsible, and insightful commander, and the possibility that stateless adventurers might cause war with Spain led him to ponder the defensive needs of his department. Indeed, he sent the War Department a five-page letter detailing Spanish troop strengths in Mexico and outlining the probable military strategy of the revolutionaries "to seize strong positions on the Gulf of Mexico, of which their privateers give them the control, and to carry on a partisan warfare on the continent. . . . Hence I apprehend a system of war which may . . . involve us in the contest, unless we have a force sufficiently powerful at this point." Such depth of analysis, attempting to assess the character of a conflict and anticipate its second- and third-order effects, was rare among American generals during this period. Ripley recognized that the Patriot forces had been recruited largely from the United States and expressed concern that an offensive against Pensacola, perhaps under Mina, would entice Americans to commit further violations of the neutrality laws. Threats to the Spanish position in the Caribbean, and American involvement therein, might produce an unexpectedly powerful reaction. In Mexico the Spanish were "scattered through an almost indefinite extent of country and could not be concentrated" without extensive preparation, but Ripley believed the Spanish could retake Pensacola from any insurgent force and "instantly possess themselves of Mobile, unless we have an imposing force to cover it."[28]

The department commander had a lot to worry about: the "heterogeneous" population of Louisiana and West Florida; the lack of effective militia in those regions; the shortage of federal troops, many of whom had enlisted in 1812 and would soon leave the army unless funds became available to reenlist them; and the poor location of many defensive positions. Always thinking of the worst case in his military estimates, Ripley believed the only way "to preserve ourselves quiet and tranquil (should such be the national policy)" was "an efficient force . . . sufficient for any contingency," and he requested two or three regiments "from the north" to bring his force to 4,000 men. This would require nearly half the army's infantry, and it would mean taking troops from Jacob Brown's Northern Division along the Canadian border. This would almost certainly weaken or delay Edmund Gaines's operations against the Creeks and Seminoles, who were much more active antagonists (and much more immediately threatened by American expansionism) than the Spanish. There was little chance the brigadier would receive such reinforcements.[29]

Commanding the Seventh Military Department (essentially Georgia and Alabama), Gaines also reported Humbert's plans to Jackson, but after fifteen years in the southern borderlands, the busy department commander cared little for any Spanish or Latin American faction. Indeed, the brigadier stressed the need for U.S. neutrality, though perhaps he did so primarily to minimize any disruption to his plans against the Seminoles. Nevertheless, Gaines abandoned Fort Scott, which he had considered so critical earlier in the year, to dispatch its garrison to guard Mobile. Meanwhile, unable to get a clear commitment from Ripley, the Patriots—or, more precisely, the New Orleans Associates—turned to Colonel William King, commander of the Fourth Infantry, for a loan of arms. King "indignantly refused" and reported their plans for a foray from Galveston to Adjutant General Daniel Parker, along with his intention to forcibly disperse any filibuster, "or more properly speaking . . . *brigand*," expedition entering the Eighth Department. The colonel doubted that such aggressive action would meet "the approbation of my superiors," but he was worried that the governor of Pensacola would call on him for assistance to protect the inhabitants from "slaughter & desolation" at the hands of the invaders. Like Ripley, King advocated a clear-cut solution: "permit the '*Star Spangled Banner*' to wave o'er the works of the Barrancas [Pensacola] & St. Augustine & the Troops of the U.S. to occupy those posts subject to the future arrangement of the two governments."[30]

Unsure how far King might go, Parker felt compelled to affirm Ripley's republican internationalism while prohibiting U.S. military intervention, whatever the motive. Parker's words to King encapsulated the neutral stance officially taken by the U.S. government, as well as the antagonism many military commanders felt toward Spanish rule: "It is the policy of our government to have nothing to do with the Patriots or the authorities of Florida. I have no doubt the Patriots will not only win possession of Florida but that all South America will soon be independent of old Spain. I wish success to the Patriots but it is determined that we shall do nothing in favor of either party." Unfortunately, King got the impression that the adjutant general thought he intended to assail Pensacola on his own initiative and demanded, how "in the name of all the Gods . . . can it be possible that the President of the U.S. . . . believes that I am so dam'd a fool as to think seriously of entering the Spanish dominions with a military force, without the orders of my government?" How indeed? King was not privy to Thomas Jesup's proposals to invade Cuba or his threat to attack Pensacola to liberate Americans held prisoner there during the autumn of 1816. Nor did King consider Clinch's operations—initiated by Gaines with Jackson's support, contrary to War Department intent—which had culminated in the bombardment and destruction of the Negro Fort sixty miles inside Spanish territory that July.[31]

Even though he sympathized with Jesup, encouraged Gaines, and ordered King to concentrate the Fourth Infantry Regiment where it could join the Seventh "towards" Pensacola, Jackson wanted to avoid upsetting President-elect Monroe, whom he expected to support future expansionist action. The division commander now assured Graham that he would "permit no act to be done to provoke war with Spain." Gaines felt no such qualms, warning a Spanish officer visiting his headquarters that he would occupy Pensacola if the rebels seized it. Few officers stationed in the borderlands truly "wish[ed] success" to the insurgents in Florida. To do so would imply recognizing the legitimacy of autonomous, self-created polities that might obstruct U.S. expansion and endanger the cohesion of the American union. The experience of the War of 1812, combined with the expansion of plantation agriculture, had convinced southern whites not to allow any other nation to control Florida.[32] Republican ideology demanded virtuous citizens, and national army officers found few virtuous Patriots. But there was a fine line between the self-restraint of republican virtue and the martial self-assertion of republican *virtú* and national territorial expansion, and a sense of American national virtue surely fed officers' hard-earned confidence in their martial *virtú*. Conduct that military officers labeled banditry among Latin insurgents and private citizens seemed natural for themselves, sanctioned by nationalism and not infrequently by the civil authorities of the nation-state—a course they believed destined, if not manifest. In a political world of popular expansionism, in the absence of unambiguous legal boundaries, the course of national glory and growth could easily take military commanders beyond the constitutional bounds of accountability to civil authority. Unfortunately, their transgressions often appeared to be sanctioned by those very civil authorities or by their inaction in the face of military adventurism.

THE FARTHER SHORE: VISIONS OF CUBA, 1816

Cuba was the most distant focal point for expansionist intrigue by army officers between 1815 and 1821. Some of these men were quite junior in both rank and time in service, and their ability to visualize themselves leading amphibious expeditionary forces of several thousand men against territories that clearly belonged to foreign nations gives us our best evidence of officers' almost boundless sense of opportunity for expansion along the nation's southern frontier before 1820.

Major Thomas Sidney Jesup, acting commander of the Eighth Military Department—principally charged with the defense of New Orleans—was the most energetic plotter during the summer of 1816, expressing the widely held view that Cuba was the "key to all Western America": under British control, the island would be "so formidable as to menace" American independence. The twenty-seven-year-old Kentuckian, an eight-year veteran, had shown decisive initiative while commanding the Twenty-fifth Infantry Regiment at the Battle of Chippewa two years before. Jesup sent Jackson his proposal for an invasion of Cuba only a week after refusing to provide Louisiana governor Claiborne with assistance to prevent filibuster preparations. In that instance, Jesup somewhat disingenuously professed concern that military action would interfere unjustifiably with civil liberties during a time of "profound peace." It is not clear whether Jesup was avoiding an unpleasant duty (hearkening back to his experience observing the Hartford Convention—when he had expressed little support for local laws and civil liberties while ostensibly recruiting for his regiment) or reacting (like so many military officers during the preceding decade) against Claiborne's efforts to assert control over federal military forces.[33]

Governor Claiborne's effort to restrain filibusters was rare and perhaps just as disingenuous as Jesup's response, but it was certainly in tune with President Madison's proclamations. Jesup, in contrast, seems to have had his belligerent military superior uppermost in his mind. Jackson had just warned the major to exercise "the most cautious vigilance" against the possibility of a Spanish offensive against Mobile, demanding "every exertion to acquire correct information" regarding Spanish intentions. Clearly, Jesup knew the sort of thing Old Hickory liked to hear. Nor did the impetuous Kentuckian report to Ripley, his immediate military superior, with whom he had been at odds since the Niagara campaign two years before. Jesup did forward his proposal to Secretary of State Monroe, with whom he had corresponded directly during the Hartford Convention, only three days after he wrote to Jackson, and he dispatched three more letters to the Republican presidential nominee within the month. Yet Jesup never sent a word about the matter to the War Department or to his civilian superior, Secretary of War Crawford, presumably because of Crawford's reputation for caution and restraint toward military adventurism derived from his well-known clashes with Jackson over the Creek and Cherokee cessions earlier in the year. Indeed, Jesup signaled his irreverence toward civilian authority by crowing to Jackson that "soldiers [were] not to be outgeneralled by politicians."[34]

Presumably, the major counted on naval support from Commodore Daniel Patterson, who was dispatching the USS *Firebrand* to convey arms to Mexican rebels at the time. But Jesup's confidence far outran his influence, for he would need civilian volunteers to raise the 3,000 to 4,000 soldiers he considered necessary. The federal troops under his command did not exceed several hundred, and to call up civilian volunteers without authorization from the president would have violated several statutes as well as the constitutional chain of command and accountability. Jesup initially assumed that he would command the invasion force himself, but he must have realized that this responsibility was a bit beyond his rank; he soon amended his proposal, suggesting that Jackson command. Wrapping himself in the prerogatives of an independent gentleman, the zealous major seems to have recognized no other military superior: "as the plan is my own, I would not be willing to yield to another."[35]

Jackson must have been pleased to find another budding Clinch, assuring Jesup that the "project against Cuba is a good one." Yet the nation's most powerful military commander repeated and extended his earlier injunction: "You will be cautious . . . & by no means provoke offensive movements" by

Thomas Sidney Jesup, later in life. (Courtesy Army
Quartermaster Museum)

Spanish troops. The precocious major then proposed that he be dispatched
on a reconnaissance mission to the island, telling the secretary of state that he
had discovered "a secret negotiation" between Britain and Spain to exchange
Florida and Cuba for British help in recovering the rest of Spain's Latin American colonies. How a major in the U.S. Army would learn of such secret international negotiations he did not say. Jesup also reported rumors that Spanish
officials were plotting to attack New Orleans, but Jackson routinely downplayed the hints of Spanish assertiveness so often reported by his restless subordinates in the Eighth Department; presumably, Sharp Knife did not want
scarce troops drawn away from operations against the Creeks and Seminoles.
(In this ability to focus and dismiss distractions, as in his attention to logistics, Jackson certainly proved himself a more capable commander than his sub-

ordinates.) Jesup's last substantial letter on the subject of Cuba during his command, sent directly to Monroe, ran on for eleven pages to stress that "the military policy of the country should be to secure every assailable point"— absolute and preclusive security. To achieve this objective, the major proposed an immediate invasion to seize the island without awaiting further "provocation," asserting that "such an act would not be inconsistent with the soundest political morality . . . an act which may be justified by every principle which governs the most upright nation." Monroe probably agreed with the major's objectives, if not with his interpretation of political morality, but he certainly did not want to provoke British intervention and apparently did not respond.[36]

Jesup's last letter about seizing Cuba was dated the day after the USS *Firebrand* returned to New Orleans from Spanish detention. The major's belligerence was soon rebuked by Secretary of War Crawford—presumably alerted by Monroe, rather than Jackson—who emphasized that Jesup should have provided the administration with the evidence of Spanish aggressiveness on which he based his claims. Crawford agreed with the major's presumption of preemption but demanded that he remain subordinate to civilian control. Given these rebukes, Jesup's continued rise to military eminence—he would be one of only four generals authorized in the army after Jackson's retirement, and one of only six to hold that rank between 1821 and 1846—may seem somewhat surprising: it is certainly worth remark. Early national leaders valued the sort of energy and initiative Jesup so often demonstrated—they had to, given the limited means of communication available. Like civilian gentlemen, frontier commanders had to be "independent"; they had to be willing to make decisions and seize the initiative, as Jesup had done on the Niagara frontier in 1814 and would do with equal decisiveness in the Creek country two decades later. The Kentuckian continued to discuss preparations in case war broke out, but he did so at the local and regional levels rather than disturbing Washington with belligerent rhetoric: later in September he asked brevet Major Henry Chotard to talk with Mississippi territorial governor William Holmes about raising 1,500 militiamen in case of war.[37]

Jesup was equally belligerent that autumn, when the governor of Pensacola imprisoned several American citizens who had entered Florida without passports. The major prepared to liberate the prisoners by force, crowing to a subordinate that "we will at least take East Florida into safekeeping" if war broke out. (Surprisingly, Jesup, a future slaveholder, had told General Gaines "there [was] nothing to be apprehended from the Negro fort.") The administration had ignored Jesup's letters to Monroe about Cuba, but his continued belligerence led acting secretary of war Graham to warn Jackson that the major's plans to rescue the prisoners exceeded his authority. The general then ordered his subordinate "to permit no act . . . to provoke war with Spain," but Jackson reaffirmed his casual standards of international relations in a letter to the War Department praising the Kentuckian's aggressiveness. According to Old Hickory, the proposed incursion "would have been easily adjusted by the two governments, and [would have] taught Spain to know that the wanton infringement of our Rights by her Officers would be met by the same measure, and [would] thus confine them to proper conduct toward their peaceful neighbors."[38]

Thomas Jesup demonstrated the farthest-ranging expansionist sentiments in the officer corps during this era. Early in 1812, as a republican internationalist and a frustrated soldier pursuing excitement and honor, he pondered resigning to serve with the South American insurgents if Congress refused to declare war on Britain. Maturity and experience diminished Jesup's internationalism but not his urge to think expansively. Serving as the army's quartermaster general three years after his Cuban proposal, he drafted a letter advocating the seizure of the Spanish port of Ceuta in Morocco, opposite the British base at Gibraltar, to give the United States a military outpost bordering on the Mediterranean. Recurring to his plans for the Western Hemisphere, the bold Kentuckian worried "very much . . . that we shall play a small game," that Congress would stop with the annexation of Florida. "It is time that this Nation should accustom itself to think and act on a great scale," he wrote. "If it be just to take possession of Florida, it is equally so to take Cuba & Mexico. . . . A plan of such magnitude would impress Europe with a respect for us, which would be worth more than an army of one hundred thousand men," and it would prevent Mexico from becoming dependent on Britain.[39]

Nor was Andrew Jackson averse to action if the circumstances were right. Though he made sure nothing was done in 1816 or 1817, his victorious campaign in Florida encouraged bolder plans. In November 1818 he requested orders to take St. Augustine, promising to add Cuba if given sufficient reinforcements. The diplomatic priority of securing the cession of Florida, combined with the political uproar caused by Jackson's invasion, precluded such measures, but the general reiterated his willingness, albeit with a new element of self-constraint, two years later, hinting to Commissary General George Gibson that he would guarantee Cuba in six months "if the Congress should will it." Jackson presented a strategic rationale for invading Cuba closely echoing the nontransfer doctrine espoused by Jefferson and Madison toward Florida and Cuba that presaged American policy toward Cuba during the 1820s. Jackson did not consider European consent necessary for U.S. expansion if the United States sought sole possession of Cuba, but his primary concern was to keep the strategically placed island out of British hands, even if that required its retention by Spain. The result was an element of self-restraint (perhaps disingenuous) that precluded precipitate action. Cuba should not be seized "with a view of Conquest, but to be held by the United States until Europe guarantees the possession to Spain, and that it shall not pass from her to any maritime power of Europe, without the full consent of America and the European powers." Much like his attitude toward Texas during these years, Jackson considered security for the plantation empire he had carved from the heart of the Southeast more urgent than further expansion around the Gulf littoral.[40]

The moment for aggression against Cuba passed when the Transcontinental Treaty was ratified, securing Florida and signaling an end to federal support for expansion at Spanish expense. Whatever the hopes of Jesup, Ripley, and Jackson, there had never been sufficient political support for aggression against Cuba. Even Jackson was unwilling to attempt such an invasion without congressional sanction, which was extremely unlikely in the aftermath of his conquest of Florida. None of these commanders, with the exception of Jesup, attempted to secure the naval support that would have been necessary to ferry and sustain an invasion force. To many American policy makers, Cuba's status as the last of Spain's Latin American colonies was an ideologically irksome geopolitical anomaly, and they worried that the island might become a British tool of aggression or constraint against the United States. Yet only a handful of soldiers suggested action to resolve these irritants during the 1820s and 1830s. Fear of Britain was the focus of their comments on the subject, but these opinions were expressed only in the context of rumored British efforts to acquire the island. Thus, these occasional commentators advocated wartime strikes to preempt British action, rather than unprovoked territorial conquest and annexation initiated by the United States. It appears that no army officers commented on the possibility of intervention to aid, forestall, or defeat the rumored Mexican and Colombian invasions against Cuba in the mid-1820s, although their fading ideological commitment to Latin American republicanism must have been outweighed, and greatly diminished, by their desire to minimize hemispheric competition against the United States.[41]

American military attention was momentarily redirected toward Cuba at the end of the 1830s, as Anglo-American relations soured during the Canadian border crises and officers became concerned over the growing commercial rivalry between the two nations. In 1839 Major William Chase, the engineer in charge of constructing fortifications at the navy's primary Gulf coast base in Pensacola, worried that "the indebtedness of Spain to Great Britain will afford a pretext for the transfer of Cuba." Chase warned that sustaining the Monroe Doctrine would ultimately require the United States to fight "a great naval battle [against Britain] in the Gulf of Mexico or the

Caribbean sea." This was virtually the only time an army officer mentioned the Monroe Doctrine in print during this era. Writing in the *Pensacola Gazette*, the slaveholder Chase appealed to southern sectional interests by warning that "the slave islands of the West Indies must, to suit the policy of England and the Abolitionists, be placed, in a very few years, on the same footing with their own free (Brigand) islands." This concern, emblematic of the tragic interdependence of black slavery and white freedom in the nation's southwestern expansion, was repeated six months later in the 1839 report of Inspector General John Ellis Wool, who warned against a threat of "servile insurrection" emanating from Cuba. Yet Chase's letter and Wool's report were intended to sway public opinion and Congress in favor of greater military appropriations, not to provide practical military planning. The expansionist impetus toward Cuba a decade later was entirely civilian and substantially southern and sectional, despite glimmers of interest from a few national military officers.[42]

James Monroe, by Robert Weir. (Courtesy Army Art Collection)

4

CONCLUDING THE QUASI-WAR WITH SPAIN

Civil-Military Tensions, the Occupation of Amelia Island, and the "First Seminole War," 1817–1818

War with Spain would wait another year. Thomas Jesup's Cuban plan was too demanding and too provocative, and the danger of filibustering against Pensacola faded as dissension grew among the "Patriots." The *Firebrand* incident was smoothed over, reflecting concern about British intervention during the change of administration, and the adjutant general's admonitions helped redirect the army's attention from the Spanish to the Seminoles, the most powerful source of resistance to American expansion remaining in Florida after the destruction of the Negro Fort. Jackson and Gaines represented settlers, be they planters or yeoman farmers; they did not represent unpredictable adventurers who challenged national sovereignty and the army's monopoly on the operational direction of American military power. Despite his long-standing interest in Texas, Jackson's focus was securing the future heartland of the cotton kingdom, and Nashville was too far from the scene for him to worry much about freebooting whites, whom his subordinates considered distractions or, at best, pretexts for action. As a true career officer, commissioned nearly two decades before, Gaines's reputation and promotion depended on his success advancing *national* expansion, so he had even more reason for antagonism toward stateless adventurers.

The hero of New Orleans showed little hesitation advising sympathetic national political leaders on the proper course of action in the southern borderlands; their responsiveness confirmed and reinforced Jackson's self-assurance. The election of James Monroe, Madison's lead man in stirring expansionist plots against Florida and Texas before the War of 1812, gave the general and his subordinates hope that stronger action might be authorized. In November 1816 Jackson advised Monroe, generally seen as more warlike and expansionist than Madison, to put the lands ceded by the southern tribes on the market for white settlement. The Virginian's response, written three days after Jackson assured the War Department that he would prevent subordinates from warring on Spain, went beyond the disposition of public lands to envision the American annexation of Florida: "As soon as our population gains a decided preponderance in those [frontier] regions, Florida will hardly be considered by Spain as a part of her dominions, and no other [European] power will accept it from her as a gift."[1]

Indeed, the president-elect offered Jackson the position of secretary of war. The general refused, but the proposal signaled that Old Hickory would face little real opposition from the new administration. (Still a political powerhouse, William Crawford moved to the Treasury, probably relieved to hand off the willful general to a potential rival.) With Monroe apparently on board for Florida, Sharp Knife laid out his vision of Indian relations for the new president on the day he was inaugurated. Well before he had finished dispatching the Spanish, Jackson began to press the policy of dispossession and ethnic cleansing that later became known as Indian removal: "I have long viewed treaties with the Indians as an absurdity. . . . The Indians are subjects of the United States . . . is it not absurd for the sovereign to negotiate by treaty with the subject[?] . . . All Indians within the territorial limits of the United States, are considered subject to its sovereignty . . . hence I conclude that Congress has the full power, by law, to regulate all the concerns of the Indians." Uniting the perspectives of frontier general, southern planter, land speculator, and entrepreneur, Jackson repeated that "the sooner . . . this [Creek] country can be brought into market the better. . . . Next to the completion of the Fortifications of [coastal] defence, I would beg leave to call your attention to strengthening that Frontier by a permanent settlement of all the Lands acquired from the Creek Indians." (Note that Jackson was prioritizing coastal fortifications over frontier settlement, however.) Indeed, the general's words presaged the expansive public land policies he would carry out as president a decade and a half later:

> Short sighted politicians [William Crawford, for example] may urge that
> by bringing too much land into market at once, it will reduce the price,
> and thereby injure the finances of the Country—others, still more blind,
> may contend that it will drain the old States of their population, to

prevent which . . . the land ought not to be brought into market for twenty years. . . . The lower country is of too great importance to the Union for its safety to be jeopardized, by such a short sighted policy—all the lands to be sold, are, in a national point of view, but as a drop in the bucket when brought into competition with the value of that Country to the Union, or when compared with the amount it would cost the United States to retake it, should it fall into the hands of an Enemy possessing a superiority on the Ocean.

Sharp Knife concluded with a reminder of the logistical advantages of having "a permanent population, able to defend [the new territory], who will by their industry afford ample supplies for an Army, [build] good roads, & improve the navigation, so as to render the transportation of every thing necessary for an Army, easy and cheap." Once this was done, "Louisiana may be considered safe, and the lower country [the Deep South] impregnable." Expansion provided security and buffers against foreign contagion and threat, while land, roads, and commerce went hand in hand with the booming market agriculture of the emerging cotton kingdom, the principal source of American exports and foreign exchange.[2]

Meanwhile, despite Jackson's victories against Crawford over the Fort Jackson cession and the Cherokee treaty, the precise timing of land settlement remained a bone of contention among officials on the frontier, repeatedly embroiling the general's chief deputy in civil-military controversy. Though eager to provide security to white settlement, Gaines wanted to avoid the toils of civil law in order to focus on the military dimensions of that goal, clearing the way by crushing the Red Sticks. In June 1815 he tried to persuade his father-in-law, federal district judge Harry Toulmin, that land disputes were purely civil responsibilities and that the army should not be deployed to eject white squatters from Indian or public lands. Yet President Madison's proclamation against squatters on public lands that December required the general to act if called on by civil authorities, and Crawford emphasized that "the destruction of [squatters'] houses must be repeated as often as necessary" to force their departure. Matters were further confused because Indians still occupied much of the "public land" on the Fort Jackson cession, and the War Department had to explain that trespassers on Indian lands were to be treated like those on public lands.[3]

Federal Indian agents blamed white encroachment for Creek and Seminole raids, and a year later Georgia governor David B. Mitchell asked Gaines to keep the Fourth Infantry at Fort Scott to prevent squatters from occupying Indian land. The brigadier sometimes appeared to view white incursions on native lands as a threat to peace or perhaps to federal control over Indian relations; he actually told one group of whites that the Indians had a right to live among them, but he certainly did not accord expelling squatters the same priority as reacting to Spanish movements or removing Indians from the Fort Jackson cession. Indeed, Gaines concealed the fact that he had ordered Fort Scott abandoned the previous month to reinforce Mobile in case of a Spanish counteroffensive against the rumored filibuster against Pensacola. The general promised to dispatch a company from distant Charleston to remove the squatters, but he told Mitchell that the long-term solution to disorder was forcibly repressing native resistance to white settlement: "Should the Seminole [or Red Stick] Indians continue to annoy our exposed settlements, I beg that I may be permitted to visit and reclaim [capture] them. It is vain to calculate upon a good understanding with those Indians without the application of force."[4]

Gaines did not let any civilian authorities know that he had abandoned the fort until Mitchell discovered it on his own early in February 1817; by that time, Red Sticks had burned the undefended post. Gaines was not reprimanded; his objective remained constant, and by April, he had begun preparing plans and pretexts for another advance into Florida, this time nearer Pensacola. At Cantonment Montpelier, Captain Enos Cutler lamented that he would have to leave his "elegant" new barracks, since whites were "continually filling the head of our General with stories of Indian atrocities and murders." Unable to command civilians as he did soldiers, Gaines still had to navigate his way through irritating distractions by white frontiersmen. Reporting to Jackson in the language of genteel irony, he praised "our white and red *people of the woods*" for remaining subordinate to national sovereignty—declining to join extralegal expeditions against Pensacola—but became annoyed with the white settlers because they disrupted his plans, especially his control over timing and tempo, against Creek resistance. By August, the brigadier was refusing aid to squatters who accused the Indians of theft in the Murder Creek area, between Fort Crawford and his headquarters at Fort Montgomery in southwestern Alabama. Reporting to the War Department, Gaines excused his reluctance to assist these citizens, observing:

> I have uniformly referred them to the civil magistrates, because I have in no case during the present year [1817] heard of any thing like an *assemblage* of *force* among the Indians in this quarter of the Territory. Nor could I see any reason why persons who had obtruded themselves

upon the public land, contrary to law, should be allowed military protection against the petty offences of which these people complained—especially as it did not appear that the civil authority had been . . . resorted to by the complainants.[5]

Jackson was not unwilling to eject whites squatting on unceded Indian lands and echoed his subordinate's frustration with the intruders. This attitude illustrates Sharp Knife's authoritarian side and his impatient demand for discipline from everyone else, aggravated by his Creek War experiences with mutinous citizen-soldiers. Indeed, the division commander recommended that squatters' cattle be confiscated and turned over to the civil authorities, noting that "it is the only way to put an end to the villainies practiced within the Indian boundaries." Yet legalism worked both ways, as Jackson recognized: "If the military is not aided by the civil authority . . . it will be useless to harass the former . . . all of the troops on the Military peace establishment" could not prevent intrusions by land-hungry white citizens. Jackson was not going to impose martial law against white frontiersmen merely to protect Indians or to support a restrictive land policy that threatened his social, political, and strategic vision.[6]

Nor did the demands of a few frontiersmen divert Gaines from his focus on Florida. Having wrestled with Spanish officials for nearly fifteen years over the navigation of the Mobile and Apalachicola Rivers, Gaines logically added the Escambia to his demands, dispatching Colonel David Brearley to Pensacola in May to gain Spanish acquiescence in supplying Fort Crawford, which the brigadier had established on the Conecuh River in U.S. territory north of the town. When Governor José Masot stipulated that Gaines would have to purchase provisions in Pensacola or through a Pensacola merchant, the brigadier angrily retorted that transit of the Escambia was "an inherent right" not subject to negotiation. Gaines also continued to urge Jackson on, claiming that British and Spanish officials "secretly countenance[d] the Seminolas." Sharp Knife backed his deputy to the hilt, pressing Gaines to renew his efforts against the Indians and telling him to punish those conducting raids within U.S. territory any way possible. Indeed, the Tennessee tornado warned the administration, "As long as I have the honor to command I will enforce justice from [all] our neighbors, whether Indian, British, or Spanish," apparently without regard for constitutional niceties. In essence, the only alternative, the only way to bring Jackson under control, was to relieve him—a move with political implications akin to President Truman's removal of Douglas MacArthur. Since Monroe shared Jackson's objectives (and there was no Soviet Union to worry about), this would not happen. Assured of Old Hickory's support, Gaines became increasingly eager "to visit the Spaniards," as he hinted to Tennessee senator John Williams in July. By August, he was simply looking for an excuse.[7]

Gaines found his pretext less than a week after he had denied hearing "any thing like an *assemblage* of *force* among the Indians" in the Murder Creek area. When a squatter was reportedly slain by Indians, the brigadier sent a lieutenant, along with two friendly Indians, to investigate and find the offenders. When the killers could not be found, Gaines took it for granted that they had "taken refuge among the Seminolas—whither they shall be pursued, if not delivered up." Dispatching soldiers to apprehend them would almost certainly mean entering Florida, and the brigadier hinted to Jackson that he would have done so already if he had been able to procure sufficient transport for supplies. Gaines promptly demanded that the Florida Indians surrender the killers and then went much further, demanding that they allow him passage to strike the maroon villages on the Suwannee in the heart of Florida, nearly 250 miles east of Pensacola and about 120 miles west of St. Augustine—villages that had nothing to do with the killing on Murder Creek.[8] If the U.S. Army could go there, it could go anywhere in the inhabited regions of Florida. The Hitchiti chief Neamathla, of the heterogeneous Fowl Towns, had maintained neutrality up to this point, but he now warned brevet Major David Twiggs not to cross the Flint River in the southwest corner of Georgia. Twenty miles to the southeast, near the lake that bears their name, the much larger concentration of Mikasuki Seminoles under the Red Stick Kinache (who had resisted Andrew Ellicott's survey of the Spanish-American boundary a generation before) had already warned Gaines that they would use force to stop Americans from passing through their territory in pursuit of black fugitives. Gaines's estimate of the situation, dispatched on October 1, must have assured Jackson of his subordinate's eagerness for a fight: "I am convinced that nothing but the application of force, will be sufficient to ensure a permanent adjustment of this affair." These words embody the views of the officer corps as a whole toward Indian relations in general and Florida in particular.[9]

ESTABLISHING U.S. HEGEMONY AGAINST NONSTATE ACTORS: THE OCCUPATION OF AMELIA ISLAND, 1817–1818

The offensive against the Seminoles was set to begin when the generals were again diverted from their objective by freebooters and filibusters. Seeking ships and men to harass Spanish commerce, groups of Latin American revolution-

Gregor MacGregor, adventurer, engraving by Lizars, in Thomas
Strangeway, *Sketch of the Mosquito Coast* (1822).

aries, expansionist American businessmen, and Napoleonic exiles often made
alliances of convenience with the stateless marauders and corsairs who roamed
the Gulf of Mexico as Spanish authority broke down during the 1810s. Thus
the self-proclaimed "Spanish Americans" and "Patriots" roaming the
Caribbean were really a diffuse collection of international adventurers bound
together more by a desire for loot than any allegiance to aspiring nation-states
or republican ideals. Although the freebooters claimed to act as legal privateers under the auspices of the Mexican or Venezuelan government, the
United States did not officially recognize the insurgent regimes until the
1820s, by which time they had effectively won their independence and Spain
had been crippled by coup, civil conflict, and French intervention. (The par-
allel with British and French acceptance of Confederate privateering during

the American Civil War is worth noting.) Nor did the freebooters exercise self-restraint to gain American approbation: given their assaults on American vessels, the presence of Haitians and black sailors feared by slaveholding Americans, and the illegal slave trading often linked to the corsairs, U.S. officials accurately saw men like Jean Laffite, Louis Aury, and Gregor MacGregor as stateless pirates, not privateers defending international republicanism.

With the Napoleonic Wars at an end, the Barbary states brought to terms by British and American naval expeditions, and international trade flourishing for the first time in a decade, fewer Americans felt much patience for depredations against international commerce by nonstate actors. In a sense, the short- and long-term interests of American coastal ports collided: outfitting privateers versus legitimate trade. On the one hand, filibusters had proved to be useful tools in pressuring Spain, and Baltimore remained a flourishing source of recruits and supplies for privateers into the 1820s. On the other hand, establishing peace, commercial order, and U.S. hegemony over the Gulf coast required the exclusion of competitor states and an end to the autonomy—the lawlessness—of nonstate actors. With Spain clearly in retreat, the U.S. government had no desire to see successor states gain control of strategic points along the nation's borders, and policy makers were determined to excise heterogeneous elements from the region, lest they provide Britain with an excuse for intervention. The United States now sought much the same monopoly over significant armed force along its maritime littoral as it did along landward borders.[10]

American military commanders therefore treated the freebooters much as they did Indian and maroon "banditti"—as rivals and competitors, if not threats, or as pretexts for the gradual "pre-occupation" of Florida that had secretly been authorized by Congress in case of imminent foreign intervention during the American incursions around Mobile in 1811. In March 1817, for example, Gaines warned a Spanish officer visiting Fort Montgomery that he would occupy Pensacola if the Patriots seized it. Nevertheless, because they were dependent on civil courts to secure piracy convictions, the U.S. Navy and the Customs Service were unable to repress piracy or privateering until the chain of civil authority became more sympathetic. Ships were robbed in U.S. territorial waters within sight of Fort St. Philip, twenty-five miles up the Mississippi estuary from the Gulf, early in 1817, and there were at least eleven privateers in New Orleans that August. Nevertheless, William Crawford, now secretary of the treasury and in charge of the Customs Service, downplayed complaints about slave smuggling from the collectors under his command: only when the army's pressure had secured the cession of Florida would serious and successful prosecutions for piracy begin.[11]

A more serious source of irritation was Amelia Island, on the Atlantic coast at the Georgia-Florida border. A group of adventurers led by Gregor Mac-Gregor, a former British officer who had served with Francisco de Miranda and was linked to Francisco Xavier Mina, seized the island from Spanish officials in June 1817. (U.S. forces had seized Amelia in 1812 in support of filibusters from Florida and Georgia, who had been stimulated by Madison's agent and former Georgia governor George Mathews. Madison disavowed Mathews, however, and U.S. troops withdrew the following year.) Among MacGregor's lieutenants were two or three erstwhile U.S. officers, one of whom acted as his second in command and led the assault on the island's port, Fernandina. Like their counterparts in the Gutiérrez-Magee and Long expeditions against Texas, these former officers had served for only a few years. James Grant Forbes, for example, had been commissioned directly as a lieutenant colonel in the Forty-second Infantry Regiment in August 1813 and was disbanded in the June 1815 reduction in force. Nevertheless, their role, combined with the precedents of the U.S. occupation of West Florida in 1810 following a rebellion there and the U.S. incursion, supposedly justified by a similar rebellion, into East Florida in 1812–1813, has led some popular accounts to suggest that MacGregor was acting as a front man for the United States.

Fall guy would be a better term. Although Monroe had helped sustain the East Florida incursion and failed to exercise sufficient oversight to restrain the Gutiérrez-Magee expedition against Texas in 1812 or Jackson's seizures of Pensacola in 1814 and 1818, as president he was most concerned about precipitating a war with Britain through unnecessary aggression against Spain. Indeed, Monroe appears to have learned from the misadventures of 1812 and 1813, sharing Secretary of State Adams's suspicion and distaste for the "double and treble treachery in the speculations of these auxiliaries to the South American revolutions," "those itinerant establishers of republics." Thus, Monroe's correspondence and messages to Congress were replete with outrage at the lawlessness of the rebels and privateers, "fugitives from justice, and absconding slaves," whatever their asserted legal status. Although their "system of buccaneering," menacing "the lawful commerce of every nation," provided the rationale for U.S. intervention, Monroe denounced insurgent and freebooter claims that the administration had permitted MacGregor to go forward after he promised to sell the island to the United States; instead, he condemned the filibusters' "interfere[ence] in our concerns" along the nation's southern periphery. Adams suspected that MacGregor served British interests, but given Monroe's eagerness for peace with Britain, it is doubtful that the administration saw the freebooters as a pretext for pressure against Spain, and

Amelia had little positive value by itself. Thus, intervention followed a series of cabinet meetings and was not sanctioned until fully three months after Louis Aury arrived on the island with armed Haitians, surely the most savage of banditti in American eyes.[12]

Though MacGregor claimed a commission from the revolutionary governments of Latin America and attempted to maintain law and order, he confiscated goods from merchants at Fernandina, and his foraging parties soon became marauding bands. MacGregor also established a prize court at Fernandina for freebooters to sell the ships they seized, creating a base that threatened trade just miles from the United States. Amelia was already a key route for smuggling slaves into Georgia, and in mid-July the navy dispatched the brig *Saranac* to the St. Mary's station to try to halt the offense. The *Saranac* promptly impounded a vessel carrying supplies to MacGregor, suggesting that no hints of support for the filibuster had been conveyed to American commanders on the scene. Two months later, after disagreements among the Patriots led to MacGregor's departure, Aury, a privateer originally from France, arrived from Galveston with more than a hundred armed Haitians and a commission and letters of marque from the Mexican revolutionary junta. The commander of the *Saranac* refused to recognize Aury through a mutual exchange of salutes, and strife soon developed among Aury, the Haitians, and the white Americans who made up most of MacGregor's original recruits. Thirty English veterans arrived that October, following a recommendation by the U.S. consul at St. Thomas (in the Danish West Indies) that they join MacGregor, and Aury reacted by seizing civil as well as military power on the island.[13]

The specter of Haitian soldiers parading across the river from the slave plantations of Georgia galvanized American policy makers, and in November, President Monroe decided to occupy Amelia under the "no-transfer" authority of secret congressional resolutions dating from 1811. The administration's primary concern was to get the corsairs to leave, not to apprehend them, which might send too strong a signal against the Patriots. Thus, new secretary of war John C. Calhoun instructed Major James Bankhead "that the evacuation should take place without the actual application of force, if possible." Gaines was ordered to the scene to oversee operations. Bankhead and navy captain James Henley arrived with 250 men a month later, and Aury quickly surrendered the island. Bankhead's attitude toward the freebooters differed little from Monroe's and Adams's, or from Gaines's and Jackson's toward the Indians of Florida: "this band of negroes and privateersmen" was "of that profligate character generally engaged in the violation or evasion of our revenue law. I shall therefore . . . enforce such regulations as may be most likely to preserve order." The major immediately confined the Haitians to Aury's ships,

James Bankhead, peacekeeper and civil-military diplomat extraordinaire, later in life, daguerreotype by Mathew Brady. (Courtesy Library of Congress, LC-USZ62-110055)

which he had to allow to depart for lack of evidence against them. Aury was arrested and tried at Charleston later in 1818 when he stopped to rally funds, supplies, and recruits, but the charges were dismissed.[14]

Bankhead's interpretation of the reaction among local civilians expressed an expansive nationalism, characteristic of military officers in this era, that blended the desire for order with contempt for Spanish government. "The [U.S.] occupation . . . has given great satisfaction to those who reside, or have property, here; and the American inhabitants in Florida, in hopes that it is the first step towards the extension of our Government to them, hail it with much joy." Sounding much like Monroe and Adams, while claiming ignorance of possible repercussions, the major asserted that "the interest, the security, and dignity of our country require[d]" the annexation of the entire province.

> The facility with which the revenue laws are evaded, while Florida is in the possession of a foreign power, the insecurity of the frontier inhabitants . . . & the refuge it affords to their runaway slaves . . . make it desirable to include [Florida] in our limits. I am well assured that the inhabitants of Florida, if they could be certain that our Govt. would extend its protection to them, would at once throw off their allegiance to Spain. They are sensible of the imbecility of the Spanish Govt., and live in dread of such marauding parties as the one lately established here. Their interest and security alike require protection.[15]

Although Aury departed in February 1818, U.S. troops remained at Amelia long after Jackson's army left Florida in the middle of the year, and Spanish sovereignty was never truly reestablished before Florida's cession in 1821. Monroe, supported by Crawford, initially worried about British reactions and intended to withdraw from Amelia once the freebooters were dispersed. Adams and Calhoun saw the island as a bargaining chip with Spain and doubted the Spanish could hold their Florida outposts against Patriots or pirates. In January 1818 Adams asked Spanish ambassador Luis de Onís "what guarantee he could give" that the "freebooters" would not return; Onís responded that the United States could demand 400 Spanish troops as a garrison, but hinted that they might take as much as a year to materialize. The Americans' predisposition to take matters into their own hands increased when Adams asked the Spanish minister about reports that MacGregor was recruiting in the Bahamas for a new sally against Florida in the spring. Onís replied that the marauders might be able to seize Pensacola but claimed that Spain could drive them out again.[16]

Reports of popular support for the occupation of Amelia seem to have clinched Monroe's decision; that week the president reported to Congress that retaining Amelia was authorized under the no longer very secret law permitting the president to preempt foreign occupation of East Florida. The chairman of the House Foreign Relations Committee cooperated by sending a draft report to Adams for suggestions; in Adams's words, MacGregor's privateering became "an attempt to occupy the said territory by a foreign power." Jackson's invasion of Florida did not lead the administration to reconsider. Indeed, Monroe ordered the troops to remain on Amelia even after Charleston residents requested their return to that city to counter slave unrest, and the necessity of occupation figured prominently in Monroe's annual message to Congress that November. Meanwhile, Adams told an emissary from the Argentine revolutionaries that the United States would not permit any nation other than Spain to hold Florida or establish a base there. The struggle for Latin American independence and international republicanism took a distant backseat to U.S. national security interests: antipathy to disorder and aversion to interstate competition not initiated by the northern nation.[17]

Describing the difficulty of restoring law and order after nearly a decade of turmoil in the area, Bankhead expressed a new level of vitriol toward freebooters, filibusters, corsairs, and pirates:

> The great number of restless & desperate men who had assembled here—men whose fortunes and principles were best suited to scenes of revolution . . . required constant vigilance and the frequent and prompt interposition of the power vested in me, to maintain anything like order or tranquility. This however I have effected, and without that violence which the spirit of our laws would forbid. The friends of freedom would despond if they could believe that the assertors of the independence of So. America were all like those I found here. I hope and believe they are not, for . . . I could not imagine a more unprincipled, desperate set of vagabonds ever met together.

The major went on to imply that incorporation into the United States might solve other, deeper problems. For instance, he blamed rumors of an Indian raid at Trader's Hill, fifty miles up the St. Mary's, on

> white men, painted like the Indians, who in order to steal negroes . . . perpetrated this savage act. . . . It is quite common for the Crackers, as the people of a particular cast on the frontier of Georgia are called, to make incursions into Florida & steal . . . negroes. The impunity with which this vice is committed, and the temptations which will be held out as long as Florida belongs to another power will make some of our citizens worse than the savages—if they are not so already. In a moral point of view we should possess the Floridas.[18]

Bankhead dispatched soldiers to the scene of the incident, but he believed that the long-term solution to crime and disorder on the peripheries of the American empire—to controlling American citizens as well as stateless persons—was to extend American law and hegemony throughout the region. This concern extended from Monroe and Adams down to junior but well-connected officers. Captain Alexander Gray, Eleazar Ripley's aide-de-camp, justified American aggression against Amelia and beyond on grounds of realpolitik, advocating the exclusion of competing polities, whether Spain or successors, from the nation's southern periphery:

> East Florida can never be a part of any government that may be established to the south without subjecting the U.S. to the same injuries that [now] exist . . . for these reasons I think it fair nay the duty of this government to seize on this country when it can do so easiest. Are we to stand by inactive and see new empires spring up around us that may hereafter be troublesome, without taking some steps to give to them . . . direction that may best suit our interest, merely because there is a Principle of abstract law that would be violated by our act?[19]

Since American citizens did not restrain their antagonism toward foreign nations, the American government would have to do so to preserve international peace. This quest for order would ultimately lead to the extension of U.S. sovereignty over contested borderlands. Yet doing so hardly resolved the underlying problems created by an individualistic, essentially self-governing citizenry that employed local, territorial, and state governments to resist constraint by the nation-state. Historian James E. Lewis observes that "increasingly, Madison and Monroe discovered that, in order to uphold their own carefully balanced definition of neutrality, they needed to extend federal power and authority over private citizens and subordinate officials." Yet, he adds, "they showed a persistent ambivalence about the appropriateness of their actions" for a republican nation. Consequently, "they often selected halfway measures," and "their efforts often seemed halfhearted," as policy makers fell back on American republicanism in the form of popular sovereignty—a plea of American exceptionalism—to claim their inability to enforce the obligations normally incurred by nation-states in international relations. These somewhat disingenuous efforts were ultimately damaging, undermining the rule of law, encouraging populist vigilantism and violence, and discouraging trust in American reliability among European policy makers. This tension between domestic democracy and international order remained an important distinguishing characteristic of the United States as a nation and a state within the international system throughout most of the nineteenth century.[20]

National military officers like Bankhead often felt pressure to pursue a balancing act by resorting to the discretion normally granted to executive officers on the spot, but they *were* on the spot, without the layers of physical distance and political insulation available to national civilian policy makers.

Military commanders were subject to orders and a system of discipline, and in the relatively rare cases when they were called on, their principal distinctive weapon was their ability to use or threaten force. In the decades to come, they would pursue a similar quest for order and peace (however inequitable) through intimidation in Indian territories disrupted by white intruders on the southern and western frontiers. On the Canadian border, twenty years after the occupation of Amelia Island, Bankhead and his comrades continued to express similar sentiments toward U.S. citizens who refused to accept the restraints of national and international law and order. Career army officers, socialized in an authoritarian hierarchy committed to the service of the national state, were generally happy to see those restraints enforced by the strong arm of British power when the U.S. Army was unable to prevent Americans from striking across the border. Lieutenant Colonel Bankhead had a long career of peacekeeping and policing ahead of him; he would face some of the same issues and dilemmas as commander of U.S. troops in Charleston during the Nullification Crisis in 1832. So did Colonel Bankhead, clearly recognized as an expert at navigating the shoals of civil strife, when he was dispatched to aid the civil authorities against filibusters along the Niagara frontier in 1838 and in Rhode Island against the Dorr rebels four years later.[21]

THE "FIRST SEMINOLE WAR": JACKSON'S
SECOND INVASION OF FLORIDA

For Edmund Gaines, the occupation of Amelia Island was a frustrating distraction from the real work at hand: the brigadier lamented his "mortification and embarrassment" at the diversion from his self-proclaimed mission to force American peace on the Florida Indians. Neither Congress nor Spain—nor, most important of all, Britain—protested much about the incursion, which constituted a casus belli for Spain under international law. Nor had any of these players complained much about the destruction of the Negro Fort eighteen months before, signaling their acquiescence, however reluctant, in U.S. military operations across international boundaries against stateless persons and nonstate actors. Indeed, senior Spanish officials already recognized the likelihood that Florida would be lost without British support; they had begun trying to secure the northern boundary of Mexico, hoping for some restraint on American recognition of the Latin rebels in return for ceding Florida to the United States. Yet in mid-January 1818 Secretary of State Adams warned Luis de Onís that between the actions of the Patriots who had seized Amelia,

Neamathla, Fowl Towns chieftain. (Courtesy Library of Congress, LC-USZ62-25702)

precipitating American intervention, and Indians hostile to the United States, Spain "would not have the possession of Florida to give [or trade to] us." Although Adams was not referring specifically to Jackson's offensive, which had not yet gotten under way, that assault would soon add real punch to the secretary's warning. Whatever the administration said, Onís could hardly avoid seeing a connection. Nor, of course, would the United States have stood by if Indians or Patriots had seized more of Florida; Monroe already had congressional authorization in the 1811 law to prevent its transfer from Spain to any other power.[22]

The U.S. occupation of Amelia—a further sign of American willingness to take advantage of the opportunities presented by nonstate actors—made the exchange of Florida for Texas seem all the more urgent to Spain. At the end of February the Spanish foreign minister unknowingly echoed Adams, lamenting to a colleague that "negotiation based on the cession of the Floridas will be useless, as we will not have them to cede." And worse was yet to come. The Amelia occupation was not a pretext for further American action; additional opportunities for military intimidation developed at the other end of the colony when overt hostilities broke out along the West Florida frontier late in 1817. Step by step, Edmund Gaines forced the Florida Indians to choose between subjection and war, first dispatching infantry to expel the inhabitants of the Hitchiti village the Americans called Fowl Town from land claimed by the United States under the provisions of the Treaty of Fort Jackson. The Indians warned Gaines to stay away, and he had enough experience to know that they would not leave without a fight.[23]

On the surface, this operation was a case of on-the-spot Indian removal in retaliation for raids against American settlements, without specific reference to Florida. Fowl Town, really a group of several multiethnic villages, was located twenty miles north of the international boundary, but the Mikasuki, perhaps the predominant ethnic group in the Fowl Towns, lived without regard to the international boundary claimed by the United States and continued to refer to Article 9 of the Treaty of Ghent to dispute U.S. possession. Major David Twiggs of the Seventh Infantry reported as many as 2,000 Seminole and Red Stick warriors mobilizing in the region of the Flint and Chattahoochee Rivers to resist U.S. authority—an unlikely figure, as that was perhaps the total of all potential Seminole and Red Stick warriors throughout the southeastern borderlands. After two and a half years on the southern frontier, Gaines probably knew this, but he accepted Twiggs's estimate without question and moved to concentrate his regulars at Fort Scott, asking Georgia governor William Rabun to mobilize the state militia. The brigadier intended to claim hot pursuit in order to attack the Seminoles in Florida. The administration continued to hesitate to enter Spanish territory, which might lead to war and British intervention, and initially forbade him to do so.[24]

Monroe's policy quickly changed, however. William Crawford had given up the War Department, and acting secretary of war George Graham, ordinarily the department's chief clerk, had none of the political strength or resolve necessary to resist powerful chieftains like Andrew Jackson. Hence, the president spent most of 1817 trying to find someone of sufficient stature to take hold of the War Department. This administrative uncertainty made it even

more difficult to resist military initiatives, but Monroe's preferences for secretary of war—Jackson himself, Henry Clay, and Isaac Shelby, a former governor of Kentucky who had resisted federal requests for assistance against
filibusters threatening New Orleans during the 1790s[25]—suggest that the president was open to more aggressively expansionist policies than his predecessor. The army's southern commanders read these cues as optimistically as
possible and pushed the policy envelope at every opportunity. By the beginning of November, Graham had authorized Gaines to eject the Creeks from
the Fort Jackson cession, including the Fowl Towns, a significant opening
down the path favored by the generals. Whatever Monroe expected—and it
is hard to believe that he could not anticipate the probable trend of events—
forcibly removing the Indians soon led to clashes that Gaines used to demand
the invasion of Florida. On November 19 Neamathla refused the brigadier's
summons to Fort Scott; the next day Gaines dispatched Twiggs with 250
infantry to sieze Neamathla and expel the Hitchiti from the Fowl Towns.
Twiggs marched overnight and attacked before dawn, a rare tactical innovation for the army during that period. After an exchange of fire that left three
or four Indians dead, the Hitchiti fled. Lieutenant Colonel Matthew Arbuckle
took a second expedition to the village to seize the Indians' corn and cattle,
which led to another skirmish and an American death. A third foray led by
Arbuckle burned the now-deserted village on November 23. Jackson claimed
to hope "that this check to the Savages will incline them to peace," but he
admonished the War Department that "unless [they] sue for peace, [the] frontier cannot be protected without entering their country"—Spanish Florida.
Nor would such peace prevent an American invasion of Florida, since the generals intended to pursue Indians accused of crimes within the United States,
destroy maroon communities, and round up fugitives from slavery.[26]

The Indians did not sue for peace, nor were they so centralized or united
that any one leader or set of leaders could have guaranteed it. On November
30 they retaliated by ambushing an American supply boat on the Apalachicola
a mile south of Fort Scott, killing Lieutenant Richard W. Scott, thirty-three
of thirty-nine soldiers, six out of seven women, and half a dozen children. The
losses were essentially half those incurred in the defeat known as "Dade's Massacre," which began the Second Seminole War eighteen years later, and they
spurred much the same uproar in the nation's newspapers. Gaines told Jackson that more than 500 hostile warriors had been sighted, including those of
"every town upon the Chattahoochee." The brigadier reported that he would
position his infantry to keep the riverine line of communications open, entering Spanish territory if necessary, for he had persuaded himself that "the order

David E. Twiggs, later in life, in Frank E. Stevens, *Black Hawk War* (1903).

of the President prohibiting an attack on the Indians below the line, has reference only to the past." Gaines then warned the Red Stick and Seminole chiefs that he was coming and no British aid could save them: "As well look for soldiers from the moon. . . . The English are not able to help themselves; how then should they help the old 'Red Sticks'"? The "First Seminole War"— deceptively titled in name as well as number—had finally begun.[27]

In Washington, President Monroe's first annual message to Congress addressed the Amelia crisis but did not mention the Florida Indian frontier. Calhoun arrived in Washington that day (December 2), began serving as secretary of war on December 8, and was confirmed by the Senate a week later. Like Monroe, Calhoun supported much more aggressive measures than Crawford or the acting secretaries had been comfortable with, and he gave Gaines discretion to pursue hostile Indians into Florida the day after he began his duties. The pace of expansion was accelerating: the brigadier now had civilian approval to attack the Indians, and Congress admitted Mississippi as the twentieth state the following day, a confirmation of earlier expropriations that must have encouraged the expansionists of the southern army. Recognizing that Gaines would take advantage of any latitude, Calhoun gave him even more affirmative authorization within the week; the sole caveat was that he should not attack Spanish installations, even if they sheltered Indians. Presumably Spain would accept an American incursion in West Florida, as it had toward the Apalachicola and Amelia Island; clearly Monroe did not expect Spain to go to war merely because its territory had been violated.[28]

By this time, Gaines had finally received the orders, already obsolete, to direct the occupation of Amelia Island. Concerned that the brigadier could not effectively command from hundreds of miles east of the theater of operations, Calhoun ordered Jackson to the border on December 26, virtually ensuring that a full-scale invasion would take place. Whether imaginative or inexperienced, the secretary also suggested that Gaines invade Florida from the St. Johns River, on the eastern side of the peninsula, "to penetrate through Florida, and co-operate in the attack on the Seminoles." Calhoun left this decision to the brigadier's discretion, and Gaines rightly considered such a move unfeasible, given the limited knowledge he had about the thickly wooded terrain. Calhoun was obviously looking to do more than clear the Fort Jackson cession of Creeks. Indeed, the secretary's orders to Jackson somehow failed to reiterate his injunction to Gaines against attacking Spanish posts, and Calhoun informed Alabama territorial governor William Bibb that the general was "authorized to conduct the war as he thought best."[29]

On December 28 the president added fuel to the fire, urging Jackson that "this is not a time for you to think of repose . . . until our course is carried through triumphantly & every species of danger . . . settled . . . you ought not to withdraw your active support from it." (The general had often spoken of retiring for health reasons.) Monroe feared war with Spain, which might lead to war with Britain, and he preferred patience, expecting Spain's position to weaken over time. Yet with encouragement like this, it is not hard to understand how imperious generals like Gaines and Jackson—members of the southern planter class who identified its interests in territorial expansion and slavery with those of the nation as a whole—could seize the opportunity to achieve their well-known objectives by intimidating Spain militarily.[30] Nor were these interests and objectives confined to the generals. Colonel William King, commander of the Fourth Infantry Regiment and formerly of Easton, Pennsylvania, had acquired an Alabama plantation. Duncan Clinch was from a planter family; he, Virginian Matthew Arbuckle, and Georgian David Twiggs all owned substantial plantations later in their military careers. For more than three decades between 1816 and 1847, these career officers advanced American expansion by destroying the Negro Fort, forcing the Seminoles from Florida, penning the Cherokee in the Indian Territory west of Arkansas, and leading divisions in the invasion of Mexico.

Historian James E. Lewis views Jackson's appointment as a means of preventing his resignation from the army (which he had often threatened), lest he be absent in the face of "challenges from privateers and European powers as well as Seminoles." But Jackson's assignment to command the incursion was much less contingent than Lewis suggests: he was the division commander, the senior officer in the southern theater, so it was his right to command; one assumes that he would have protested had the command not been offered to him, and it seems quite unlikely that he would have refused it. The challenge from privateers at Amelia Island was minimal enough that a captain, a company, and a couple of naval vessels could control it; the challenge from European powers was a constant, but it was hardly greater at that point than in 1815 or 1816, and Jackson certainly would have rejoined the army if war had actually materialized. Whether from an institutional or a borderlands perspective, the principal contingency leading to Jackson's appointment was Gaines's deployment to Amelia. Monroe could hardly send Gaines away from a theater of active operations against resistant Indians without calling on his superior, the leading political-military figure in the South, to command those operations.

If anything, one wonders why the administration sent Gaines to Amelia when Bankhead and the navy could handle the weak force of freebooters so easily. Whether that decision was an overreaction or not, it virtually necessitated Jackson's assignment to command against the Seminoles. It is hardly necessary to suggest that Monroe was sending "a veiled authorization to attack Spanish forts," as Lewis characterizes such arguments. It is enough that Monroe and Calhoun sent Jackson to Florida without clear constraints on his actions—"rules of engagement," in today's terms—because they should have known that he would take advantage of such latitude. It was impossible to restrain the general "after his intentions became clear," as Lewis suggests:

he never clearly communicated his intention to attack the Spanish forts at St. Marks and Pensacola, and the six- to eight-week turnaround in the mail made it unlikely that Calhoun or Monroe could have stopped him in time if he had.[31]

These were the same dynamics that enabled the generals to ignore Crawford and attack the Negro Fort eighteen months before. Monroe and Calhoun, to say nothing of Crawford, knew what had happened then, and they knew how and why. What was the balance between intention and ignorance? The issue is ultimately whether the administration should have known that it needed to be as explicit as possible if it wanted to restrain Jackson in Florida. Jackson's unauthorized assault on Pensacola in 1814, his language regarding the Negro Fort, and the consistent tenor of his communications on southern frontier issues should have been clear evidence that the administration needed to do so. Such restraints were hardly unheard of, nor were they impossible in the face of genteel sensitivity about honor. Calhoun cannot be excused because he somehow imagined that he did not need to repeat to Jackson the most important element of his orders to Gaines, or because he assumed that Jackson would know better than to attack Spanish posts. At that point, administrative inexperience descends to the level of negligence, and given the presumed urgency of avoiding any pretext for British intervention, one must judge Calhoun derelict. An army officer who failed to communicate orders of such significance would be court-martialed.

Nor is it easy to understand how Monroe could so greatly misunderstand Jackson's intentions. In late December, Calhoun remembered to send the division commander copies of Gaines's orders forbidding aggression against Spanish posts, but Jackson was already seeking more explicit sanction for occupying Florida. He wrote directly to the president on January 6, urging that the United States take East Florida "as an indemnity for the outrages of Spain upon the property of our Citizens," primarily a reference to Spanish privateering during the decade after 1798. Strategically, the general believed that by seizing the initiative and Florida, he could forestall future wars, inevitable if Florida remained a source of Indian raids, U.S. retaliation, and opportunities for European intervention. Jackson proclaimed his willingness to accept the responsibility and condemnation such an invasion would incur: "This can be done without implicating the Government; let it be signified to me . . . and in sixty days it will be accomplished." The general then advised "that the arms of the United States must be carried to any point within the limits of East Florida, where an Enemy is permitted." This meant striking the Spanish if they provided sanctuary to the natives: "if our troops enter the Territory of Spain . . . all opposition that they meet with must be put down."[32]

Although Monroe routinely carried on a direct correspondence with Jackson, neither the president nor the secretary of war responded with explicit instructions forbidding Jackson to attack the Spanish positions in Florida. Monroe later claimed he had been ill and gave the letter to Calhoun without reading it. The secretary read it and suggested that Monroe do so as well, but the president later swore that he did not read the letter until that autumn; he may have mislaid it in the interim. The administration was not exercising anything remotely close to the oversight necessary to restrain its most aggressive general, who had already invaded Florida once before, contrary to War Department intent, during Monroe's tenure as secretary of war in 1814. Perhaps Calhoun said enough about the letter to cause the president concern, for on January 30 Monroe finally got around to directing the secretary to explicitly order Jackson not to assault posts occupied by the Spanish, lest he "bring the allied powers on us." Yet Calhoun still failed to do so, later claiming that he thought sending copies of Gaines's orders, which included this prohibition, would be sufficient: the Carolinian would come to know Jackson much better in years to come.[33] Calhoun authorized the general to call on the governors of Georgia and Alabama for militia, and Jackson did so. But the general preferred his own Tennesseans and bypassed the civil authorities to quickly raise a substantial force of volunteers from that state, many of whom had already served under him in the Creek War. (Although Congress later criticized this action, it got lost amidst the issue of the war as a whole.) Remembering his difficulties with Georgia militia in the Creek War, Sharp Knife told John Coffee, "If I can get 1200 mounted gunmen from Tennessee with my regular force—[and the] Georgians should mutiny, I can put [the Georgians] down, & drive into the Gulf all the Indians and [their] adherents be them who they may." To Jackson, Indian "adherents" meant Britons, blacks, and Spaniards alike.[34]

Jackson's offensive met little armed resistance, but the campaign did not go as smoothly as he had expected. The government's continued reliance on poorly compensated but politically connected civilian supply contractors, who proved unable to finance the necessary collection and distribution, aggravated the logistical situation at Fort Scott. It remained tenuous until Jackson arrived with the main body of Tennesseans and forced the nearby Indians to cease their harassment. Until then, it often seemed as if the post was under siege. In mid-January Lieutenant Colonel Arbuckle reported that he would be compelled to abandon the fort unless he was resupplied. Other officers responded more aggressively. A month later Lieutenant Colonel William Trimble, commanding the Eighth Department while Eleazar Ripley went on a lobbying trip to Washington, advised Jackson to seize the Spanish coastal post at St. Marks, halfway between the Apalachicola and Suwannee Rivers, to relieve the pressure, presumably by opening a new depot for American supplies. Trimble, a Kentucky-born expansionist who usually focused on Texas, did not explain why the United States could not establish a depot of its own, and it is unclear whether he wanted an excuse to strike against Spain or was simply attracted by the infrastructure of an existing post.[35]

Colonel Trimble had already dispatched Lieutenant Richard K. Call (the future governor of Florida) to Pensacola to discuss supply shipments up the Escambia; he also charged Call and another lieutenant with finding out whether Spanish officials were supplying the Indians. Trimble received encouragement from General Ripley's aide, Captain Alexander Gray, who observed "that a settled determination on the part of our Govt. . . . to possess itself of all east Florida under some pretext or other, and hold it as they do West Florida subject to future negotiation . . . is the only way by which we can get it without declaring war. It will not be long before our interference is necessary at Pensacola to make peace there." The colonel took a contingent of regulars and Alabama militia on a sweep from Fort Crawford toward Pensacola, but Alabama territorial governor William Bibb had ordered him to "avoid any act of hostility towards the Spanish Authorities." These clear, direct instructions from a governor to a lieutenant colonel prevented Trimble from anticipating Jackson.[36] But Sharp Knife needed no encouragement from a lieutenant colonel, and Bibb's restraint meant little to veteran Indian fighters and rabid expansionists like Gaines and Jackson. Faced with the choice of abandoning Fort Scott or going forward, Gaines counseled Calhoun that the army could not halt its offensive, lest the Seminoles gain the initiative. The brigadier saw "no prospect of peace without beating them into a conviction of the danger . . . of war with the United States," advising Georgia governor Rabun that "there will be no peace until those Indians are severely chastized." Three weeks later Gaines proposed joining the troops from Amelia Island and Fort Scott to "enable us . . . to seize upon all the red and black warriors" of the Suwannee "and put down all hostility among them."[37]

Yet Gaines had strong reason to believe that some federal civil officials in the area—particularly the Creeks' agent, former Georgia governor David B. Mitchell—thought peace was possible, and the generals may have been worried that they would be called back if their belligerence became too public. Gaines's letter to Rabun was reprinted in the *Knoxville Register* and *Niles' Weekly Register*, and Jackson immediately fired off a letter to the governor demanding that he prevent leaks to the press about prospective operations. Sharp Knife criticized "the publicity which has been given by the Journalists of

Foundations at St. Marks, photographer unknown. (Courtesy Wakulla County Chamber of Commerce)

this State to all communications from the Army": "Whatever is to be effected against the Seminoles must be done secretly & expeditiously . . . if all our movements and intentions are made public, we are ourselves defeating the very objects we wish to effect. Surely our citizens can restrain their curiosity, or are willing to remain ignorant for a time . . . when necessary for the general good."[38]

By early March, Jackson had concentrated his troops at Fort Scott and advanced south into Spanish territory, where he built Fort Gadsden (named for his principal aide-de-camp) on the sight of the old maroon fort at Prospect Bluffs, overlooking the Apalachicola. On April 1 he drove the Mikasuki from their villages, which he burned on April 2. Claiming that Spanish officials had supplied the Indians, he seized St. Marks without combat on April 7. He then continued southeast and destroyed Bowlegs' Town on the Suwannee River, the chief refuge for maroons who had escaped the Negro Fort disaster in 1816, after inconclusive exchanges of fire with a force that included as many as 500 fugitives from American slavery. Indeed, blacks far outnumbered Indians in the population of Bowlegs' Town. The following day (April 17) Jackson was appointed one of the commissioners to negotiate a land treaty with—in effect, a seizure from—the Chickasaw. Although this appointment was made before officials in Washington knew about the general's seizure of St. Marks, it throws the essential congruity between Jackson's objectives and those of his civilian superiors, and their estimation of his political popularity and intimidation value, into bold relief.[39]

Jackson's ultimatum to the Spanish commander at St. Marks reiterated familiar themes from his justifications for destroying the Negro Fort two years earlier: "Under existing treaties . . . The King of Spain is bound to preserve in peace . . . all Indian Tribes residing within his territory." When Spain failed to meet this obligation, and Spanish officials sheltered and perhaps supplied Indians who were hostile to the United States, Sharp Knife took the offensive per "that universal principal [*sic*] of self defence . . . to chastise a savage foe" and "a lawless band of Negro brigands" for their "cruel and unprovoked war against the Citizens of the U States." President Monroe had just assured Congress that the southern "general-in-chief" had been ordered to respect Spanish posts, but this was not yet known on the southern frontier, and Jackson led the Spaniard to believe that Monroe had authorized his actions, which the imperious general had some reason to believe. Jackson later justified his undiplomatic conduct to Secretary of War Calhoun by claiming that St. Marks had served as a refuge and supply depot for the Indians and was essential to meet his own logistical needs. Spanish sovereignty remained irrelevant to the Tennessee tornado: Spanish "personal rights and private property [have] been respected, & the commandant and garrison furnished with transportation to Pensacola." Coming from Jackson, that was mercy indeed.[40]

Such propriety was available only to those the general deemed harmless. Several British citizens—Indian traders and erstwhile military officers suspected of arming the Seminoles—had been captured during the incursion. Though he lacked clear authority or jurisdiction under the law or in his position as field commander (particularly without a declaration of war), Jackson had two of them tried by court-martial, essentially as stateless persons and presumably unlawful combatants or spies, and they were executed at St. Marks without any reference to higher authority in Washington. (Federal law required presidential review in such cases.) Eighteen days passed between the initial capture and the court-martial; Jackson advised the War Department of the prisoners but conveniently neglected to explain what he intended to do with them. He might have held the Britons prisoner and asked for advice from Washington while he was advancing against Bowlegs' Town, but he reported the executions after the fact, on May 5, in the same report that announced his intention to occupy Pensacola.

One of the Britons, Alexander Arbuthnot, was an elderly Scottish merchant who had supported Seminole resistance to American expansion. The previous

July, Gaines had labeled him the "prime director of the Seminola Indians" in their relations with the United States; clearly, the brigadier remained obsessed with British threats to American autonomy and could not credit autonomous Indian opposition to American encroachment. Robert Ambrister, a former British lieutenant associated with Edward Nicholls and George Woodbine— who was then leading maroons in the region near Tampa Bay as a private citizen—was actively engaged in the struggle for Indian and maroon freedom when he was captured near the Suwannee after the destruction of Bowlegs' Town. Violating established court-martial procedure, Jackson ignored the sentence (fifty lashes) handed down by the court and unilaterally imposed the death sentence—the punishment Sharp Knife had promised for whites who aided blacks or Indians nearly three years before.[41]

This was the second time in three years that Jackson had overruled his protégé Gaines in the latter's capacity as president of a court-martial instituted by his commander against civilians. In March 1815 Gaines had dismissed most of Jackson's charges against Louisiana state senator Louis Louaillier during Sharp Knife's reign of martial law in New Orleans, but Jackson disapproved of Louaillier's acquittal and kept him imprisoned. In 1818 neither Ambrister nor Arbuthnot had the official connections to provide the kind of assistance the Indians hoped for from Britain; the Mikasuki-Seminole struggle was set back far more when Jackson hung two of the principal Red Stick leaders— Hillis Hadjo (or Haya), aka Josiah Francis or Francis the Prophet, and Homathle Micco—at St. Marks without any trial whatsoever. Despite three weeks of debate over Jackson's conduct the following winter, no congressman complained about the Indians' killings.[42]

British sensibilities meant no more to Jackson than Spanish ones. Indeed, the general claimed, "There is no room to doubt but that [the British] Government had a knowledge of their [Arbuthnot's and Ambrister's] assumed character and was well advised of the measures which they had adopted to excite the Negroes & Indians in East Florida to war against the U States." Sharp Knife intended to send a message that neither British nor Spanish assistance to the Indians, whether overt or covert, would be permitted to retard American expansion or threaten its security. "The execution of these two unprincipled villains will prove an awful example to the world, and convince the Government of Great Britain as well as her subjects that certain . . . retribution awaits those unchristian wretches who by false promises delude & excite a[n] Indian tribe to all the horrid deeds of savage war." Thus Jackson's war against Indians and maroons united with the general campaign against nonstate actors threatening U.S. hegemony in the Gulf borderlands. Secretary of State Adams wove them all together in the justification he sent to Spain; he repeatedly denounced the Spanish for failing to restrain the "mingled horde of lawless Indians and negroes" urged on by "foreign white incendiaries" (meaning the British), whom Adams blamed for every American conflict with the Indians.[43]

The executions gave England cause for war, as many British newspapers urged, but when Jackson's evidence was sent to Lord Castlereagh, the foreign minister did not attempt to refute it. By 1818, the British government had come to see men like Ambrister as inconvenient and therefore stateless adventurers or messianic cranks who hindered the improvement of Anglo-American relations; when push came to shove, Britain merely protested and left the Indians and Spanish to shift for themselves. Though Jackson did not know it, Monroe and Adams had seen evidence of this shift early in 1818, before Jackson began his operations. That winter, Spain asked Britain to mediate its disputes with the United States, precisely the sort of opening Britain might have seized on to restrain American expansionism. Yet British ambassador Charles Bagot told Adams that Britain "must accommodate her policy to the nature of things," accepting the reality of American power in the Gulf borderlands, and vowed that his country hoped for "the best understanding" with the United States. Bagot added that he had warned Luis de Onís that Britain would not "support Spain in any extravagant pretensions" and that he had refused British support for MacGregor's seizure of Amelia Island. Recognizing British reluctance to intervene after several years of diplomatic and commercial reconciliation, Monroe's cabinet rejected the halfhearted British offer of mediation four days after Bagot proposed it; the British were not unhappy to avoid disrupting their rapprochement with the United States.[44]

British policy did not change after Jackson's hanging of Ambrister and Arbuthnot. That November, after Britain had frustrated French and Russian projects to intervene on Spain's side against the Latin revolutionaries at the conference of European powers at Aix-la-Chapelle, Adams justified the executions to Bagot, linking the dead men to Woodbine and maintaining that "the execution . . . was justifiable according to the ordinary laws of war." Adams had changed his mind about hanging "white m[e]n . . . found in arms with the enemy" (Jackson's order to Gaines in 1815) since the preceding spring, when he had spoken against it upon hearing the news that the Indians had been hung. (Ironically, given his clash with Jackson, William Crawford had once proposed doing so.) Persuaded by evidence or diplomatic necessity, Adams came to agree with the ferocious Tennessean, advising Albert Gallatin that "the necessity of a signal example was urgent and indispensable" to prevent European adventurers from leading the Indians astray. Indeed, the secretary claimed that doing so was "the only possible means of redeeming them from the alternative, otherwise unavoidable, of their utter extermination." Most important, Bagot responded to Adams's assertion by showing him correspondence disavowing Nicholls and, by implication, Ambrister and Arbuthnot. The British ministry delayed parliamentary discussion of the executions until May 1819, well after the furor had abated. Jackson and Adams made quite a team.[45]

Nor did France provide much help to Spain, even after the full range of Jackson's aggression became clear. In July, French ambassador Hyde de Neuville tried to let the administration off the hook by telling Adams that he did not believe Jackson's seizure of the Spanish posts had been authorized; unwilling to let it go at that, the secretary declared that Monroe would approve Jackson's conduct. Whatever Neuville thought of this, he consistently communicated Spanish fears to Adams, opining two days later that Spain would cede Florida to the United States and reminding the secretary (in Adams's words) that Spain was "extremely anxious to preserve peace." That November, Neuville hinted that he had refused to give Onís a note in support of Spanish claims; Adams felt confident enough to warn the French ambassador that doing so would be counterproductive.[46]

Jackson posed a far more immediate threat to U.S. relations with Spain, but Spain mattered to American policy makers only if it became a pretext for British, French, or Russian intervention. Evidence found at St. Marks convinced the general that Spanish officials had given his opponents aid and refuge beyond the natives' ability to extort by threats of force. On April 27 Lieutenant Call, now serving as Jackson's aide-de-camp, observed that "the Genl is quite [angered] against the Spanish Commandants and I believe [that if he] can find an excuse for it he will relieve all their garrisons in this Country." The following day division adjutant Robert Butler ordered Captain Abraham Sands to prepare siege artillery and collect intelligence about the Spanish fortifications at Pensacola, cautioning that "you cannot be too circumspect." A week later Jackson authorized a general offensive, ordering Gaines to seize any Spanish posts where hostile natives sought shelter. Gaines closed the circle of self-deception and aggression by failing to remind his superior of Calhoun's orders not to do so. Neither of the two men who knew of this restriction attempted to communicate it to Jackson, who had been "authorized to conduct the war as he thought best." Under these circumstances, Sharp Knife was going to use his professional discretion to the fullest, whether to facilitate defensive operations or to send a message of intimidation. Any hope that the general would restrain himself because he had not been granted explicit authority to attack Spanish posts was foolishness unworthy of Monroe's experience and Calhoun's intellect.[47]

After St. Marks, Sharp Knife moved against Pensacola, the capital of Spanish West Florida, hinting to Calhoun that he might treat the Spanish governor like Ambrister and Arbuthnot. Killing official representatives commissioned by the Spanish sovereign almost certainly would have led to a declaration of war, however ineffectual, by Spain. Jackson further justified his actions by the Spaniards' assertions of hostility toward the Indians, which allowed the general to claim that Spain should have aided him and closed its posts to the Seminoles. As usual, Spanish aid meant allowing the United States use of the rivers flowing through Spanish territory into the Gulf of Mexico. On March 25, the same day Monroe assured Congress that Jackson would not attack the Spanish, the general warned Colonel José Masot, the governor of Pensacola, that "I wish to be distinctly understood that any attempt to interrupt the passage of my transports [up the Escambia to Fort Crawford] cannot be received in any other light than as a hostile act." Masot had not prohibited American traffic, but he had refused to allow American supply vessels to pass without paying tolls, in accordance with Spanish regulation and law; after Jackson's ultimatum, he relented.[48]

Distinctions and concessions meant little to the Tennessee tornado, who seized Pensacola for the second time in less than four years on May 24, five weeks after he had first hinted to Calhoun that he would make "a reconnoisance [*sic*] . . . at Pensacola point." Jackson made his intentions clear in his May 5 report, but he did not wait for the secretary's response. Masot, who was apparently more eager for news from Washington, alerted the general to Monroe's March 25 statement to Congress, but Jackson did not hesitate. Instead, Sharp Knife threatened the Spanish commander that "if the peaceable surrender be refused, I shall enter Pensacola by violence." Jackson would "put to death every man found in arms"—a clear violation of the customs of war normally accepted by European and American military professionals—if American vessels were fired upon. The general warned Masot that "my resolution is fixed—& I have strength enough to enforce it." The garrison at Fort Barrancas surrendered four days later after a short blockade and artillery duel.[49]

Satisfied with his victory, Jackson did not carry out his savage threat, but he repeated his contention that the president had authorized the assault and proclaimed to the inhabitants that "the immutable laws of self-defense [have] compelled the American Government to take possession of [those] parts of the Floridas in which the Spanish authority could not be maintained." He then appointed Colonel William King of the Fourth Infantry Regiment as civil and military governor and declared American revenue laws in effect; he made his aide-de-camp and protégé, engineer captain James Gadsden, customs collector. King was supposed to follow Spanish civil law, and local civilians were appointed to most offices, but if taxation is sovereignty, Sharp Knife was declaring Florida an American possession. Indeed, as Jackson boasted to the War Department, "The articles [of surrender] . . . amount to a complete cession . . . of that portion of the Floridas."[50]

John Quincy Adams, engraving by Asher B. Durand after Thomas Sully. (Courtesy Library of Congress, LC-DIG-ppmsca-15717)

5

JACKSON AND GAINES GET THEIR WAY

Civil-Military Friction over the Invasion of Florida, Indian Relations, and Filibustering against Texas, 1817–1821

Congressional criticism of the invasion has always obscured the fundamental congruity between Jackson's actions and most Americans' support for expansion. Much, though certainly not all, of the criticism was motivated by personal and factional political rivalry rather than opposition to the general's actions or objectives per se. Knowing this, Jackson was quick to point out the benefits of his actions to his civilian superiors in the executive branch. Having demobilized the militia, volunteers, and native auxiliaries and returned to Nashville, Old Hickory closed his military campaign and opened his political one with letters to the president and secretary of war that encapsulate the arguments and objectives of expansion-minded officers on the southern frontier: "The Seminole War may now be considered at a close. Tranquility [is] again restored . . . and as long as a cordon of military posts is maintained along the Gulf of Mexico [i.e., within Spanish territory] America has nothing to apprehend from either foreign or Indian hostilities."[1] The aggressively self-righteous general responded to Monroe's mild reproof by asserting that without instructions beyond those given to Gaines—to "penetrate the Seminole Towns through the Floridas"—he had been free to undertake any measures he saw fit to achieve the executive's long-term objectives. None of the cabinet officers mentioned Secretary Calhoun's injunction against attacking Spanish posts. Jackson, the military commander on the scene, declared that he had represented, and had been compelled to represent, "the American Government" on the Florida frontier, pursuing the inalienable rights granted by the "immutable" natural law of necessity to maintain order in an apparent power vacuum exploited by the Seminoles. He then recurred to the army officer's standard nostrum for future peace: a generous dose of military preparedness. In practice, preparedness often meant preemption: that same day, Jackson's adjutant general, Colonel Robert Butler, ordered Gaines to pursue Peter McQueen, the most prominent Red Stick leader remaining, if he returned to the Suwannee. Sharp Knife's vision of international relations came down to kill or be killed.[2]

Jackson's invasion of Florida illustrates the tension between a subjective sense of responsibility for national defense and a formal and ultimately objective—at least insofar as the beliefs of the military officer are considered irrelevant to the constitutional decision-making process—sense of accountability to the authority of civilian political structures. The invasion also suggests the danger of relying on the discretion of officers socialized in gentry autonomy and command rather than impersonal bureaucratic professionalism—that is, accountability within a centralized, hierarchical chain of command devoted to a specific sphere of competence and level of focus. Given genteel diffidence, inadequate long-distance communication technologies, and hesitation in the face of Jackson's peculiar sensitivity, civilian policy makers in the executive branch failed to effectively communicate their directives or intentions to the military commanders on the frontier. Nor did they send agents to advise the imperious generals, as the State Department had sometimes done during Madison's administration (though usually to stir up or coordinate with filibusters, as in East and West Florida and Texas between 1810 and 1813). Once Louisiana became a state and William C. C. Claiborne became a state governor rather than a territorial one, the only federal civil officials in the region remotely comparable to Jackson and Gaines were the territorial governor of Alabama, the Indian agents, and the various Indian treaty commissioners. Yet the commissioners were temporary appointees, many of them friends and allies of Jackson who had often been chosen on his recommendation, largely for their aggressiveness toward the Indians. Apart from Return J. Meigs, the longtime Cherokee agent, none of the Indian agents had the generals' experience; none had anything close to Old Hickory's political stature.

Not surprisingly, Secretary of War Calhoun and his predecessor Crawford (now secretary of the treasury) believed that Jackson had been bent on war and sought his censure for insubordination. Secretary of State Adams observed that the general would resign if repudiated, and Calhoun grudgingly accepted that Jackson's popularity made it "inexpedient to punish him." Monroe, as usual, sought a middle ground, writing to the Tennessean that he recognized the need for commanders' discretion and accepted the general's actions as "measure[s] of necessity." (Monroe was the only member of the cabinet with significant military experience, albeit dating to the Revolutionary War.) The president cautioned Jackson that the nation must be united if it had to fight, so there could be no constitutional controversies over who had initiated war. Nor did Monroe want to face a united Europe, even if this consisted only of privateering against American commerce. Yet he assured Jackson that the invasion would "furnish a strong inducement to Spain to cede the territory, provided we do not wound too deeply her pride by holding it."[3] Adams bolstered Monroe's support for the general, arguing that "if the question was dubious, it was better to err on the side of vigor than of weakness—on the side of our own officer, who had rendered the most eminent services to the nation, than on the side of our bitterest enemies, and against him." Three days later, Monroe cautioned Thomas Jefferson that putting the general on trial for disobedience of the orders against attacking Spanish posts would be "improper," given the need for operational autonomy in frontier commanders. Diplomatically, trying Jackson would send a signal of hesitation that would "confirm [Spain] in the disposition not to cede Florida." Monroe was concerned that Britain might act to support Spain, but he believed in the general's integrity, accepted his authority to act as he did under the circumstances, and resolved to make the best of it.[4]

Old Hickory saw nothing to apologize for or compromise about. In August 1818 he tacitly rejected the president's request that he provide more evidence of Spanish complicity with the Indians, asserting that "my order [from Calhoun] was as comprehensive as it could be [under the circumstances], and contained neither minute original instructions, nor a reference to others, previously given, to guide and govern me. The fullest discretion was left with me." The general was in error here, for his instructions *had* included reference to those given to Gaines, but the administration had certainly aggravated the problems posed by granting its executive officers discretionary authority. Calhoun would significantly improve the War Department's capacity for systematic communications and effective command and control, but he was much too new at the helm to do so during the Florida conflict. Only action by the president could have halted Jackson or ensured his sanction after the war, and Monroe shared the popular Tennessean's objectives.[5] Nevertheless, although Jackson was acting on policies pursued by the executive branch since 1810, his ferocity threatened war with Britain, the only power that could halt U.S. expansion. More important in the long run, the generals' actions clearly violated the letter and spirit of the Constitution, demonstrating a deplorable lack of accountability to both the idea and the process of civilian control over the military. Yet it is difficult to judge Jackson or Gaines by constitutional standards alone, for the Monroe administration was clearly complicit in their actions, or at least negligent in restraining them. Indeed, the generals' actions were extreme examples of the sort of unrepublican and, by previous Republican standards, unconstitutional measures that Republican nationalists and War Hawks like Monroe and Calhoun had come to deem acceptable in the service of American expansion, beginning with the Louisiana Purchase fifteen years before.

One must wonder whether the administration allowed Old Hickory to go into Florida knowing that he was popular enough to take the heat, whatever he might do. Gaines was not so well known, and it would have been far more difficult for anyone to envision the invasion as his own handiwork. Gaines probably would have gone just as far as Jackson (apart from executing Ambrister and Arbuthnot, and perhaps Josiah Francis and Homathle Micco), but he needed more political cover, a more explicit sanction than the administration was willing to provide. With Jackson, Republican congressmen had someone other than the administration to blame for its policies or their excesses. Crawford's supporters could do so without overtly condemning the Republican president they wanted to challenge, satisfying constituents who were fearful of executive threats to the Constitution, while securing Florida and maintaining the surface appearance of partisan unity—so important after a generation of divisive factionalism. Yet whatever functions, political or psychological, he served for Republicans who were loath to admit their lust for expansion and office, Sharp Knife had usurped the authority of the elected civilian legislature, which represented the nation as a whole, to declare war. His actions in Florida posed the most egregious challenge to civilian control, the culmination of the autonomous foreign policy he and Gaines had crafted along the Gulf frontier since 1814.

Apart from Adams, the Monroe administration sat on the sidelines while Jackson's allies defeated congressional efforts to censure him. The majority report of the House Military Affairs Committee condemned his proceedings against Ambrister and Arbuthnot, but after three weeks of debate, the House voted down all the resolutions critical of Jackson, including one that would have condemned the seizure of the Spanish forts as unconstitutional. The administration completely escaped reproof, while Jacksonians successfully appealed to the separation of powers and the principle of executive discretion for justification. The votes were fundamentally personal and factional rather than sectional or ideological, with supporters of Jackson and the president aligned against those of their rivals, Crawford and Clay. (Neither Adams nor Calhoun were significant factional players in 1818, but their deeds would soon

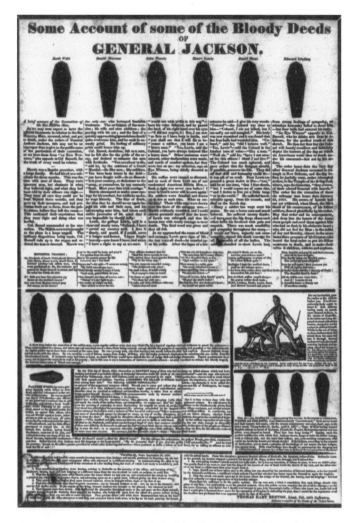

"Some account of some of the bloody deeds of General
Jackson," 1828 campaign handbill by John Binns. (Courtesy
Library of Congress, LC-USZ62-43901)

make them so.[6]) Thus, proponents of territorial expansion, especially in the
South and West, were as divided as any other group, if not more so. Two
weeks later, Senator Abner Lacock of Pennsylvania submitted the report of
his investigative committee, denouncing a wide range of Jackson's acts, including raising volunteers without following the proper procedure and appointing a military officer as governor of occupied Pensacola. However, the Senate

voted unanimously to ratify the Adams-Onís Treaty the same day, tabling Lacock's report. After all the shouting, Congress accepted the utility of Jackson's acts and sent further messages of hostility and determination to Spain. Addressing Congress on the state of the union that autumn, President Monroe blamed stateless adventurers (implicitly Ambrister and Arbuthnot) for the Indians' resistance and thus the war. For a majority in Congress, as well as the executive branch, the end had justified the means. Everyone, except the Spanish and Indians, got to have their cake and eat it too.[7]

Meanwhile, Gaines took the offensive to carry the expansionist standard in a civil-military controversy outside the halls of Congress. This complex quarrel highlights shifting military relations with state governors, state and national political factions, Indian agents and the operators of government trading posts, and factions among the Creeks, as well as the army's occasional role enforcing laws against smuggling slaves into the United States. On the surface, the conflict appears to have been a policy dispute within the War Department between Gaines and federal Indian agent David B. Mitchell, but the fault lines intersected with factional politics in Georgia and the Republican Party and affected the presidential potential of both Crawford and Jackson. The clash began in 1817 and continued into the 1820s, showing again that Jackson's lack of respect for civil authority was not idiosyncratic or unique or simply attributable to military authoritarianism. Mitchell was one of William Crawford's leading supporters in Georgia, where he had been governor since 1812. Mitchell resigned that post and was appointed federal Indian agent to the Creeks by President Madison, through Crawford's patronage, after Benjamin Hawkins's death in 1816. Gaines and Mitchell apparently worked together well enough in 1815 and 1816, but after 1815, the Crawford faction played a new role among Georgians, demanding restraint in land sales and opposing Jackson's coercive treaties. This shift had much more to do with Crawford's desire to supplant Monroe (in 1816 and even 1820), his concern over Jackson's popularity as a future presidential rival, and elite Georgian interests in frontier land speculation (which went back to the 1780s) than his belief in classical republicanism or any sudden sympathy for Native Americans. By 1825, the stars would return to their normal alignment in Georgia and Gaines would be engaged in another dispute with the next Crawfordite governor, defending federal authority against Georgia's lust for the remaining Creek lands. (That crisis, during which the Georgians threatened civil war, is explored in my second volume.)

Sharp Knife had feuded with his civilian superior throughout 1816. Although Jackson emerged victorious and Crawford moved on to the Treasury Department in the Monroe administration, the ever-present tensions between military officers and Indian agents became increasingly serious as patronage became a covert form of advancing or undermining presidential candidates during the "Era of Good Feelings" (a period of superficial harmony within the Republican Party, when overt federalism was disappearing). These tensions often began as petty disputes over resources—whether officers would allow troops to help build trading posts (then called factories) and other agency buildings, and who would control land reserved for public use around military posts like Fort Hawkins (near modern-day Macon)—but they quickly took on significant policy implications. Military reluctance to employ soldiers on fatigue details that were not directly related to military facilities was multiplied by the perception, extending from Jackson on down, that the civilian factors and Indian agents (though often former officers) were too closely linked and too sympathetic to the natives the army was preparing to fight. Duncan Clinch, for example, reportedly remarked that if former major Daniel Hughes, the factor at Fort Mitchell, wanted help, "let him call on the Indians or his red brethren & he would be more likely furnished with aid than from the Military."[8]

Indeed, expansionist sympathies and military officiousness went so far that some officers apparently permitted settlement on public reservations before it had been opened for sale, reversing their unhappy traditional role of ejecting trespassers from native and public lands. Post commanders had some discretion to authorize temporary settlement on the "military reservations" around their posts, but this became confusing when forts were no longer used militarily (as at Fort Hawkins) or when the reservations encompassed land miles from the forts. Indeed, post commanders usually discouraged settlement on military reservations in order to keep alcohol away from their soldiers. But during the spring of 1817, civil officials began to complain that military commanders were encouraging settlement in advance of survey and sale by allowing sutlers—civilians, commonly former officers, who sold goods to soldiers in garrison, as regulated by their commanders—to trade with the Indians in violation of the nonintercourse laws. Neither side cared anything for the Indians. The civilian complaints were rooted in commercial rivalry, for Indian agents were forbidden to trade with their charges, but both Mitchell and his successors did so, using Creek leaders or relatives as front men.[9]

Civil-military friction along the Florida frontier came to a head when Gaines and Mitchell clashed over the possibility of peace with the Seminoles and the employment of Creeks as auxiliaries during the war. The brigadier had the upper hand from the beginning, partly because of his position within the federal bureaucracy, but primarily because his objectives were so clearly in tune with popular pressure for Indian removal. Mitchell complained (not without

David B. Mitchell, governor of Georgia, federal agent to the Creeks, and Edmund Gaines's antagonist. (Photograph by Edwin Jackson, courtesy Georgia Archives, Georgia Capitol Museum Collection)

reason) that Gaines's withdrawal from Fort Scott had encouraged Red Stick violence during the winter of 1817, but the agent seemed just as eager as the general "to compel them to a more reasonable course of conduct." Toward that end, Mitchell told the general he had alerted the allied Creeks that the United States wanted their aid, and he offered to help mobilize them. A month later, in November 1817, as Gaines prepared to drive the Creeks from the Fort Jackson cession, acting secretary of war George Graham informed Mitchell that he needed to communicate with Gaines if removal would threaten any arrangements the agent was making with the Creeks.[10]

This hierarchy, in which the War Department's military operations trumped its civil diplomacy with the Indians, seems to have come as a shock to the former governor, who had held command authority over the Georgia militia, much like the president's over the national army. Mitchell quickly advised Secretary Calhoun that Gaines had launched an unnecessary war. Mitchell did so on the very day that Jackson dispatched the "Rhea letter" to President Monroe, offering to seize Florida without implicating the administration. Meanwhile, Gaines cautioned Calhoun and Georgia governor William Rabun—a member of the anti-Crawford faction in state politics—not to hope for peace. (The dispute between Jackson and Rabun over the Chehaw Massacre of friendly Creeks by Georgia militia the following spring did not threaten the fundamental solidarity between federal generals and state governors in support of white expansion. Jackson's rage over that incident was both personal— his own honor and authority had been offended—and pragmatic—he feared his Creek auxiliaries would desert or change sides.) Calling attention to many Creeks' allegiance to the United States and their anger at the assault on the Fowl Towns, Mitchell next demanded an official War Department policy statement, asserting that Gaines had "brought upon himself the embarrassment and difficulties he now experiences, and the loss he has sustained." In effect, Mitchell was trying to blame Gaines for the Scott massacre, the only U.S. defeat of the First Seminole War. Yet nothing about the administration's policy suggested that the agent would receive satisfaction; the die had long been cast, and he only aggravated the generals.[11]

Mitchell's motives may have been both partisan—to help Crawford blame the war on Jackson, and perhaps Monroe—and pecuniary—to maintain peaceful conditions in which to carry on his trade with the Indians and keep land values high—but the agent provided a sobering voice against military belligerence. It is difficult to see how Mitchell so completely misjudged the balance of political forces as to believe that public opinion would sustain him against Andrew Jackson during an Indian war, but greed and anger led the agent well beyond the bounds of propriety. Indeed, Mitchell publicly condemned the Tennessean's destruction of the Fowl Towns in a speech to friendly Creeks who had gathered to join the offensive into Florida. Gaines could now tar the agent with a brush that utterly obscured anything valuable in his advice. On January 12 the brigadier began his counteroffensive. In a skillful campaign of insinuation, he demonstrated that, as Thomas Sidney Jesup had boasted during a dispute with William Claiborne, "soldiers [were] not to be outgeneralled by politicians" on the southern frontier. The war enabled Gaines to avoid facing up to the racial-ethnic competition for southern land, and he blamed the growing militancy among previously friendly Creeks on "some evil disposed persons . . . engaged in smuggling negroes into the U.S. from East Florida. Two considerable droves . . . I am credibly informed, have been taken into the immediate vicinity of the Creek agency."[12]

The brigadier's accusations were soon reinforced by news from William Trimble that significant numbers of slaves were about to be smuggled into the United States via Galveston and East Florida. Thomas McKenney, the superintendent of Indian trade in Washington, added his censure against Mitchell's "avaricious" business arrangements, observing that the agent's establishment of a trading post in partnership with Creek leader William McIntosh, competing with the official factory run by Daniel Hughes, had fostered great hostility among the Creeks. Despite clashes of his own with commanders like Clinch, Hughes piled on with accusations against Mitchell that amounted to conflict of interest, if not fraud. Indeed, the Trade and Intercourse Acts prohibited agents from selling goods to Indians, although no one seems to have called Mitchell on that. That summer, the apparently incorrigible agent purchased cattle from McIntosh and other Creek leaders. (Jackson had ordered the cattle, captured from the Seminoles, distributed among his Creek allies to help compensate for their losses during the Creek War.) Secretary of War Calhoun ordered the cattle confiscated from Mitchell and sold, presumably at auction. Most important, Old Hickory joined with John Clarke, Rabun's successor as governor of Georgia, to weigh in against the outnumbered agent with President Monroe, taking full advantage of the opportunity to incriminate Crawford in Mitchell's appointment.[13]

Realizing that he had miscalculated Gaines's support, Mitchell attempted to counter the charges against him. The Georgian maintained that the men who had claimed a group of slaves at his agency were "gentlemen of respectability" with letters of introduction from the brigadier himself. They may have possessed such letters, but it seems highly unlikely the general would have provided his imprimatur had he known the recipients were engaged in slave smuggling, and the reputed letters were never produced. Opening another front, Colonel David Brearley, New Jersey–born commander of the Seventh Infantry Regiment, changed sides in the dispute. Brearley, who had initially provided a deposition implicating Mitchell, quarreled with Gaines over institutional military matters and joined the agent's counterattack by charging Gaines with negligence for failing to prevent the destruction of Lieutenant Scott's party on the Apalachicola. Once again the generals' opponents miscalculated. Coming two years after the event, when Congress had already refused to censure Jackson's conduct, Brearley's spurious charges went nowhere against Sharp Knife's favorite subordinate. Facing a life of harassment from Jackson in the army, Brearley resigned in March 1820, but he still had connections. Six years later, he found a new federal position: agent to the Creeks who had migrated west under pressure from Georgia governor George Troup, another Crawford ally who warred with Gaines.[14]

By September 1818, Gaines demanded to "be excused from having any intercourse whatsoever" with "the negro smuggling agent." Gaines and Jackson continued to hammer away at Mitchell until he was dismissed in 1821. In fact, Gaines was able to have much of his argument inserted in a congressional report originally intended to examine Jackson's mobilization of volunteers without the required congressional authorization. In the meantime, historians have discovered that Mitchell "managed to pocket virtually the entire annuity income of the [Creek] nation." Indeed, historian Francis Paul Prucha observes that improving the financial accountability of Indian agents was Calhoun's most important motive for advocating the abolition of the "factory" system of government trading posts, as demanded by their private competitors. Yet Mitchell's case was only the most egregious and best publicized incident of peculation by Indian agents during these years. This suggests that the innovative factory system, praised by historians for its comparatively fair dealings with the Indians, was damaged as much by the repercussions of civil-military controversy as by criticism from the advocates of limited government or by competition from private enterprise.[15]

Whatever Mitchell's role, the illegal importation of slaves became even more of a problem after the United States intervened in Florida. Persistent disorder, combined with American access to Amelia Island, afforded smugglers even greater facilities than before. Gaines reported that he had forbidden the movement of slaves between Spanish Florida and Amelia Island, and Calhoun authorized the army to seize slaves being smuggled "to places in our possession" (which presumably included Amelia). The United States then had to dispose of the slaves in question, and they were not going to be granted their freedom in 1819: the captives were sold at auction, making a mockery of the nation's halfhearted laws against the international slave trade.[16] Nor were the slavers satisfied to circumvent national law and international sentiment: Calhoun had to reassure James Bankhead that the U.S. district attorney would defend officers in lawsuits against their impounding of slaves being smuggled through East Florida prior to the territory's cession to the United States. Indeed, U.S. policy contributed even more directly to the increased availability of slaves in the borderland: even as Lieutenant Colonel Matthew Arbuckle assured the War Department that he would prevent the Apalachicola from becoming a route for smugglers, U.S. officers required surrendering Indians to give up any blacks they held for adjudication between claimants. This policy, intended to restore the "property" of American slaveholders taken by native marauders, soon became the basis for all sorts of claims, against blacks of all statuses, by speculators and planters (often one and the same) both white and Creek, much as it would during the Second Seminole War two decades later.[17]

Jackson's institutional position and personal determination to secure the southern borderlands made him the nation's principal strategist, civil or military, for that region, much as James Wilkinson had been during the Jefferson administration. His justifications for the land cessions he demanded from the southern Indians routinely included broad strategic considerations, similar to those of senior commanders on the northern frontier, where a comparable process was unfolding, and among the board of officers planning coastal fortifications. Jackson's strategy for securing the southern borderlands integrated military operations, diplomacy—from the position of strength those operations had produced—and economic development. Well before the Seminole War, Old Hickory believed that the long-term solution to American security concerns in the southern borderlands lay in the growth of white population and settlement. Expansion and security went hand in hand. His second invasion of Florida confirmed these views. The unwavering general drew an analogy between his objectives in Florida and those during the Creek War of 1813–1814, explaining that in each case he had acted to close avenues for British offensives from the Gulf coast. The key remained isolating the natives from European aid:

> So long as the Indians within the territory of Spain are exposed to . . .
> the poison of foreign intrigue; so long as they can receive ammunition
> . . . from pretended Traders, or Spanish commandants it will be
> impossible to restrain their outrages. . . . Resupplied by Spanish
> Authorities they may concentrate or disperse at will, and keep up a
> lasting predatory warfare against the Frontiers of the U States, as
> expensive as [it is] harassing to her Troops. The Savages must therefore
> be made dependent on us, & cannot be kept at peace without [being]
> persuaded of the certainty of chastisement . . . [up]on the commission of
> the first offence.[18]

Enforcing this dependence required the continued presence of American regulars in Florida: "so long as Spain has not the power, or will to enforce the treaties . . . no security can be given to our Southern Frontier without occupying a cordon of Posts along the Sea Shore." Again and again Jackson returned to the theme of a power vacuum that endangered American settlement and demanded federal action: Spanish "territory will always provide an asylum to the disaffected and restless savage, as well as to a more dangerous population [black maroons], unless some energetic government can be established to controul or exclude these Interlopers." It is not clear whether the general was referring specifically to Spaniards, Indians, or maroons as interlopers; he no doubt had all three in mind, plus Britons like Ambrister and Arbuthnot. He therefore sought the retention of St. Marks, Fort Gadsden, and the Barrancas, "so Essential to the peace & security of our frontier, and the future welfare of our country," after the conclusion of his campaign. Similarly, "the hordes of negro Brigands" who had fled to Tampa Bay had to be captured or kept in flight; once this was done, Jackson felt certain that "sound national Policy will dictate holding Possession [of Florida as a whole] as long as we are a republick."[19]

The administration chose a course of political and diplomatic compromise. In March 1818 Monroe had rejected suggestions that he seek legislative authorization to retain the Floridas, lest doing so produce war with Spain and then Britain. Yet even after news of the seizure of St. Marks arrived in May, the cabinet tentatively recommended keeping U.S. troops in Florida once the Seminoles had been defeated. Jackson himself had promised to restore Pensacola to the Spanish, a provision of the agreement under which the town had surrendered, but Secretary of State Adams advised the president to retain Pensacola until the Spanish could guarantee that they would restrain the Indians. Monroe again took a middle ground, ordering the return of Pensacola and the retention of St. Marks until a Spanish garrison arrived.[20] Yet Jackson saw his agreement to return Pensacola as merely a means to an end. That August he lectured Secretary Calhoun—a smart young man, but still inexperienced by Old Hickory's standards—that "it is alone, by a just & a bold course of conduct that we can expect to obtain & ensure respect from Europe[,] & not from a timid, temporizing policy. . . . I therefore conclude that the [Florida] Posts [should] never be surrendered" unless on American terms. "The security of the western States renders it necessary that they should be held—the voice of the people will demand it." This overtly political argument was atypical of the officer corps; few officers possessed the Tennessean's political instincts or leverage. But Jackson's belligerent conclusions were not atypical; nor did he intend to relent. That November he asked for a regiment of reinforcements from Jacob Brown's Northern Division to seize St. Augustine, which would have extended the dormant Spanish-American conflict to the capital of East Florida. His ardor mounting, the southern general promised to take Cuba if he were given a second regiment.[21]

Jackson felt no qualms about his aggressive course of action and was quick to call on his acute perception of the popular will to justify it, admonishing Calhoun that a responsible "Government will never jeopardize the safety of the Union or the security of our frontier by surrendering these posts." Three months later, facing congressional inquiry into his belligerence, the general again defended his conduct: "My only apprehensions are that my operations were not sufficiently extensive to ensure permanent tranquility." Jackson displayed no sense whatsoever of the danger of war with Spain or that it might lead to war with Britain, although the British were doing their best to prevent Spain from carrying matters that far. Indeed, he informed a friend, the American minister to Russia, "All I regret is that I had not stormed the works [of Pensacola,] captured the Gov [Masot,] put him on trial for the [Indian] murder of Stokes and his family and hung him for the deed." Increasingly conscious of American military superiority, the general derided the possibility of Spanish action along the Sabine River boundary with Louisiana as a distraction raised by timid locals. Sharp Knife advocated decisive offensive measures to clear the remainder of the Florida peninsula of hostile forces while the moment was still ripe. "If unmolested they may acquire confidence . . . and prove a destructive Enemy to our Frontier settlers—They should be pursued, before they recover from the panic of our last operations." The specter of armed refugees from slavery also commanded Jackson's attention, and he recommended twin amphibious offensives for the following spring: against the maroons and Red Sticks at Tampa Bay on the Gulf coast, and from the Atlantic up the St. Johns River to Picolata. These campaigns would establish bases and move inland to scour the Suwannee region and north-central Florida from the east while crossing the middle of the peninsula from the west, destroying "Woodbynes negro establishment" but otherwise "deviating only where Indian villages or settlements . . . invite their attention."[22]

Jackson believed these inviting detours—destroying the natives' homes and food supplies in order to starve them—would "finally [crush] Savage hostilities in the south" while "affording active service to some of our Regiments who have grown sluggish from the inactivity of garrison duties." American vigor would be gained at the expense of native hunger and decline, life from death. Nor did Jackson's plans end with blacks or Indians, for he repeatedly advocated the seizure of St. Augustine and Cuba, deeming them "essential to the security of our southern frontier and to our commerce [during] a state of war." These points could "be taken by a Coup de Main whenever thought necessary." A regiment of reinforcements with light naval support "would insure Ft St augusteen," and with "another Regt. and one Frigate . . . I will insure you Cuba in a few days." Presumably, the general's Florida experience had taught him that Spain would back down; otherwise, the actions he proposed would cause the state of war he professed concern for. The irresponsibility of Jackson's plans seemed to grow in train with their scope, for he mentioned nothing about the war with England that this disturbance of the balance of power in the Caribbean would likely incur—Old Hickory probably welcomed another opportunity to ply his switch against aristocratic British abolitionists.[23]

Sharp Knife was never alone in his belligerence, nor was military pugnac-

Next target: Castillo de San Marcos, St. Augustine. (Courtesy Library of Congress, HABS FLA, 55-SAUG, 1–2)

ity limited to West Florida. The day after the general took Pensacola, James Bankhead proposed to "risque my life and reputation" to seize St. Augustine, since doing so with 300 men "would tend to sustain the reputation of our Army" more than Jackson's doing so with 3,000. Like his boss, Gaines continued to plan the conquest of Florida throughout his tenure in command on the southern frontier. With Jackson back in Nashville, Gaines again became the de facto theater commander. In July 1818 he wrote to Jackson proposing an assault on St. Augustine; on August 7 Sharp Knife told the brigadier to go ahead, assuming that an enterprising expansionist like his deputy would have no difficulty finding evidence "that the hostile Indians have been fed and furnished from the garrison. . . . This evidence being obtained, you will . . . permit nothing to prevent you from reducing Fort St. Augustine except a positive order from the Dept. of War." Jackson then noted his expectation that the brigadier had already destroyed any Indians who had returned to the Suwannee; surprisingly, Gaines had not done so, probably owing to a lack of supplies. Jackson attempted to justify this escalation "not on the [specific legal] ground that we are at War with Spain" but "on the [abstract, universalist, and ultimately absolute] ground of [preemptive] self-defence, bottomed on the broad basis of nature and of nations, and justified by giving peace and security to our frontier"—almost exactly the language Gaines used. Given white aggression and the decentralization of Native American societies, there were always some Indian depredations to underpin these assertions, but tying the havoc to the Spanish was predicated on an absolutist, virtually preclusive concept of security that would ultimately mean U.S. domination over the North American continent.[24]

Jackson alerted his civilian superiors to these ambitions three days later, advising the president that he hoped Gaines had begun operations. Facing public criticism for allowing the generals such free rein, the War Department countermanded Jackson's authorization to Gaines almost immediately, warning Jackson that war with Spain could mean war with Britain, but this did not prevent Gaines from repeatedly, almost continuously, recommending operations in Florida. In mid-September he reported from Fort Hawkins, Georgia, that "I shall repair to Amelia Island and endeavor to do what can be done . . . to secure that frontier, and pursue the savages," advocating an advance up the St. Johns and across the peninsula to Tampa Bay.[25] This was even more ambitious than the offensive Secretary of War Calhoun had suggested at the beginning of the year, but Gaines's confidence had grown with the army's victories. Calhoun had already anticipated the brigadier's loss of hearing, warning Monroe and Jackson that their subordinate was exaggerating the number of natives and the threat they posed in Florida. Indeed, the secretary cautioned Gaines against active operations at least five times between late September and late November: a flurry of communication that might have prevented the seizure of Pensacola and St. Marks. Calhoun did renew the brigadier's authority to enter Florida in pursuit of hostile Indians, assuring him of supplies and reinforcements if Gaines thought them necessary, but he admonished the general that "you should not commence hostility, unless it should be forced on you." This guidance dissuaded Gaines from launching large-scale operations and restarting the war against Spain.[26]

Gaines began to back away from his incessant reports of native hostility and suggested an attempt to mollify the Seminoles who had surrendered by providing them rations, but the administration never really convinced the generals that it was preferable to wait on diplomacy, and they continued to grasp at opportunities to initiate hostilities. In November 1818 Jackson used a skirmish between volunteers and Indians to reaffirm his stance and to call for another offensive. "The fact that the news of the restoration of Pensacola to Spain has revived [the Seminoles'] hopes and again excited them to war is an additional evidence of the propriety of my operations in the Floridas, and has confirmed me in my unalterable opinion that the Seminole conflict could not have been terminated by any other means than [were] there adopted. My only apprehensions are that my operations were not sufficiently extensive to assure permanent tranquility in the South."[27]

No longer willing to trust the generals' discretion, Calhoun promptly admonished Gaines against proceeding without explicit War Department orders. Before the secretary's letter arrived, Gaines requested permission to liberate a sergeant (Augustus Santee, who was on leave at the time) and two civilians taken prisoner by a Spanish party—reportedly led by an American deserter—while pursuing an American civilian fugitive in Spanish territory on the St. Johns. Claiming that Spanish officials had supplied the Indians (and maroons) at Tampa with ammunition and urged them to attack, the brigadier vowed to "hold myself in readiness . . . and . . . strike at any force that may present itself."[28] Completely unable to take a hint, Gaines again reminded Calhoun that he would be happy to seize St. Augustine, where the three men were being held, and asked for a battalion of reinforcements. The prisoners were released before the general could initiate hostilities. Ironically, a soldier who had accompanied Gaines's emissary demanding the prisoners' release deserted while in St. Augustine; the Spanish governor promised to return the deserter, but the general vowed to pursue deserters into Florida. (Nothing came of this, and it is not clear whether the governor sent the deserter back to Gaines.) Nor was the Tennessee brigadier alone in his belligerence: early in 1819 the normally moderate Major Abraham Eustis expressed his hope that leading Bostonians would support Jackson's approach; a year later, Major Bankhead repeated his demand for a role in the conquest of St. Augustine.[29]

As for West Florida, the president decided in August 1818 to withdraw from Pensacola but to retain St. Marks until sufficient Spanish forces arrived to secure it against Indian control. "Sufficient" was left to Gaines's judgment, and he suggested 250 men as a reasonable number. However, the brigadier left the final decision—the implementation of national policy—to the commander on the spot, a mere captain. St. Marks was returned to Spanish control in April 1819; other places seized from or formerly inhabited by stateless "banditti," such as Amelia Island, were not given up. In the same letter that cautioned against provoking war, Calhoun observed that Fort Gadsden—established on the site of the erstwhile Negro Fort at Prospect Bluffs, overlooking the Apalachicola deep in Spanish Florida—appeared to be "a very commanding position, and ought not to be evacuated . . . so long as there is any danger." U.S. troops apparently remained there at least until December 1820, sending another message to Spain that its days on the North American continent were numbered. Indeed, Calhoun's order permitted Gaines to maintain U.S. forces in Florida east of the Apalachicola without stipulating their precise location, a dangerous grant of autonomy to the bellicose general: the only Spanish post remaining east of the river was St. Augustine.[30]

The furor over Jackson's incursion, combined with the return of St. Marks and Pensacola, dismayed many officers, but only temporarily. Indeed, they possessed far more confidence and far less sense of contingency than most historians or modern military officers would wish for or expect. Military commanders also recognized the influence of factional politics in the uproar, but they accurately assessed its limits as a restraint on national expansion. In September 1818 George Mercer Brooke, major of the Fourth Infantry stationed at the Barrancas, expressed his satisfaction at the course of events, assuring Old Hickory:

> I am happy to see that the Executive have approved of your conduct, though they intend to give [Florida] back. I cannot understand exactly the conditions [for Spanish forces to reoccupy the forts] . . . [but] the province may be considered as virtually ours. . . . I expect Congress will make a good deal of noise about this business, and the party which has been forming (the head of it [Henry Clay] from Kentucky) against the present administration, will make it a point to disapprove, for the purpose of throwing all the odium possible on the Government and its officers.

Like several other commanders, Brooke promised Jackson that he could secure depositions stating that the Spanish had armed the Indians, in case the people's representatives needed to be reassured of the general's good intentions.[31]

Gaines must have been encouraged by the news dispatched by Duncan Clinch—the lieutenant colonel who commanded the expedition against the Negro Fort—two days after Monroe's decision to withdraw from Florida: "The President speaks in the highest terms of the conduct of Gen'l Jackson, and of the army of the South." Indeed, Monroe had praised Gaines in "unqualified terms of approbation." Promoted to colonel in 1819, Clinch remained an ardent expansionist, looking "anxiously" to "the ratification of the Treaty—should it not be ratified, I hope the Government will not hesitate in taking possession. St. Augustine will be a delightful place under our Government." The Florida frontier made a profitable career for Clinch. Early in 1820 he advised the adjutant general on the economics of planting and slave reproduction in the region; Clinch purchased plantations of his own on Amelia Island and the St. Johns River. He rose to the rank of brevet brigadier general (as high as he could reasonably expect) and commanded troops in the

John C. Calhoun, by John Wesley Jarvis. (Courtesy Army Art Collection)

region until 1836. Yet his career, like Gaines's, suggests the complexity of the army's mission on the frontier: Clinch resigned because of Jacksonian criticism during the initial campaign of the Second Seminole War, finishing his public service as a Whig congressman opposed to the Jacksonians a decade later.[32]

Military commanders were not alone in advocating more aggressive pressure against Spain. In November, John Quincy Adams advised Monroe to seek congressional authorization to hold the Spanish posts until Spain agreed to resume negotiations. When the president refused, Adams recommended securing congressional sanction for the seizure of Florida if the Indians renewed hostilities; Monroe again counseled patience, awaiting news from the conference of European powers at Aix-la-Chapelle. But the ability to counsel patience depended on the assumption that Spain could not hold out against American pressure—pressure rooted in the threat created by Jackson. Thus, Adams's letter to the U.S. ambassador to Spain, justifying Jackson's actions, vowed that "Spain must immediately make her election, either to place a force in Florida adequate . . . to the protection of her territory, and to the fulfillment of her engagements, or cede [Florida] to the United States." The secretary concluded that if the United States felt compelled to invade Florida again, it would never leave. The following February, Adams told French ambassador Hyde de Neuville that if Spanish ambassador Onís did not accept American terms at the negotiating table, the administration would ask Congress for the authority to seize Florida, and Spain would face American terms at Jackson's hands. Onís capitulated three days later; within a fortnight, Monroe wrote that "by the pressure on Spain we have obtained" Florida. That pressure came from Andrew Jackson and the U.S. Army, not from civilian settlers, frontiersmen, filibusters, or even the persistent diplomacy of John Quincy Adams.[33]

Like Adams and Monroe, diplomatic historian William Weeks observes that the invasion of Florida "proved decisive in the making of the Transcontinental Treaty." In addition to securing the cession of Florida, which Onís had proposed to Adams in January 1818, before Jackson's assault on Pensacola and St. Marks, Jackson's menace helped spur Spain to accept a transcontinental boundary line extending to the Pacific Ocean. Spain dropped its demands, however unrealistic, for a Mississippi River boundary, and the United States got everything it might have asked for, save Texas. The situation in Florida remained confused while negotiations continued, but Sharp Knife had served the administration, southern whites, and ultimately the army and the nation well, cutting the Gordian knot that had frustrated American expansionists for more than a generation. Britain recognized the new reality and preferred mutual peace and profit, ratifying the Anglo-American Convention of 1818 despite the lynchings of Ambrister and Arbuthnot. Looking to penetrate Latin American markets and restrain the growth of conservative hegemony in Europe, Britain prevented Spanish attendance at the congress of European powers held at Aix-la-Chapelle that September, where the British blocked French and Russian proposals for military intervention against the Latin revolutions.[34]

As historian Michael Fitzgerald observes, these actions "announced

Britain's acquiescence in the limited [though ultimately quite extensive] expansion of the United States in North America . . . the message to Spain was unequivocal." That October, Spain gave Onís carte blanche to negotiate a settlement, which could only mean the cession of Florida. The United States gave up its rather artificial claim to Texas and accepted a Sabine River boundary, and the fundamental congruity between Jackson and the administration was demonstrated when Monroe directed the secretary of state to consult the popular general on the prospective treaty. Among members of the cabinet, only the expansionist Adams had defended Jackson's invasion, using much the same language as the general, and the two men met for the first time to discuss the boundaries delineated by the treaty. Though Jackson would later claim Texas as president, the diplomat and the general had no difficulty agreeing on the Sabine boundary in 1819.[35]

The Adams-Onís Treaty was signed in Washington in February 1819, but Spanish domestic politics delayed ratification, and that November, Monroe sought congressional authorization to seize Florida unless Spain ratified the cession. Once again, Jackson's violence would provide the sharp edge to back Adams's diplomacy—a diplomacy that depended on the force exerted by the Southern Division commander. The following month, preparations for an invasion began in earnest: the War Department requested reports from Chief Engineer Walker K. Armistead and Quartermaster General Thomas Sidney Jesup, as well as Gaines and Jackson, on the strength of the Spanish troops and fortifications, the most opportune moment to begin operations, and how much time would be required to secure the province. Returning to a proper tactical caution, Jackson warned his superiors against investing or assaulting St. Augustine with insufficient force, which might lead to a reversal that would damage public support for the conquest—a good example of the general's political insight and an awareness rarely expressed so explicitly by career officers. The day before Christmas, Calhoun asked Jackson for a plan of operations, and on the last day of the year, the secretary outlined their course of action if Congress were to approve a forcible occupation.[36]

Although the financial panic and the crisis over Missouri posed political obstacles, and the administration backed off from preparations after receiving French and Russian requests for restraint, Jackson hinted to a War Department staff officer that "if [Congress] will authorize the measure, the Floridas shall be in the possession of the United States in three months." None of the administration's concerns—fiscal, political, or diplomatic—were evident among army officers, whose narrower perspective encouraged continued expressions of expansionism. Spain could hardly ignore the threat posed by the Tennessee typhoon, and without European support, its prospects for defense were virtually untenable. Spain was then beset by a military coup of its own when soldiers refused to embark for the reconquest of the American colonies, leading to a liberal government and threats of invasion by France. Spain finally ratified the Transcontinental Treaty in October 1820, but the cession did not mean that Florida would become a peaceful place; Jackson had always known the Indians were the real obstacles to the expansion of American landholding and staple crop production. The following May he cautioned Calhoun that the work of American expansion remained incomplete: "One thing is certain. As long as [the Indians] are permitted to remain . . . the Floridas . . . will be a receptacle for rogues, murderers, and runaway negroes." There was little likelihood that a middle ground could emerge under such circumstances: the U.S. government would spend the next forty years alternating between policies of reservation and removal toward the Seminoles. As for fugitives from slavery, a large party of Creeks, spurred by white slave dealers, raided the maroons who had fled to Sarasota and Tampa Bay (today the headquarters for U.S. Special Operations Command) the very month Jackson wrote these words, enslaving about 300 men, women, and children.[37]

HINTS OF A NEW ACCOUNTABILITY ON THE LOUISIANA FRONTIER: RIPLEY, BEARD, AND A FINAL WAVE OF FILIBUSTERS AGAINST TEXAS, 1819–1820

Apart from William Trimble and Eleazar Ripley, Texas was rarely much of a consideration for even the most expansionist officers. Indeed, once the French émigrés left, the War Department instructed Trimble to focus his energies on restraining American encroachment rather than invading or "exploring" Spanish territory himself. (This restraint, plus his defeat in a court-martial aimed at Edmund Gaines, probably accounts for Trimble's departure from the army early in 1819, when he accepted election to the Senate from Ohio.) Andrew Jackson repeatedly pooh-poohed reports of Spanish activity along the Sabine: "There cannot exist any serious apprehension of an invasion . . . in that quarter." Jackson, who as Southern Division commander was actually in command of the entire frontier from Florida to the Missouri River, would have been happy to annex Texas, to secure the nation's boundaries to the west. In December 1820, before Spain's final ratification of the treaty was known, he remarked to Calhoun that "if we do not possess the Floridas, I have supposed we would take possession of Texas and extend our Garrisons to our Territorial Limits; by which we would overawe the Indians under Spanish influence, and form a cordon of posts from the Mandan Villages south west to the Rio Grande or Del Norte, or at least as far West as Galvestown."[38]

Spanish officials feared an American invasion of Mexico and tacitly bargained away Florida to keep Texas and Mexico secure from U.S. assault. Nevertheless, this foremost of American expansionists believed that "Texas for the present we can do well without—But without the Floridas our lower country cannot be made secure, and our Navy cannot afford protection to it in time of war. The idea of invading our Territory through the province of Texas, is to me absurd. Should it be attempted, a vigilant General . . . could cut [off] the Invaders in the rear and destroy or capture the whole. No military man would hazard such a step with a view to conquer New Orleans." Indeed, Jackson cautioned John Quincy Adams against demanding Texas in his negotiations with Onís, lest he jeopardize the primary strategic objective of securing Florida and the nation's southern flank. This attitude shaped the general's reaction when Spanish soldiers captured part of a filibuster expedition led by James Long—son-in-law of former commanding general James Wilkinson— in East Texas during the summer and fall of 1819. This obscure incident, and its ambiguous civil-military and diplomatic dynamics, is significant because of the contrast with earlier policy and military attitudes on that frontier. These new dynamics presaged the dilemmas and responses of army officers along the Canadian border two decades later, along with those of many officers toward Texan aggression against Mexico—and New Mexico and Native Americans within Texas—between 1835 and 1860.[39]

With Trimble no longer in the army, brevet Captain William C. Beard, an average junior officer with seven years' experience, was the federal commander at Fort Claiborne and Cantonment Jesup, on the edge of the Neutral Ground halfway between Natchitoches and the Sabine River, when a group of 200 freebooters seized Nacogdoches in June 1819. The political and diplomatic situation had changed dramatically since Beard had entered the army in 1812, the year of the Gutiérrez-Magee expedition. The executive's inability to restrain filibusters and privateers had gradually become so notorious, so embarrassing to U.S. claims to uphold international law, that President Madison finally sought a new neutrality law, which was passed in 1817. Yet the new law added little to its predecessor: juries remained sympathetic to privateers, and enforcement by local civil officials, including federal appointees, was so sluggish that, according to historian James E. Lewis, "popular activity in support of the revolutionaries continued almost unhampered."[40]

Nevertheless, reversing the expansionist approaches of his superiors Trimble and Ripley and of Wilkinson, Wollstonecraft, and Pike before them,

Beard's first reaction was to offer the local magistrate—a former aide-de-camp to José Alvarez de Toledo during the Gutiérrez-Magee expedition—aid against the filibusters under the provisions of the 1817 law. Beard proffered his subordination but hinted that he spoke as an official representative of the United States: "as the subject is one in which the honor and interest of our country may be deeply involved I hope I shall receive the advice and aid of the civil authority." Sounding much like Major Jacint Laval trying to restrain filibusters on the East Florida border opposite Amelia Island in 1812, Beard explained his concerns to the federal marshal on the scene, warning that the expedition "may lead our country into war, and is at all events a disgrace to our citizenry." He then reported the situation to his department commander, Ripley, stressing obedience to law as the measure of the national integrity he was bound by oath to protect: "Viewing . . . such conduct as a disgrace to the country and a violation of the laws and national faith, I have thought it my duty to make every exertion to put a stop to their proceedings." But Beard's dilemma continued to grow, for the lukewarm response of the local civil authorities, including several men who had condoned the Gutiérrez-Magee expedition, indicated that "they are more inclined to favour than to obstruct" the foray.[41]

Other military commanders reacted even more energetically. At St. Louis, remembering the trouble Aaron Burr had caused him more than a decade before, brevet Brigadier General Daniel Bissell immediately dispatched Captain Robert Coombs into the Neutral Ground, to Crow's Ferry on the Sabine, with orders to prevent anyone crossing from the American side. The delicate political situation that followed Jackson's invasion of Florida spurred Beard's chain of command to respond even more carefully, in language full of constitutional precision: "You will act in all cases in subordination to the civil authority . . . without their calls . . . make no military movement," read Ripley's order of July 9. The only exception would be an invasion of U.S. territory, presumably by Spanish soldiers attempting to preempt or pursue the marauders. Caught between congressional criticism and his unwillingness to jeopardize U.S. chances to secure Florida, Jackson approved these instructions: "the military being subordinate to the civil power [they] cannot act in the present case, unless their services are required" by the appropriate civil officials. Beard could not act decisively because the civil officials in Natchitoches sympathized with the filibusters, but an attempt was made to arrest Long at his headquarters in Natchez, army officers impounded a supply vessel in Louisiana, and a group of filibuster recruits was later arrested outside New Orleans.[42]

Threatened directly, without voters to appease, the Spanish authorities reacted much more energetically, dispersing the Long expedition and retaking Nacogdoches that October with a contingent between 300 and 1,000 soldiers strong. Yet American commanders no longer worried that the Spanish would threaten Louisiana. Instead, on October 31, Beard moved forward to Coombs's position on the Sabine, naming it Camp Ripley, and attempted to mediate between the Spanish commander and the American civilian population on both sides of the river. The captain provided food and shelter to refugee women and children while negotiating for the release and repatriation of American farmers he thought innocent of filibustering, though it is not clear how he made this determination. Beard also asked the Spanish to deliver any American deserters found among the captured filibusters to his custody, where they would reinforce U.S. power to restrain freebooters or intimidate Spain. Indeed, the Spanish commander's report suggests that Beard asked for the repatriation of all American prisoners, "on the ground that they had been engaged in making a living [albeit in Spanish territory] and were innocent of aggression against the Spaniards." The Spanish colonel, Ignacio Pérez, initially refused and responded with his own query about the reason for Beard's presence in the Neutral Ground. Beard replied that his orders were to arrest Long and to prevent Spanish soldiers from pursuing him across the river into the Neutral Ground: the U.S. Army had entered the demilitarized zone to prevent its Spanish counterpart from doing so. Beard dispatched Lieutenant George Spencer and a civilian, T. P. Taylor, to help Pérez determine which individuals should be released; Pérez withdrew his troops westward and returned eighteen of his thirty prisoners in exchange for guarantees that they would not reenter Spanish territory.[43]

Beard's ability to constrain these filibusters was limited by the operation of due process under American civil law: fifty-three men were charged with violations of the Neutrality Act as a consequence of the Long expedition, but only four were actually put on trial in the sympathetic civilian courts. The captain tried to draw a clear line separating freebooters from ordinary American emigrants, disavowing the former and interceding solely "for the industrious and peaceable American settlers who are not blameable for the outrageous conduct of a set of desperate adventurers." Yet Beard's criteria for classifying the floating populace on the Sabine frontier were highly artificial, for the men he called peaceful farmers were trespassing on Spanish territory without proper legal title. Whether they were recruited in New Orleans and Natchez or East Texas and the Neutral Ground, the motives of Long's men were not much different from those of the Americans already there. Anglo-Americans on the frontier had few scruples about how they gained their land or wealth in general, and it would have been easy to confuse the soldiers in Long's force with other Americans—all of them armed—who had been hunting, trapping, and farming in East Texas for several years. Beard's distinctions had little meaning for Pérez: the American squatters had welcomed Long's secessionist plot and would provide a pool of recruits for similar plots in the future. Hence, Pérez was prepared to drive the squatters out of East Texas along with those Americans specifically identified as filibusters. In contrast, Beard had to enforce his nation's official policy of neutrality while remaining sensitive to popular demands for American expansion, pressures that might embarrass the administration and hinder his future advancement should he overreact.[44]

Beard enjoyed only mixed success resolving the contradictions of his position, but his reactions to the Long expedition are significant when compared with those of other officers in this period. Apart from Jacint Laval in East Florida seven years before, Beard's counterparts and superiors had shown few scruples about intervening in, or even initiating, actions designed to add new territory to the United States during the 1810s. Jackson's sudden emphasis on the supremacy of local civilian authority along the Sabine River undoubtedly stemmed from political considerations in the aftermath of his invasion of Florida. Indeed, the Tennessean warned Secretary of War Calhoun, "This expedition has been planned by designing men who from feelings of personal hostility are desirous of involving the [president] in political difficulty and furnishing matter for declamatory discussion at the next session of Congress." Needless to say, Jackson's own actions in Florida had done just that: Jackson could never see that he was sometimes his own worst enemy.[45]

Eleazar Ripley was less concerned than either Jackson or Beard. Returning from an extended lobbying trip in Washington to take command of the Eighth Military Department in the summer of 1818, Ripley shared William Trimble's desire for military preparedness along the Texan frontier. Yet his work in the capital had done little to remedy recruiting shortfalls during the postwar economic boom, and any reinforcements were siphoned off to Gaines's occupation of northern Florida, so Ripley found his command in much the same state as before he left. That October, facing "a black population so strong as continually to excite alarm" in Louisiana, his total force, supposedly three to four regiments, amounted to no more than 630 soldiers, less than a single regiment at full strength. Yet "with the Spaniards [reportedly 500 in number] moving up to our frontier," spying in Natchitoches, "and already menacing our thin population," troops had been transferred from his department to Gaines's forces in Florida.[46]

The Eighth Infantry Regiment was left with only 144 of the more than 800 soldiers authorized by law, and Ripley feared that "this Regt. will be struck . . . from the rolls of the Army unless it be concentrated organized and disciplined." Nor was there any "disposable [meaning deployable] militia force of any kind" in Louisiana to supplement the regulars, and Ripley reported that the New Orleans branch of the Bank of the United States was demanding an unusually high discount on his official drafts. Sounding a note of dismay rarely heard among the confident veterans of the southern frontier, the brigadier made his demoralization manifest: "I actually am sickened with a State of service where every hope is defeated and every calculation disappointed." Yet the combination of Spain's inability to resist American advances in Florida and widespread public approval for Jackson's incursion also seems to have encouraged a new confidence and belligerence in the cautious brigadier, who sought funding for posts on the Red and Sabine Rivers within the demilitarized Neutral Ground. (He had hinted at establishing such posts as early as March.) Granted discretionary authority by Calhoun, Ripley reported that "the Government & Inhabitants of Louisiana are greatly alarmed" by Spanish movements and the lack of troops. He then advanced the 360 soldiers of the First Infantry to the Sabine, within the Neutral Ground, at the end of October 1818 and requested a loan of the Fourth Infantry, then occupying Pensacola, from Gaines's department. Indeed, Ripley may have been planning his own thrust against Spain: in November he advocated building a road from the Mississippi River to Natchitoches, advising Calhoun that it would "turn a pretty strong current of population towards the Sabine & up Red river and would do more than Posts and fortifications to cover that portion of our country."[47]

Early in 1817 Ripley had expressed antipathy for smugglers operating along the Gulf coast, but his personal interests and connections in the Southwest must have evolved as he became more familiar with the opportunities available on the frontier. He had missed the First Seminole War while lobbying in Washington, and August 1818 found him lamenting that there was no "prospect of kicking up a dust. . . . Under these circumstances we have nothing left but simply to vegetate." Unable to win glory in the nation's standing army, embroiled in disputes with Major General Jacob Brown and many of the leading officers who had participated in the 1814 Niagara campaign, Ripley worked to develop personal and financial contacts with the New Orleans Associates. Early in 1819, rumors appeared in northern newspapers that he was concentrating a force at Baton Rouge to invade Texas. That June, he sought a six-month furlough to settle his accounts. By this time, Ripley and Jackson had begun arguing over the brigadier's failure to complete a road he had been assigned to build from Bay St. Louis, on the Gulf coast west of Mobile, back in 1817. Ripley had put fewer than a hundred soldiers to work on the project, and when a lack of supplies reduced them to "a state of star-vation," they raided private cornfields to eat. After two years, no more than seventy miles of road had been cut, and public complaints were mounting. Ripley repeatedly failed to respond to Jackson's demands for clear reports, and Old Hickory vowed, "There must be some neglect [a court-martial offense] somewhere." The brigadier's request for furlough was considered, probably correctly, a prelude to his resignation; whatever Ripley's motives, Jackson's friend Robert Butler, the Southern Division adjutant general, gave Ripley the final push, indicating that he would accept the brigadier's resignation.[48]

Complaining that "this command has been difficult laborious and embarrassing," Ripley dispatched his letter of resignation the following month, telling Calhoun it was a step he had "contemplated for a long period." In September he was ordered to Washington to settle his accounts; his resignation was formally accepted in December and took effect February 1, 1820. By June 1820, he had become sufficiently tired of "the repose and quiet I now enjoy as a Citizen" to accept election by Long's Supreme Council as president of the "Republic of Texas," with a magnificent salary of $25,000 per year—far more than that paid to any general in the army. He subsequently worked to facilitate Long's second invasion of Texas, raising funds and gathering supplies through his extensive network of connections—developed as department commander—in Louisiana and the Southwest, but he never received his salary and apparently did not enter Texas himself.[49]

Military responses to Ripley's performance during his final year as department commander provide further glimpses of the dissension in the higher ranks of the officer corps, of the persistent relationships between military commanders and national politics, and of Jackson's priorities. Ripley had always complained about a lack of funds, and Jackson hinted to Calhoun that the brigadier had left his department "in an entire state of disorganization . . . the most deplorable condition, without order discipline or subordination." Jackson had tried to prevent Ripley's transfer from the Northern Division to his command in 1816, recognizing that the brigadier would be accompanied by faction, controversy, and dissension wherever he went. He now asserted that Ripley had sown disorder "with a view of aiding those in [the political] opposition, who are unfriendly to the Army," indicating that he would probably prefer court-martial charges against the brigadier because of his failure to report on the progress of the military road he was supposed to be building. President Monroe still preferred to avoid controversy, however, and rejected

Jackson's request for a court of inquiry, since Ripley's resignation had already been accepted.[50]

Lieutenant Colonel Zachary Taylor seconded the division commander's assessment when he complained to Thomas Jesup, now quartermaster general for the entire army, about the state of the Eighth Infantry, which was "without organization, subordination, or discipline, and without harmony among the officers" due to "the want of arrangement & system from the head of the dept down." Indeed, even Perrin Willis, Ripley's assistant adjutant general, reported to Adjutant General Parker on the "loose manner in which General Ripley conducted . . . the business of the Department," charging that "from some cause, perhaps to conceal his own conduct, [Ripley] preferred moving in turbid water." The Treasury sued Ripley for thousands of dollars in expenses, but military accountability to law went only so far: none of the military critics mentioned the brigadier's ties to the filibusters who violated American neutrality laws. When it came to military hierarchy and civilian control, form still trumped motive—or perhaps some motives were so widely shared that only deviations from form could raise military eyebrows. Indeed, Ripley retained his connections in the world of southwestern affairs and served as congressman from Louisiana between 1835 and 1837—the years of the Texas Revolution, which figured prominently among his concerns. But Ripley turned out to be the exception to a new rule. The army did act against Long, and Beard was rewarded with a cushy recruiting assignment in Philadelphia. Although some local civil officials sympathized with Long, and former Indian agent John Sibley even joined him, the new Indian agent at Natchitoches derided the plot. Apart from Ripley, who never actually went to Texas, it appears that only two former officers joined the marauders. Typical of American soldiers who chose filibustering, these men were short-service veterans of the War of 1812 who had been discharged in 1815 (see appendix A).[51]

Upholding Spanish and American sovereignty by enforcing domestic and international laws against filibustering were departures for Republican administrations: aside from Wilkinson's belated operations against Burr, the Long expedition was the first such foray launched from U.S. territory that faced effective opposition by federal officials during the Jeffersonian era. Army operations against the West Florida rebels—after they seized Baton Rouge—and the Amelia corsairs enabled the United States to extend its sovereignty under cover of restoring law and order, while Jacint Laval's opposition to filibustering against East Florida was overcome when an officer more sympathetic to the insurgents took command. Indeed, apart from the Burr conspiracy, federal military power had not been deployed specifically to halt filibustering, to uphold the sovereignty of the nation-state over its citizens and maintain international peace without absorbing some new territory, since the Federalist period. The Transcontinental Treaty, Mexico's eagerness to attract American settlers, and the pursuit of Indian lands within U.S. boundaries produced nearly a generation of quiet along the nation's new borders after 1818. The government did little to halt individuals and groups reinforcing the Texan revolutionaries in 1835 and 1836, but military deployments became one of the federal government's principal means of combating filibustering from 1837, with the advent of incursions against Canada, until the Civil War. In the interim, a generation of socialization in conservative nationalism, legalism, and statism that began when most future lieutenants spent four years at West Point caused career army officers to adopt Beard's attitude, much like Bankhead's at Amelia Island or Laval's at Point Petre opposite Amelia in 1812, upholding law, social order, national sovereignty, and international stability. No longer fellow citizens in the eyes of national military officers, filibusters became "desperate adventurers," mentally deranged "violators of all Law," nineteenth-century sociopaths.[52]

There were many reasons for this shift, which would not become clear until the resurgence of filibustering in the late 1830s. Beard's actions did not precipitate the change, although they certainly presaged it. Most important, the United States had nearly achieved its expansionist objectives: Sharp Knife had intimidated Spain in Florida, and U.S. military preparations were continuing in case further pressure was required. Why not open a second front by proxy in Texas, as the Gutiérrez-Magee expedition had done in 1812? First, Texas had always been secondary to Florida in most U.S. policy makers' calculations. Thus, the tacit bargain of the Adams-Onís Treaty had been Florida for Texas: the United States would acknowledge the Sabine and the Red as its legal boundaries. Once he was satisfied that Florida would remain American, President Jackson would revive the claim to the Rio Grande, but this lay a decade in the future. Second, Texas threatened to open an empire for slavery just as the crisis over Missouri statehood was erupting, whereas the administration could portray the annexation of Florida as a means of closing off the illegal slave trade.[53] Whether because of the perceived climate and terrain or the anticipated national security benefits, the potential expansion of plantation slavery in Florida did not stir much debate at the time. Third, Jackson's actions had aroused so much controversy that further military adventurism was out of the question. Fourth, the opportunities presented by "imperial flux" no longer appeared so alluring: the wave of filibustering under Latin American auspices between 1815 and 1817, combined with the activities of Napoleonic exiles and stateless freebooters and pirates like Aury and Laffite, seemed to be a more direct threat to U.S. sovereignty and future expansion than the decaying rule of Spain. The Panic of 1819 and the depression that followed aggravated all these concerns, intensifying sectional tensions and fueling the demands for military retrenchment that would produce the reduction in force two years later. The dynamics of westward expansion were changing—in large part due to Jackson's success—and filibustering went out of style for a generation.

Though often irresponsible and even insubordinate in its belligerence, the army officer corps served the underlying territorial and economic interests of the white American nation well during the decade after the War of 1812. Jackson's methods pose significant questions for the study of military professionalism and civil-military relations, however, particularly that of balancing substantive responsibility, or an officer's subjective sense of that responsibility, with the more objective demands of formal legal and constitutional accountability. As diplomatic historian Ernest May observes, "To a large extent . . . [early national] foreign policy approximated whatever consensus obtained among a majority of the interested electorate"—an electorate narrowly defined by race and gender. In 1818 Andrew Jackson probably represented the views of that majority as well as any civilian officeholder.[54]

Conversely, the imperious general blatantly disregarded the representative mechanisms established by the Constitution to convey the majority's wishes, substantiating the criticism, however politically motivated, that he was a potential Bonaparte impatient to substitute his own will for that of the electorate. Fortunately for the future of American civil-military relations, law, and democracy, circumstances would change after 1820, and Jackson would prove exceptional in will, stature, and action. Populist Caesarism did not find fertile soil among his successors. His high-handed assault on Florida represents an end rather than a beginning in the development of civil-military relations along the borders and frontiers. The autocratic general's reluctance to subordinate himself to the legal direction and restraints of the nation-state represented by his civilian superiors was not uncommon among the cocky, hard-bitten veteran officers of the immediate postwar army; they demonstrated a similar and closely related resistance to the demands and constraints of an institutionalized organizational hierarchy. Jackson's willfulness and political stature made him difficult if not impossible to restrain; he more than any other American military leader then or since, believed himself a tribune for the citizens he served. Jackson was the ultimate political general: the erstwhile Tennessee politician saw the white settlers of the Southwest as his true constituency, regardless of national elections, the national legislature, or the national constitution. These characteristics distinguish Jackson from any other military officer of this era and perhaps from any other in American history—even Douglas MacArthur or Winfield Scott (who was a candidate for the presidency while on active duty).

Nevertheless, filibustering plots by less senior officers like Ripley and Jesup—who remained in the army as quartermaster general and was one of the top commanders in the second set of Creek and Seminole wars during the 1830s—demonstrate that Jackson was not unique in his belligerence, and he was almost universally acclaimed by the officers of his division. His civilian commander in chief, James Monroe, offered him the ultimate compliment, however full of ironies for the Spaniards and Seminoles. If Jackson remained in the army, the president suggested, his presence—essentially meaning the threat of unrestrained violence the Tennessean embodied—would "have a tendency to prevent" war and preserve "order along our frontiers." Political rivalries doomed Jackson to retirement from the army in the 1821 reduction, but Monroe still saw his general in the same light. Offering Sharp Knife the civilian governorship of Florida (which both men undoubtedly considered a transitional post), the president proclaimed that "smugglers and slave traders will hide their heads, pirates will disappear, and the Seminoles will cease to give us trouble" with Jackson in charge. Monroe would never admit it, and perhaps he shied away from consciously recognizing it, but he was relying on the threat of unlimited military violence as his trump card to impose order in the borderlands.[55]

In 1820 the U.S. Army officer corps was much like the British in its attitudes toward expansion and empire—full of belligerent glory seekers eager to substitute colonial adventures (or individual duels), often on exaggerated pretexts, for the excitement, fame, and potential political advancement of wars now past.[56] Indeed, Jackson and Gaines used their commissions to act almost as independently of civilian control as former British officers Nicholls, Ambrister, and Woodbine, though the Americans were certainly much more in tune with the thrust of their nation's policy. But in 1821 the Transcontinental Treaty settled the Florida question, the sectional tensions roused by the Missouri crisis precluded action against Texas, and British power deterred both U.S. aggression against Canada and European intervention in America. With the breakup of the Spanish empire, the most chaotic period of "imperial flux" in the Western Hemisphere was over; opportunities for expansion at Mexican expense would take another generation to become "manifest," and by that time, a much more settled border had replaced the unregulated borderlands of Spanish-American competition.

Although the officer corps always pined for martial glory, its attitudes toward international relations would change during the next decade. Many War of 1812 veterans, particularly those of Jackson's Southern Division, left the officer corps for growing opportunities in planting, politics, and commerce in the southern borderlands they had helped conquer. Afterward, the officer corps' authoritarianism was increasingly directed at whites, citizens who challenged national sovereignty through practices like filibustering along the borders and frontiers. Meanwhile, the army became increasingly subordinate and responsive to the national government with which it identified. Volume 2 will show the development of a less belligerently expansionist body of commanders who reacted with growing accountability to constitutional civilian control—itself increasingly responsible to international norms—when faced with turmoil in the nation's borderlands.

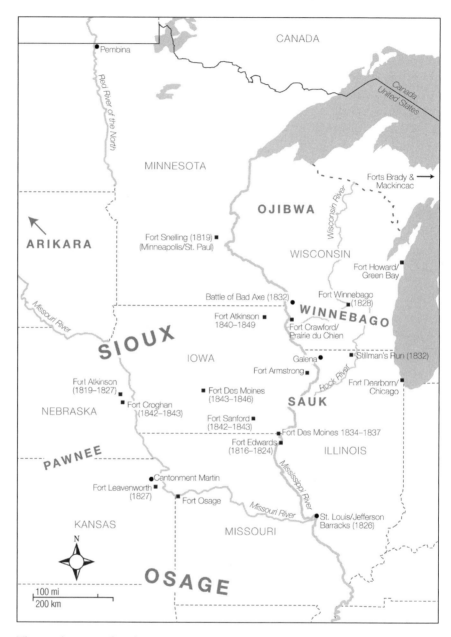

CANADA

Pembina

Red River of the North

Canada
United States

MINNESOTA

OJIBWA

Forts Brady &
Mackincac →

Fort Snelling (1819)
(Minneapolis/St. Paul)

WISCONSIN

Wisconsin River

ARIKARA

Fort Howard/
Green Bay

Missouri River

Battle of Bad Axe (1832)

Fort Winnebago
(1828)

Fort Atkinson
1840–1849

WINNEBAGO

Fort Crawford/
Prairie du Chien

SIOUX

IOWA

Galena

Stillman's Run (1832)

Fort Armstrong

Rock River

Fort Atkinson
(1819–1827)

Fort Croghan
(1842–1843)

Fort Des Moines
(1843–1846)

SAUK

Fort Dearborn/
Chicago

NEBRASKA

Fort Sanford
(1842–1843)

Fort Des Moines 1834–1837

Fort Edwards
(1816–1824)

ILLINOIS

PAWNEE

Mississippi River

Cantonment Martin

Fort Leavenworth
(1827)

Fort Osage

Missouri River

St. Louis/Jefferson
Barracks (1826)

KANSAS

MISSOURI

N

100 mi
200 km

OSAGE

The northwestern frontier.

6

ASSESSING NATIONAL MILITARY EXPANSION ON THE WESTERN FRONTIER TO 1825

Political and Diplomatic Ebb and Flow in Army Operations on the Plains

Facing limited threats to the Atlantic and Gulf frontiers during the generation following the Transcontinental Treaty—with its Atlantic flank covered by the British navy, one might say—the army's principal operational concern lay in the inland zone of contact with Native Americans being displaced by aggressive white expansion. Despite the federal government's lack of a long-range strategic planning process, the nation's de facto policy along its landward frontiers was territorial expansion, whatever its pace at any specific moment. Occasional proposals to restrain white settlement within specific territorial boundaries never became law or policy; indeed, the trade and intercourse acts that attempted to regulate white movement in Indian lands, first passed in 1790 and repeated through 1834, were widely ignored by white citizens. Although the officer corps collectively preferred to prepare to defend against European opponents whose defeat would bring romantic glory and public acclaim, civilian and military policy makers recognized that their most common antagonists were Indians resisting white encroachment within the national borders already recognized by the European powers. This process of "internal" pacification, colonialism, and dispossession—the nation's "western" policy of expropriation and ethnic cleansing, usually referred to then and now as "Indian removal"—was clearly the dominant thrust of executive policy and western security strategy long before its legislative assertion in the Indian Removal Act of 1830.

The Winnebago and Black Hawk "wars" of 1827 and 1832 (explored in my second volume) were only the most overtly coercive events in a persistent pattern of expansion and expropriation that asserted, extended, and finally consolidated U.S. hegemony, forcing Amerindians from the prairies of Illinois and the forests of southern Wisconsin. Though none of these conflicts involved sustained, large-scale combat, this policy, along with the growth in white population that precipitated it, fostered endemic friction along the inland frontier. This required a state of constant military readiness and frequent intervention to deter, prevent, restrain, contain, or resolve hostilities. Indeed, the "wars" against northwestern Indians were really extensions of the policing, peacekeeping, and peace enforcement—internal pacification to extend the sovereignty of American (white) national law and consolidate the monopoly on the legitimate use of force asserted by the white nation-state— that characterized the multitude of routine operations and shows of force intended to intimidate the Indians and facilitate white expansion. As ethnohistorian John Hall recently observed, "diplomacy between Indians and the United States would take place in a distinctly military milieu."[1]

This chapter provides a national and theater-level overview of the army's interaction with Native America between the Treaty of Ghent in 1815 and the army's withdrawal from the Middle and Upper Missouri River Valley a decade later. It focuses on contexts and constraints; the army's roles and missions; its significance in the process of territorial expansion in comparison with civilians, citizen-soldiers, and civil government; and the general trajectories and outcomes for whites and Indians, rather than the details of operations per se. Given the general consensus in U.S. politics in favor of white territorial expansion, there were few philosophical or ideological debates over long-term goals. Rather, the physical dynamics of scale and scope—the long distances involved and the ratio of soldiers to space—and the costs they entailed were the primary determinants of military strategy—the means and methods of implementing national policy—in the West. Given the natives' hostility to white expansion, the nation's western policy required a continual military presence to lend physical force to diplomacy and protect the trade that gave the United States growing economic, cultural, and political sway among the Indians. The permanence of this mission demanded standing military forces that could be deployed and sustained for extended periods, rather than state or territorial militias, which were too expensive to maintain, both politically and economically (they were commonly estimated to cost twice as much as regulars).[2]

During the years between the Peace of Ghent and the Transcontinental Treaty, the army's regiments were roughly evenly deployed along the nation's

many borders and frontiers. Between the annexation of Florida and the outbreak of the Second Seminole War fifteen years later, between four and a half
and six and a half of the army's eleven (after 1832, twelve) regiments—40 to
60 percent of the army—were deployed along the landward frontier. The
western commitment was generally 50 percent greater than that devoted to
Florida and the southeastern Indians (three to four regiments) and three to
four times the average commitment on the Canadian border (one and a half
regiments); at most, one or two regiments actually garrisoned the Atlantic
coastal fortifications. (The army's four artillery regiments were commonly
deployed in Florida and in the southeastern Indian removal operations
explored in volume 2, as well as in deterring slave unrest and South Carolina's
attempt to nullify federal law in 1832.) Every border and frontier was denuded
during the Second Seminole War, but the priority of the inland frontier was
restored once victory was declared in 1842; a year later, there were nine regiments in the West, two in Florida, and three along the Atlantic and Canadian
frontiers.[3]

Given widespread citizen opposition to the taxation necessary to support
the national standing army or pay for repeated militia mobilizations, cost was
the principal practical issue in western security policy: how far to push, and
thus how much to spend doing so, at any specific point in time. The issue of
cost was in turn a question of politics: what would Congress pay for, in an era
when legislators frequently investigated government expenses? The expeditions to extend American power up the Mississippi and Missouri valleys to
exclude British influence between 1815 and 1825, plus Henry Leavenworth's
punitive expedition against the Arikara on the middle Missouri in modern
South Dakota in the summer of 1823, are the major case studies of military
frontier diplomacy in this chapter. The Missouri River Valley expeditions were
exceptional in planning, scope, and sustained duration among army operations during the era between the wars with Britain and Mexico, and they
ended in 1825 due to budgetary pressures and lack of popular demand. After
Congress halted the Missouri expeditions, variants of coercive diplomacy and
peacekeeping in support of pacification and eventual conquest became the
norm for army operations in the West until the onset of widespread warfare
during the 1850s. (These missions are explored in volume 2.)

The first priority, logical and chronological, of American national policy in
the West was security from European intervention. This would be achieved
by isolating the Indians from British influence or support and keeping peace
among the Indians, lest their wars spill over onto the white frontier. During
the 1810s and 1820s, this meant establishing new forts well ahead of significant white settlement. The assertion of U.S. sovereignty gradually turned

imperial borderlands, "native grounds," and multiethnic "middle grounds" into national borders through geostrategic isolation and internal pacification. This was only a prelude, though perhaps a prerequisite, to the extension of white agrarian settlement. The ultimate goal was always national expansion and growth—envisioned as a social, political, and economic safety valve that would avert excess population buildup, social stress, and disorder in the East, permitting the replication of a relatively egalitarian republican society westward and in the nation as a whole. Yet expansion had to be paced against costs: fiscal costs, in a nation of increasingly reluctant taxpayers; international costs, given the potential friction with Britain and damage to the nation's reputation among European policy makers skeptical of American "civilization"; and social and economic costs, should the opportunities presented by expansion disrupt or depopulate established eastern communities, fostering entropy.[4] Unrestrained expansion might also accelerate centrifugal political trends, further decentralizing the country and diminishing national cohesion and capability, perhaps leading to the formation of new western polities that might invite European intervention or sectional conflict for their allegiance. Even without European competitors like those in Florida, Texas, and the Gulf borderlands, American expansion fostered complex dilemmas and uncertainty; the outcome easily could have been less than the sum of the parts.[5]

The nation's political structure and ideology—that is, the combination of constitutional federalism and growing liberal democracy—effectively secured autonomy for the citizens of its many parts but precluded a national policy of conserving energy, such as planning or restraining territorial expansion in order to focus on intensive growth and development in the East. Such a policy could only have been directed from the top or center. Whether in Jefferson's "empire for liberty" or Jackson's "area of freedom," security was intended to open and release individual energy, not to bind, concentrate, or conserve. Thus, the direction and extent of expansion most desirable or efficient for the nation as a whole were rarely obvious or generally agreed on. Local demand, measured through white population growth, was translated into public opinion through a free press and representative democracy, which tended to pull, if not drive, national policy. Shaped by the interplay of many complex factors, the tempo of settlement varied widely from region to region. As a result, as historian Bruce Vandervort observes in his broad-ranging survey, "the army's role was . . . by and large, a reactive one, foisted upon the soldiers by [citizens] . . . clamoring for protection." In the Northwest, Illinois was rapidly filling with white farmers by the mid-1820s, but Indian power and the supposed aridity of the Plains—highlighted by the assertions of army topographical engineer Stephen H. Long—appeared to set an ecological limit

White Cloud, an Ioway chief.
(Courtesy Library of Congress,
LC-USZC4-4752)

on extensive white agricultural expansion into Iowa or from Missouri into Kansas for another decade. Indeed, national policy generally set aside the region west of Missouri and Arkansas as "Indian country" for the natives being driven—or "removed," in the contemporary euphemism—from areas of more populous settlement and greater political pressure in Georgia, the Old Northwest, and the Old Southwest.[6]

Yet apart from a few missionaries and reformers, few whites ever truly intended "Indian country" to be more than a temporary expedient to ease the expropriation of native land in the East. Nor did national military commanders want their troops permanently tied to posts that were located largely based on pressure from civilian frontiersmen; their ultimate preference was to concentrate units to improve training for conventional combat against the nation's most dangerous potential enemies—European powers like Britain. Thus, when generals wrote about "a chain of forts" like the one Andrew Jackson recommended between Mobile and the Georgia border in 1815, they meant only a temporary screen to secure the advance of white farmers via the separation of Anglos and Indians.[7]

The army pushed westward in four conscious stages between 1815 and 1846, each roughly corresponding with a decade of that era. Prompted by senior civil officials, the first phase, occurring in the years immediately after the War of 1812, focused on securing the upper Mississippi and combating British influence among the Indians, whose warfare against American frontier settlements did not immediately cease with the Treaty of Ghent. As historian Colin Calloway observes, "Before the War of 1812 the United States had barely challenged British influence among the tribes of the upper Great Lakes and upper Mississippi River." The Indians and British had seized most of the positions the Americans had established before the war, and although the British withdrew, Indian raids against the Missouri and Illinois frontier continued through 1815.[8] That summer approximately half the army's infantry (the Third, Fifth, Sixth, and Rifle Regiments)—twice the number of regiments immediately available to Gaines and Jackson along the Florida frontier— deployed west. These numbered several thousand soldiers at most, and they were spread from the Missouri to the Great Lakes. Nevertheless, the combination of American advance and Britain's retreat from trading with and providing assistance to the northwestern Indians (which we now recognize as near complete), led to peace treaties with representatives of the Omaha, Potawatomi, and four bands of Sioux at Portages des Sioux that July. In September treaties were signed at Portages des Sioux and Detroit with representatives of nearly a dozen tribes: the Ojibwa (or Chippewa), Ottawa, and Wyandot; the Delaware, Miami, and Shawnee; the Iowa (commonly referred to as Ioway), Kickapoo, and Osage; and the Missouri River Sauk and Fox. An October treaty with the Kansa left only the Mississippi or Rock River Sauk and Fox overtly hostile.

The army continued to advance up the Mississippi the following spring, building Fort Armstrong at Rock Island, Fort Crawford at Prairie du Chien at the juncture of the Wisconsin and Mississippi Rivers, rebuilding Fort Dearborn at the future site of Chicago, and Fort Howard at Green Bay. (Cantonment Davis became Fort Edwards, near modern-day Warsaw, Illinois.) The remaining Sauk and Fox, the Ho-chunk (Winnebago), the Menominee, and eight more Sioux bands accepted peace treaties with the United States during 1816. Although ethnohistorians, eager to assert Indian agency, often question whether these treaties represent U.S. dominance over the tribes in question, they did lead to a general peace. The tribes remained local and regional military powers for a generation to come, but the peace was broken only by sporadic thefts and less frequent assaults and murders, despite growing white settlement and competition for natural resources. The vast majority of Native American violence was directed toward other Indians; conflict on the scale of the War of 1812 did not recur until the United States challenged the Sioux in the 1850s and 1860s. With such a benign security situation, posts established during the 1790s in the Wabash and Ohio River Valleys to the east, such as Forts Wayne, Harrison, and Knox in Indiana and Forts Clark and Massac in Illinois, were abandoned soon after 1815.[9]

Two years later, Major Stephen H. Long reconnoitered the Wisconsin region to assist War Department planning. The following year, Jacob Brown, commanding the army's Northern Division, recommended maintaining posts at Detroit, the Chicago River (Fort Dearborn), and Green Bay (Fort Howard); establishing a fort at the outlet of Lake Superior (Sault Ste. Marie); and abandoning Mackinac. Brown's plan would have been sufficient to secure the principal ports and choke points on the western Great Lakes in case of war with Britain, but Secretary of War Calhoun sought an advance far up the Missouri to enhance American trade and authority with the Indians while excluding the British east of the Rocky Mountains. To do so, the secretary demanded a more extensive network of inland posts, maintaining Forts Howard, Crawford, and Armstrong between Lake Michigan and the Mississippi. Troop shortages and budgetary constraints, compounded by the First Seminole War and the start of the first major expedition up the Missouri, precluded the establishment of the posts Calhoun proposed at the heads of the St. Croix and Minnesota Rivers. Nevertheless, Cantonment New Hope (renamed Fort Snelling, after the colonel of the Fifth Infantry Regiment, six years later) added the most forward post to the northwestern chain at the juncture of the Minnesota (then known as the St. Peters) and Mississippi Rivers, opposite the modern site of St. Paul, in 1819. En route, hard-nosed Colonel Henry Leavenworth, wounded in the bloodbath at Lundy's Lane and twice brevetted for gallantry in the Niagara campaign in 1814, asserted U.S. domination over the nation's newest Northwest. When a Ho-chunk warrior declared that "the Lake is locked," Leavenworth responded by waving his musket and vowing, "This is the key, and I shall unlock it." Nevertheless, Ho-chunk warriors fired on U.S. troops after the latter refused to pay a toll for traversing the Fox River.[10]

The priorities of theater-level (western) military strategy changed after the army enhanced frontier security by projecting a military presence into the Upper Mississippi and Missouri Valleys and along the western borders of Arkansas and Missouri, but the long-term national objectives and policy of expansion did not. This extension of national sovereignty, combined with the conquest of Florida and Anglo-American rapprochement (or at least the cessation of active British support to the Indians), transformed the upper Mississippi and the lower Missouri (the Missouri River watershed within the state of that name) into national frontiers rather than imperial borderlands in surprisingly short order, permitting the military reduction in force of 1821. Nevertheless, the Middle and Upper Missouri Valley, west of the state of Missouri,

A romantic rendition of Fort Snelling, one of the more imposing western forts, by Seth Eastman. (Courtesy Army Art Collection)

remained a "native ground" that was increasingly dominated by the Sioux, and the Upper Mississippi Valley remained a multiethnic "middle ground," where most whites were trappers or traders, for the next generation.

Though Secretary of War Calhoun joined the army's generals in advocating further initiatives to extend the national presence up the Missouri, the decline of British influence among the Indians east of the Rockies, combined with a backlash against the expansive National Republican vision of activist government, brought U.S. military expansion to a halt in the Upper Missouri Valley for several decades. The army's growing insulation from partisan intervention in institutional administration and officer selection did not mean autonomy from congressional financial oversight, which repeatedly curtailed major initiatives on the frontier. (Prior to the Civil War, Congress exercised extremely close control over appropriations for specific military operations. However, it is worth noting that Congress was less interested in the substance of the western operations it chose to fund than it had been when its authority was challenged by Jackson's invasions of Florida.) Lack of funding, combined with lack of settlement and a lack of military belligerence, prevented significant U.S. military challenges to the Sioux, the most powerful Indians in the plains, prairies, and forests between the Mississippi and the Missouri, prior to the 1850s.[11]

MILITARY DIPLOMACY FAR BEYOND THE SETTLEMENT
FRONTIER: HENRY ATKINSON AND THE MISSOURI
EXPEDITIONS, 1818–1825

The second substantial thrust in the westward extension of U.S. sovereignty
was intended to achieve familiar objectives—influence over the Indians and
exclusion of the British, for both military and commercial reasons—in the
northern Great Plains through the establishment of a strong military presence
in the Upper Missouri Valley. Treaties were made with the Otoes, Poncas, and
Pawnee west of the Missouri in 1817 and 1818, and a series of expeditions
up the river began during the latter year. In 1819 these produced a significant
post (later named Fort Atkinson, after the expedition's commander) at Council Bluffs, at the junction of the Missouri and Platte Rivers near the site of
modern-day Omaha, replacing the intermittently occupied Fort Osage east
of present-day Kansas City.

Senior commanders usually envisioned frontier forts as pivot points that
were useful principally as bases to house and supply the troops and impress
nearby Indians with a military presence ready to punish transgressions against
white citizens and American law. This mission was usually carried out by expeditionary forces, whether on a regimental scale of regional campaigns or a
squad or company scale of local or long-range patrols. (Volume 2 discusses
these dynamics in greater depth.) Brevet Brigadier General Henry Atkinson,
commander of the Ninth Military Department (the inland frontier north of
Louisiana) under Andrew Jackson from 1819 to 1821 and of the Right Wing
(the northern half) of the Western Department afterward, was the army's leading exponent of large-scale, long-distance campaigns to demonstrate American
power on the landward frontier during the 1810s and 1820s.

Atkinson proposed that the army advance far beyond the agrarian settlement frontiers of Missouri and Illinois, into a region that was not even organized as a territory. This was true "Indian country," where the only whites
were migratory trappers and traders dependent on native goodwill for survival. Like Jackson, Atkinson appealed to the nation's long-term security strategy, emphasizing the need to demonstrate U.S. power and protect American
fur traders so they could woo the Indians away from the British companies
that still dominated trade in the Canadian-American borderlands. Like the
engineers planning coastal fortifications, the brigadier recognized the incremental, substantially economic character of peacetime international competition, warning in 1820 that "if our traders do not make establishments among
[the Indians] . . . they will be so far drawn away by British influence that it
may be impossible to recall them."

Monroe and Calhoun intended the dual movements up the Mississippi and Missouri to extend American power so far north and west that the British would be permanently excluded from U.S. territory east of the Rocky Mountains. (Oregon was jointly occupied but largely under the sway of the Hudson's Bay Company, a problem the Americans would have to deal with in the future.) A borderland, fraught with the potential for imperial competition, would become a border. Calhoun hoped to establish an outer line of posts—at the Mandan villages on the upper Missouri, near the modern site of Bismarck; at the head of the St. Croix River, near the site of present-day Duluth; at the mouth of the Minnesota River; and at the head of that river, near the site of modern-day Fargo—that would dominate "the most valuable fur trade in the world." The secretary ordered the first step in March 1818: 250 men would move to the mouth of the Yellowstone River, about 1,200 miles beyond the most advanced U.S. post. Calhoun expected "every opposition" from British officials and directed that "no pains must be spared to counteract them," whereas he ordered that "no effort . . . [be] spared to conciliate the [Upper Missouri Valley] Indians . . . particularly the powerful bands of the Sioux."[12]

Colonel Thomas Smith of the Rifle Regiment, Atkinson's predecessor as departmental commander, responded two months later by suggesting the immediate erection of a post at the Mandan villages to anticipate and forestall any British opposition. Lack of professional commitment then obtruded when Smith (a fifteen-year veteran) was appointed receiver of money for the public land office in Missouri. He resigned from the army that November, leaving a mere captain to command the army's principal field operation. Supply problems, aggravated by Smith's divided attention and resignation, delayed the movement, and by the end of 1818, the first detachment had been compelled to make its winter camp, Cantonment Martin, just past the Missouri's northward bend at Cow Island (near the later site of Fort Leavenworth), only a hundred miles upriver from Fort Osage. American authority had made little progress since 1815: during the spring and summer of 1819, Rifle Regiment hunting parties endured attacks by the Kansa, Ioway, and Otoes, while the Pawnee shot at Stephen Long's exploring party nearby. The army's most effective response was to provide ammunition for the Osage Indians and help them cross the Missouri to attack the Otoes and Ioway.[13]

With anger from the War of 1812 and the Seminole War still fresh, officers frustrated by logistical constraints and the sluggish pace of operations sometimes gave in to outbursts of rage against the Indians and their supposed British sponsors. Jackson's reaction could have been anticipated: despite a year of criticism of his invasion of Florida and his hanging of British citizens, Sharp

Knife hoped to quash potential resistance in the Northwest by using the same sort of violence. In May 1819 Jackson observed to Atkinson that "the British Traders . . . ought in my opinion to be hung where ever they are found among the Indian Tribes within our Territory . . . [A] few examples would be sufficient . . . but the overly cautious policy of the Executive has directed that they only be arrested. . . . This instead of put[t]ing down the[ir] influence . . . will have a different effect." Junior officers expressed similar fury during the plodding trek north: surgeon John Gale hoped that aid from the Otoes would enable the United States "to exterminate" the Kansa. This rage slowly paled as it became clear that logistical obstacles rather than Indian hostilities or British subversion were the greatest impediment to the army's advance. By January, Gale realized that Kansa "numbers are too inconsiderable to excite much alarm," but he was loath to abandon his fears altogether, expecting "powerful opposition from the tribes situated higher up this river, among whom there are many British emissaries." The following year, Jackson advised Atkinson to arrest any foreign nationals found among the Indians on territory claimed by the United States, a lawful act unless they could display passports per the Trade and Intercourse Act. Nevertheless, Sharp Knife cautioned the brigadier to follow instructions from Washington in order to avoid the sort of controversy his own actions had caused in Florida.[14]

During the spring of 1819 the Fifth Infantry moved west from Detroit and established the future Fort Snelling, without significant hostilities or conciliation, on the upper Mississippi. Meanwhile, Major Long of the topographical engineers prepared for an extensive exploratory expedition over the plains west of the Missouri. The army's main effort was less successful. Calhoun wanted the full-scale Missouri expedition to go all the way to the Yellowstone. Atkinson took personal command, but he was unable to get much farther than he had in 1818. The problem was primarily logistical, so Quartermaster General Thomas Jesup was dispatched to St. Louis to sort things out, but politics intervened: the contracts for the expedition's rations were held by the brother of Richard M. Johnson, chairman of the House Military Affairs Committee. Despite growing congressional pressure for retrenchment, Calhoun felt compelled to work with Johnson, even though there were constant cost overruns and failures to deliver necessary quantities of supplies on time. Transportation problems and delays supplying the expedition prevented it from going past Council Bluffs, the first point intended as an intermediary post, and Fort Atkinson was built a thousand miles short of the objective. More than 150 soldiers died of scurvy that winter, a disaster in soldier health unmatched between 1815 and 1834.[15]

Calhoun's visionary plan was defeated by the operational friction—the accumulating delays—caused by the contractor's greed and inefficiency. The situation can be partially excused by the difficulty businessmen faced securing credit amid the financial panic of that year, but Johnson and his agents managed to commit virtually every possible defalcation. The troops got fed, but the supply controversy resulted in an investigation that gave congressmen hostile to the administration and its expansionist plans the excuse they needed to cancel funding for the advance beyond Council Bluffs as part of a general retrenchment the following April. Fort Atkinson became the most forward post on the Missouri, while the proposed forts at the Mandan villages and the head of the St. Croix were never built, and the Kansa Indians harassed the unmounted troops with near impunity. A House committee later recommended that the government go to court to recover its costs from the contractor, but the campaign was long over. The budget cuts also curtailed Long's exploratory plans, leading to an abbreviated trip directly over the western Plains, along the Platte River to the foot of the Rockies, and back via the Arkansas and Canadian Rivers, where Long observed sand dunes. The result was Long's famous map labeling the area the "Great American Desert," discouraging agrarian settlement for a generation.[16]

Failure in 1819 did not deter the architects of the Missouri policy. Atkinson's concern about British sway over the northwestern Indians was shared by most senior commanders and civilian decision makers, who recognized that influence as a tool of cold war and containment that had been waged against the United States since 1783. Depredations encouraged by British officials had been a principal cause of the War of 1812 in the Northwest, and British negotiators had unsuccessfully demanded the creation of a native buffer state in the Northwest during the talks leading to the Treaty of Ghent. Although the Convention of 1818 established a clear international border along most of the Canadian-American frontier, the Hudson's Bay Company had long dominated the trapping and Indian trade west of the upper Missouri, and U.S. policy makers continued to worry about British clout there. Near the close of 1819, Secretary Calhoun reported to the chairman of the House Military Affairs Committee (a general during the War of 1812 who was frequently critical of administration policy), "This intercourse is the great source of danger to our peace; and until [it] is stopped our frontiers cannot be safe." Almost simultaneously, Southern Division Inspector General Arthur P. Hayne alleged that there were "not less than *15,000* . . . well armed and mounted" Amerindian warriors in the upper Missouri region "completely under the control of the British Companies," which were "incessantly Cabaling to induce" them to oppose American settlement. Like his commander, Andrew Jackson, Hayne considered the British "our *implacable* enemies" and feared that "if a respectable & well appointed [U.S.] force is not kept in that country [the Indians] will be induced to become hostile."[17]

Their views unchanged, senior military leaders continued to call for further expeditions in pursuit of the same objectives. Hayne used his 1819 report on Atkinson's department to urge the establishment of posts at the Mandan villages and the mouth of the Yellowstone, with regular mounted patrols from the new posts to "promptly . . . punish any Depredations." Each of these forward operating bases would mount three such patrols at any time, with a hundred men (a company) apiece. Anticipating Atkinson's later success supplying his department by using soldiers as farmers, the inspector general suggested that hunting by patrols, combined with gardening by the company that remained at each post, would enable the forts to subsist without long supply lines down the Missouri that could easily be interdicted by Indians or weather. The combination of posts and patrols would enable U.S. troops to maintain "our respectable standing"—which may have been in question after the failure of the 1819 expedition—and sustain the authority of the United States in the eyes of the Indians. In effect, Hayne was proposing base camps for cavalry patrols and reconnaissance in force, like those conducted from the central Plains during the 1830s and 1840s, but at a more routine tempo akin to those conducted on the Plains during the 1870s and 1880s. Strategically, Hayne intended for the Mandan post to watch the Hudson's Bay Company establishments to the north, while the Yellowstone contingent would somehow communicate overland with Fort Smith and other posts on the Arkansas River to "detect any insidious attempt from that Quarter by the Spaniards" from Santa Fe.[18]

In November 1820 Atkinson suggested a compromise between large-scale campaigns and routine patrol bases in the form of smaller expeditions up the Missouri each year, remarking that "it will not cost more to subsist the troops . . . than it would if they were to remain in quarters" near St. Louis. Indeed, he thought that "such trips would become rather excursions of pleasure to the soldiery," much as Hayne expected the troops to be "rendered expert, by attending solely to the duties of Soldiers." These duties clearly included their own logistical support: as early as 1820, Atkinson demonstrated his logistical and administrative acumen, along with the penchant for system and order common among career soldiers, by suggesting that a single regiment (presumably his own) could garrison all the posts on the upper Missouri in order to facilitate supply, communications, and the coordination of mutual support. Aggressive commanders always faced the burden of demonstrating their fiscal economy to Congress, and Atkinson showed a keen appreciation of logistics and expense in all his expeditionary plans, promising that "no additional expenses [would] be incurred" in the Yellowstone expedition. Indeed, not a single soldier died on that expedition, despite the constant potential for accidents on the river: drowning was a routine source of casualties in military operations on the frontier, including that against the Arikara in 1823, which employed many of the same troops as Atkinson's campaign. The organization, health, and efficiency of Atkinson and his veteran soldiers demonstrated their professional development of accountability and attention to duty and detail, as well as some medical experience acquired since the scurvy epidemic they suffered in the winter of 1818–1819. In contrast, an epidemic halved the strength of Henry Leavenworth's first dragoon expedition over the central Plains in 1834; that campaign was conducted by raw recruits, and half of the officers had been commissioned directly from civilian life (though they were supposedly veteran frontiersmen) only a year or two before.[19]

Atkinson demonstrated his sense of mission and duty and his desire for autonomy as a commander by refusing the premier staff post of adjutant general during the 1821 reorganization, remaining in command of the Sixth Infantry Regiment and the Missouri project. Atkinson was compelled to sacrifice his lineal rank as brigadier (although he still held that rank by brevet) but retained the principal field command in the Western Department and, indeed, in the army as a whole after the cession of Florida. The apparent failure of Leavenworth's expedition against the Arikara in 1823, intended to retaliate for attacks on American trappers several hundred miles north of Council Bluffs, along with worries about British mercantile influence over the Indians, spurred Atkinson to resubmit his proposal for an expeditionary campaign farther up the Missouri the following year. Such an expedition would "prove to the Indians our ability to traverse their country at pleasure and punish them for offences at any point however remote. Establishing a permanent post [at the Mandan villages or the Yellowstone, without sending an expedition through Indian country first] would diminish this belief and lessen their idea of our capacity to move with celerity. . . . The plan will moreover greatly benefit the troops as it will render them highly efficient and make the duty not only pleasant to both officers and men, but envious. And again it will require a much smaller force" than establishing a permanent post farther upriver.[20]

Historian J. Wendel Cox observes that "in 1824, the American political and military presence on the northern Plains remained as limited as it had been on the eve of the War of 1812." Atkinson aimed to change that, warning, "I deem it of the highest importance that an imposing force should . . . be shown to the upper Tribes [meaning those beyond the Mandan bend in the future Montana country, like the Blackfeet], who know nothing of our character or strength, that a favorable and lasting impression may be made on their minds." The strategy for doing so was still being debated, however. Responding to pressure from fur trade companies and related interests, Jacob Brown authorized the brigadier to establish a post with four or five companies, if he felt it necessary and feasible. Atkinson's regimental major, Abram Woolley, added an unusually ambitious recommendation (bypassing his unsympathetic commander and writing directly to Brown) for forts to connect the Missouri and Columbia Rivers, justifying this permanent invasion of Indian lands with European examples: "the British have done as much in Bengal, Russia in Tartary and the Spanish a vast deal more in South America." Secretary Calhoun seized the opportunity to reassert his desire for a post at the Mandan villages that would control the fur business and exclude British traders, and Congress created an "Indian Peace Commission" to try to conciliate the upper Missouri tribes.[21]

As one of the peace commissioners and the most influential American on the spot, Atkinson led the Sixth Infantry, reinforced by part of the Third, upriver in 1825. As noted earlier, the first Missouri expedition had never advanced more than a few miles past Council Bluffs, where the establishment of Fort Atkinson reflected that failure. Supported by new logistical procedures that dispensed with civilian supply distribution, the 1825 Yellowstone expedition pushed nearly 1,800 miles from St. Louis and more than 100 miles beyond its official objective in just a couple of months—the farthest western advance by so substantial a body of American troops until the war with Mexico. No Indians openly challenged the movement. Atkinson and a civilian peace commissioner signed treaties with sixteen Indian bands, including the Arikara, Cheyenne, Crow, Hidatsa, Mandan, Ponca, and elements of six major divisions of the Sioux. All promised to accept U.S. "protection" and "supremacy," not to trade with whites unless they had U.S. licenses, and to keep the peace with American traders and trappers and among themselves.

By the end of the summer, Atkinson came to doubt that a permanent post in the Yellowstone country was necessary because British influence had proved much weaker than expected. Indeed, the logistical problems of the Missouri campaigns had taught Atkinson that forts could not provide protection where it was truly necessary; their distance from St. Louis would make the cost of supplies prohibitive no matter who oversaw their distribution. Instead, the brigadier articulated a general principle for strategy and operations on the western frontier, maintaining that "an occasional show of an imposing military force in an Indian country produces . . . a better effect than a permanent location of troops among them." In lieu of a post on the Yellowstone, he

Henry Leavenworth, by Samuel Sartain. (Courtesy Frontier Army Museum, Fort Leavenworth)

urged a scaled-back version of his standard expeditionary proposal, recommending an advance by 300 to 400 troops (roughly a regiment) to the falls of the Missouri every three or four years—a regular repetition of the Yellowstone campaign.[22]

Neither approach (forts or expeditions) was implemented. Another wave of Old Republican attacks against National Republican activism, strengthened by the growing Jacksonian movement against John Quincy Adams, brought the Missouri project to an end. In 1827 the troops at Council Bluffs were withdrawn south to establish Fort Leavenworth as a more central position on the Plains and a stepping-stone toward Santa Fe and the Southwest. It would be seven years before large-scale expeditions were again dispatched to Indian country for diplomatic purposes during peacetime, and before the 1850s, none would last as long or involve as many troops. In the meantime, the regiments in Atkinson's department were concerned primarily with operations to quell Indian resistance to white expansion in the Illinois-Wisconsin-Iowa triangle and maintain peace along the arc between the Missouri and Red Rivers (all discussed in volume 2). Drawing on his extensive operational experience, Atkinson adroitly used the theater reserve at Jefferson Barracks to quell unrest among the Winnebago with minimal bloodshed in 1827 and to pursue and trap the Sauk and Fox Indians under Black Hawk five years later.

HENRY LEAVENWORTH AND PUNITIVE DIPLOMACY: THE ARIKARA WAR, 1823

As men with national orientations, comparatively extensive administrative and command experience, and organized armed power at their backs, professional military officers were often employed as diplomats (or "commissioners") in negotiations for land and peace and as mediators among rival tribes. Indeed, modern ethnohistorians, like contemporary army officers, often credit the army with greater diplomatic efficacy than civilian agents and commissioners; the latter's eagerness to negotiate land cessions, and their willingness to use bribes to do so, was obvious to the Indians. Native American leaders, particularly those along the western frontier, were usually warriors or former warriors themselves, and they "afford[ed] greater respect to military officers," who represented concrete physical power. Recognizing that American military display was a sign of respect for Indian power, "Indians themselves preferred . . . military setting[s]" for diplomacy.[23]

Nor are these claims mere valorizations of the army or essentialist reifications of native culture as warlike and primitive. Given the transparent self-interest of civilian treaty commissioners—often locally prominent white officeholders and former officeholders who had gained election by promising Indian dispossession—the decreasing experience and very specific tribal affiliations (and sometimes allegiances) of Indian agents, and those agents' reliance on military force to coerce or protect the Indians, it is not surprising that military commanders appeared more objective and more authoritative. Indeed, civilian agents commonly wore military uniforms and affected military (often militia) ranks. Yet an agent in uniform without soldiers to command, or an agent whose rank was known to derive from the militia (since the Indians near a post could easily differentiate between an agent and an officer who commanded regular soldiers there), was projecting either very little authority or a very threatening one given the indiscipline and indiscriminate violence of citizen-soldiers. Neither extreme was conducive to negotiation. With the army, both sides laid their cards on the table; military officers might hope to intimidate the Indians, but even if that failed, the Indians felt respected by the Americans' show of power.

Nor was civilian legal authority clear. Even when the Supreme Court deemed Native American tribes "domestic dependent nations" subject to U.S. sovereignty in 1831, the precise points of intersection between Indian relations and the federal system often remained unclear, resulting in jurisdictional confusion between local and national officials. (The Court's reassertion of native sovereignty in *Worcester v. Georgia* the following year was famously ignored by President Jackson and had little immediate effect on the mid-nineteenth-century frontier.) The federal court system rarely penetrated far onto the frontier; district courts were few and far between, and circuit courts had vast distances to cover. As Illinois, Missouri, and Arkansas became states, their courts assumed jurisdiction over cases involving whites and Indians within their boundaries, yet this was less of a change than might be supposed, since their federal territorial courts had been staffed largely by local appointees, or men who quickly developed local attachments and allegiances. Practical material circumstances—the product of scale, distance, and popular opposition to government spending—also played a significant role: given the rarity of civilian jails, responsible military commanders like Atkinson often felt compelled to hold Indian prisoners, as well as citizens accused of encroaching on Indian lands in violation of the trade and intercourse acts. Those citizens usually secured writs of habeas corpus from local magistrates and were released; native prisoners often languished while waiting for some American authority to take charge of their cases.[24]

Keeping peace between Indians was an almost exclusively federal task, in which Indian agents were handicapped by the factors already noted. Army peacekeeping efforts among the Indians present both an example of intercultural military diplomacy and a study in the larger dynamics of political-legal rationalization. In a process analogous to its imposition of private property, the United States demanded that the Indians follow legal processes intended to clarify the guilt of individuals and uphold U.S. control over the use of force to protect or punish. This required that the Indians give up their customs of personal retaliation (by the injured individual) and collective retaliation (often essentially indiscriminate, against relatives or tribesmen of the injurer, which could mean virtually any white in cases in which whites had injured Indians). The Indians justified these customs as the age-old natural order and as the equivalent of international war. The Americans rightly believed that retaliation and revenge meant recurrent war, a virtual state of nature, and they forbade the practice in most treaties. Instead, tribal councils (and in some southeastern tribes, tribal police) were to identify and punish criminals in cases occurring within Indian nations; these councils would turn aggressors over to the United States when the depredations crossed ethnic lines, whether between tribes or against whites. Indian leaders were supposed to return property stolen from whites, and the United States was supposed to compensate Indians for property stolen by whites. In effect, the United States demanded that justice, and the legitimate use of force to ensure justice, be centralized in its hands. As veteran dragoon commander Philip St. George Cooke put it in 1857, "The main object of our troops . . . [is] to awe the Indians—to *prevent* depredations and war, and to repress their morbid inclinations for internal aggressions, to *preserve peace*, and further the design of civilization."[25]

The United States was unwilling to expend the resources to make this a reality, however. Military commanders routinely demanded the surrender of Indians accused of crimes against whites, and under the direction of civil officials, they sometimes took citizens accused of crimes against Indians into custody; however, an 1817 statute contradicted most treaties by declaring Indians accused of crimes against other Indians, in areas regarded as "Indian country," as being outside U.S. jurisdiction. Legally unable to use force, frequently ignorant of the specific circumstances of violence between Indians, and often quick to attribute that violence to irremediable savagery, experienced professional officers were happy to avoid the diplomatic complexities, stress, and potential political complications of yet another peacekeeping mission and rarely pressed demands for justice in clashes between Indians. Indeed, at the beginning of 1832, Edmund Gaines recommended to Willoughby Morgan, colonel of the First Infantry, that the United States should interfere in Indian affairs only when necessary to protect its own citizens. Colonel Josiah Snelling had intervened in favor of the Ojibwa against the Sioux in 1827, contradicting and undermining U.S. policy by encouraging Indian violence; however, this had been an understandable reaction to the affront to American sovereignty when the Sioux attacked their enemies just outside Snelling's fort. Zachary Taylor's reluctance to interpose between Sioux and Ojibwa when he took over the First Infantry in 1833 was more characteristic of harassed frontier commanders.[26]

Like whites, Indians were usually transferred to local judicial custody for trial, but the executive branch often preferred to rely on national military officers rather than civilian agents, state or local, to capture offenders. This was partly a matter of limited civilian capability—neither the U.S. Marshals nor the Customs Service had the necessary manpower to execute the laws themselves (they lacked the substantial police personnel they have today)—but primarily a matter of reliability and discretion, accountability to national legal standards, and at least the shadow of due process for Native Americans in the face of local and frontier-wide attitudes of white supremacy. Employing local sheriffs and posses or militiamen, who often exhibited little more discipline than vigilante mobs, threatened to aggravate tensions and turn individual incidents based on personal quarrels and miscommunication into full-scale war, ethnic cleansing, and massacre.

In most instances (much as in twenty-first-century stability and support operations), federal military officers acted in conjunction with and in effective subordination to civilian officials, whether federal or local. In moderating but executing the demands of frontier citizens, they provided the limited civilian agencies of the government with the administrative, logistical, and coercive capacity necessary for effective diplomacy and territorial expansion. Absent this military capacity and military accountability—responsibility and subordination to civilian objectives and direction—the conquest would have been even more chaotic and bloody, less ethnic cleansing than outright genocide. The atrocities in California during the 1850s, effectively amounting to genocide, and those in the trans-Mississippi West during the Civil War provide an instructive contrast: in each case, state and territorial civil officials, driven by the values of white supremacy and majoritarian democracy, gained effective control over Indian relations, enabling citizen-soldier volunteers and militias to strike out with little restraint. As the aristocratic Cooke observed:

> An irregular, ill-armed force, composed of individuals who have never acknowledged the common restraints of society, who confound insubordination with a boasted equality, who cannot endure the wholesome action of discipline, or even obedience, cannot be considered comparable for these objects, with a force whose perfect discipline insures an absence of all offensive irregularities, whose complete and perfect arms are the tokens of strength, whose accurate evolutions, responding to a guiding will, are emblematic of power, whose very uniforms have an imposing moral effect, investing them to Indian eyes, with the character of direct representatives of a great nation which they dread.[27]

The military vision of responsibility stemmed from feelings of superiority and the desire for control, as well as sympathy, reflecting soldiers' beliefs that Indians were treacherous or, at best, drawn into conflicts by a childlike impulsiveness that could be restrained only through force or intimidation. The coercive foundation of American relations with the Indians was evident in commanding general Alexander Macomb's 1834 instructions to brevet Brigadier General Henry Leavenworth: seize Indian hostages when whites were killed or plundered, "until acceptable satisfaction shall have been made by the offending tribe." Leavenworth needed no such reminders from Macomb. After two soldiers were murdered in 1820, he seized Ho-chunk (Winnebago) hostages to secure the surrender of those accused, vowing that "it would have been better to have *executed*" the murderers before trial, because "if they are *tried* they must be *executed* [to set an example of American determination] or we shall feel the weight of the Winnebago Tomahawk."

Ho-chunk leaders turned over the culprits. Leavenworth had the case prosecuted in a civil court, and two of the three Indians were sentenced to death. Other military leaders less closely involved contributed greater perspective to that decision and a better sense of the objectivity, integrity, and honor the officer corps normally valued. Inspector General John Wool, touring the northwestern posts, recommended to Jacob Brown "that for the honor of the army as well as the nation, [Leavenworth] will be induced to change his determination" to execute the Ho-chunks. Brown apparently passed Wool's views on to Secretary of War Calhoun, who asked Leavenworth's opinion about granting the Indians clemency. The colonel responded that Amerindians knew "no other motives but *want* and *fear*," and they would attribute a pardon to fear on the part of the government. Just as significantly, the colonel worried that if the law was not enforced by the federal government, the frontiersmen would "take the sword of justice into their own hands & thereby jeopardize the peace of the country." Leavenworth warned that as long as "a mischievous spirit prevails amongst the Rock River band, . . . it may . . . be well to make an example of [the convicted Indians]," for he was convinced that "the *certainty* of punishment is the best preventative of crime." Abandoning his usual moderation, Atkinson agreed: "If a suitable punishment is not inflicted on the offenders . . . we may expect similar occurrences." Ultimately, one of the Ho-Chunks was hung, another died in jail, and the third was released.[28]

To this point, Leavenworth's conduct embodied the image of the authoritarian military commander. Yet his command of the expeditionary force that tried to punish Arikara attacks on American trappers three years later highlights the complexities of military diplomacy with the Indians. The Transcontinental Treaty, the joint British and American use of Oregon as agreed on in the Convention of 1818, and the termination of the government trading post system in 1822 reopened the way for American companies to trap beaver in the Rockies and the Pacific Northwest. "Brigades" of trappers headed far up the Missouri, hoping to bypass the Indians who had traditionally sold pelts to the fur companies. After two years of peace, the Indians of the northern Plains realized that the Americans were disrupting their trade patterns and taking resources without compensation, leading angry bands of Sioux, Crow, Blackfeet, and Assiniboine to rob trappers and traders. Tensions among the Indians themselves, rooted in competition for access to American trade and the aggressive expansion of the Sioux, also led to confrontations with whites. Frustrated Arikara warriors attacked two trading posts on the Missouri in 1820, and in March 1823 they robbed Missouri Fur Company trappers and attacked their trading post. Three months later, a mixture of white transgressions and miscommunication ended in an Arikara assault that killed fourteen trappers of the American Fur Company, led by Missouri lieutenant governor William Ashley, at the Arikara villages two-thirds of the way up the Missouri River.[29]

When news of the slaughter arrived at Fort Atkinson on June 18, Leavenworth, now lieutenant colonel of the Sixth Infantry, acted without seeking orders (which would have taken at least two weeks to arrive) and departed with 230 regulars only four days later. Supplies and three cannon had to be poled upriver on keelboats, and the march to the Arikara villages 300 miles north of Fort Atkinson took nearly seven weeks. The colonel was joined by Missouri Fur Company employees and picked up Ashley and his surviving trappers, together numbering about eighty. Contrary to some historians, this was not Leavenworth's first independent command. Indeed, there were probably few officers of his rank with equal experience on the western frontier. Gaines, who had the greatest experience by far, was on leave when the news reached Fort Atkinson. Atkinson was in temporary command of the Western Department, but he was stationed farther downriver at Fort Belle Fontaine, near St. Louis. Unlike Leavenworth, who was wounded in the firestorm at Lundy's Lane in 1814, Atkinson had not seen significant combat during the War of 1812 (although he did fight a duel); he also had less practice leading active operations, having come to the Missouri expedition after its initial problems in 1818 and facing a less dangerous environment than that Leavenworth confronted in Wisconsin and Minnesota. As commander at Cantonment New Hope (the future Fort Snelling and the most advanced army post in the Northwest) in 1819 and 1820, Leavenworth had worked to establish peace between the Sioux and Ojibwa and developed "considerable proficiency" in some Siouan dialects. In 1823 the colonel's diplomacy seemed to pay dividends: between 500 and 750 Sioux warriors joined the expedition against the Arikara, eager to seize the riches the river Indians had accumulated in their villages.[30]

Yet upon arriving at the Arikara villages on August 9, Leavenworth quickly felt compelled to adopt a more cautious stance. Remarkably, the Arikara drove off the Sioux in a mounted skirmish, but the Arikara withdrew into their palisaded villages when the regulars advanced. Though some of the U.S. infantry penetrated one of the stockades, Leavenworth drew back. The next day his cannon bombarded the villages, and a company of riflemen led by Captain Bennet Riley surged inside the upper village, but the Arikara held on to the cabins inside the wall. Although Ashley did not challenge Leavenworth's leadership, several of the colonel's subordinates and the Missouri Fur Company trappers led by Joshua Pilcher (whose trading post had been attacked by the Arikara earlier in the spring) urged that the assault continue. No soldiers had been killed and only one had been wounded, but the bombardment had used most of the expedition's cannon shot. In addition, one of the Sioux leaders began to talk about joining the Arikara to plunder the Americans. Even though the regulars could probably hold the Indians off, the colonel feared that his regiment might be stranded hundreds of miles from reinforcement or subjected to weeks of harassment if they were compelled to retreat downriver. However small the risk of disaster, the possibility that an embarrassing outcome would encourage native hostilities all along the frontier appeared to outweigh any possible benefits of success. Leavenworth began negotiations, demanding that the Arikara turn over five hostages, return any property taken from Ashley's party, and stop attacking Americans.[31]

The Missouri Fur Company trappers were outraged and threatened the Arikara leaders. Shots were fired during the parley, and the Sioux began to depart. The following day (August 11), a series of officers sent to parley inside the villages returned and reported their vulnerability, but Leavenworth remained more concerned about his own exposure and that of the fur trade in the future. Though he and the trappers disagreed over how best to secure that trade, the colonel was certainly thinking at a strategic level appropriate for the nation's most powerful representative in the upper Missouri watershed. Leavenworth concluded that, given "my small force—the strange and unaccountable conduct of the Sioux, and the even greater probability of their joining the Aricaras against us—and also considering the importance of saving to our country the expense and trouble of a long Indian warfare, and the importance of securing the Indian trade, I thought it proper to accept the terms." In contrast, Captain Riley reportedly "became allmost furious and swore that he demande the prviledge . . . that they had been laying at garison at Council Bluffs for 8 or 10 years doeing nothing but eating pumpkins and now a small chance for promotion occurred and it was denied him and might not ocurr again for the next ten years."[32]

Leavenworth's calculations illustrate the mixture of personal and diplomatic considerations he was trying to reconcile, and they show that he had learned much about frontier diplomacy since his haughty treatment of the Winnebago in 1820. Emotion and policy clashed: the colonel felt that "my reputation and the honor . . . of the expedition required that I should gratify my troops and make a charge, but I also thought that sound policy and the interest of my Country required that I should not." Leavenworth chose the nation's interest over his own reputation. He knew that no one wanted a full-scale war with or among the Plains Indians, and since he also knew that the Sioux would take advantage of a successful assault to massacre the Arikara, he believed "that the Government would be better pleased to have those Indians corrected than exterminated." Nor could he have been eager to eliminate the Arikara from the balance against the Sioux. Above all, the colonel recognized the political-operational dilemma of the situation. Dispersing the Arikara would almost certainly cause more problems than coming to an agreement, however weak, with them as a group. "If we succeeded in our charge, all that we could expect was to drive the Indians from their villages and perhaps kill a few more of them. The remainder would be left in the Country in a confirmed state of hostility to every white man. We could not expect to overtake them nor had we provisions sufficient to enable us to pursue them."

Knowing the Sioux were already dissatisfied, the colonel settled for trying to reestablish peace by granting clemency to the Arikara and maintaining the balance of power among the Indians along the Missouri. Yet the unreliability of citizen-soldiers and nonstate actors hampered Leavenworth's ability to conclude the conflict. His moderation did not convince the Arikara to trust his ability to restrain the trappers; the Indians fled their villages during the night of August 11–12, taking refuge farther upriver with the Mandan. Four days later, the Americans returned downriver, but some of the Missouri Fur Company trappers sneaked back to burn the villages, ensuring ongoing Arikara enmity. Leavenworth estimated fifty Arikara dead, mostly from the bombardment; he had lost seven soldiers drowned but only one wounded in action. Safe at home in Missouri, the trappers immediately mounted a newspaper campaign against the colonel, branding the wounded veteran of Lundy's Lane a coward.[33]

Whatever their private qualms about the colonel's strategic choices, the army hierarchy quickly rallied to his defense when the institution's honor came under attack. Henry Atkinson, usually an advocate of diplomacy and forbearance, expected the Arikara to recommence hostilities at the first opportunity and thought the Sioux might be emboldened to do so as well, so he advocated sending 600 or 700 troops to the Yellowstone in 1824. The often aggressive

Bennet Riley, impetuous frontier infantry officer. (Courtesy Kansas State Historical Society)

Edmund Gaines, Atkinson's superior, had supported Leavenworth's claim to promotion to a permanent colonelcy in an artillery regiment the previous year; he rejected the Missouri Fur Company's criticism and made the best of the situation by emphasizing the colonel's discretionary authority as the executive agent on the scene, applauding his "enlightened and virtuous" moderation.[34]

Jacob Brown, Leavenworth's commander at the bloody battles of Chippewa and Lundy's Lane in the Niagara campaign against the British in 1814, concurred with Gaines, expressing his "high satisfaction with the success of the expedition & his approbation" for "the zeal & activity" of the colonel and his subordinates. (Brown's reports of the Niagara campaign had contained little mention of Leavenworth, who had been wounded before the climactic firefight atop the ridge at Lundy's Lane. Leavenworth had offered some support to Eleazar Ripley in that general's postwar quarrel with Brown, so the commanding general's praise may have been an attempt at reconciliation.) In contrast, Brown censured the trappers of the Missouri Fur Company, who "so illy seconded the efforts of Colo. Leavenworth to bring the affair to a[n] . . . amicable termination." The general condemned the burning of the Arikara villages as "very much to be regretted" and a danger to future peace, and he ordered a halt to any preparations for an immediate follow-up. The expedition's junior officers recognized that any imputations of cowardice against Leavenworth would ultimately trickle down to them, and seven joined in sending a letter to the *St. Louis Enquirer* "to contradict . . . so base a calumny." However, they limited their refutation to Leavenworth's conduct "during the engagement," which might have implied their disagreement with his decision to withdraw. The impetuous Riley—whom Leavenworth recommended for a brevet promotion, albeit for "good conduct and efficiency" rather than bravery—believed the expedition had been "disgraced" by the withdrawal, but Riley knew where his bread was buttered and signed the letter to the *Enquirer*.[35]

Vilified by trappers its officers rightly considered greedy and lawless, the army took care of its own, an example of its insulation and autonomy from political influence and its recognition of strategic wisdom and moral and physical courage. In 1824 Leavenworth received a brevet promotion to brigadier general for ten years' service as a brevet colonel (an honor he had gained at Lundy's Lane); "ten-year" brevets were customary but hardly mandatory if the Monroe administration had wanted to censure the colonel. In 1825 Leavenworth's seniority earned him the permanent lineal rank of colonel and commander of the Third Infantry Regiment; the army's most advanced post in the central area of the western frontier was named after him when the army withdrew downriver from Fort Atkinson two years later. Both Atkinson and Gaines planned campaigns to follow Leavenworth's. Gaines ordered a regiment from Baton Rouge and Pensacola to St. Louis and prepared to send a second regiment if other tribes joined the Arikara. Together, the generals advanced nearly an entire regiment forward to Fort Atkinson, but these troops would go up the Missouri to try to intimidate the Blackfeet and show American strength in the Yellowstone country under Atkinson's command, rather than pursuing the Arikara. The latter found the Sioux a greater and more persistent threat than the Americans after fleeing their villages.[36]

Leavenworth's bitter experience with the trappers changed his perspective about the frontier; under attack, his reports soon went beyond defending his caution during the expedition to point out the dubious ethics of the fur trade and the dilemmas it created for the United States. Outraged by the burning of the Arikara villages, the colonel advised that "it will be impossible for the military force of our Country to preserve peace between the Indians and our Citizens (and there is nothing else to do it) if traders or citizens can with impunity burn the villages and towns of Indians whenever they choose to do so." Indeed, the authoritarian colonel hinted that only his subordination to the legal constraints of due process had prevented him "from taking such measures on the subject as would readily have occurred to the mind of every military man"—a thinly veiled reference to summary court-martial and execution. Although Leavenworth initially praised Ashley and the American Fur Company for their "zeal and efficiency," while blaming the Missouri Fur Company, that November he warned Atkinson that trappers had taken "the beaver of the Indians without consideration or compensation of any kind," urging that "the interests of the nation require that this trapping business should be fully and completely suppressed." His views were echoed by eastern newspapers like the *New York American*, where Leavenworth probably had connections from his term as a New York state legislator immediately after the War of 1812. That newspaper recognized the fundamental congruity among trappers, filibusters, and freebooting marauders. Soon, even western papers like the *Detroit Gazette* condemned the trappers for lawlessly breaking the peace.[37]

While the trappers blamed British influence for native depredations, Leavenworth denied that the British were active in the region. Instead, he held the American fur companies responsible for conflict because they were less fair to the Indians than was the Hudson's Bay Company. Thus, the colonel's vision for the 1824 campaign season was an expedition up the Missouri River to establish peace by expelling trappers, American as well as British, and intimidating Indians. How he expected to do the former was not clear, unless the fur companies were denied licenses by federal civil authorities and the army was tasked with enforcement. The government had no intentions of destroying the fur trade, which it saw as an essential instrument of American influence—perhaps greater than that of the army—in the contest with Britain for Indian loyalties. Indeed, the fundamental disingenuousness of U.S. Indian policy became evident in the 1834 Trade and Intercourse Act, which intoned that no whites were permitted to hunt or trap in Indian country except for personal subsistence. A year later, Captain Benjamin Bonneville received leave to undertake a trapping expedition. Nevertheless, the War Department and the army chain of command continued to entrust important diplomatic and peacekeeping efforts (discussed in volume 2) to Leavenworth, against the

Jacob Jennings Brown, commanding general, *Portfolio* (1814).

Winnebago in 1826 and in the first major dragoon expedition onto the southern Plains eight years later, when the brigadier presided over a series of treaties and died of fever after twenty-two years' service.[38]

On the whole, American fear of British influence over the Indians of the Mississippi River and the Great Lakes declined significantly after 1820. As early as June 1815, the British officer commanding at Mackinac observed that "the whole of the Western Indians are completely hemm'd in, thoroughly in the power of the Americans, & their assistance in any future war, *hopeless.*" As the army advanced, Congress created a legal basis for excluding British merchants from the Indian country. An 1816 law authorized the army to arrest foreigners found in Indian country without passports granted by state or territorial governors or military commanders and to seize goods from foreigners trading with the Indians, with or without passports. Two years later, after the calming in Anglo-American relations and the Convention of 1818, Secretary of War Calhoun reported to House Speaker Henry Clay that "helplessness" had replaced "independence" among the western Indians: "they neither are, in fact, nor ought to be, considered as independent nations." In 1823, as commanding general after the reduction in force, Jacob Brown again recommended no more than an exterior line of posts for the arc from the Missouri to the Lakes—Forts Howard, Crawford, Snelling, Atkinson, and Brady (at Sault Ste. Marie)—probably in order to concentrate soldiers in larger units for more effective training, one of his principal objectives.[39]

Calhoun still had to answer frontier demands for protection against possible Indian threats, highlighted by the Arikara "war" that summer, so he rejected Brown's minimalist proposal. However, the decline of British antagonism and influence, combined with growing demands for retrenchment by Old Republicans and Jacksonians, led to the army's withdrawal from the middle Missouri when Fort Atkinson was closed in 1827. Economizing also led to the temporary abandonment of Forts Crawford and Towson in 1826 and 1829, although each was reestablished two years later. Fort Edwards, at the junction of the Mississippi and Des Moines, had already been deemed redundant and closed in 1824. Brown made the best of the situation and took advantage of the contraction to concentrate most of the First and Sixth Regiments at the juncture of the Mississippi and Missouri, where Jefferson Barracks replaced Fort Belle Fontaine near St. Louis in 1826. There they could serve as theater reserves, moving more quickly against the growing threat of intertribal conflicts west of Arkansas or against the Winnebago, whose anger with white lead miners became a short-lived "war" in 1827. Even more important for Brown, the concentration of twenty-two companies—a fifth of the entire army—at Jefferson Barracks allowed the establishment of an infantry school to enhance troop training.

His lack of any western experience notwithstanding, the commanding general felt no doubt that the army could dominate the Great Plains, claiming that there was "no policy so effectual, as to send forth from these strong posts . . . well organized parties of troops to penetrate the retirements of the savages, and awe them by a salutary exhibition of our power." According to Brown, the open topography of the Plains was advantageous for the projection of conventional military power: "The country between the Missouri and the Rocky Mountains is of such a nature that large bodies of savages cannot find a secure retreat within its limits. . . . It would not require a large command [probably meaning no more than two regiments] of well trained mounted infantry, with a few pieces of light or flying artillery, to disperse any force of savages which might be collected to oppose them." Unlike Leaven-worth facing the Arikara villages or Gaines facing Black Hawk in 1831, Brown did not seem to worry about what the Indians would do once dispersed. Nor, of course, did the army have two regiments of mounted troops.[40]

The forts established in the first two phases of the army's westward expansion during the 1810s and 1820s formed the basis of the line of western defense for the rest of the period before the Mexican War. Western military deployments continued to change according to diplomatic, strategic, and operational circumstances, however. Several temporary posts were established during the third phase of military expansion in the 1830s and 1840s, as the dragoon regiments created during the former decade mounted patrols to show American power over larger areas along the edge of the Great Plains. (They also mounted several battalion expeditions across the Plains in 1834, 1835, and 1845, which are examined in volume 2.) Fort Des Moines was built in 1834 near the site of modern-day Montrose to keep peace between the Sauk and the Sioux, although the post was closed two years later during the redeployments necessitated by the second set of Creek and Seminole wars. Fort Coffee, established just west of Fort Smith in 1834, never became more than a temporary dragoon post to enforce the trade and intercourse laws and support the peaceful resettlement of Indians driven from the Southeast amidst the tribes native to the area. In 1838 its garrison was shifted to the new Fort Wayne, sixty miles northeast of Fort Gibson on the Arkansas state line, to restrain conflict between rival Cherokee factions and counter the rumored formation of a Pan-Indian confederation.[41]

The withdrawal from Fort Atkinson and the Upper Missouri Valley represented a retreat unprecedented in the history of U.S.-Indian relations and territorial expansion. Yet evaluating the significance of this withdrawal depends largely on one's expectations of the army's impact in the region. Atkinson's force had effectively provided for its own subsistence, proving the army's ability to sustain itself far from logistical depots. But without mounted troops, it was unable to catch hostile Indians or conduct the routine peacekeeping operations and patrols necessary to establish an effective American presence in the region. In other words, the army possessed the capability to project power at the strategic level but lacked the resources and tactical capability necessary to give that strategy consistent operational force. More important, none of the army's strategic missions in the Upper Missouri Valley remained national priorities by the mid-1820s. British influence declined because the 1821 merger of their two principal fur trading companies reduced their need for competition in marginal or peripheral areas of beaver pelt production within U.S. territory, leading Atkinson to report that the British and the Indians of the upper Missouri no longer visited each other. Persistent friction between American fur traders and the military came to a head after Leavenworth's punitive expedition retreated from the hostile Arikara villages in 1823; protecting trappers then seemed irrelevant because the Arikara conflict and attacks by the Blackfeet farther west drove the mountain men to use overland routes to the south during the mid-1820s. Indeed, not until after 1830 did the American Fur Company resume the traditional European practice of paying Indians for pelts, finally giving the tribes of the northern Plains the incentive to trade with Americans that Atkinson had hoped to create a decade before. This enabled the company to make peace and trade with the Blackfeet without the assistance of national military power, an outcome neatly in tune with decentralized Jacksonian liberalism.[42]

Roger L. Nichols, Atkinson's biographer, concludes that the army proved ineffective in the Upper Missouri Valley. I would argue that the army's principal mission was to keep conflict among the Indians from leading to attacks on white farmers along the settlement frontier, which was far to the east of the upper Missouri watershed. Inter-Indian wars, plus the ability to avoid decimation by epidemic diseases brought by whites, greatly enhanced Sioux power, perhaps making possible their later challenges to U.S. expansion. But most hostilities among the Indians weakened the tribes and enhanced their dependence on supplies of guns and ammunition, which were now obtained almost entirely from American traders. Keeping peace among the Indians usually meant post facto punishment rather than preemptive action and never really amounted to anything more than a means to achieving other strategic objectives. Nichols concludes that "by 1830 the valley had reverted to the Indians, who retained most of it until settlers began moving into the region in large numbers several decades later." Of course, the region had never actually been in U.S. hands: Fort Atkinson was a strategic island, with no significant white settlement within more than a hundred miles. Thus, J. Wendel Cox, who like Nichols emphasizes the limits of American military power in the Missouri Valley, observes that the power projection efforts of the Missouri expeditions were no longer considered necessary to national security. Factors external to the army—the rise of the Jacksonian movement, calling for retrenchment as the nation strove to recover from economic depression, the rapprochement with Britain, and the shift in policy emphasis from countering British influence to preparing for Indian removal—rather than institutional incapacity per se precluded appropriations sufficient to mount troops and sustain extended expeditionary campaigns.[43]

Without such appropriations, the army could lead but could not secure American territorial expansion in the trans-Mississippi West. Indeed, the army unintentionally contributed to this dilemma when Stephen Long's explorations fostered the impression that the Plains were a desert inhospitable to agriculture. Just as ironic, the proponents of retrenchment were largely the same Jacksonians who would soon be crying out for renewed territorial expansion. Indeed, the Jacksonians would create two regiments of dragoons—an increase of more than 20 percent in the army's troop strength—to patrol the borderland between "Indian country" and the white settlement frontier in 1833 and 1836, along with a regiment of mounted riflemen to protect the Oregon Trail a decade later. These regiments, particularly the First Dragoons, proved crucial to American peacekeeping and power projection on the Plains and in the Iowa forests and prairies during the 1830s and 1840s, and they formed the core of the Army of the West that secured California in 1847. In the meantime, the army waited a generation for agrarian settlement to catch up with its far western posts. To do otherwise would have been strategic irresponsibility, whether driven by civil or military policy makers.

The range (and perhaps confusion) of historiographical judgments on the army's impact in the Upper Missouri Valley is illustrated by Frederick Hoxie, who observes that "the power of the United States [was] laughable in 1825, but clearly greater than it had been in 1805 and capable of orchestrating the efforts of both fur traders and military men." Hoxie, a student of the Crow, notes that Atkinson had a hard time finding the Indians with whom he sought to negotiate, yet Crow leaders "could see that the Americans were potential allies and dangerous foes. . . . In the future, they would have to gauge their actions with increasing reference to the military strength of the United States." In other words, the Plains Indians (northern, central, and southern) could largely, but not completely, ignore the Americans during the 1820s. Nevertheless, although it would require two or three generations of explosive white population growth, the United States would ultimately be able to back up its assertions of supremacy as Spain and France had not. Perhaps France and Spain never intended to do so, but the demography of their empires did not permit such an alternative. British Canada, in contrast, provides perhaps the best control case: as in the United States, white migration led to Indian subordination there, perhaps undergirded by the military actions of the United States during the 1860s and 1870s. Jackson's destruction of the Seminole, Red Stick, and Mikasuki villages in Florida should make it clear, if only to historians in retrospect, that the army's power was hardly laughable, but during the 1820s, the nation's priorities, as expressed in Congress, lay elsewhere.

Meanwhile, the friction between military commanders and fur company employees during and after the Arikara conflict so poisoned relations between the national military and private enterprise that the orchestration to which Hoxie refers was no more than a temporary attachment of trappers and traders to Atkinson's military expedition.[44]

Thus, the American impact on the Crow, as on the other tribes of the upper Missouri watershed, lay primarily in relations among the Indians themselves— giving them access to weapons and trade goods needed to sustain tribal leadership and unity or to ward off other tribes. Atkinson's treaties did not stop northern Plains Indians from warring with one another, but this did not bother American policy makers. Without a settlement frontier to protect or police, the army did not return to the region—aside from the movement of the Mounted Rifles to Oregon and the establishment of Forts Kearny and Laramie on the Platte hundreds of miles south in 1849 and Forts Randall and Pierre on the Missouri in 1855—until the middle of the 1860s, after the passage of the Homestead Act. With agrarian settlement so far behind the fur trade and trapping frontier, there was little congressional interest in paying for efforts to pacify, "civilize," or conquer the Indians of the upper Plains and the Rocky Mountain slope. As Cox points out, the United States made only one additional treaty with the natives of the northern Plains before midcentury. One might say much the same of U.S. forays to the Southwest: dragoon expeditions toured the southern Plains, successfully treating with the Pawnee, Wichita, and Comanche in 1834 and 1835, but they were not repeated until 1844, as Indian raids against Mexico increased and the United States looked toward annexing Texas. The Comanche did not become a danger to U.S. citizens until the annexation of Texas; the government responded to Texan demands for military assistance against the Comanche during the 1850s, though its military officers demonstrated much the same skepticism they had toward earlier calls for aid.[45]

The U.S. government, particularly the executive agencies, did not pursue unconstrained expansion and aggression without heed to cost; it commonly deferred expansionist initiatives until white settlement and demands for protection reached a politically critical mass. Unlike Andrew Jackson on the Florida frontier, western military commanders did not initiate operations to attack the Indians on their own authority; they sometimes did so in response to pressure from settlers, but they were reluctant to intervene and were usually able to avoid doing so unless whites had actually been slain (which was remarkably rare). As a result, combat between the army and the western Indians was surprisingly uncommon prior to the American surge across the Plains into the Southwest, California, and the Pacific Northwest during the 1850s—after the army had defeated Mexico and opened those lands to American claims of sovereignty.

U.S. relations with the Sioux, the Crow, the Ojibwa, or any other tribe cannot be understood independent of the contingent circumstances and objectives of each encounter. Indeed, one could argue that the United States played the Ojibwa and the Sioux (or the Sauk and the Sioux) against each other (or at least took advantage of clashes between them) in the Upper Mississippi Valley during the 1820s and 1830s, much as the Osage were weakened by conflict with the Cherokee and the Pawnee by the Sioux. Though I have found no evidence to suggest that officials saw it this way, the United States and the Sioux enjoyed a symbiotic relationship: the Sioux provided the violence that made the Ojibwa, Sauk, and Pawnee vulnerable to American inducements. Although it asserted sovereignty and demanded peace, the United States took advantage of the flux along its peripheries to limit its expenses while waiting for the Indians to wear themselves down. The United States did not lack power to deploy to the West prior to the Civil War; it lacked sufficient interest to deploy the power necessary to secure hegemony so long as its citizens were not assailed, and this was not a serious problem prior to substantial agrarian settlement. With Mexicans or other Indians to raid, the Sioux and Comanche did not strike at the white frontier; the Osage did so only in small bands of thieves—on a criminal rather than national scale—after being driven to desperation by the Cherokee and other Indians deported into Osage territory by the United States.

More precisely, most of the substantial agencies of organized power, whether public or private, were busy in the East: they had higher priorities. We can reasonably identify the absence of U.S. hegemony in one region or another, or over one tribe or another, as a contingent objective reality for that region or tribe, but we should be careful not to extrapolate some general ceiling to U.S. power, any more than we should presume the inevitability of white settlement. The critical question was when national power, normally latent, would be mobilized and directed against a particular tribe or region, and this was essentially a political question among U.S. citizens and their representatives, the outcome determined by the dynamics of federalism and racialized democracy. Sadly, that contingency lay as much in the timing and extent of white intrusion as in native agency.

Soldiers of the Rifle Regiment, 1814, by H. Charles McBarron. (Courtesy Army Art Collection)

The officer's ideal of leadership and war: Fort George, 1813, from Richardson, *Messages and Papers of the Presidents* (1903).

7

THE GROWTH OF PROFESSIONAL ACCOUNTABILITY DURING THE 1820S AND 1830S

Contexts, Policies, and Causation— Domestic and International

The year 1821 marked a critical juncture for the development of the regular army and its officer corps. The final implementation of the Transcontinental Treaty with Spain removed the most urgent potential threats to U.S. expansion and national security, enabling a reduction in force of approximately 40 percent that summer. The annexation of Florida and the confirmation of the nation's western boundaries, combined with the end of Spanish rule in Mexico and decades of sociopolitical tumult there, effectively minimized any international threat along the nation's southern and western arcs, while a gradual rapprochement with Britain diminished the threat along the northern border. Budgetary constraints, intensified by the depression that followed the Panic of 1819, slowed the construction of the "third system" of coastal fortifications proposed by the army-led Board of Engineers for Fortifications between 1816 and 1821. Yet other developments made it clear that the United States had less to fear from the Continental powers of Europe than ever before. Anglo-American rapprochement culminated in 1823 with the British proposal of a military entente against European intervention in the Western Hemisphere, and France's Polignac memorandum of the same year stipulated that Louis XVIII had no plans to intervene. Indeed, historian Jeremy Black suggests that "the North American Question had been settled by the War of 1812": the United States would not be a British satellite, but it lacked the strength to challenge Britain without allies; meanwhile, maintaining the European balance of power required Britain to focus its attention on that side of the Atlantic. North America became no more than a tertiary priority for

Britain, far less important than the "Eastern Question": the defense of India and competition with France and Russia over the decaying Ottoman Empire. Without European support, the decentralized North American Indians were ultimately helpless against nationally organized white power and normally did no more than harass isolated settlers or small parties of soldiers.[1]

As a result of these dynamics, the national standing army engaged in only four campaigns (or "wars") involving unit combat engagements in the seventeen years between the two Seminole wars. Two of these, against the Arikara in 1823 and the Comanche in 1829, involved only a single engagement and a few army casualties; a third, the Winnebago "war" of 1827, was really no more than an armed sweep to intimidate resistance, like most army operations against Indians, and did not involve any combat by soldiers. Native resistance turned back U.S. thrusts into the upper Missouri basin and delayed white settlement in the Upper Mississippi Valley during the 1820s and 1830s, but this was possible only because of disagreements and other priorities, and a consequent lack of focus and effort toward the Northwest, among U.S. policy makers. In this overtly peaceful era, the army's missions and force structure were shaped less by threats—potential, perceived, or actual—than by national means, dictated by objectives that were less imperative and more open to popular and congressional debate. This chapter provides a broad context for the army's frontier diplomacy and constabulary operations between 1821 and 1846; volume 2 presents the archival evidence and the narrative of operations.

The resources the nation was willing to devote to standing military forces shrank along with the threats to its security. The Panic of 1819 aggravated fiscal scarcity, but growing political divisions over national objectives proved to be a more lasting constraint. Economic recovery and the coalescence of the National Republican "American system" of more activist government did not lead to a corresponding revival in the military budget during the mid-1820s. Instead, the superficial National Republican consensus embodied in the "Era of Good Feelings" dissipated in the resurgence of traditionalist, decentralizing republicanism that began with the "Old Republicans" of the 1810s, flourished among those termed "radicals" during the years of financial panic and depression, and culminated in the Jacksonian movement. Even though these blocs often employed the authority of national military power in pursuit of territorial expansion, they resisted efforts to increase government revenue and challenged the regular army's claim to monopoly over the direction of organized armed force.[2] Fortunately for the army and its officers, the de facto postwar consensus—however diffuse, diverse, or disputed by dissenters—in favor of territorial expansion (whether on grounds of "security" or for expansion per se) now became a de facto consensus supporting the maintenance of national sovereignty and white supremacy in the newly acquired regions. Thus, although Secretary of War Calhoun famously proclaimed that the army's purpose was to prepare for war, its primary operational mission shifted from readiness for conventional conflict with Britain or Spain, or even relatively large-scale war with the Red Sticks and Seminoles, to the constabulary duties of armed diplomacy, peacekeeping, and domestic law enforcement along international borders and territorial frontiers.

While as much as 40 percent of the officer corps served in staff positions developing administrative, logistical, and ordnance systems that would bolster the army's expansion in case of future wars, constabulary operations provided a raison d'être that Old Republicans—mostly southerners dedicated to sustaining, if not expanding, the system of plantation slavery—and Jacksonians could accept. Jackson's invasion of Florida demonstrated the political path to institutional survival, and contemporary senior officers probably recognized this. Southern political leaders who were suspicious of large military staffs and federal aid for internal improvements (civilian transportation projects) did not complain when plantation slavery was advanced and secured by the annexation of Florida and the expropriation of Indian tribes within the emerging cotton heartland—the future Black Belt of Georgia, Alabama, and Mississippi. Nevertheless, "selling" the army to the public—highlighting these services while maintaining the army's staff cadre and countering radical critiques of standing military forces—was a difficult, multifaceted, never-ending process that continues in new forms even in the twenty-first century. Historian Robert Wooster provides unusually specific details about the reasons why the army sometimes received bad press, beyond the rhetorical excesses of Jacksonian oratory. In particular, Secretary of War Calhoun, like his military subordinates, was focused on conventional European threats and failed to emphasize frontier defense, much less westward expansion, in his 1821 expansible army plan. An easterner with little personal contact with or empathy for the frontier, mindful of the strategic pause embodied in the Transcontinental Treaty and enforced by the Missouri crisis, Calhoun did not make a case for an expansive military role to balance the reduced need to defend against European threats.[3]

In these things, the secretary was not unrepresentative of the army's officers, who were mostly easterners (like most of the population) and aspiring gentlemen whose seminal military experience was the War of 1812 against Britain. (The officers of the Left Division of the Northern Army, who had led close-order assaults in the American victory at Chippewa and the fiercely contested bloodbath at Lundy's Lane in the Niagara campaign in 1814, were disproportionately retained in the army after the reduction in force the following year.) Nor did Stephen Long's reports of a "Great American Desert" on the

Plains suggest that there was much for an army to explore or defend. Nevertheless, despite all the friction, tension, and uncertainty, the military's utility to diverse sectional, ideological, and sectoral interests enabled the national standing army to maintain an unusually large proportion of career officers, sustain a more stable force structure, and enhance its primacy in the operational direction of American armed force.[4]

The demand for military accountability came from three sources, each involving fiscal, political (meaning responsiveness to the policies chosen by Congress and the executive), and practical dimensions. The first source was a parsimonious Congress, which could always gain votes by appealing to a public that was antagonistic to taxation and jealous of political privilege yet demanded a variety of expensive tasks that no existing civilian agency could undertake; the public also demanded a rigorous accounting of public funds while preserving the army's war-fighting capability. Second were the logistical needs of the organization itself and its officers and enlisted soldiers, who had suffered severely from the inefficiency and corruption of civilian contractors before and during the War of 1812, leading the army to assume greater inspection and distribution responsibilities afterward. Third were the demands of U.S. foreign policy for a capable force responsive to national civilian authorities. All three sources were joined in the development of a military force capable of projecting effective power over international distances—a capability the United States lacked in 1815 or 1820. After a quarter century of reform, the regular army provided this capability, which enabled the conquest of northern Mexico and the incorporation of California into the United States; during the Civil War, the regular army's administrative and logistical skills did the same for national reunification. The vaunted volunteers provided plentiful manpower but lacked the regulars' logistical and tactical expertise, or even their fiscal accountability and sensitivity to civil-military relations. Ultimately, Congress focused its inquiries on expenditures, and populist congressional critics aimed their ire at the monopolies Congress had effectively granted to West Point and the regular army, rather than closely scrutinizing the conduct of specific constabulary operations in the borderlands.[5]

Substantial continuities remained between the periods before and after 1821. The international state system remained fundamentally competitive rather than cooperative, a balance of power that often failed to balance power before damage was done to smaller states. The international system remained generally hostile to republicanism, liberalism, and democracy. North American Indian relations were still characterized by white agrarian expansionism fueled by the continuing surge in the white American population, which nearly doubled each decade. Despite growing white racialism (supposedly justified by science), the normative language of Indian relations remained that of Jeffersonian and Enlightenment philanthropy, of nurture rather than nature, of acculturation (albeit more segregated than before) rather than annihilation or extinction. The U.S. government remained federal and decentralized, its politics sectional but not critically so, amid a growing movement in favor of white male democracy throughout most of the nation. Despite Jackson's invasions of Florida, the foundation of American civil-military relations remained civilian supremacy and military subordination to constitutional civil authority, whether that of statute, due process, congressional oversight, or executive officials at the federal, state, and local levels.

Conversely, the threats and influence of the international system were much less urgent than before. Many historians have challenged the concept of "free security" for the immediate postwar period (approximately 1815–1820), but few have done so for the periods after 1820, 1823, or 1825. Although policy makers, including military commanders, continued to worry about the potential for international conflict, it is difficult to deny that the United States enjoyed a substantial period of international calm, a full fourteen years between the proclamation of the Monroe Doctrine and the Canadian border crisis that broke out at the end of 1837. Diplomatic historians have pointed out that few Americans pressed the Monroe Doctrine prior to the mid-1840s, and the only serious Euro-American diplomatic crisis between 1823 and 1838 was President Jackson's demand that France pay American claims related to shipping seized during the Napoleonic Wars—an overblown spat that was resolved without real difficulty in 1836.[6]

Rarely did civil or military policy makers publicly proclaim worst-case scenarios in Anglo-American relations; even more rarely did they do so with any fervor, and the same was true of federal policy makers and Indian relations until the mid-1830s. Whatever fears policy makers occasionally expressed about the disposition of Cuba or Oregon in the mid and late 1820s or during the French claims crisis in 1835, historians must abdicate their critical judgment to discover threats analogous to those of the immediate postwar era in the years between 1820 and 1837. To report occasional instances of concern as if they were just as intense as before the Transcontinental Treaty is to narrate rather than analyze or assess. Nor, as most civil and military policy makers recognized at the time, did the Mexican invasion of rebel Texas threaten the United States, either directly or by stirring up Indian resistance to white expansion. And although military commanders and executive officials occasionally returned to fretting about British influence in the trans-Mississippi Northwest, it requires the suspension of critical judgment to envision this influence—declining and recognized as such by civil and military policy makers as the 1820s went on—as a significant threat to U.S. security or national interests.

Absent such threats, the contingent unity of the Republican Party (which had become increasingly national in orientation as the anticolonial struggle against Britain was aggravated by the French Revolution and Napoleonic Wars) foundered amid competing ideological, sectional, and sectoral interests. The nationalist program of 1816—the revived national bank, protective tariff, and military buildup, plus growing calls for nationally sponsored internal improvements—soon sparked a reaction among traditionalist, locally minded Republicans and populist "radicals" who favored strict constitutional construction and the decentralization of government power. (We should not forget that these libertarians were often slaveholders, however.) By 1820, this backlash was intensified by the Marshall Court and the Panic of 1819, which many blamed (not entirely without reason) on manipulation by the Bank of the United States. The Old Republicans had always been strongest in the South, and the panic struck hardest at the cash-poor cotton South and the underfinanced West; the Missouri crisis completed the equation for discord. Interpretations that stress western concern for state sovereignty in the Missouri crisis and the future direction of American territorial expansion—the "surrender" of Texas in the Transcontinental Treaty—may be exaggerated, but the panic and crisis made the discordant sectional implications of the National Republican program abundantly clear.

Regardless of whether one views the 1820 crisis as fundamentally political or essentially economic, the rapidly growing commercialization of American life fostered a volatility in political culture and class structure; capital, credit, and resource flows; and production and distribution that differentiated, liberalized, and politicized American society as never before. Liberalization and politicization—the coordinate rise of interest-group politics and the backlash against it—were embodied in the "venturesome conservatives" of the Jacksonian movement and the democratization (however uneven) of political organization and culture they represented and advanced. These developments effectively eliminated any chance that an elite leadership—such as the National Republicans or later the Whigs—would be able to plan and direct the nation's development. Although the National Republicans of the 1820s (and later the Republicans of the 1860s and 1870s) would implement specific programs that favored particular economic sectors, along with banking and currency innovations that provided greater predictability to the financial system, the American political nation would not accept coordinated national development until the Great Depression a century later. Thus, among historians of American politics and the early national state, Richard R. John and Ronald P. Formisano have observed that growing administrative capacity in federal civilian executive agencies was curtailed and substantially reversed by the Jacksonian backlash against political centralization after 1828, producing "state regression" and "an end to state development." L. Ray Gunn and John L. Larson have suggested that decentralizing libertarian republicanism and liberal individualism became the dominant ideologies of nineteenth-century American political economy and governance during the Jacksonian period (rather than the Revolution or the Jeffersonian era), in reaction to National Republican efforts at state building and central planning embodied in Henry Clay's "American system" during the 1820s.[7]

Yet a blanket assertion of "state regression" goes too far, given the growth in federal expenditures during the Seminole and Mexican wars, evidence that the national state remained active in funding territorial expansion. Indeed, federal spending on internal improvements (roads, canals, railroad surveys, harbor and river clearance) increased during the Jackson administration, and the provision of military aid to private enterprise (at War Department direction) authorized in the General Survey Act of 1824 was not revoked by Congress until financial panic combined with war to render it necessary.[8] Federal courts, marshals, revenue cutters (ancestors of the Coast Guard), lighthouses, post offices, Indian agents, and customs collectors continued to operate; the Indian Bureau established within the War Department in 1824 was much more active during the removal and reservation eras than the federal government factory system (for regulated Indian trade) had been prior to its abolition in 1822. Clearly, these agencies were much less autonomous from partisan influence under the Jacksonian spoils system. Nevertheless, the partisan attractions of expanding patronage, combined with the practical needs of a rapidly growing and more widely dispersed population, led to a growth in the number of federal civil employees: by more than 50 percent per decade between 1821 and 1841, by 46 percent between 1841 and 1851, and by 40 percent between 1851 and 1861. Between 1821 and 1861, federal civilian employment multiplied more than fivefold, while the population grew only threefold.[9]

The "early democratization" (early in comparison to Europe) that Formisano and political scientist Martin Shefter see as constraining American state development did not provide reliable—militarily capable, fiscally accountable, and nationally responsible—armed forces to answer constituents' demands for territorial expansion. Nor did democracy resolve the international security tensions aggravated by American liberalism and decentralization. The antistatist backlash of the Jacksonian era did not reverse the development of bureaucratic institutions and a professional ethos—a blend of insulation from partisan control and accountability to national civilian authority—within the officer corps of the Jacksonian army. The size and administrative complexity of that army far exceeded that of most full-time private entities and all government entities except the post office (and most postal employees, like ministers in the private sector, were part-timers who supplied their own food, clothing, and housing). Thus, the small size of the War Department was possible precisely because the army had a committed, comparatively experienced, and highly accountable administrative cadre composed of its commissioned officer corps, particularly the staff officers of the quartermaster, commissary, ordnance, and adjutant general departments. Experienced military officers, subject to military discipline and increasingly trained in administrative procedures and habits of accountability at the Military Academy, filled many of the roles civil servants performed (or were not present to perform) in other government agencies. As historian Mark Wilson observes about the Civil War, "the [army] quartermaster department was already the best-qualified organization in America to handle complex . . . logistical problems." The statist project of career national military officers was unparalleled elsewhere in Jacksonian and antebellum America, and the officer corps survived the Jacksonian imposition of rotation in office within the civilian executive agencies (which so damaged the nonpartisanship and bureaucratic capability of the post office) almost unscathed, with significantly greater autonomy than before.[10]

Despite some sympathy for Native Americans among National Republicans, Whigs, and evangelical Christians, most American citizens and policy makers supported the notion of white supremacy, whether envisioned as paternalistic, dominative, or exclusive. This de facto consensus helped the army and its officers avoid the sectional conflict promoted by debates over commercialization and political economy. Apart from a few abolitionists, no whites wanted slave unrest or rebellions, and nearly every white American had some interest in the army's service as a peacekeeping force on the Indian frontiers, whether this meant the restraint of whites (and the expensive wars their excesses fostered) or the repression and expulsion of Indians. Despite the Missouri crisis and sectional hackles raised by the invasion and annexation of Florida, the nation's interest in preventing British or Spanish aid to the southern Indians and subversion among the slaves was so self-evident that no substantial opposition, either sectional or ideological, coalesced to prevent the ratification of the Transcontinental Treaty. Yet during the decade and a half that followed, the nation's focus on commercial depression and recovery, political-economic debate, democratization, and the sectional tensions brought to prominence by the Missouri controversy minimized the likelihood of further territorial expansion.

The army's most important influence on national development since Jefferson's election and the Louisiana Purchase—if not since its occupation of the Mississippi Territory in 1797 and 1798—had been as an instrument of southern territorial expansion and the extension of plantation slavery. After 1820 the army lost much of this sectional association as it turned to constabulary missions, enhancing and consolidating sovereignty over territory the United States already claimed rather than extending it to new regions. During the 1830s much of this "internal pacification" was performed in the Southeast—essentially making the "Old Southwest" into the nation's Southeast through Indian removal (explored in volume 2). Yet the army first undertook similar tasks in the Northwest, where repressing Indian resistance to white commercial expansion led to two of the army's three significant combat campaigns during the 1820s: the Arikara "war" of 1823 and the Winnebago "war" of 1827 (also examined in volume 2). These operations occurred during the National Republican administrations of James Monroe and John Quincy Adams, hinting that they shared the fundamental expansionism and, when under popular pressure, commitment to Indian removal of the Jacksonians, particularly in regions adjoining British Canada.[11]

In the Southeast, Jackson's protégé Edmund Gaines now commanded the new Western Department—in effect, the southern and western frontiers as far north as the Illinois prairies, including the internal Indian frontiers of Georgia, Mississippi, and Alabama. Gaines faithfully—indeed, zealously—carried out Adams's orders to prevent conflict between the state of Georgia and the Creeks remaining inside its boundaries. Doing so initially meant restraining or intimidating Georgians, led by erstwhile Old Republicans, who had seized the banner of white supremacist democracy and planned to dismember the Creek territories under the guise of state sovereignty. Gaines struggled against radical populist decentralization until Adams himself gave up the fight; then the general turned subtly but decisively toward a strategy of pressuring the Creeks to depart (a story traced in volume 2).

This trajectory was repeated in Alabama; with the Cherokee in Georgia, North Carolina, and Tennessee; and ultimately in Florida against the Seminole. It culminated in the military execution of President Jackson's Indian removal policy, leading to the nation's longest single war against a single native tribe or polity: the Second Seminole War (explored in volume 2). This process ensnared the army in the most significant civil-military friction in a generation. Yet the tension that developed was less between military commanders and northern Whigs or National Republicans (both found Indian removal distasteful) than between officers and frontiersmen, particularly those steeped in Jacksonian individualism, egalitarianism, and decentralization. In the end, Whigs and National Republicans found military professionalism and its associated values—essentially specialization and hierarchy—too attractive, while the Democrats elected to national office found a standing military force too valuable for populist Jacksonian assaults on the army's legitimacy to damage its force structure or undermine its professional development. In practice, Democratic congressmen voted for the army almost as much as Whigs did.[12] Flexibly adapting to serve a variety of interests and execute a variety of assignments, the army was able to develop and preserve a degree of autonomy in force structure (particularly officer selection and socialization) and professional development. It crafted a professionally accountable balance in both expertise and responsibility (mission and jurisdiction) that allowed its specialist cadre to develop greater conventional war-fighting expertise while infantry, artillery, and dragoon officers conducted the constabulary operations demanded by politicians and the public. After a wave of retrenchment efforts in 1829 and 1830, the Jacksonians expanded the army and accepted greater operational expenses in response to the growing tempo of Indian removal, so there was no need to rely solely on Whig support to gain appropriations.

The military legislation passed in July 1838—the most important of its kind between 1821 and the Civil War—clearly expressed the army's dual utility and the more general drives toward functional specialization and territorial expansion characteristic of the Jacksonian era. The law distinguished and enlarged the specialist administrative and logistical staffs and provided enhanced promotion opportunities, added a new infantry regiment, and increased the size of companies and the army as a whole to their largest since 1821. Jackson and Van Buren had both recommended a larger standing army with more professional staff officers to complete Indian removal and uphold national sovereignty along the Canadian border, and the law gave the army almost everything its leaders sought. Indeed, the statute provided every officer except generals "an additional ration per diem" for each five years of service: this meant two rations for most first lieutenants, three or more for most captains, and five or six for the many field-grade officers (majors and colonels) who had entered the army in 1808 and 1812. These rations were commonly converted into monetary payments, providing a general pay raise in response to officer complaints about inflation.[13]

SELF-SELECTION AND WEEDING OUT: CHANGES IN CIVILIAN OCCUPATIONAL PATTERNS, COMMISSIONING SOURCES, AND OFFICER CHARACTERISTICS AND COMMITMENT

During the 1820s and 1830s the international concerns that had ultimately dominated American military policy from the Revolution through the immediate post–War of 1812 era were eclipsed by domestic currents. The external structural factors—the competitive international state system, the representative nature of American government and civil-military relations, and white supremacy—remained, despite shifts in the form and weight of issues. Military agency—the values and objectives of the officer corps as a body and the internal factors in the army's institutional development—flourished, moving toward greater power and autonomy. The persistence of external influences precluded anything like real military isolation from civil society, but the lack of international urgency and the range of problems facing civil society created space for institutional and professional innovation that was relatively insulated from and autonomous of civilian influence or direction. The military reform initiatives of 1816 and 1817—the creation of a permanent logistical and administrative staff structure composed of military officers rather than civilians, and the assignment of Sylvanus Thayer as superintendent of the Military Academy at West Point, with a mandate for reform and revitalization—were sustained and enhanced during the ensuing decade and retained by the Jacksonians. Indeed, John C. Calhoun, President Monroe's fourth choice for secretary of war, turned out to be the most significant innovator and reformer in the nineteenth-century War Department and perhaps in nineteenth-century American government as a whole, given his firm support of increased professional education and bureaucracy.

Calhoun became the initial connecting point in the synthesis between internally and externally based reform, linking mission and structure. Like most officers, he espoused preparation for future conventional war as the regular army's principal raison d'être, a crucial focus during a generation in which further territorial expansion, and the possibility of actual war, seemed unlikely. Like other National Republicans, he valued the army for its utility as an instrument of national action, whether that meant exploration and reconnaissance, strategic power projection (the Missouri and Yellowstone expeditions) and peacekeeping in the service of westward agrarian expansion, or surveying roads, railroads, and canals in support of eastern commercial development. Through transport, commerce, and communications, he hoped to knit tighter the "bonds of union"—a mission that reinforced nationalism within the officer corps, as well as the association between the army and the nation in the public mind. This association would eventually aggravate radical Jacksonian attacks on the national standing army, but it also encouraged an institutional shift away from the southern sectional affinities developed in the army's expansionist missions during the Jeffersonian era.[14]

Calhoun's union of military preparation and civilian nationalism was most evident, and perhaps ultimately most significant, in the War Department's personnel policies during the second Monroe administration, which created a virtual monopoly on commissions for West Point graduates. The board of general officers that conducted the 1815 reduction in the officer corps had emphasized gallant or meritorious combat experience over all but moral criteria. The result was a veteran officer corps, but not one that was particularly well educated, truly subordinate, or socially adept. Only a seventh of the officers retained in 1815 were graduates of the Military Academy; an approximately equal number were former enlisted soldiers who had been hardened by battle but were often unaccustomed to the genteel civilian society with which they would associate while garrisoned in or near urban centers like New Orleans, St. Louis, and Detroit. Between 1815 and 1820, entrants to the officer corps came from a variety of sources: wartime officers discharged in 1815 (who made up the majority of entrants until 1817), cadets from the Military Academy, men from the enlisted ranks (normally sergeants with wartime experience), and civilians, though the latter often had experience as wartime volunteers. There were no consistent standards for selection and appointment. Nor was there much incentive for officers to stay in the army, so they came and went; their resignations were as frequent, and their careers as short and dysfunctional, as those of their prewar counterparts during the Jeffersonian era. (There were no official provisions for retirement until the Civil War.[15])

Such an officer corps had little claim to superior qualifications beyond combat experience, which would fade over time. Fortunately for the regular army and the nation's future, this instability in officer selection and retention ended during the 1820s. The transformation cannot be ascribed to changes in the domestic political landscape, for the Old and Radical Republicans remained critics and grew in strength with the Jacksonian movement. Factionalism increased among National and mainstream Republicans, and there was significant danger that the army would be too closely identified—whether by its officers' affinities or in public perception—with Calhoun in the 1824 presidential contest, encouraging further attacks. Commanding general Jacob Brown adeptly shifted his support to John Quincy Adams and worked closely with the new president to minimize perceptions of military involvement in politics and civil affairs. Yet Brown's northern origins and affinities, combined with the clash between Gaines (following Adams's orders) and the state of Georgia, led by a Crawfordite and future Jacksonian (a crisis treated in volume 2), gave ample ammunition to southern sectionalists in the Jackson movement, creating a new opening for partisan and ideological assault.[16]

International change provides a powerful but essentially negative and ultimately insufficient explanation for the stabilization of officer selection and retention, and of officer commitment, during the 1820s. There were no temporary crisis-driven surges in demand necessitating a reliance on citizen-soldier or volunteer candidates. The decline in international threats and opportunities might have produced a decline in the potential supply of officers and thus in competition for commissions from the militia and other sources outside West Point: the 1820s presented much less chance of military glory to be won by war with Britain, or of political reputation to be gained by conquest against the Indians. Yet had diminishing threats been the sole or primary factor, and had antagonism to standing armies been as great as many historians claim, the regular army presumably would have been abolished in favor of locally controlled volunteers or militia or reduced to a Jeffersonian level, fostering constant uncertainty in officers' careers. Monroe could have allowed the Military Academy to sink back into the obscurity and confusion of the Madison years, relying on meritorious veterans or appointments directly from civilian life on the grounds of political reliability, as had been the norm before 1815.

Instead, the most important effect of the international scene lay in the mixed memories of the Jeffersonian era and the War of 1812. Despite the triumphalism New Orleans fostered in poetry, rhetoric, and song, the war's trials and tribulations provided nationalist Republicans sufficient warning to ensure the retention of a combat force capable of a single expeditionary campaign, whether against Florida, Cuba, or a more weakly defended Canada, along with the staff bureaus and the skeleton of an expansible force to guard the nation's coast or for an extended war with a European power. Although the ordnance branch was reinserted into the artillery and several other staff positions were eliminated, the staff re-created between 1812 and 1816 was essentially retained in the force reduction of 1821; in contrast, the system of contracting supply distribution to civilian businesses, a source of immense logistical problems and professional frustration since 1802, was abolished. The army's authorized strength was reduced from 10,000 to 6,000 soldiers, and three of eleven regiments were eliminated; however, the artillery was reorganized from two regiments (one with four battalions) into four, leaving the same total number of regiments (eleven) and a more flexible artillery structure. Although the artillerists usually lacked the proper complement of cannon due to their cost, they frequently served in Indian and squatter removal operations during the 1820s and 1830s and made up the majority of the regular troops during the first year of the Second Seminole War.[17]

The Transcontinental Treaty was intended to settle the country's disputed boundaries and reduce potential security threats. The permanence of this settlement depended on the army's efforts to stem privately organized military expeditions and the officer corps' allegiance to national priorities and policy—above all, to centralized, national control over American foreign relations and the use of armed power. The decline in filibustering among officers after 1820 and among civilians between 1820 and 1835 is best attributed to the changing national and international context, the settlement of boundary disputes, and the availability of land and opportunities in the United States and Texas during the boom years from the mid-1820s to the mid-1830s. The resurgence of filibustering among American civilians after 1835 can be attributed to the reappearance of international boundary questions and the lack of economic opportunities during the depression that followed the Panic of 1837, combined with the Jacksonian culture of individualist, populist disdain for institutions and law.

When that happened, in Texas in 1836 and along the Canadian border between 1837 and 1842, the officer corps of the standing army no long proved so eager for territorial expansion or so belligerent toward Britain. The army was no more supportive of nonstate actors during the 1830s and 1840s than it had been at Amelia Island or against the Long filibusters circa 1820, nor did senior military commanders try to take advantage of the opportunities filibustering and crisis presented against a weak Mexico. Indeed, the army played a crucial, perhaps decisive role as the only national force available to stem the filibuster tide during the Canadian crises—likely the most dangerous point in Anglo-American relations after 1815. After a moment of expansive romantic sympathy for the Canadian rebels, officers' reactions quickly turned to distaste and repression as lawless American citizens sought to invade Canada and entrap the United States in a potentially disastrous war with Britain. Would this reaction have been the same had the crisis occurred in 1821 or 1825, when the officer corps still consisted largely of men commissioned directly from civilian life, without some socialization in professional ethics?

External forces of international security and domestic politics were united with internal institutional factors in a third phenomenon: a shift in career choices and structure that encompassed both the civilian and military spheres circa

1820. Military and civil officeholding had often overlapped, whether con-currently or consecutively, in the governments of the federal territories in the Federalist and Jeffersonian West. This reflected the ease with which the early national gentry shifted between leadership positions, without much sense of specialization or institutional career commitment. Most significant civilian officials in the Northwest Territory (1787–1803), from the governor down, were Continental Army veterans, as were some of those in the Southwest Ter-ritory, which became Tennessee in 1796. The Orleans (Louisiana) and Louisiana (which actually meant Missouri) Territories were initially governed, at least outside their capitals, by regular army commanders or men temporar-ily clothed in military rank.

William Henry Harrison and William Hull, the first governors of the Indi-ana and Michigan Territories in 1800 and 1805, respectively, were former army officers. Hull had last served in the Revolutionary War, however, and Harrison resigned his War of 1812 commission in 1814, the month after Jack-son took up his commission. Because Orleans had sufficient population, and because the Mississippi Territory had such limited space available to white set-tlers prior to the 1820s, military and regular army veteran influence in civil governance and officeholding diminished rapidly there, after being very sig-nificant in the initial American occupations in 1798 (Mississippi) and 1804–1805 (Louisiana). I have not investigated the civil officership of the Alabama and Mississippi Territories during the late 1810s; although there were probably many War of 1812 veterans, population growth was so rapid, and the transition to statehood so quick, that any overt military influence or con-nections quickly dissipated. Thus, by the 1820s, active-duty military officers no longer held territorial civil offices, and the role of former officers was decreasing in the more thickly populated territories. Nevertheless, we should remember that military men (including the de facto commanding general, James Wilkinson) governed Missouri directly until 1807, and former regular army officers did so between 1807 and 1809 (Meriwether Lewis), 1813 and 1820 (William Clark), and 1828 and 1832 (War of 1812 veteran John Miller). Indeed, two-thirds (twelve of eighteen) of the field-grade officers (majors, lieutenant colonels, and colonels) who left the army between 1816 and 1821 received federal civil posts, mostly in territorial government (see appendices B and C).

Looking to larger trends in American occupational patterns, we can see that the social and sectional composition and attitudes of the officer corps were changing as American society became more economically and occupa-tionally specialized. Growing opportunities, including the rise of more organized political parties, encouraged volunteer and wartime soldiers to make more enduring career choices, enabling the remaining officers to serve for significantly longer periods than their predecessors in the Federalist and Jeffersonian eras. Indeed, a similar process of occupational specialization and differentiation was developing in the political realm and within the federal government itself. As population densities grew and communications improved, territories became states with elected civilian officeholders, and the federal government turned to prominent local civilians or former officers rather than serving commanders for its civil agents. Fewer opportunities for civilian officeholding among career officers meant that their roles were less overtly political than they had sometimes been before 1820.

This process appears to have been especially significant among the southern planter class that had led the nation's expansion prior to 1820, particularly given the virtual monopoly on commissions by West Point graduates during the following decade. The strictly limited size of the army, its growing bureaucratization and rigid seniority system of promotion, and the de facto requirement that officer candidates spend four years at the Military Academy deterred or excluded established gentlemen planters of the sort who had been commissioned through social and political influence directly from civilian life under the less rigid conditions prevailing before 1821. Tighter academic and disciplinary standards meant that fewer southerners, especially those from frontier areas, were able to pass through the Military Academy—probably the most rigorous institution of higher education in the United States at the time—and enter the officer corps.[18]

Military careers also became less attractive to southern elites and men of ambition as they concentrated their energies on seeking personal independence through economic opportunities in the Old Southwest they had helped conquer. With the growth of export markets after the War of 1812, the southern planter class turned the weight of its energies from a mixture of part-time activities, including land speculation and active military leadership, to the full-time cultivation of cotton and other cash crops as the primary basis of its wealth. Concerned with maintaining a sectional balance in commissions that matched that of the citizen population as closely as possible, Calhoun's successors gradually instituted a system of congressional nominations for vacancies at West Point. By 1830, the sectional origins of the officer corps had become much more balanced, at least between North and South. Thus, although the southern states regained disproportionate representation at West Point through the operation of the three-fifths clause and commissions from civilian life by Democratic administrations between 1836 and 1855, the southern presence on the 1830 Army Register was significantly weaker than in 1815 or 1820. Yet officers drawn from the nation's frontier and borderland regions, North or South, remained disproportionately underrepresented in 1860 as well as 1830, suggesting that the corps gained little sensitivity to the values of those areas through its professional socialization, diminishing its potential sympathy for frontier claims and grievances.[19]

Because they served a national institution and were posted less according to sectional origin than institutional circumstance (driven by national territorial expansion and security considerations), numerous officers born in the North spent their careers, military and postmilitary, in the South. This phenomenon was hardly new: Eleazar Ripley was not the first Massachusetts man to settle in Louisiana after he left the army, nor was he the first to command a militia, practice law, and serve in local and state offices. Several of the officers who directed the occupation and initial government of Louisiana in 1804 and 1805 settled there and served in local civil government, most notably Edward Turner and Bartholomew Shaumburgh in Natchitoches and Henry Hopkins in Attakapas. Nor was this pattern limited to Louisiana: several of the officers who led the occupation of Mississippi in 1798 settled there after being discharged by President Jefferson in the reduction of 1802, including planter Isaac Guion and printer Andrew Marschalk.

This transition from national military officer to southern man of affairs—planter, lawyer, and sometime land speculator—was much more pronounced after the War of 1812, when a much larger officer corps faced a much deeper reduction in force amid a surging export market, particularly in southern cotton. A fair number of these commanders, including Ripley, William Allen Trimble, and Robert C. Nicholas, had an additional reason to leave the army: they felt they had received insufficient credit for their service in the Niagara campaign. Thus the rigidity of genteel, and especially military, conceptions of honor, the zero-sum clash of reputations, spurred capable men who were full of pride and ambition to reenter civilian life in search of wider horizons than those available in the small army retained in 1821. These men had the initiative and, in many cases, the connections to go far, regardless of their military careers and reputations, but their courageous military service had garnered them national fame, and this was much less disputed in civilian quarters than among jealous fellow commanders. Their military assignments took them far from their home regions, introducing them to the full opportunities of the expanding nation and drawing them from the settled shore to the frontiers of commercial enterprise.

Many of these men turned to politics around 1820. Resigning in 1819 after his dispute with Edmund Gaines over his role in the defense of Fort Erie five years before, William Trimble was almost immediately selected a U.S. senator from Ohio and served until his death in 1821 from complications of the wound he received in that battle. Robert Carter Nicholas, whom Jacob Brown blamed for the First Infantry Regiment's disordered rebuff at Lundy's Lane, was promoted colonel by seniority and retained to command the Eighth Infantry (with Trimble as his subordinate) in 1815, but he preferred tending to his plantations in Virginia and Kentucky and left the army the same year as Trimble. His Virginia connections secured him a lucrative post as U.S. agent to the Chickasaw in 1821, but his principal interest soon became his sugar plantation in Louisiana; he served as U.S. senator from Louisiana from 1836 to 1841, while Ripley was serving in the House of Representatives. During those years, fully half of Louisiana's congressional delegation were disgruntled veterans of the Niagara campaign.

This individual transition from military command to civilian leadership was equally apparent in the other trans-Mississippi frontier territories and states, particularly Arkansas and Missouri. Half of Missouri's 1837 congressional delegation had been regimental commanders in the War of 1812, and from 1819 to 1828, at least eight Arkansas territorial officials, including the first two governors, were former officers. Major William Bradford ran twice for the position of territorial delegate to Congress while still in uniform but was defeated by a former officer. He resigned from the army in 1824—the only field-grade officer to resign between 1822 and 1829—to serve as a general in the territorial militia, a post held by two other former officers. Andrew Jackson served as Florida's first territorial governor, drawing on several former subordinates from his "military family" of aides and staff officers for his administration. For these men, departure from the army was usually more choice than compulsion, and federal office smoothed their transition to civil life. Yet besides Bradford, only one other field-grade officer (John McNeil) appears to have resigned to enter the federal civil service between 1821 and 1846, when my study ends. Indeed, only nine field-grade officers resigned from the combat arms regiments between 1822 and the end of 1840—averaging one every other year out of a pool of between thirty-three and forty-two officers.[20]

The decade between 1815 and 1825 became a sorting-out period for the army, as men who were less certain of or less committed to a military future departed for greener pastures. For the officers who remained, however, the army offered a fixed salary that was not subject to the erratic fluctuations of the business world, and the army never went "out of business": barring dismissal for misconduct, it was virtually impossible for a regular officer to lose his commission between 1821 and 1865. Indeed, the officers of the regular army escaped reduction after the war with Mexico, and another generation passed before the composition of the officer corps was fundamentally altered by the integration of veteran volunteers after the Civil War. Soldiers who sought greater opportunities for upward mobility resigned to participate in the growing market economy, but resignations declined precipitously as the great majority stayed in the service, often because they felt unsuited for the instability of business life. The officers who remained were almost by definition more committed to national military careers.[21]

Put together, these developments contributed to the formation of an increasingly committed, increasingly professional officer corps whose primary political loyalties and identity were national rather than sectional or local. This nationalism—indeed, statism—enabled an otherwise weak government to employ the army as a reliable means of restraining filibusters, maintaining national sovereignty over the borderlands, and conducting U.S. foreign relations along the landward frontiers. The officers who remained increasingly saw themselves as career public employees dedicated to the full-time service of an established national institution, with the same distinctive objectives as an occupational interest group, rather than as men of affairs free to pursue personal, sectoral, or sectional interests like civilians or their predecessors before 1820. Reflecting these changes, officers began to respond to threats to slavery and to policies and conflicts to promote its extension as practical military questions (as in the Second Seminole War) or as personal ones (as on the Rio Grande in 1846), rather than issues of sectional defense and expansion. In significant contrast to southern civilians, few if any officers of the 1830s and 1840s advocated territorial aggrandizement in order to spread or defend plantation slavery. This hesitance led officers of the Jacksonian era into conflict with Florida settlers, where their predecessors had worked together in pursuit of the same goals twenty years before.

Ultimately, the *sufficient* factor in the institutional stabilization of the army between 1816 and about 1832 was internal: the sense of professional mission and motivation that most captains, majors, senior commanders, and leading staff officers shared with Secretary of War Calhoun. The urgency and impetus for this commitment to institutional reform and professional development were derived largely from the frustrating and dangerous (both personally and nationally) experience of unpreparedness and disorganization during and for several years after the War of 1812. Indeed, much the same experience, rooted in the Revolutionary War and threats to American sovereignty from Britain and France, had driven Federalist policy makers during the 1790s. The difference was that reform after the War of 1812 did not dissipate due to, or in the face of, decentralizing political ideology, as had been the case under President Jefferson. By 1815, the wave of officers commissioned in 1808 had experienced seven years of service and informal professional socialization, and they had gained some prestige among the nation's gentlemen, encouraging an emotional sense of mission and commitment. The new urgency of the post-1815 professional vision intensified officers' efforts not only to retain the wartime staff structure but to enhance it through the development of systematic standard operating procedures, to create effective bureaucracies in the expert, functionally specialized sense associated with Max Weber. The most important consequence came in the procedures established in the staff bureaus during the 1820s and 1830s, but this vision also prompted Brown and Quartermaster General Thomas Sidney Jesup to join Calhoun in advocating a school of artillery practice followed by a school of infantry practice, which were established in 1824 and 1826.

Yet an emphasis on combat experience and proficiency rooted in wartime experience might not have had the impact on officer selection that actually transpired. Unlike the politically driven force reductions of 1800 and 1802, which Presidents Adams and Jefferson conducted with little advice from experienced military commanders, those of 1815 and 1821 provided the army with an almost unprecedented opportunity for conscious, comprehensive self-shaping, an opportunity over which its officers exercised greater control than ever before. In both years the War Department established selection boards of senior officers and asked commanders to report on the efficiency, morals, and merit of all their regimental officers. The boards then evaluated regimental officers, using these reports, and regimental commanders, through reports obtained from the commanders of divisions and geographic districts. The criteria were broad enough that the evaluating officers were able to employ language that expressed collective values and priorities, and the boards, largely consisting of the same men in both years, were able to assess changes in the army's needs. Major Willoughby Morgan's commendation of his subordinates in the Twelfth Infantry Regiment serves as a fitting summary of the sort of officers and expertise the army hierarchy sought at the conclusion of the War of 1812:

> This regiment, with some exceptions, is finely officered, the officers generally having served upon the lines during almost the whole period of

the war, besides the merit of . . . having frequently encountered the enemy have acquired much practical knowledge and experience. In general they unite the Soldier and the Gentleman—some [perhaps meaning the West Pointers] add the embellishment of science and literature. Among officers professing such qualifications it is painful to discriminate: a discrimination must, however, be made.

Morgan went on to draw particular attention to Second Lieutenant Joseph Shommo, a Virginian whose early education had been neglected: "I recommend him because he is distinguished by the most fearless gallantry and active attention to duty . . . and well acquainted with the routine of police and discipline. I am convinced he will improve daily, being fond of the profession and ambitious of distinction."[22]

Morgan was right in one sense but wrong in another: Shommo was retained and rose to captain, but he resigned in 1820. (Morgan was retained through both reductions and rose to the rank of colonel before his death in 1832.) Though we do not know his motives, Shommo's decision exemplified the limits to the professionalism of the battle-hardened officer corps forged in the War of 1812. Despite their experience—or perhaps because of it, due to their ambitions and the contrast between wartime glory and peacetime drudgery—many members of this group lacked the commitment to make the peacetime army their career. Indeed, the officer corps retained in 1815 proved deficient or dysfunctional in several respects. Financial accountability, especially the timely submission of complete and accurate supply and strength returns, remained a significant problem for much of the following decade, and troops frequently went unpaid and wore ragged uniforms for as much as six months or a year at a stretch. Despite a financial panic and economic depression in 1819, desertion by enlisted soldiers continued at a level, often exceeding 20 percent per annum, that Secretary of War Calhoun warned "threatens the service." The commanders of the geographic military departments, as well as their subordinates, often ignored the correct reporting chains, writing directly to higher echelons and often failing to distribute orders to lower ones. Numerous company officers (captains and lieutenants) were absent without leave or never reported to their units.[23]

The resulting friction told on tempers across the army and was part of the background to Andrew Jackson's celebrated challenge to the War Department's authority to send orders directly to subordinates within his command. When the belligerence of their honor-bound gentry culture was aggravated by veteran confidence and disputes over wartime accomplishments, junior officers often engaged in acrimonious, sometimes violent disputes among themselves or with civilians. Nor did senior commanders set much of an example: similar controversies played out among general and senior field-grade officers such as Winfield Scott (versus Andrew Jackson, after Scott condemned Jackson's challenge to the War Department), Jacob Brown and Thomas Sidney Jesup (versus Eleazar Ripley), Edmund Gaines (versus William Trimble), and Alexander Macomb (versus Joseph Lee Smith, commander of the Third Infantry). (The last three cases were resolved by resignation of the junior officer in question.) Backbiting, duels, and retaliatory courts-martial flourished, driving capable combat veterans incapable of emotional self-discipline to resign. Under these circumstances, it was hardly unfair for the people's representatives in Congress to question the officer corps' accountability to the republican norms of disinterested virtue that its members professed.

On-the-job training may have worked for combat during the war, but it did not do so afterward. The army's problem was how to enhance the professional socialization of the officers commissioned in 1808 or during the war and how to develop it among new officers without damaging the institution while these men tried to get it right (or resigned if they could not). The solution was the United States Military Academy. As changing international circumstances made combat readiness less urgent, the army's senior leaders tacitly identified internal indiscipline as the principal threat to its survival. Recognizing that the inevitable decline in officer combat experience was accelerating due to indiscipline and resignations by veterans, the army's commanders implicitly adopted a collective vision of officership that stressed education, habituation to accountability, and genteel sociability to maintain and develop future professional expertise while enhancing accountability to the norms of civilian elites. Thus, the idiom of gallantry in combat that was almost universally espoused in 1815 shifted to privilege education, gentility, and collegiality in the evaluations made six years later. These were the qualities Sylvanus Thayer was endeavoring to develop in his reform of the Military Academy, and West Pointers were disproportionately retained in 1821, while former enlisted soldiers and officers commissioned directly from civilian life were disproportionately discharged. Combined with the West Point commissioning monopoly instituted by Calhoun and Monroe that year, the proportion of Military Academy graduates in the army officer corps surged, from 15 percent in 1817 to 40 percent six years later and 60 percent in 1830. More important, the junior officer corps of West Pointers and long-service veterans retained in 1821 demonstrated a substantially greater sense of commitment to the army than that retained in 1815, for the resignation rate declined precipitously, from an average of about 10 percent a year before the reduction to about 4 percent between 1821 and 1860.[24]

This sea change in officer selection, socialization, and retention was eased and heralded by the instability and departure of many wartime veterans during the preceding half decade, but it was confirmed and cemented by deliberate policy choices made in the 1821 reduction and by the Monroe, Adams, and even Jackson administrations. During the second Monroe administration, Calhoun made the postwar preference for West Point graduates a settled policy, admitting only a handful of aspirants to the officer corps who had not passed through the Military Academy. Adams's secretaries of war, James Barbour and War of 1812 volunteer commander Peter B. Porter, sustained this commissioning policy. Indeed, although Jackson proved more aggressive than previous presidents and secretaries of war in reinstating dismissed cadets or commissioning them as officers, no significant cracks appeared in the Military Academy monopoly on new commissions until the creation of the Battalion of Mounted Rangers after the Black Hawk War, near the end of his first term. This battalion, officered by men appointed from civil life in the western states and territories, became the First Dragoon Regiment the following year; yet only half of its officers—less than a fifth of all those commissioned in 1832—remained in service when the battalion was renamed, and most of their places were filled by West Pointers. Otherwise, Military Academy graduates retained their monopoly until 1836, when the Second Dragoon Regiment was established.

West Point neatly satisfied the army's need for new officers through the 1820s. Few brevet second lieutenants—"surplus" officers, above the number Congress had authorized by statute in 1821—were kept on the rolls (and paid) while awaiting permanent commissions after graduating from the Military Academy. But that number nearly tripled between 1828 and 1829, when the Army Register listed thirty-eight such men—an entire regiment's complement of officers and half as many men as all the second lieutenants required by the regiments of either infantry or artillery. This surplus persisted—and Congress allowed it to persist, essentially recognizing West Point graduates' claim to commissions—until 1835. Perhaps as a result of this surplus, the Jacksonians did not abandon the West Point–only commissioning policy for existing regiments until 1838, after several years of mushrooming resignations due to a combination of economic boom times and a frustrating, distasteful war against the Seminoles in Florida. (This "resignation crisis" is examined at length in volume 2.)

In 1838 officers had to be commissioned directly from civilian life, without Military Academy socialization or training, because West Point was too small (averaging about forty graduates a year) to do more than replace the normal rate of attrition from death and resignations in a year when a new infantry regiment was formed and the staff was increased. Yet that shift to direct commissions lasted only two years: after a decade in power, the Jacksonians still did not use the opportunity to do away with the Military Academy monopoly through the appointment of deserving enlisted soldiers or partisan patronage appointments from civilian life. In 1840, resignations had shrunk to the smallest proportion in army history due to the departure of uncommitted officers and the depression that followed the Panic of 1837; in fact, officers who had resigned in 1836 and 1837 were clamoring to be reinstated. As a result, the Military Academy regained its de facto monopoly on initial officer selection for the regular army. West Pointers maintained this dominance, with the exception of the additional officers needed for the new Regiment of Mounted Riflemen in 1846 and four new regiments (which West Point graduated too few officers to supply) in 1855, until the mass national mobilization of the Civil War. Indeed, despite all these injections from civilian life, by 1860, more than 75 percent of the army's officers—the historical peak—were Military Academy graduates, providing a professional education and socialization more pervasive and consistent than in any major European army, any American civilian profession, or the navy's officer corps.[25]

This persistence of Military Academy dominance over officer commissions should not be taken as a given. Indeed, historians have traditionally made a great deal of Jacksonian criticism of the West Point monopoly. How can we explain the dissonance among rhetoric, interpretation, and reality? Facing little cohesive opposition in Congress throughout Jackson's first term, the administration had several options for democratizing the officer corps, if the Jacksonian coalition had truly wanted to do so in a sense that went beyond merely partisan patronage. Yet since the 1960s, historians have recognized that there was little real difference in economic class between Jacksonian and Whig leaders or between Jacksonian civil service appointments and National Republican or Whig ones, and this was probably true of their followers as well.[26] Reforms in officer accessioning would have saved money (a significant priority in Jackson's first administration); decreased the number of officers available for detached service away from their regiments, especially those providing a de facto government subsidy to private companies by surveying railroads and canals; and reduced the West Point monopoly on commissions—all subjects of strident complaint among the more egalitarian Democrats. The most direct solution would have been to end the retention of brevet (super-numerary) second lieutenants; given the rarity of resignations, this would have ended the need for new officers from the Military Academy between 1829 and 1835. Indeed, the administration could have implemented this solution under existing constitutional authority, though not without a political firestorm, simply by refusing to submit new graduates' commissions for con-sent by the Senate. Jackson could have justified this action as strict adherence to statutory law, which was hardly unfair to men who had already received an education at taxpayer expense. Less immediately, but with more egalitarian socioeconomic (as well as partisan) impact, Jackson could have replaced resign-ing officers with men commissioned directly from civilian life or with enlisted soldiers, as the House Military Affairs Committee observed in 1831.[27]

Aside from creating the Battalion of Mounted Rangers, Jackson did none of these things. Indeed, in his first annual message to Congress, he praised the Military Academy as "one of the safest means of national defense" that had "exercised the happiest influence upon the moral and intellectual charac-ter of our army."[28] The Jacksonians did not attempt to democratize the army except by appointing their own constituents and relatives to the Military Acad-emy and commissioning about a regiment and a half's worth of mounted ranger and dragoon officers directly from civilian life in 1832, 1833, and 1836, when the creation of new units presented the opportunity to do so without stirring controversy by dismissing officers who already held commis-sions. Nor did the men the Jacksonians added to the officer corps make it more representative of the middle classes or of the nation as a whole. (The officers of the Battalion of Mounted Rangers *were* mostly westerners—rare in the officer corps at that time—but most of these men resigned within half a decade, in part *because* they clashed with the West Point graduates commis-sioned into the First Dragoon Regiment.)

About half the nation, including its middle class, consisted of farmers, yet the sons of farmers accounted for only about a quarter of the officer corps in both 1830 and 1860. The proportion of sons of professionals, largely from urban centers, increased between 1830 and 1860, from 23 to 26 percent of the officer corps; the proportion of sons of government officials (civil and mil-itary) rose from 20 to 22 percent. In other words, the sons of men in occu-pations amounting to 3 percent of the free male population held nearly half the commissions in the national standing army. The proportion of sons of arti-sans and nonagricultural laborers—like the farm sector, accounting for about 45 percent of the free male population in the 1850 census—increased from 5 to 6 percent of the officer corps. This was not an aristocracy in the European sense, but it was certainly a dramatic example of privilege extended and sustained by the government to particular sectors of the upper middle class. Nor did the Jacksonians substantially change the sectional distribution of cadets and officers to benefit the largely Jacksonian states of the South and West. The informal system of congressional nominations to West Point prevented them from doing so, especially since National Republicans, "anti-Jacksonians," and Whigs constituted nearly half of Congress throughout this era. Thus, the three-fifths clause in the Constitution was the southern states' and, indeed, the Jacksonians' principal advantage; the more thinly populated western states and territories benefited from direct commissions into the dragoon regiments, but half or more of these men resigned within several years of commissioning and were usually replaced by West Pointers.[29]

The surplus of brevet second lieutenants that developed at the end of the 1820s, averaging nearly an additional officer per company (a 25 percent augmentation over the number authorized by statute), created dilemmas for everyone except the congressmen who nominated cadets. Each company of forty soldiers needed no more than two officers for garrison or combat operations, yet artillery companies were authorized five apiece, and infantry companies were authorized three. Secretary of War Calhoun had recognized the need for additional officers to undertake "detached" or staff service—recruiting, commissary, quartermaster, ordnance, fortification construction, and West Point teaching and disciplinary duties outside their companies and regiments—to maintain the army, develop its expertise, and supplement or stand in for branches Congress had reduced or eliminated in 1821. There were also "special duties" assigned directly by the War Department, such as surveying railroad and canal routes under the General Survey Act of 1824 or administering Indian removal, to say nothing of the positions that had to be filled due to court-martial duty, personal leaves, individual travel to new assignments, and sickness. Thus, when President Jackson first issued General Order 48, instructing officers on detached service to return to duty with their regiments in 1833, the result was an even greater surplus of officers on regimental duty. Yet the administration did nothing to reduce the surpluses or to reconcile populist ideological rhetoric criticizing these officers and their roles supporting army administration and national development with the realities of institutional logistics and diverse mission requirements.[30]

The disparity between the size of the officer corps and its missions came to a head because of numerous resignations—nearly a sixth of the entire officer corps—in 1836, spurred in part by two more general orders (43 and 69) against detached service or extended leaves amid the frustrating Seminole war.

These resignations left the infantry and artillery short of officers—the artillery lost nearly a third of its second lieutenants—as the majority of the army deployed to Florida. Due to general orders and resignations, ordnance, engineer, and topographical (transportation survey) duty disappeared from the infantry and artillery regiments on the 1837 Army Register, fully eighteen months before the 1838 army law forbade officers from serving on transportation projects for private companies.[31] Some of the resigning officers were probably tired of military discipline and did not need the war to stimulate their departure. With civilian opportunities abounding in the economic boom of the mid-1830s, and with few wars to fight and little glory to win against "savage" Indians and Mexicans, the quasi-aristocratic motives of glory, reputation, and gentility inherited from European officer corps were unlikely to hold restless, individualistic Americans under the constraints of military discipline long enough to develop professional commitment. Yet the surge in resignations during the mid-1830s was very short-lived, lasting not much more than a year. The officer corps' long-term rate of career persistence—a median career of over twenty years among officers on the 1830 and 1860 Army Registers—was unparalleled in any other institution, organization, occupation, or profession in the United States at that time and probably exceeded that of most European officer corps.[32]

Even though about a sixth of the officer corps resigned between 1835 and 1837, the resignation rate for the decade as a whole actually averaged only thirty-six officers a year, or 6 percent. On average, West Point graduated forty-four cadets per year during this period, enabling the Academy to fill most slots opened by resignation or death. Although the resignation rate for the 1830s was 50 percent greater than the "normal" rate of 4 percent a year between 1821 and 1860, only in 1836 and 1837 did it actually exceed 6 percent. The economic boom peaked in 1836, the year the Second Seminole War began in earnest, promising arduous service in malarial swamps with little prospect of martial glory or public thanks. Between 1839 and 1844 the resignation rate was only 1.5 percent—less than half the normal percentage—even though the "thankless" and "inglorious war" in Florida continued until 1842, breeding growing frustration, and sometimes demoralization, in the officer corps.[33] Ultimately, officers' absence from their companies was a false positive, a sign of the army's adaptive success in self-administration and self-sustainment. The "resignation crisis" of the mid-1830s was a historical aberration. Focusing on these issues—as most historians of the Jacksonian army and civil-military relations have done at some point—leads to interpretive distortion. Historians should ask not only why there was a crisis but why it ended and was not repeated before 1860. (Although many officers who became famous in the Civil War left the army during the economic boom of the early to mid-1850s, they actually constituted a very small proportion of the officer corps as a whole.) In effect, the surge in resignations between 1835 and 1837 was the exception that proves the rule of professional commitment and career persistence among West Point graduates and regular army officers.

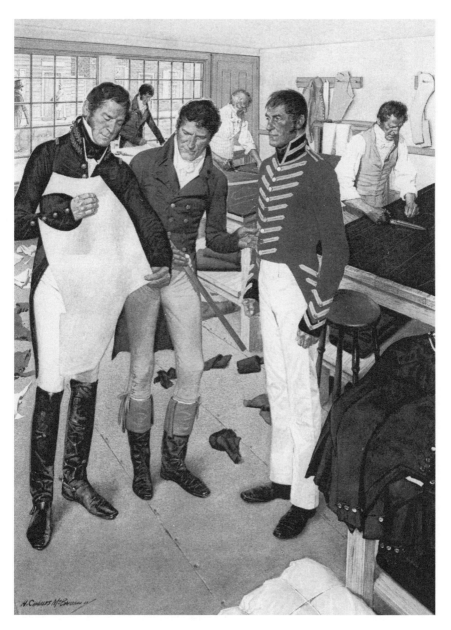

Accountability: *Clothing the Troops*, by H. Charles McBarron. (Courtesy Army Art Collection)

West Point cadet monument. (Photograph by the author)

CONCLUSION

THE SOLDIER AND THE JACKSONIAN STATE

The Military Academy, Army Missions, and Political Acceptance in an Age of Democratization

The essence of post–War of 1812 military reform, and the ultimate roots of American military professionalism, lay in successfully imbuing future officers at the Military Academy with the principles later embodied in the motto "Duty, Honor, Country." Probing beyond the slogan, analysis suggests that these words articulated essential prerequisites for the creation of a capable military leadership accountable to national civilian authority. *Duty* meant subordination and acceptance of the tasks assigned by a constitutionally authorized and delegated command; *honor* meant performing one's duties with selfless integrity in the defense of law rather than the belligerent defense of personal reputation, regardless of right or wrong; and *country* provided the focus of graduates' service—to the nation rather than self, class, or section. After four years of consciously practicing these principles, working together toward a common goal under the mentorship of officers who had experienced the same process as cadets themselves, graduates had developed a strong sense of their duty to serve the nation responsibly and accountably—the moral and emotional basis for professional commitment.

To paraphrase historian Leonard White, the Military Academy fostered the first organized, professional body in the nation's service. Indeed, West Point and the regular army officer corps became the basis for an informal national administrative cadre in the Weberian sense of a body organized both hierarchically, to ensure subordination and accountability to control by national authority, and along lines of functional specialization, to ensure responsibility and effectiveness in the execution of specific missions and duties. At West

Point, merit was determined by constant, standardized, and systematic—in officers' words, "regular"—evaluation and competition under conditions of formal equal opportunity and clearly delineated lines of specialized expertise and authority. Such competition habituated aspiring officers to functional specialization, subordination to legally constituted hierarchies of authority, and accountability to public values and expectations. Although the Military Academy experience of meritocracy implicitly clashed with the seniority system that was the norm for most company and field-grade promotions, officers accepted the seniority system as a compromise between experience (representing meritorious service) and institutional stability. They knew that merit could be rewarded through postings, a variety of staff assignments, or the occasional opportunity to bypass the seniority process when new positions were authorized by Congress. Thus, during the 1820s the Military Academy became one of the principal forces in the development of a distinctive professional ethos of disinterested public service, encouraging career army officers to view their posts as impersonal offices and their perquisites as privileges. Officers still disputed the perquisites and recognition due to specific ranks and offices, and they maintained a strong sense of their "rights" as officers and gentlemen, but they increasingly demonstrated an understanding that these rights were derived from the duties of their offices rather than inherent in the individuals holding them. This sense of impersonal public service, open to public observation and political inquiry, was essential for effectiveness and accountability in public administration and, beyond that, for responsibility to republican government and society.[1]

Allied with values of system, instrumental rationality, and order, specialization and standardization became hallmarks of the officer corps, enhancing its engineering, logistical, and administrative aptitude while encouraging officers to respond to the demands of civilian supremacy with laudable accountability. Responding accountably to the pressures of politics and public opinion, the officers of the national standing army became republicans as well as professionals—indeed, they united republicanism and professionalism in their distinctive ethos of duty and service. Together, effectiveness and accountability enabled the Military Academy, the officers it produced, and the army they led to secure the institutional and professional monopoly they sought, with far-reaching and ultimately positive consequences for the character of American expansion, foreign relations, and union. By the 1840s, socialization in the professional ethic of duty, honor, and country had fostered a nationally oriented commitment and institutional cohesion that made army officers more reliable public servants than ever before. As such, the regular army officer corps served as one of the few forces for cohesion and connection between center and periphery in the early- to mid-nineteenth-century American borderlands. These officers displayed leadership far beyond narrow military spheres and played crucial roles implementing federal policy far from the capital. Military Academy training in mathematics, science, and engineering imparted the skills necessary for exploration and infrastructure development, which was difficult for the inconsistently trained (because inconsistently funded) private sector to undertake. Whether acting as peacekeepers or conquerors, the national standing army of the 1820s, 1830s, and 1840s proved far more reliable than the unstable force of the 1790s, 1800s, and 1810s. Professional in both subordination and capability, the army supported the nation's territorial expansion, population movement, and economic development while maintaining national sovereignty and helping to avoid war with Britain through law enforcement and on-scene diplomacy during crises along the Canadian border.

This process began with the Military Academy's reform under the superintendency of Captain Sylvanus Thayer between 1817 and 1833. Before 1817, the Academy graduated few officers, and most of them left the army just as quickly as men commissioned directly from civilian life. Each of the first three superintendents—Colonel Jonathan Williams, Colonel Joseph G. Swift, and Captain Alden Partridge—resigned for selfish personal reasons in disputes over command, setting examples of impatience and insubordination rather than dutiful, disinterested commitment to national service. Arriving at West Point after fifteen years of inattention, confusion, and recurrent disorder there, Thayer believed that the primary purpose of American higher education was the inculcation of mental discipline—an instrumental rationality that was particularly essential for what Swift labeled "a corps of instructed administrative officers to serve as a nucleus upon which may be predicated any necessary force." As such, West Pointers formed the cadre for the expansible army established in the reduction in force of 1821.[2]

Thayer's intent is often summarized as the creation of a school for civil engineers, but this explanation puts the cart before the horse. Thayer realized that no curriculum could possibly do all the valuable things proposed by his predecessors and in the reports of the Boards of Visitors. He therefore chose to pursue depth rather than breadth, fearing that the latter would degenerate into superficiality, regardless of subject. Thayer shared his predecessors' desire to develop the Corps of Engineers as an elite intellectual cadre, and he sought to diffuse the knowledge of fortification design he had encountered at the French Ecole Polytechnique, but his first concern was to foster a military milieu of discipline, subordination, and habituation to duty. This, as much as any specific desire to teach engineering, was the reason for the emphasis on mathematics and the physical sciences, and it accounts for Thayer's initial resis-

Sylvanus Thayer, by Thomas Sully. (Courtesy West Point Museum)

tance to incorporating civil engineering into an already overstretched curriculum. (He regarded French and English grammar as essential to an understanding of the art of fortification and to communicating with others, and he was required by law to maintain the course in history, geography, and ethics, despite its somewhat cursory character.) Yet regardless of Thayer's intent or who actually initiated the shift, the introduction of civil engineering into the curriculum in 1824 was indispensable to the implementation of the General Survey Act of that year, which eventually demanded dozens of officers to survey railroad and canal routes.[3]

Military Academy training and education did three basic things to prepare graduates for all the various missions they were called on to perform. First, the lack of opportunities to learn tactics under fire meant that new lieutenants needed a school where they could learn the drill on which nineteenth-century tactics were based. Drill at West Point gave future officers firsthand experience of the limits and possibilities of contemporary tactics, from the school of the individual soldier up to the battalion and sometimes (albeit in miniature) the brigade, simulating exercises of several hundred to a thousand soldiers. This training was followed by smaller-scale drill in their companies and supplemented between the mid-1820s and mid-1830s by assignment to the regiment-sized schools of infantry and artillery at Jefferson Barracks (outside St. Louis) and Fortress Monroe (at Hampton Roads), providing a foundation for officers' military competence. Supplemented by the discipline of unit drill in garrison and the experience of small-unit leadership and tactical initiative in the Second Seminole War, this expertise gave American units superior combat power in the war with Mexico and won regular officers recognition as troop trainers, plus rapid promotion to command large volunteer forces, at the outset of the Civil War.[4]

Second, by 1820, engineer, ordnance, and artillery officers were learning far more of their trade at the Military Academy than they had ever learned in their units before the War of 1812. By 1825, graduates in these branches made up about two-fifths of the officer corps, and they planned and directed the construction of the extensive coastal fortification system—one of the principal elements of American defense against European attack throughout the nineteenth century (however irrelevant in retrospect). Military Academy graduates led surveys of U.S. international boundaries throughout this era, and under the General Survey Act, uniformed graduates conducted canal and railroad surveys and oversaw some construction until the act was repealed in 1838. Many more graduates continued to perform these activities after leaving the army into the 1850s and beyond, while the Jacksonians continued to employ serving officers on river and harbor improvement projects. West Point–trained ordnance officers designed and tested new weapons and munitions and oversaw the national arsenals and armories where the "American system of manufactures" (employing interchangeable parts) was first developed, building and maintaining weapons for the expansible army and eventually developing the rifles and artillery used in the Civil War. Such men urgently needed technical training of the sort unavailable at civilian colleges and universities but increasingly emphasized at the Military Academy after 1820.[5]

Third, technical training in mathematics, science, and engineering helped foster a mind-set of instrumental rationality, or what officers labeled a sense of "system and regularity." Some modern scholars have criticized this training (as the Radical Republicans did in the 1860s), which was far more rigid than a modern liberal education, arguing that the Military Academy produced inflexible thinkers who were unable to adjust to the changing battlefields of the Civil War. Yet all Civil War commanders—volunteers as well as regulars, amateurs as well as professionals—faced problems in exercising effective battlefield and operational command. These difficulties were due to the scale of the conflict (unprecedented in American experience), officers' lack of experience in employing new technologies (the rifled musket, the railroad, the telegraph) on such a scale, and their lack of opportunities to practice large-scale command in the small prewar army.

The limits or absence of postgraduate or staff schools notwithstanding, most students of the Jacksonian army—both modern scholars and contemporaries like commanding generals Jacob Brown and Winfield Scott—have identified the dispersion of troops into company-sized posts as the principal factor limiting training opportunities and command experience. This dispersion, which Brown and Scott tried to minimize by establishing central reserves and posts for brigade-level training, was dictated by the army's constabulary missions policing the borders and frontiers. Even if there had been staff schools, the army was far too small (given the limited threat from overseas) for officers to practice large-scale maneuvers of the sort they would conduct after 1861. Yet regular officers, mostly West Pointers, were generally more tactically and strategically effective than their volunteer counterparts (usually nongraduates), and civil society clearly accepted them as such, for Academy graduates eventually held virtually all of the operational and strategic—army- and theater-level—commands on both sides in the Civil War, as well as most of the larger unit commands (over corps and divisions). The Radical Republican critique ultimately proceeded from political concerns about the West Pointers' commitment to total war rather than defects in their military competence per se, and as the war went on, Academy graduates such as Ulysses S. Grant and Henry W. Halleck were able to replace amateur generals with West Point–trained ones in most senior commands.[6]

The habits of mental discipline and accountability that became the heart of the Military Academy's socialization process under Thayer proved invaluable, and probably indispensable, to administering and supplying the nation's largest, most centralized, yet most specialized and farthest flung full-time organization. That army was the strongest and most autonomous federal presence on the nation's frontiers, the only willing and capable force available to restrain private incursions into neighboring countries and to keep some degree of peace between whites and Indians. As such, West Point ultimately proved to be one of the most—and perhaps one of the few—successful efforts in the early republic at creating a new, nationally oriented social body, a triumph of the nationalist visions and "comprehensive programs" that so often came under fire during the years between the Revolution and the Civil War and have so often been neglected by historians.

Modern indictments of Military Academy training and army staff work take the twentieth century as a baseline, a less historical approach than using the War of 1812 (the army's baseline at the time). From that perspective, army logistics and administration must be recognized as among the most advanced and effective in pre- and early industrial America. Academy training instilled the numeracy, detail orientation, mental discipline, and precision necessary for surveying, building, and accounting. Buttressed by endless drill and inspections, the mathematical rationality instilled at West Point encouraged timeliness and a habituation to and integrity in reporting—the regularity and, more broadly, the accountability by which officers often judged one another and were judged by Congress. Though limited in abstraction and rarely very critical, this outlook encouraged officers to think about how their actions in one sphere influenced actions and consequences in others. However primitive, this sense of perspective helped officers to think more systematically—and systemically—than most civilians, to recognize the interactions involved in complex systems and the interdependence of modern society.[7]

These qualities were an essential starting point not only for the army's technical branches but for the junior officers now tasked with supply duties, which had been handled very inefficiently by civilian contractors before the establishment of a permanent staff structure within the army after the War of 1812. The inadequacy of American logistical support is a common theme in histories of the war with Mexico, an interpretation based largely on Lieutenant D. H. Hill's venomous letters to the *Southern Quarterly Review*. Examining the operations of the Quartermaster Department throughout the war tells a different story of comparative and in fact decisive effectiveness amid very difficult circumstances. Even the most superficial comparison with the experience of the War of 1812—when the United States was unable to mount an effective offensive to Montreal, much less Quebec—shows a profound improvement in army supply.

This transformation was certainly due in great part to steam and naval power—the ability to move supplies by rail and sea to New Orleans and by sea to Corpus Christi, the mouth of the Rio Grande, and Veracruz. Yet the right supplies still had to be transported in sufficient quantities overland by animal power to the arid Mexican interior—a problem not unlike that encountered in the wilderness of upstate New York and Ohio in 1812—or purchased locally by the West Point–educated commissary officers, who were now called on to supply regiments, brigades, and divisions on the move rather than static posts of a couple hundred men—their usual experience before the war. Despite the inevitable difficulties of adapting to the new scale of operations, army logisticians had developed far greater capability through experience (generally lacking among the newly commissioned staff officers of 1812); the creation of uniform standards, regulations, and procedures; and a professional culture and subculture of affinity for and habituation to these specialized duties. It is impossible to imagine the army of 1812–1815 sending hundreds of men thousands of miles across the plains, mountains, and desert to Santa Fe, Chihuahua, California, and Oregon, as it did in 1846 and 1847. The logistical capability developed during the 1820s and 1830s and West Pointers' intolerance of depredations against the local populace were prerequisites for Winfield Scott's strategy of conciliating the Mexican people, inhibiting popular insurgency, and easing the peace process once he won a military victory against the armed forces of the Mexican government.[8]

The junior officer corps of the Jacksonian era was tempered in the forge of Thayer's Military Academy, a testing ground where respectability, authority, and honor were claimed on the basis of socialization, formal education, and habituation to accountability rather than military skill, gallantry, or experience on the field of battle.[9] This corps proved more enduring than that which had fought the War of 1812. The remaining field-grade and general commanders enhanced institutional continuity by leading the army's peacetime rationalization, while junior officers commissioned from West Point implemented new standard operating procedures that enhanced administrative capability and fiscal accountability and led their companies to victories in Florida and Mexico. The army benefited professionally from senior leaders' wartime experience and from the example of battlefield leadership and courage they set for their young subordinates. This continuity of effort and example, along with the institutional stability and accountability it encouraged, distinguished the army as an organization and officership as a profession from most of their civilian counterparts in the early United States. Though the armywide officer evaluation process was not repeated until after the Civil War, the 1821 officer evaluations provided the basis for a more socially and culturally aware, yet more politically and sectionally neutral, standard of officership. This vision, combined with the new socialization experience at West Point, was a harbinger of the growing institutionalization—meaning both insulation and interdependence—of army, officers, government, and society, a functional specialization and operational autonomy in the division of labor without social isolation or political alienation.

The army's institutional stabilization was a complex process, the product of many interrelated dynamics. These included declining international ten-

Winfield Scott as he imagined himself, engraving after Amos Alonzo Chappel. (Courtesy Library of Congress, LC-USZ62-57637)

sions and the 1821 reduction in force, the sorting out of civil and military career paths and the stable force structure that followed, the standardized criteria for initial officer accession, plus the professional socialization institutionalized in the Military Academy. With so many forces at work, it is difficult to isolate any single causally primal factor. However, the internal drive—the agency of experienced senior and field-grade officers who were veterans of a generation of institutional instability, unpredictability, and insecurity, as well as international instability, insecurity, and war—proved crucial. When the influence of external structures and dynamics reached a certain balance with the influence of military values and agency, contingencies on both sides came together to foster institutional and professional reform. Reform was achieved in both force structure (while under populist assault from Old Republicans, radicals, and Jacksonians) and ethos—values, ideas, and attitudes. The result was a more professional officer corps, one that was more expert, more committed and cohesive, and above all, more accountable to the nation's constitutional civilian authorities.

The Jacksonian assault would have been stronger and more convincing if army administration were still as poor as it had been before and during the War of 1812. The principal reasons for its new efficiency were the managerial reforms—the creation of armywide general regulations and specialized systems for logistical accountability—initiated by young but veteran senior officers like Winfield Scott and Quartermaster General Thomas Sidney Jesup, both in their late twenties at the end of the war. Given the sluggishness of promotion (almost universally by seniority), the lack of any system of mandatory retirement, and the army's small size, no West Point graduate attained general officer rank before 1860. (Promotion by seniority, which we tend to view as an impediment to a merit-based system, was not widely questioned by contemporaries: the meaning of *merit* was subjective and open to politicization, whereas *seniority* was clear, impartial, and predictable.) Yet reform requires execution as well as command, and non–West Pointers like Scott and Jesup applauded the ability of Military Academy graduates to implement those reforms through timely, accurate reporting to their superiors and to Congress. Accountability demands the ability to count, and few Americans were better at this than West Point graduates. Most officers spent substantially more time filling out forms than drilling troops: with the possible exception of the navy, the army was by far the largest, farthest flung, most internally articulated, and most expensive full-time organization in the United States before 1877. It required more constant logistical maintenance and disbursed more funds than any other organization in the country, public or private. It intermittently launched active operations to project power on a greater scale than any other organization in the continental United States. The fur companies were minuscule in comparison, and their employees supplied themselves with most necessities. Post office workers fed themselves, and the vast majority were part-time, often short-term employees because of the partisan nature of their appointments. Following the postrevolutionary disestablishment, similar economic dynamics applied in most churches, particularly evangelical ones.

The army required greater administrative rationality and managerial capability than any other organization in the nation, and education and socialization at West Point were the primary means of consciously developing this aptitude among officers. Indeed, historians of American accounting have traced the origins of an accounting mind-set to the Military Academy of this era, and President Jackson's seventh annual message to Congress suggests his agreement: the varied duties discharged by army officers "embrace very heavy expenditures of public money and require fidelity, science, and business habits in their execution. . . . That this object has been in a great measure attained by the Military Academy is shown by the . . . prompt accountability which has generally followed the necessary advances."[10]

Jacksonian criticism did not lead to the catastrophic consequences—wholesale reduction, the Academy's disbandment, or West Pointers' replacement by former enlisted men or Democratic partisans from civilian life—anticipated by some officers or implied by some scholars, given the populist, anti-institutional rhetoric so common among Jacksonian politicians. Although Thayer resigned as superintendent in 1833, he continued to serve as a fortification engineer and an important adviser to future superintendents. After several years of relative laxity (cadets still slept on mattresses on the floor), Jackson reasserted disciplinary standards and stopped intervening in cadet dismissals. The disappearance of the infantry and artillery schools in the early 1830s was due to operational needs, the confluence of the Black Hawk War, the Nullification Crisis, Indian and squatter removal, and ultimately the Second Seminole War, rather than Democratic criticism.

The new officer corps proved more cohesive and enduring than ever before. This was not because of compression in its missions or skill sets. Indeed, the army's younger intellectual leaders, such as Dennis Hart Mahan and Henry Halleck, tended to encourage a damaging dichotomy between preparation for conventional war and the armed diplomacy that most officers actually engaged in on the borders and frontiers. Like some officers in the late twentieth century, they privileged conventional warfare as more difficult, more essential, and more glamorous than peacekeeping or coercive diplomacy. Yet, though the institutional army did little to develop standards, doctrine, or training for constabulary missions or even for Indian fighting, the army's senior leaders—

the general officers, regimental commanders, and staff bureau chiefs—proved more flexible and adaptable than some of their ambitious subordinates, accepting a dual role consisting of immediate national service as a constabulary as well as preparation for international war. The irony is that Halleck and Mahan are better known today, especially to army officers seeking antecedents for the large-scale conventional warfare of the Civil War and the twentieth century, than are any of the army's commanders except for Zachary Taylor (commonly derided as a military simpleton) and Winfield Scott (known primarily for his conventional campaign in Mexico).

The growth of interest-group—or, per historians, distributive—politics was at the core of the decentralizing movements of the Jacksonian era. This liberalism aggravated the dilemmas posed by federalism, demonstrating the negative as well as positive sides to Madison's vision in *Federalist Number 10*. All major social and economic formations represented in American politics were supposed to gain something and could balance their objectives and gains against one another; this might temporarily obscure or ameliorate sectional and sectoral friction, but at a risk to national power and cohesion in Indian and international relations. Nevertheless, preparing for conventional international warfare provided officers with a culturally glamorous sense of mission and a distinctive raison d'être. This bolstered a firmer professional identity and a claim to a superior expertise that would ultimately enable long-serving regular officers to secure an effective monopoly on higher-level (operational, theater, and strategic) commands in the Seminole, Mexican-American, and Civil Wars. Each of the army's several distinct missions provided political utility to some element among politically powerful constituencies, which was crucial to warding off the Jacksonian assault on the army's legitimacy. These constituencies included southern and western whites, yeomen as well as planters; although they were otherwise Jacksonian partisans and antagonists to institutions, they preferred that the standing army do the fighting and dying necessary to seize the Native American lands they desired.[11] Regardless of their constituents' interests or constitutional issues, few congressmen who were not from frontier areas believed that the majority of citizens and taxpayers, living far from the frontiers, would be willing to surrender effective national sovereignty—control over war and peace—to a small minority of frontiersmen who were often typecast as reckless, greedy ruffians. Despite their salience in contemporary popular culture, neither Congress nor the executive accepted impetuous frontiersmen as representatives of American republicanism or national sovereignty.[12]

This choice, so contrary to facile assumptions about the omnipotence of populism and popular sovereignty in mid-nineteenth-century America, may have been due to distinctions between classical liberalism and classical republicanism, between democracy by whites and democracy for whites, between domestic and interethnic power and coercion. Classical liberal individualism, ultimately even more decentralizing and antistatist than republicanism, came to share the ideological spotlight with American democracy during the first half of the nineteenth century. The "Market Revolution" of that era was (for white men) primarily libertarian and individualist rather than republican, in the sense of politics addressing or expressing the public affairs of a relatively homogeneous and generally united community, or democratic, in a more egalitarian sense that might have promoted further planning and regulation by the state. Yet libertarian individualism did not effectively address national security dilemmas or the means, processes, and outcomes of territorial expansion; nor, apart from the mass popular mobilization for civil war, did populist democracy. Decentralizing liberalism and racialized democracy presented reasonably effective (though often brutally one-sided) answers to domestic disorder, but filibusters, vigilantes, and volunteers proved inadequate to repress significant Indian resistance, and citizen-soldiers required central direction and coordination, conducted largely by officers of the national standing army, to achieve effective power projection during the war with Mexico and the Civil War.

Of the principal ideologies in early American politics—republicanism, liberalism, and democracy—republicanism was most overtly concerned with power, which republicans defined politically rather than economically. It was especially concerned with concentrated power, which republicans identified most directly with the central government and most specifically in the military, that supreme tool of coercion. Politics is fundamentally about power, and the nation-state has been the ultimate power center in modern and early modern politics—however much academics, mazed by visions of decentralization rooted in the egalitarianism of social history, may deplore it. For most historians, early American republicanism has meant an apparently unyielding antagonism to standing armies and aristocratic military placemen, yet the United States maintained a standing military force that was increasingly commanded by career professionals, under the control of the central government, without any real pause from 1775 forward. The fear of concentrated power was a core component of classical republicanism, but republicanism was also an ideology of community and public duty, of communal virtue and martial *virtú*, of individual integrity, faith, and honor. Republican independence and community traditionally meant an antipartisanship congenial to national military officers, though civilian advocates of partisanship began to turn this argument around during the 1820s. Thus, despite its pervasiveness, the republican reaction against concentrations of power took different forms in different situations, particularly when supplemented and contested by Jacksonian liberalism, partisanship, and desire for territorial expansion. Revolutionary republicans may have seen executive military power as the most extreme danger to liberty, but under the Constitution, the imperatives of foreign relations and national security encouraged greater cohesion among civil and military, executive and legislative nation-state actors, imposing a filter between civil officials and legislators and their usual sensitivity to public opinion.[13]

Republican fears of standing armies were based in large part on their subservience to government, but for those serving in government, this subordination was a virtue. Republican independence and social gentility were expected of officers; they were men of honor and integrity who received sufficient compensation to make additional part-time labor unnecessary. But neither the nation nor the state sought military commanders or military forces that were independent of its control. Indeed, a dependent standing army beholden to the nation-state perfectly suited civilian executive branch officials, whatever their party or ideological perspective. They needed a reliable force to back up the thinly spread, often locally oriented federal civil officials in the enforcement of national law and sovereignty and the implementation of national policy along the frontiers. For sixty years, every president, of every party, realized this and acted accordingly. Many historians have observed that, as presidents, Jefferson and Jackson were comfortable with institutions and powers they had previously decried, and the standing army proved no exception. Although Jefferson reduced the army and navy and cut their logistical staffs to the bone, neither he nor Jackson spoke seriously of replacing national standing military forces with state militias or short-term volunteer forces. Both accepted the basic principle that war is a complex affair that requires specialized expertise—the foundation stone of military professionalism.

Whigs and National Republicans, members of the commercial middle classes, and advocates of functional specialization and orderly institutional development could appreciate the army as an embodiment of their values while they enjoyed its concrete economic contributions. These included clearing rivers and harbors of obstacles, exploring or surveying transportation routes, and providing markets for food and materials for the construction of coastal fortifications. Such undertakings were certainly much less liable to financial failure in the depression of the late 1830s than private ventures or those funded by state bonds. Indeed, these goods were probably proportionally more beneficial to southern and western constituencies than to northern ones, yet populist politicians concentrated in these regions voted to end the army's role in planning and constructing internal improvements in 1838. (No one can accuse Jacksonian politicians of a sophisticated understanding of economic development. Fortunately, they had much less impact on the army than on the financial system and the national economy.[14])

The reforms begun between 1815 and 1817 as a result of international tension and the nationalist moment permitted a new departure in officer socialization, bolstering and extending values of specialization and centralization that had long competed with officers' sectional and sectoral interests and values during the Federalist and Jeffersonian eras. The National Republican nation-state sponsored and indeed promoted the emerging military professionalism and a new civil-military dynamic. This dynamic involved a limited insulation of standing national military forces from full or direct control by populist egalitarianism, despite continued subordination to representative civilian control—an affinity, allegiance, and control more national than ever before. The return of populist decentralization in the Jacksonian movement, whether in the form of antimonopolist, antistatist egalitarianism or sectionalist states' rights, did not reverse this transformation. Indeed, part of the impetus for this enhancement of the army's professional autonomy was the Jacksonians' own need for some force to moderate or restrain the often entropic impact of white supremacist democracy, if only as a humanitarian cover to protect the reputations of politicians and the nation in the court of public and international opinion.

Another source of public acceptance was the Jacksonians' desire for someone else to do their dirty work. Federal pay in hard currency drew willing participants for only short periods in actual time of war. But the critical reason the army gained and maintained its new autonomy from partisan control was the professional socialization and commitment developed among senior and field-grade officers during the 1810s and sustained among newly minted junior officers throughout the 1820s—a commitment instilled in each sectionally diverse cohort of aspiring officers at the national Military Academy. The 1820s brought a pause in territorial expansion, a breathing space in the international tensions that expansion usually aggravated. An entire generation's worth of officers were socialized in the values and practice of nationalism, stability, hierarchy, and order; they were schooled in professional independence, (relative) objectivity, and integrity while performing their duty to their country. These men had to learn patience, responsibility, self-restraint, and accountability with regard to expenditures, personal behavior (facing periodic waves of command pressure against drunkenness and the mistreatment of enlisted men), and the growing body of standardized regulations that governed ever-greater dimensions of their duties and lives.

Fort Taylor in the Gulf of Mexico, part of the system of coastal fortifications, by army officer Seth Eastman. (Courtesy Army Art Collection)

Between the mid-1820s and the mid-1830s, generals, field-grade commanders, and their West Point–educated subordinates continually stood against the entropic demands of Jacksonian individualism, racist populism, and state sovereignty in conflicts over squatter and Indian removal and nullification. In later variations along the Canadian border between 1838 and 1841, in the Texas borderlands, and in the Dorr War between citizen factions in Rhode Island, they consistently acted to maintain national sovereignty and authority against decentralizing parochial interests. They often did so at the risk of former political ties: in 1836 Jackson clashed with three of his four active theater commanders—Duncan Clinch in Florida, John Wool in the Georgia Cherokee country, and Edmund Gaines in Texas—all former protégés or Democratic partisans. Indeed, the Whig Winfield Scott, who was repressing the Creeks in Alabama, was the only theater commander that Jackson or his War Department did not reprimand or censure that year, although Thomas Jesup (a Democrat and Scott's subordinate in Alabama) publicly disparaged Scott's sluggish performance. Jacksonian civilian officials at every level were quick to blame the deep-running tensions of federalism on the military commanders sent to mediate and ameliorate them. Yet national military officers remained the most consistent and certainly the most powerful champions of nationalist values and national cohesion on the frontiers, which were otherwise dominated by the centrifuge of racialized democracy. After Jackson left office, they were sustained by Whig and Democratic administrations alike.

THE LIMITED IMPACT OF CULTURAL, TECHNOLOGICAL, AND MILITARY CHANGE

Specific institutional, political, social, and international changes—largely deliberate policies (U.S. or foreign) or their second- and third-order effects—influenced the army's development far more than general technological or cultural changes or specifically military technical ones. The great technological inventions of the era—the railroad and the telegraph, the standard-bearers of transformations that American historians have labeled the Transportation and Communications Revolutions—had perhaps the least direct impact. The telegraph did not appear until 1844, near the end of the period explored in this book, and its military significance would not become apparent until the Crimean War. Although officers frequently applauded the growing speed of transportation and communications and the quickening tempo of life, they took the utility of the railroad for granted, leaving little specific comment on its military value. The speed of steamships and railroads did spur debate over the value of the coastal fortification program begun in 1816, but the Corps of Engineers was able to ward off critics until the Civil War. The railroad's greatest effect was in politics and civil-military relations, providing the army with a constituency because of its efforts supporting private transportation projects under the General Survey Act of 1824; however, these efforts gradually roused populist antagonism against the assistance its officers extended to particular companies, trade routes, and localities.[15]

The growth of mass media was potentially much more influential. As sociologist Michael Mann points out, under the Constitution, federal government "offices were intended as a full-fledged bureaucracy [in the positive, ideal-typical Weberian sense, emphasizing accountability and efficiency through specialization], the only one in the world for at least another fifty years." Although specialization facilitated insulation, American representative democracy usually meant more openness to public observation and inquiry than in European bureaucracies. Indeed, as political scientist Samuel Finer observes, the publicity of the American political system, the presence of active legislative oversight accountable to the voters, "*forces* the military not only to speak out but to establish relationships with political forces," not unlike civilian interest groups. Yet the third significant technological innovation of the Jacksonian era, the penny press (made possible by more efficient printing presses), had remarkably little effect on the army's missions, structure, or operations prior to the Civil War. It extended the reach of the news, increased the frequency of its publication, and accelerated the news cycle, intensifying the publicity of American political life, but its impact depended primarily on the content of the news itself and hence on developments in other spheres of human endeavor. We cannot understand the army's acceptance by civilian society, and hence its personnel monopoly and operational autonomy, without recognizing and assessing the threats to its reputation for accountability, which often originated within its own ranks. Dysfunctional military behaviors such as drunkenness, sexual liaisons with Indian women, and dueling injured that reputation, threatening officers' claims to disinterested virtue and undermining their assertions of gentility and social superiority over civilian frontiersmen. Yet these vices were more of a problem for Whiggish and proto-Victorian reformers, who found the army appealing as an agent and example of rationality and order, than for Jacksonians and frontiersmen, who ardently acclaimed the priority of white male independence, with its characteristic excesses of alcoholism and violence.[16]

Frontiersmen sometimes accused military officers of conflicts of interest and misuse of official resources or information, particularly through insider access to public lands, whether as surveyors or because of their control over land reserved for military use around forts. But these critiques seem to have been based more on Jacksonian perception and rhetoric, shaped by the individualist and populist antiauthoritarianism and antimonopoly beliefs so prominent in Jacksonian ideology, than reality. Army officers, like many other Americans, took advantage of information they gained in the course of their duties, usually related to resources and land quality. They may well have benefited from their acquaintance with land office agents, although the value of those relationships probably depended on who had appointed the agents, many of whom were locally prominent patronage appointees who were more sympathetic to settlers and frontier businessmen than to national military officers. Although the land agents may have seen army officers as valuable allies, as social and political connections to Washington and continued patronage, the pattern is one of an intermingled or aspiring elite that used these connections to improve their income and status. Individual officers undoubtedly profited from inside information, contrary to their professional service ethic, but they did so as individuals (sometimes in collusion with civilians), not as a distinct body or interest group.[17]

The ire of frontiersmen and Jacksonians was directed largely at military elitism and authoritarianism or at the army's disdain for citizen-soldiers and its lack of support for frontier expansionism—two additional expressions of elitism. Populist critics sometimes reproached officers for hypocrisy, but they were much more concerned about censuring antidemocratic military attitudes than about the immoral behaviors that went hand in hand with racism and patriarchy. The behavior of soldiers, particularly professionals, had always been disparaged, and the penny press may have made these ills more visible, but the press was not yet sufficiently national in scope and organization that incidents on military posts became national scandals. Any examination of appointments and contracting in any department of the Jackson administration would show far more egregious patterns of venality. By using their knowledge for speculative purposes, officers partook of the individualism of Jacksonian America. While asserting their independence as gentlemen in that Jacksonian milieu on frontiers far from their families, they did not always live up to their claims of disinterested republican virtue. But no major constituency or public actor found the army objectionable across the board: Jacksonians forgave individual vices, of which they themselves were often guilty, and they ultimately forgave even military authoritarianism because the army served their expansionist goals. Whigs forgave individual vices because they recognized the army as a significant force for their values of stability, hierarchy, and cohesion along the frontiers.[18]

Operationally, the location of constabulary efforts enhanced military commanders' insulation from media influence. Most operations in response to incidents or crises occurred so far from media centers that communications remained sluggish, and the press had little impact on the operational decision cycle of frontier peace enforcement and mediation. In more drawn-out peacekeeping and Indian or squatter removal operations, the tempo of policy execution was conditioned by the gradual character of conciliation and diplomacy. This gradualism often spurred denunciation by Democratic and frontier newspapers that were dissatisfied with the army's willingness to coerce whites and accommodate Indians, but military commanders normally ignored such disparagement and were able to do so without being called to account. There is very little evidence from any of the western frontiers or from the Canadian and Texan borders that officers took media condemnation into account in creating, revising, or executing plans—a significant indication of the army's growing operational autonomy.[19] As an extreme example, William Worth withdrew federal military protection from the St. Lawrence border with Canada in 1839, despite the censure that might bring (an incident explored in volume 2). Army officers also recommended deploying federal military forces during the Dorr

War in Rhode Island, near the very center of the emerging national media, although that counsel was given within the executive branch and remained undisclosed until a later congressional inquiry.[20]

Apart from John Wool's tenure overseeing the Cherokee country in 1836 (discussed in volume 2), it does not seem likely that media outcry led civilian executive branch officials to put significantly greater pressure on military commanders than they otherwise would have done. Yet Wool and his subordinates gave back as good as they got, replying or posting correspondence in local newspapers themselves. Though doing so led to further censure from the War Department and President Jackson, it reminds us that the press was as multifaceted as Jacksonian politics: Whiggish newspapers like the *National Intelligencer* provided outlets for military officers (usually writing anonymously) and their civilian supporters, who were usually politicians or politically connected gentlemen. Indeed, Wool used the publicity of the U.S. government to turn the tables on his detractors by demanding a court of inquiry, at which his accusers failed to appear, and was vindicated by friendly fellow officers, including his own chief of staff and his successor in the Cherokee command. Wool's assertions of national sovereignty over Indian affairs through the Constitution's treaty power were ignored by the Van Buren administration, but they were published by Congress, potentially for all to see.[21]

If newspapers and party politics constrained the operational autonomy of military commanders, Wool did not show it. He acted just as objectively and independently of political pressure, just as much in accordance with his professional sense of personal, institutional, and national duty, on the Canadian border in 1838, less than a year after his court of inquiry. But this time he responded to newspaper criticism in private correspondence, turning to his array of genteel social and elite political connections to explain his actions and express his frustration. Though still a Democrat, Wool's distancing from Jackson probably helped his promotion to brigadier general vice Winfield Scott under a new Whig administration in 1841, despite claims of greater service and seniority from a number of regimental commanders. (The seniority principle did not determine general officer promotions, although politicians accepted its corollary—experience—to exclude citizen-soldiers from direct entry to field and general officer ranks during peacetime.) Admittedly, the principal claimants were older men in poor health, such as Henry Atkinson, while Zachary Taylor, a quiet Whig, was junior to Wool and under a cloud as a result of his disparagement of the Missouri volunteers under his command at the Battle of Lake Okeechobee. Wool went on to command one of the five principal campaigns in the war with Mexico. Commanding in San Francisco and the Pacific Northwest during the mid-1850s, Wool was again censured by a Democratic administration pandering to local sentiment in favor of illegal enterprises; he again accepted the censure and continued to serve, although he resumed his public disputation in newspapers. Indeed, Wool was the only officer of his generation to serve actively in the Civil War, commanding the capture of Norfolk in 1862 and overseeing the Middle Department, including Maryland and Pennsylvania, before his retirement in 1863. Battling nearly every Democratic president did not hurt Wool's military career, though it surely damaged his political prospects, if he ever held any aspirations in that direction.[22]

Nor did publicity ever deter Edmund Gaines from performing his duty as he saw it. Instead, the zealous brigadier took advantage of the new media, attending the "southern commercial convention" in Nashville in 1845 and going on tour with his second wife, a famous advocate for international peace, to advance his views on railroads, steam gunboats, and the coastal fortification program supervised by the Corps of Engineers. Apart from Gaines, commanders on the frontier actually became *more* skeptical of white claims about Indian threats as newspapers multiplied the rumors that seemed to echo across the frontier every time a cow was stolen or a couple of Indians from different tribes met. Newspaper calumnies did not deter federal military officers from criticizing state volunteers and militia throughout the course of the Second Seminole War, and Philip St. George Cooke weathered media censure after he forcibly disarmed Texan marauders operating in U.S. territory along the Santa Fe Trail in 1843. When the State Department responded to Texan protests by seeking an explanation of Cooke's actions, he was promptly supported and shielded by Gaines, Stephen W. Kearny, and other officers in his chain of command (an incident explored in volume 2).

Army officers felt capable of resisting media pressure because the army had developed substantial institutional insulation and operational autonomy. Nevertheless, media disparagement undoubtedly contributed to officers' sense of irritation and disenchantment with civilian politics. Yet they continued to read partisan newspapers, including Democratic ones among officers with Democratic affinities (about half of those whose preferences we know). Federal military officers were hardly isolated, either physically or mentally, from civil society, and they had enough defenders there that terms like *alienated* distort their relationship with the media, politicians, and civil society as a whole. If we want one word to characterize the form of this civil-military relationship, it should be *insulated*; if we want one word to encapsulate the consequences in the field, it should be *autonomy*; if we want one word to sum up the outcome for American civil-military relations, it should be *accountablility*, resulting from the combination of professional socialization and civilian oversight.

Soldiers drill at the artillery school, 1827, by H. Charles
McBarron. (Courtesy Army Art Collection)

Military technological changes were no more significant. Nineteenth-
century European armies faced a continual and pervasive conflict between
ideals and epistemologies of "character," commonly tied to elite social status,
political influence, and merit demonstrated through experience in the field or
at school. Despite the start of the Industrial Revolution, applied military technology remained essentially unchanged between the end of the Napoleonic
Wars and the onset of the Crimean conflict. Political reliability was a more
urgent consideration than specific military expertise in the era of Chartism,

aristocratic reaction, and the July Days, to say nothing of 1848. The otherwise intangible ideal of character seemed to be an eminently practical qualification, encompassing both the experience or heritage of command shared by gentlemen and an assumed correlate (if not source) of courage and selflessness. This conflict, and its usual resolution in favor of social ascription, permeated questions of initial selection, promotion, and access to privileged positions and opportunities of all sorts: elite regiments, military schools, and branches of service (usually the cavalry); furloughs, detached service, and staff posts; choice operational commands or the chance to avoid service on distant or uncomfortable stations.

The beginnings of the Industrial Revolution did not fundamentally alter American warfare or military institutions. The U.S. Army was one of the international leaders in the development of firearms—both cannon and shoulder arms, including breech-loading rifles—as early as the 1810s. Yet the expense and unreliability of these early models were too great to permit their general adoption, and issues related to logistics and rate of fire led Winfield Scott to limit the use of Model 1841 percussion cap and rifled muskets during the war with Mexico.[23] The artillery systems developed by a series of ordnance boards during the 1830s and 1840s had some impact on the efficiency of American artillery in that war. However, their impact was much less than that of the new horse artillery doctrine—effectively the first combined-arms doctrine in U.S. history—and the thorough training instilled by experienced junior officers in the horse artillery batteries. Indeed, U.S. artillery regiments normally drilled and fought as infantry and were organized in companies rather than batteries through the Mexican-American War. The most significant weapons system innovation in this era, the percussion cap introduced to American service in 1841, did not transform tactics or the dynamics of battle.[24]

Changes in the form and character of American warfare were incremental at most. No new threat, whether technological or international, called for dramatic innovations. Indeed, the central features of Napoleonic warfare—its greater scale, scope, and speed—had little relevance and little actual impact in the United States prior to the Civil War. The principal maneuver forces of the War of 1812 (like the American Left and Right Divisions along the Canadian border) were no larger than Napoleonic divisions or brigades—North American field "armies" were one-fifteenth the size of those at Austerlitz, Jena, and Friedland between 1805 and 1807 or one-thirtieth the size of those at Wagram, Borodino, and Dresden between 1809 and 1813. None of the strategic or operational developments that made Napoleonic-era warfare revolutionary in military history existed in North America before the Civil War. There was no *leveé en masse*, no conscription, no corps system, no *battalion carré* (the movement of Napoleon's corps on separate roads for mutual support and operational maneuver distributed along multiple axes). Indeed, the campaigns of Simon Bolivar and the wars of Latin American independence, virtually unknown to American military historians, probably provide more significant examples of military innovation and expertise than those of the War of 1812.

Heirs to a tradition that privileged private property, American commanders rejected French Revolutionary and Napoleonic-style foraging (theft from the civilian populace) as a standard means of food supply. Supplies in Mexico were purchased locally or drawn by wagon train from depots along the coast. This was what made Winfield Scott's move to Mexico City so daring—not just that he left no line of communications, except posts at Puebla and Jalapa to help guard wagon trains from the coast, but that his army did not subsist by foraging. Indeed, it actually came close to running out of rations when supplies on its wagon trains were nearly exhausted during the maneuvering around Mexico City. This shortage was a significant factor in Scott's decision to pursue a truce—an operational as well as a political pause—after seizing Contreras and Churubusco. Facing equally limited opponents, lacking the numbers to form multiple corps in a single theater of operations, and absent the will (or, given their scale, the need) to forage for supplies, U.S. armies did not conduct "distributed operations"—the essence of Napoleonic warfare and the nineteenth-century operational art—until the Civil War.[25]

In sum, prior to 1861 (or really 1862), American battles and campaigns looked much like those of the Revolution: armies of no more than 10,000 soldiers (usually far less) moving together (or sequentially down a single road) as a unit, organized tactically for battle rather than operationally to set up and exploit victory in battle. When they fought, they did so almost entirely as infantry, with a few skirmishers, or in loose linear formations akin to European skirmish deployments if they found themselves in difficult terrain. Artillery, which was crucial in many battles of the war with Mexico, was limited to a few batteries armed with cannon, while four-fifths or more of each artillery regiment served as infantry. Cavalry was virtually nonexistent either because terrain forced it to dismount (as was often the case with the Second Dragoons in Florida) or because battle commanders had little idea how to use it effectively. This was true even of Winfield Scott, the army's foremost tactician, who was certainly familiar with European cavalry employment yet failed to use it effectively in most of his battles en route to Mexico City. Nor was the cavalry's mounted performance in battle, at Resaca de la Palma in Texas and San Pascual in California, particularly competent. (In fairness, the American cavalry was greatly outnumbered.) The horse artillery of the Mexican-

American War was the only arm of the service that thought in anything approximating combined-arms terms: the infantry did what it did and hoped for artillery support; the cavalry acted almost entirely independently, when it acted at all. American campaigns looked much like those of pre-Napoleonic warfare: apart from a few supporting detachments, one army advanced on one objective, fighting whatever enemy forces stood in the way—a "strategy of a single point" rather than distributed maneuver. As brilliant as Scott's tactical execution (his reconnaissances, turning movements, and envelopments) or his temporary willingness to cut loose from his supply lines may have been, his advance from Veracruz to Mexico City closely fits this description.[26]

Imperial responsibilities demanded a form of expertise, or skill sets, distinct from that of conventional war fighting. This expertise was in diplomacy, logistics, and small-unit or at least small-scale tactics, rather than the maneuver of large forces. The standard campaign or operation went like this: military officers, often the only federal (or European) officials on the scene, attempted to prevent crisis through diplomacy. (We can call this the strategic stage.) If this failed, the next skill in demand was logistics (moving to the operational stage): the ability to project power into areas with limited resources and transportation networks, often in difficult terrain. In both stages, the premium was on adaptability. Finally, if the successful deployment of force failed to compel submission through show (displaying the flag, graduated shows of force), the operation proceeded to tactical employment: perhaps battle (albeit often on the scale of skirmishes), but more often the destruction of dwelling places, crops and food supplies, and other resources, using logistics as tactics.

Regular army officers embraced technological change but resisted the general cultural shift from Enlightenment rationalism to emotive romanticism, whether in its sentimental, populist, racist, or evangelical religious form. Officers often expressed themselves sentimentally, but their values and actions were not driven by the attitudes or tropes of sentimentalism. Some were evangelical Christians, but most were moderate Episcopalians or Presbyterians or remained outside of or indifferent to denominational religion. (There were probably substantially more Catholics, of a moderate, socially genteel sort, than there were evangelicals.) Though they probably dreamed of—but rarely recorded their longings for—individual Byronic heroism and subscribed to the ideal of individual genius, their epistemology was experiential and rooted in professional education as much as or more than any other occupational group in the nation: they knew they could not rely on genius for everyday administration. Their experiences with the passionate individualism, populism, and anti-institutionalism of the Jacksonians, particularly on the frontier, pushed them toward Whiggish elitism and institutionalism and the defense of moderation, order, and stability. The most significant modification in the army officers' relationship with their parent culture was the shift from an essentially eighteenth-century gentility to a proto-Victorian "respectability" in social self-description. Yet the significance of this mutation lay primarily in the continuities it maintained and extended—the search for hierarchical order and the expression and reality of hierarchical stratification.[27]

Using historian Gordon Wood's terms, early national, Jacksonian, and pre–Civil War army officers fit the transitional "republican" mold of the late eighteenth century much better than the "democratic" (egalitarian) mold of the era they lived in. Lest that characterization prove confusing, given the widely varied meanings scholars assign to republicanism, we can more specifically categorize career army officers and the Military Academy as participants in what historian Henry May labels the "Didactic Enlightenment": an attitude skeptical of human perfectibility that was most influential in the form of Scottish Common Sense philosophy. May identifies the Didactic Enlightenment as a blend of the "Moderate Enlightenment"—that is, "the defense of balance and order in all things"—and moderate Calvinism, neither antiscientific nor cynical toward religion. This was very much the sort of perspective generally held by army officers. The qualities of discipline and restraint of passion, first in self and then in society, that this philosophy sought to inculcate had their analogues in the calm and coolness under fire required of leaders in battle or the disciplined integrity of administrators responsible for public funds. Indeed, they were frequently evident in the language commanders used to evaluate their subordinates in the reductions of 1815 and 1821.[28]

Unlike many (perhaps most) nineteenth-century Americans, and unlike many cadets upon their arrival at the Military Academy, most graduates and officers espoused some variant of the eighteenth-century concept of society as a stable, orderly, and balanced system governed by rational laws, a sociopolitical ideal they learned at the Academy and consistently pursued in their actions as government agents. However religious some of them became, few military officers shared the faith in the perfectibility of human nature and society that spread among evangelicals during the Second Great Awakening. Frustrating experiences while mediating between competing interests in the nation's borderlands reinforced their skepticism about human nature. Thus, while romanticism, perfectionism, evangelical religion, and the cultures of sentiment and reform can be found among officers, their impact was limited. Most officers pursued a cautious quest for national order, improvement, and stability through the rationalization of social relationships—a Whiggish search that anticipated the Progressive ideal of a putatively apolitical order transcending and, in many respects, consciously or unconsciously concealing or repressing social and cultural conflict. In this sense of quasi-utilitarian social rationalization, the officer corps and the Military Academy remained bulwarks of at least some elements of Enlightenment sensibility long after the emotions of romanticism, sectionalism, and the Second Great Awakening had absorbed or supplanted the rationalistic Enlightenment qualities present in early national culture.[29]

Finally, although increasingly comprehensive commercialization—the phenomenon American historians label the Market Revolution—was the most transformative and perhaps most destabilizing process in the early- and mid-nineteenth-century United States, the army and its officers seem to have adjusted to this upheaval without serious disruption. Flourishing commercialization did not alter the army's core mission of advancing and sustaining national territorial expansion; if anything, the Market Revolution eventually contributed to reaccelerating expansion after the "strategic pause" of the 1820s and 1830s. Regular army officers praised and took advantage of industrialization—the acceleration of transportation and the heightened time sense these developments encouraged—of commercialization, regional economic specialization, and social interdependence. Many officers invested in land and bank and factory stock, although there is much less evidence that they invested in retail or wholesale commerce. The army's logistical bureaus and staff officers benefited by the greater speed, larger scale, and lower cost of the production and distribution of the supplies necessary to equip and sustain the army; they benefited from a society that was increasingly organized along lines of specialization and interdependence, broadly analogous to those that characterized the army itself.[30]

The consequent social density and complexity—the swelling range and variety of social organization and hierarchy—also benefited the army, or at least the officer corps. The new middle classes increasingly recognized specialized expertise as a criterion of success and authority, while impoverished immigrants became available to swell the ranks of enlisted recruits. Cultural prejudices against the latter damaged the army's public reputation, though independence-loving Americans had never held "hireling" soldiers, subject to slave-like discipline, in high regard. Conversely, the advent of greater economic interdependence and specialization played much the same role that Enlightenment rationality had earlier served in justifying the officer's authority, whether epistemologically as an expert specialist or, at least in Whig and National Republican eyes, as a representative and agent of the national polity and social order. The gap between officers and enlisted soldiers remained as great as, if not greater than, that in George Washington's army. Barely literate Irish Catholic immigrants or German Catholics who spoke no English had little prospect of gaining Whig sympathies. The officer's authority was rooted in his education in functionally specialized expertise, and the hierarchical disciplines of the army buttressed that same socially functional purpose and specialization. Together, these could provide a model for industrial discipline that was more politically acceptable to the northern middle class than that emanating from southern plantation fields.[31]

In effect, army officers accepted most of the transformations of the Market Revolution and benefited from many of them. Their values and attitudes fit comfortably within the range of middle-class civilian attitudes and values that composed the emerging culture of Victorianism. Regular army officers were neither alienated social critics nor a reactionary elite analogous to many of their European counterparts. Yet the officer corps did become a distinct social, or sectoral, formation in the American class structure and the economic division of labor. On the one hand, we should be careful not to exaggerate: regular officers were too few in number and shared too many values from the past to be characterized as a "new class" similar to the "new men" of the Market Revolution. On the other hand, we gain little by characterizing service in the officer corps simply as an occupation, as a mere fragment of a larger class, whether the professional and officeholding upper middle class, the southern planter aristocracy, a new middle class, or the protean, amorphous American middle class as a whole. Instead, with Military Academy socialization as a mediating force, the officer corps was a relatively open social formation, its status, roles, authority, and sometimes even its existence contested both ideologically and politically, with a professional and social consciousness linked to but distinct from that of other sectors of the American bourgeoisie.[32]

In sum, the impact of greater instability in the economic, political, and social spheres of American life was outweighed by greater international and institutional stability. International stability largely shielded the regular army from the influence of social, political, and economic change, allowing institutional developments to mature: more extensive, articulated, and effective bureaucratic and educational structures; more stable and standardized selection and retention, both in criteria and in actual numbers; and more extensive and effective professional socialization. The result was a less sectional, less partisan or politicized, and more professional officer corps. Each of these qualities was further tempered and confirmed by the difficult experience of civil-military and federal-local tension in the army's efforts to mediate national policy in the borderlands. This experience, the subject of my second volume, led gradually, unevenly, but surprisingly quickly to a far greater accountability to national civilian authority than the army had demonstrated before 1820 or than most contemporary European officer corps demonstrated on their imperial frontiers. This accountability was fraught with complexity and friction, and a few senior officers, such as Winfield Scott, managed to burrow even deeper into the webs of partisan civilian politics. Yet the outcome was an army officer corps that actually approached social science standards of professional responsibility, setting the tone for the regular army officer corps ever since.

Taken as a whole, 1822 to 1835 (or at least 1822 to 1832) was a time of essential continuity for the regular army and its officer corps. No transformations in Indian relations, civilian or military technology, or general culture shaped or reshaped the army's institutional development or the officer corps' professional development. Nor did the resurgence of ideological conflict and the rise of the Second Party System do so. The shifts in social and sectional origins, career paths, and officer selection and socialization (initiated largely by the military and the War Department) evident during the 1820s transformed the army, but they had already begun before 1821. The changes in American foreign relations and the army's strength and structure that occurred in or around 1821 were crucial but quickly became sources of continuity and stability. Nor were missions, force structure, technology, or officer selection and socialization fundamentally altered by the surge in operational demands in and after 1832: the Black Hawk War, the Nullification Crisis, the French war scare in 1834, the Seminole War from the end of 1835, and the second "Creek War" and the Texas Revolution in 1836, in addition to Cherokee and other Indian removal efforts. The number of regiments was increased by almost a third, the number of soldiers almost doubled, and operational mobility and tactical capability were vastly enhanced by the creation of mounted regiments for the Plains, but the army remained hard-pressed to execute the constabulary missions it was assigned. The West Point monopoly on commissions ended for several years during the 1830s, but the great majority of officers continued to develop professional commitment and cohesion, nationalism and a statism rare in nineteenth-century America, habituation to duty and service, and a basis for developing administrative expertise before graduating from the Military Academy. West Point regained its virtual monopoly on new commissions even before the Whigs took power in 1841, and the "resignation crisis" of the mid-1830s actually strengthened the professional commitment and cohesion of the officer corps when those less committed to national service on the frontiers sought civilian employment.

Continuity did not mean certainty. One of the principal problems for historians of the army during this period, as for historians in general, is distinguishing between perception and reality and identifying the relations between them. Regular officers feared that domestic or international political change would destabilize the army's structure or create a gap between missions and means. Domestically, this usually meant fear of another reduction in force, especially as populist Republicans grew in strength and the Jacksonian coalition rose to power. Internationally, officers worried that the army was far too small to deal with any significant European military threat. As a result, the army's officers often felt little of the stability that is evident in hindsight. But as historians, we must recognize that there *was* an underlying stability to this period: changes in U.S. relations with Native Americans and Europe were limited, and major changes were unlikely; without war, there was little chance of a rush to arms or a quest for commissions by civilians; and deep, pervasive, enduring change rarely takes place overnight. Implicitly or explicitly, officers recognized these dynamics: there was remarkably little competition—far less than Democratic rhetoric or some officers' correspondence suggests—over the direction of nationally organized armed force during the Jacksonian era.

The upsurge of majoritarian democracy and partisanship did not produce an egalitarian, democratic, or Democratic army or officer corps—nor did it produce an actively Whig one, antagonistic to the Democratic Party or elected Democratic officials.[33] These political transformations did not lead to commissions for significant numbers of former enlisted men or prevent the development of a near monopoly on commissions by graduates of the Military Academy. The appointment of officers directly from civilian life was limited even during the Jackson and Van Buren administrations. Neither national security policy and strategy nor the army's tactics and operations were transformed by technology, nor did more than a small fraction of the officer corps anticipate such a transformation. The army's probable missions or opponents did not change, so it was unlikely, as officers recognized, that the army would increase substantially in size.

Change and military professionalization were certainly incremental, but this does not mean they were insignificant. Stability in missions, force structure, and officer selection, socialization, and careers enabled the army and its officer corps to make decisive strides toward an effective professionalism. The army's ability to retain a de facto monopoly over the operational direction of American military force during these years of partisan denunciation and international peace put it in a position to do so during the Mexican-American and Civil Wars. The army developed artillery and supply systems—systems that were primarily tactical and administrative, human rather than technological—

The Wood Monument and the Plain, by George Catlin. (Courtesy West Point Museum)

and it retained young officers with experience in Florida as well as a core of older veterans from the War of 1812. These men and systems enabled the army to win the first battles of the war with Mexico and to supply and direct the strategic, operational, and tactical projection of power that won that war. That victory enhanced and confirmed the prestige, and thus the legitimacy and authority, of the now relatively professional national standing army. As a result, its officers were able to maintain the operational and in large part the strategic direction of the far larger military effort of the Civil War. "Political generals" notwithstanding, officers devoted to careers in the profession of arms—a profession they did as much to define as their civilian masters— became the dominant force directing the operational application of organized American military power, and they have remained so ever since.

APPENDICES

APPENDIX A

Ex-Army Officers Who Joined the Gutiérrez-Magee and Other Expeditions against Spanish Texas, Mexico, and Florida, 1812–1820, or the Texan Revolution, 1835–1836

Post-1820 data based on George W. Cullum, comp., *Biographical Register of the Officers and Graduates of the United States Military Academy at West Point, N.Y., from Its Establishment, in 1802, to 1890*, 3 vols. (Boston: Houghton Mifflin, 1891), entries for 1820, 1825, 1830–1840, and 1845.

GUTIÉRREZ-MAGEE EXPEDITION AGAINST SPANISH TEXAS (SUMMER 1812–FALL 1813)

Ex-Captain Augustus Magee (Mass.)—West Point graduate in early 1809 (after one year's schooling), resigned June 1812; leader of American forces in Gutiérrez-Magee expedition: three and a half years' service after graduation. (Note: Magee was the only serving officer who resigned to join a filibustering expedition prior to 1836; that year, two others did so.)

Anthony Campbell (Pa.)—commissioned 1802, resigned 1805: three years' service.

Samuel D. Forsythe—surgeon's mate, 1807–1808 (resigned); artillery commander in expedition: one year's service.

Nathan Kennedy—surgeon's mate, 1806–1807: one year's service.

Zachariah Nettles (S.C.)—commissioned 1799, disbanded 1800: one year's service, in Federalist "New Army."

Samuel Noah (N.Y., born in England)—West Point graduate, December 1807 (after less than a year's schooling), resigned March 1811; artillery commander in expedition: three years' service.

Reuben Smith (Ga.)—commissioned 1803, resigned 1806; brother of officer and future brigadier general Thomas A. Smith; artillery commander in expedition: three years' service.

Joseph B. Wilkinson (Md.)— surgeon's mate, 1800–1802, disbanded owing to reduction in force (RIF); Brigadier General James Wilkinson's third son; acted as aide-de-camp to José Alvarez de Toledo; reported on situation to State Department agent William Shaler: two years' service.

Henry Perry (La.)—not an officer—perhaps confused by some sources with Henry Peire (see below). Perry was with Gutiérrez-Magee, volunteered at New Orleans December 1814–June 1815 (disbanded), and was with the New Orleans Associates in 1815; in the fall of 1815 he was on the Sabine with 150 filibusters, and in November 1815 he moved to Bolivar Point and joined and then split with Francisco Xavier Mina. Perry was killed in action or committed suicide in Texas in June 1817.

Reuben Ross—despite being mentioned in secondary sources, Ross cannot be found in army biographical registers—not an officer.

Summary: There were eight regular army officers with less than seventeen years' regular army service; only two had more than three years' service, and three had one year's service (or less). There were three surgeons and two West Pointers.

THE NEW ORLEANS ASSOCIATES, FRANCISCO XAVIER MINA (AGAINST TEXAS AND FLORIDA)

Ross Bird (Pa.)—commissioned 1791, disbanded 1796, commissioned 1808, resigned from Seventh Infantry Regiment (stationed at New Orleans) in October 1813: five years' continuous service, served with Mina.

Henry D. Peire (La.)—volunteer aide-de-camp to James Wilkinson 1812; commissioned 1813, major Forty-fourth Infantry Regiment; commanded Seventh Infantry Regiment at Battle of New Orleans; disbanded in 1815 RIF: two years' wartime service, with Toledo and Mina.

Guilford D. Young (N.Y.)—New York militia major, commissioned 1813; disbanded in 1815 RIF: two years' wartime service, with Mina. Henry P. Walker's suggestion that Young was at the Battle of Alazan in June 1813 seems unlikely, since he was commissioned a major in the Twenty-ninth Infantry Regiment (which served in New York) in February and was promoted to lieutenant colonel in April 1813.

Abner L. Duncan (La. businessman)—not an officer. Volunteer aide-de-camp to Jackson, December 1814–January 1815; leader of the New Orleans Associates; involved with Toledo and Mina 1815–1817.

Note: Secondary sources mention Abner L. Duncan, Henry Perry, and Reuben Ross as "army quartermasters," but they are not mentioned as such in army biographical registers. In these cases, "quartermaster" likely refers to someone who merely provided supplies for the army; both Duncan and Perry may have done so as aides to Andrew Jackson in the defense of New Orleans.

ASSOCIATED WITH THE LONG EXPEDITIONS AGAINST SPANISH EAST TEXAS, 1819–1820

Hamlin Cook (Ga.)—commissioned 1812, staff (major, assistant inspector general); disbanded in 1815 RIF: three years' service.

Isaac T. Preston (Va.)—commissioned 1813, captain 35th Infantry; disbanded in 1815 RIF: two years' service.

Brigadier General Eleazar Wheelock Ripley (Mass.)—commander of Eighth Military Department (Sabine and New Orleans); commissioned 1812, resigned 1820; accepted Long's offer of the "presidency of the republic of Texas": eight years' military service. Does not appear to have entered Texas.

ASSOCIATED WITH GREGOR MACGREGOR (SEIZED AMELIA ISLAND IN SPANISH FLORIDA, 1817)

Major (deputy quartermaster general) Samuel Champlin (Conn.)—West Point 1807; staff appointments 1811–1816; Charleston connections; dropped from rolls May 1816.

James Grant Forbes (N.Y.)—commissioned 1813 as lieutenant colonel in Forty-second Infantry Regiment (no combat); disbanded in 1815 RIF: two years' service.

Note: There was also an "Irwin," probably John from Georgia, who was a volunteer in 1813. James Irwin of Pennsylvania served as a volunteer in 1812 and 1813; Matthew Irwin (state unknown) was a purchasing officer from 1813 to 1815; and Charles Irwin of New York was a lieutenant in 1814 and 1815. None of these men were career officers.

PRECISE FILIBUSTER SERVICE UNKNOWN

First Lieutenant John W. Holding (state of origin unknown)—entered army 1813 as sergeant; adjutant and brigade major for Miller's brigade at Fort Erie; promoted by brevet to captain (December 1816) for distinction at Lundy's Lane; aide-de-camp to Ripley; with Patriots and/or pirates June 1817–September 1818; dropped from rolls November 1818: four years' service before joining filibusters. Lieutenant Colonel Henry Leavenworth sought his formal dismissal from the army.

Note: Average time in service for all officers who joined filibusters from 1812 to 1821, discounting Champlin, Ripley, and Bird's first service, was about two years.

TEXAS, 1835–1836

All of the following were lieutenants and West Point graduates and had an average of 4.7 years' service:

Albert Sidney Johnston, 1826–1834 (Ky.)
Joseph Cadle, 1824–1830 (N.Y.)
William Shaler Stillwell, 1827–1833 (N.Y.)
John T. Collinsworth, 1830–1836 (Tenn.)
George B. Crittenden, 1832–1833 (Ky.)
Hugh McLeod, 1835–1836 (N.Y.)

Note: No officers joined the filibusters against Canada between 1837 and 1842. One officer (William L. Crittenden, 1845–1849) joined the Narciso Lopez filibuster against Cuba, and one (Philip Roots Thompson, 1835–1855) joined William Walker.

Officers Who Became Civilian Territorial or Senior Federal Executive Branch Officials, 1814–1846

Name	Dates and Highest Rank as Regular Officer	Civilian Positions and Dates
William Clark	1792–1796, 1804–1807; lieutenant (Senate rejected Jefferson's nomination as lieutenant colonel)	Missouri territorial governor, 1813–1820; federal superintendent of Indian affairs, St. Louis, 1822–1838 (died)
John Miller	1812–1818; colonel (Ohio, distinguished at Fort Meigs, 1813)	Public land registrar, Missouri, 1818–1825; state governor, 1828–1832; House of Representatives, 1837–1843
Thomas A. Smith	1803–1818; colonel (commanded Ninth Military Department in St. Louis)	Public land office receiver of money, Missouri, 1818–
Richard Keith Call	1814–1822; captain (Jackson protégé)	Florida territorial council, 1822; territorial militia general, 1823; territorial delegate, 1823–1825; U.S. receiver of public lands in west Florida, 1825; territorial governor, 1835–1839 and 1841–1845

(*continued*)

Name	Dates and Highest Rank as Regular Officer	Civilian Positions and Dates
Robert Butler	1812–1821; adjutant general, Southern Division (Jackson), declined reduction to lieutenant colonel	U.S. surveyor general of public lands, Florida, 1824–1849
James Gadsden	1812–1821; inspector general, Southern Division (Jackson), Senate rejected nomination as adjutant general	Florida territorial council, 1824; treaty commissioner to Seminoles, 1823 and 1832; chief negotiator for land purchase from Mexico, 1853
Joseph Lee Smith	1812–1821; colonel (Conn.), disbanded after dispute with Alexander Macomb	Superior court of east Florida, 1822–
John McNeil	1812–1830; colonel (N.H.), hero at Lundy's Lane	U.S. surveyor, Port of Boston, 1830–1850 (died) (only field-grade officer who resigned to enter federal civil service, 1821–1846)
John McIntosh	1808–1820; major (Ga.)	U.S. Customs collector, Darien, Ga., 1824–
Charles Mason	West Point, 1829–1831; lieutenant (first in class)	Chief justice, superior court of Iowa territory, 1838–1847
James Miller	1808–1819: colonel (Mass.), hero at Lundy's Lane	Arkansas territorial governor, 1819–1825; U.S. Customs collector, Salem, Mass., 1825–1851 (died)
George Izard	1794–1803, 1812–1815; major general	Arkansas territorial governor, 1825–1828 (died)
Robert Crittenden	1814–1815; lieutenant	Arkansas territorial secretary and acting governor, 1819–1829 (brother of Senator John J. Crittenden)

William Bradford	1812–1824; major (only field-grade officer who resigned, 1822–1830)	Ran twice for Arkansas territorial delegate to Congress while still in uniform; Arkansas territorial militia general, 1824–
Henry Conway	1812–1820; lieutenant (related to Sevier political family)	Defeated Bradford for Arkansas territorial delegate, 1823–1827 (mortally wounded by Crittenden in 1827 duel)
William O. Allen	1812–1818; captain	Arkansas territorial militia general, 1820–
John Nicks	1808–1821; lieutenant colonel, Seventh Infantry Regiment (stationed in Ark.)	Arkansas territorial militia general, 1827–
Joseph Selden	1812–1820; brevet lieutenant colonel	Federal judge in Arkansas (killed in 1824 duel)

Data drawn from army biographical sources and state political histories. Note that the terminal dates for many civil offices are not given in the army sources. I included states of origin when these were relevant to federal civil appointments.

These cases show the movement from federal military service to civilian federal executive branch employment between 1815 and 1821. Their average military service was 9.3 years; only seven of these eighteen men exceeded 9 years in the army. Only two left the army after 1822, and one of them (Bradford) was the only field-grade officer to resign from the entire line of the army (infantry and artillery) between 1822 and 1830. Six of these men were first appointed to civil office by James Monroe, two by John Quincy Adams, and one (McNeil) by Andrew Jackson. McNeil was the only field-grade officer to resign his army commission to enter the federal civil service between 1821 and 1846, after he supported a newspaper backing Jackson in 1828. Bradford and McNeil were two of only six field-grade officers in the line who resigned between 1822 and 1837.

These men's practical significance was as territorial governors (commanders of territorial militias) and as generals of militia, and in the acquisition and sale of public lands from Indians and to whites, above all in Florida, where Jackson's influence was critical.

APPENDIX C

Army Officers Who Served as Indian Agents, 1814–1846

Agency	Name	Dates as Regular Officer	Dates as Agent
Apalachicola (Florida)	(Captain) John Phagan	1813–1815	1826–1833
Caddo	(Lieutenant) Jehiel Brooks	1818–1820	1830–1834
Cherokee (West)	(Colonel) David Brearley	1808–1811, 1812–1820	1820–1823
	(Captain) George Vashon (ex-Delaware and Shawnee)	1812–1819	1830–1834
	(Lieutenant) Pierce M. Butler	1819–1820	1841–1845
Chickasaw (East)	(Colonel) Robert Carter Nicholas	1808–1819	1820–1823
Chickasaw (West)	(Lieutenant) Gaines P. Kingsbury (West Point graduate)	1832–1836	1837–1839
Choctaw (West)	(Captain) F. W. Armstrong	1812–1817 (U.S. marshal, Alabama, 1823–1827)	1831–1835
Creek (West)	Brearley (ex-Cherokee West)	1820–1821	1826–1829
	(Lieutenant) Wharton Rector	1836–1842, paymaster (exchanged with Harney for LTC 2nd Dragoons)	1835–1836

Agency	Name	Dates as Regular Officer	Dates as Agent
Delaware and Shawnee	Vashon	—	1829–1830
Green Bay	(Colonel) John Bowyer	1792–1815	1816–1821
Osage	(Lieutenant) John F. Hamtramck (West Point graduate)	1819–1822	1826–1830
Prairie du Chien (Fort Winnebago subagency)	Three serving officers	—	1834–1837
Sault Ste. Marie	(Captain) Waddy V. Cobbs	1813–1848	1834–1837 (acting)
Seminole	(Lieutenant Colonel) Gad Humphreys	1808–1821	1822–1830
	Phagan (also Apalachicola)	—	1830–1833
Upper Missouri (Sioux subagency)	(Lieutenant) George Kennerly	1813–1819; 1823, sutler (Fort Atkinson); 1828–1842 (Jefferson Barracks); 1846–1848, assistant quartermaster	1824–1828
Totals and averages	13 total, not including acting agents: 3 colonels, 1 lieutenant colonel, 3 captains, 6 lieutenants	Average, 6.5 years (5.5 minus Bowyer); average date of separation, 1820	Average, 4 years

Data drawn from comparison of army biographical sources with Edward E. Hill, *The Office of Indian Affairs, 1824–1880: Historical Sketches* (New York: Clearwater Publishing, 1974).

Thirteen was a significant number of agents, but it was only a small minority of the total number and a very small minority of the officers who were disbanded in 1815 or 1821 or who resigned. In contrast, former officers figured prominently as agents for tribes being removed to the West and for those in Florida. Only two of the thirteen left the army after 1821; they were also the only West Pointers among the thirteen. None of these men became career officials in the Indian service: only three of the thirteen served more than the four-year average. Only three received their appointments after 1831, and only three served after 1836, suggesting that former officers were no longer a significant constituency for federal patronage after Jackson's first administration.

APPENDIX D

The Spectrum of Coercive Diplomacy and Deterrence

Here I suggest a schematic range of actions and intended consequences to clarify some of the confusion surrounding phrases such as "constabulary operations," "operations other than war," "military operations other than war," "stability operations," "stability and support operations," "gunboat diplomacy," and "coercive diplomacy" (a concept invented in analyses of Cold War diplomatic crises). As a historian, I am much more interested in the specific action or form of deployment and the message it was intended to convey than in precise definitions of specific concepts, so I do not distinguish sharply between deterrence and coercive diplomacy or between peacekeeping and peace enforcement, except that in each pairing, the latter is more active and perhaps more aggressive. I also accept the general distinction that deterrence and peacekeeping are intended to prevent actions, whereas coercion (sometimes referred to as "compellance") and peace enforcement are intended to change existing behavior.

Above all, the following list is intended to show a spectrum from passivity to violence, from indirection to direction, from implication to action, from generally small scale to larger scale, and from lesser to greater demands on the targeted populace, using specific historical deployment types as examples. I do not attempt to make moral distinctions, because virtually all army officers justified these actions as law enforcement and expressed their moral qualms privately.

1. Simply being garrisoned in an area—passive presence. This constitutes a passive form of point or "wide area" security, in today's terms, but it implies the potential for more active power projection: "We are here."
2. Showing the flag more actively, through small-scale (squad- to company-sized) presence patrols or the presence (usually in the guise of guards, on a small scale) at negotiations.

3. Focused movements, usually to specific places of political significance—usually Indian or squatter villages. This represents a move from peace-keeping to the potential for peace enforcement.

    A. More specifically, and thus implicitly more aggressively, showing the flag—an implied threat: "We know where you are, and we can reach you."

    B. A more explicit show of threat intended to intimidate, but still passive coercion, such as warnings to leave an area or otherwise change behavior.

4. Active coercion, via larger and more extended or more frequently sustained expeditions, often couched in terms of peacekeeping or peace enforcement, but potentially culminating in conquest, either overt or de facto. These actions can be "punitive" or "law enforcement" in nature (in both cases, retaliating for individual incidents or for several incidents or a pattern thereof).

    A. Remove Indians or squatters from a village or from an area.

    B. Detain them.

    C. Burn their crops and/or dwellings.

    D. Do so with the authority (usually implied in orders to "use your discretion") to employ lethal force if resisted.

NOTES

ABBREVIATIONS

Note that the document collections cited here are not included in the bibliography.

AFS   *Armed Forces and Society*

AGOLR   Letters Received by the Office of the Adjutant General, M 566 and M 567, RG 94 (only the author is cited, unless the adjutant general was not the addressee)

AGOLS   Letters Sent by the Office of the Adjutant General (Main Series), 1800–1890, M 565, RG 94 (only the addressee is cited, unless the adjutant general was not the author)

AJ   Andrew Jackson

ANC   *Army and Navy Chronicle* (a weekly newspaper published in Baltimore and Washington, D.C., between 1835 and 1842)

ASPFR   *American State Papers: Documents, Legislative and Executive, of the Congress of the United States, Class I, Foreign Relations.* 4 vols. (Washington, D.C.: Gales and Seaton, 1832–1861) (available online)

ASPIA   *American State Papers: Documents, Legislative and Executive, of the Congress of the United States, Class II, Indian Affairs.* 2 vols. (Washington, D.C.: Gales and Seaton, 1832–1861) (available online)

ASPMA   *American State Papers: Documents, Legislative and Executive, of the Congress of the United States, Class V, Military Affairs.* 7 vols. covering the years 1794–1836 (Washington, D.C.: Gales and Seaton, 1832–1861) (available online)

BHC   Burton Historical Collection, Detroit Public Library

CAJ   John Spencer Bassett, ed., *Correspondence of Andrew Jackson*, vol. 2, *May 1, 1814 to December 31, 1819* (Washington, D.C.: Carnegie Institution of Washington, 1927)

DH   *Diplomatic History*

DPP	Daniel Parker Papers, HSP (Parker is the addressee unless otherwise noted)
Entry	Collection number in the RG inventories published by the NA
EPG	Edmund P. Gaines
FHQ	*Florida Historical Quarterly*
GAHQ	*Georgia Historical Quarterly*
GLSR	Edmund P. Gaines, Letters Sent and Received, 1814–1815 and 1817–1819, RG 98, Entry 78
HA	Henry Atkinson
HL	Henry Leavenworth
HQALS	Letters Sent by the Headquarters of the Army (Main Series), 1828–1903, M 857, RG 108 (only the addressee is cited, unless the commanding general was not the author)
HSP	Historical Society of Pennsylvania, Philadelphia
JAH	*Journal of American History*
JCC	John C. Calhoun
JER	*Journal of the Early Republic*
JMH	*Journal of Military History*
JW	James Wilkinson
LAHQ	*Louisiana Historical Quarterly*
LBWCCC	Dunbar Rowland, ed., *Official Letter Books of W. C. C. Claiborne, 1801–1816*, vols. 5 and 6 (Jackson, Miss.: State Department of Archives and History, 1917)
LC	Library of Congress
"M" followed by a number: microfilm number for the relevant NA collection	
MJQA	Charles F. Adams, ed., *Memoirs of John Quincy Adams, Comprising Portions of His Diary from 1795 to 1848*, vols. 3 and 4 (Philadelphia: J. B. Lippincott, 1874–1877)
MPP	James D. Richardson, comp., *Compilation of the Messages and Papers of the Presidents*, vols. 1–3 (New York: Bureau of National Literature, 1897)
MVHR	*Mississippi Valley Historical Review*
NA	National Archives (Archives I), Washington, D.C.
NYPL	New York Public Library, New York City
OHS	Ohio Historical Society, Columbus
PAJ	Harold D. Moser et al., eds., *The Papers of Andrew Jackson*, 7 vols. to date (Knoxville: University of Tennessee Press, 1980–)
PJCC	Robert L. Meriwether and W. Edwin Hemphill, eds., *The Papers of John C. Calhoun*, vols. 2–9 (Columbia: University of South Carolina Press, 1963–1976)
PJM	J. C. A. Stagg et al., eds., *The Papers of James Madison, Presidential Series*, vols. 2–5 (Charlottesville: University Press of Virginia, 1992–2004)

PLDU	Perkins Library, Duke University
RG	Record Group
SWHQ	*Southwestern Historical Quarterly*
SWLR: IA	Letters Received by the Office of the Secretary of War Relating to Indian Affairs, 1800–1823, M 271, RG 107 (only the author is cited, unless the secretary of war was not the addressee)
SWLR: Reg	Letters Received by the Secretary of War, Registered Series, 1801–1870, M 221, RG 107 (only the author is cited, unless the secretary of war was not the addressee)
SWLR: Unreg	Letters Received by Secretary of War, Unregistered Series, 1789–1861, M 222, RG 107 (only the author is cited, unless the secretary of war was not the addressee)
SWLS	Letters Sent by the Secretary of War Relating to Military Affairs, 1800–1889, M 6, RG 107 (only the addressee is cited, unless the secretary of war was not the author)
THS	Tennessee Historical Society, Nashville
TP	Clarence E. Carter and John P. Bloom, eds., *The Territorial Papers of the United States*, 28 vols. (Washington, D.C. : U.S. State Department and National Archives, 1934–1975) (available online)
USMA	United States Military Academy Library, Special Collections, West Point, N.Y.
WCCC	William C. C. Claiborne
WHQ	*Western Historical Quarterly*
WJM	Stanislaus Murray Hamilton, ed., *The Writings of James Monroe*, vols. 5 and 6 (New York: G. P. Putnam's Sons, 1898–1903)
WJQA	Worthington Ford, ed., *Writings of John Quincy Adams*, vols. 5–7 (New York: Macmillan, 1913–1917)
WLC	William L. Clements Library, University of Michigan, Ann Arbor
WMQ	*William and Mary Quarterly*, 3rd ser.
WS	Winfield Scott
ZT	Zachary Taylor

INTRODUCTION: THE SOLDIER AND THE NINETEENTH-CENTURY AMERICAN STATE

1. *Nonstate actor* can mean anyone not acting under the authority of the nation-state, although it usually refers to actions in the international arena, such as in frontiers and borderlands. The modern term *nongovernmental organization* (NGO) has a similar meaning, but it usually refers to a group acting peacefully (for example, working in disaster relief, poverty assistance, and economic development), whereas in present-day usage, *nonstate actor* tends to refer to an armed person not under nation-state authority. Indians were, almost by definition, nonstate actors, but I use the term

primarily to refer to whites, whether U.S. citizens (usually frontiersmen) or European or Latin American adventurers, who were usually armed, aggressive, and not acting under the authority of internationally recognized nation-states. Indeed, most of their significant actions were contrary to national or international law (or at least its evolving customs and principles), much like criminals, pirates, and terrorists today. The movement of American farmers (usually armed) across international boundaries without passports was considered invasion under international custom; Native Americans saw intrusion onto their lands the same way, and U.S. federal law actually sided with the Indians, however inadequately it was enforced.

2. Prussian and Russian officers were almost always nobles or aristocrats, so their sense of "national" security was ultimately based as much on social (domestic or, crudely put, class) interests as on military (international) ones. See Gordon A. Craig, *The Politics of the Prussian Army, 1640–1945* (New York: Oxford University Press, 1955); John Shelton Curtiss, *The Russian Army under Nicholas I, 1825–1855* (Durham, N.C.: Duke University Press, 1965); John L. H. Keep, *Soldiers of the Tsar: Army and Society in Russia, 1462–1874* (Oxford: Clarendon Press, 1985); and Brian D. Taylor, *Politics and the Russian Army: Civil-Military Relations, 1689–2000* (Cambridge: Cambridge University Press, 2003). The growing autonomy—civilian policy makers' acceptance of expertise and jurisdiction—and accountability of the Jacksonian army are summarized in Samuel Watson, "How the Army Became Accepted: West Point Socialization, Military Accountability, and the Nation-State during the Jacksonian Era," *American Nineteenth-Century History* 7 (June 2006): 217–249. The European officer corps were far more intimately involved in politics, both social (class-based) politics and electoral and partisan politics; apart from American officers' support for the advancement and maintenance of white supremacy, their European counterparts were far less autonomous—whether from the politics of social stratification, personal patronage, or ideology—than were U.S. Army officers. The army was not infrequently deployed to counter rumors of slave unrest, but prior to the Civil War, federal military forces were virtually never called on to repress unrest among white workers or strife between native and immigrant, Protestant and Catholic, despite the extensive urban rioting of the Jacksonian and antebellum eras. Nor did officers form a specifically "military interest" in American politics, as is sometimes said of Britain, and they did not exercise significant influence on civilian political issues, legislation, policy making, or the dynamics of the American social structure.

British officers often sought and won election to Parliament (where officers were the largest occupational or professional group represented in the House of Commons between the mid-eighteenth and mid-nineteenth centuries) before and after the electoral reforms of 1832 and 1867, to say nothing of the aristocratic officers, whose proportion in the House of Lords more than tripled between 1837 and 1898. Gwyn Harries-Jenkins, *The Army in Victorian Society* (London: Routledge and Kegan Paul, 1977), chap. 7, 218–220. See also Edward M. Spiers, *The Army and Society, 1815–1914* (London: Longman, 1980), and Hew Strachan, *The Politics of the British Army* (Oxford: Clarendon Press, 1997). Military officers constituted 10 to 20 percent of the Chamber of Deputies in France, and 30 to 40 percent of the peers were generals. Paddy Griffith, *Military Thought in the French Army, 1815–1851* (Manchester: Manchester University Press, 1989), 14. The Bourbon Restoration tried to isolate officers as well as enlisted soldiers from political engagement after the fall of Napoleon, repressing leftist plots among noncommissioned officers and enlisted men during the 1820s, but the army failed to halt the July Revolution in 1830. Then, in Algeria, it developed a deeper isolation and alienation from civilian values that facilitated its use to repress citizens in 1848. Ultimately, the army's resurgent sense of itself as the embodiment of the French nation, combined with institutional self-interest, encouraged its return to Bonapartism by overthrowing the Second Republic in 1851, much as it had done in tandem with Napoleon I half a century before. See Douglas Porch, *Army and Revolution: France, 1815–1848* (London: Routledge and Kegan Paul, 1974) (which actually deals only with events to 1836 and the effective end of military dissent); Anthony Thrall Sullivan, *Thomas-Robert Bugeaud, France, and Algeria, 1784–1849: Politics, Power, and the Good Society* (Hamden, Conn.: Archon Books, 1983); Richard Holroyd, "The Bourbon Army, 1815–1830," *Historical Journal* 14 (September 1971): 529–552; and Richard D. Price, "The French Army and the Revolution of 1830," *European Studies Review* 3 (July 1973): 243–267.

3. For officers' attitudes toward foreign relations, see William B. Skelton, *An American Profession of Arms: The Army Officer Corps, 1784–1861* (Lawrence: University Press of Kansas, 1992), chap. 17. There is no detailed work on officers' views of Indian warfare before the Civil War to match those for the post–Civil War era in Sherry L. Smith's *The View from Officers' Row: Army Perceptions of Western Indians* (Tucson: University of Arizona Press, 1990) or the sources collected in Peter Cozzens, ed., *Eyewitnesses to the Indian Wars, 1865–1890*, vol. 5, *The Army and the Indian* (Mechanicsburg, Pa.: Stackpole Books, 2005); see Andrew J. Birtle, *U.S. Army Counterinsurgency and Contingency Operations Doctrine, 1860–1941* (Washington, D.C.: Center of Military History, 1998), chap. 1, for a synopsis. My article "Knowledge, Interest, and the Limits of Military Professionalism: The Discourse on American Coastal Defense, 1815–1860," *War in History* 5 (Fall 1998): 280–307, begins with a broad discussion of early national officers' views about American national security and how they conceptualized strategy; see also Jamie W. Moore, *The Fortifications Board 1816–1828 and the Definition of National Security* (Charleston, S.C.: The Citadel, 1981), and Brian M. Linn, *The Echo of Battle: The Army's Way of War* (Cambridge, Mass.: Harvard University Press, 2007), chap. 1.

4. See Gordon S. Wood, *The Radicalism of the American Revolution* (New York: Alfred A. Knopf, 1992), and Robert H. Wiebe, *The Opening of American Society: From the Adoption of the Constitution to the Eve of Disunion* (New York: Alfred A. Knopf, 1984), especially pt. 1 on gentility; see Richard L. Bushman, *The Refinement of America, 1750–1850: Persons, Houses, Cities* (New York: Alfred A. Knopf, 1993), for an analysis of what might be called "the gentrification of the American middle class" during this era, highlighting the survival of genteel and aristocratic values in the early republic. Army officers fit much more comfortably into what Wood labels the "repub-

lican society" of the early national period than the "democratic" or liberal, individualist one of the Jacksonian era; their professional socialization and the practice of military discipline and institutional hierarchy served as a powerful mechanism of social distancing and differentiation, engendering both elite and working-class formation through the operation of negative stereotyping and distinctions. See Scott Hughes Myerly, *British Military Spectacle: From the Napoleonic Wars through the Crimea* (Cambridge, Mass.: Harvard University Press, 1996), for an examination of the sociopolitical role played by the performance of command in Britain.

Rigid discipline was not the only model available for officers' relationships with enlisted men, but it was the dominant one. Historian Ronald Spiller has observed that "for most . . . officers, leadership [meant] the process of enforcing discipline" ("From Hero to Leader: The Development of Nineteenth Century American Military Leadership" [Ph.D. diss., Texas A&M University, 1993], 89). For the variety of relationships between officers and enlisted soldiers, see also Samuel J. Watson, "Professionalism, Social Attitudes, and Civil-Military Accountability in the U.S. Army Officer Corps, 1815–1846," 2 vols. (Ph.D. diss., Rice University, 1996), chaps. 6, 10; Samuel J. Watson, "Bureaucrats and Aristocrats Encounter the Labor Market: Market Relations between Army Officers and Enlisted Men in the Age of Jackson" (paper presented to the Society for Historians of the Early American Republic, July 21, 1995); Skelton, *An American Profession of Arms*, chap. 14; and especially Dale R. Steinhauer, "'Sogers': Enlisted Men in the U.S. Army, 1815–1860" (Ph.D. diss., University of North Carolina, 1992). Few noncommissioned officers served more than the standard five-year enlistment, in contrast to the officer's average twenty-plus years of service (Steinhauer, "'Sogers,'" 325, 346–347).

5. Watson, "Professionalism, Social Attitudes, and Civil-Military Accountability," chaps. 3–10. Robert P. Wettemann Jr., *Privilege vs. Equality: Civil-Military Relations in the Jacksonian Era, 1815–1845* (Westport, Conn.: Praeger Security International, 2009), provides a wide-ranging, balanced assessment that emphasizes the complex interplay of civil society and military institutions but is focused almost entirely on civilian perspectives. Marcus Cunliffe, *Soldiers and Civilians: The Martial Spirit in America, 1776–1865*, 2nd ed. (New York: Free Press, 1973), is more balanced in coverage but is fundamentally more anecdotal than analytical (or at least very inconsistent in its approach to analysis). See also Matthew Warshauer, *Andrew Jackson and the Politics of Martial Law: Nationalism, Civil Liberties and Partisanship* (Knoxville: University of Tennessee Press, 2006), which is more narrowly focused. The 1850s have received no explicit treatment; the student must look for snippets in Cunliffe's and Skelton's work; in biographies, especially of Winfield Scott and John Wool; and in Durwood Ball's *Army Regulars on the Western Frontier, 1848–1861* (Norman: University of Oklahoma Press, 2001), a superb history of operations that exaggerates partisanship, politicization, and sectionalism both in commissioning and promotions and among officers themselves. See Samuel Watson, "Continuity in Civil-Military Relations and Expertise: The U.S. Army during the Decade before the Civil War," *JMH* 75 (January 2011): 221–250 (a literature review), for the most recent and comprehensive attempts

at synthesis. Thomas S. Langston, *Uneasy Balance: Civil-Military Relations in Peacetime America since 1783* (Baltimore: Johns Hopkins University Press, 2003), provides the only historically accurate examination by a political scientist, but he devotes only a chapter to the period between 1815 and 1861.

6. See Samuel Watson, "The U.S. Army to 1900," in *The Blackwell Companion to American Military History*, ed. James C. Bradford (Oxford: Wiley-Blackwell, 2009), for a comprehensive synopsis of the historiography of the army's professional development, the balance between regulars and citizen-soldiers in force structure and action, and the debate between their advocates. See also Samuel J. Watson, comp., introduction to *The International Library of Essays in Military History: Warfare in the USA, 1784–1861* (Burlington, Vt.: Ashgate Publishing, 2005).

7. By populist, I mean both egalitarian and committed to a more direct process of majority rule. Whatever the virtues of populism today or throughout the course of American history, during the Jacksonian era, it was commonly based on racist and patriarchal hierarchies and exclusions and was employed to support violent individualism and local, regional, or sectional self-interest. In doing so, it diluted or undermined the checks and balances of representative government, which the Constitution intended to calm and reduce the clash of local and sectional interests. As federal mediators, officers clearly understood this destabilizing dynamic and bore much of the burden of ameliorating its disruptive impact on the nation's borders and frontiers.

8. The debate over the timing of professionalization in the U.S. armed forces has been a hardy perennial for American military historians. By 1960 a general consensus had emerged, rooted in the work of Emory Upton and his followers among historians of the U.S. Army and codified in Samuel P. Huntington's *Soldier and the State: The Theory and Practice of Civil-Military Relations* (Cambridge, Mass.: Harvard University Press, 1957). This work set the timing of professionalization in the late nineteenth century, during the eras of national economic integration and Progressive reform, which put a premium on specialization and expertise. Huntington's principal interpretive rival, sociologist Morris Janowitz, challenged his assumptions and conclusions but did not address the historical process or trajectory of professionalization that Huntington articulated. Historian Russell F. Weigley's *History of the United States Army* (New York: Macmillan, 1967), the first history of the army truly based on archival research, contradicted the timing of Huntington's trajectory, but most readers pay less attention to his chapter titled "The Professionalization of the Regular Army, 1821–1846" than they do to the chapters on the army's professional development between 1877 and 1900. As a result, Weigley's work is commonly assumed to confirm Huntington and the Uptonians, or it is ignored by those who prefer Huntington's assertions to Weigley's evidence. Although focused on the army's social history rather than on professionalism or professionalization per se, Edward M. Coffman's widely read book *The Old Army: A Portrait of the American Army in Peacetime, 1784–1898* (New York: Oxford University Press, 1986) presents a portrait more in tune with Huntington's; Allan R. Millett, *Military Professionalism and Officership in America* (Columbus, Ohio: Mershon Center, 1977), also follows Huntington.

John M. Gates, "The Alleged Isolation of the U.S. Army Officers in the Late Nineteenth Century," *Parameters* 10 (Spring 1980): 32–45, is critical of assertions that the officer corps was physically or mentally isolated; Terrence J. Gough, "Isolation and Professionalization of the Army Officer Corps: A Post-Revisionist View of the *Soldier and the State*," *Social Science Quarterly* 73 (June 1992): 420–436, focuses on the late nineteenth century and tries to strike a balance; David J. Fitzpatrick, "Emory Upton and the Citizen Soldier," *JMH* 65 (April 2001): 355–389, revises the stereotype of Upton on which much twentieth-century historiography was based. More generally, Donald Connelly, *John M. Schofield and the Politics of Generalship* (Chapel Hill: University of North Carolina Press, 2006), and James L. Abrahamson, *America Arms for a New Century: The Making of a Great Military Power* (New York: Free Press, 1981), demonstrate the manifold yet complex connections between soldiers and society, showing that they were not physically or mentally isolated, despite their frustration with many aspects of American individualism (meaning capitalism, or at least its effects, as well as democracy).

9. As Michael Holt observes, "One of the most striking omissions from the literature on the party period [of American politics, between c. 1835 and the 1890s] . . . is any serious consideration of federalism and its evolution in the nineteenth century" (*Political Parties and American Political Development, from the Age of Jackson to the Age of Lincoln* [Baton Rouge: Louisiana State University Press, 1992], 99). Forrest McDonald, *States' Rights and the Union: Imperium in Imperio, 1776–1876* (Lawrence: University Press of Kansas, 2000), is a rare exception.

10. Michael Mann, *The Sources of Social Power: The Rise of Classes and Nation-States, 1760–1914* (Cambridge: Cambridge University Press, 1993), 81–82, 445, 459; Mark R. Wilson, *The Business of Civil War: Military Mobilization and the State, 1861–1865* (Baltimore: Johns Hopkins University Press, 2006), 209. Even today, Leonard D. White's books *The Federalists*, *The Jeffersonians*, and *The Jacksonians* (New York: Macmillan, 1948–1959) remain the most detailed analyses of the federal executive branch for the period 1789 to 1850—remarkable and lamentable evidence of the loss of interest in the nineteenth-century state since the 1960s. The significance of state power and employment to professional development in Europe can hardly be overestimated. The best illustration of this is that the civil service bureaucracy was (and is) considered a profession in its own right throughout Europe. See Gerald L. Geison, ed., *Professions and the French State* (Philadelphia: University of Pennsylvania Press, 1984); Geoffrey Cocks and Konrad H. Jarausch, eds., *German Professions, 1800–1950* (New York: Oxford University Press, 1990); Charles E. McClelland, *The German Experience of Professionalization: Modern Learned Professions and Their Organizations from the Early Nineteenth Century to the Hitler Era* (Cambridge: Cambridge University Press, 1991); Harold J. Perkin, *The Rise of Professional Society: England since 1880* (London: Routledge, 1989); A. G. Fielding and D. Portwood, "Professions and the State: Towards a Typology of Bureaucratic Professions," *Sociological Review* 28 (February 1980): 23–54.

11. Morton Keller, *Affairs of State: Public Life in Late Nineteenth-Century Amer-*

ica (Cambridge, Mass.: Harvard University Press, 1977); Stephen Skowronek, *Building a New American State: The Expansion of National Administrative Capacities, 1877–1920* (Cambridge: Cambridge University Press, 1982), 24 ("state of courts and parties"); Martin Shefter, *Political Parties and the State: The American Historical Experience* (Princeton, N.J.: Princeton University Press, 1994); Daniel P. Carpenter, *The Forging of Bureaucratic Autonomy: Reputations, Networks, and Policy Innovation in Executive Agencies, 1862–1928* (Princeton, N.J.: Princeton University Press, 2001). Keller and Skowronek have moved on to other periods and projects. Shefter continued to assert the weak-state and the state of courts and parties theses as recently as 2002, although he never demonstrated significant archival research in the antebellum period; see Martin Shefter, "War, Trade, and U.S. Party Politics," in *Shaped by War and Trade: International Influences in American Political Development*, ed. Ira Katznelson and Martin Shefter (Princeton, N.J.: Princeton University Press, 2002).

12. Peter J. Kastor, *The Nation's Crucible: The Louisiana Purchase and the Creation of America* (New Haven, Conn.: Yale University Press, 2004), presents a more recent example of neglect in the study of the early nineteenth century. Kastor claims to focus on governance and observes that "as much as any institution, the military and paramilitary bodies in Louisiana became the instruments for three of the most vital facets of [Louisiana's] incorporation" into the American polity, proving "crucial to implementing the legislation of 1805–1808"(90). So far so good, but apart from the defense of New Orleans, Kastor barely mentions the actions of the army, which administered most of Louisiana during the first year of American occupation (and for the first three years in Missouri), paying far more attention to the agency of red, white, and black Louisianans. Thus, when caught between his theses of "governance" and "local diplomacy," the agency embodied in the latter triumphs; his "incorporation" and "attachment" proceed via inclusion, resulting in pluralism, at least among whites. In effect, Louisianans rather than parties capture the state; their agency drives its governance. This is certainly a more accurate interpretation than a purely binary one in which U.S. authorities impose a foreign order on the French Louisianans amid constant ethnocultural conflict with new American settlers, as many previous accounts suggested. Nevertheless, the great majority of Kastor's examples of governance are of Louisianans proposing or petitioning and receiving rhetoric or legislation in response, rather than physical actions by the government—a rather attenuated conception of governance. Nor do recent reassessments of the nineteenth-century state, such as Brian Balough, *A Government Out of Sight: The Mystery of National Authority in Nineteenth-Century America* (Cambridge: Cambridge University Press, 2009), overcome the ahistorical distinction between civil government and the military with sufficient attention to the latter.

13. Richard L. McCormick, "The Party Period and Public Policy: An Explanatory Hypothesis," *JAH* 66 (September 1979): 279–298; Richard L. McCormick, *The Party Period and Public Policy: American Politics from the Age of Jackson to the Progressive Era* (New York: Oxford University Press, 1986); Charles C. Bright, "The State in the United States in the Nineteenth Century," in *Statemaking and Social Movements: Essays*

in History and Theory, ed. Charles C. Bright and Susan Harding (Ann Arbor: University of Michigan Press, 1984); Joel H. Silbey, *The Partisan Imperative: The Dynamics of American Politics before the Civil War* (New York: Oxford University Press, 1985). For a strong critique of these interpretations, particularly of McCormick, see Richard R. John, "Farewell to the Party Period: Political Economy in Nineteenth-Century America," *Journal of Policy History* 16 (April 2004): 117–125, and "Ruling Passions: Political Economy in Nineteenth-Century America," *Journal of Policy History* 18 (January 2006): 1–20.

14. William B. Skelton, "Samuel P. Huntington and the American Military Tradition," *JMH* 60 (April 1996): 325–338; Louis Hartz, *The Liberal Tradition in America: An Interpretation of American Political Thought since the Revolution* (New York: Harcourt, Brace, and World, 1955). Like many historians, political scientists (particularly Huntington) took the classically liberal rhetoric Hartz identified at face value as both an accurate and a comprehensive description of American social reality across the nineteenth century. The more specialized political historiography of the 1940s and 1950s also argued that Jacksonian America was a highly egalitarian society antagonistic to specialization, institutions, and elites, which implied that there was no social or institutional precedent or desire for an autonomous army. The years 1945–1960 saw at least four major interpretive works on Jackson and his followers, whereas the first studies of the Whigs beyond the state level did not appear until the late 1970s. Without a tradition of aristocracy or a powerful state, how could American military officers claim authority and autonomy, whether in relation to subordinates, politicians, or society as a whole? Although historians rapidly turned from liberalism to republicanism as their principal explanatory device for nineteenth-century politics during the 1960s and 1970s, their continued emphasis on ideology—always considered antagonistic toward concentrated power—reinforced these tendencies. See Daniel Walker Howe, *The Political Culture of the American Whigs* (Chicago: University of Chicago Press, 1979); Thomas Brown, *Politics and Statesmanship: Essays on the American Whig Party* (New York: Columbia University Press, 1985); Lawrence Frederick Kohl, *The Politics of Individualism: Parties and the American Character in the Jacksonian Era* (New York: Oxford University Press, 1989); and Michael F. Holt, *The Rise and Fall of the American Whig Party* (New York: Oxford University Press, 1999). See Burton J. Bledstein, *The Culture of Professionalism: The Middle Class and the Development of Higher Education in America* (New York: W. W. Norton, 1976), for an early recognition of Jacksonian era specialization and institutionalism outside the realm of political history, and Wiebe, *The Opening of American Society,* chap. 15, for a discussion of interdependence and institutions. Howe presents a Whiggish perspective on the era as a whole in *What Hath God Wrought? The Transformation of America, 1815–1848* (New York: Oxford University Press, 2007). As *Jackson's Sword* will show, many Democrats who were otherwise antagonistic to centralized institutions had their own uses—Indian removal, the conquest of northern Mexico—for the standing army and were much less critical than stereotypes about Jacksonian

egalitarianism would imply; Skelton found evidence for this in congressional voting (*An American Profession of Arms*, 295).

15. Skowronek, *Building a New American State*, 19; Keller, *Affairs of State*, 13; William E. Nelson, *The Roots of American Bureaucracy, 1830–1900* (Cambridge, Mass.: Harvard University Press, 1982), 5. Although Keller and Skowronek recognize that American overseas imperialism provided a major impetus for governmental change, neither addresses the West or the army's role in the West. Downplaying the nineteenth-century state runs counter to the widespread recognition among western historians that the frontier and the West have always depended heavily on aid and support from the federal government. Indeed, leading western historian Richard White refuted the application of Skowronek's arguments to the West almost point for point, simultaneously rejecting dicta privileging private and nonstate actors (settlers and frontiersmen) over state power in the conquest of the West. White observes that the national government often preceded and shaped significant settlement; that the militia rarely proved to be a capable force in the West; that federal bureaucracies were especially active and influential there; and that those executive agencies were increasingly professional, not merely instruments of partisan patronage. Richard White, *"It's Your Misfortune and None of My Own": A New History of the American West* (Norman: University of Oklahoma Press, 1991), especially 57–59.

16. Joel H. Silbey, "'To One or Another of These Parties Every Man Belongs': The American Political Experience from Andrew Jackson to the Civil War," in *Contesting Democracy: Substance and Structure in American Political History, 1775–2000*, ed. Byron E. Shafer and Anthony Badger (Lawrence: University Press of Kansas, 2001), 77–78; Ira Katznelson, "Flexible Capacity: The Military and Early American State-Building," in Katznelson and Shefter, *Shaped by War and Trade*, 86. Despite portents in Matthew A. Crenson, *The Federal Machine: The Beginnings of Bureaucracy in Jacksonian America* (Baltimore: Johns Hopkins University Press, 1975), and Richard H. Kohn, *Eagle and Sword: The Federalists and the Creation of the Military Establishment in America, 1783–1802* (New York: Free Press, 1975), the historical reassessment of the early national state largely began with Richard R. John, *Spreading the News: The American Postal System from Franklin to Morse* (Cambridge, Mass.: Harvard University Press, 1995), and William J. Novak, *The People's Welfare: Law and Regulation in Nineteenth-Century America* (Chapel Hill: University of North Carolina Press, 1996).

See also Richard R. John, "Governmental Institutions as Agents of Change: Rethinking American Political Development in the Early Republic, 1787–1835," *Studies in American Political Development* 11 (Fall 1997): 347–380; Richard F. Bensel, *Yankee Leviathan: The Origins of Central State Authority in America, 1859–1877* (Cambridge: Cambridge University Press, 1990); Richard F. Bensel, *The Political Economy of American Industrialization, 1877–1900* (Cambridge: Cambridge University Press, 2000); Max M. Edling, *A Revolution in Favor of Government: Origins of the U.S. Constitution and the Making of the American State* (New York: Oxford University

Press, 2003), which examines the Confederation and Federalist periods; Laura Jensen, *Patriots, Settlers, and the Origins of American Social Policy* (Cambridge: Cambridge University Press, 2003), which explores the early republic and the antebellum era; Robert Angevine, *The Railroad and the State: War, Politics and Technology in Nineteenth-Century America* (Stanford, Calif.: Stanford University Press, 2004); Wilson, *The Business of Civil War*, and Mark R. Wilson, "The Politics of Procurement: Military Origins of Bureaucratic Autonomy," *Journal of Policy Studies* 18 (January 2006): 44–73. Apart from Angevine, who misreads the sources and trajectory of American military professionalism, and John's student Wilson, little of this linkage has filtered to American military history.

17. Ronald Formisano, "State Development in the Early Republic: Substance and Structure, 1780–1840," in Shafer and Badger, *Contesting Democracy*, 26; Katznelson, "Flexible Capacity," 91–93 (statistics), 101; Keller, *Affairs of State*, 13; Wilson, *The Business of Civil War*. Ironically, just as a growing number of historians have questioned the concept of statelessness in the early republic, a leading historian of the colonial era has attempted to revive it. See the roundtable on the nation, the state, and the states in *WMQ* 64 (April 2007): 235–286, in which eminent colonial historian Jack Greene reasserts the preeminence of the states over the nation or the nation-state in early American history. Although Greene's points about continuities between the colonial and early national periods are significant, his eagerness "to subvert the parochial mentality implicit in the national state focus" (286) in favor of the states appears willful or even perverse, if not a polemical case of special pleading or disciplinary aggrandizement in favor of his own chronological period and subject. In Greene's case, the nonspecialist is projecting his biases forward into the early republic, rather than backward as the political scientists do, but with much the same errant conclusions about a "weak state." Adam Rothman, a student of American territorial expansion in the early Southwest, provides the strongest critique of Greene's arguments and the weak-state thesis within this roundtable. Indeed, Greene's emphasis on the big-picture continuities of Anglo-American territorial expansion, aggression, and empire building actually complements the recognition of the growing role of the state by students of the early republic, since the shift from British "benign neglect," or from the Proclamation of 1763, was so profound. Greene appears to believe that territorial expansion occurred almost entirely through nonstate actors (settlers), a myth I hope *Jackson's Sword* will help dispel.

18. In *The Old Army*, Coffman used chapter titles—"Buried in Oblivion," "Companions of Our Exile"—that conveyed an overwhelming sense of isolation, but his emphasis on the social experience of the frontier army presented that isolation primarily in physical terms or as a matter of civilian neglect, leaving the implications for civil-military relations unclear. Thus William Skelton was the first scholar to address the question of isolation for the antebellum army in significant depth and context. Skelton focused on the development of a cohesive, committed occupational group that was largely educated and socialized together at West Point. They married one another's relatives; served long careers, often at frontier outposts with few civilian inhabitants;

and developed similar institutional and occupational foci and attitudes, distinct from those of civilians. These mutually reinforcing experiences led officers not just to bipartisanship or nonpartisanship but to antipartisanship, an apolitical stance that sometimes became at least rhetorically antipolitical, as in officers' frequent denunciations of politicians as demagogues. Thus, "by the eve of the Civil War, the officer corps had developed into a distinct subculture that was partially isolated, both physically and intellectually, from the main currents of the civilian world" (Skelton, *An American Profession of Arms*, 181). In 2006 Skelton observed that "officers' widespread sense of alienation from the civilian mainstream and their commitment to a unique and supposedly [morally] superior service ethic provided an important function for the emerging military profession, a means to preserve its identity and cohesion in the face of the disintegrating forces of America's democratic culture." William B. Skelton, "The Commanding Generals and the Question of Civil Control in the Antebellum U.S. Army, 1821–1841," *American Nineteenth-Century History 7* (June 2006): 155.

Recent works by Robert Angevine and Robert Wettemann focusing on army efforts in support of civilian transportation projects argue that the army became more isolated from civilian society after 1838 due to legislation passed that year that prohibited officers' assignment to duty with civilian transportation surveys. Combined with the move west during the 1840s and 1850s, which supposedly produced a "physically isolated army," Wettemann maintains that this disengagement from civilian engineering encouraged "new ideas of martial service" and a concentration on "purely martial duties"— a new professionalism. Yet these arguments, so similar to Huntington's vision of professionalism or to Weigley's analysis of the post–Civil War era, fail the proportionality test: Angevine and Wettemann rely on the behavior of 5 to 10 percent of the officer corps—those engaged, while on leave or on duty, in aiding private railroad and other transportation companies under the General Survey Act between 1824 and 1838—to explain a change they consider armywide. During the 1820s and 1830s, as well as the 1840s and 1850s, the army's identity—as expressed in personal correspondence, official reports, professional journals, public ceremonies, and institutional efforts to develop expertise, commitment, and cohesion—was rooted in memories of the War of 1812, preparation for conventional combat with European powers, and frontier duties, however frustrating officers found them. See Angevine, *The Railroad and the State*, chap. 5; Robert P. Wettemann Jr., "A Part or Apart? The Alleged Isolation of Antebellum U.S. Army Officers," *American Nineteenth-Century History 7* (June 2006): 209–210.

Concluding that the army was partially isolated is not an unreasonable assessment. Nor is Skelton's functionalist interpretation of professional self-differentiation and identity building through distancing from negative reference groups unreasonable; it accounts for societal trends in politics and culture, individual psychological dynamics, and the self-interest of institution and occupation. In *Privilege vs. Equality* (90), Wettemann acknowledges the limited number of officers working on civilian transportation projects and thus the disproportion between cause and effect in his previous interpretation (which may help explain declining Jacksonian criticism of the army). Recognizing these problems, he concludes that the army was "anything but isolated from the civilian realm" (128). Wettemann makes this statement in reference to Jacksonian criticism of the West Point and regular army monopolies, rather than army attitudes, but see his quotation (127) from "The Army of the United States," *North American Review* 28 (October 1826): 274. Mark R. Grandstaff presents the most accurate interpretation, identifying two waves of professionalization in the nineteenth-century army: the first a wave of commitment and cohesion during the Jacksonian era, as identified by Skelton, and the second a wave of institutions for developing conventional war-fighting expertise after Reconstruction. See Mark R. Grandstaff, "Preserving the 'Habits and Usages of War': William Tecumseh Sherman, Professional Reform, and the U.S. Army Officer Corps, 1865–1881, Revisited," *JMH* 62 (July 1998): 521–545.

19. This circle is especially evident in Weigley, *History of the United States Army*, chap. 12.

20. The southern, central, and eastern European monarchies proved to be routinely as well as ultimately dependent on military force, from Naples and Spain in 1820 to the revolutions of 1848. See Eric Christiansen, *The Origins of Military Power in Spain, 1800–1854* (Oxford: Clarendon Press, 1967); Alan Sked, *The Survival of the Hapsburg Empire: Radetsky, the Imperial Army, and the Class War, 1848* (London: Longman, 1979); and, more generally, Geoffrey Best, *War and Society in Revolutionary Europe, 1770–1870* (New York: St. Martin's Press, 1982); Geoffrey Wawro, *Warfare and Society in Europe, 1792–1914* (London: Routledge, 2000); and Arno J. Mayer, *The Persistence of the Old Regime: Europe to the Great War* (New York: Pantheon, 1981). Even Britain employed national standing forces, against political radicals in the 1810s and Chartist workers in the 1830s and 1840s, on a scale unknown in the United States prior to the Civil War; see Anthony Babington, *Military Intervention in Britain: From the Gordon Riots to the Gibraltar Incident* (London: Routledge, 1990), for a survey. In these states, where the sovereign was normally a monarch, national security meant the defense of social privilege as much as the defense of national sovereignty against other states. Even in Britain, the army—which was led by aristocrats, although the junior officer corps was increasingly middle class—used the prerogative of the sovereign, Queen Victoria, as a tool to deflect accountability to Parliament. This effectively undermined and limited civilian control, since the queen hardly represented civilian authority in any meaningful sense. Whether the defense of prerogative was conducted primarily in the army's institutional interests or as part of the more general defense of aristocracy "to counteract the growth of the Democratic Power"—as Wellington tellingly, and approvingly, maintained (quoted in Strachan, *The Politics of the British Army*, 61)—it limited military subordination to civil authority when that civil authority asked the military to accept change. As a result, historian Hew Strachan labels the idea of "dual [Parliamentary and monarchical] control" a myth (ibid., 73), but he still considers the British army professional because of its extensive experience—a rather diminished concept of professionalism.

21. Spiers, *The Army and Society*, 2. See Best, *War and Society in Revolutionary Europe*; David Gates, *Warfare in the Nineteenth Century* (New York: Palgrave, 2001); Wawro, *Warfare and Society in Europe*; Azar Gat, *The Origins of Military Thought, from the Enlightenment to Clausewitz* (Oxford: Clarendon Press, 1989); and Azar Gat, *The Development of Military Thought: The Nineteenth Century* (Oxford: Clarendon Press, 1992), for background on the social, cultural, and intellectual influences on nineteenth-century European military thought and institutions. The most significant "revisionist" works (stressing the extent of reform and its origins within armies) are Hew Strachan, *Wellington's Legacy: The Reform of the British Army, 1830–1854* (Manchester: Manchester University Press, 1984), and Paddy Griffith, *Military Thought in the French Army, 1815–1851* (Manchester: Manchester University Press, 1989), but they are less critical or innovative than they appear because of their acceptance of the contemporary emphasis on practical experience and moral considerations, along with subjective or ideological (i.e., social and cultural rather than solely institutional) civilian control and complex systems of constitutional checks and balances.

In *The Politics of the British Army*, Strachan consistently downplays the role of social (or ideological) interests and values in the political behavior of British military commanders. Yet he just as frequently provides evidence, including quotations from senior military leaders such as Lord Wellington, that clearly demonstrates that British military politics was not merely the politics of the army as an institution—like the "army politics" identified by Skelton (*An American Profession of Arms*, chap. 15) in the antebellum U.S. officer corps—or as a professional interest group seeking resources. Strachan seems to be on reasonable ground in downplaying partisan politics, arguing that the army was conservative, not Conservative or Tory, because neither major British party was antagonistic to the interests of the military as an institution (35), but he shows no sense of the social or ideological beliefs, which were fundamentally antidemocratic and against representative civilian control, of the senior officers he quotes.

Strachan's dismissal of social politics appears to be rooted in his refusal to accept that social origins are relevant to the form and character of military professionalism. Having effectively demonstrated that the British officer corps was not overwhelmingly aristocratic, Strachan goes on to portray the roots of British military professionalism wholly as a matter of war-fighting experience: the British army was professional because it got a lot of practice at warfare (largely in the British Empire). He rejects the rather commonsense view that the standard practice of purchasing commissions constrained professional development, implies that half-pay officers were no less professional than those employed full-time (23), and presents as evidence of professional development the statistic that 31 percent of the colonels (essentially, regimental commanders) between 1714 and 1763 had served more than fifteen years (24). Strachan has a point that these phenomena did not preclude professionalism, but surely any profession (including the military) is more expert when its practitioners enter through institutions of professional education and socialization rather than buying their way in. Surely full-time practitioners are more focused and more expert than reservists, and what truly professional army would want 69 percent of its regimental commanders to have less than fifteen years' service when appointed to that position?

This depiction of professionalism goes hand in hand with Strachan's tacit dismissal of subordination, accountability, and responsibility to civilian (or client) control as a core characteristic, or value, of professionalism (military or otherwise). In other words, he takes empire as Britain's core national interest, says virtually nothing about the use of the army against the Chartists, and does not see anything unprofessional about the army's use of the royal prerogative as a foil against control by or accountability to representative government (a practice he explicitly recognizes on page 69). Rather than asserting that "dual control was really tripartite control . . . allow[ing] the army to play off royal prerogative against ministerial authority" (73), I would argue that effective civilian control was intermittent at best, particularly in the empire, where Strachan as well as students of British India observe a process of militarization of the government. If the monarch was not truly a civilian and certainly not representative, and if the army used that false front to ward off accountability to representative civilian government, then to the extent the military succeeded, civilian control was lost.

22. The concept of shirking duties demanded by the civilian authority, rather than actively or overtly opposing civil control, is emphasized in Peter D. Feaver, *Armed Servants: Agency, Oversight, and Civil-Military Relations* (Cambridge, Mass.: Harvard University Press, 2003); see also Peter D. Feaver, "The Civil-Military Problematique: Huntington, Janowitz, and the Question of Civilian Control," *AFS* 23 (Winter 1996): 149–178. Though less focused on historical examples than Huntington's *Soldier and the State*, Samuel E. Finer's *The Man on Horseback: The Role of the Military in Politics* (1964; rev. ed., Boulder, Colo.: Westview Press, 1988) provides a more structured and comprehensive exploration of the historical range of civil-military relations than either Huntington or sociologist Morris Janowitz, with whom Huntington is usually contrasted. Janowitz's *The Professional Soldier: A Social and Political Portrait* (New York: Free Press, 1960) is the most present-minded, least historical, and, in many ways, most narrowly focused of these three classic analyses, but he recognizes the utility of and demand for constabulary operations (or operations other than war) rather than privileging high-intensity conventional warfare as the most important military skill set.

Finer lays out a range of military insubordination to civilian control: shirking or refusing duties, tying the government's hands by threatening to do so (blackmail), intimidating the government directly, and displacing the government by refusing to defend it or by siding with rebels—all short of a coup by the military for the military. In 1913, for example, British commanders up to the highest levels sought to prevent the implementation of Irish home rule by refusing to defend Ireland against Unionist lawbreakers, either tying the hands of the ministry or blackmailing it with the threat to do so. This behavior (the "Curragh mutiny") could have displaced the ministry by forcing a vote of confidence and general elections if sufficient members of Parliament felt the ministry could not implement its policies. In 1830 the French army effectively displaced Louis XVIII by refusing to defend him; in 1848 the French army defended the Second Republic from further revolution from below; and in 1851 part of the military proved crucial to the coup by Louis Bonaparte.

23. Andrew Abbott, *The System of Professions: An Essay on the Division of Expert Labor* (Chicago: University of Chicago Press, 1988). Following Huntington's rival Janowitz, political scientist Thomas Langston observed in *Uneasy Balance* that successful American postwar civil-military settlements have depended on a balancing of military demands for greater war-fighting capability—reforms to address the problems that appeared during the war—with social-political demands for a greater variety of services from the armed forces. The most historically nuanced approach might be that of former officer Donald Connelly, who observes that the key question in American civil-military relations is to which civilian authority (the executive or Congress) the military has been more responsive. See Donald Connelly, *John M. Schofield and the Politics of Generalship* (Chapel Hill: University of North Carolina Press, 2006), xii, for a summary assessment of the relationship between officers and American politics (nineteenth century and today) that accords well with my own. Samuel Huntington (and perhaps Hew Strachan) considered this "dual control" a weakness that hindered professional development. See the many works of Dennis Showalter, such as *The Wars of Frederick the Great* (London: Longman, 1996), 1–2, for trenchant critiques of Whig and Calvinist teleologies among military historians.

24. Michael Geyer, "The Past as Future: The German Officer Corps as Profession," in *German Professions, 1800–1950*, ed. Geoffrey Cocks and Konrad H. Jarausch (New York: Oxford University Press, 1990), 187.

25. Wilson, *The Business of Civil War*; Ball, *Army Regulars on the Western Frontier*; Wayne Wei-siang Hsieh, *West Pointers and the Civil War: The Old Army in War and Peace* (Chapel Hill: University of North Carolina Press, 2009); Mark A. Smith, *Engineering Security: The Corps of Engineers and Third System Defense Policy, 1815–1861* (Tuscaloosa: University of Alabama Press, 2009). Hsieh, Smith, Wilson, and I all emphasize the professionalization of the army before the Civil War, and we all earned our doctorates since the publication of Skelton's *An American Profession of Arms*. Ball did not and comes from a different perspective as a western historian, although he has begun to emphasize the army's professionalism and autonomy in his work on Edwin Vose Sumner, one of its principal commanders in peacekeeping operations during the 1850s.

26. Jeremy Black has been especially important in calling attention to the frequency, extent, and significance of domestic policing and internal security missions, rather than conventional combat between large symmetrical forces, for military institutions and warfare. See Black's *War: Past, Present, and Future* (New York: St. Martin's, 2000); *Western Warfare, 1775–1882* (Bloomington: Indiana University Press, 2001); *War in the Nineteenth Century, 1800–1914* (Cambridge: Polity Press, 2009); and his and Dennis Showalter's essays in *European Warfare, 1815–2000*, ed. Jeremy Black (New York: Palgrave, 2002).

27. Jefferson's first inaugural, March 4, 1801, *MPP*, 1:311.

28. Skowronek, *Building a New American State*, 86; Timothy D. Johnson, *A Gal-*

lant Little Army: The Mexico City Campaign (Lawrence: University Press of Kansas, 2007), appendix 2. The three volunteer regiments were larger than their regular counterparts, and the majority of the army's enlisted soldiers were wartime recruits, but the officer corps at Mexico City was disproportionately composed of career regulars who held all the key staff positions. Volunteers did make up the great majority of troops holding the line of communications from Mexico City to Veracruz, though they were often under regular command.

29. Cass, annual report, November 21, 1831, *ASPMA*, 4:712.

30. Arthur P. Wade, "Roads to the Top—An Analysis of General-Officer Selection in the United States Army, 1789–1898," *Military Affairs* 40 (December 1976): 157–163; William B. Skelton, "High Army Leadership in the Era of the War of 1812: The Making and Remaking of the Officer Corps," *WMQ* 51 (April 1994): 253–274; William E. Birkhimer, *The Law of Appointment and Promotion in the Regular Army of the United States* (New York: A. G. Sherwood, 1880). I am not arguing that it was a good idea to draw a quarter of the officer corps directly from civilian life, but these officers soon acquired as much experience as the "ninety-day wonders" who entered the officer corps on a far larger scale (both in absolute numbers and proportionally) during the world wars. Moreover, their tasks were simpler, and they enjoyed closer supervision by the three-quarters of the officers who made the army their career.

31. Skelton, *An American Profession of Arms*, 138–139. See Thomas J. Goss, *The War within the Union High Command: Politics and Generalship during the Civil War* (Lawrence: University Press of Kansas, 2003), and Andrew J. Polsky, "'Mr. Lincoln's Army' Revisited: Partisanship, Institutional Position, and Union Army Command, 1861–1865," *Studies in American Political Development* 16 (Fall 2002): 176–207. Paul A. C. Koistinen, *Beating Ploughshares into Swords: The Political Economy of American Warfare, 1606–1865* (Lawrence: University Press of Kansas, 1996), tacitly echoes the weak-state thesis through his emphasis on the success of decentralized mobilization in the North and the limits of centralization in the Confederacy. Students of Civil War mobilization should look first to Wilson, *The Business of Civil War*, and then to Paul D. Escott, *Military Necessity: Civil-Military Relations in the Confederacy* (Westport, Conn.: Praeger Security International, 2006), although Koistinen remains valuable for his thorough detail.

32. Wilson, *The Business of Civil War*; Wilson, "Politics of Procurement." I make this link in my 1996 dissertation. See Skelton, *An American Profession of Arms*, 182–183, 213–216, for statistics on officer commissioning sources, career length, and resignation rates prior to 1861.

33. For a summary of naval diplomatic operations, see David F. Long, *Gold Braid and Foreign Relations: Diplomatic Activities of U.S. Naval Officers, 1798–1883* (Annapolis, Md.: Naval Institute Press, 1988).

34. Richard White, *The Middle Ground: Indians, Empires, and Republics in the Great Lakes Region, 1650–1815* (Cambridge: Cambridge University Press, 1991); Leonard Thompson and Howard Lamar, "The North American and South African Frontiers," in *The Frontier in History: North America and Southern Africa Compared,*

ed. Howard Lamar and Leonard Thompson (New Haven, Conn.: Yale University Press, 1981), 38. Eric J. Hinderaker, *Elusive Empires: Constructing Colonialism in the Ohio Valley, 1673–1800* (Cambridge: Cambridge University Press, 1997), presents a similar conclusion, as does Kathleen Du Val, *The Native Ground: Indians and Colonists in the Heart of the Continent* (Philadelphia: University of Pennsylvania Press, 2006). Patricia Nelson Limerick, *The Legacy of Conquest: The Unbroken Past of the American West* (New York: W. W. Norton, 1987), is focused primarily on legacies rather than the process of conquest itself; the federal government plays an important part in her interpretation, but she devotes virtually no attention to the army. See Daniel J. Herman, "Romance on the Middle Ground," *JER* 19 (Summer 1999): 279–291, for a powerful early critique suggesting that the middle-ground concept reasserts American exceptionalism as multicultural adaptation; see "Forum: The Middle Ground Revisited," *WMQ* 63 (January 2006): 3–96, for a discussion of the divergence, tensions, and paradox in historians' use of the concept. Jerome Adelman and Stephen Aron, "From Borderlands to Borders: Empires, Nation-States, and the Peoples in between in North American History," *AHR* 104 (June 1999): 814–841, is the most widely cited essay on the borderlands concept.

35. Anthony Giddens, *The Nation-State and Violence: Volume Two of a Contemporary Critique of Historical Materialism* (Berkeley: University of California Press, 1985), 49–50. See Peter Sahlins's pathbreaking book *Boundaries: The Making of France and Spain in the Pyrenees* (Berkeley: University of California Press, 1989), for one of the most nuanced analyses available.

36. John Darwin, "Imperialism and the Victorians: The Dynamics of Territorial Expansion," *English Historical Review* 112 (June 1997): 634–640; Ronald Hyam, *Britain's Imperial Century, 1815–1914: A Study of Empire and Expansion* (New York: Palgrave Macmillan, 2002), 2, 280–283, 288, 317–319; R. E. Robinson and J. A. Gallagher, *Africa and the Victorians: The Official Mind of Imperialism* (London: Macmillan, 1961).

37. Giddens, *Nation-State and Violence*, 160; Norbert Elias, *The Civilizing Process, Part I: The History of Manners*, trans. Edmund Jephcott (1939; reprint, New York: Urizen Books, 1978); Norbert Elias, *The Civilizing Process, Part II: Power and Civility*, trans. Edmund Jephcott (1939; reprint, New York: Pantheon, 1982); Hans Gerth and C. Wright Mills, eds., *From Max Weber: Essays in Sociology* (New York: Oxford University Press, 1946), 201; Skelton, *An American Profession of Arms*, 71. See Steven C. Bullock, *Revolutionary Brotherhood: Freemasonry and the Transformation of the American Social Order, 1730–1840* (Chapel Hill: University of North Carolina Press, 1996), for a stimulating examination of the links among cosmopolitan learning, ambition, gentility, respectability, and nonsectarian nationalism among the Freemasons, links that were commonly present among officers as well.

38. Alexander Saxton, *The Rise and Fall of the White Republic: Class Politics and Mass Culture in Nineteenth-Century America* (London: Verso, 1990); Roy Harvey Pearce, *Savagism and Civilization: A Study of the Indian and the American Mind*, 2nd ed. (Berkeley: University of California Press, 1988); Michael Paul Rogin, *Fathers and*

Children: Andrew Jackson and the Subjugation of the American Indian (New York: Alfred A. Knopf, 1975); Robert F. Berkhofer, *The White Man's Indian: Images of the American Indian from Columbus to the Present* (New York: Alfred A. Knopf, 1978); Ronald T. Takaki, *Iron Cages: Race and Culture in Nineteenth-Century America* (New York: Alfred A. Knopf, 1979); Richard Drinnon, *Facing West: The Metaphysics of Indian-Hating and Empire-Building* (Minneapolis: University of Minnesota Press, 1980); Reginald Horsman, *Race and Manifest Destiny: The Origins of American Racial Anglo-Saxonism* (Cambridge, Mass.: Harvard University Press, 1981).

   39. Robert Wooster, *The American Military Frontiers: The United States Army in the West, 1783–1900* (Albuquerque: University of New Mexico Press, 2009), xv; V. G. Kiernan, *Colonial Empires and Armies, 1815–1960* (Phoenix Mill, U.K.: Sutton Publishing, 1998); Douglas Porch, *Wars of Empire* (London: Cassell, 2000); Bruce Vandervort, *Wars of Imperial Conquest in Africa, 1830–1914* (Bloomington: Indiana University Press, 1998); J. A. deMoor and H. L. Wesseling, eds., *Imperialism and War: Essays on Colonial Wars in Asia and Africa* (Leiden, Netherlands: Brill, 1989); Anthony Clayton, *France, Soldiers, and Africa* (London: Brassey's, 1988); C. M. Andrew and A. S. Kanya-Forstner, "Centre and Periphery in the Making of the Second French Empire, 1815–1920," *Journal of Imperial and Commonwealth History* 16, 3 (1988): 9–34; Sullivan, *Thomas-Robert Bugeaud, France, and Algeria*; A. S. Kanya-Forstner, *The Conquest of the Western Sudan: A Study in French Military Imperialism* (Cambridge: Cambridge University Press, 1969); Strachan, *The Politics of the British Army*; Ian Beckett, *The Victorians at War* (London: Hambleton and London, 2003); Ian Hernon, *Britain's Forgotten Wars: Colonial Campaigns of the 19th Century* (London: Sutton Publishing, 2003); Byron Farwell, *Eminent Victorian Soldiers: Seekers of Glory* (New York: W. W. Norton, 1985); Douglas M. Peers, *Between Mars and Mammon: Colonial Armies and the Garrison State in Early Nineteenth-Century India* (London: I. B. Tauris, 1995); Robert A. Huttenback, *British Relations with the Sind, 1799–1843: An Anatomy of Imperialism* (Berkeley: University of California Press, 1962); H. T. Lambrick, *Sir Charles Napier and Sind* (Oxford: Clarendon Press, 1982); E. Willis Brooks, "Nicholas I as Reformer: Russian Attempts to Conquer the Caucasus, 1825–1855," in *Nation and Ideology: Essays in Honor of Wayne S. Vucinich*, ed. Ivo Banac et al. (New York: Columbia University Press, 1981), 245; David Mackenzie, "Russian Expansion in Central Asia: St. Petersburg versus the Turkestan Generals," *Canadian Slavic Studies* 3 (1969): 293–311; David Mackenzie, *The Lion of Tashkent: The Career of General M. G. Cherniaev* (Athens: University of Georgia Press, 1974); and, from an earlier era, Stephen Saunders Webb, *The Governors-General: The English Army and the Definition of Empire, 1569–1681* (Chapel Hill: University of North Carolina Press, 1979).

   40. Stephen Peter Rosen, "Alexander Hamilton and the Domestic Uses of International Law," *DH* 5 (Summer 1981): 183–198; Kinley J. Brauer, "The Great American Desert Revisited: Recent Literature and Prospects for the Study of American Foreign Relations, 1815–1860," *DH* 13 (Summer 1989): 395–417; William Earl Weeks, "New Directions in the Study of Early American Foreign Relations," *DH* 17 (Winter 1993): 73–95; Jay Gitlin, "Private Diplomacy to Private Property: States,

Tribes, and Nations in the Early National Period," *DH* 22 (Winter 1998): 85–99; Adelman and Aron, "From Borderlands to Borders"; Nathan J. Citino, "The Global Frontier: Comparative History and the Frontier-Borderlands Approach in American Foreign Relations," *DH* 25 (Fall 2001): 677–693; Peter J. Kastor, "'Motives of Peculiar Urgency': Local Diplomacy in Louisiana, 1803–1821," *WMQ* 58 (October 2001): 819–848.

41. R. R. Davies, *The First English Empire: Power and Identities in the British Isles, 1093–1343* (New York: Oxford University Press, 2000), 173; Adams to William H. Crawford, September 14, 1814, *WJQA*, 5:140. Historians blinded to the virtues of the nation-state by love of diversity and antagonism toward hierarchy should be thankful they do not live in the failed states of the world. See Jeremi Suri, *Liberty's Surest Guardian: American Nation-Building from the Founders to Obama* (New York: Free Press, 2011), for a recognition that nation-states continue to wield great power today—in some respects, more than they did in the late twentieth century.

CHAPTER ONE: CONFIDENCE, BELLIGERENCE, AND INSUBORDINATION

1. Privateers were nonstate actors who gained "letters of marque" from nation-states or revolutionaries authorizing them to attack shipping. They were usually businessmen—armed entrepreneurs—who attacked other businessmen (merchants). See Charles C. Griffin, *The United States and the Disruption of the Spanish Empire, 1810–1822* (New York: Columbia University Press, 1937); James J. Auchmuty, *The United States Government and Latin American Independence, 1810–1830* (London: P. S. King, 1937); Arthur P. Whitaker, *The United States and the Independence of Latin America, 1800–1830* (Baltimore: Johns Hopkins University Press, 1941); John J. Johnson, *A Hemisphere Apart: The Foundations of United States Policy toward Latin America* (Baltimore: Johns Hopkins University Press, 1990); Lester D. Langley, *The Struggle for the American Mediterranean: United States–European Rivalry in the Gulf-Caribbean, 1776–1904* (Athens: University of Georgia Press, 1976), chaps. 1, 2; and Rafe Blaufarb, "The Western Question: The Geopolitics of Latin American Independence," *AHR* 112 (June 2007): 742–763.

2. For the army's constabulary role between 1784 and 1810, see James Ripley Jacobs, *The Beginning of the U.S. Army, 1783–1812* (Princeton, N.J.: Princeton University Press, 1947); William B. Skelton, *An American Profession of Arms: The Army Officer Corps, 1784–1861* (Lawrence: University Press of Kansas, 1992), chap. 4; Francis Paul Prucha, *The Sword of the Republic: The United States Army on the Frontier, 1783–1846* (New York: Macmillan, 1969), chaps. 2–5; Richard H. Kohn, *Eagle and Sword: The Federalists and the Creation of the Military Establishment in America, 1783–1802* (New York: Free Press, 1975); William H. Guthman, *March to Massacre: A History of the First Seven Years of the United States Army, 1784–1791* (New York: McGraw-Hill, 1975); John P. Huber, "General Josiah Harmar's Command: Military

Policy and the Old Northwest, 1784–1791" (Ph.D. diss., University of Michigan, 1968); Alan S. Brown, "The Role of the Army in Western Settlement: Josiah Harmar's Command, 1785–1790," *Pennsylvania Magazine of History and Biography* 93 (April 1969): 161–178; Gayle Thornbrough, ed., *Outpost on the Wabash, 1787–1791: Letters of Brigadier General Josiah Harmar and Major John Francis Hamtramck and Other Letters and Documents Selected from the Harmar Papers in the William L. Clements Library* (Indianapolis: Indiana Historical Society, 1957); Richard C. Knopf, ed., *Anthony Wayne, a Name in Arms: Soldier, Diplomat, Defender of Expansion Westward of a Nation: The Wayne-Knox, Pickering-McHenry Correspondence* (Pittsburgh: University of Pittsburgh Press, 1960); Wiley Sword, *President Washington's Indian War: The Struggle for the Old Northwest, 1790–1795* (Norman: University of Oklahoma Press, 1985); Alan D. Gaff, *Bayonets in the Wilderness: Anthony Wayne's Legion in the Old Northwest* (Norman: University of Oklahoma Press, 2004); and Theodore J. Crackel, *Mr. Jefferson's Army: Political and Social Reform of the Military Establishment, 1801–1809* (New York: New York University Press, 1987).

3. On June 14, 1810, after conferring with President Madison in Washington, Louisiana territorial governor William C. C. Claiborne wrote to Louisiana parish judge and militia commander William Wykoff, asking explicitly that he stimulate rebellion in West Florida and seek U.S. intervention, preferably through a convention of the inhabitants (*LBWCCC*, 5:31–34). Secretary of State Robert Smith then asked Georgia senator William H. Crawford to find an agent to undertake similar efforts; on June 20 Crawford selected George Mathews, the governor of Georgia during the filibusters against East Florida during the mid-1790s (*TP*, 9:883–885). Madison approved Claiborne's plan for subversion and intervention and prepared for further contingencies on July 17, ordering Secretary of State Smith to have Mississippi territorial governor David Holmes mobilize his militia for intervention against "foreign [British] interference" or "internal convulsions" in West Florida (*PJM*, 2:419). Smith told Holmes that Claiborne's letter to Wykoff had been "written under a sanction from the president" (*PJM*, 2:420n4). See James A. Padgett, ed., "Official Records of the West Florida Revolution and Republic," *LAHQ* 21 (July 1938): 685–805; James A. Padgett, ed., "The West Florida Revolution of 1810, as Told in the Letters of John Rhea, Fulwar Skipwith, Reuben Kemper, and Others," *LAHQ* 21 (January 1938): 76–202; Isaac J. Cox, *The West Florida Controversy, 1798–1813: A Study in American Diplomacy* (Baltimore: Johns Hopkins University Press, 1918); Stanley C. Arthur, *The Story of the West Florida Rebellion* (St. Francisville, La.: St. Francisville Democrat, 1935); *PJM*, 2:305–320; David A. Bice, *The Original Lone Star Republic: Scoundrels, Statesmen, and Schemers of the 1810 West Florida Rebellion* (Clanton, Ala.: Heritage Publishing Consultants, 2004); Frank L. Owsley Jr. and Gene A. Smith, *Filibusters and Expansionists: Jeffersonian Manifest Destiny, 1800–1821* (Tuscaloosa: University of Alabama Press, 1997), chap. 4; Andrew McMichael, *Atlantic Loyalties: Americans in Spanish West Florida, 1785–1810* (Athens: University of Georgia Press, 2008); and J. C. A. Stagg, *Borderlines in Borderlands: James Madison and the Spanish-American Frontier, 1776–1821* (New Haven, Conn.: Yale University Press, 2009), chap. 2.

4. Mathews's instructions are in Monroe to Mathews and John McKee, January 26, 1811, *ASPFR*, 3:571. The most thorough accounts of Mathews's operations are J. C. A. Stagg, "James Madison and Geo Mathews: The East Florida Revolution of 1812 Reconsidered," *DH* 30 (January 2006): 23–55; J. C. A. Stagg, "George Mathews and John McKee: Revolutionizing East Florida, Mobile, and Pensacola in 1812," *FHQ* 85 (Winter 2007): 269–296; and Stagg, *Borderlines in Borderlands*, chap. 3. The most thorough narrative of the East Florida conflict is James G. Cusick, *The Other War of 1812: The Patriot War and the American Invasion of East Florida* (Gainesville: University Press of Florida, 2003), which replaces Rembert W. Patrick, *Florida Fiasco: Rampant Rebels on the Georgia-Florida Border, 1810–1815* (Athens: University of Georgia Press, 1954), a pathbreaking book but short on citations. See also Wanjohi Waciuma, *Intervention in the Spanish Floridas, 1801–1813: A Study in Jeffersonian Foreign Policy* (Boston: Branden Press, 1976). Cusick maintains that the "Patriot" movement was largely indigenous to East Florida rather than an outright invasion from Georgia (as had been the case during the mid-1790s), but the rebels were aided by slave hunters and marauders from Georgia.

5. John Quincy Adams to Alexander Hill Everett, March 16, 1816, and to John Adams, February 29, 1816, *WJQA*, 5:537, 522; John Quincy Adams to Secretary of State Monroe, April 30, 1816, *WJQA*, 6:22. See Charles K. Webster, *The Foreign Policy of Castlereagh, 1815–1822* (London: G. Bell and Sons, 1925), and Bradford Perkins, *Castlereagh and Adams: England and the United States, 1812–1823* (Berkeley: University of California Press, 1964).

6. Neutrality Act of June 5, 1794, secs. 5, 7, 1 *Stat.* 384; Neutrality Act of April 20, 1818, 3 *Stat.* 447–450. The second act added nothing significant to federal authority. The Neutrality Act of March 10, 1838 (5 *Stat.* 212–214), authorized the preventative seizure of weapons, ammunition, and ships "which may be provided or prepared for" such filibusters.

7. Cushing, April 24, 1810, file C-126, SWLR: Reg. In general, see Villasana Haggard, "The Neutral Ground between Louisiana and Texas," *LAHQ* 28 (October 1945): 1001–1128.

8. Donald Jackson, ed., *The Journals of Zebulon Montgomery Pike, with Letters and Related Documents* (Norman: University of Oklahoma Press, 1966), 2:95–97, 288, 360–361, 379–380.

9. Capt. Charles Wollstonecraft to Col. Thomas Cushing, June 12 and July 21, 1810, file C-191, SWLR: Reg. See also G. P. Whittington, "Dr. John Sibley of Nacogdoches, 1757–1837," *LAHQ* 10 (October 1927): 467–512. Although the American filibusters entered Texas at the invitation of indigenous revolutionaries like Gutiérrez, I refer to them as filibusters because that was their status (private individuals operating outside or in violation of the law) under the U.S. neutrality law of 1794 and under all international norms and customs.

10. JW to Jefferson, September 1, 1808, Thomas Jefferson Papers, LC; Félix D. Almaráz Jr., *Tragic Cavalier: Governor Manuel Salcedo of Texas, 1808–1813* (Austin: University of Texas Press, 1971), 29–31, 55–56; Carlos Castañeda, *The Mission Era:*

The End of the Spanish Regime, 1780–1810 (Austin, Tex.: Von Boeckmann-Jones, 1942), 393–395.

11. Castañeda, *Mission Era*, 392; Cushing, April 24, file C-126 and enclosures, Wollstonecraft to Cushing, June 12, file C-191, and enclosures to Cushing, September 12, file C-217, all 1810, SWLR: Reg; *PAJ*, 3:136. Today's military doctrinal term for such an operation is "combined," but I assume most readers will find "joint" easier to understand. The exact chain of transmission is not clear; Salcedo wrote to American justice of the peace John C. Carr, who referred him to Claiborne, but the latter had already departed for Washington, where he would plot rebellion by American settlers against Spain in West Florida.

12. Peter J. Kastor, *The Nation's Crucible: The Louisiana Purchase and the Creation of America* (New Haven, Conn.: Yale University Press, 2004), 121; Peter J. Kastor, "'Motives of Peculiar Urgency': Local Diplomacy in Louisiana, 1803–1821," *WMQ* 58 (October 2001): 819–848. See Almaráz, *Tragic Cavalier*, 62–64, 75, on U.S. Army deserters who entered Texas in May 1810 but were returned to Louisiana (where they were presumably received by U.S. officers for punishment) by the Spanish that summer.

13. Kastor, *The Nation's Crucible*, 119.

14. Marietta M. LeBreton, "A History of the Territory of Orleans, 1803–1812" (Ph.D. diss., Louisiana State University, 1969), 402–404; Almaráz, *Tragic Cavalier*, 142; Sibley to ?, July 17, 1811, deposition of John Garniere, September 19, 1811, Sibley to Attorney General Edmund Randolph, September 23, 1811, and Sibley to Eustis, December 31, 1811, and April 24 and June 24, 1812, in Julia K. Garrett, ed., "Dr. John Sibley and the Louisiana-Texas Frontier, 1803–1814," *SWHQ* 49 (July 1945–January 1946): 116–119, 291, 399–400, 407–408; WCCC to Monroe, November 19, 1811, *LBWCCC*, 5:383. Menchaca may have been a double agent or an agent provocateur.

15. Carr to WCCC, July 4, 1811, WCCC to Secretary of State Robert Smith, December 19, 1811, and memorial, January 4, 1812, *TP*, 9:943, 961, 976–977; WCCC to Hampton, January 20, 1812, *LBWCCC*, 6:34–36.

16. Hampton to WCCC, January 23, 1812, *TP*, 9:990; Hampton to Pike, February 6, 1812, file H-213, SWLR: Reg (also in *TP*, 9:998–1000). See Hampton, January 3 and 19, 1811, files H-278 and 294, and Hampton to WCCC, February 9, 1811, enclosure, file C-362, SWLR: Reg, for their clash over control of operations near Mobile during the U.S. incursion there. Most of the secondary literature cites the commander of Natchitoches as *John* Overton, perhaps thinking of Andrew Jackson's friend, but Charles K. Gardner, comp., *A Dictionary of the Officers of the Army of the United States* (New York: G. P. Putnam, 1860), makes it clear that there was no such officer in the army in 1812, whereas Walter H. Overton was a captain stationed at Natchitoches in that year. As so often happens, authors without access to the army biographical dictionaries mistook names or assumed an identity with a more famous individual of the same name, and other historians followed their lead.

17. Hampton to Pike, February 6, 1812, file H-213, SWLR: Reg; Pike to King, Montero, and Simón de Herrera (the top Spanish military commander in Texas), Feb-

ruary 26, to Hampton, March 2, and to Magee, March 3, 1812, file H-213, SWLR: Reg. The law in question was passed March 3, 1807 (2 *Stat.* 445–446). Like most Jeffersonian legislation, it authorized the president to direct action by civil subordinates (federal marshals) and to employ military force. Privileging strict constitutional scruples at the expense of effective law enforcement, Jeffersonians usually interpreted this to mean that the president had to issue a specific order for a specific situation—essentially a presidential warrant—rather than relying on subordinates' initiative or discretion.

18. Pike to Magee, March 3, to Hampton, March 2, and to Overton, March 16, 1812, and Magee to Pike, March 18, 1812, file H-213, Overton to Montero, March 27, 1812, and undated response, enclosure in Hampton, April 14, 1812, file H-238, SWLR: Reg; Almaráz, *Tragic Cavalier*, 137; Haggard, "The Neutral Ground between Louisiana and Texas," 1067–1068. Several secondary accounts assert that Magee whipped two bandits and placed hot coals on their backs during one of his expeditions into the Neutral Ground, but they do not provide sources.

19. Julia K. Garrett, *Green Flag over Texas* (Dallas: Cordova Press, 1939), 85–88 (Overton to JW, October 21, 1811, quoted on 87).

20. Ibid., 110, 155 (second quotation from Overton to JW, August 25, 1812); Pike, October 28, 1811, file P-13, SWLR: Reg; Sibley to ?, July 17, 1811, in Garrett, "Dr. John Sibley and the Louisiana-Texas Frontier," 118; Roy F. Nichols, *Advance Agents of American Destiny* (Philadelphia: University of Pennsylvania Press, 1956). Some sources refer to Shaler as "captain," but he never served in the regular army. Most historians have followed Harris Gaylord Warren, *The Sword Was Their Passport: A History of American Filibustering in the Mexican Revolution* (Baton Rouge: Louisiana State University Press, 1943), in arguing that the Madison administration lent its sympathy, as well as some financial support, to Gutiérrez and Toledo. See Owsley and Smith, *Filibusters and Expansionists*, chap. 3, for the argument that Shaler was intended to play much the same expansionist role as George Mathews and other Jeffersonian covert agents provocateurs, although Shaler did not have to stir up a rebellion. David E. Narrett, "Liberation and Conquest: John Hamilton Robinson and U.S. Adventurism toward Mexico, 1806–1819," *WHQ* 40 (Spring 2009): 23–50, emphasizes the explicit strictures against filibustering in Monroe's instructions to Shaler and Robinson (as U.S. emissary to Nemecio Salcedo, in Monroe to Robinson, July 1, 1812, Correspondence Relating to Filibustering Expeditions against the Spanish Government of Mexico, 1811–1816, microcopy T286, RG 59, NA) and that Monroe initiated legal action against Robinson's filibustering schemes in 1814 (34–35), but he acknowledges that these emissaries acted in ways that could easily be perceived as U.S. support for filibustering.

J. C. A. Stagg disputes the Warren-Owsley-Smith interpretation in "The Madison Administration and Mexico: Reinterpreting the Gutiérrez-Magee Raid of 1812–1813," *WMQ* 59 (April 2002): 449–480; in his editorial note "Madison and the Problem of Mexican Independence: The Gutiérrez-Magee Raid of August 1812," *PJM*, 5:235–245; and in *Borderlines in Borderlands*. Stagg has the best access to sources and the greatest familiarity with Madison's policies, but he takes his sources almost entirely at face value, relying heavily on the letter of Shaler's formal instructions rather than on his actions; this creates overly rigid distinctions that obscure U.S. government sympathy for and connections with Gutiérrez. In particular, labeling the Gutiérrez-Magee expedition a raid, as Stagg consistently does, clouds reality: the forces that Gutiérrez and Magee led into Texas seized the capital at San Antonio de Bexar and remained there for more than a year, until they were defeated by royalist troops at the Battle of Medina. Nor does Stagg acknowledge that Madison's encouragement of Mexican independence—the very motive for Shaler's mission—meant encouraging rebellion, a violation of Spanish sovereignty by any standard.

In my view, the combination of Monroe's explicit efforts to foment rebellion in West Florida; Shaler's mission; Monroe's meetings with and payments to Gutiérrez and Toledo in Washington; the presence of Joseph B. Wilkinson, one of the general's sons, as a liaison to the expedition; the lack of effort by federal civil and military officials to enforce the neutrality act against the expedition; and the possibility that federal officials were involved in weapons transfers suggest that Warren, Owsley, and Smith have the better argument. Madison and Monroe consistently failed to exercise effective oversight over their agents in the borderlands: in East Florida, where U.S. troops remained for an entire year, despite the administration's disavowal of Mathews; in Pensacola, which Jackson seized twice; and in Texas in 1812 and 1813. A competent administration would not have to continually disavow its agents on every disputed front, as Madison did between 1812 and 1814. To what extent was Madison overwhelmed—and allowed himself to be overwhelmed—because he was convinced that the United States had a right to the territories in question and would eventually gain them, regardless of Spain? Madison seems to have been convinced that history would work the way he wanted, whereas Monroe sometimes felt that history needed some help, and there were plenty of Americans eager to make that "destiny" reality.

21. Wollstonecraft to JW, July 10, 1812, enclosure to JW, August 10, 1812, file W-303, SWLR: Reg. Wollstonecraft's August 2 letter (enclosure to JW, August 17, 1812, file W-304, SWLR: Reg) notes that the filibusters "have several swivels [cannon], one 9 pdr [pounder]," distinct from the guns he left with Overton. Republican scruples about strict constitutional interpretation and national standing armies compelled the Jefferson administration to secure a law authorizing the president to employ federal military forces, as well as militia, to repress insurrection "or obstruction to the laws" (March 3, 1807, 2 *Stat.* 443)—just in time for Jefferson's Embargo, which constitutional scholar Leonard W. Levy maintains was "the most repressive and unconstitutional legislation ever enacted by Congress in time of peace" (*Jefferson and Civil Liberties: The Darker Side*, 2nd ed. [Chicago: Ivan R. Dee, 1989], 139).

22. Wollstonecraft, August 2 and 3, enclosure to JW, August 17, 1812, file W-304, SWLR: Reg; WCCC to JW, August 9, to Monroe, August 10, to Carr, August 12 and 14, and to Judge Steele (at Baton Rouge), August 17, 1812, *LBWCCC*, 6:151–152, 159–165; JW, August 10, 1812, file W-303, SWLR: Reg; Ted Schwarz, *Forgotten Battlefield of the First Texas Revolution: The Battle of Medina, August 18, 1813* (Austin, Tex.: Eakin Press, 1985), chap. 1. Schwarz has Wollstonecraft returning to Baton

Rouge on August 13, but JW, August 17, 1812, file W-304, SWLR: Reg, encloses a letter from the captain at Baton Rouge dated August 6. Whether because of Claiborne's support during the Burr crisis or because the governor and the general now shared expansionist sentiments without any of the complications Wilkinson had felt in 1806, the general had much more praise for Claiborne than he had a decade before: though troubled by "mauvais subjects" in New Orleans, Wilkinson believed the governor would "rise above his enemies, because he is honest and patriotic" (JW, August 10, 1812, file W-303, SWLR: Reg). After two years of Wade Hampton, Claiborne probably saw Wilkinson in a more positive light as well.

23. Isaac J. Cox, "The Pan-American Policy of Jefferson and Wilkinson," *MVHR* 1 (September 1914): 212–239; Pike to Monroe, June 19, 1812, in Jackson, *Journals of Zebulon Montgomery Pike*, 2:379–387; Harold A. Bierck Jr., "Dr. John Hamilton Robinson," *LAHQ* 25 (July 1942): 644–669; Narrett, "Liberation and Conquest." I think the sum of the evidence shows that Stagg's emphasis on Madison's concentration on Florida—where agent George Mathews had embroiled the army in an undeclared war with Spanish troops outside St. Augustine—and the War of 1812 is accurate, but this did not prevent Madison's subordinates, from Monroe on down, from expressing sympathy, looking the other way, and providing varying degrees of assistance to this first major American filibuster against Texas. As shown in the first three chapters of *Jackson's Sword*, the Jeffersonians hardly made an adequate effort to restrain filibustering. Were they culpable, derelict in their constitutional duty to enforce the laws, or merely negligent? Or was Jeffersonian administration so deficient—in comparison to that of the Federalists, who immediately preceded the Jeffersonians—that the United States lacked effective sovereignty over its borders, its citizens, and even its own agents?

24. Sibley to Eustis, July 14, 1812, in Garrett, "Dr. John Sibley and the Louisiana-Texas Frontier," 118, 411; Garrett, *Green Flag over Texas*, 142; JW, August 4 and 10, October 12, and November 11, 1812, files W-286, 303, 361, and 387, SWLR: Reg. I have not researched enlisted desertions from Fort Claiborne because counting deserters would be meaningless unless we could find their names in the scant records of the expedition, and it would be difficult to prove any link between desertion and official tolerance or policy. Poorly paid and brutally disciplined enlisted men needed little official encouragement to take up filibusters' offers of personal independence and opportunity. See Bill Walraven and Marjorie K. Walraven, "The 'Sabine Chute': The U.S. Army and the Texas Revolution," *SWHQ* 107 (April 2004): 573–601, for the most thorough examination of army desertion in this situation. Robert E. May also suggests the significance of army deserters for filibuster recruitment during the 1840s and 1850s in *Manifest Destiny's Underworld: Filibustering in Antebellum America* (Chapel Hill: University of North Carolina Press, 2002).

25. Magee, June 22, 1812, AGOLR; Schwarz, *Forgotten Battlefield*, 59; William C. Davis, *The Pirates Laffite: The Treacherous World of the Gulf Corsairs* (New York: Harcourt, 2005), 394, 408. The number eight is based on a comparison of every name in the sources listed herein with those in the army biographical dictionaries. There may have been other filibusters who served as officers, but the small number identified thus

far suggests that there were few, and the sources are fragmentary enough that ex-officers said to have been in one filibuster expedition may in fact have been in another. Another problem in identification lies in the common use of military ranks by men not in the regular army: scholars must beware of assuming that the two were synonymous. Indeed, most filibusters identified as holding military ranks (whether in filibuster forces or simply by claiming such rank) cannot be found in the army biographical dictionaries or registers. No doubt many held some sort of militia rank; in other cases, common names such as Smith and Brown do not allow positive correlation without further evidence. If anything, I have erred on the side of filibustering, assuming a common identity if filibusters' names were also present in the biographical sources (aside from Smiths and Browns), even without positive evidence to that effect.

26. Overton to JW, October 22, enclosure to JW, November 23, 1812, file W-407, SWLR: Reg; see also JW, October 18 and November 11, and Overton, October 3, 1812, files W-379 and 387.

27. Eustis to JW, August 26 and September 21, 1812, SWLS; WCCC to Madison, October 23, 1813, *PJM*, 6:708; *PJM*, 6:679n3.

28. Spanish efforts to maintain their American empire can be followed in John Lynch, *The Spanish-American Revolutions, 1808–1826* (New York: W. W. Norton, 1973); Timothy E. Anna, *Spain and the Loss of America* (Lincoln: University of Nebraska Press, 1983); Jaime E. Rodriguez O., *The Independence of Spanish America* (Cambridge: Cambridge University Press, 1998); Robert Harvey, *Liberators: Latin America's Struggle for Independence, 1810–1830* (Woodstock, N.Y.: Overlook Press, 2000); Christon I. Archer, ed., *The Wars of Independence in Spanish America* (Wilmington, Del.: Scholarly Resources, 2000); Michael P. Costeloe, *Response to Revolution: Imperial Spain and the Spanish American Revolutions, 1810–1840* (Cambridge: Cambridge University Press, 1986); and Romeo Flores Caballero, *Counterrevolution: The Role of the Spaniards in the Independence of Mexico, 1804–1838*, trans. Jaime E. Rodriguez O. (Lincoln: University of Nebraska Press, 1969). Margaret L. Woodward, "The Spanish Army and the Loss of America, 1810–1824," *Hispanic American Historical Review* 48 (November 1968): 586–607, provides a concise examination of Spanish military deficiency, rooted in political division and lack of motivation as much as economic weakness.

29. Patrick, *Florida Fiasco*, 255, 259–265; Cusick, *The Other War of 1812*, 257–270; Flournoy to Madison, October 6, 1813, *PJM*, 6:678.

30. Provisions against piracy were included in the omnibus federal crime law of April 30, 1790, 1 *Stat.* 113–115.

31. Davis, *Pirates Laffite*, 42, 50, 54–55, 75–78, 83–85; Jane Lucas de Grummond, *The Baratarians and the Battle of New Orleans* (Baton Rouge: Louisiana State University Press, 1961), 4–21, 40–47.

32. Hampton, February 14, 1812, file H-170, and Ballinger to JW, October 19, 1812, enclosure, file W-380, SWLR: Reg.

33. Holmes to Wollstonecraft, November 20, 1812, enclosure, file W-107, SWLR: Reg.

34. Davis, *Pirates Laffite*, 87, 91–94, 111–115, 126; WCCC to JW, March 17, 1813, *LBWCCC*, 6:216–217.

35. Davis, *Pirates Laffite*, 126, 134–139, 182–191; Madison, June 29, 1814, *MPP*, 2:529; Robert C. Vogel, "Patterson and Ross' Raid on Barataria, Sept., 1814," *Louisiana History* 33 (Spring 1992): 157–170; Wilbur S. Brown, *The Amphibious Campaign for West Florida and Louisiana, 1814–1815: A Critical Review of Strategy and Tactics at New Orleans* (University: University of Alabama Press, 1969), 33–42. The soldiers attacked in October 1813 appear to have been under the command of Captain Ferdinand Amelung of the Louisiana volunteers, who later entered the U.S. Army. Ross had commanded the volunteers who joined Hampton against the German Coast slave uprising in Louisiana in January 1811.

36. AJ, proclamation, September 21, and to WCCC, September 30, 1814, *CAJ*, 2:57–63; Davis, *Pirates Laffite*, 195–210; de Grummond, *The Baratarians and the Battle of New Orleans*, 12, 23; Owsley and Smith, *Filibusters and Expansionists*, 164–175; LeBreton, "History of the Territory of Orleans," 33. See also John Sugden, "Jean Lafitte and the British Offer of 1814," *Louisiana History* 20 (Spring 1979): 159–167, and Robert C. Vogel, "Jean Laffite, the Baratarians, and the Battle of New Orleans: A Reappraisal," *Louisiana History* 41 (Summer 2000): 261–276. The Baratarians received letters of marque from the insurgent government of Cartagena, in modern Colombia, soon after that city rebelled in 1811.

CHAPTER TWO: THE ARMY ASSERTS AMERICAN HEGEMONY ON THE FLORIDA FRONTIER

1. Ethnohistorians have recently begun to explore and dissect the European practice of naming indigeneous aboriginal groups for political purposes, usually to aid in their division, subjugation, and dispossession. Recognizing the artificial construction, charged meaning, and ethnopolitical privileging inherent in the naming of Amerindian enthocultural groups, I have varied my practice according to my intent and the perspective I am adopting at the moment of labeling. See especially J. Leitch Wright Jr., *Creeks and Seminoles: The Destruction and Regeneration of the Miscogulge People* (Lincoln: University of Nebraska Press, 1986), whose work on these complex issues is especially stimulating. For analyses of officers' attitudes toward Amerindians, see William B. Skelton, *An American Profession of Arms: The Army Officer Corps, 1784–1861* (Lawrence: University Press of Kansas, 1992), chap. 16. Skelton's conclusion that "the army's relationship with Indians was intensely adversarial" through the War of 1812 (306) can be applied to the Florida frontier during the next half decade as well. Although Gaines and Jackson sometimes tried to protect friendly Indians from direct violence by whites, on the whole, they were virulent partisans of white supremacy and expansion. James W. Silver depicts a more benign Gaines in "A Counter-Proposal to the Indian Removal Policy of Andrew Jackson," *Journal of Mississippi History* 4 (October 1942): 207–215, but his evidence is primarily from the late 1820s and 1830s, after

the Florida frontier had been secured for white settlement; the evidence he gives for 1815–1821 seems to contradict his overall argument. U.S. Army officers shared many of their British counterparts' attitudes toward Indians, those rooted in their association with the nation-state as well as those rooted in ethnocentrism; see Colin G. Calloway, *Crown and Calumet: British-Indian Relations, 1783–1815* (Norman: University of Oklahoma Press, 1987).

2. Robert V. Remini, *Andrew Jackson and the Course of American Empire, 1767–1821* (New York: Harper and Row, 1977), 191.

3. AJ, December 16, 1817, file J-1, SWLR: Reg.

4. JW, July 13 and 22, 1812, files W-259 and 265, SWLR: Reg.

5. JW, July 28 and August 4, 1812, files W-267 and 286, SWLR: Reg; February 12, 1813, 3 *Stat.* 472; Gene A. Smith, "'Our Flag Was Display'd within Their Works': The Treaty of Ghent and the Conquest of Mobile," *Alabama Review* 52 (January 1999): 3–20.

6. Monroe to AJ, October 21, AJ to Secretary of War John Armstrong, June 27, Benton to Flournoy, July 5, 1814, *PAJ*, 3:171, 83–85, 100; Flournoy to Madison, October 6, 1813, *PJM*, 6:678.

7. AJ to Manrique, July 12, Manrique to AJ, July 26, 1814, *PAJ*, 3:86, 95–96.

8. AJ to Manrique, August 24 and September 9, report by Lt. (brevet Captain) John Gordon, July 29, Armstrong to AJ, July 18, 1814, *PAJ*, 3:120–21, 129–131, 98–99, 90.

9. Parker to Monroe, August 29 [1814], DPP; WCCC to AJ, August 12, and AJ to Armstrong, August 25, 1814, *PAJ*, 3:116, 122.

10. AJ to John Reid, August 27, to Monroe, October 10, and to Coffee, October 20, Monroe to AJ, October 21, AJ to Monroe, October 26 and November 20, and AJ to Manrique, November 6, 1814, *PAJ*, 3:125, 131n8, 151n2, 155, 169, 171, 173, 193, 180; Brian R. Rucker, "In the Shadow of Jackson: Uriah Blue's Expedition into West Florida," *FHQ* 73 (January 1995): 325–338. Jackson described the assault in letters to Willie Blount and Rachel Jackson (*PAJ*, 3:184–88). The closing reference is to Jackson's famous "Rhea letter," AJ to Monroe, January 6, *PAJ*, 4:165–167. For the strategic and operational situation, see Frank L. Owsley Jr., *The Struggle for the Gulf Borderlands: The Creek War and the Battle of New Orleans* (Gainesville: University Press of Florida, 1981), chaps. 9, 10; Nathaniel Millett, "Britain's 1814 Occupation of Pensacola and America's Response: An Episode of the War of 1812 in the Southeastern Borderlands," *FHQ* 84 (Fall 2005): 229–255; and, more generally John K. Mahon, "British Strategy and the Southern Indians," *FHQ* 44 (April 1966): 285–305; John Sugden, "The Southern Indians in the War of 1812: The Closing Phase," *FHQ* 60 (January 1982): 273–312; and C. J. Bartlett and Gene A. Smith, "'A Species of Milito-Nautico-Guerilla-Plundering Warfare': Admiral Cochrane's Naval Campaign against the United States, 1814–1815," in *Britain and America Go to War: The Impact of War and Warfare in Anglo-America, 1754–1815*, ed. Julie Flavell and Stephen Conway (Gainesville: University Press of Florida, 2004), 173–204.

11. Remini, *Andrew Jackson and the Course of American Empire*, 191. See, among

many such examples, AJ to Big Warrior, August 7, 1814, to John Coffee, August 10, 1814, and to Secretary of War William Crawford, December 17, 1815, *PAJ*, 3:110, 113, 396, and Commissioners (led by Jackson) to Crawford, September 20, 1816, *PAJ*, 4:66–67. See also Karl Davis, "'Remember Fort Mims': Reinterpreting the Origins of the Creek War," *JER* 22 (Winter 2002): 611–636; H. S. Halbert and T. H. Ball, *The Creek War of 1813 and 1814* (1895; reprint, University: University of Alabama Press, 1969); James W. Holland, *Andrew Jackson and the Creek War: Victory at the Horseshoe* (University: University of Alabama Press, 1968); Owsley, *Struggle for the Gulf Borderlands*; David S. Heidler and Jeanne T. Heidler, *Old Hickory's War: Andrew Jackson and the Quest for Empire* (Mechanicsville, Pa.: Stackpole Books, 1996), chaps. 1, 2; Robert V. Remini, *Andrew Jackson and His Indian Wars* (New York: Viking, 2001), chap. 4; Wright, *Creeks and Seminoles*, chap. 6; and Claudio Saunt, *A New Order of Things: Property, Power, and the Transformation of the Creek Indians, 1733–1816* (Cambridge: Cambridge University Press, 1999), chap. 11.

12. Bradford Perkins, *Castlereagh and Adams; England and the United States, 1812–1823* (Berkeley: University of California Press, 1964), 284; Gallatin to Monroe, May 2 and 8, 1813, in *The Writings of Albert Gallatin*, ed. Henry Adams, 3 vols. (Philadelphia: J. B. Lippincott, 1879), 1:539–540, 545.

13. Treaty of Ghent, *ASPFR*, 3:745–748. See Robert S. Allen, *His Majesty's Indian Allies: British Indian Policy in the Defense of Canada, 1774–1815* (Toronto: Dundurn, 1992), for the British perspective.

14. James E. Lewis Jr., "Quieting the Southern Frontier: President Madison, General Jackson, and the Southern Indians after the War of 1812" (unpublished paper used by permission of the author), 34n21. See Leonard J. Sadosky, *Revolutionary Negotiations: Indians, Empires, and Diplomats in the Founding of America* (Charlottesville: University Press of Virginia, 2009), 196–205, for an interpretation paralleling that herein.

15. January 25, 1816, *MJQA*, 3:290–291; Adams to Monroe, February 8, 1816, *WJQA*, 5:503. Rafe Blaufarb, "The Western Question: The Geopolitics of Latin American Independence," *American Historical Review* 112 (June 2007): 755, states that this was "the only hint ever dropped that Britain might counter American designs on the Spanish borderlands by force." See Lester D. Langley, *The Struggle for the American Mediterranean: United States–European Rivalry in the Gulf-Caribbean, 1776–1904* (Athens: University of Georgia Press, 1976); William W. Kaufmann, *British Policy and the Independence of Latin America, 1804–1828* (New Haven, Conn.: Yale University Press, 1951); J. Fred Rippy, *The Rivalry of the United States and Great Britain over Latin America, 1808–1830* (Baltimore: Johns Hopkins University Press, 1929); William Spence Robertson, *France and Latin American Independence* (1939; reprint, New York: Octagon Books, 1967); Russell H. Bartley, *Imperial Russia and the Struggle for Latin American Independence, 1808–1828* (Austin: University of Texas Press, 1978); and, more generally, Edward H. Tatum, *The United States and Europe, 1815–1823: A Study in the Background of the Monroe Doctrine* (Berkeley: University of California Press, 1936). The diplomatic struggle for Florida is discussed in Philip C.

Brooks, *Diplomacy and the Borderlands: The Adams-Onís Treaty of 1819* (Berkeley: University of California Press, 1939); Samuel Flagg Bemis, *John Quincy Adams and the Foundations of American Foreign Policy* (New York: Alfred A. Knopf, 1949), chaps. 15, 16; Perkins, *Castlereagh and Adams*; George Dangerfield, *The Awakening of American Nationalism, 1815–1828* (New York: Harper and Row, 1965), chap. 2; and William Earl Weeks, *John Quincy Adams and American Global Empire* (Lexington: University Press of Kentucky, 1992). Bemis (284) suggests that Canning, the previous British foreign minister, would have been less conciliatory than Castlereagh, but fundamental British interests would not have been different.

16. James E. Lewis Jr., *The American Union and the Problem of Neighborhood: The United States and the Collapse of the Spanish Empire, 1783–1829* (Chapel Hill: University of North Carolina Press, 1998), 68; Adams to Joseph Hall, September 9, 1815, *WJQA*, 5:372; Rembert W. Patrick, *Florida Fiasco: Rampant Rebels on the Georgia-Florida Border, 1810–1815* (Athens: University of Georgia Press, 1954), chap. 22; Michael S. Fitzgerald, "'Nature Unsubdued': Diplomacy, Expansion and the American Military Buildup of 1815–1816," *Mid-America* 77 (Winter 1995): 11. James A. Carr, "The Battle of New Orleans and the Treaty of Ghent," *DH* 3 (Summer 1979): 273–282, remains the most accurate explanation of British considerations and intent.

17. Henry Clay, cited in James A. Field Jr., "1789–1820: All Oeconomists, All Diplomats," in *Economics and World Power: An Assessment of American Diplomacy since 1789*, ed. William H. Becker and Samuel F. Wells (New York: Columbia University Press, 1984), 39; Lewis, *The American Union and the Problem of Neighborhood*, 57, 59, 76–77; Dallas to AJ, May 22, 1815, *CAJ*, 2:206. Lewis (56–68) stresses the pessimism of policy makers pondering the lessons of the War of 1812. Like Lewis, Michael S. Fitzgerald, "Europe and the United States Defense Establishment: American Military Policy and Strategy, 1815–1821" (Ph.D. diss., Purdue University, 1990), stresses the diplomatic uncertainty of the immediate postwar era and the danger that U.S. expansion against Spain might precipitate British intervention. However, Fitzgerald's dismissal of the Treaty of Ghent—that there was "absolutely no indication that the English nation desired a settlement . . . or intended to improve relations" (47)—and of the mercantile convention of 1815—that it "merely" restored provisions from the Jay Treaty (122), which the United States had abandoned a decade before—seems extreme. Britain did cease military operations against the United States: this may have been due to American defensive victories at Baltimore, Plattsburgh, and New Orleans, or it may have been because there was no serious reason for war after the defeat of Napoleon. In any case, peace constitutes a physical improvement in relations. And, as Fitzgerald notes (78–79), some Americans (albeit Federalists like Timothy Pickering, perhaps because they recognized the power of trade) accurately foresaw the increasingly pacific trajectory of postwar Anglo-American relations. In other words, American fears of continuing British hostility were fundamentally self-created. The caution of worried civilian policy makers was certainly responsible, but it is ironic that they, rather than military leaders, so often thought in terms of worst-case scenarios. Indeed, Fitzgerald also dismisses the Rush-Bagot agreement of 1817 (199) before referring to

a "developing détente between Britain and the United States" that year (257). Since he and Lewis focus on the fears of American policy makers, neither pays much attention to the rapprochement that did occur. Nor can the defensive caution of civilian policy makers explain the belligerence of senior military commanders and their subordinates on the southern frontier throughout this era. Though generally emphasizing the uncertainty and danger of the postwar period, Fitzgerald has also stressed Monroe's aggressiveness; see "'Nature Unsubdued,'" 10–13, 30–32, and "James Monroe and the Conduct of American Foreign Policy" (paper presented to the Society for Historians of the Early American Republic, July 17, 1998).

18. Crawford to AJ, March 8, 1816, *CAJ*, 2:235; Lewis, *The American Union and the Problem of Neighborhood*, 69. See also Fitzgerald, "Europe and the United States Defense Establishment." There is no good biography of Crawford as secretary of war or, indeed, for any other post-Federalist, pre–Civil War secretaries of war except for Calhoun and Jefferson Davis. Chase C. Mooney, *William H. Crawford, 1772–1834* (Lexington: University Press of Kentucky, 1974), provides less than fifteen uncritical pages on his tenure there.

19. Heidler and Heidler, *Old Hickory's War*, 32; Fitzgerald, "'Nature Unsubdued'"; Fitzgerald, "James Monroe and the Conduct of American Foreign Policy."

20. See the map in Daniel Walker Howe, *What Hath God Wrought? The Transformation of America, 1815–1848* (New York: Oxford University Press, 2007), 224, for communications times. Although the map uses New York rather than Washington as its basis for calculation, the difference was only a couple of days.

21. See *PJCC*, 2:xxxi–xl, for the circumstances of Calhoun's entry into the War Department. The chief clerk of the department was well connected and had full authority to conduct policy while acting as secretary, but he simply did not have the political stature of a Monroe when dealing with Jackson or other war heroes like Gaines. Federal district judge Harry Toulmin—Gaines's father-in-law—was an unusual exception, in part because he had been in the Southwest so long: his influence was less federal than local in origin. Territorial governors had authority over the territorial militia and, implicitly, over the standing army as a federal military force when it was within their jurisdictions; Arthur St. Clair had exercised such authority while commanding a major expedition against the Ohio Indians in 1791. Although James Wilkinson held his own against Claiborne in southwestern military command before 1812 and was himself the civil governor of "Louisiana" (actually meaning Arkansas and Missouri) between 1804 and 1807, less senior officers often deferred to Claiborne and other territorial governors. In 1812 Claiborne became the state governor of Louisiana, but he lost that position in 1816 and died prior to taking his Senate seat. Gaines and Jackson cooperated with the governors of Georgia and Alabama, but neither was as forceful or expansionist as Claiborne had been. Insulated between Alabama and Louisiana, the territorial and state governors of Mississippi had never been major players in southern borderlands diplomacy and became even less so as the action moved east along the Florida frontier. Alabama was so new that its governors had little leverage. This meant that Georgia was the only state bordering Florida whose governor had the political or

electoral weight to influence the generals. Yet the factionalism of Georgia politics and its links to factionalism in the national Republican Party, embodied in Crawford, seems to have diminished the generals' regard for the state executives.

22. Kenneth Bourne, *Britain and the Balance of Power in North America, 1815–1908* (Berkeley: University of California Press, 1967), 11; Owsley, *Struggle for the Gulf Borderlands*, 174–194. More generally, see Mark F. Boyd, "Events at Prospect Buff on the Apalachicola River, 1808–1818," *LAHQ* 15 (October 1937): 55–96, and Saunt, *New Order of Things*, chap. 12.

23. Robin Reilly, *The British at the Gates: The New Orleans Campaign in the War of 1812* (New York: Putnam, 1974), 174–175, 342–343; Wilbur S. Brown, *The Amphibious Campaign for West Florida and Louisiana, 1814–1815: A Critical Review of Strategy and Tactics at New Orleans* (University: University of Alabama Press, 1969), 166–169; Monroe to AJ, March 13, 1815, SWLS; EPG, May 14, 1815, enclosure to file G-126, SWLR: Reg.

24. EPG to AJ, June 20, 1815, enclosure to file G-136, SWLR: Reg.

25. Hawkins, August 16, 1814, file H-49, SWLR: Reg; register entry for Hawkins, August 16, 1814, SWLR: Reg; Hawkins to Allied Creeks, in *Letters, Journals and Writings of Benjamin Hawkins*, ed. C. L. Grant, 2 vols. (Savannah, Ga.: Beehive Press, 1980), 2:731–739; *ASPFR*, 4:553–554; Florette Henri, *The Southern Indians and Benjamin Hawkins, 1796–1816* (Norman: University of Oklahoma Press, 1986), chap. 12.

26. Hawkins to AJ, May 5, to Dallas, May 5, and to Thomas Pinckney, May 12, 1815, in Grant, *Letters, Journals and Writings of Benjamin Hawkins*, 2:725–726; EPG, May 22 and 14, 1815, file G-126 and enclosure, SWLR: Reg.

27. EPG to AJ, May 14, file G-136, EPG, May 22, file G-126, and EPG to Chamberlain, May 29, enclosure to EPG, June 2, 1815, file G-129, SWLR: Reg.

28. AJ to Big Warrior, August 7, 1814, *PAJ*, 3:110; Dallas to AJ, June 12, 1815, *TP*, 15:62; AJ to Dallas, June 20 and July 11, 1815, *CAJ*, 2:210–211 and *PAJ*, 3:372.

29. EPG, June 20, 1815, SWLR: IA.

30. AJ to Big Warrior, August 7, 1814, *PAJ*, 3:110.

31. EPG to McDonald, July 20 and 24, 1815, file G-164 and enclosure to file G-206, SWLR: Reg; AJ to the Creek chiefs, September 4, 1815, *PAJ*, 3:283; EPG, September 12 and October 8, 1815, files G-205 and 190, SWLR: Reg; EPG to Georgia governor Peter Early, and Crawford to EPG, October 13 and 24, 1815, Telamon Cuyler Collection, University of Georgia Libraries, cited in John and Mary Lou Missall, *Victims of Empire: The Scott Massacre and the Quest to Control Florida* (University Press of Florida, forthcoming).

32. EPG, October 14, November 14, and December 12, 1815, files G-192, 213, and 226, SWLR: Reg; EPG, October 22, 1815, SWLR: Unreg; James W. Silver, *Edmund Pendleton Gaines: Frontier General* (Baton Rouge: Louisiana State University Press, 1949), 58.

33. Nicholls to Benjamin Hawkins, June 12, 1815, *CAJ*, 2:211n3; EPG to Harry Toulmin, undated, cited in Silver, *Edmund Pendleton Gaines*, 55n6; William R. Man-

ning, ed., *Diplomatic Correspondence of the United States: Canadian Relations*, vol. 1, *1784–1820* (Washington, D.C.: Carnegie Endowment, 1940), 734–735, 788; Heidler and Heidler, *Old Hickory's War*, 57–59; Remini, *Andrew Jackson and His Indian Wars*, 84–88, 96–100; Adams to Monroe, September 9, 1815, *WJQA*, 5:385; November 30, 1818, *MJQA*, 4:184. Article 9 of the Treaty of Ghent is reproduced in *ASPFR*, 3:748; the Treaty of Fort Jackson is in Charles J. Kappler, comp., *Indian Affairs: Laws and Treaties*, vol. 2 (Washington, D.C.: Government Printing Office, 1904), 107–110. See Perkins, *Castlereagh and Adams*, chap. 6, and Frank L. Owsley Jr., "Prophet of War: Josiah Francis and the Creek War," *American Indian Quarterly* 9 (Summer 1985): 286, for British policy makers' lack of interest in upholding Article 9 or sustaining Indian resistance.

34. EPG, June 8, 1815, file G-130, and EPG to AJ, June 20, 1815, enclosure to file G-136, SWLR: Reg. See Wright, *Creeks and Seminoles*, for the variety of Creek social and political alignments.

35. Madison, December 12, 1815, *MPP*, 2:557–558; AJ to Coffee and to George Colbert, February 13, 1816, *PAJ*, 4:11–13; law against intrusion on public lands, March 3, 1807, 2 *Stat.* 445–446.

36. AJ to Monroe, May 12 (quotations), to James Gadsden, May 30, and to Crawford, June 4, 1816, *PAJ*, 4:29, 34–38; Crawford to AJ, May 20 and July 1, 1816, *PAJ*, 4:32–33, 48–49.

37. Southern Division Adjutant General Richard Butler to brevet Brigadier General Thomas A. Smith, July 3, 1816, and to Houston, October 22, 1816 (see also January 9 and February 5, 1817), Division of the South, Letters Sent, 1816–1821, Entry 72, RG 98, NA; AJ to Campbell, November 22, 1816, *PAJ*, 4:75–76. For Jackson's views on settling the public lands, see AJ to Monroe, October 23 and November 12, 1816, and January 6 and March 4, 1817, *PAJ*, 4:69–70, 73–74, 80, 93–96. The acts regulating trade and intercourse with the Indians are in July 22, 1790, 1 *Stat.* 137–138; May 19, 1796, 1 *Stat.* 469–474; March 3, 1799, 2 *Stat.* 39–40; March 30, 1802, 2 *Stat.* 139–146; and April 29, 1816, 3 *Stat.* 332–333.

38. Commissioners to Crawford, September 20, 1816, *PAJ*, 4:66–67; AJ, December 9, 1816, DPP; AJ to Monroe, October 23, 1816, *PAJ*, 4:69–70. See *PAJ*, 4:176–177, concerning Jackson's personal investments in the ceded lands. See Remini, *Andrew Jackson and His Indian Wars*, chaps. 6, 7, on Jackson's efforts to press the Indians into further cessions, including his role as commissioner. Lewis, "Quieting the Southern Frontier," 17–18, 22–24, maintains that the administration's decision to give way to Jackson on the Cherokee and other claims was not motivated by the general's political influence or that of the westerners; rather, it was based on the need to have the frontiersmen available as a reliable military force, subject to restraint by the administration, in case tensions escalated into war. This seems reasonable as a statement of Madison's motivation, but support for Jackson meant escalating tensions with the Cherokee, and securing reliable support from the southern militia was an inherently political matter, with inevitable political consequences: Lewis and I are emphasizing different sides of the same coin. The administration assumed that the Indians would

not initiate war without European support, so the United States could get away with angering them. If tensions led to war with Spain, the southern militia might be useful, if only as part of the effort to ensure popular support; Madison would be able to remind Jackson and the militia that he had supported them over the Indian cessions, allowing him to call them back and facilitate a settlement once they captured Pensacola and St. Augustine.

39. AJ to EPG, March 12, 1816, *PAJ*, 4:31; AJ, May 21, 1816, SWLR: IA; AJ to Crawford, June 9, 1816, *PAJ*, 4:44.

40. EPG to Clinch, May 23, 1816, *ASPFR*, 4:558; EPG to War Department, December 4, 1817, *ASPMA*, 1:688. See former quartermaster Christopher Van Deventer, May 20, 1817, DPP, for another example of military belligerence toward Spain; the well-connected Van Deventer had always been a fire-eater and was soon appointed chief clerk of the War Department.

41. Capt. Mann P. Lomax, February 2, 1816, AGOLR; Capt. Ferdinand Amelung to AJ, June 4, 1816, *ASPFR*, 4:557.

42. AJ to EPG, September 30, 1815, Andrew Jackson Papers, LC.

43. EPG to AJ, March 20, 1816, enclosure to AJ to EPG, April 8, 1816, file J-94, SWLR: Reg; EPG to acting Secretary of War Dallas, May 14 and 22, 1815, AGOLR; Heidler and Heidler, *Old Hickory's War*, 64, chap. 3. See also Nathaniel Millett, "Slave Resistance during the Age of Revolution: The Maroon Community at Prospect Bluff, Spanish Florida" (Ph.D. diss., Cambridge University, 2002), the most complete account; Nathaniel Millett, "Defining Freedom in the Atlantic Borderlands of the Revolutionary Southeast," *Early American Studies* 5 (Fall 2007): 367–394; Saunt, *New Order of Things*, chap. 12; James W. Covington, "The Negro Fort," *Gulf Coast Historical Review* 5 (1990): 78–91; Frank J. Owsley and Gene A. Smith, *Filibusters and Expansionists: Jeffersonian Manifest Destiny, 1800–1821* (Tuscaloosa: University of Alabama Press, 1997), chap. 6; and Benjamin W. Griffith Jr., *McIntosh and Weatherford: Creek Indian Leaders* (Tuscaloosa: University of Alabama Press, 1988), 172–177.

44. Crawford to AJ, March 15, 1816, *CAJ*, 2:236–237; AJ to EPG, April 8, 1816, file J-94, SWLR: Reg.

45. Ibid.

46. Ibid.; AJ to Crawford, April 24, 1816, *PAJ*, 4:26; AJ to Governor Mauricio de Zuniga, April 23, Zuniga to AJ, May 26, Capt. Ferdinand Amelung to AJ, and AJ to Crawford, June 15, 1816, *ASPFR*, 4:556–557. See also David S. Heidler and Jeanne T. Heidler, "Between a Rock and a Hard Place: Allied Creeks and the United States, 1814–1818," *Alabama Review* 50 (October 1997): 267–289. During the War of 1812 the Spanish informed both Britain and the United States that they considered the Apalachicola settlements Creek territory rather than their own; they changed their position at the end of the war, when it seemed that they might be able to restore some sovereignty over the region. See Owsley, *Struggle for the Gulf Borderlands*, 183–184.

47. EPG to AJ and Benjamin Hawkins to AJ, May 14 and April 21, 1816, Jackson Papers, LC; Little Prince to AJ, April 26, 1816, *PAJ*, 4:428; EPG, April 30, file G-48, and Clinch to EPG, May 9, enclosure to EPG, May 24, 1816, file G-55, SWLR: Reg.

See also Hawkins to Crawford, April 2 and May 3, 1816, in Grant, *Letters, Journals and Writings of Benjamin Hawkins*, 2:779–781, 783–785. James W. Covington, *The Seminoles of Florida* (Gainesville: University Press of Florida, 1993), 38, gives the impression that Gaines was less belligerent than Clinch, but this was only a matter of using different means to gain the same objectives.

48. AJ, May 12, 1816, file J-92, SWLR: Reg; EPG, May 27, 1816, SWLR: IA; EPG, July 1, 1816, SWLS.

49. Ibid.; Madison to Crawford, June 21, 1816, SWLR: Reg; Lewis, "Quieting the Southern Frontier," 22–25.

50. Clinch report to Col. (Southern Division adjutant general) Robert Butler, published in *Niles Weekly Register*, November 20, 1819; Capt. James M. Glassell to Clinch, December 26, 1816, EPG to Clinch, May 6, 1817, and AJ to Clinch, September 6, 1816, all reprinted in the *Savannah Georgian*, April 19, 1819, and cited in Rembert W. Patrick, *Aristocrat in Uniform: General Duncan L. Clinch* (Gainesville: University of Florida Press, 1963), 33–36. See also Clinch's reports to Butler, July 28, 1817, Jackson Papers, LC, and August 2, 1817, *PAJ*, 4:440, and the correspondence collected in *ASPFR*, 4:555–561. I call them "Seminoles" because that was the term used most often by U.S. commanders; the Indians were probably a combination of Red Stick Creek refugees, Mikasuki from the west, and Seminoles from the east.

51. C. A. Bayly, *Imperial Meridian: The British Empire and the World, 1780–1830* (London: Longman, 1989); Douglas M. Peers, *Between Mars and Mammon: Colonial Armies and the Garrison State in India, 1819–1835* (London: I. B. Tauris, 1995); Hew Strachan, *The Politics of the British Army* (Oxford: Clarendon Press, 1997), chap. 3. Lewis, "Quieting the Southern Frontier," helps explain the gradual, hesitant, and contingent shift from caution and self-restraint among national civilian policy makers, and I find persuasive his hypothesis that Madison was worried about maintaining control over organized American military force, whether against the Indians, Spain, or Britain. The president's dilemma was to balance the imperatives of expansion (however gradual or far in the future) against the need to control his military subordinates. The emergence of a less rambunctious officer corps, a process delineated in chapter 7 and the conclusion, made this much easier twenty to thirty years later.

52. Lewis, "Quieting the Southern Frontier."

CHAPTER THREE: THE TENSIONS OF AGGRESSION AND ACCOUNTABILITY

1. John S. Galbraith, "The 'Turbulent Frontier' as a Factor in British Expansion," *Comparative Studies in Society and History* 2 (January 1960): 150–168; R. E. Robinson and J. A. Gallagher, *Africa and the Victorians: The Official Mind of Imperialism* (London: Macmillan, 1961); R. E. Robinson, "Non-European Foundations of European Imperialism: Sketch for a Theory of Collaboration," in *Studies in the Theory of Imperialism*, ed. R. Owen and B. Sutcliffe (Harlow, U.K.: Longman, 1995), 117–140;

Ronald Hyam, *Britain's Imperial Century, 1815–1914: A Study of Empire and Expansion* (New York: Palgrave Macmillan, 2002), 9, 287, 330; Bruce Vandervort, *Wars of Imperial Conquest in Africa, 1830–1914* (Bloomington: Indiana University Press, 1998).

2. James E. Lewis Jr., *The American Union and the Problem of Neighborhood: The United States and the Collapse of the Spanish Empire, 1783–1829* (Chapel Hill: University of North Carolina Press, 1998), 78–79.

3. Lawrence S. Kaplan, *Entangling Alliances with None: American Foreign Policy in the Age of Jefferson* (Kent, Ohio: Kent State University Press, 1987), 178, chap. 12; Christopher Van Deventer, May 20, 1817, DPP. See Alfred Hasbrouck, *Foreign Legionaries in the Liberation of Spanish South America* (New York: Columbia University Press, 1928); Matthew Brown, *Adventuring through Spanish Colonies: Simon Bolivar, Foreign Mercenaries, and the Birth of New Nations* (Liverpool: Liverpool University Press, 2007); and Ben Hughes, *Conquer or Die! Wellington's Veterans and the Liberation of the New World* (Oxford: Osprey, 2010), for the role of British expatriates in the Patriot struggles. See Timothy E. Anna, *The Forging of Mexico, 1821–1835* (Lincoln: University of Nebraska Press, 1998), for a discussion of the social politics of the Mexican Revolution.

4. This is not to say that officers along the Canadian border were not self-confident and hostile to their recent British adversaries; however, their mission was much less complicated by nonstate actors—potential filibusters were deterred by British power, and Canadians had become more loyal to Britain because of American invasion—and military aggressiveness toward Britain and Canada was tempered by British strength and the reality that Britain was the United States' largest trading partner. Volume 2 provides further analysis.

5. Richard W. Van Alstyne, "The American Empire Makes Its Bow on the World Stage," in *From Colony to Empire: Essays in the History of American Foreign Relations*, ed. William Appleman Williams (New York: J. Wiley, 1972), 45.

6. Van Deventer, May 20, 1817, DPP; Clay speech, January 24, 1817, in *The Papers of Henry Clay*, ed. James F. Hopkins and Mary W. M. Hargreaves (Lexington: University Press of Kentucky, 1961), 2:290. Van Deventer was an 1809 graduate of West Point; he resigned from the army in August 1816 but became chief clerk of the War Department, replacing George Graham, in 1817 and remained intimately involved in military affairs for the next decade.

7. Charles Winslow Elliott, *Winfield Scott: The Soldier and the Man* (New York: Macmillan, 1937), 203–204; WS to Secretary of State James Monroe, March 19, 1816, from Liverpool, England, Winfield Scott Papers, USMA. See also WS to Monroe, November 18, 1815, ibid.

8. WS to Secretary of State Monroe, March 19, 1816, Scott Papers, USMA; Jefferson to Monroe, February 4, 1816, in *The Writings of Thomas Jefferson*, 10 vols., ed. Paul L. Ford (New York: G. P. Putnam's Sons, 1892–1899), 10:19. See also Harris Gaylord Warren, "The Origins of General Mina's Invasion of Mexico," *SWHQ* 42 (July 1938): 1–20; Curtis A. Wilgus, "Some Notes on Spanish-American Patriot Activ-

ity along the Atlantic Seaboard, 1816–1822," *North Carolina Historical Review* 4 (April 1927): 172–181; and Curtis A. Wilgus, "Some Notes on Spanish American Patriot Activity along the Gulf Coast of the United States, 1811–1822," *LAHQ* 8 (April 1925): 193–215.

9. See William C. Davis, *The Pirates Laffite: The Treacherous World of the Gulf Corsairs* (New York: Harcourt, 2005), 260–325; Julia K. Garrett, ed., "Dr. John Sibley and the Louisiana-Texas Frontier, 1803–1814," *SWHQ* 49 (July 1945–January 1946): 116–119, 290–292, 399–431; G. P. Whittington, "Dr. John Sibley of Nacogdoches, 1757–1837," *LAHQ* 10 (October 1927): 467–512; Harold A. Bierck Jr., "Dr. John Hamilton Robinson," *LAHQ* 25 (July 1942): 644–669; David E. Narrett, "Liberation and Conquest: John Hamilton Robinson and U.S. Adventurism toward Mexico, 1806–1819," *WHQ* 40 (Spring 2009): 23–50. Note that the four former officers said to be linked to the Friends of Mexican Emancipation do not match up with the three I identified in the Mina expeditions of the New Orleans Associates. Of course, the four former officers may be visible in the record because of their prominence in the filibuster; there may have been others, such as former lieutenants disbanded in the large reduction in force, but such men would have had no more than a couple years' service. The critical point is how few of these men there were and how short their socialization in the national army officer corps. Dick Steward, *Frontier Swashbuckler: The Life and Legend of John Smith T* (Columbia: University of Missouri Press, 2000), 140, cites a Captain James Luckett and a James T. Johnson as army officers connected to Toledo in April 1814, but there is no James Luckett in the biographical sources, and the two James Johnsons (neither identified as James T. Johnson) were a lieutenant with one year's service and a former lieutenant who resigned in 1810 after eighteen months' service. John Roger Nelson Luckett, a lieutenant connected to the Burr conspiracy in 1806, remained in the army but died early in 1813. Given the rarity of field-grade officers—no more than 200, even counting all the regiments raised for the War of 1812—those who left the army (about 150 of those 200 in the postwar reduction in force) would have been hard to miss if they became filibusters. And of course, about three-quarters of the wartime field-grade officers had been commissioned only in 1812 or 1813 and were no more representative of the career officer corps than captains or lieutenants.

10. Davis, *Pirates Laffite*, 147, 150–151, 220, 276, 232–248, 259–264; Jane Lucas de Grummond, *The Baratarians and the Battle of New Orleans* (Baton Rouge: Louisiana State University Press, 1961), 12, 23; Frank L. Owsley Jr. and Gene A. Smith, *Filibusters and Expansionists: Jeffersonian Manifest Destiny, 1800–1821* (Tuscaloosa: University of Alabama Press, 1997), 164–175; Marietta M. LeBreton, "A History of the Territory of Orleans, 1803–1812" (Ph.D. diss., Louisiana State University, 1969), 33. Davis, *Pirates Laffite*, 260, suggests that Governor Claiborne hinted at sympathy for Toledo; see ibid., 261–263, 276, 299, 310–312 for Patterson's complicity with the associates.

11. Davis, *Pirates Laffite*, 261; WCCC to Monroe, July 26, 1815, *LBWCCC*, 6:359–360; WCCC to Monroe, July 20, 1815, quoted in Davis, *Pirates Laffite*, 267.

12. Madison, September 1, 1815, *MPP*, 2:546–547.

13. Lewis, *The American Union and the Problem of Neighborhood*, 79–85; Adams to Monroe, March 30, 1816, WJQA, 5:553. See Dwight F. Henderson, *Congress, Courts, and Criminals: The Development of Federal Criminal Law, 1801–1829* (Westport, Conn.: Greenwood Press, 1985), chap. 7, on privateering and piracy connected to the South American revolutions.

14. Davis, *Pirates Laffite*, 261–263, 299, 310–312; Harris Gaylord Warren, "The *Firebrand* Affair: A Forgotten Incident of the Mexican Revolution," *LAHQ* 21 (January 1938): 203–212; Maury Baker, "The Spanish War Scare of 1816," *Mid-America* 45 (April 1963): 67–78; "Instructions Prepared for the Navy Department," c. October 19, 1816, in *Letters and Other Writings of James Madison*, 4 vols., ed. William C. Rives and Philip R. Fendall (Philadelphia: J. B. Lippincott, 1965), 3:10–11.

15. Ted Schwarz, *Forgotten Battlefield of the First Texas Revolution: The Battle of Medina, August 18, 1813* (Austin, Tex.: Eakin Press, 1985), 121; Major Joseph Selden to Jesup, September 17, 1816, Jesup Papers, LC. For Galveston, see Davis, *Pirates Laffite*, chaps. 16–20, and Harris Gaylord Warren, ed., "Documents Relating to the Establishment of Privateers at Galveston, 1816–1817," *LAHQ* 21 (October 1938): 1086–1109.

16. Only five of the fifty regular army infantry and rifle regiments—the Second, Third, Seventh, Thirty-ninth, and Forty-fourth—were deployed in the Gulf borderlands during the war, so a proportional reduction in the officer corps left few veterans of the New Orleans campaign. Jackson and Gaines were appointed members of the board that considered wartime officers for retention or discharge during the spring of 1815, but neither was able to attend its meetings in Washington. Indeed, Gaines had earned his wartime distinction and promotion (from captain at the beginning of 1812) in the North, during the Niagara campaign; though he missed the battles of Chippewa and Lundy's Lane while overseeing the defense of the important naval base at Sacketts Harbor, he was wounded and brevetted to major general for gallantry in the defense of Fort Erie. Jacob Brown and Winfield Scott became the principals on the reduction board, and veterans of Brown's Left Division formed the core of the officer corps for the next generation.

17. The principal accounts are Warren, "The Origin of General Mina's Invasion"; Harris Gaylord Warren, "Xavier Mina's Invasion of Mexico," *Hispanic American Historical Review* 23 (February 1943): 52–76; and Davis, *Pirates Laffite*, 315–338. See also Fane Downs, "Governor Antonio Martinez and the Defense of Texas from Foreign Invasion, 1817–1822," *Texas Military History* 7 (Spring 1968): 27–43. Harris Gaylord Warren, "Pensacola and the Filibusters, 1816–1817," *LAHQ* 21 (July 1938): 817, asserts that Mina's expedition was "largely made up of former American army officers," a statement that takes the logic out of "largely." Warren, "Xavier Mina's Invasion of Mexico," 53, suggests that "many adventurous young men . . . [who] had held commissions in the United States army" joined Mina, but Warren does not present any substantial evidence to support this assertion. Indeed, later (68) he suggests that another ex-officer, Hamlin Cook, was killed with Perry, but Warren has Cook with James Long on the Sabine in 1819 in *The Sword Was Their Passport: A History of*

American Filibustering in the Mexican Revolution (Baton Rouge: Louisiana State University Press, 1943), 234, 236, 244. Reuben Ross is not in any of the army biographical dictionaries; authors unfamiliar with the army's organizational structure sometimes mistake temporary civilian supply contractors for quartermasters with permanent commissions in the national standing army.

18. See the letters to Toledo (referred to as "General Toledo") that autumn in Division of the South, Letters Sent, 1816–1821, Entry 72, RG 98, NA.

19. Lewis, *The American Union and the Problem of Neighborhood*, 89; AJ, July 9, 1816, SWLS (Confidential and Unofficial); Jesup to Trimble, April 1, 1817, William A. Trimble Papers, OHS. Jesup was born in western Virginia in 1788 and moved to Kentucky at age four. Far from the scene, Captain John Michael O'Connor also expected war with Spain, but he thought it would be bungled like that with Britain, and so Texas would remain Spanish (June 1, 1816, DPP). See Samuel J. Watson, "Thomas Sidney Jesup: Soldier, Bureaucrat, Gentleman Democrat," in *The Human Tradition in the Early Republic*, ed. Michael A. Morrison (Wilmington, Del.: Scholarly Resources, 2000), for elaboration; Samuel J. Watson, "Soldier, Expansionist, Politician: Eleazer Wheelock Ripley and the Dance of Ambition in the Early American Republic," in *Nexus of Empire: Loyalty and National Identity in the Gulf Borderlands, 1763–1835*, ed. Gene A. Smith and Sylvia L. Hilton (Gainesville: University Press of Florida, 2009), 321–346, for an exploration of Ripley's career; and John D. Morris, *Sword of the Border: Major General Jacob Jennings Brown, 1775–1828* (Kent, Ohio: Kent State University Press, 2000), for an extended analysis of the controversy between Ripley and Brown more favorable to the latter than I think is accurate. There is no agreement on the spelling of Ripley's first name: the Army Register spells it Eleazer, but the *Biographical Dictionary of Congress* spells it Eleazar; the two biographies before mine differ, as does his own signature.

20. Trimble to Jesup, May 6, 18, and 20, 1817, Jesup Papers, LC; Trimble to Major (assistant adjutant general) Reynolds M. Kirby, March 17, and to Ripley, March 17, April 22, and June 4, 1817, Trimble Papers, OHS; William Trimble to Allen Trimble, March 17, 1817, Allen Trimble Papers, Western Reserve Historical Society (notes on documents taken by and received from William B. Skelton). See Thomas W. Kavanaugh, *The Comanches: A History, 1706–1875* (Lincoln: University of Nebraska Press, 1996), 165–172, on American trade with the Texan Indians.

21. John Jamison (U.S. Indian agent at Natchitoches) to Trimble, April 2, 1817, Trimble to Kirby, April 8, to Riddle, April 2, to Selden, April 25, and to AJ, December 13, 1817, and unaddressed draft, January 26, 1818 (quotations), Trimble Papers, OHS. See also Trimble, October 16, 1818, SWLS (Confidential); Jamison to Trimble, March 25, 1817, "A Statistical Account of the Country between the Head of the Red River of Louisiana and the Colorado of the Province of Texas" (n.d.), "A Statistical Table of Indian Tribes Residing on the Waters of the Red River between Said River and the Rio del Norte" (n.d.), and other lists of Indians in Texas and between the Red and Arkansas Rivers in box 4, folders 2 and 3, Trimble Papers, OHS. Trimble was born in Kentucky in 1786 and migrated to Ohio as a youth.

22. William Earl Weeks, *John Quincy Adams and American Global Empire* (Lexington: University Press of Kentucky, 1992), 58–64; Trimble to Monroe, January 26, 1818, *PJCC*, 2:95; JCC to AJ, December 12, and AJ to JCC, December 30, 1817, *PJCC*, 2:12, 46; Davis, *Pirates Laffite*, 142–143; Capt. John Jones to Jesup, February 12, 1817, Jesup Papers, LC. Apart from Davis—the best researched account—the most comprehensive treatment of the Galveston freebooters is Stanley Faye, "Commodore Aury," *LAHQ* 24 (July 1941): 611–697; see also Stanley Faye, "The Great Stroke of Pierre Lafitte," *LAHQ* 23 (July 1940): 733–826; Lyle Saxon, *Lafitte the Pirate* (New York: The Century, 1930); and Stanley Clisby Arthur, *Jean Lafitte: Gentleman Rover* (New Orleans: Harmanson, 1952). Davis presents the most persuasive evidence for the spelling of Laffite.

23. Adams to Peter Paul Francis deGrand, September 28 and November 13, 1817, *WJQA*, 6:204n1; November 9, 1817, *MJQA*, 4:18–19; Rafe Blaufarb, *Bonapartists in the Borderlands: French Exiles and Refugees on the Gulf Coast, 1815–1835* (Tuscaloosa: University of Alabama Press, 2005), 94–102.

24. Trimble to AJ, March 24, 1818, Trimble Papers, OHS; Trimble to AJ, October 20 and November 27, 1818, files T-20 and T-45, SWLR: Reg.

25. Blaufarb, *Bonapartists*, 95–97, 109–110; May 16, 1818, *MJQA*, 4:97. Contrary to Blaufarb, Graham was not a career military officer (he is not listed in any of the biographical dictionaries or the Army Register); he was chief clerk of the War Department and acting secretary of war.

26. Blaufarb, *Bonapartists*, 110–114; Graham to Laffite, August 26, 1818, in Harris Gaylord Warren, "Documents Relating to George Graham's Proposals to Jean Laffite for the Occupation of the Texas Coast," *LAHQ* 21 (January 1938): 217; George Mason Graham, "Political Occurrences on the Island of Galvezton in 1818," *Tyler's Historical and Geneological Magazine* 27 (April 1946): 255–273; November 20, 1818, *MJQA*, 4:175; *New York Spectator*, June 1 and 8, 1820 (cited in Davis, *Pirates Laffite*, 433). Edmund Gaines advised a group of French immigrants on good locations in Alabama; see James W. Silver, *Edmund Pendleton Gaines: Frontier General* (Baton Rouge: Louisiana State University Press, 1949), 68. In addition to Blaufarb, see Davis, *Pirates Laffite*, 350–384; Ines Murat, *Napoleon and the American Dream*, trans. Frances Frenaye (Baton Rouge: Louisiana State University Press, 1976), 111–114, 122–144; Kent Gardien, "Take Pity on Our Glory: Men of Champ d'Asile," *SWHQ* 87 (January 1984): 241–268; and Roger G. Kennedy, *Orders from France: The Americans and the French in a Revolutionary World, 1780–1820* (Philadelphia: University of Pennsylvania Press, 1990), 343–346, 360–373, regarding the Bonapartist exiles on the Trinity.

27. Joseph B. Lockey, "The Florida Intrigues of Jose Alvarez de Toledo," *FHQ* 12 (Fall 1934): 145–178; Warren, "Pensacola and the Filibusters"; Warren, *The Sword Was Their Passport*, 123, 126, 129, 135–136; Baker, "The Spanish War Scare of 1816"; Ripley, January 6, 1817, file R-28, SWLR: Reg, enclosing Ripley to Humbert, January 2, 1817.

28. Ripley, January 18, 1817, file R-73, SWLR: Reg.

29. Ripley, February 5, 1817, file R-47, SWLR: Reg.

30. EPG to AJ, February 14, 1817, Jackson Papers, LC; David S. Heidler and Jeanne T. Heidler, *Old Hickory's War: Andrew Jackson and the Quest for Empire* (Mechanicsburg, Pa.: Stackpole Books, 1996), 78; King, January 25, 1817, DPP.

31. Parker to King, February 23, 1817, file P-32, SWLR: Reg; King, February 27, 1817, SWLS (Confidential and Unofficial); King, April 2, 1817, DPP. See surgeon Tobias Watkins, April 29, 1817, DPP, for another example of an officer's support for "the perfect emancipation of all Spanish America."

32. Southern Division adjutant general Richard Butler to King, October 28, 1816, Division of the South, Letters Sent, 1816–1821, Entry 72, RG 98, NA; AJ to Graham, December 11, 1816, *CAJ*, 2:265; Warren, "Pensacola and the Filibusters," 816–817. See also Butler to King, January 21, 1817, Division of the South, Letters Sent.

33. Jesup to AJ, August 18, 1816, Jesup Papers, LC; Jesup to WCCC, August 10, 1816, Jesup Papers, PLDU.

34. AJ to Jesup, August 1, 1816, Jesup to Monroe, September 8, 1816, and Jesup to AJ, August 12, 1816, Jesup Papers, LC. Universally applauded for his ability, and with plenty of senior patrons, Jesup overcame his McChrystal moment to serve forty-two years as quartermaster general. See Chester L. Kieffer, *Maligned General: A Biography of Thomas S. Jesup* (San Rafael, Calif.: Presidio Press, 1979), 42–49, for Jesup's mission reporting on the Hartford Convention and his legal problems with Connecticut authorities while recruiting in the antiwar state.

35. Jesup to Commodore Daniel Patterson, August 19, and to AJ, August 18 and 21, 1816, Jesup Papers, LC.

36. AJ to Jesup, September 6, 1816, *PAJ*, 4:60; Jesup to AJ, August 21, and to Monroe, August 21 ("Confidential"), September 3, September 5 ("Confidential"), and September 8, 1816, Jesup Papers, LC.

37. AJ, September 27 and November 5, 1816, SWLS (Confidential); Jesup to Chotard and to Holmes, September 26, 1816, Jesup Letterbook, 1816–1817, Jesup Papers, PLDU. Despite his professed fears about Spanish offensives against Mobile, Brigadier General Ripley shared Jesup's belief that Havana was vulnerable to attack. He did not explain why he thought Spain would launch a counteroffensive powerful enough to recover West Florida but not Cuba—a much more valuable province—but pointing this out would have been contrary to his career interests in securing command over a larger force and leading an expansionist offensive. Ripley therefore echoed Jesup's proposals when he arrived in the Eighth Military Department in 1817, suggesting to the War Department that he could easily take Cuba with a force of 3,000 soldiers, although he made it clear that he would not attempt to do so unless the two nations went to war. Nor were Ripley and Jesup (who returned to acting command of the First Infantry Regiment when Ripley arrived) likely to cooperate on such a venture. Ripley, January 18, 1817, file R-73, SWLR: Reg.

38. Jesup to Many, October 4, and to EPG, June 11, 1816, Jesup Letterbook, 1816–1817, Jesup Papers, PLDU; AJ, November 5, 1816, SWLS (Confidential); AJ,

December 11, 1816, file J-19, SWLR: Reg; Heidler and Heidler, *Old Hickory's War*, 76–77. See also Jesup to AJ, August 18 and 21, and to Monroe, "Private and Confidential," September 5, 1816, Jesup Papers, LC.

39. Jesup to Judge Ethan A. Brown, February 7, 1812, and to an unnamed general, November 7, 1819 (unsent draft), Jesup Papers, LC. The general may have been Jacob Brown, under whom Jesup had served in 1814 (and to whom he owed his rapid advancement to quartermaster general), but Brown rarely expressed the ardent passion for expansion that Jesup so loquaciously shared with Jackson.

40. AJ, November 28, 1818, file J-71, SWLR: Reg; AJ to Gibson, February 1, 1820, *PAJ*, 4:356.

41. See Donald R. Hickey, "America's Response to the Slave Revolt in Haiti, 1791–1806," *JER* 2 (Winter 1982): 361–379, and Lester D. Langley, *The Struggle for the American Mediterranean: United States–European Rivalry in the Gulf-Caribbean, 1776–1904* (Athens: University of Georgia Press, 1976), 40, regarding official concerns about the region's social and ethnic stability. See Langley, *Struggle for the American Mediterranean*, 43, 48, and Douglas M. Astolfi, *Foundations of Destiny: A Foreign Policy of the Jacksonians, 1824–1837* (New York: Garland, 1989), 8, 27, regarding the negative American response to rumors of Cuban revolt and Latin invasion.

42. William Chase, "Harbor of Pensacola," *Pensacola Gazette*, March 21, 1839, in *ANC* 8 (April 18, 1839): 244; Wool, report of October 23, 1839, reprinted in *ANC* 13 (February 12, 1842): 49. See also Lt. H[enry] J[ames] Feltus to Capt. Rufus Lathrop Baker, January 19, 1827, Rufus Lathrop Baker Papers, USMA; this is the only commentary (and an insubstantial one, at that) I have found on Cuba between the early 1820s and late 1830s. See Louis A. Perez, *Cuba and the United States: Ties of Singular Intimacy* (Athens: University of Georgia Press, 1990), chap. 2, and J. Fred Rippy, *The Rivalry of the United States and Great Britain over Latin America, 1808–1830* (Baltimore: Johns Hopkins University Press, 1929), chap. 3, regarding American policy toward Cuba in the 1820s. Mary W. M. Hargreaves, *The Presidency of John Quincy Adams* (Lawrence: University Press of Kansas, 1985), chaps. 4–7, deals with American foreign relations during the Adams administration (on Cuba, see especially 137–143). See Ernest R. May, *The Making of the Monroe Doctrine*, 2nd ed. (Cambridge, Mass.: Harvard University Press, 1992); Samuel Flagg Bemis, *John Quincy Adams and the Foundations of American Foreign Policy* (New York: Alfred A. Knopf, 1949), chaps. 17–19; and Dexter Perkins, *The Monroe Doctrine, 1823–1926* (Cambridge, Mass.: Harvard University Press, 1932), regarding American policy toward the newly independent states of Latin America and the conception of the Monroe Doctrine. For British policy, see Harold W. Temperley, *The Foreign Policy of Canning, 1822–1827: England, the Neo–Holy Alliance, and the New World* (London: G. Bell and Sons, 1925), and William W. Kaufmann, *British Policy and the Independence of Latin America, 1804–1828* (New Haven, Conn.: Yale University Press, 1951); for French policy, see William Spence Robertson, *France and Latin American Independence* (1939; reprint, New York: Octagon Books, 1967).

Frederick Merk (with the collaboration of Lois Bannister Merk), *The Monroe Doctrine and American Expansionism, 1843–1849* (New York: Alfred A. Knopf, 1966), 16, notes several rumors during the late 1830s and early 1840s that Britain would assume control over Cuba as compensation for Spanish debts. See Robert E. May, "Young American Males and Filibustering in the Age of Manifest Destiny: The United States Army as a Cultural Mirror," *JAH* 78 (December 1991): 879–880, and Charles H. Brown, *Agents of Manifest Destiny: The Lives and Times of the Filibusters* (Chapel Hill: University of North Carolina Press, 1980), 45–48, for evidence of some officers' sympathy for filibusters against Cuba after the Mexican War. Neither of the principal officers sought by the filibusters—William Worth and Captain (brevet colonel) Robert E. Lee—took up their offer; the only officer known to have done so was William L. Crittenden, an 1845 West Point graduate who resigned in 1849 and filibustered to Cuba with Narciso Lopez, where he was captured and executed by the Spanish authorities in 1851. See Tom Chaffin, "'Sons of Washington': Narciso Lopez, Filibustering, and U.S. Nationalism, 1848–1851," *JER* 15 (Spring 1995): 79–108, regarding American filibustering against Cuba, and Robert E. May, *The Southern Dream of a Caribbean Empire, 1854–1861* (1973; reprint, Athens: University of Georgia Press, 1989), for pro-slavery expansionism in the Caribbean during the late 1840s and 1850s.

CHAPTER FOUR: CONCLUDING THE QUASI-WAR WITH SPAIN

1. AJ to Monroe, November 12, and Monroe to AJ, December 14, 1816, *CAJ*, 2:263–266.

2. AJ to Monroe, March 4, 1817, *PAJ*, 4:93–98.

3. EPG to Judge Harry Toulmin, June 1, 1815, cited in James W. Silver, *Edmund Pendleton Gaines: Frontier General* (Baton Rouge: Louisiana State University Press, 1949), 56; Crawford to AJ, January 27, 1816, *CAJ*, 2:228; EPG, January 27, 1816, SWLS.

4. Mitchell to EPG, January 6, 1817, AGOLR; EPG to the inhabitants of Murder Creek, July 12, 1817, *ASPMA*, 1:684; Clinch to EPG, December 26, 1816, AGOLR; EPG to Mitchell, February 5, 1817, *ASPMA*, 1:681. Mitchell referred to "Fort Crawford" in his letter because Fort Scott had originally been known as Camp Crawford. In early 1817 the actual Fort Crawford was the new post on the Conecuh, a tributary of the Escambia, north of Pensacola.

5. Lt. Richard Sands, February 2, 1817, *ASPMA*, 1:681; Mitchell to acting secretary of war George S. Graham, March 30, 1817, *ASPMA*, 1:681–683; Cutler, April 7, 1817, DPP; EPG to AJ, April 2, 1817, *PAJ*, 4:106; EPG, August 25, 1817, file G-134, SWLR: Reg.

6. AJ to Graham, July 22, 1817, *PAJ*, 4:128.

7. EPG to Masot, May 12, enclosure in EPG, May 28, 1817, file G-86, SWLR: Reg; EPG to AJ, April 6, 1817, Jackson Papers, LC; AJ, April 29, 1817, file J-94, SWLR: Reg; EPG to Sen. John Williams, July 12, 1817, AGOLR; EPG, August 25,

1817, file G-134, SWLR: Reg. Junior as well as senior officers saw the pretext afforded by the use of the rivers and the need to control them in order to supply American operations against the Indians; see former captain Christopher Van Deventer, May 20, 1817, DPP, regarding Fort Scott and the Apalachicola. See Major James Bankhead, July 20, 1817, DPP, for another officer's interest in seizing Florida. Colonel William King asked Adjutant and Inspector General Daniel Parker whether the rumors of a forthcoming war with the Seminoles were true; his main concern was that it be conducted after the hot season to minimize casualties to disease (King, August 28, 1817, DPP).

8. Lt. George Leftwich to EPG, July 28, 1817, *ASPMA*, 1:684; EPG to AJ, August 31, 1817, *CAJ*, 2:323; EPG "to the Seminole chief" (Kinache), undated [August 1817], *ASPMA*, 1:723.

9. Twiggs to EPG, August 11, 1817, Jackson Papers, LC; Mikasuki (actually Fowl Towns) Indians to EPG, September 17, enclosure in Twiggs to EPG, September 18, 1817, AGOLR; Kinache response to EPG, undated [August 1817], *ASPMA*, 1:723; EPG to AJ, October 1, 1817, *CAJ*, 2:326; David S. Heidler and Jeanne T. Heidler, *Old Hickory's War: Andrew Jackson and the Quest for Empire* (Mechanicsburg, Pa.: Stackpole Books, 1996), 97–100. Kinache is sometimes incorrectly referred to as Tom Perryman, a mixed-blood factor and onetime father-in-law to William Bowles; see James W. Covington, *The Seminoles of Florida* (Gainesville: University Press of Florida, 1993), 22–25, for the most detailed clarification. Contemporary American sources commonly refer to him as "King Hatchy" or the like. The Mikasuki, who were Hitchiti rather than Muskogee speakers, lived around Lake Miccosukee and were not directly related to the Seminoles of the Alachua (or Payne's) Prairie near modern Gainesville; the latter came from the Cowkeeper or Sehoya lineage of Creeks who immigrated to Florida during the eighteenth century.

10. William Earl Weeks, *John Quincy Adams and American Global Empire* (Lexington: University Press of Kentucky, 1992), 57–58, emphasizes the legitimacy of the privateers' commissions and letters of marque, but this is open to question, since neither the United States nor any other sovereign state had recognized the governments from which they came. Although the Latin American revolutionaries had to rely on the privateers to project naval power, and the privateers ordinarily respected vessels flying the American flag, their presence threatened free trade, and their forces were hardly as disciplined as those of nation-states. Weeks is correct that U.S. policy makers wanted to prevent Spain's replacement by more secure sovereignties, but it seems unlikely that the privateers could provide a solid basis for such polities.

11. Harris Gaylord Warren, "Pensacola and the Filibusters: 1816–1817," *LAHQ* 21 (July 1938): 816–817; William C. Davis, *The Pirates Laffite: The Treacherous World of the Gulf Corsairs* (New York: Harcourt, 2005), 342–344.

12. Monroe to Jefferson, December 23, 1817, and to Madison, February 13, 1818, *WJM*, 6:47–48; January 19, 1818, *MJQA*, 4:43; Adams to Peter Paul Francis deGrand (regarding the Frenchmen under Lallemand), January 21, 1818, *WJQA*, 6:290; "Suppression of Piratical Establishments," draft of House Foreign Affairs Committee report

revised by Adams, January 1818, *WJQA*, 6:287 (final version in *ASPFR*, 4:132); Monroe, annual message to Congress, November 16, 1818, *WJM*, 6:76–77; Adams to Charles Collins, December 31, 1817, *WJQA*, 6:285.

13. See T. Frederick Davis, "MacGregor's Invasion of Florida," *FHQ* 7 (July 1928): 3–71 (the most thorough account of the Amelia imbroglio); Stanley Faye, "Commodore Aury," *LAHQ* 24 (July 1941): 611–697; *Narrative of a Voyage to the Spanish Main in the Ship "Two Friends,"* introduction by John W. Griffin (1819; reprint, Gainesville: University Press of Florida, 1978). Rufus Kay Wyllys, "The Filibusters of Amelia Island," *GAHQ* 12 (Fall 1928): 297–305, and Frank L. Owsley Jr. and Gene A. Smith, *Filibusters and Expansionists: Jeffersonian Manifest Destiny, 1800–1821* (Tuscaloosa: University of Alabama Press, 1997), chap. 7, provide more concise accounts.

14. EPG to the War Department, December 15, 1817, *ASPMA*, 1:689; Bankhead, November 12, SWLS (Confidential and Unofficial), December 12, SWLS, and to George Graham, December 24, 1817, *ASPFR*, 4:141–144; JCC to Bankhead, December 16, 1817, *PJCC*, 2:20; Davis, "MacGregor's Invasion of Florida," 41–44, 47, 51–56, 67.

15. Bankhead's report, June 20, 1818, file B-255, SWLR: Reg; Bankhead, July 27, 1818, SWLS; EPG, May 7, 1820, file G-254, SWLR: Reg; Bankhead to Christopher Van Deventer, January 15, 1818, Christopher Van Deventer Papers, WLC. Bored by peacetime routine in Boston, Lieutenant Colonel Abraham Eustis offered his battalion for the seizure of Amelia or Galveston (December 8, 1817, AGOLR).

16. Harry Ammon, *James Monroe: The Quest for National Identity* (New York: McGraw-Hill, 1971), 417–418; January 10 and 14, 1818, *MJQA*, 4:38, 42.

17. Monroe, January 13, 1818, *MPP*, 2:592–594; 3 *Stat.* 471–472; "Suppression of Piratical Establishments," January 1818, *WJQA*, 6:287 (final version in *ASPFR*, 4:132); Bankhead, June 20, 1818, file B-255, SWLR: Reg; JCC to Bankhead, July 27, 1818, *PJCC*, 2:427; Monroe, November 16, 1818, *MPP*, 2:609–611 (see also 582–583); May 8, 1818, *MJQA*, 4:89.

18. Bankhead to Christopher Van Deventer, January 15, 1818, Van Deventer Papers, WLC. See also Bankhead to George Graham, December 24 and 27, 1817, *ASPFR*, 4:142.

19. Gray to Lt. Col. William A. Trimble, January 14, 1818, Trimble Papers, OHS.

20. James E. Lewis Jr., *The American Union and the Problem of Neighborhood: The United States and the Collapse of the Spanish Empire, 1783–1829* (Chapel Hill: University of North Carolina Press, 1998), 82–83.

21. A Virginian commissioned in 1808, Bankhead was sufficiently well connected to serve as an assistant adjutant general, and then as one of several adjutants general, from 1813 to 1815. He also participated in the Second Seminole War and the removal of the Cherokee; he earned a brevet to brigadier general for gallantry at the siege of Veracruz in 1847 and died nine years later, after forty-eight years of service. His deployment in most of the army's major constabulary operations was due primarily to his position in an artillery regiment that was stationed in coastal fortifications along the Atlantic seaboard, more easily deployed than infantry regiments stationed along the

western frontier. However, his efforts also attracted the attention and patronage of senior leaders. Nullification brought him onto Winfield Scott's radar screen, which probably contributed to his deployment in the Cherokee removal, Canadian border, Dorr War, and Veracruz operations, all commanded or overseen by Scott.

22. EPG to AJ, January 12, 1818, GLSR; Weeks, *John Quincy Adams and American Global Empire*, 68–69; January 14, 1818, *MJQA*, 4:42; January 15, 1811, 3 *Stat.* 471–472.

23. Spanish foreign minister Pizarro to the minister of war, February 26, 1818, quoted in Philip C. Brooks, *Diplomacy and the Borderlands: The Adams-Onís Treaty of 1819* (Berkeley: University of California Press, 1939), 92.

24. Twiggs to EPG, August 11, 1817, Jackson Papers, LC, and *CAJ*, 2:323–324n1; EPG to Graham and to AJ, November 9, 1817, *ASPMA*, 1:686; EPG to Rabun, November 9, 1817, cited in Heidler and Heidler, *Old Hickory's War*, 102–103; Graham to Indian agent David B. Mitchell, November 3, 1817, *TP*, 18:186–187. Most sources label Neamathla and the Fowl Towns as Mikasuki; J. Leitch Wright Jr., *Creeks and Seminoles: Destruction and Regeneration of the Muscogulge People* (Lincoln: University of Nebraska Press, 1986), identifies them as Hitchiti, although he observes that Hitchiti was an ethnolinguistic rather than a political category (220–221). The confusion probably arose because the army associated Fowl Town (or, as Wright points out, the Fowl Towns) with the nearby Mikasuki towns to the southeast, on the shores of what is today Lake Miccosukee. Spellings vary, and the modern tribe is labeled the Miccosukee. Covington, *Seminoles of Florida*, refers to the eighteenth- and nineteenth-century tribe as Mikasuki. Since *micco* means chief, the modern spelling may be a modern adoption, or it may accurately reflect nineteenth-century usage.

25. *PJCC*, 2:xxxiii; Archibald Henderson, "Isaac Shelby and the Genet Mission," *MVHR* 6 (March 1920): 452; Sylvia Wrobel, *Isaac Shelby: Kentucky's First Governor and Hero of Three Wars* (Danville, Ky.: Cumberland Press, 1974).

26. Graham to EPG, October 30, 1817, *ASPIA*, 2:159; Graham to Mitchell, November 3, 1817, *TP*, 18:186–187; EPG to Twiggs, November 20, and Twiggs to EPG, November 21, 1817, *CAJ*, 2:333–334; EPG to AJ, November 21, 1817, *PAJ*, 4:150–151; Capt. George Birch, "Private Journal," undated entry, Birch Family Papers, HSP; EPG to AJ, October 23 and November 26, 1817, Jackson Papers, LC; Capt. John N. McIntosh to Senator Abner Lacock, February 5, 1819, *ASPMA*, 1:747; AJ, December 16, 1817, file J-1, SWLR: Reg. Most sources put the U.S. force at the Fowl Towns at 250; a larger force seems unlikely, given the speed with which the expedition was launched and moved.

Lewis, *The American Union and the Problem of Neighborhood*, 96–98, walks a fine line in observing that the Monroe administration balanced continuing concerns about war and British intervention with "a dramatic . . . shift" in the influence of "active unionists" such as Adams, Clay, and Calhoun during 1817 and 1818. Lewis labels Monroe, along with Madison and Jefferson, a "passive unionist," meaning that he believed that the power of voluntary citizen action made centralization or activist federal government unnecessary and that he opposed strong restraints on the behavior of

American citizens toward foreign nations. Yet ultimately, Madison and Monroe accepted most of the "active unionist," or nationalist or National Republican, measures opposed by traditionalist or "Old" Republicans after the War of 1812: a new Bank of the United States, protective tariffs, a national system of coastal fortifications, a "general staff" (though not in the later Prussian sense) for the army, an expansible skeleton army with a disproportionate number of officers in the 1821 reduction in force, and the General Survey Act of 1824 authorizing federal support for surveys of transportation routes. Monroe seems less passive than Madison, demonstrating a more aggressive expansionism both before and after the War of 1812; see Michael S. Fitzgerald, "'Nature Unsubdued': Diplomacy, Expansion and the American Military Buildup of 1815–1816," *Mid-America* 77 (Winter 1995): 10–13, 30–32, and "James Monroe and the Conduct of American Foreign Policy" (paper presented to the Society for Historians of the Early American Republic, July 17, 1998), for interpretations stressing Monroe's activism and aggressiveness. In any case, it seems clear that the shift toward greater influence by "active unionists" did not go "largely unnoticed" (Lewis, 97) among army officers. Nor should we forget an earlier name for several of these active unionists: War Hawks.

27. EPG to AJ, December 2, 1817 (quotations), *PAJ*, 4:153–154; EPG, enclosure, December 2, 1817, *ASPFR*, 4:598. Gaines was right: that April, British foreign minister Lord Castlereagh told the Spanish ambassador that Britain would not fight the United States in defense of Spanish Florida; see Charles C. Griffin, *The United States and the Disruption of the Spanish Empire, 1810–1822* (New York: Columbia University Press, 1937), 94–95. The most comprehensive primary source for the First Seminole War is the correspondence collected in *ASPMA*, 1:681–769. See also Heidler and Heidler, *Old Hickory's War*; Robert V. Remini, *Andrew Jackson and His Indian Wars* (New York: Viking, 2001), chaps. 8, 9; and Wright, *Creeks and Seminoles*, chap. 7.

28. Monroe, December 2, 1817, *MPP*, 2:582–583; JCC to EPG, December 9 and 16, 1817, *PJCC*, 2:8, 20. In contrast to the policy makers' perceptions he stresses in *The American Union and the Problem of Neighborhood*, in *John Quincy Adams: Policymaker for the Union* (Wilmington, Del.: Scholarly Resources, 2001), 46, James E. Lewis observes that by 1817 there was little likelihood of an Anglo-American war, unless it was precipitated by U.S. aggression against Spain. Clearly, Calhoun did not think pursuing the Indians in Florida was likely to cause a war with Spain, which suggests he had a good sense of the limits of British support for Spanish sovereignty. See Michael S. Fitzgerald, "Europe and the United States Defense Establishment: American Military Policy and Strategy, 1815–1821" (Ph.D. diss., Purdue University, 1990), 256–257, for the same recognition.

29. EPG to the War Department, December 15, 1817, *ASPMA*, 1:689; JCC to EPG and to AJ, December 26, 1817, *PJCC*, 2:39–40; Thomas Hart Benton, *Thirty Years View, or, a History of the Working of the American Government for Thirty Years, from 1820 to 1850* (New York: D. Appleton, 1854–1856), 1:170.

30. Monroe to AJ, December 28, 1817, James Monroe Papers, NYPL; Ammon, *James Monroe*, 417; Monroe to Jefferson, December 23, 1817, *WJM*, 6:47.

31. Lewis, *The American Union and the Problem of Neighborhood*, 246–247n92. Jackson hinted at his intentions in a letter he sent to Calhoun on March 25 (*ASPMA*, 1:698).

32. JCC to AJ, December 11, 17, and 26, 1817, *PJCC*, 2:10, 24, 39; Heidler and Heidler, *Old Hickory's War*, 117; AJ to Monroe, January 6, 1818, *PAJ*, 4:165–167. For further analysis, see Daniel Feller, "The Seminole Controversy Revisited: A New Look at Andrew Jackson's 1818 Florida Campaign," *FHQ* 88 (Winter 2010): 309–325.

33. Monroe, sworn statement, June 19, 1831, *WJM*, 7:234–236; Monroe to JCC, May 19, 1830, *PJCC*, 11:165, and January 30, 1818, *PJCC*, 2:104.

34. Monroe to JCC, January 30, 1818, *PJCC*, 2:104; Remini, *Andrew Jackson and His Indian Wars*, 137–140; AJ to John Coffee, January 14, 1818, *PAJ*, 4:169–170. Jackson later argued that the volunteers were the equivalent of militia, though he had no authority to muster the latter into service either; see *ASPMA*, 1:758–759, and *PAJ*, 4:168, for related citations.

35. Trimble to AJ, February 12, 1818, Jackson Papers, LC. The following officers wrote to Jackson about Fort Scott and the Apalachicola supply route: Arbuckle, December 19, 1817, January 12, February 15, and March 5, 1818; Commissary General George Gibson, February 2 and 12, 1818; Trimble, February 4, 1818; and EPG, February 22, 1818 (all in Jackson Papers, LC). Jackson summed up these problems in his letters to Calhoun, February 26, 1818, *ASPMA*, 1:698, and to John Coffee, March 26, 1818, Jackson Papers, THS. He mentioned his later supply problems in his report to Calhoun of April 20, 1818, *PAJ*, 4:193–196. The William A. Trimble Papers, OHS, contain extended discussions of supply efforts from New Orleans and Mobile to Fort Crawford, north of Pensacola.

36. Trimble to Call, February 1, Trimble to Call and Lt. W. [William] Arnold, "Confidential," February 1, and Gray to Trimble, January 8, 1818, Trimble Papers, OHS; Governor William Bibb to JCC, and Bibb, order, April 30, 1818, *TP*, 18:317–320. See Capt. John McCrary to Capt. Josiah Jones, January 25, 1818, Trimble Papers, for a report of another patrol from Fort Crawford that burned an Indian village.

37. EPG to JCC, January 23, 1818, *PJCC*, 2:90 (also in GLSR); EPG to AJ, January 31, 1816, GLSR.

38. EPG to Rabun, quoted in Silver, *Edmund Pendleton Gaines*, 77n76; AJ to Rabun, February 10, 1818, *PAJ*, 4:174.

39. Wright, *Creeks and Seminoles*, 204–207. See Remini, *Andrew Jackson and His Indian Wars*, chap. 10, for Jackson's performance as commissioner to the Chickasaw.

40. AJ to Francisco Caso y Luengo, April 6, 1818, *PAJ*, 4:186–187; Monroe, March 25, 1818, *MPP*, 2:601; AJ, April 8, 1818, file J-84, SWLR: Reg. Jackson's reports to the War Department are in *ASPFR*, 4:572–573, 600 (March 25, April 26); *PAJ*, 4:189–190 (April 8), 193–196 (April 20), and 197–200 (May 5); and Col. Robert Butler (adjutant general, Southern Division) to Adjutant and Inspector General Daniel Parker, May 3, 1818, *ASPMA*, 1:703–704.

41. AJ to JCC, April 8 and May 5, 1818, *PAJ*, 4:190, 199; EPG to AJ, July 10, 1817, *CAJ*, 2:305–306; AJ to EPG, September 30, 1815, Jackson Papers, LC; Wright, *Creeks and Seminoles*, 194–197, 212–214; Heidler and Heidler, *Old Hickory's War*, chap. 6; Frank L. Owsley Jr., "Ambrister and Arbuthnot: Adventurers or Martyrs for British Honor?" *JER* 5 (Fall 1985): 289–308.

42. Matthew Warshauer, *Andrew Jackson and the Politics of Martial Law: Nationalism, Civil Liberties, and Partisanship* (Knoxville: University of Tennessee Press, 2006), 37; Frank L. Owsley Jr., "Prophet of War: Josiah Francis and the Creek War," *American Indian Quarterly* 9 (Summer 1985): 273–293. Some sources identify Homathle Micco as Homathlemico; the person was the same. Hillis Haya (also spelled Hallaya or Hadjo) means medicine man, which Francis was, as well as a trader. See Wright, *Creeks and Seminoles*, 29–30, on the variety of names one individual Creek or Seminole might hold, according to different dimensions of his identity.

43. AJ to JCC, May 5, 1818, *PAJ*, 4:199; Adams to U.S. ambassador to Spain George Washington Erving, November 28, 1818, *WJQA*, 6:498, 482, 486, 488, 501 (see 493–495, linking Ambrister, MacGregor, and Woodbine). See also Adams to Onís, November 30, 1818, *WJQA*, 6:505–509, which refers to the Negro Fort and asks why the Spanish permitted Arbuthnot to operate in Florida when they were normally so zealous in regulating trade. The Erving letter is examined in depth in William Earl Weeks, "John Quincy Adams's 'Great Gun' and the Rhetoric of American Empire," *DH* 14 (Winter 1990): 25–42.

44. January 27 and 31, 1818, *MJQA*, 4:50–51; Adams, memo refusing British mediation, February 2, 1818, *WJQA*, 6:294–298; Ammon, *James Monroe*, 419.

45. Adams to Gallatin, November 30, 1818, *WJQA*, 5:513; May 4, November 24 and 30, 1818, *MJQA*, 4:87, 179–180, 184; Bradford Perkins, *Castlereagh and Adams: England and the United States, 1812–1823* (Berkeley: University of California Press, 1964), chap. 15; Weeks, *John Quincy Adams and American Global Empire*, 130, 148. See *ASPMA*, 1:721–734, for records of the Ambrister and Arbuthnot courts-martial, and *ASPMA*, 1:757–758, for Jackson's defense of his proceedings, an intriguing topic in light of twenty-first-century debates about "unlawful enemy combatants." For legal analysis, see Deborah A. Rosen, "Wartime Prisoners and the Rule of Law: Andrew Jackson's Military Tribunals during the First Seminole War," *JER* 28 (Winter 2008): 559–595.

46. July 8, 10, and 16, August 9, and November 9, 1818, *MJQA*, 4:105–106, 110, 124, 169.

47. Call to Trimble, April 27, 1818, Trimble Papers, OHS; Butler to Sands, April 28, 1818, Abraham L. Sands Papers, Sterling Memorial Library, Yale University; AJ to EPG, May 5, 1818, *ASPMA*, 1:708.

48. AJ to JCC, May 5, 1818, *PAJ*, 4:197–200; AJ to Masot, March 25, 1818, *CAJ*, 2:355; Masot to AJ, April 15, 1818, *ASPFR*, 4:562. See also AJ to Masot, April 27, 1818, *ASPFR*, 4:562–563.

49. AJ to JCC, April 20 and May 5, to Gov. José Masot, May 23 and 25, and to Lt. Col. Luis Piernas, May 24, 1818, *PAJ*, 4:195, 199–200, 206–211.

50. AJ, proclamation, May 29, and AJ to JCC, June 2, 1818, *CAJ*, 2:375, 380. See *ASPFR*, 4:562–578, for the exchanges between Jackson and the Spanish authorities and for Jackson's justifications to the administration. Masot complained to Major White Youngs, April 27, 1818, *ASPFR*, 4:563, that U.S. troops had murdered several peaceful Indians, including women and children. Jackson later rationalized his imposition of American revenue laws as a means to end smuggling, but he could not keep from adding his desire "to admit the American merchant to an equal participation in trade, which would have been denied under the partial operations of the Spanish commercial code" (*ASPMA*, 1:757).

CHAPTER FIVE: JACKSON AND GAINES GET THEIR WAY

1. AJ to Monroe, "private," June 2, 1818, *PAJ*, 4:213–215; AJ to JCC, June 2, 1818, *CAJ*, 2:379–381. Small-scale patrols and raids continued against the Seminoles and Red Sticks until at least September, however; see Major George Mercer Brooke to AJ, September 15, 1818, *PAJ*, 4:239, and EPG to AJ, with enclosures, September 16, 1818, Jackson Papers, LC.

2. AJ to Monroe, "private," June 2, 1818, *PAJ*, 4:213–15; Butler to EPG, June 2, 1818, GLSR.

3. JCC to Charles Tate, September 5, 1818, *PJCC*, 3:105–106; Monroe to AJ, July 19, 1818, *WJM*, 6:58–59.

4. July 13, 16, 20, and 21, 1818, *MJQA*, 4:107, 109, 113, 115; Monroe to Jefferson, July 22, 1818, *WJM*, 6:63; see also Monroe to Madison, July 10, 1818, ibid., 53–54.

5. Monroe to AJ, July 19, 1818, *PJCC*, 2:400; AJ to Monroe, August 19, 1818, *PAJ*, 4:236–238. Fiscal accountability aside, administrative capacity can only be judged subjectively. The early Monroe administration was certainly more capable, even with a temporary secretary of war, than the early Madison administration; the Jefferson administration had some capable heads, such as Albert Gallatin. Despite the Republican factionalism of the Monroe era, Monroe's eventually became the most administratively capable of the Republican presidencies, with Calhoun's War Department leading the way. In 1817 and 1818 the administration was still finding its sea legs, however.

6. House reports, January 12, 1819, *ASPMA*, 1:735–739; House debate, January 18–February 8, 1819, in *Annals of Congress*, 15th Cong., 2nd sess., 527–530, 583–1138.

7. Lacock report, February 24, 1819, *ASPMA*, 1:739–743; Norman K. Risjord, *The Old Republicans: Southern Conservatives in the Age of Jefferson* (New York: Columbia University Press, 1965), 188; David S. Heidler, "The Politics of National Aggression: Congress and the First Seminole War," *JER* 13 (Winter 1993): 526–527; David S. Heidler and Jeanne T. Heidler, *Old Hickory's War: Andrew Jackson and the Quest for Empire* (Mechanicsburg, Pa.: Stackpole Books, 1996), 213–219; Monroe, Novem-

ber 16, 1818, *MPP*, 2:609–610. The administration did order commanders to refer the fate of future British captives to Washington; see AJ to HA, May 15, 1819, *PJCC*, 4:63, amid planning for Atkinson's expedition up the Missouri River.

8. AJ to Crawford, September 20, 1816, *PAJ*, 4:65; Daniel Hughes (factor at Fort Mitchell, and an army major until 1815) to Thomas L. McKenney (superintendent of Indian trade), February 10 and 26, 1817, and Clinch quoted in William Bowen to Hughes, January 22, 1817, *TP*, 18:47–52.

9. Hughes to McKenney, May 28, 1817, *TP*, 18:279–282; section 11, Intercourse Act of March 30, 1802, 2 *Stat.* 143. See also McKenney to Hughes, June 21, 1817, *TP*, 18:115.

10. EPG to JCC, October 17, 1819, *ASPMA*, 2:127, citing letters from Mitchell; Mitchell to the secretary of war, March 30, 1817, *ASPIA*, 2:156; Mitchell to EPG, October 17, 1817, *ASPMA*, 2:132 (quotation); Graham to Mitchell, November 3, 1817, *TP*, 18:187.

11. Mitchell to JCC, January 6 and February 3, 1818, *ASPIA*, 2:152, and *PJCC*, 2:114–118 (quotation at 118); EPG to JCC, January 23, 1818, *PJCC*, 2:90; EPG to Rabun, quoted from the January 27, 1818, *Milledgeville Journal* in James W. Silver, *Edmund Pendleton Gaines: Frontier General* (Baton Rouge: Louisiana State University Press, 1949), 77n76. See Heidler and Heidler, *Old Hickory's War*, and *PAJ* vol. 4 regarding the Chehaw massacre. See Major George Mercer Brooke to AJ, September 18, 1818, *PAJ*, 4:239–240, for condemnation of the lynching of five captured Creeks by white Alabamans that July; this atrocity led Brooke to detain eight other Indians at Pensacola rather than exposing them to danger by sending them to Montgomery.

12. Jesup to AJ, August 12, 1816, Thomas Sidney Jesup Papers, LC; EPG to JCC, January 12, 1818, *PJCC*, 2:68; Benjamin W. Griffith Jr., *McIntosh and Weatherford: Creek Indian Leaders* (Tuscaloosa: University of Alabama Press, 1988), 184–186. The account in Heidler and Heidler, *Old Hickory's War*, 103, 109–110, 114, 132, 191, is less unfavorable to Mitchell, but the agent's course wavered enough that it is hard to see a consistent policy direction. Having told Gaines in October that he would help the general "compel" the Seminoles, it seems rather disingenuous to complain about the attack on the Fowl Towns a month later. It is possible that the agent regarded the Fowl Towns Indians as innocents who were mistaken for the Mikasuki, Seminole, or Red Sticks, but if one accepts the legitimacy of the Treaty of Fort Jackson, as Mitchell surely did, Gaines and Jackson appear to have had better evidence about the Fowl Towns' role in violence along the frontier.

13. Trimble to Monroe, January 26, 1818, *PJCC*, 2:95; McKenney to JCC, March 28, 1818, enclosing Hughes to McKenney, December 28, 1817, *TP*, 18:279, 282–284; JCC to AJ, July 28, EPG to Arbuckle, October 24, and AJ to JCC, February 14, 1818, GLSR; AJ to Monroe, September 29, 1819, *PAJ*, 4:330–332. Hughes, Mitchell's successor John Crowell, and Crowell's successor David Brearley all had conflicts of interest—Hughes as the government factor (head of the government-run trading post), Crowell because his brother ran a store that traded with the Creeks, and Brearley in employing his son and profiteering at Creek expense. See Griffith, *McIntosh*

and Weatherford, 195–200, 217–218, and Roley McIntosh and other Creeks to AJ, March 7, 1829, *PAJ*, 7:83–85.

14. Mitchell to JCC, February 3, 1818, *PJCC*, 2:117; EPG, March 19, 1820, file G-212, Major Milo Mason, March 12, 1820, file M-195, and AJ, November 5, 1819, file J-153, SWLR: Reg; JCC to EPG, February 21, 1820, *PJCC*, 4:674–675; Brearley's deposition, October 18, 1818, SWLR: IA, 2:528–558. See also AJ to Monroe, September 29, 1819, *PAJ*, 4:329–332. Gaines had Brearley court-martialed in June 1818, apparently over purely military matters, but the colonel was found not guilty (*ASPMA*, 2:110–116). However, hints of malfeasance continued to dog him: in 1831 Congress passed a private bill compensating Seventh Infantry Regiment sutler John Nicks for a bad check Brearley had written during removal operations (March 3, 1831, 6 *Stat.* 465).

Jackson also sought the opportunity to associate Crawford with the illegal slave trade; see *CAJ*, 2:416–421, for his correspondence with John Clarke, Crawford's principal rival in Georgia, who searched for evidence sufficient to implicate the treasury secretary. Gaines's most comprehensive rebuttal of Mitchell's charges, along with his own countercharges, came in his response to the critique of his operations during the autumn of 1817 (and Jackson's the following spring) by the Senate committee under Abner Lacock; see EPG, October 17, 1819, file G-103, SWLR: Reg (reprinted in *ASPMA*, 2:125–130). Most of the letter is devoted to proving the belligerence of the Fowl Towns Indians and the virtue of the white population on the frontier. The administration's final report on Mitchell is Attorney General William Wirt, "Slaves Imported by the Indian Agent Contrary to Law," January 21, 1821, communicated to the Senate, May 4, 1822, in *ASPMA*, 2:957–975; see also Dwight F. Henderson, *Congress, Courts, and Criminals: The Development of Federal Criminal Law, 1801–1829* (Westport, Conn.: Greenwood Press, 1985), 188–192; Royce G. Shingelton, "David Brydie Mitchell and the African Importation Case of 1820," *Journal of Negro History* 58 (July 1973): 327–340; and Griffith, *McIntosh and Weatherford*, 196, 198.

15. EPG to JCC and to AJ, September 8, 1818, GLSR; EPG to JCC, October 17, 1819, *ASPMA*, 2:129; Griffith, *McIntosh and Weatherford*, 199–200; Michael D. Green, *The Politics of Indian Removal: Creek Government and Society in Crisis* (Lincoln: University of Nebraska Press, 1982), 56–57 (second quotation); Francis Paul Prucha, *American Indian Policy in the Formative Years: The Indian Trade and Intercourse Acts, 1790–1834* (Cambridge, Mass.: Harvard University Press, 1962), 93–94. See also William S. Belko, "John C. Calhoun and the Creation of the Bureau of Indian Affairs: An Essay on Political Rivalry, Ideology, and Policymaking in the Early Republic," *South Carolina Historical Magazine* 105 (July 2004): 170–197.

16. EPG, May 1, 1819, and March 19, 1820, files G-13 and 212, SWLR: Reg; EPG to Creek chiefs, September 16, and to Arbuckle, October 22, Lt. Daniel Burch (Gaines's aide-de-camp) to post commanders, September 17, and JCC to EPG, September 30, 1818, GLSR.

17. Bankhead, June 21, 1822, SWLS; Arbuckle, November 5, 1818, file A-13, SWLR: Reg. On October 26, 1818, Calhoun ordered Mitchell to prevent the entry

of blacks from Florida (GLSR). See also JCC to EPG, January 25, 1820, *PJCC*, 4:603. See Hazel Akehurst, "Sectional Crises and the Fate of Africans Illegally Imported into the United States, 1806–1860," *American Nineteenth-Century History* 9 (June 2008): 97–122, regarding the status and disposition of enslaved persons brought into the United States after Congress outlawed the importation of slaves in 1807. More generally, see W. E. B. DuBois, *The Suppression of the African Slave Trade to the United States of America, 1638–1870* (1896; reprint, New York: Oxford University Press, 2007), and Ernest Obadele-Starks, *Freebooters and Smugglers: The Foreign Slave Trade in the United States after 1808* (Fayetteville: University of Arkansas Press, 2007).

18. Jamie W. Moore, *The Fortifications Board 1816–1828 and the Definition of National Security* (Charleston, S.C.: The Citadel, 1981); Samuel J. Watson, "Knowledge, Interest, and the Limits of Military Professionalism: The Discourse on American Coastal Defense, 1815–1860," *War in History* 5 (Fall 1998): 280–307; AJ to JCC, August 10, 1818, *ASPMA*, 1:744–745, and May 5, 1818, *PAJ*, 4:200 (block quotation).

19. AJ to JCC, May 5, 1818, *PAJ*, 4:200; AJ, November 28, 1818, file J-71, SWLR: Reg.

20. March 23, May 13, and July 11 and 17, 1818, *MJQA*, 4:66–67, 91, 106, 111.

21. AJ to JCC, August 10, 1818, *ASPMA*, 1:744–745; AJ to George W. Campbell, October 5, 1818, *CAJ*, 2:296; AJ, November 28, 1818, file J-71, SWLR: Reg.

22. AJ to JCC, August 10, 1818, *ASPMA*, 1:744–745; AJ, November 28, 1818, file J-71, SWLR: Reg (and last quotation); AJ to George W. Campbell, October 5, 1818, *CAJ*, 2:397.

23. AJ, November 28, 1818, file J-71, SWLR: Reg. See Brig. Gen. Eleazar Wheelock Ripley (commander of the Eighth Military Department, including the Sabine frontier) to AJ, October 31, 1818, *PAJ*, 4:252, 518, concerning Spanish movements in Texas.

24. Bankhead, May 25, 1818, DPP; EPG to AJ, July 17, 1818, AGOLR; AJ to EPG, August 7, 1818, *CAJ*, 2:384.

25. AJ to Monroe, August 10, 1818, *CAJ*, 2:385; JCC to EPG, September 1, and to AJ, September 8, 1818, *PJCC*, 3:85–86, 111; EPG, September 20, 1818, file G-106, SWLR: Reg.

26. JCC to Monroe, September 21, and to AJ, September 24, 1818, *PJCC*, 3:148–149, 158; JCC to EPG, September 23, October 2 and 26 (quotation), and November 3 and 25, 1818, *PJCC*, 3:152, 185, 234–235, 252, 299. On September 1, Calhoun wrote to a civilian friend (*PJCC*, 3:88) that war with Britain was unlikely because the British appreciated the consequences; it matters little whether Calhoun changed his mind during the ensuing week or was only trying to restrain the generals.

27. EPG to JCC, November 14, 1818, GLSR; AJ, November 28, 1818, file J-71, SWLR: Reg.

28. JCC to EPG, January 19, 1819, *PJCC*, 3:507; EPG, December 29, 1818, file G-72, SWLR: Reg; Capt. A. C. W. Fanning to EPG, November 27, 1818, *ASPMA*,

1:752; EPG to Gov. José Coppinger, December 28, 1818, and January 24, 1819, and Coppinger to EPG, January 3 and 5, 1819, GLSR.

29. EPG, January 12, 1819, file G-81, SWLR: Reg; Eustis, January 5, 1819, and Bankhead, January 10, 1820, DPP. See ex–quartermaster general James R. Mullany, October 7, 1819, file M-128, SWLR: Reg, and Capt. James M. Glassell, March 12, 1820, DPP, for further examples of military interest in invading Florida. Historians sympathetic to the Florida maroons have taken American claims of Spanish arms shipments to the Seminoles at face value, an interesting inversion of past tendencies to assume that U.S. officials were fabricating justifications for aggression; see Cantor Brown Jr., "Tales of Angola: Free Blacks, Red Stick Creeks, and International Intrigue in Spanish Southwest Florida, 1812–1821," in *Go Sound the Trumpet! Selections in Florida's African-American History*, ed. Donald H. Jackson Jr. and Canter Brown Jr. (Tampa, Fla.: University of Tampa Press, 2005), 10. Desertion was apparently not as much of a problem in Florida after 1814 as it had been in West Florida before 1810, as it remained in the Neutral Ground until 1821, or as it was along the Canadian border throughout most of the period covered by this book. Presumably, the growth of hostilities—from the "Patriot" rebellion and the U.S. incursion into East Florida and the Creek War onward—made it difficult for American deserters to reach Florida, and it was unsafe even if they made it.

30. JCC to EPG, August 14, and to AJ, September 8, 1818, *PJCC*, 3:29–30, 110; EPG to JCC, May 2, 1819, *PJCC*, 4:47; Capt. A. C. W. Fanning, December 13, 1820, DPP; EPG to Fanning, September 16, 1818, GLSR.

31. Brooke to AJ, September 15, 1818, *PAJ*, 4:240.

32. Clinch to EPG, August 16, 1818, cited in Rembert W. Patrick, *Aristocrat in Uniform: General Duncan L. Clinch* (Gainesville: University of Florida Press, 1963), 41; Clinch, August 2, 1819, and April 14, 1821, DPP.

33. November 10 and 20, 1818, *MJQA*, 4:170, 175; Adams to George Washington Erving, November 30, 1818, *WJQA*, 6:487–488, 501–502; February 19, 1819, *MJQA*, 4:268; Monroe to Robert Rush, March 7, 1819, *WJM*, 6:91.

34. William Earl Weeks, *John Quincy Adams and American Global Empire* (Lexington: University Press of Kentucky, 1992), 106, 74; James E. Lewis Jr., *The American Union and the Problem of Neighborhood: The United States and the Collapse of the Spanish Empire, 1783–1829* (Chapel Hill: University of North Carolina Press, 1998), 122–123.

35. Michael S. Fitzgerald, "Europe and the United States Defense Establishment: American Military Policy and Strategy, 1815–1821"(Ph.D. diss., Purdue University, 1990), 260; Heidler, "Politics of National Aggression," 506, 508; *MJQA*, 4:239; John Quincy Adams to George Washington Erving, November 28, 1818, *WJQA*, 6:487–488; February 1 and 3, 1819, *MJQA*, 4:238–239.

36. Christopher Van Deventer (chief clerk of the War Department) to AJ, confidential, November 22, 1819, *PJCC*, 4:426; Monroe to AJ, December 12, 1819, *CAJ*, 2:448; Armistead, December 15, and Jesup, December 14, 1819, files A-51 and J-124, SWLR: Reg; AJ to Monroe, December 10, 1819, Monroe Papers, NYPL; AJ to

JCC, December 11, and JCC to AJ, December 24 and 31, 1819, *PJCC*, 4:477, 505, 530. The planning and preparations for another invasion can be followed in *PJCC*, 4:477, 484, 489, 499, 505, 512, 530, 588, 602, 623, 706, 743; a note on p. 411 indicates that planning began in October if not before. See also Major (assistant adjutant general) James M. Glassell to Major James E. Dinkins, January 12, 1820, and EPG, confidential circular, January 12, 1820, Letters Sent by Brevet Major General Edmund Pendleton Gaines and Staff, 1819–1826, RG 393, Entry 5806, NA.

37. Adams to William Lowndes, December 21, 1819, *WJQA*, 6:563–564; Message to Congress, March 27 and May 9, 1820, *WJM*, 6:118, 126; Charles C. Griffin, *The United States and the Disruption of the Spanish Empire, 1810–1822* (New York: Columbia University Press, 1937), 218–224, 231–241; AJ to Commissary General George Gibson, February 1, 1820, *PAJ*, 4:356; AJ, May 26, 1821, file J-307, SWLR: Reg; Canter Brown Jr., "The 'Sarazota, or Runaway Negro Plantations': Tampa Bay's First Black Community, 1812–1821," *Tampa Bay History* 12 (Fall–Winter 1990): 14–17.

See James W. Covington, *The Seminoles of Florida* (Gainesville: University Press of Florida, 1993), 47–48, for a summary of Seminole and Red Stick movements after Jackson's invasion, generally to the east (to the Alachua region)and southward down the Gulf coast side of the Florida peninsula. Historians of American-Indian relations have always emphasized the late nineteenth century as the "reservation" era, often citing policies in California during the 1850s as the first example, but this reflects a focus on the Plains and perhaps a desire to distinguish between removal and reservation. The reality was very much a continuum; the term *reservation* was used as early as the 1820s, if not before, originating in the sense of land "reserved" for some specific purpose under an agreement, such as the Western Reserve of Ohio or the "military reservations" that surrounded army posts. The parallels between African American maroons and Seminole refugees are evident when we note that *Seminole* was probably etymologically related to *cimarron*, the Spanish word for "wild and untamed" and the root of *maroon*. *Isti simanole* also means "wild and untamed" and "runaway." See J. Leitch Wright Jr., *Creeks and Seminoles: Destruction and Regeneration of the Muscogulge People* (Lincoln: University of Nebraska Press, 1986), 4.

38. Trimble, October 16, 1818, Confidential SWLS; Trimble to JCC, February 1, 1819, *PJCC*, 2:537; AJ, November 28, 1818, file J-71, SWLR: Reg; AJ to JCC, December 21, 1820, *PAJ*, 4:409.

39. *PAJ*, 4:410; Philip C. Brooks, *Diplomacy and the Borderlands: The Adams-Onís Treaty of 1819* (Berkeley: University of California Press, 1939), 155; February 3, 1819, *MJQA*, 4:239; Douglas M. Astolfi, *Foundations of Destiny: A Foreign Policy of the Jacksonians, 1824–1837* (New York: Garland, 1989), 59. See Gary C. Anderson, *The Conquest of Texas: Ethnic Cleansing in the Promised Land, 1820–1875* (Norman: University of Oklahoma Press, 2005), and my second volume for army officers' attitudes toward Texans.

40. Lewis, *The American Union and the Problem of Neighborhood*, 84–85. Beard was wounded in a skirmish at Ogdensburg, New York, in February 1813, but he held

his brevet as compensation because he had been demoted from captain to first lieutenant in the postwar reductions in force.

41. Beard to Natchitoches district judge Henry Adams Ballard, June 14, 1819, to U.S. marshal John C. Carr, June 18, 1819, and to Ripley, June 22, 1819, all enclosures to AJ, July 24, 1819, file J-55, SWLR: Reg. Ballard was a state official, not a federal appointee; as Ballard's predecessor in 1812, Carr had done little to discourage the Gutiérrez-Magee expedition. The filibusters in 1819 also included Edmund Gaines's brother James, a civilian businessman; their backers included the usual suspects, such as the Kemper brothers. See Edward A. Bradley, "Fighting for Texas: Filibuster James Long, the Adams-Onis Treaty, and the Monroe Administration," *SWHQ* 102 (January 1999): 336–337; Edward A. Bradley, "Forgotten Filibusters: Private Hostile Expeditions from the United States into Spanish Texas, 1812–1821" (Ph.D. diss., University of Illinois at Urbana-Champaign, 1999); William C. Davis, *The Pirates Laffite: The Treacherous World of the Gulf Corsairs* (New York: Harcourt, 2005), 393–436; and, from the Spanish perspective, Alfred B. Thomas, "The Yellowstone River, James Long, and Spanish Reaction to American Intrusion into Spanish Dominions, 1818–1819," *New Mexico Historical Review* 4 (April 1929): 164–187. The struggle over control of the national armed forces on the border of East Florida in 1812 is discussed in James G. Cusick, *The Other War of 1812: The Patriot War and the American Invasion of East Florida* (Gainesville: University Press of Florida, 2003), and Rembert W. Patrick, *Florida Fiasco: Rampant Rebels on the Georgia-Florida Border, 1810–1815* (Athens: University of Georgia Press, 1954).

42. Beard to Coombs, June 9, Ripley to Beard, July 7, and AJ to Ripley, July 24, 1819, enclosures to AJ, July 24, 1819, file J-55, SWLR: Reg; Bradley, "Fighting for Texas," 338. Bissell commanded the Ninth Military Department, in Jackson's Southern Division, in St. Louis.

43. Beard to the Officer Commanding, Eighth Military Department (Ripley), October 10, 1819, and AJ, January 23, 1820, file J-181, SWLR: Reg; quotations from Pérez in Harris Gaylord Warren, *The Sword Was Their Passport: A History of American Filibustering in the Mexican Revolution* (Baton Rouge: Louisiana State University Press, 1943), 244–245; Beard, October 2, enclosure in AJ, January 23, 1820, file J-181, SWLR: Reg.

44. Curtis A. Wilgus, "Some Notes on Spanish American Patriot Activity along the Gulf Coast of the United States, 1811–1822," *LAHQ* 8 (April 1925): 214; Beard to Perez, n.d. (probably early November 1819), enclosure to AJ, January 23, 1820, file J-181, SWLR: Reg.

45. AJ, January 23, 1820, file J-181, SWLR: Reg; Wilgus, "Some Notes on Spanish American Patriot Activity," 206; AJ, July 24, 1819, file J-55, SWLR: Reg.

46. Ripley to Trimble, March 15 and April 16, 1818, Trimble Papers, OHS; Ripley, October 31, 1818, file R-46, SWLR: Reg.

47. Ripley, October 31 and September 9, 1818, files R-48 and 30, SWLR: Reg; Ripley to Trimble, March 15 and April 16, 1818, Trimble Papers, OHS; Ripley, October 20, SWLS; Ripley, October 31 and November 30, 1818, files R-48 and 72, SWLR:

Reg. Ripley had command over the First and Eighth Infantry, a battalion of artillery normally serving as infantry, and sometimes elements of the Third Infantry.

48. Ripley to Jesup, February 28, 1817, Jesup Papers, LC; Ripley to Christopher Van Deventer, "Private," August 15, 1818, Christopher Van Deventer Papers, WLC; *New Hampshire Sentinel*, January 9, 1819, and *American Advocate and Kennebec Advertiser*, February 13, 1819, Readex Early American Newspapers online database; Ripley to Butler, June 6, AJ to Ripley, July 31, and Butler to Ripley, July 16, 1819, *PAJ*, 4:536, 305, 539.

49. Ripley to JCC, August 20, 1819, *PJCC*, 4:260; Butler to Ripley, September 11, and Parker to Butler, December 22, 1819, *PAJ*, 4:545, 554; Ripley to Van Deventer, November 14, 1819, *PJCC*, 4:408; Warren, *The Sword Was Their Passport*, 250–251; Charles A. Gulick Jr. et al., eds., *The Papers of Mirabeau B. Lamar: Edited from the Original Papers in the Texas State Library*, 6 vols. (1920–1927; reprint, Austin, Tex.: Pemberton Press, 1968), 2:82, 94–98, 103–104. Jackson's July 31 letter contains the clearest discussion of the road question. Longtime filibuster leader Fulwar Skipwith wrote to Secretary of War Calhoun that Ripley said the United States would purchase land from him to build an arsenal (July 24, 1818, *PJCC*, 2:423).

50. AJ, January 17, 1820, file J-178, SWLR: Reg; AJ to Crawford, April 24, 1816, *PAJ*, 4:24–26; AJ to JCC, September 7, 1819, *PJCC*, 4:306; JCC to AJ, January 22 and February 5, 1820, *PJCC*, 4:591, 635–636.

51. ZT to Jesup, April 20, 1820, Zachary Taylor Papers, LC; Willis to Parker, August 23, 1820, Eighth Military Department, Letters Sent, RG 98, Entry 75, NA; Agent John Jamison, August 25, 1819, file J-58, SWLR: Reg. Former Natchitoches Indian agent John Sibley may have been associated with Long as well. See Samuel Watson, "Soldier, Expansionist, Politician: Eleazer Wheelock Ripley and the Dance of Ambition in the Early American Republic," in *Nexus of Empire: Loyalty and National Identity in the Gulf Borderlands, 1763–1835*, ed. Gene A. Smith and Sylvia L. Hilton (Gainesville: University Press of Florida, 2009), 321–346, for a synopsis of Ripley's career after 1821. In 1835 the U.S. District Court at New Orleans granted Ripley a settlement of $20,000 for his expenses as department commander; *New Bedford Mercury*, June 26, 1835, Readex Early American Newspapers online database.

52. Major (assistant adjutant general) Perrin Willis to Col. John McNeil, May 23, 1820, Eighth Military Department, Letters Sent ("desperate adventurers"); Beard to Col. Daniel Bissell, November 10, 1819, enclosure to Bissell to AJ, January 7, 1820, enclosure to AJ, January 23, 1820, file J-181, SWLR: Reg.

53. This is not to say that Americans, particularly westerners and southerners, did not want Texas. However, the administration feared the sectional irritation it would foster; see Monroe to Jefferson, May 1820, and to AJ, May 23, 1820, *WJM*, 6:119–120, 128. Some historians have suggested that the most important gain the United States achieved in the treaty was the delineation of the boundary to the Pacific. This may have been true in the long run, and John Quincy Adams may have seen it that way, but most contemporaries saw the treaty primarily as the cession of Florida. See Lewis, *The American Union and the Problem of Neighborhood*, chap. 5, and Robert

Pierce Forbes, *The Missouri Compromise and Its Aftermath: Slavery and the Meaning of America* (Chapel Hill: University of North Carolina Press, 2007).

54. Ernest R. May, *The Making of the Monroe Doctrine*, 2nd ed. (Cambridge, Mass.: Harvard University Press, 1992), 257.

55. Monroe to AJ, May 23, 1820, and May 23, 1821, *WJM*, 6:130, 185.

56. See the works cited in note 41 in the introduction; C. A. Bayly, *Imperial Meridian: The British Empire and the World, 1780–1830* (London: Longman, 1989); and Ronald Hyam, *Britain's Imperial Century, 1815–1914: A Study of Empire and Expansion* (New York: Palgrave Macmillan, 2002), 282–283, 288. V. G. Kiernan, *Colonial Empires and Armies, 1815–1960* (Phoenix Mill, U.K.: Sutton Publishing, 1998), 135, asserts that British officers at imperial stations were "always avid for a smell of powder, and would nearly always deem the most unjust war better than the most just peace." See Richard Cobden, *How Wars Are Got Up in India: The Origin of the Burma War* (London: William and Frederick G. Cash, 1853), for a contemporary critique.

CHAPTER SIX: ASSESSING NATIONAL MILITARY
EXPANSION ON THE WESTERN FRONTIER TO 1825

1. John W. Hall, *Uncommon Defense: Indian Allies in the Black Hawk War* (Cambridge, Mass.: Harvard University Press, 2009), 36. The Yellowstone and dragoon expeditions were all acts of intimidation without physical combat, as were the operations mounted to remove the Cherokee and Choctaw and to sustain American sovereignty along the Mexican border in 1819 and 1836–1837. There were several small firefights during the initial stages of the Missouri expedition in 1818 and 1819 and the operations against the Patriot filibusters along the Canadian border during the late 1830s, but the rarity of actual combat during this period is remarkable, in contrast to the eras both before and afterward. By *pacification*, I mean the process of becoming peaceful, of being restrained from the routine use of violence to solve personal and community problems. This process was certainly a coercive as much as a cultural one, as much the product of hard power as of soft, and it should not be understood to mean that official U.S. "civilization" policies (essentially, efforts to Christianize and teach agriculture) succeeded or played a dominant role in pacification. The coercive means and pacific ends of pacification also involve the repression of resistance to the power asserting its hegemony (or *supremacy*, in the idiom employed by contemporary American officials). I use the terms *policing*, *peacekeeping*, and *peace enforcement* loosely, as suits the predoctrinal nineteenth century. By *policing*, I mean daily operations, such as presence patrols, or operations to enforce domestic laws like the trade and intercourse acts—for example, statutes against whites selling whiskey or cutting wood in Indian country—or to aid civilian law enforcement officials in making arrests and executing writs, which was usually done by squad-sized elements (ten or twelve soldiers led by a noncommissioned officer or junior lieutenant). By *peace enforcement*, I mean keeping the peace after an agreement ending an armed conflict, whether among Indians or

between Indians and whites. By *peacekeeping*, I mean the wide range of efforts to prevent violence in the aforementioned situations and between American citizens (acting as filibusters) and foreign nations. No modern social science definitions or implications are intended.

2. See, for example, Rep. Richard M. Johnson, House Military Affairs Committee, "On Converting the Corps of Mounted Rangers into a Regiment of Dragoons," November 28, 1832, *ASPMA*, 5:126.

3. These numbers were derived from a variety of sources, particularly the annual reports of the secretary of war. See also Francis Paul Prucha, *The Sword of the Republic: The United States Army on the Frontier, 1783–1846* (New York: Macmillan, 1969), and Henry P. Beers, *The Western Military Frontier, 1815–1846* (1935; reprint, Philadelphia: Porcupine Press, 1975). The plan presented by commanding general Macomb to Michigan territorial governor Lewis Cass, August 19, 1828, HQALS, provides a good sense of military priorities between the First and Second Seminole Wars (1818 and 1836): one infantry regiment (the Fourth) in Florida, one (the Second) along the Canadian border, and five from the Louisiana border to the Great Lakes. With the exception of a few companies, the four artillery regiments were deployed in the Atlantic and Gulf coastal fortifications and in squatter and Indian removal operations in the southeastern interior when required. See also the table in Ruth A. Gallaher, "The Military-Indian Frontier, 1830–1835," *Iowa Journal of History and Politics* 15 (July 1917): 396–399.

4. Historians usually associate these views with the Federalists, but see Rush Welter, *The Mind of America, 1820–1860* (New York: Columbia University Press, 1975), chap. 12, and Rush Welter, "The Frontier West as Image of American Society: Conservative Attitudes before the Civil War," *MVHR* 46 (March 1960): 593–614. Army officer Zebulon Montgomery Pike saw the arid Plains as a restraint on sectionalism and disunion; see Brian DeLay, *War of a Thousand Deserts: Indian Raids and the U.S.-Mexican War* (New Haven, Conn.: Yale University Press, 2008), 10.

5. See especially Drew R. McCoy, *The Elusive Republic: Political Economy in Jeffersonian America* (Chapel Hill: University of North Carolina Press, 1980), and Thomas R. Hietala, *Manifest Design: Anxious Aggrandizement in Late Jacksonian America* (Ithaca, N.Y.: Cornell University Press, 1985). See William F. Deverell, "To Loosen the Safety Valve: Eastern Workers and Western Lands," *WHQ* 19 (August 1988): 269–285, for a perspective from the left of the nineteenth-century spectrum.

6. Reginald Horsman, "The Dimensions of an 'Empire for Liberty': Expansion and Republicanism, 1775–1825," *JER* 9 (Spring 1989): 1–20; Bruce C. Vandervort, *The Indian Wars of Mexico, Canada, and the United States, 1812–1900* (London: Routledge, 2006), 37. See Brian W. Dippie, *The Vanishing American: White Attitudes and U.S. Indian Policy* (Middletown, Conn.: Wesleyan University Press, 1982), chap. 4, for the origins and evolution of the idea of an "Indian country."

7. AJ, December 17, 1815, file J-366, SWLR: Reg. See Inspector General John Wool to Secretary of War Lewis Cass, February 29, 1836, *ASPMA*, 6:184, for characteristic arguments against the establishment of permanent posts, and Earl A. Shoe-

maker, *The Permanent Indian Frontier: The Reason for the Construction and Abandonment of Fort Scott, Kansas, during the Dragoon Era* (n.p.: National Park Service, 1986). David G. McCrady, *Living with Strangers: The Nineteenth-Century Sioux and the Canadian-American Borderlands* (Lincoln: University of Nebraska Press, 2006), 9–11, discusses British trade with the Sioux, primarily in British territory, between the 1810s and the 1830s. McCrady notes that the opposition of the Ojibwa was a significant constraint on Sioux access to British goods. However, regardless of Ojibwa opposition, and despite the paranoia of some U.S. officials about any news of British trade with Indians, Britain was no longer supplying the Indians with weapons and ammunition on the scale necessary for war against the United States.

8. Colin G. Calloway, "The End of an Era: British-Indian Relations in the Great Lakes Region after the War of 1812," *Michigan Historical Review* 12 (Fall 1986): 4. See Robert S. Allen, *His Majesty's Indian Allies: British Indian Policy in the Defense of Canada, 1774–1815* (Toronto: Dundurn, 1992), and Timothy D. Willig, *Restoring the Chain of Friendship: British Policy and the Indians of the Great Lakes, 1783–1815* (Lincoln: University of Nebraska Press, 2008), for background.

9. Monroe to the Senate Military Affairs Committee, February 22, 1815, *WJM*, 5:325; acting secretary of war Alexander J. Dallas to Northern Division commander Jacob Brown, May 17, 1815, Brown Letterbooks, LC; Dallas to AJ, May 22, 1815, *CAJ*, 2:206; Dallas to Secretary of State James Monroe, June 1, 1815, Monroe Papers, LC; Jacob Brown to Dallas, August 7, 1815, Brown Letterbooks, LC; Robert L. Fisher, "The Treaties of Portages des Sioux," *MVHR* 19 (March 1933): 495–508; Southern Division Adjutant General Robert Butler to brevet Brigadier General Thomas A. Smith, April 24, 1816, Division of the South, Letters Sent, 1816–1821, Entry 72, RG 98, NA. The treaties are in *ASPIA*, 2:1–25. General narratives include Edgar B. Wesley, *Guarding the Frontier: A Study of Frontier Defense from 1815 to 1825* (Minneapolis: University of Minnesota Press, 1925); Prucha, *Sword of the Republic*, chap. 7; and Robert Wooster, "Military Strategy in the American West, 1815–1860" (M.A. thesis, Lamar University, 1979). Francis Paul Prucha, *A Guide to the Military Posts of the United States, 1789–1895* (Madison: State Historical Society of Wisconsin, 1964), provides a thorough listing of forts; the essays in William E. Whittaker, ed., *Frontier Forts of Iowa: Indians, Traders, and Soldiers, 1682–1862* (Iowa City: Iowa University Press, 2009), examine forts outside the current state, including Crawford and Atkinson. Officers frequently referred to posts by their names only, rather than as Fort X or Y; I have adopted this custom for aesthetic reasons.

10. Long to Thomas A. Smith, May 12, 1818, in *The Northern Expeditions of Stephen H. Long: The Journals of 1817 and 1823 and Related Documents*, ed. Lucile M. Kane, June D. Holmquist, and Carolyn Gilman (n.p.: Minnesota Historical Society Press, 1978), 333–351; Beers, *The Western Military Frontier*, 40–41; Marcus L. Hansen, *Old Fort Snelling, 1819–1858* (Minneapolis: Ross and Haines, 1958), 21; Hall, *Uncommon Defense*, 43. Brown's recommendations, which he believed would provide a preclusive defense against Indian attacks, are in Brown to JCC, February 5, 1818, Brown Letterbooks, LC; Calhoun's response of October 17, 1818, is in *PJCC*,

3:14–16. See also "Memorandum of Tribes of Indians in the North-west, Furnished by Messrs. Crooks & Stewart, of the South-western Company," August 31, 1819, Brown Letterbooks, LC. Fort Snelling was situated at the Falls of St. Anthony; the river was the St. Peters, however.

11. See Kathleen Du Val, *The Native Ground: Indians and Colonists in the Heart of the Continent* (Philadelphia: University of Pennsylvania Press, 2006), for the concept of "native grounds" dominated by Indian concerns and power; she focuses on the Osage and Quapaw in what is now Arkansas and Missouri during the periods of French and Spanish colonialism. Like Richard White dealing with the "middle ground" around the Great Lakes, Du Val recognizes that this native ground disappeared rather quickly once large-scale American settlement began, protected by the national standing army. Nevertheless, her concept remains a valuable shorthand for describing situations in which Indian power remained dominant, as it did with the Sioux in the northern and central Plains and the Comanche in the southern Plains until the 1870s.

Farther south, the United States tried in vain to keep peace between (and thus assert its dominion over) the Osage and the Indians who had come from the East, most prominently the Cherokee, but the Cherokee gradually wore down Osage hegemony in the eastern half of modern Oklahoma. The army's role in the conflicts between the Osage and the Cherokee, and in other peacekeeping and domestic law enforcement efforts in the Southwest, was too extensive for me to treat in depth. See Willard H. Rollings, *The Osage: An Ethnohistorical Study of Hegemony on the Prairie-Plains* (Columbia: University of Missouri Press, 1992), chaps. 8, 9; Brad Agnew, *Fort Gibson: Terminal on the Trail of Tears* (Norman: University of Oklahoma Press, 1980), chaps. 2–4; Edwin C. Bearss and Arrell M. Gibson, *Fort Smith: Little Gibraltar on the Arkansas* (Norman: University of Oklahoma Press, 1969), chap. 3; Grant Foreman, *Advancing the Frontier, 1830–1860* (Norman: University of Oklahoma Press, 1933), chaps. 6–7; Grant Foreman, *Indians and Pioneers: The Story of the American Southwest before 1830* (New Haven, Conn.: Yale University Press, 1930); and David LaVere, *Contrary Neighbors: Southern Plains and Removed Indians in Indian Territory* (Norman: University of Oklahoma Press, 2000).

12. HA, November 24, 1820, file A-38, SWLR: Reg; JCC to Smith, March 16, and to Jacob Brown, October 17, 1818, *PJCC*, 2:194–195, 3:216. See Francis Paul Prucha, *American Indian Policy in the Formative Years: The Indian Trade and Intercourse Acts, 1790–1834* (Cambridge, Mass.: Harvard University Press, 1962), chap. 5, for the use of licenses for the fur and Indian trade as a diplomatic tool; see Francis Paul Prucha, "The Army and the Fur Trade," in *Indian Policy in the United States: Historical Essays* (Lincoln: University of Nebraska Press, 1981), for a survey of their relationship. See William R. Swagerty, "'The Leviathan of the North': American Perceptions of the Hudson's Bay Company, 1816–1846," *Oregon Historical Quarterly* 104 (Winter 2003): 478–517, for perceptions from fur traders; Swagerty does not cite any army officers apart from western explorers Benjamin Bonneville (who was on a leave of absence as a fur trader) and John C. Frémont, both junior officers and both exceptional in their individual initiatives in the West. See John S. Galbraith, *The*

Hudson's Bay Company as an Imperial Factor, 1821–1869 (Toronto: University of Toronto Press, 1957), for the British perspective. Frederick Merk, "The Snake Country Expedition, 1824–1825: An Episode of Fur Trade and Empire," *MVHR* 21 (June 1934): 49–62, shows that Hudson's Bay Company initiatives in the Oregon region came from local officials; those at company headquarters rejected intrusions into U.S. territory.

13. Smith, May 16, 1818, file S-139, SWLR: Reg; JCC to HA, March 27, 1819, *PJCC*, 3:695–696; Greg Olson, *The Ioway in Missouri* (Columbia: University of Missouri Press, 2008), 63, 76. For a firsthand account, see Roger L. Nichols, ed., *The Missouri Expedition, 1818–1820: The Journal of Surgeon John Gale with Related Documents* (Norman: University of Oklahoma Press, 1969).

14. AJ to HA, May 15, 1819, *PAJ*, 4:298; Gale to brevet Major Daniel Baker, November 10, 1818, and January 15, 1819, Daniel Baker Papers, BHC; AJ to HA, February 27, 1820, file J-200, SWLR: Reg. See also AJ to Secretary of War Graham, April 22, 1817, *PAJ*, 4:111; JCC to AJ, August 22, 1818, *PJCC*, 3:60–61; Macomb's recommendations regarding army organization and reduction, September 30, 1820, file M-122, SWLR: Reg; Col. John L. Smith, January 5, 1820, file S-167, SWLR: Reg; Michigan governor Lewis Cass to acting secretary of war Alexander Dallas, July 20, 1815, cited in Prucha, *Sword of the Republic*, 125; and ibid., 135–137, in general. Gaines reportedly viewed the Winnebago as enemies before the commencement of hostilities in 1827 because of their former affinity for the British; see Calvin Reese, "The United States Army and the Indian: Low Plains Area, 1815–1854" (Ph.D. diss., University of Southern California, 1963), 176. The British perspective is explored in Reginald Horsman, "British Indian Policy in the Northwest, 1807–1812," *MVHR* 45 (June 1958): 51–66; Calloway, "The End of an Era"; and, more generally, Colin G. Calloway, *Crown and Calumet: British-Indian Relations, 1783–1815* (Norman: University of Oklahoma Press, 1987).

15. Virgil Ney, *Fort on the Prairie: Fort Atkinson, on the Council Bluff, 1819–1827* (Washington, D.C.: Command Publications, 1978), 60; Sally A. Johnson, "The Sixth's Elysian Fields: Fort Atkinson on the Council Bluffs," *Nebraska History* 40 (March 1959): 1–38; Mary Ellen Rowe, "'A Respectable Independence': The Early Career of John O'Fallon," *Missouri Historical Review* 90 (July 1996): 403. Atkinson's instructions from Jackson, which emphasized "security," "caution," and peaceful relations with the Indians and anticipated stopping at Council Bluffs for the winter, are in Southern Division Adjutant General Robert Butler to HA, March 7, 1819, Division of the South, Letters Sent, 1816–1821, Entry 72, RG 98, NA. Indeed, despite hostilities by the Kansa against the troops encamped at Cantonment Martin on Cow Island during the winter of 1818–1819, Jackson's instructions conveyed surprisingly little of the urgency one would expect from him: perhaps he did not want to be blamed for further hostilities after congressional criticism of his invasion of Florida.

16. Connie Woodhouse, "Droughts for the Future, Implications for the Past," in *The Future of the Southern Plains*, ed. Sherry L. Smith (Norman: University of Oklahoma Press, 2003), 104; Roger L. Nichols, *General Henry Atkinson: A Western Mil-*

itary Career (Norman: University of Oklahoma Press, 1965), chaps. 4, 5; Prucha, *Sword of the Republic*, chap. 8; Roger L. Nichols, "Martin Cantonment and American Expansion in the Missouri Valley," *Missouri Historical Review* 64 (October 1969): 1–17; Edgar B. Wesley, "A Still Larger View of the So-called Yellowstone Expedition," *North Dakota Historical Quarterly* 5 (July 1931): 219–238; Richard G. Wood, *Stephen H. Long, 1784–1864: Army Engineer, Explorer, Inventor* (Glendale, Calif.: Arthur H. Clark, 1966); Roger L. Nichols and Patrick L. Halley, *Stephen Long and American Frontier Exploration* (London: Associated University Presses, 1980). The Missouri expedition's supply difficulties are discussed in Erna Risch, *Quartermaster Support of the Army: A History of the Corps, 1775–1939* (Washington, D.C.: Quartermaster Historian's Office, 1962), 188–193; see also HA to JCC, April 20, 1819, file A-96, SWLR: Reg, and *PJCC*, vol. 4. Woodhouse notes that 1820 was a drought year on the southern Plains. Zebulon Montgomery Pike had referred to the Arkansas River region in similar terms in 1806; see Dan Flores, "Loving the Plains, Hating the Plains, Restoring the Plains," in Smith, *Future of the Southern Plains*, 221.

17. JCC to Rep. Alexander Smyth, December 29, 1819, *ASPMA*, 2:33–34; Hayne, Confidential Inspection Report for the 9th Military Department, October 1819, Adjutant General's Office, Confidential Inspection Reports, 1812–1826, RG 159, NA.

18. Ibid.

19. HA, November 24, 1820, April 5, 1821, and May 12, 1820, files A-38, A-97, and A-1, SWLR: Reg; Hayne, Confidential Inspection Report, October 1819; Nichols, *General Henry Atkinson*, 108.

20. HA, January 6, 1824, file A-116, SWLR: Reg. For similar proposals, see HA, April 12, 1821, file A-87, and January 25, 1822, file A-78, SWLR: Reg. Atkinson exercised his brevet rank for most of the next twenty years as de facto theater commander of the Missouri and Upper Mississippi Valleys, with several regiments under his command. His arguments for the disciplinary and training benefits of annual campaigning were echoed, probably by a junior officer, a decade later, just before the outbreak of the Second Seminole War, in "Nothing to Do [pseud.]," "The Army," *Military and Naval Magazine of the United States* 6 (December 1835): 305. Superintendent of Western Indian Affairs William Clark was the most prominent western official to express concern about the British; see Clark to JCC, September 18, 1823, and March 29, 1824, *PJCC*, 8:272, 605–606. Edmund Gaines wanted 600 or 700 troops sent to the Yellowstone to punish the Blackfeet, who had robbed American traders; see EPG to JCC, October 16, 1823, *ASPMA*, 2:596.

21. J. Wendel Cox, "A World Together, a World Apart: The United States and the Arikaras, 1803–1851" (Ph.D. diss., University of Minnesota, 1998), 113; HA, July 14, 1824, file A-61, SWLR: Reg; Brown to HA, July 21, 1825, Brown Papers, LC; Woolley to Jacob Brown, June 20, 1825, Sixth Infantry Regiment Letters Sent, 1824–1833, Entry 1204, RG 391, NA; JCC to Sen. Thomas Hart Benton, February 23, 1824, *ASPIA*, 2:448–449.

22. HA to Brown, November 23, 1825, *ASPIA*, 2:605–608, 656–657; Nichols, *General Henry Atkinson*, chap. 6. The treaties are in Charles J. Kappler, ed., *Indian*

Affairs: Laws and Treaties, 4 vols. (Washington, D.C.: Government Printing Office, 1903–1929), 2:225–246.

23. Hall, *Uncommon Defense*, 49–50.

24. *Cherokee Nation v. Georgia*, 30 U.S. 1; *Worcester v. Georgia*, 31 U.S. 515. See Deborah A. Rosen, *American Indians and State Law: Sovereignty, Race, and Citizenship, 1790–1880* (Lincoln: University of Nebraska Press, 2007), regarding the extension of state jurisdiction over Native Americans.

25. Philip St. George Cooke, *Scenes and Adventures in the Army, or, the Romance of Military Life* (Philadelphia: Lindsay and Blakiston, 1857), 223. See the trade and intercourse acts and the treaties in Kappler, *Indian Affairs: Laws and Treaties*, 2:225–246, for examples of these provisions.

26. 3 *Stat.* 383; EPG to Col. Willoughby Morgan, January 23, 1832, cited in Reese, "The United States Army and the Indian," 182; Hall, *Uncommon Defense*, 58; K. Jack Bauer, *Zachary Taylor: Soldier, Planter, and Statesman of the Old Southwest* (Baton Rouge: Louisiana State University Press, 1985), 65.

27. Cooke, *Scenes and Adventures*, 223. For context, see Frederick S. Calhoun, *The Lawmen: United States Marshals and Their Deputies, 1789–1989* (Washington, D.C.: Smithsonian Institution, 1989), and Dwight F. Henderson, *Congress, Courts, and Criminals: The Development of Federal Criminal Law, 1801–1829* (Westport, Conn.: Greenwood Press, 1985). See Prucha, *American Indian Policy*, 193–198, for a summary of military confinement of Indians.

28. HL, February 19, 1834, HQALS; HL to Adjutant General Daniel Parker, June 10, 1820, DPP; Martin Zanger, "Conflicting Concepts of Justice: A Winnebago Murder Trial in Frontier Illinois," *Journal of the Illinois State Historical Society* 73 (Winter 1980): 263–276; Wool to Brown, June 18, 1820, Brown Papers, WLC; HL, June 27, 1821, file L-174, and HA, November 24, 1820, file A-38, SWLR: Reg. Surprisingly, the only attempt at a scholarly biography of this important officer is Henry S. Parker, "Henry Leavenworth: Pioneer General," *Military Review* 50 (December 1970): 56–68. See Arbuckle to Adjutant General Charles J. Nourse, November 4, 1824, *TP*, 19:719, for a case in which the local commander recommended clemency for Osage leaders surrendered as hostages and sentenced to death by a white civilian court.

29. Roger L. Nichols, "Backdrop for Disaster: Causes of the Arikara War of 1823," *South Dakota History* 14 (Summer 1984): 93–114.

30. Parker, "Henry Leavenworth," 62–63. The best analytical narrative is William R. Nester, *The Arikara War: The First Plains Indian War, 1823* (Missoula, Mont.: Mountain Press Publishing, 2001); chaps. 2 and 3 deal with the trappers, and chap. 4 covers the Arikara assault on Ashley's party. See also Cox, "World Together, World Apart," chap. 4.

31. Nester, *Arikara War*, 168, 173–176; HL to HA, August 23, 1823, *ASPMA*, 2:593 (casualty statistics). It is notable that British assaults against Maori *pah* (stockades) also failed on occasion, despite the use of artillery and rockets, but the British followed up because they were less distant from succor than Leavenworth and less irritated by the civilians whose immediate interests they were serving. See James Belich,

The New Zealand Wars and the Victorian Interpretation of Racial Conflict (Auckland, New Zealand: Auckland University Press, 1986).

32. Nester, *Arikara War*, 176–179; Leavenworth's official report to HA, October 20, 1823, quoted in Dale L. Morgan, ed., *The West of William H. Ashley* (Denver: Old West Publishing, 1964), 54; Riley's outburst (with his misspellings) quoted in Linda M. Hasselstrom, ed., *James Clyman: Journal of a Mountain Man* (Missoula, Mont.: Mountain Press Publishing, 1984), 18. If Clyman's report was accurate, Captain Riley had a poor sense of time, since the army had been at Fort Atkinson (or Cantonment Martin before it) for only five years. Nor was he likely to gain any promotion besides a brevet—which Leavenworth recommended for him—given the army's system of promotion by seniority.

33. HL to HA, October 20, 1823, in Doane Robinson, ed., "Official Correspondence of the Leavenworth Expedition of 1823 into South Dakota for the Conquest of the Ree [Arikara] Indians," *South Dakota Historical Collections* 1 (1902): 197, 199, 213, 218, 220–223, 230; HL to HA, August 23, 1823, *ASPMA*, 2:593. See Roger L. Nichols, "The Army and the Indians, 1800–1830—A Reappraisal: The Missouri Valley Example," *Pacific Historical Review* 41 (May 1972): 163, 165, regarding Leavenworth's calculations.

34. Nester, *Arikara War*, 185–188; John E. Sunder, *Joshua Pilcher: Fur Trader and Indian Agent* (Norman: University of Oklahoma Press, 1968), 48–54; Richard M. Clokey, *William H. Ashley: Enterprise and Politics in the Trans-Mississippi West* (Norman: University of Oklahoma Press, 1980), 114–118; HA to EPG, September 13, and EPG's orders, September 21, 1823, *ASPMA*, 2:594–596; EPG to JCC, September 28, 1822, *PJCC*, 7:286–287, and October 16, 1823, *ASPMA*, 2:596. Sunder observes that Indian agent Benjamin O'Fallon, who was appointed Atkinson's civilian counterpart as a federal treaty commissioner in the 1825 Yellowstone expedition, continued to criticize Leavenworth and Atkinson nearly a year later, albeit in personal letters to them (59). Pilcher was unable to secure a position with that expedition, but he developed political connections that enabled him to succeed William Clark as superintendant of Indian affairs at St. Louis in 1839, five years after Leavenworth's death.

35. Assistant Adjutant General Edmund Kirby (for Brown) to EPG and EPG to HL, October 10 and 24, 1823, Sixth Infantry Regiment Letters Sent and Received, 1817–1824, RG 391, Entry 1202, NA; *St. Louis Enquirer*, January 20, 1824. Riley had been disenchanted with Leavenworth before the expedition and remained bitter afterward; see the correspondence in James S. Hutchins, ed., "'Dear Hook': Letters from Bennet Riley, Alphonso Wetmore, and Reuben Holmes, 1822–1833," *Bulletin of the Missouri Historical Society* 36 (1980): 205–210 (quotation, March 31, 1824, at 209).

36. HL to HA, September 7, 1823, *ASPMA*, 2:596; Nester, *Arikara War*, 163–164; EPG to JCC, September 22, 1823, *ASPMA*, 2:592; Richard White, "The Winning of the West: The Expansion of the Western Sioux in the Eighteenth and Nineteenth Centuries," *JAH* 65 (September 1978): 319–343.

37. HL to HA, October 20, 1823, in Robinson, "Official Correspondence," 232;

HL to HA, August 30, 1823, *ASPMA*, 2:593 ("zeal and efficiency"); HL to HA, November 22, 1823, in Morgan, *The West of William H. Ashley*, 65–66; Clokey, *William H. Ashley*, 115.

38. HL to HA, November 22, 1823, cited in Cox, "World Together, World Apart," 139–141; letter quoted in Sunder, *Joshua Pilcher*, 49n24; section 8, law of June 30, 1834, 4 *Stat.* 730.

39. Col. Robert McDouall to Sir George Murray, June 1815, quoted in Beers, *The Western Military Frontier*, 37; 3 *Stat.* 332–333; JCC to Clay, December 5, 1818, *PJCC*, 3:342, 350; Brown to JCC, March 21, 1823, *PJCC*, 7:534–536.

40. Brown to HA, November 25, 1825, *ASPIA*, 2:656; Brown to Barbour, January 11, 1826, *ASPMA*, 3:216. See EPG to Brown, July 18, 1826, file G-131, SWLR: Reg, for calculations regarding Forts Atkinson and Leavenworth and, more generally, Ray H. Mattison, "The Military Frontier on the Upper Missouri," *Nebraska History* 37 (September 1956): 159–182. For the infantry school, see Brown to Secretary of War James Barbour, December 8, 1825, Brown Letterbooks, LC; Brown to Barbour, annual report communicated to Congress by the president, December 4, 1826, *ASPMA*, 3:332–333; EPG to Adjutant General Roger Jones, February 11, 1826, quoted in Stuart R. Carswell, "Infantry School of 1826," *Infantry Journal* 24 (March 1924): 263; and, more generally, Byron B. Banta Jr., "A History of Jefferson Barracks, 1826–1860" (Ph.D. diss., Louisiana State University Press, 1981), and Marc E. Kollbaum, *Gateway to the West: The History of Jefferson Barracks from 1826–1894*, 2 vols. (St. Louis: Friends of Jefferson Barracks, 2002).

Michigan territorial governor Lewis Cass, August 19, 1828, HQALS, shows that Brown was more successful in concentrating the army than secondary accounts usually suggest, and that his successor sought to maintain that concentration. On that date, there were sixteen infantry posts outside Florida, averaging nearly four companies per post—or nearly a battalion in contemporary terms (in theory, as few as two companies, but usually meaning three to six). Two posts, Fort Leavenworth and Jefferson Barracks in St. Louis, had a regiment or close to it; six posts held four companies; and the other eight held two companies. Given the small companies authorized in 1821, four companies still meant no more than about 150 soldiers, minus any sick, absent without leave, or under arrest, but these were hardly the minuscule garrisons sometimes found in the coastal fortifications or in the many temporary forts that would dot Florida during the Second Seminole War. From another perspective, how many plantations or factories had 150 workers in that era?

41. Foreman, *Advancing the Frontier*, chaps. 4, 5; Beers, *The Western Military Frontier*, 139–140, 143–144.

42. John C. Ewers, *The Blackfeet, Raiders on the Northwestern Plains* (Norman: University of Oklahoma Press, 1958), 53–59, 64. See also Ted Binnema and William A. Dobak, "'Like the Greedy Wolf': The Blackfeet, the St. Louis Fur Trade, and War Fever, 1807–1831," *JER* 29 (Fall 2009): 411–440.

43. Nichols, "The Army and the Indians," 161–162, 167; Cox, "World Together, World Apart," 148; see also Secretary of War Peter B. Porter to President John Quincy

Adams, November 24, 1828, *ASPMA*, 4:2. For the Sioux, see White, "Winning of the West," and Jeffrey Ostler, *The Plains Sioux and U.S. Colonialism from Lewis and Clark to Wounded Knee* (Cambridge: Cambridge University Press, 2004). See also Clyde W. Dollar, "The High Plains Smallpox Epidemic of 1837–38," *WHQ* 8 (January 1977): 15–38. Binnema and Dobak's "'Like the Greedy Wolf'" appears to be the only work apart from my own that explicitly recognizes the limits of U.S. interest as well as U.S. power. Nichols does note that, under the circumstances, "it seems unreasonable to expect the soldiers to have accomplished much more than they did" ("The Army and the Indians," 168). His larger message—that an "imperial school" of military and frontier historians exaggerated the army's role as "an orderly purveyor of civilization" or an "agent of empire," "the cutting edge and holding power of white government" and expansion (ibid., 151–152, 168)—is a reasonable caveat, but it must be understood as a point on a historiographical spectrum. Nichols was responding specifically to Francis P. Prucha, *Broadax and Bayonet: The Role of the Army in the Development of the Northwest, 1815–1860* (Madison: State Historical Society of Wisconsin, 1953), viii ("orderly purveyor"); Prucha, *Sword of the Republic*, 319 ("agents of empire"); and Don Rickey Jr., *Forty Miles a Day on Beans and Hay* (Norman: University of Oklahoma Press, 1963), 350 ("cutting edge"). Nichols also cites William H. Goetzmann, *Army Exploration in the American West* (New Haven, Conn.: Yale University Press, 1959), who appraised the army topographical engineers as "a central institution of Manifest Destiny" (4).

Many western histories (military and otherwise) written before the 1970s were deeply ethnocentric in their language of "civilization." Yet one can acknowledge that ethnocentrism and the army's limitations as an agent of empire but still recognize the army as one of the few forces for national cohesion on the disordered frontier of white individualism. Certainly the communities that western and frontier historians emphasize were often much farther from orderly civilization than military posts. As a final example, Nichols cites Bearss and Gibson, *Fort Smith:* the "Army was a primary force in opening the Southwestern wilderness" to permanent white settlement (3). This seems a rather unexceptionable statement to me: it was not *the* primary force or the dominant force, but it was *one* of the primary forces involved.

Nichols's call for additional case studies of the army's impact and effectiveness as an expansionist force, in comparison with settlers or other factors, has not been taken up in his critical spirit. Rather, a mass of studies by frontier and western historians has demonstrated the army's significance in the nineteenth-century western economy and its efforts and achievements as "an orderly purveyor of civilization" in the nineteenth-century sense of liberal capitalist individualism that most Americans still accept today. See especially Michael L. Tate, *The Frontier Army in the Settlement of the West* (Norman: University of Oklahoma Press, 1999), who provides a thorough bibliography, and Harvey Meyerson, *Nature's Army: When Soldiers Fought for Yosemite* (Lawrence: University Press of Kansas, 2001). As a result, scholars have not clarified whether the U.S. state or American civil society led white expansion westward. The folk wisdom—part of Frederick Jackson Turner's "frontier thesis" and a core ingredient in Americans' belief in their exceptional character as a nation—is that families and individuals (nonstate actors) did so, and government followed to build or restore social and political order and cohesion. Indeed, this article of faith has been replicated in the majority of recent scholarship, in its emphasis on demography, the extension of the railroads by private enterprise, or the destruction of the buffalo, whether by whites or Indians. The extensive historiography of Russian expansion east from the Moscow-Volga core provides an instructive contrast, though Russian historiography has faced and presented many of the same elements of cultural chauvinism and exceptionalism, and modern critical scholarship has generally been published in the United States. See my second volume for further discussion and historiography.

44. Frederick A. Hoxie, *Parading through History: The Making of the Crow Nation in America, 1805–1935* (Cambridge: Cambridge University Press, 1995), 65. See James Belich, *Replenishing the Earth: The Settler Revolution and the Rise of the Anglo-World, 1783–1939* (Oxford: Clarendon Press, 2009), for a masterful exploration of large-scale demographic and economic dynamics, replete with numerous case studies from the United States and Canada. See also D. W. Meinig, *The Shaping of America: A Geographical Perspective on 500 Years of History*, vol. 3, *Transcontinental America, 1850–1915* (New Haven, Conn.: Yale University Press, 1998).

45. Raymond W. Settle, ed., *March of the Mounted Riflemen, from Fort Leavenworth to Fort Vancouver, May to Oct., 1849* (1940; reprint, Lincoln: University of Nebraska Press, 1989); Cox, "World Together, World Apart," 157, 164, 207.

CHAPTER SEVEN: THE GROWTH OF PROFESSIONAL
ACCOUNTABILITY DURING THE 1820S AND 1830S

1. Jeremy Black, *The War of 1812 in the Age of Napoleon* (Norman: University of Oklahoma Press, 2009), 228. See Ronald Hyam, *Britain's Imperial Century, 1815–1914: A Study of Empire and Expansion* (New York: Palgrave Macmillan, 2002), 64–69, 231–235, both for an emphasis on the "American problem" in nineteenth-century British grand strategy and for the conclusion that Britain resolved that problem by gradually but steadily backing down from American challenges in order to focus on Europe and Asia. Kenneth Bourne, *Britain and the Balance of Power in North America, 1815–1908* (Berkeley: University of California Press, 1967), takes a similar perspective, although he recognizes the arguments made by historians of the Royal Navy that Britain hoped to overawe and deter the United States by threatening to bombard American ports. See, for example, C. J. Bartlett, *Great Britain and Seapower, 1815–1853* (Oxford: Clarendon Press, 1963), and, more recently, Howard Fuller, *Clad in Iron: The American Civil War and the Challenge of British Naval Power* (Westport, Conn.: Praeger Security International, 2008).

2. See especially James E. Lewis Jr., *The American Union and the Problem of Neighborhood: The United States and the Collapse of the Spanish Empire, 1783–1829* (Chapel Hill: University of North Carolina Press, 1998); John L. Larson, *Internal Improve-*

ment: National Public Works and the Promise of Popular Government in the Early United States (Chapel Hill: University of North Carolina Press, 2001); and John L. Larson, *The Market Revolution: Liberty, Ambition, and the Eclipse of the Public Good* (Cambridge: Cambridge University Press, 2010), which go far beyond their titles in discussing early national political ideology and culture.

3. Robert Wooster, *The American Military Frontiers: The U.S. Army in the West, 1783–1900* (Albuquerque: University of New Mexico Press, 2009), 60–70.

4. The growing autonomy—essentially civilian policy makers' acceptance of its expertise and jurisdiction—and accountability of the Jacksonian and antebellum army are explored in William B. Skelton, *An American Profession of Arms: The Army Officer Corps, 1784–1861* (Lawrence: University Press of Kansas, 1992); Mark R. Wilson, *The Business of Civil War: Military Mobilization and the State, 1861–1865* (Baltimore: Johns Hopkins University Press, 2006); Mark A. Smith, *Engineering Security: The Corps of Engineers and Third System Defense Policy, 1815–1861* (Tuscaloosa: University of Alabama Press, 2009); and, most explicitly, Samuel J. Watson, "How the Army Became Accepted: West Point Socialization, Military Accountability, and the Nation-State during the Jacksonian Era," *American Nineteenth-Century History* 7 (June 2006): 217–249. Samuel J. Watson,"The U.S. Army to 1900," in *The Blackwell Companion to American Military History*, ed. James C. Bradford (Oxford: Wiley-Blackwell, 2009), provides a comprehensive synopsis of the historiography of the army's professional development, the balance between regulars and citizen-soldiers in force structure and action, and the debate between their advocates.

5. I may have seriously underestimated congressional inquiry into and criticism of the army's frontier operations. Like populist criticism of West Point or efforts to reduce officer compensation, these inquiries worried officers and fostered resentment toward civilian politics and politicians. However, there is little evidence of such criticism, or of its actually having a concrete effect on officers' careers, in their public or private papers. The *ASPMA* and the Congressional Serial Set contain the best, and often very thorough, after-action reports available for these operations. Still, officers' papers, combined with the titles and tone of the congressional documents, suggest that Congress was primarily concerned with fiscal restraint (which of course influenced the army's force structure, means, and available methods) and protecting the frontier, rather than the methods the army used to do so. Indeed, substantial congressional investigations, like those into Jackson's invasion of Florida, were not conducted into operations on the western frontier, although pressure by southern states, especially Georgia, led to significant inquiries into Indian and squatter removal operations between 1825 and 1838, and the Second Seminole War produced massive documentation (for that era) due to its early disasters and persistence. All these cases are explored in my second volume.

6. See more generally Reginald C. Stuart, *War and American Thought from the Revolution to the Monroe Doctrine* (Kent, Ohio: Kent State University Press, 1982), and Reginald Horsman, "The Dimensions of an 'Empire for Liberty': Expansion and Republicanism, 1775–1825," *JER* 9 (Spring 1989): 1–20. Kinley J. Brauer has been

the most active historiographer of recent work on nineteenth-century American foreign relations; see his "The Great American Desert Revisited: Recent Literature and Prospects for the Study of American Foreign Relations, 1815–1860," *DH* 13 (Summer 1989): 395–417, and "The Need for a Synthesis of American Foreign Relations, 1815–1861," *JER* 14 (Winter 1994): 467–476. See also Bradford Perkins, "Interests, Values, and the Prism: The Sources of American Foreign Policy," *JER* 14 (Winter 1994): 458–466.

7. Marvin Meyers, *The Jacksonian Persuasion: Politics and Belief* (New York: Vintage, 1957); Richard R. John, "Affairs of Office: The Executive Department, the Election of 1828, and the Democratic Party," in *The Democratic Experiment: New Directions in American Political History*, ed. Meg Jacobs, William J. Novak, and Julian E. Zelizer (Princeton, N.J.: Princeton University Press, 2003); Ronald P. Formisano, "State Development in the Early Republic: Substance and Structure, 1780–1840," in *Contesting Democracy: Substance and Structure in American Political History, 1775–2000*, ed. Byron E. Shafer and Anthony Badger (Lawrence: University Press of Kansas, 2001), 21–26; L. Ray Gunn, *The Decline of Authority: Public Economic Policy and Political Development in New York, 1800–1860* (Ithaca, N.Y.: Cornell University Press, 1988); Larson, *Internal Improvement*; Larson, *Market Revolution*. Formisano acknowledges that the army may have escaped this subordination to ideology and partisanship, citing my article "U.S. Army Officers Fight the 'Patriot War': Responses to Filibustering on the Canadian Border, 1837–1839," *JER* 18 (Fall 1998): 487–521. See Stephen J. Rockwell, *Indian Affairs and the Administration State in the Nineteenth Century* (Cambridge: Cambridge University Press, 2010), for a perspective that emphasizes the autonomy and effectiveness of Indian policy, albeit from a political scientist with limited archival evidence who tends to dismiss the army's role in favor of civilian Indian agents. Richard R. John, "Ruling Passions: Political Economy in Nineteenth-Century America," *Journal of Policy History* 18 (January 2006): 1–20, and Robert Fishman, "Federalism and National Planning: The Nineteenth-Century Legacy," in *The American Planning Tradition: Culture and Policy*, ed. Robert Fishman (Baltimore: Johns Hopkins University Press, 2000), provide balanced long-range perspectives on the nineteenth-century American state.

8. In other words, ideological opposition alone was never sufficient to repeal this act. See Robert P. Wettemann Jr., "'To the Public Prosperity': The U.S. Army and the Market Revolution, 1815–1844" (Ph.D. diss., Texas A&M University, 2001), and Robert P. Wettemann Jr., "West Point, the Jacksonians, and the Army's Controversial Role in National Improvements," in *West Point: Two Centuries and Beyond*, ed. Lance A. Betros (Abilene, Tex.: McWhiney Foundation Press, 2004), for works stressing Jacksonian attacks on the army's role in implementing the General Survey Act.

9. Rhodri Jeffreys-Jones and Bruce Collins, eds., *The Growth of Federal Power in American History* (De Kalb: Northern Illinois University Press, 1983), 45.

10. Martin Shefter, *Political Parties and the State: The American Historical Experience* (Princeton, N.J.: Princeton University Press, 1994); Formisano, "State Development in the Early Republic"; Wilson, *The Business of Civil War*, 66.

11. See especially Reginald Horsman, *The Origins of Indian Removal, 1815–1824* (Lansing: Michigan State University Press, 1970). U.S. troops did not engage in combat (direct exchanges of fire) in the Winnebago "war," but they did maneuver to do so. Their commanders understood that the deployment was likely to result in combat, unlike most of the army's coercive operations, which were expected to work through intimidation rather than the actual application of force. The third engagement came against the Comanche, who attacked a merchant caravan escorted by a battalion of the Sixth Infantry on the Santa Fe Trail in 1829.

12. Skelton, *An American Profession of Arms*, 295.

13. July 5, 1838, 5 *Stat.* 256–260. An 1827 law had also increased officers' compensation by granting each captain and lieutenant a second ration; officers serving in command of companies were granted $10 per month, regardless of their rank (March 2, 1827, 4 *Stat.* 227). Thomas S. Langston, *Uneasy Balance: Civil-Military Relations in Peacetime America since 1783* (Baltimore: Johns Hopkins University Press, 2003), is the most historically informed work by a political scientist on American civil-military relations; see especially 28–32 for the significance such mission balances have had in stabilizing civil-military relations in the aftermath of major wars, particularly during calls for military retrenchment and reductions in force. See Watson, "How the Army Became Accepted," for a more detailed exploration of this process in the officer corps after 1820.

Jackson's final annual message, December 5, 1836, *MPP*, 4:1473–1475, recommended increasing the number of enlisted soldiers and staff officers and increasing army pay. Van Buren's first annual message, December 5, 1837, *MPP*, 4:1607, recommended increasing the number of enlisted soldiers and staff officers and increasing the service obligations of West Pointers to three years after graduation. The 1838 law authorized eighty additional staff officers, including six assistant adjutant generals (temporarily detailed from regiments and ranked as captains and majors by brevet), who would also serve as assistant inspector generals; five commissary officers; nine engineers; twelve quartermasters (to be transferred from regiments within the army); twenty-two ordnance officers (transferred from the artillery); and twenty-six topographical engineers, transferred from the line or (in six cases) commissioned from civil life. (Seven of the new topographical engineers had resigned in 1836 and were recommissioned.) Most of these men had already been working in these positions, which now became permanent. Note that only six of these eighty men were commissioned directly from civilian life without any past experience as army officers. The officers of the Eighth Infantry Regiment were drawn almost entirely from existing infantry regiments. In sum, after accounting for adjustments in the artillery, seventy-five new officers were needed. West Point produced forty-five new officers in 1838 and thirty-one more in 1839. In terms of overall statistical effect, the Military Academy filled the slots created by the 1838 law; men had to be commissioned directly from civilian life to fill the places of those who resigned in 1836. Staff officers received the higher pay of dragoon officers, as well as a variety of new allowances for ordnance and engineer officers in charge of arsenals and fortification construction. Enlisted pay was increased, with a

160-acre bounty after ten years' service. The army's only objective not answered by the law was to increase the number of infantry regiments to ten; the Ninth and Tenth Infantry Regiments were placed on the peacetime establishment in 1855.

14. The impact of federal military action, or its absence, on sectional interests and attitudes is explored with great insight in Andrew R. L. Cayton, "'Separate Interests' and the Nation-State: The Washington Administration and the Origins of Regionalism in the Trans-Appalachian West," *JAH* 79 (June 1992): 39–67.

15. See Skelton, *An American Profession of Arms*, 137–139, and Samuel J. Watson, "Evaluating the Early National Officer Corps: Social, Cultural, and Professional Considerations in Officer Retention during the Army Reductions of 1815 and 1821" (paper presented to the Southwestern Historical Association, March 20, 1998). For instability in the Jeffersonian army, see Skelton, *An American Profession of Arms*, chaps. 1–3, and Samuel J. Watson, "Federal Diplomats: The U.S. Army Officer Corps in the Borderlands of the Early Republic, 1784–1814" (unpublished ms.).

16. See Brown Letterbooks, LC; Brown Papers, Massachusetts Historical Society; and Brown Papers, WLC.

17. See Roger J. Spiller, "Calhoun's Expansible Army: The History of a Military Idea," *South Atlantic Quarterly* 79 (Spring 1980): 189–203. Michael S. Fitzgerald, "Rejecting Calhoun's Expansible Army Plan: The Army Reduction Act of 1821," *War in History* 3 (Summer 1996): 161–185, is primarily about the reasons for the reduction; it does not address the actual impact on the army's force structure or capability. Scholars have long debated the exact form and intent of Calhoun's plan for an "expansible army." Was it a mere skeleton, with each regiment to be filled out to raise an expeditionary army several times larger than the peacetime one? Was it to be truly expansible, growing in number as well as size of units? Was Calhoun's real objective to provide the basis for a larger enlisted force, or was it to maintain a cadre of experienced officers who would be able to develop further professional expertise in preparation for future war? Most secondary accounts suggest, often tendentiously, that the reduction was a defeat for military professionalism. Spiller does not take a clear stand, observing that the plan was remembered as a model for professional military development; however, because Congress substituted its own plan, requiring greater reductions in the officer corps, he states that Calhoun's "plan foundered," "failed to win the support of Congress," and was "stillborn" (200, 202, 203). These statements are factually correct but convey a fundamentally inaccurate sense of the outcome and consequences. The reduction in 1821 was about 20 percent of the officer corps (versus approximately 80 percent in 1815) and between a half and a third of the enlisted ranks (depending on whether one counts authorized or actual strength). The army lost three of fourteen regiments or battalions (in which artillery had been organized between 1815 and 1821) and the officers to match, but the number of officers per company and regiment was not reduced. Although the Ordnance Corps and several much smaller staff organizations were disbanded, each artillery company was authorized four lieutenants. It could be argued that this was due to the dispersion of artillery regiments in a large number of coastal forts, but the excess lieutenants enabled the army to main-

tain an ordnance organization and provide additional officers for topographical engineer work under the General Survey Act of 1824.

Thus, whatever the specific legislation and consequent numbers, the post-1821 army *was* expansible in terms of potential combat power, it *was* expanded by increasing the authorization of enlisted men for each company in 1838, and it *did* provide a cadre for the development of greater war-fighting capability. Calhoun's vision, largely developed (as Spiller points out) by veteran regular officers, was thereby sustained. Congress rejected only one specific version of expansible military organization, while the new system effectively maintained and developed a cadre of expert professionals. Though often criticized by Jacksonian demagogues for not serving with troops in the field, these cadre officers—today we would call them the "institutional army"—taught others at West Point and in the infantry and artillery schools established in the mid-1820s; planned and supervised the construction of the system of coastal fortifications, the centerpiece of American defense planning; maintained the army logistically and developed administrative experience essential for projecting power on a larger scale in Mexico and the Civil War; and performed civil duties sought by the public by surveying transportation routes, providing the army with an additional raison d'être during the peaceful 1820s.

18. This differentiation is also evident in Cooper Kirk, *William Lauderdale: General Andrew Jackson's Warrior* (Fort Lauderdale, Fla.: Manatee Books, 1982). Jackson found it much more difficult to mobilize volunteers from his home state for the Second Seminole War (1835–1842) than for the First (1817–1818), or for the Creek War of 1813–1814. It is debatable whether West Point candidates from the South were actually less prepared than others; assuming that the class composition of candidates from North and South were about the same, and that most of the candidates were of middle-class or elite backgrounds, it is doubtful that the lack of public primary schooling in the South would have had much of an effect: most upper-middle-class and elite children had access to private schooling in some form. See James L. Morrison Jr., *"The Best School in the World": West Point in the Pre–Civil War Years, 1833–1866* (Kent, Ohio: Kent State University Press, 1986), 132.

19. Theodore J. Crackel, *West Point: A Bicentennial History* (Lawrence: University Press of Kansas, 2002), 115; Skelton, *An American Profession of Arms*, tables 2.1 (19) and 9.1–9.3 (155–157). Planters increasingly tended to move to the lands they purchased, rather than trying to resell as speculators or rent to yeomen (as George Washington had done). William B. Skelton, "High Army Leadership in the Era of the War of 1812: The Making and Remaking of the Officer Corps," *WMQ* 51 (April 1994): 258 (table II), surveys the geographic origins of the army's field and general officers appointed between 1808 and 1815. The proportion of appointments to these grades from Federalist New England during this period was 88 percent of that region's representation in the nation's free population in 1810, that from the Mid-Atlantic states was 82 percent, and the proportion from the Republican South Atlantic and western states was 120 percent. In other words, although the figures for all these regions, except for the West, were relatively close (86 to 93 percent) to their proportion of U.S.

representatives (i.e., to apportionment as adjusted by the three-fifths clause of the Constitution), the South Atlantic states enjoyed a dramatic advantage over their northern brethren in the allocation of senior officer appointments. The West—meaning Tennessee, Kentucky, Ohio, and the Indiana and Michigan Territories—appears to have enjoyed the largest advantage, with appointments totaling 225 percent of its representation in the House, but the absolute numbers remained small because of the much smaller populations there. Although many of these men came from nonslaveholding areas, they shared the aggressive expansionism and commercial ambitions of their counterparts in the coastal South; indeed, western support for expansion against Canada obviously accounts for much of this disparity in appointments.

Skelton, *An American Profession of Arms*, table 9.1 (155), provides an assessment of the geographic origins of the officers on the 1830 and 1860 Army Registers. With congressional appointments to the Military Academy (and thus the operation of the three-fifths clause on cadet nominations) a recent innovation, North and South were represented in proportions equal to their percentages of the free population in 1830, but this equality represented a significant decline for the South since 1815. Indeed, whether because they better survived the intellectual and disciplinary rigors of West Point or because of greater career persistence, the number of northern officers was approximately 112 percent the proportion of that region's representation in the House, while that of southerners was 84 percent and that of men from the South Atlantic region was only 75 percent (the Mid-Atlantic had the same proportion of the free population, and of officers, as the South). The frontier Northwest and Southwest suffered the most from the higher entrance requirements at West Point and were severely underrepresented on the 1830 list, with their officer representation amounting to only about 40 percent of their free population.

In 1860 the proportions of officers relative to both the free population and representation in the House had changed dramatically. Northern officers accounted for only 80 percent of their section's proportion of the free population and 92 percent of its share of the House, while for southern officers, the figures were 139 percent and 110 percent, respectively; the South Atlantic states had more than double their share of officers based on the free population. New England remained disproportionately represented, but at about 133 rather than 150 percent of the free population, and with about the same absolute number of officers as in 1830. The Mid-Atlantic remained proportionately represented, but officers from the Northwest were still less than half their percentage of the free population, which was about equal to that of the entire South; the northwestern states had produced only about one-third the officers of the southern states. The Mid-Atlantic, South Atlantic, and western regions had each produced between 273 and 295 officers, or 26 to 28 percent of the officer corps; New England was down from 28 to 16 percent. The number of officers from Washington, D.C., was seventeen times its proportion of the population in 1830 and twenty times that proportion in 1860. Presumably, the disproportionate commissioning of southerners directly from civilian life, overseen by Secretary of War Jefferson Davis during the army expansion of 1855, accounts for some of the shift. Indeed, Skelton's table

9.3 (157) shows that the southern proportions of infantry, medical, and paymaster officers had all increased—by about 20 percent in the infantry (from 34 to 41 percent of its officers)—which can easily be explained by the operation of the three-fifths clause in nominations to West Point, better education in the South (and thus fewer failures at the Military Academy), and two new regiments authorized in 1855. The proportion of paymasters (commonly appointed directly from civilian life and given the honorary rank of major—the most overt use of patronage in officer accessions) from the South had nearly doubled, to a near majority. The five mounted regiments, all created by Democratic administrations since 1830, had received half their officers directly from civilian life, and 60 percent were southern; the four artillery regiments (with about the same number of officers as the mounted branch) and the staff remained more than 60 percent northern.

20. Lonnie J. White, *Politics on the Southwestern Frontier: Arkansas Territory, 1819–1836* (Memphis, Tenn.: Memphis State University Press, 1964), especially 41–43; S. Charles Bolton, *Arkansas, 1800–1860: Remote and Restless* (Fayetteville: University of Arkansas Press, 1998), chap. 2. See also appendices B and C. I did not have access to the Army Registers for 1842–1844; those for 1845–1847 show no field-grade officer resignations.

21. See Skelton, *An American Profession of Arms*, tables 11.1–11.4 (182–183, 194, 213), for median career lengths, promotion rates (time in grade), and means of attrition. The median career length for all officers on the 1830 and 1860 Army Registers was twenty-two to twenty-three years; for those who reached field grade (majors and above), it was thirty-nine to forty-one years. Approximately 40 percent of all officers served for at least thirty years, and as many as 23 percent served for forty, even though promotion to captain normally took about thirteen years during this period, and promotion to major took twenty-six to twenty-eight years. Of the officers on the Army Register of 1830, 37 percent resigned, 47 percent died while still in service (overwhelmingly of natural causes), and 12 percent lived to retire during and after the Civil War, when Congress first provided pensions in an effort to unclog the ranks and remove men who were physically unable to command. I addressed some of the psychosocial dimensions of these career choices and dynamics in Samuel J. Watson, "Flexible Gender Roles in the Era of the Market Revolution: Family, Friendship, Marriage, and Masculinity among U.S. Army Officers, 1815–1846," *Journal of Social History* 29 (Fall 1995): 81–106; see also William B. Skelton, "The Army Officer as Organization Man," in *Soldiers and Civilians: The U.S. Army and the American People*, ed. Garry D. Ryan and Timothy K. Nenninger (Washington, D.C.: National Archives and Records Administration, 1987).

22. Morgan, report on officers of the Twelfth Infantry Regiment, April 2, 1815, SWLR: Unreg.

23. JCC to Major General Jacob Brown, July 29, 1818, Brown Letterbooks, Brown Papers, LC. For extensive examples of the army's administrative dysfunction between 1815 and 1821, see DPP and the letterbooks of the Fifth and Eighth Military Departments, Letters Sent, RG 98, Entry 75, NA, although the correspondence of any offi-

cer provides examples. See Dale R. Steinhauer, "'Sogers': Enlisted Men in the United States Army, 1815–1860" (Ph.D. diss., University of North Carolina, 1992), chap. 5, for the most comprehensive exploration of desertion, and the War Department Annual Report for 1891, 9, cited in Edward M. Coffman, *The Old Army: A Portrait of the American Army in Peacetime, 1784–1898* (New York: Oxford University Press, 1986), 193, for the longest-ranging statistical study. Alan Taylor, *The Civil War of 1812: American Citizens, British Subjects, Irish Rebels, & Indian Allies* (New York: Alfred A. Knopf, 2010), chap. 12, provides an outstanding account of the disorder among officers as well as enlisted soldiers in the American camps along the Canadian border in 1813 and 1814, which postwar garrisons commonly replicated on a smaller scale.

24. See Skelton, *An American Profession of Arms*, 137–139, figure 11.1 (216), and Watson, "Evaluating the Early National Officer Corps." Two hundred eleven enlisted men received commissions during the War of 1812; only twenty-eight (about 12 percent, in comparison to about 20 percent of the entire officer corps) were retained in 1815, and most of these were discharged in 1821. By 1835, only eight remained in the army; by 1845, three. Thirteen enlisted men were commissioned between 1815 and 1821; only six served five or more years. See Steinhauer, "'Sogers,'" 299–300, chap. 7. Of the 136 West Point graduates in the army, 130 were retained in the 1821 reduction in force. Military Academy graduates made up 18 percent of the regular army officer corps (not counting medical officers and paymasters) after the reduction in force in 1815, 15 percent in 1817 (after some former officers were reappointed in the interim), 29 percent in 1821, 40 percent in 1823, 64 percent in 1830, and 70 percent at the end of 1835, despite the commissioning of officers directly from civilian life into the Mounted Rangers and First Dragoon Regiment in 1832 and 1833. In 1860 the proportion was 76 percent. These statistics were drawn primarily from George W. Cullum, comp., *Biographical Register of the Officers and Graduates of the U.S. Military Academy*, 2 vols. (New York: D. Van Nostrand, 1868); Charles K. Gardner, comp., *A Dictionary of the Officers of the Army of the United States* (New York: G. P. Putnam, 1860); William A. Gordon, comp., *A Compilation of Registers of the Army of the United States, from 1815 to 1837* (Washington, D.C.: James C. Dunn, 1837); and Francis B. Heitman, comp., *Historical Registry and Dictionary of the United States Army, from Its Organization, September 29, 1789 to March 2, 1903*, 2 vols. (Washington, D.C.: Government Printing Office, 1903).

25. Skelton, *An American Profession of Arms*, 138–139. Most of these commissions were for lieutenants. Usually graduating about 40 (between 30 and 55) cadets per year, West Point was unable to supply enough lieutenants (40 second lieutenants) for the four new regiments in 1855, as well as replacing those lost by attrition (due to resignation, death, and the rare dismissal) in the fifteen existing regiments. Each second lieutenant already in the army (mostly West Pointers) who was promoted to first lieutenant in the new regiments required a replacement, as did first lieutenants promoted to captain. In other words, the army had to come up with 120 new captains and lieutenants with only 34 West Point graduates. This meant graduating West Pointers early, and setting a precedent for diluting their socialization and expertise;

commissioning civilians (after passing an examination); or commissioning enlisted soldiers. One might wonder why the last option was not preferred, but both officers and civilian politicians generally regarded enlisted men as lacking the education and, more important, the social polish for officership. See Samuel J. Watson, "Professionalism, Social Attitudes, and Civil-Military Accountability in the U.S. Army Officer Corps, 1815–1846," 2 vols. (Ph.D. diss., Rice University, 1996), chaps. 1, 15, for more detailed comparisons with European officer corps and American civilian professions. For the U.S. Navy, see ibid., chap. 14; Christopher McKee, *A Gentlemanly and Honorable Profession: The Creation of the U.S. Naval Officer Corps, 1794–1815* (Annapolis, Md.: Naval Institute Press, 1991); William P. Leeman, *The Long Road to Annapolis: The Founding of the Naval Academy and the Emerging American Republic* (Chapel Hill: University of North Carolina Press, 2010); and Charles Todorich, *The Spirited Years: A History of the Antebellum Naval Academy* (Annapolis, Md.: Naval Institute Press, 1984).

26. Edward Pessen, "The Egalitarian Myth and American Social Reality: Wealth, Mobility, and Opportunity in the 'Era of the Common Man,'" *AHR* 76 (October 1971): 989–1034; Edward Pessen, *Riches, Class, and Power before the Civil War* (Lexington, Mass.: D. C. Heath, 1973); Douglas T. Miller, *Jacksonian Aristocracy: Class and Democracy in New York, 1830–1860* (New York: Oxford University Press, 1967); Sidney H. Aronson, *Status and Kinship in the Higher Civil Service: Standards of Selection in the Administrations of John Adams, Thomas Jefferson, and Andrew Jackson* (Cambridge, Mass.: Harvard University Press, 1964), 82, 90. Robert P. Wettemann Jr., whose dissertation and early work stressed Jacksonian antimonopolism, now recognizes that the Jacksonians' reputation as advocates of equality is "illusory at best"; see Wettemann's *Privilege vs. Equality: Civil-Military Relations in the Jacksonian Era, 1815–1845* (Westport, Conn.: Praeger Security International, 2009), xi.

Nineteenth-century America democratized politically, but it did not do so to the same degree socially or economically. Detailed work remains to be done, but no one can read the Army Registers without noting the Clays, Berriens, Van Burens, and other sons and nephews of prominent politicians from both sides of the partisan aisle. Nor should this be surprising. Many politicians, Democrat as well as Whig, came from socially prominent families despite growing social mobility and congressional turnover, and nominations to West Point were commonly made in consultation with members of Congress, probably as early as Calhoun's term as secretary of war. Indeed, it is clear that senior military commanders, as well as Calhoun and his successors, saw bipartisan (and multisectional) nominations as a means of moderating political attacks on the Military Academy and the army, and it seems reasonable to conclude that they succeeded. In 1843, when Congress mandated that nominations to West Point come primarily from congressmen (March 1, 1843, 5 *Stat.* 606), the legislature recognized that democratization—at least in the sense of having an officer corps whose initial opportunity to pursue commissions reflected voting patterns—could be achieved incrementally, without granting excessive influence to any one person, section, or party. Given patterns of political influence then and now, this would produce a more middle-class officer corps, but never one that was truly representative of the American people as a whole.

27. Wettemann, *Privilege vs. Equality*, 59, notes that a bill to dismiss any new graduates without permanent commissions waiting for them in the regiments was introduced in the committee early in 1831 but was not acted on; this would have ended the accession of new brevet second lieutenants but would not have dismissed those already commissioned (*ASPMA*, 4:683). At that point, even before the graduation of the class of 1831, there were eighty-three brevet second lieutenants in the army—nearly half the number of permanent officers of artillery, and nearly one-fifth of all permanent infantry and artillery officers. And with the Black Hawk War, the Nullification Crisis, and the next national elections at least a year away, the moment would have been opportune, although several years of slave unrest, culminating in Nat Turner's rebellion, may have deterred the Jacksonians. Ninety brevet second lieutenants were included on the 1832 Army Register, where they were listed in a separate table for the first time; eighty-five were listed in 1833, sixty-three in 1834, sixty-eight in 1835, and sixty-nine in 1836, before the resignations of that year provided permanent commissions for all those remaining. (At the beginning of 1830 there were sixty-five; during the Adams administration, there were twenty-three in 1826, forty-two in 1827, fourteen in 1828, and thirty-eight in 1829.) During these years, the average West Point graduate waited two years for a permanent commission; between 1829 and 1835, virtually all of each year's graduating class entered the army with brevet commissions.

28. AJ, December 8, 1829, *MPP*, 3:1018–1019. Jefferson did not mention the Military Academy in any annual or inaugural address; Madison did so in four out of eight annual messages (once implicitly); Monroe in three (1822–1824) during his second term; and Adams in three out of five, including his inaugural (the only mention of the Academy in an inaugural during this era). Jackson praised the regular army in seven of his eight annual messages. The Military Academy was thus mentioned in nine of the twenty-eight annual messages between 1801 and 1828; see especially Madison, December 5, 1815, Monroe, December 3, 1822, and December 7, 1824, and Adams, December 6, 1825, *MPP*, 2:553, 757–758, 823–824, 871–872. Indeed, West Point was the only example of effective national support for higher education that Daniel Walker Howe cited—or could have cited—in his 2001 presidential address to the Society for Historians of the Early Republic: "Church, State, and Education in the Young American Republic," *JER* 22 (Spring 2002): 3.

29. Skelton, *An American Profession of Arms*, tables 9.4 and 9.5 (159–160). The Jacksonians' own social positions and networks prevented fundamental change or democratization. Thus, the sons of government officials (civil and military) made up only (!) 14 percent of West Point graduates between 1844 and 1860, and sons of professionals accounted for 23 percent; 28.5 percent of West Point graduates between 1844 and 1860 were the sons of farmers, compared with only 22 percent of the officers on the 1830 and 1860 Army Registers. The sons of artisans and nonagricultural laborers made up 7 percent of graduates—the same proportion as the sons of lawyers—and thus had little effect in increasing their representation in the officer corps. Despite

the great number of postal officials and their prominent role in partisan patronage, their sons accounted for 5 percent of West Point graduates at most (and probably much less, since that number included all federal civil servants). Indeed, the sons of military officers increased their representation in the officer corps—from 9 to 14 percent between 1830 and 1860—although they constituted only 9 percent of Military Academy graduates. The largest occupational groups of officers' fathers were thus military officers, lawyers, and merchants or shopkeepers, each at 12 to 14 percent of the officer corps.

The numbers for the sons of military officers appear anomalous, given the substantial and growing majority of Military Academy graduates among officers (64 percent in 1830, 75 percent in 1860). Skelton could find evidence for only 70 percent of the officers on the 1830 and 1860 registers (still far greater than most samplings, and well beyond the demands of statistical accuracy), but the numbers can still be accounted for by the aging of the officer corps as men commissioned before 1844 remained in service, since most officers who resigned did so during the first decade of their careers. The sons of nonagricultural businessmen decreased from 35 to 28 percent of the officer corps as a whole, though they increased to account for 31 percent of West Point graduates. It would be worthwhile to look at the social origins of the officers commissioned directly from civilian life by the Democrats in 1833, 1836, 1838–1840, 1846, and 1855, although these men resigned their commissions in proportions far greater than Military Academy graduates and thus composed an even smaller percentage of the officer corps in 1860 than officers commissioned directly from civilian life had in 1830.

30. General Order 48, May 18, 1833, General Orders and Circulars, AGO, 1809–1860, M1094, reel 3, RG 94, NA. Robert P. Wettemann Jr., "A Part or Apart? The Alleged Isolation of Antebellum U.S. Army Officers," *American Nineteenth-Century History* 7 (June 2006): 206, asserts that Jackson used his "best efforts" to compel officers working on civil engineering projects and other detached (noncompany) service to return to their units, but he cites only the orders, not efforts to enforce them. General Order 48 allowed exceptions, and Jackson never court-martialed an officer for failing to return to duty under these orders. The relevant statistics are drawn primarily from the Army Registers; "Letter of the Adjutant General" (to the secretary of war), in *ANC* 4 (February 16, 1837, originally November 26, 1836): 97–99; and "Statement of the Number of Company Officers of the Army in Service against the Creek and Seminole Indians in Florida in 1836, etc.," February 28, 1837, *ASPMA*, 7:110–115. See also Coffman, *The Old Army*, 52–54, and Skelton, *An American Profession of Arms*, 216–217.

General Order 48 did have an effect: only eight officers of infantry and artillery were listed as being on duty surveying for civilian transportation projects on the next (1834) Army Register. Thus, the order did reduce the assignment of national military officers to assist private civilian entities, although the War Department granted some exceptions. Yet all these orders were flawed in concept and execution, with ideology and appearance triumphing over mission requirements and necessary army administration. General Order 48 allowed the commanding general to make exceptions, and all three orders used confusing language. General Order 69 made exceptions for "those employed in the military service proper or upon some duty of the public service strictly speaking"; officers on engineering duty were normally building coastal fortifications, which was presumably "some duty of the public service," if not "military service proper." Jackson presumably intended "military service" to mean company duty with troops, but "some duty of the public service" actually encompassed every detached assignment, including the transportation surveys assigned through the War Department. Only 15 to 20 percent of the officers on detached duty, and less than 4 percent of the officer corps as a whole, were engaged in civilian transportation projects under the General Survey Act, and all officer assignments, detached or otherwise, required War Department approval. Yet the order went on to list officers on engineering, ordnance, and "special" duty (which usually meant the Indian removal demanded by the administration) as those who were ordered to return to their companies. These officers had been assigned to these duties with the sanction of the secretary of war, and the president certainly had the authority to order them back to their companies. But if he did, who would conduct Indian removal, fortification construction, and ordnance development and maintenance? In fact, as discussed in volume 2, the army continued to remove captured or surrendered Creeks and Seminoles, and it would have done so with the Cherokee had President Van Buren not granted John Ross the authority to conduct their actual movement to the West after the army rounded them up.

31. General Orders 43 and 69, June 28 and October 15, 1836, General Orders and Circulars, AGO, 1809–1860, M1094, reel 4, RG 94, NA. General Order 69 also mandated that no more than two artillery and one infantry officer per company be permitted to serve on detached duties, but this was already the norm. When more officers were absent from company duty, it was usually due to leave (granted by the War Department, usually because of long separation from family, urgent personal financial issues, or perhaps political influence—influence among the Jacksonians), temporary court-martial duty, or sickness. Similarly, field-grade officers were ordered to their regiments unless they had been excepted by previous General Order 58 (issued August 27). In effect, this latter provision addressed only officers on leave. Given that there were only thirty-nine regimental field-grade officers, few of whom were not with the troops of their regiments (although several were serving as regional commanders at recruiting and communications centers like Detroit and St. Louis), this amounted to a handful of men at most. Nineteen officers on transportation surveys were ordered back to their companies, and the twenty-eight officers on engineering or ordnance duty could certainly be spared for their companies. Yet until the ordnance department and the Corps of Engineers were increased in 1838, the implementation of General Order 69 provided only an average of four officers per regiment (0.5 officer per company at best) to the field army, and the vast majority of them were lieutenants, not captains (company commanders). Ultimately, these orders were expressions of egalitarian ideology rather than substantive reforms.

There was no law or regulation that prohibited officers from working for private enterprise while on leave, nor did the 1838 law change this, contrary to Wettemann, *Privilege vs. Equality*, 94. Officers did not merely wander off duty in pursuit of private employment—that would constitute absence without leave, a violation of the Articles of War and the General Regulations. Either they were on leave, as formally authorized by the War Department, or they were assigned to surveying duties through their chains of command, normally at the request of private companies. Such requests were normally routed through the War Department and were subject to civilian scrutiny before officers were issued orders. Although some new West Point graduates never showed up at their regiments, this was ultimately because the War Department failed to end their postgraduate leaves. The key was enforcement—refusing to extend leaves and then sanctioning officers who remained absent without leave—but enforcing the law was not a strength of the Jacksonians, unless it applied to the president's enemies. Whatever the precise circumstances, officers had to secure War Department sanction to work on transportation projects while they were not on leave. A few officers were able to use their political connections—presumably Jacksonian—to work directly for commercial enterprises or to escape service in Florida, but that handful was hardly characteristic of the army officer corps, except in the eyes of Jacksonian ideologues, who preferred to blame others for the favoritism of their own leaders. The War Department could have refused to grant exceptions to President Jackson's orders for officers to return to their regiments, and it could have conducted courts-martial or dismissed delinquent officers from the army, but it did neither. Martin Van Buren did not object when his son Abram, a lieutenant who graduated from West Point in 1827, served as commanding general Alexander Macomb's aide between 1829 and 1836. Most important, if all officers had returned to their regiments from ordnance, quartermaster, commissary, and recruiting duties, the army would have collapsed in short order because the force established in 1821 depended on company officers (lieutenants and a few captains) from the combat arms regiments to fill those critical logistical positions. Only the paymaster and medical departments were fully staffed with permanently assigned personnel.

32. Skelton, *An American Profession of Arms*, tables 11.1 and 11.2 (182–183); Skelton, "Army Officer as Organization Man." See Gwyn Harries-Jenkins, *The Army in Victorian Society* (London: Routledge and Kegan Paul, 1977); Edward M. Spiers, *The Army and Society, 1815–1914* (London: Longman, 1980); Douglas Porch, *Army and Revolution: France, 1815–1848* (London: Routledge and Kegan Paul, 1974); John Shelton Curtiss, *The Russian Army under Nicholas I, 1825–1855* (Durham, N.C.: Duke University Press, 1965); and John L. H. Keep, *Soldiers of the Tsar: Army and Society in Russia, 1462–1874* (Oxford: Clarendon Press, 1985), for the principal European officer corps. There is no adequate study in English of the Prussian officer corps (apart from civil-military relations) between 1815 and 1860, though there are valuable tidbits in Arden Bucholz, *Moltke and the German Wars, 1864–1871* (New York: Palgrave, 2001).

33. Skelton, *An American Profession of Arms*, figure 11.1, table 11.4 (216, 213); "A Subaltern," "Florida War, No. 4," *ANC* 8 (April 4, 1839): 220 ("thankless");

"Florida War," *ANC 7* (August 16, 1838): 105 ("inglorious"); "Quasi Major," "The Seminole War" [a public letter addressed to the secretary of war], *ANC 7* (October 18, 1838): 249; "A Subaltern of the 7th," "The Seventh Infantry," *ANC 9* (August 22, 1839): 116.

CONCLUSION: THE SOLDIER AND THE JACKSONIAN STATE

1. Leonard D. White, *The Jeffersonians: A Study in Administrative History, 1801–1829* (New York: Macmillan, 1959), 259. For further context, see Matthew A. Crenson, *The Federal Machine: The Beginnings of Bureaucracy in Jacksonian America* (Baltimore: Johns Hopkins University Press, 1975). Promotion by seniority would also appear to constrain the professional autonomy of the army's senior leaders, but institutional stability and the perception of fairness were more important to them, given the difficulty of distinguishing among meritorious junior officers. Promotion to general, the creation of new units, and the expansion of existing ones still provided some critical opportunities to reward and employ outstanding merit, as in Thomas Jesup's selection for quartermaster general, John Wool's for inspector general, and William Worth's promotions to major (into the revived ordnance branch in 1832) and colonel (as commander of the revived Eighth Infantry Regiment in 1838). Indeed, today's U.S. Army promotes officers by time in grade, with only limited provisions for accelerating or delaying promotion (almost never occurring more than a year early at each field-grade rank). Although officers move "up or out," with forced retirement when they are not promoted, the promotion and retention rate during times of need (such as the last decade) has been as high as 90 percent to major and 80 percent to lieutenant colonel.

2. Chief Engineer Joseph G. Swift, diary, March 10, 1814, in *The Memoirs of General Joseph G. Swift, L. L. D., U.S. Army, with a Genealogy of His Family*, ed. Harrison Ellerly (n.p., 1890), 125.

3. Peter M. Molloy, "Technical Education and the Young Republic: West Point as America's Ecole Polytechnique, 1802–1833" (Ph.D. diss., Brown University, 1975); James W. Kershner, "Sylvanus Thayer: A Biography" (Ph.D. diss., University of West Virginia, 1975); Theodore J. Crackel, *West Point: A Bicentennial History* (Lawrence: University Press of Kansas, 2002), 96–98; April 30, 1824, 4 *Stat.* 22–23. The mathematics, military engineering, and drawing taught before and after 1824 were certainly of use to future civil engineers, but Crackel shows that no course in civil engineering was taught until that year, when the combination of a new engineering professor interested in civil engineering and the imminent passage of the General Survey Act led the Academic Board (the department heads and the superintendent) to mandate its addition to the curriculum. For Thayer's correspondence, see Cindy Adams, ed., *The West Point Thayer Papers, 1808–1872* (West Point, N.Y.: Association of Graduates, 1965; reprint, Brookhaven Press, 2001), now available online in the USMA Library catalog.

4. William B. Skelton, *An American Profession of Arms: The Army Officer Corps,*

1784–1861 (Lawrence: University Press of Kansas, 1992), 137–139. See James L. Morrison Jr., *"The Best School": West Point in the Pre–Civil War Years, 1833–1866*, 2nd ed. (Kent, Ohio: Kent State University Press, 1986), 94–101, and Samuel J. Watson, "Professionalism, Social Attitudes, and Civil-Military Accountability in the U.S. Army Officer Corps, 1815–1846," 2 vols. (Ph.D. diss., Rice University, 1996), chap. 3, for thorough treatments of military training at West Point before 1846. For a comprehensive assessment of the character, state, and evolution of army troop training, drill, and combat readiness during this era, see ibid., chaps. 5–7. The contemporary perception (sometimes repeated even today) that the Mexican army was equally or better trained proved illusory. That army lacked the leadership, discipline, and morale to maintain unit cohesion and execute its drills, however often it practiced on the parade ground—and that frequency has been exaggerated by repetition of the observations made by a few travelers. See William A. DePalo Jr., *The Mexican National Army, 1822–1852* (College Station: Texas A&M University Press, 1997), for the best treatment.

5. For the fortification system, see Robert S. Browning, *Two if by Sea: The Development of American Coastal Defense Policy* (Westport, Conn.: Greenwood Press, 1983); Russell Reed Price, "American Coastal Defense: The Third System of Fortification, 1816–1864" (Ph.D. diss., Mississippi State University, 1999), which focuses on the technology of the system; and Mark A. Smith, *Engineering Security: The Corps of Engineers and Third System Defense Policy, 1815–1861* (Tuscaloosa: University of Alabama Press, 2009), which includes substantial attention to congressional politics. Brian M. Linn has argued the centrality of coastal defense to nineteenth-century officers' visions of American national security policy; see *"The American Way of War* Revisited," *JMH* 66 (April 2002): 508–509, and *The Echo of Battle: The Army's Way of War* (Cambridge, Mass.: Harvard University Press, 2007), chap. 1. For broad strategic considerations, see Jamie W. Moore, *The Fortifications Board 1816–1828 and the Definition of National Security* (Charleston, S.C.: The Citadel, 1981), and Samuel J. Watson, "Knowledge, Interest, and the Limits of Military Professionalism: The Discourse on American Coastal Defense, 1815–1860," *War in History* 5 (Fall 1998): 280–307, which also addresses the influence of civilian political culture and the economy. For ordnance, see Merritt Roe Smith, *Harpers Ferry Armory and the New Technology: The Challenge of Change* (Ithaca, N.Y.: Cornell University Press, 1977). For officers and exploration, see (among many works) William H. Goetzmann, *Army Exploration in the American West* (New Haven, Conn.: Yale University Press, 1957); for officers and internal improvements, see Forest G. Hill, *Roads, Rails, and Waterways: The Army Engineers and Early Transportation* (Norman: University of Oklahoma Press, 1957); Robert G. Angevine, "The Railroad and the State: War, Business, and Politics in the United States to 1861" (Ph.D. diss., Duke University, 1999); and Robert P. Wettemann Jr., "'To the Public Prosperity': The U.S. Army and the Market Revolution, 1815–1844" (Ph.D. diss., Texas A&M University, 2001). For context, see John L. Larson, *Internal Improvement: National Public Works and the Promise of Popular Government in the Early United States* (Chapel Hill: University of North Carolina Press,

2001), and Drew R. McCoy, *The Elusive Republic: Political Economy in Jeffersonian America* (Chapel Hill: University of North Carolina Press, 1980).

6. See Mark E. Neely Jr., *The Union Divided: Party Conflict in the Civil War North* (Cambridge, Mass.: Harvard University Press, 2002), for the best synopsis of the Radical Republican critique of strategy during the Civil War. In 1865 all the army-level commanders (commanders of the Army of the Potomac, the Army of the Tennessee, etc.) on both sides were graduates, as were nearly all corps commanders and the majority of division commanders. Every one of the sixty largest battles of the war was commanded by a graduate on at least one side, and in fifty-four cases by graduates on both sides. Crackel, *West Point*, 135. See Andrew J. Polski, "'Mr. Lincoln's Army' Revisited: Partisanship, Institutional Position, and Union Army Command, 1861–1865," *Studies in American Political Development* 16 (Fall 2002): 176–207, for the most thorough study of Union general officer appointment practices in print, and Thomas W. Goss, *The War within the Union High Command: Politics and Generalship during the Civil War* (Lawrence: University Press of Kansas, 2003).

7. Robert H. Wiebe, *The Opening of American Society: From the Adoption of the Constitution to the Eve of Disunion* (New York: Alfred A. Knopf, 1984), chap. 11. For critics, see Morrison, *"The Best School in the World,"* and Matthew Moten, *The Delafield Commission and the American Military Profession* (College Station: Texas A&M University Press, 2000). See Edward L. Hagerman, *The American Civil War and the Origins of Modern Warfare: Ideas, Organization, and Field Command* (Bloomington: Indiana University Press, 1988), for an analysis of the organizational, tactical, operational, and logistical problems American officers faced in that conflict and their responses, which were much more innovative than the critics have concluded.

8. Daniel H. Hill, "The Army in Texas," *Southern Quarterly Review* 9 (April 1846): 434–457, and 14 (July 1848): 183–197; Timothy D. Johnson, *Winfield Scott: The Quest for Military Glory* (Lawrence: University Press of Kansas, 1998). For the army's logistical structure, see Watson, "Professionalism, Social Attitudes, and Civil-Military Accountability," chap. 8; Erna Risch, *Quartermaster Support of the Army, 1775–1939*, rev. ed. (Washington, D.C.: Center of Military History, 1988); Cynthia Ann Miller, "The United States Army Logistics Complex, 1818–1845: A Case Study of the Northern Frontier" (Ph.D. diss., Syracuse University, 1991); and Chester L. Kieffer, *Maligned General: The Biography of Thomas Sidney Jesup* (San Rafael, Calif.: Presidio Press, 1979). Charles R. Shrader, ed., *United States Army Logistics, 1775–1992: An Anthology*, vol. 1 (Washington, D.C.: Center of Military History, 1997), provides selected primary documents that support both favorable and unfavorable interpretations.

9. See Crackel, *West Point*, chap. 4, and Samuel J. Watson, "Developing 'Republican Machines': West Point and the Struggle to Render the Officer Corps Safe for America," in *Thomas Jefferson's Military Academy: Founding West Point*, ed. Robert M. S. McDonald (Charlottesville: University Press of Virginia, 2004).

10. Keith W. Hoskin and Richard H. Macve, "The Genesis of Accountability: The West Point Connections," *Accounting, Organizations, and Society* 13, 1 (1988), 37–73;

AJ, December 7, 1835, *MPP*, 3:1388–1389. For the postal system, which underwent similar processes of rationalization, see Richard R. John, *Spreading the News: The American Postal System from Franklin to Morse* (Cambridge, Mass.: Harvard University Press, 1995). See Patricia Cline Cohen, *A Calculating People: The Spread of Numeracy in Early America* (Chicago: University of Chicago Press, 1982), chap. 4, for the role mathematics was expected to play in disciplining the minds of republican citizens, and chap. 5 for its role in early national state formation and public administration.

11. Scholars should always remember the problems Jackson had with militiamen in the Creek War. He understood from hard personal experience the wide range of forces and reliability encompassed in references to "citizen-soldiers," and it is an error to assume that he intrinsically preferred their use, whatever his political followers might have wished. Jackson probably doubted that many volunteers were as aggressive as the Tennesseans who served under him in the Creek and Seminole Wars.

12. Martin Shefter, *Political Parties and the State: The American Historical Experience* (Princeton, N.J.: Princeton University Press, 1994). Ronald P. Formisano, "State Development in the Early Republic: Substance and Structure, 1780–1840," in *Contesting Democracy: Substance and Structure in American Political History, 1775–2000*, ed. Byron E. Shafer and Anthony Badger (Lawrence: University Press of Kansas, 2001), suggests a similar thesis.

13. See Michael Wallace, "Changing Concepts of Party in the United States: New York, 1815–1828," *AHR* 74 (December 1968): 453–491; Richard Hofstadter, *The Idea of a Party System: The Rise of Legitimate Opposition in the United States, 1780–1840* (Berkeley: University of California Press, 1969); Thomas Brown, *Politics and Statesmanship: Essays on the American Whig Party* (New York: Columbia University Press, 1985); Marc W. Kruman, "The Second American Party System and the Transformation of Revolutionary Republicanism," *JER* 12 (Winter 1992): 509–537; Major L. Wilson, "Republicanism and the Idea of Party in the Jacksonian Period," *JER* 8 (Winter 1988): 419–432; and Major L. Wilson, "The 'Country' versus the 'Court': A Republican Consensus and Party Debate in the Bank War," *JER* 15 (Winter 1995): 619–647, on changes and continuities—the continued emphasis on virtue and community consensus, now bolstered and expressed through parties to buttress republicanism—in republican values and rhetoric during the 1830s. Army officers, in contrast, seem to have partaken of the "disengaged belief," "engaged disbelief," and "vernacular liberalism" explored by Glenn C. Altschuler and Stuart M. Blumin in *Rude Republic: Americans and Their Politics in the Nineteenth Century* (Princeton, N.J.: Princeton University Press, 2000);"'Where Is the Real America?' Politics and Popular Consciousness in the Antebellum Era," *American Quarterly* 49 (June 1997): 225–267; and "Limits of Political Engagement in Antebellum America: A New Look at the Golden Age of Participatory Democracy," *JAH* 84 (December 1997): 855–885. See also Samuel J. Watson, "What Do We Mean by Partisan? Army Officers and Politics during the Evolution of the Second Party System" (paper presented to the Southwestern Historical Association, April 1, 1999).

14. See Thomas S. Langston, *Uneasy Balance: Civil-Military Relations in Peace-time America since 1783* (Baltimore: Johns Hopkins University Press, 2003), 12, chap. 1, especially 19–21, 28–32; and Daniel Walker Howe, *The Political Culture of the American Whigs* (Chicago: University of Chicago Press, 1979), chaps. 5, 8.

15. See George Rogers Taylor, *The Transportation Revolution, 1815–1860* (New York: Holt, Rinehart, 1951); John, *Spreading the News*; David M. Henkin, *The Postal Age: The Emergence of Modern Communications in Nineteenth-Century America* (Chicago: University of Chicago Press, 2006); Daniel Walker Howe, *What Hath God Wrought? The Transformation of America, 1815–1848* (New York: Oxford University Press, 2007), chaps. 6, 17; Robert Angevine, *The Railroad and the State: War, Politics and Technology in Nineteenth-Century America* (Stanford, Ca.: Stanford University Press, 2004), chap. 3; E. G. Campbell, "Railroads in National Defense, 1829–1848," *MVHR* 27 (December 1940): 361–378; Wettemann, "'To the Public Prosperity'"; Robert P. Wettemann Jr., "West Point, the Jacksonians, and the Army's Controversial Role in National Improvements," in *West Point: Two Centuries and Beyond*, ed. Lance A. Betros (Abilene, Tex.: McWhiney Foundation Press, 2004); Watson, "Knowledge, Interest, and the Limits of Military Professionalism"; and Smith, *Engineering Security*, who considers my critical evaluation of the fortification program ahistorical, along with virtually all other scholarly analyses. I believe that Smith takes the arguments of the Corps of Engineers too much at face value, fails to consider the officer's responsibility to anticipate the trajectory of future change, and dismisses the critiques made by contemporary officers, both inside and outside the Corps of Engineers, too hastily. The proposals made by the critics were often unrealistic, but that is not evidence that the Corps of Engineers' program was realistic or cost-effective. Like Wettemann, Hill's *Roads, Rails, and Waterways*, focuses on army support for civilian railroad survey and construction, not military thought about their military uses.

16. Michael Mann, *The Sources of Social Power: The Rise of Classes and Nation-States, 1760–1914* (Cambridge: Cambridge University Press, 1993), 457–458; Samuel E. Finer, *The Man on Horseback: The Role of the Military in Politics* (1964; rev. ed., Boulder, Colo.: Westview Press, 1988), 130. See also Leonard D. White, *The Federalists: A Study in Administrative History, 1789–1801* (New York: Macmillan, 1948), 268, 278–284, 512–514. See Howe, *What Hath God Wrought?* chap. 7, on the John Quincy Adams administration as "the improvers"; see Howe, *The Political Culture of the American Whigs*, chaps. 7, 8, and Brown, *Politics and Statesmanship*, chap. 4, on the Whigs' proto-Victorian dedication to "improvement" and reform. The extensive unpublished research of Walter Bachman demonstrates that many officers claimed an official allowance for servants (often slaves) but did not have any, or they shared servants but claimed the full allowance. The War Department permitted this practice and apparently considered these allowances de facto supplements to officers' pay. More seriously, Bachman (personal correspondence, 2008–2011) has evidence that most officers stationed in slaveholding states either became slaveholders or hired slaves from their masters as servants, and Dred Scott was not the only slave to be held in free states or territories by army officers. I believe officers justified this on the grounds that army

posts were federal property, and neither Bachman nor I have found any evidence of disapproval from either local civilians or fellow officers. Still, these officers clearly violated the spirit of state antislavery laws and federal territorial codes, beginning with the Northwest Ordinance. This participation in slavery, and the officer corps' abhorrence of abolitionism, provides a further example of officers' authoritarian predisposition.

17. Robert Wooster, *The American Military Frontiers: The United States Army in the West, 1783–1900* (Albuquerque: University of New Mexico Press, 2009), 66–67, refers specifically to civilian claims that officers at Fort Snelling (essentially, modern Minneapolis) created an excessively large military reservation (the area around the post reserved for military training or, more commonly, established to keep taverns and liquor dealers away from the troops) to protect their private land claims. This was certainly possible, in the sense that officers could wait for civilian competitors to leave an area and then purchase land when the military reservation was reduced or eliminated. This would take time, however, and an officer's claim to land formerly within a reservation was no greater than that of any civilian. An officer might be able to use "insider knowledge" to be first in line to buy the land, but the increase or decrease of reservations was closely watched and commonly publicized in local newspapers. Nor was the creation or reduction of the reservation a decision made solely by the commanding officer of a post. Reservations had to be authorized by the War Department, and local civilians commonly complained at every stage of this process.

In the specific case of Fort Snelling, the Wisconsin territorial assembly complained that a group of speculators, including the post commander, had repeatedly extended the reservation in order to drive settlers from landings along the Mississippi River. This reduced competition for lumber mills and transfer points onto the river, where the speculators had made claims outside the reservation. In doing so, they not only sought a monopoly but also repeatedly and arbitrarily drove "peaceful and enterprising citizens" from land they had already improved with buildings and crops, pushing the settlers too far from the fort for it to provide them with any protection. The petitioners labeled the commander's conduct "oppressive" and "derogatory to the principles of common honesty and justice," questioning how far the military's power should extend and how much justification it should have to offer. They further claimed that the territory was essentially a state in waiting and that the assembly's legislative powers should trump military authority to claim a reservation. Resolutions of the Assembly of Wiskonsin [*sic*], March 16, 1840, House Document 144, 26th Cong., 1st sess. (serial 365), 3, 4.

The assembly's material case appears to have been well-founded, and its concerns for the separation of powers and federalism were reasonable, apart from the egregious assertion that the territory was a de facto state. Yet fundamentally (and beyond this case), the problem was not individual officers' profiteering but a clash of cultures. The army commonly set off large tracts of valuable land—for example, at the junction of rivers—without regard for the commercial interests of civilian frontiersmen. For military commanders, military discipline (primarily keeping liquor away from soldiers) trumped commercial utility. Civilians complained about this sense of priorities, regardless of officers' individual land dealings. The Wisconsin assembly argued that no distance "will prevent soldiers from getting [liquor] when so inclined," and it not infrequently joined general and specific complaints or threw one in to buttress the other, whether either or both were true or false. See Edwin C. Bearss and Arrell M. Gibson, *Fort Smith: Little Gibraltar on the Arkansas* (Norman: University of Oklahoma Press, 1969), chap. 9, and Tony R. Mullis, *Peacekeeping on the Plains: Army Operations in Bleeding Kansas* (Columbia: University of Missouri Press, 2004), chap. 5, for the most extended analyses of these situations available. Mullis does find significant conflict of interest, but scholars should be conscious of the dynamics discussed above.

18. The record of Jacksonian politics—with the spoils system (so open to corruption and so much in contrast with the army's precommissioning socialization and de facto tenure) and Indian removal as prime examples—demonstrates a much more consistent venality (as one would expect in a much more partisan system), with fewer sanctions. Rather than additional studies of Jacksonian ideology, historians would profit greatly by rigorous studies of the match, or mismatch, between Jacksonian political rhetoric and the reality of Jacksonian governance: of the ways in which Jacksonian political culture fostered a spiral of rhetorical escalation, ultimately pandering to the most egregious complaints and the most extreme prejudices, with little regard for the truth. Indeed, few historians have remarked on the degree to which the Jacksonian spoils system of civilian officeholder patronage (from which the army remained immune) came to approximate the sale of offices—a common practice in the European ancien régime that the United States had managed to avoid for several generations after the Revolution. See White, *The Federalists*, 514.

19. See Culver H. Smith, *The Press, Politics, and Patronage: The American Government's Use of Newspapers, 1789–1875* (Athens: University of Georgia Press, 1977); Thomas C. Leonard, *The Power of the Press: The Birth of American Political Reporting* (New York: Oxford University Press, 1986); John C. Nerone, "The Mythology of the Penny Press," *Critical Studies in Mass Communication* 4 (1987): 376–404; Gerald J. Baldasty, *The Commercialization of News in the Nineteenth Century* (Madison: University of Wisconsin Press, 1992); Jeffrey L. Pasley, "*The Tyranny of Printers*": *Newspaper Politics in the Early American Republic* (Charlottesville: University Press of Virginia, 2001); and John L. Brooke, "To Be 'Read by the Whole People': Press, Party, and Public Sphere in the United States, 1789–1840," *Proceedings of the American Antiquarian Society* 110 (2002): 89–118. Pasley's work focuses primarily on the period before 1815, but chaps. 13 and 14 provide an outstanding analysis of the role of newspaper editors during the "reconstruction of party politics" in the mid-1820s. My future work on the Second Seminole War should help illuminate the relationship among the media, perceptions of public opinion, and military operations.

20. WS, April 25, 1842, SWLR: Unreg; Col. James Bankhead, June 27, 1842, AGOLR.

21. A court of inquiry was an investigative body without punitive authority; it could have as few as three members. In contrast, a court-martial would find guilt or innocence and recommend sanctions to the president; it required more participants,

usually of a rank at least equal to that of the accused (very difficult to find for any field-grade or general officer). The members of the court were probably chosen by commanding general Macomb, who did not want to stir up trouble among his leading subordinates; however, Van Buren or Secretary of War Poinsett could have changed its composition had they wanted a better chance of punishing Wool.

22. See Durwood Ball, *Army Regulars on the Western Frontier, 1848–1861* (Norman: University of Oklahoma Press, 2001), chap. 5, and Harwood P. Hinton, "The Military Career of John Ellis Wool, 1812–1863" (Ph.D. diss., University of Wisconsin, 1960), chaps. 6–9.

23. Richard Bruce Winders, *Mr. Polk's Army: The American Military Experience in the Mexican War* (College Station: Texas A&M University Press, 1997), 97. The Minié ball had not yet been invented, so the 1841 rifled musket had the slow rate of fire normal in muzzle-loading rifles before the 1850s—half or a third that of smoothbores. Scott's aversion to mixing percussion caps with flintlocks in the same regiment was probably an exaggerated case of adherence to the principles of standardization and uniformity he had tried to inculcate in the army. See Dennis Showalter, "Infantry Weapons, Tactics, and the Armies of Germany," *European Studies Review* 4 (April 1974): 119–140, and Geoffrey Wawro, "An 'Army of Pigs': The Technical, Social, and Political Bases of Austrian Shock Tactics, 1859–1866," *JMH* 59 (July 1995): 407–435, on the difficulties in tactical understanding and doctrinal development posed by the revolutionary technological changes occurring after 1850. See Michael Howard, *The Franco-Prussian War: The German Invasion of France, 1870–1871* (New York: Dorset Press, 1961), and Dennis Showalter, *Railroads and Rifles: Soldiers, Technology, and the Unification of Germany* (Hamden, Conn.: Shoestring Press, 1975), for classic discussions of the impact of the revolutionary technological changes that occurred between 1850 and 1870.

24. See Lester R. Dillon Jr., *American Artillery in the Mexican War, 1846–1847* (Austin, Tex.: Presidial Press, 1975); Watson, "Professionalism, Social Attitudes, and Civil-Military Accountability," 396–403, 463–466; and Wayne Hsieh, "The Old Army in War and Peace: West Pointers and the Civil War Era, 1814–1865" (Ph.D. diss., University of Virginia, 2004), 93–102.

25. James J. Schneider, "The Loose Marble—and the Origins of Operational Art," *Parameters* 19 (March 1989): 85–99, provides the most succinct analysis and a useful conceptualization of the evolution of the components of nineteenth-century operational art, both before and after the Civil War. For elaboration, see Robert M. Epstein, "Patterns of Change and Continuity in Nineteenth-Century Warfare," *JMH* 56 (July 1992): 375–388; Robert M. Epstein, "The Creation and Evolution of the Army Corps in the American Civil War," *JMH* 55 (January 1991): 21–46; and Hagerman, *American Civil War and Origins of Modern Warfare*. Napoleonic experts will point out that the French armies often operated like their eighteenth-century predecessors, sending commissary officers ahead to arrange for large-scale purchases or to levy "contributions" from communities, rather than allowing individual soldiers or small groups to forage at the expense of individual farmers. The implication is that the reduced bur-

dens of Napoleonic logistics were really little more than the product of the eighteenth century "Agricultural Revolution" and a denser road network in western Europe. Yet Napoleonic armies did move faster and farther, on a more sustained basis, than their predecessors: something in the pace of operations changed fundamentally.

26. Russell F. Weigley provides a reasonably accurate analysis in *The American Way of War: A History of American Military Strategy and Policy* (New York: Macmillan, 1973), chap. 4. For a survey of army expertise, see Skelton, *An American Profession of Arms*, chap. 13; for extended explorations, see Watson, "Professionalism, Social Attitudes, and Civil-Military Accountability," chaps. 4–7, and Hsieh, "The Old Army in War and Peace."

27. Richard L. Bushman, *The Refinement of America, 1750–1850: Persons, Houses, Cities* (New York: Alfred A. Knopf, 1993); Daniel Walker Howe, "Victorian Culture in America," in *Victorian America*, ed. Daniel Walker Howe (Philadelphia: University of Pennsylvania Press, 1976). See Howe, *The Political Culture of the American Whigs*, chap. 9; Howe, *What Hath God Wrought?* 583–584; and Brown, *Politics and Statesmanship*, chap. 3, for Whig conservatism rooted in skeptical assessments of human nature and contemporary American social trends. I normally capitalize *Whiggish* to recognize the partisan potential of these more comprehensive affinities.

Despite their exercise of authoritarian command and their periodic engagement in personal violence during war, I believe career officers manifested more of what Amy Greenberg labels genteel or "restrained masculinity" than the "aggressive masculinity" she identifies as characteristic of frontiersmen and filibusters. See Amy S. Greenberg, *Manifest Manhood and the Antebellum American Empire* (Cambridge: Cambridge University Press, 2005); she does not discuss the army, apart from the war with Mexico. Officers also shared the slaveholder's predicament of exercising authoritarian power without losing self-control; see Steven M. Stowe, *Intimacy and Power in the Old South: Ritual in the Lives of the Planters* (Baltimore: Johns Hopkins University Press, 1987); Kenneth S. Greenberg, *Masters and Statesmen: The Political Culture of American Slavery* (Baltimore: Johns Hopkins University Press, 1985); and Kenneth S. Greenberg, *Honor and Slavery* (Princeton, N.J.: Princeton University Press, 1996). See Samuel J. Watson, "Flexible Gender Roles in the Era of the Market Revolution: Family, Friendship, Marriage, and Masculinity among U.S. Army Officers, 1815–1846," *Journal of Social History* 29 (Fall 1995): 81–106, for a more detailed examination.

See the following for important explorations of early- to mid-nineteenth-century American culture: John Allen Krout and Dixon Ryan Fox, *The Completion of Independence, 1790–1830* (New York: Macmillan, 1944); Perry Miller, *The Life of the Mind in America: From the Revolution to the Civil War* (New York: Harcourt, Brace, and World, 1966); John Higham, *From Boundlessness to Consolidation: The Transformation of American Culture, 1848–1860* (Ann Arbor, Mich.: William L. Clements Library, 1969); David J. Rothman, *The Discovery of the Asylum: Social Order and Disorder in the New Republic* (Boston: Little, Brown, 1971); Rush Welter, *The Mind of America, 1820–1860* (New York: Columbia University Press, 1975); Richard D. Brown, *Mod-*

ernization: The Transformation of American Life, 1600–1865 (New York: Hill and Wang, 1976); Wiebe, *The Opening of American Society*; Steven Watts, *The Republic Reborn: War and the Making of Liberal America, 1790–1820* (Baltimore: Johns Hopkins University Press, 1987); Jean V. Matthews, *Toward a New Society: American Thought and Culture, 1800–1830* (Boston: Twayne, 1991); Gordon Wood, *The Radicalism of the American Revolution* (New York: Alfred A. Knopf, 1992); Lewis Perry, *Boats against the Current: American Culture between Revolution and Modernity, 1820–1860* (New York: Oxford University Press, 1993); and Daniel Walker Howe, *Making the American Self: Jonathan Edwards to Abraham Lincoln* (Cambridge, Mass.: Harvard University Press, 1997).

28. Wood, *The Radicalism of the American Revolution*; Henry F. May, *The Enlightenment in America* (New York: Oxford University Press, 1976), 340, 358, 359. See also Howe, *Making the American Self*; Donald H. Meyer, *The Instructed Conscience: The Shaping of the American National Ethic* (Philadelphia: University of Pennsylvania Press, 1972); and Ethan S. Rafuse, "'To Check . . . the Very Worst and Meanest of Our Passions': Common Sense, 'Cobbon Sense,' and the Socialization of Cadets at Antebellum West Point." *War in History* 16 (Fall 2009): 406–424, on the influence of Common Sense philosophy and its cousin, moral philosophy, in antebellum America and the antebellum Military Academy. See Watson, "Professionalism, Social Attitudes, and Civil-Military Accountability," chap. 6, for an assessment of these qualities as they were sought after and praised in contemporary army officers.

29. See Magali Sarfatti Larson, *The Rise of Professionalism: A Sociological Inquiry* (Berkeley: University of California Press, 1977), for an insightful analysis of the political implications (putatively apolitical) of late-nineteenth-century professionalism and progressivism. See Harvey Meyerson, *Nature's Army: Why Soldiers Fought for Yosemite* (Lawrence: University Press of Kansas, 2001), for a superb exploration of the persistence of these attitudes and values among army officers throughout the century.

30. See Wiebe, *The Opening of American Society*, chaps. 13 and 15, regarding interdependence; Charles Sellers, *The Market Revolution: Jacksonian America, 1815–1846* (New York: Oxford University Press, 1991), for a negative perspective; Howe, *What Hath God Wrought?* for a positive one; and John L. Larson, *The Market Revolution: Liberty, Ambition, and the Eclipse of the Public Good* (Cambridge: Cambridge University Press, 2010), for a skeptical balance. See also special issues of the *Journal of the Early Republic*: *JER* 12 (Winter 1992) on Sellers's book, and *JER* 16 (Summer 1996) on capitalism in the early republic.

31. Burton J. Bledstein, *The Culture of Professionalism: The Middle Class and the Development of Higher Education in America* (New York: W. W. Norton, 1976); Watson, "Professionalism, Social Attitudes, and Civil-Military Accountability," chap. 10; Samuel J. Watson, "Bureaucrats and Aristocrats Encounter the Labor Market: Market Relations between Army Officers and Enlisted Men in the Age of Jackson" (paper presented to the Society for Historians of the Early American Republic, July 21, 1995). Howe, *What Hath God Wrought?* 607, observes that the Whigs saw themselves as the "party of the middle class," in the larger sense of their dedication to order, stability,

self- and social discipline and improvement, and a certain degree of cosmopolitanism. See Howe, *The Political Culture of the American Whigs*; Brown, *Politics and States-manship*; and Lawrence Frederick Kohl, *The Politics of Individualism: Parties and the American Character in the Jacksonian Era* (New York: Oxford University Press, 1989), chap. 4, for elaboration.

32. Stuart M. Blumin, "The Hypothesis of Middle-Class Formation in the Nineteenth Century: A Critique of Some Proposals," *AHR* 90 (April 1985): 299–338.

33. See especially William B. Skelton, "Officers and Politicians: The Origins of Army Politics in the United States before the Civil War," *AFS* 6 (Fall 1979): 22–48, and Skelton, *An American Profession of Arms*, chap. 15. The army did not side with the Whigs or vote for them as a block, even after friction with the Jackson administration led to disenchantment during his second term (as it did among so many Americans, leading to the re-formation of the National Republicans as Whigs). Indeed, a slight majority of the officers whose views are known (about the same proportion as among civilian voters) favored the Democrats (Skelton, *An American Profession of Arms*, 295).

SELECTED BIBLIOGRAPHY

In the notes, I cited documents in the sources where I initially found them, but many official letters are duplicated in several places, including *American State Papers*, published National Historical Publications and Records Commission editions, and multiple National Archives record groups. Researchers will find the *Papers of Andrew Jackson*, particularly its calendar of documents, useful for identifying alternative sources of these documents; often, several copies were made for the adjutant general as well as for the secretary of war. Similarly, the *Papers of John C. Calhoun* may be easier for researchers to access than the National Archives microfilm. Note that many documents cited in the registers of letters received by the War Department (M 222) are not preserved in the microfilm of the letters themselves (M 22). Many of my citations to National Archives records are listed in the abbreviations section at the beginning of the endnotes.

NATIONAL ARCHIVES, WASHINGTON, D.C.

Records of the State Department, RG 59
  Correspondence Relating to the Filibustering Expedition against the Spanish
    Government of Mexico, 1811–1816, Microfilm Publication T 286
Records of the Office of the Adjutant General, RG 94
  Confidential Inspection Reports, 1812–1826, Entry 20
  General Orders and Circulars of the War Department and General Headquarters
    of the Army, 1809–1860, M 1094
  Letters Received by the Office of the Adjutant General, 1805–1821, M 566
Records of United States Army Commands, 1784–1821, RG 98
  Division of the South, Letters Sent, 1816–1821, Entry 72
  Edmund P. Gaines, Letters Sent and Received, 1814–1815 and 1817–1819,
    Entry 78
  5th Military Department, Letters Sent, 1815–1821, Entry 67
  8th Military Department, Letters Sent, 1817–1821, Entry 75

Records of the Office of the Secretary of War, RG 107
  Confidential and Unofficial Letters Sent by the Secretary of War, 1814–1847,
    M 7
  Letters Received by Secretary of War, Unregistered Series, 1789–1861, M 222
  Registers of Letters Received by the Office of the Secretary of War, Main Series,
    1800–1870, M 22
Records of the Office of the Inspector General, RG 159
  Inspection Reports, 1814–1842, M 624
Records of U.S. Regular Army Mobile Units, 1821–1942, RG 391
  Sixth Infantry Regiment Letters Sent and Received, 1817–1824, Entry 1202

MANUSCRIPT COLLECTIONS

Robert Alves, Greenwich, Connecticut (private collection)
  Thomas Sidney Jesup
Burton Historical Collection, Detroit Public Library
  Daniel Baker
  Hugh Brady
  Lewis Cass
  Macomb Family Papers
  Macomb Letterbook, 1807–1819
  John Mason
  Winfield Scott
  Zachary Taylor
  Henry Whiting
  William Woodbridge
William L. Clements Library, University of Michigan, Ann Arbor
  Jacob Brown
  Lewis Cass
  H. A. S. Dearborn
  Amos B. Eaton
  Maskell C. Ewing (Ewing Family Papers)
  Thomas Sidney Jesup
  John Michael O'Connor
  Winfield Scott
  Alexander R. Thompson
  Christopher Van Deventer
Manuscript Division, Library of Congress, Washington, D.C. (many in the
    Miscellaneous Manuscripts Collection)
  Robert Anderson
  Jacob Brown

Sylvester Churchill
Duncan Lamont Clinch
George Croghan
James B. Dyer
Edmund Pendleton Gaines
Samuel P. Heintzelmann
Ethan Allen Hitchcock
Andrew Jackson
Thomas Sidney Jesup
Roger Jones
Alexander Macomb
George Brinton McClellan
Montgomery C. Meigs
Alfred Mordecai
James K. Polk
Eleazar Wheelock Ripley
Winfield Scott
Zachary Taylor
Martin Van Buren
Massachusetts Historical Society, Boston (microfilm courtesy of John Morris)
    Jacob Brown
New Jersey Historical Society, Newark
    Winfield Scott
New York Public Library, New York City
    James Monroe
New York State Library, Albany
    Charles Kitchel Gardner
Ohio Historical Society, Columbus
    William Allen Trimble
Old Colony Historical Society, Taunton, Mass.
    Francis Baylies Papers (letters to and from John E. Wool)
Historical Society of Pennsylvania, Philadelphia
    Military Papers of Captain Thomas J. Baird, Edward Carey Gardiner Collection
    Birch Family
    Cadwalader Family
    Edmund Pendleton Gaines
    Nauman Family
    Daniel Parker
William R. Perkins Library, Duke University
    Edward G. W. Butler
    Andrew Jackson
    Thomas Sidney Jesup

Southern Historical Collection, University of North Carolina, Chapel Hill
Alexander Macomb
Edward Brett Randolph Diary
Edmund Kirby Smith
Sterling Memorial Library, Yale University
Abraham L. Sands
Earl Gregg Swem Library, College of William and Mary
Patrick Henry Galt letters, in Galt Family Papers II
Tennessee Historical Society, Nashville
Edmund Pendleton Gaines (John W. Gaines Papers)
United States Army Military Historical Institute, Carlisle, Pennsylvania
William T. H. Brooks
Abraham Eustis
Maskell C. Ewing
Charles J. Nourse
Edwin Vose Sumner (Carlisle Papers)
Lucius B. Webster
Charles E. Woodruff
United States Military Academy Library, Special Collections, West Point, New York
Edmund Brooke Alexander
Robert Allen
Charles Benjamin Alvord
Robert Anderson
Jacob W. Bailey
Rufus Lathrop Baker
Philip Norbourne Barbour
Alexander H. Bowman
Braxton Bragg
William Chapman
Thomas Jefferson Cram
Napoleon Tecumseh Dana
Dialectic Society Journal, 1840–1844
James Duncan
William Dutton
Charles Winslow Elliott Collection, Winfield Scott Papers
Maskell C. Ewing
William Frazer
Ulysses S. Grant
Henry Wager Halleck
Robert Hazlitt
George W. Hazzard
Abner Riviere Hetzel
Ethan Allen Hitchcock

Washington Hood
Joseph F. Irons
Abraham Robinson Johnston
Gouveneur Kemble
Minor Knowlton
Alexander Macomb
Dennis Hart Mahan
John K. F. Mansfield
Morris Smith Miller
John Michael O'Connor
Charles Petigru
John Pope
Samuel H. Raymond
Jeremiah Mason Scarrit
James Wall Schureman
Winfield Scott
Charles Ferguson Smith
Frederick Augustus Smith
Isaac Ingalls Stevens
Alexander J. Swift
Joseph Gardner Swift
Sylvanus Thayer
Joseph G. Totten
William Jenkins Worth

BOOKS, ARTICLES, AND DISSERTATIONS

Abbott, Andrew. *The System of Professions: An Essay on the Division of Expert Labor.* Chicago: University of Chicago Press, 1988.

Abernethy, David B. *The Dynamics of Global Dominance: European Overseas Empires, 1492–1980.* New Haven, Conn.: Yale University Press, 2000.

Abrahamson, James L. *America Arms for a New Century: The Making of a Great Military Power.* New York: Free Press, 1981.

Abrahamsson, Bengt. *Military Professionalization and Political Power.* Beverly Hills, Calif.: Sage, 1972.

Abrams, Philip. "Notes on the Difficulty of Studying the State." *Journal of Historical Sociology* 1 (March 1988): 58–89.

Adelman, Jeremy, and Stephen Aron. "From Borderlands to Borders: Empires, Nation-States, and the Peoples in between in North American History." *American Historical Review* 104 (June 1999): 814–841.

Adler, William D., and Andrew J. Polsky. "The State in a Blue Uniform." *Polity* 40 (July 2008): 348–354.

Albers, Patricia, and Jeanne Kay. "Sharing the Land: A Study in American Indian Territoriality." In *A Cultural Geography of North American Indians*, ed. Thomas E. Ross and Tyrel G. Moore. Boulder, Colo.: Westview Press, 1987.

Allen, Robert S. *His Majesty's Indian Allies: British Indian Policy in the Defense of Canada, 1774–1815*. Toronto: Dundurn, 1992.

Almaráz, Félix D., Jr. *Tragic Cavalier: Governor Manuel Salcedo of Texas, 1808–1813*. Austin: University of Texas Press, 1971.

American State Papers: Documents, Legislative and Executive, of the Congress of the United States. Washington, D.C.: Gales and Seaton, 1832–1861.

Anderson, David M., and David Killingray, eds. *Policing the Empire: Government, Authority, and Control, 1830–1940*. Manchester: Manchester University Press, 1991.

Anderson, Gary C. *Kinsmen of Another Kind: Dakota-White Relations in the Upper Mississippi Valley, 1650–1862*. Lincoln: University of Nebraska Press, 1984.

Andrew, C. M., and A. S. Kanya-Forstner. "Centre and Periphery in the Making of the Second French Empire, 1815–1920." *Journal of Imperial and Commonwealth History* 16, 3 (1988): 9–34.

Angevine, Robert. *The Railroad and the State: War, Politics and Technology in Nineteenth-Century America*. Stanford, Calif.: Stanford University Press, 2004.

Anna, Timothy E. *Spain and the Loss of America*. Lincoln: University of Nebraska Press, 1983.

Aron, Stephen. "Lessons in Conquest: Towards a Greater Western History." *Pacific Historical Quarterly* 63 (May 1994): 125–147.

Aronson, Sidney H. *Status and Kinship in the Higher Civil Service: Standards of Selection in the Administrations of John Adams, Thomas Jefferson, and Andrew Jackson*. Cambridge, Mass.: Harvard University Press, 1964.

Ashworth, John. *"Agrarians" and "Aristocrats": Party Political Ideology in the United States, 1837–1846*. Atlantic Highlands, N.J.: Humanities Press, 1983.

Astolfi, Douglas M. *Foundations of Destiny: A Foreign Policy of the Jacksonians, 1824–1837*. New York: Garland, 1989.

Atkinson, James R. *Splendid Land, Splendid People: The Chickasaw Indians to Removal*. Tuscaloosa: University of Alabama Press, 2004.

Babington, Anthony. *Military Intervention in Britain: From the Gordon Riots to the Gibraltar Incident*. London: Routledge, 1990.

Baker, Jean H. *Affairs of Party: The Political Culture of Northern Democrats in the Mid-Nineteenth Century*. Ithaca, N.Y.: Cornell University Press, 1983.

Baker, Maury. "The Spanish War Scare of 1816." *Mid-America* 45 (April 1963): 67–78.

Baldwin, Peter. "Beyond Weak and Strong: Rethinking the State in Comparative Policy History." *Journal of Policy History* 17 (January 2005): 12–33.

Balough, Brian. *A Government Out of Sight: The Mystery of National Authority in Nineteenth-Century America*. Cambridge: Cambridge University Press, 2009.

Banner, Stuart. *How the Indians Lost Their Land: Law and Power on the Frontier*. Cambridge, Mass.: Harvard University Press, 2005.

Barbuto, Richard V. *Niagara 1814: America Invades Canada*. Lawrence: University Press of Kansas, 2000.

Barfield, Thomas J. *The Perilous Frontier: Nomadic Empires and China*. Oxford: Basil Blackwell, 1989.

Barr, Daniel P., ed. *The Boundaries between Us: Natives and Newcomers along the Frontiers of the Old Northwest Territory, 1750–1850*. Kent, Ohio: Kent State University Press, 2006.

Baud, Michiel, and Willem Van Schendel. "Toward a Comparative History of Borderlands." *Journal of World History* 8 (Fall 1997): 211–242.

Bauer, K. Jack. *Zachary Taylor: Soldier, Planter, and Statesman of the Old Southwest*. Baton Rouge: Louisiana State University Press, 1985.

Baumann, Robert F. *Russian-Soviet Unconventional Wars in the Caucasus, Central Asia, and Afghanistan*. Fort Leavenworth, Kans.: U.S. Army Combat Studies Institute, 1993.

Bayly, C. A. *Empire and Information: Intelligence-Gathering and Social Communication in India, 1780–1870*. Cambridge: Cambridge University Press, 1990.

———. *Imperial Meridian: The British Empire and the World, 1780–1830*. London: Longman, 1989.

Bearss, Edwin C., and Arrell M. Gibson. *Fort Smith: Little Gibraltar on the Arkansas*. Norman: University of Oklahoma Press, 1969.

Beckett, Ian. *The Victorians at War*. London: Hambleton and London, 2003.

Beers, Henry P. *The Western Military Frontier, 1815–1846*. 1935. Reprint, Philadelphia: Porcupine Press, 1975.

Belich, James. *The New Zealand Wars and the Victorian Interpretation of Racial Conflict*. Auckland, New Zealand: Auckland University Press, 1986.

———. *Replenishing the Earth: The Settler Revolution and the Rise of the Anglo-World, 1783–1939*. Oxford: Clarendon Press, 2009.

Belko, William S., ed. *America's Hundred Years' War: U. S. Expansion to the Gulf Coast and the Fate of the Seminole, 1763–1858, Essays in Honor of J. Leitch Wright, Jr*. Gainesville: University Press of Florida, 2010.

Belohlavek, John M. *"Let the Eagle Soar!" The Foreign Policy of Andrew Jackson*. Lincoln: University of Nebraska Press, 1985.

Beltman, Brian W. "Territorial Commands of the Army: The System Refined but Not Perfected, 1815–1821." *Journal of the Early Republic* 11(Summer 1991): 185–218.

Bemis, Samuel Flagg. *John Quincy Adams and the Foundations of American Foreign Policy*. New York: Alfred A. Knopf, 1949.

Bensel, Richard F. *Yankee Leviathan: The Origins of Central State Authority in America, 1859–1877*. Cambridge: Cambridge University Press, 1990.

Berkeley, George E. *The Democratic Policeman*. Boston: Beacon, 1969.

Berkhofer, Robert F. *The White Man's Indian: Images of the American Indian from Columbus to the Present*. New York: Alfred A. Knopf, 1978.

Best, Geoffrey. *War and Society in Revolutionary Europe, 1770–1870*. New York: St. Martin's Press, 1982.

Binnema, Ted, and William A. Dobak. "'Like the Greedy Wolf': The Blackfeet, the St. Louis Fur Trade, and War Fever, 1807–1831." *Journal of the Early Republic* 29 (Fall 2009): 411–440.

Black, Jeremy. *America as a Military Power: From the American Revolution to the Civil War.* Westport, Conn.: Praeger, 2002.

———. *War in the Nineteenth Century, 1800–1914.* Cambridge: Polity Press, 2009.

———. *Western Warfare, 1775–1882.* Bloomington: Indiana University Press, 2001.

Blaufarb, Rafe. *Bonapartists in the Borderlands: French Exiles and Refugees on the Gulf Coast, 1815–1835.* Tuscaloosa: University of Alabama Press, 2005.

———. "The Western Question: The Geopolitics of Latin American Independence." *American Historical Review* 112 (June 2007): 742–763.

Bledstein, Burton J. *The Culture of Professionalism: The Middle Class and the Development of Higher Education in America.* New York: W. W. Norton, 1976.

Blumin, Stuart M. *The Emergence of the Middle Class: Social Experience in the American City, 1760–1900.* Cambridge: Cambridge University Press, 1989.

———. "The Hypothesis of Middle-Class Formation in the Nineteenth Century: A Critique of Some Proposals." *American Historical Review* 90 (April 1985): 299–338.

Bolton, S. Charles. *Arkansas, 1800–1860: Remote and Restless.* Fayetteville: University of Arkansas Press, 1998.

Bond, Brian, ed. *Victorian Military Campaigns.* New York: Praeger, 1967.

Bourne, Kenneth. *Britain and the Balance of Power in North America, 1815–1908.* Berkeley: University of California Press, 1967.

Boyd, Mark F. "Events at Prospect Buff on the Apalachicola River, 1808–1818." *Louisiana Historical Quarterly* 15 (October 1937): 55–96.

Bradford, James C., ed. *Command under Sail: Makers of the American Naval Tradition, 1775–1850.* Annapolis, Md.: Naval Institute Press, 1985.

———. *The Military and Conflict between Cultures: Soldiers at the Interface.* College Station: Texas A&M University Press, 1997.

Bradley, Edward A. "Fighting for Texas: Filibuster James Long, the Adams-Onis Treaty, and the Monroe Administration." *Southwestern Historical Quarterly* 102 (January 1999): 323–342.

———. "Forgotten Filibusters: Private Hostile Expeditions from the United States into Spanish Texas, 1812–1821." Ph.D. diss., University of Illinois at Urbana-Champaign, 1999.

Bradley, Jared W. "W. C. C. Claiborne and Spain: Foreign Affairs under Jefferson and Madison, 1801–1811." *Louisiana History* 12 (Autumn 1971): 297–314 and 13 (Winter 1972): 5–26.

Brantlinger, Patrick. *Rule of Darkness: British Literature and Imperialism, 1830–1914.* Ithaca, N.Y.: Cornell University Press, 1988.

Brauer, Kinley J. "The United States and British Imperial Expansion, 1815–1860." *Diplomatic History* 12 (Winter 1988): 19–37.

Bright, Charles C. "The State in the United States in the Nineteenth Century." In

Statemaking and Social Movements: Essays in History and Theory, ed. Charles C. Bright and Susan Harding. Ann Arbor: University of Michigan Press, 1984.

Brooke, John L. "To Be 'Read by the Whole People': Press, Party, and Public Sphere in the United States, 1789–1840." *Proceedings of the American Antiquarian Society* 110 (2002): 89–118.

Brooks, Philip C. *Diplomacy and the Borderlands: The Adams-Onís Treaty of 1819.* Berkeley: University of California Press, 1939.

Brower, Benjamin Claude. *A Desert Named Peace: The Violence of France's Empire in the Algerian Sahara, 1844–1902.* New York: Columbia University Press, 2009.

Brower, Daniel R., and Edward J. Lazzerini, eds. *Russia's Orient: Imperial Borderlands and Peoples, 1700–1917.* Bloomington: Indiana University Press, 1997.

Brown, Alan S. "The Role of the Army in Western Settlement: Josiah Harmar's Command, 1785–1790." *Pennsylvania Magazine of History and Biography* 93 (April 1969): 161–178.

Brown, Canter, Jr. "The 'Sarazota, or Runaway Negro Plantations': Tampa Bay's First Black Community, 1812–1821." *Tampa Bay History* 12 (Fall–Winter 1990): 14–17.

Brown, Richard D. *Knowledge Is Power: The Diffusion of Information in Early America, 1700–1865.* New York: Oxford University Press, 1989.

Brown, Richard Maxwell. "Western Violence: Structure, Values, Myth." *Western Historical Quarterly* 24 (February 1993): 4–20.

Brown, Thomas. *Politics and Statesmanship: Essays on the American Whig Party.* New York: Columbia University Press, 1985.

Brown, Wilbur S. *The Amphibious Campaign for West Florida and Louisiana, 1814–1815: A Critical Review of Strategy and Tactics at New Orleans.* University: University of Alabama Press, 1969.

Bullock, Steven J. *Revolutionary Brotherhood: Freemasonry and the Transformation of the American Social Order, 1730–1840.* Chapel Hill: University of North Carolina Press, 1996.

Burbank, Jane, Mark von Hagen, and Anatolyi Remnev, eds. *Russian Empire: Space, People, and Power, 1700–1930.* Bloomington: Indiana University Press, 2007.

Burroughs, Peter. "Imperial Defence and the Victorian Army." *Journal of Imperial and Commonwealth History* 15, 1 (1986): 55–72.

Burt, A. L. *The United States, Great Britain, and British North America, from the Revolution to the Establishment of Peace after the War of 1812.* New Haven, Conn.: Yale University Press, 1940.

Bushman, Richard L. *The Refinement of America, 1750–1850: Persons, Houses, Cities.* New York: Alfred A. Knopf, 1993.

Byler, Charles. *Civil-Military Relations on the Frontier and Beyond, 1865–1917.* Westport, Conn.: Praeger Security International, 2006.

Byman, Daniel, and Matthew Waxman. *The Dynamics of Coercion: American Foreign Policy and the Limits of Military Power.* Cambridge: Cambridge University Press, 2002.

Caballero, Romeo Flores. *Counterrevolution: The Role of the Spaniards in the Inde-*

pendence of Mexico, 1804–1838, trans. Jaime E. Rodriguez O. Lincoln: University of Nebraska Press, 1969.

Cain, P. J., and A. G. Hopkins. *British Imperialism: Innovation and Expansion, 1688–2000*. London: Longman, 2001.

Calhoun, Daniel H. *Professional Lives in America: Structure and Aspiration, 1750–1850*. Cambridge, Mass.: Harvard University Press, 1965.

Calhoun, Frederick S. *The Lawmen: United States Marshals and Their Deputies, 1789–1989*. Washington, D.C.: Smithsonian Institution, 1989.

Calhoun, John C. *The Papers of John C. Calhoun*, vols. 2–9, ed. Robert L. Meriwether and W. Edwin Hemphill. Columbia: University of South Carolina Press, 1963–1976.

Calloway, Colin G. *Crown and Calumet: British-Indian Relations, 1783–1815*. Norman: University of Oklahoma Press, 1987.

———. "The End of an Era: British-Indian Relations in the Great Lakes Region after the War of 1812." *Michigan Historical Review* 12 (Fall 1986): 4–20.

Callwell, C. E. *Small Wars, Their Principles and Practice*, 3rd ed. 1906. Reprint, Lincoln: University of Nebraska Press, 1996.

Cannadine, David. *Ornamentalism: How the British Saw Their Empire*. New York: Oxford University Press, 2001.

Carp, E. Wayne. *To Starve the Army at Leisure: Continental Army Administration and American Political Culture, 1775–1783*. Chapel Hill: University of North Carolina Press, 1984.

Carpenter, Daniel P. *The Forging of Bureaucratic Autonomy: Reputations, Networks, and Policy Innovation in Executive Agencies, 1862–1928*. Princeton, N.J.: Princeton University Press, 2001.

Carroll, Francis M. *A Good and Wise Measure: The Search for the Canadian-American Boundary, 1783–1842*. Toronto: University of Toronto Press, 2001.

Cayton, Andrew R. L. "'Separate Interests' and the Nation-State: The Washington Administration and the Origins of Regionalism in the Trans-Appalachian West." *Journal of American History* 79 (June 1992): 39–67.

Cayton, Andrew R. L., and Fredrika J. Teute, eds. *Contact Points: American Frontiers from the Mohawk Valley to the Mississippi, 1750–1830*. Chapel Hill: University of North Carolina Press, 1998.

Cell, John W. *British Colonial Administration in the Mid-Nineteenth Century: The Policy-making Process*. New Haven, Conn.: Yale University Press, 1970.

Champagne, Duane. "A Multidimensional Theory of Colonialism: The Native North American Experience." *Journal of American Studies of Turkey* 3 (1996): 3–14.

Childress, David T. "The Army in Transition: The United States Army, 1815–1846." Ph.D. diss., Mississippi State University, 1974.

Christiansen, Eric. *The Origins of Military Power in Spain, 1800–1854*. Oxford: Clarendon Press, 1967.

Cipolla, Carlo M. "The Professions: The Long View." *Journal of European Economic History* 2 (Spring 1975): 37–52.

Citino, Nathan J. "The Global Frontier: Comparative History and the Frontier-Borderlands Approach in American Foreign Relations." *Diplomatic History* 25 (Fall 2001): 677–693.

Clayton, Anthony. *France, Soldiers, and Africa.* London: Brassey's, 1988.

Coakley, Robert W. *The Role of Federal Military Forces in Domestic Disorders, 1789–1878.* Washington, D.C.: Center of Military History, 1988.

Cobden, Richard. *How Wars Are Got Up in India: The Origin of the Burma War.* London: William and Frederick G. Cash, 1853.

Coffman, Edward M. *The Old Army: A Portrait of the American Army in Peacetime, 1784–1898.* New York: Oxford University Press, 1986.

———. *The Regulars: The American Army, 1898–1941.* Cambridge, Mass.: Harvard University Press, 2004.

Cohen, Eliot A. "The Unequal Dialogue: The Theory and Reality of Civil-Military Relations and the Use of Force." In *Soldiers and Civilians: The Civil-Military Gap and American National Security,* ed. Peter D. Feaver and Richard H. Kohn. Cambridge, Mass.: MIT Press, 2001.

Cole, Donald B. *The Presidency of Andrew Jackson.* Lawrence: University Press of Kansas, 1993.

Colley, Linda. *Britons: Forging the Nation, 1707–1837.* New Haven, Conn.: Yale University Press, 1992.

Collins, Bruce. "The Ideology of the Ante-bellum Northern Democrats." *American Studies* 11 (April 1977): 103–121.

Connelly, Donald. *John M. Schofield and the Politics of Generalship.* Chapel Hill: University of North Carolina Press, 2006.

Connor, John. *The Australian Frontier Wars, 1788–1838.* Sydney: University of New South Wales Press, 2002.

Cook, Hugh. *The Sikh Wars: The British Army in the Punjab, 1845–1849.* London: Leo Cooper, 1975.

Cooke, Philip St. George. *Scenes and Adventures in the Army, or, the Romance of Military Life.* Philadelphia: Lindsay and Blakiston, 1857.

Cooper, Jerry M. *The Army and Civil Disorder: Federal Military Intervention in Labor Disputes, 1877–1900.* Westport, Conn.: Greenwood Press, 1979.

Corning, Charles R. "General Eleazar Wheelock Ripley." *Granite Monthly* 17 (July 1894): 1–10.

Corrigan, Philip, and Derek Sayer. *The Great Arch: English State Formation as Cultural Revolution.* Oxford: Basil Blackwell, 1985.

Costeloe, Michael P. *Response to Revolution: Imperial Spain and the Spanish American Revolutions, 1810–1840.* Cambridge: Cambridge University Press, 1986.

Covington, James W. "The Negro Fort." *Gulf Coast Historical Review* 5 (1990): 78–91.

———. *The Seminoles of Florida.* Gainesville: University Press of Florida, 1993.

Cox, J. Wendel. "A World Together, a World Apart: The United States and the Arikaras, 1803–1851." Ph.D. diss., University of Minnesota, 1998.

Crackel, Theodore J. *Mr. Jefferson's Army: Political and Social Reform of the Military Establishment, 1801–1809*. New York: New York University Press, 1987.

———. *West Point: A Bicentennial History*. Lawrence: University Press of Kansas, 2002.

Craig, Gordon A. *The Politics of the Prussian Army, 1640–1945*. New York: Oxford University Press, 1955.

Crenson, Matthew A. *The Federal Machine: The Beginnings of Bureaucracy in Jacksonian America*. Baltimore: Johns Hopkins University Press, 1975.

Cress, Lawrence Delbert. *Citizens in Arms: The Army and the Militia in American Society to the War of 1812*. Chapel Hill: University of North Carolina Press, 1982.

Crowder, Michael, ed. *West African Resistance: The Military Response to Colonial Occupation*. London: Hutchinson, 1971.

Cullum, George W., comp. *Biographical Register of the Officers and Graduates of the U.S. Military Academy*. 2 vols. New York: D. Van Nostrand, 1868.

Cunliffe, Marcus. *Soldiers and Civilians: The Martial Spirit in America, 1776–1865*, 2nd ed. New York: Free Press, 1973.

Currie, David P. "Rumors of War: Presidential and Congressional War Powers, 1809–1829." *University of Chicago Law Review* 67 (Winter 2000): 1–40.

Curtiss, John Shelton. *The Russian Army under Nicholas I, 1825–1855*. Durham, N.C.: Duke University Press, 1965.

Dandeker, Christopher. *Surveillance, Power, and Modernity: Bureaucracy and Discipline from 1700 to the Present Day*. New York: St. Martin's Press, 1990.

Daniel, Donald C. F., Patricia Taft, and Sharon Wiharta, eds. *Peace Operations: Trends, Progress, and Prospects*. Washington, D.C.: Georgetown University Press, 2008.

Danziger, Raphael. *Abd al-Qadir and the Algerians: Resistance to the French and Internal Consolidation*. New York: Holmes and Meier, 1977.

Darwin, John. "Imperialism and the Victorians: The Dynamics of Territorial Expansion." *English Historical Review* 112 (June 1997): 634–640.

Davis, Karl. "'Remember Fort Mims': Reinterpreting the Origins of the Creek War." *Journal of the Early Republic* 22 (Winter 2002): 611–636.

Davis, T. Frederick. "MacGregor's Invasion of Florida." *Florida Historical Quarterly* 7 (July 1928): 3–71.

———. *MacGregor's Invasion of Florida, 1817*. Jacksonville: Florida Historical Society, 1928.

Davis, William C. *The Pirates Laffite: The Treacherous World of the Gulf Corsairs*. New York: Harcourt, 2005.

Dawson, Graham. *Soldier Heroes: British Adventure, Empire, and the Imagining of Masculinities*. London: Routledge, 1994.

Dawson, Joseph G., III. *Army Generals and Reconstruction: Louisiana, 1862–1877*. Baton Rouge: Louisiana State University Press, 1982.

Debo, Angie. *The Road to Disappearance*. Norman: University of Oklahoma Press, 1941.

D'Elia, Donald J. "The Argument over Civilian or Military Indian Control, 1865–1880." *Historian* 24 (February 1962): 207–225.

Deloria, Philip J. *Playing Indian.* New Haven, Conn.: Yale University Press, 1998.

Demeter, Karl. *The German Officer Corps in State and Society,* rev. ed. New York: Praeger, 1965.

deMoor, J. A., and H. L. Wesseling, eds. *Imperialism and War: Essays on Colonial Wars in Asia and Africa.* Leiden, Netherlands: Brill, 1989.

DePalo, William A., Jr. *The Mexican National Army, 1822–1852.* College Station: Texas A&M University Press, 1997.

Deudney, Daniel. "Binding Sovereigns: Authorities, Structures, and Geopolitics in Philadelphian Systems." In *State Sovereignty as Social Construct,* ed. Thomas J. Biersteker and Cynthia Weber. Cambridge: Cambridge University Press, 1996.

Diehl, Paul F. *Peace Operations.* Cambridge: Polity Press, 2008.

Dippie, Brian W. *The Vanishing American: White Attitudes and U.S. Indian Policy.* Middletown, Conn.: Wesleyan University Press, 1982.

Donnelly, Alton S. *The Russian Conquest of Bashkiria, 1552–1740.* New Haven, Conn.: Yale University Press, 1968.

Dowd, Gregory Evans. *A Spirited Resistance: The North American Indian Struggle for Unity, 1745–1815.* Baltimore: Johns Hopkins University Press, 1991.

Downs, Fane. "Governor Antonio Martinez and the Defense of Texas from Foreign Invasion, 1817–1822." *Texas Military History* 7 (Spring 1968): 27–43.

Drinnon, Richard. *Facing West: The Metaphysics of Indian-Hating and Empire Building.* Minneapolis: University of Minnesota Press, 1980.

Drinnon, Richard F. "The Metaphysics of Empire-Building: American Imperialism in the Age of Jefferson and Monroe." *Massachusetts Review* 16 (Autumn 1975) 666–688.

Duffy, Christopher. *The Military Experience in the Age of Reason.* New York: Atheneum, 1988.

Durkheim, Emile. *Professional Ethics and Civic Morals,* trans. Cornelia Brookfield. London: Routledge and Kegan Paul, 1957.

Du Val, Kathleen. *The Native Ground: Indians and Colonists in the Heart of the Continent.* Philadelphia: University of Pennsylvania Press, 2006.

Dyer, Brainerd. *Zachary Taylor.* Baton Rouge: Louisiana State University Press, 1946.

Earle, Carville, and Changyong Cao. "Frontier Closure and the Involution of American Society, 1840–1890." *Journal of the Early Republic* 13 (Summer 1993): 163–179.

Eblen, Jack Ericson. *The First and Second United States Empires: Governors and Territorial Government, 1784–1912.* Pittsburgh: University of Pittsburgh Press, 1968.

Edling, Max M. *A Revolution in Favor of Government: Origins of the U.S. Constitution and the Making of the American State.* New York: Oxford University Press, 2003.

Elias, Norbert. *The Civilizing Process. Part I: The History of Manners,* trans. Edmund Jephcott. 1939. Reprint, New York: Urizen Books, 1978.

————. *The Civilizing Process. Part II: Power and Civility*, trans. Edmund Jephcott. 1939. Reprint, New York: Pantheon, 1982.

————. *The Court Society*, trans. Edmund Jephcott. 1969. Reprint, Oxford: Basil Blackwell, 1983.

Elliott, Charles Winslow. *Winfield Scott: The Soldier and the Man*. New York: Macmillan, 1937.

Elliott, Philip. *The Sociology of the Professions*. New York: Herder and Herder, 1972.

Ellis, Steven G. *Tudor Frontiers and Noble Power: The Making of the British State*. Oxford: Clarendon Press, 1995.

Emmons, David M. "Constructed Province: History and the Making of the Last American West." *Western Historical Quarterly* 25 (Winter 1994): 437–459.

Epstein, Robert M. "Patterns of Change and Continuity in Nineteenth-Century Warfare." *Journal of Military History* 56 (July 1992): 375–388.

Escott, Paul D. *Military Necessity: Civil-Military Relations in the Confederacy*. Westport, Conn.: Praeger Security International, 2006.

Ewers, John C. *The Blackfeet: Raiders on the Northwestern Plains*. Norman: University of Oklahoma Press, 1958.

Farwell, Byron. *Eminent Victorian Soldiers: Seekers of Glory*. New York: W. W. Norton, 1985.

Faye, Stanley. "Commodore Aury." *Louisiana Historical Quarterly* 24 (July 1941): 611–697.

Feaver, Peter D. *Armed Servants: Agency, Oversight, and Civil-Military Relations*. Cambridge, Mass.: Harvard University Press, 2003.

————. "The Civil-Military Problematique: Huntington, Janowitz, and the Question of Civilian Control." *Armed Forces and Society* 23 (Winter 1996): 149–178.

Feld, Maury D. *The Structure of Violence: Armed Forces as Social Systems*. Beverly Hills, Calif.: Sage, 1977.

Feller, Daniel. *The Jacksonian Promise: America, 1815–1840*. Baltimore: Johns Hopkins University Press, 1995.

————. "Politics and Society: Toward a Jacksonian Synthesis." *Journal of the Early Republic* 10 (Summer 1990): 135–161.

————. "The Seminole Controversy Revisited: A New Look at Andrew Jackson's 1818 Florida Campaign." *Florida Historical Quarterly* 88 (Winter 2010): 309–325.

Ferguson, R. Brian, and Neil L. Whitehead, eds. *War in the Tribal Zone: Expanding States and Indigenous Warfare*. Santa Fe, N.M.: School of American Research Press, 1992.

Field, James A., Jr. "1789–1820: All Oeconomists, All Diplomats." In *Economics and World Power: An Assessment of American Diplomacy since 1789*, ed. William H. Becker and Samuel F. Wells. New York: Columbia University Press, 1984.

Field, Peter S. *The Crisis of the Standing Order: Clerical Intellectuals and Cultural Authority in Massachusetts, 1780–1833*. Amherst: University of Massachusetts Press, 1998.

Fielding, A. G., and D. Portwood. "Professions and the State: Towards a Typology of Bureaucratic Professions." *Sociological Review* 28 (February 1980): 23–54.

Finer, Samuel E. *The Man on Horseback: The Role of the Military in Politics.* 1964. Rev. ed., Boulder, Colo.: Westview Press, 1988.

Fitzgerald, Michael S. "Europe and the United States Defense Establishment: American Military Policy and Strategy, 1815–1821." Ph.D. diss., Purdue University, 1990.

———. "'Nature Unsubdued': Diplomacy, Expansion and the American Military Buildup of 1815–1816." *Mid-America* 77 (Winter 1995): 5–32.

———. "Rejecting Calhoun's Expansible Army Plan: The Army Reduction Act of 1821." *War in History* 3 (Summer 1996): 161–185.

Foley, William E. *The Genesis of Missouri from Wilderness Outpost to Statehood.* Columbia: University of Missouri Press, 1989.

Foreman, Carolyn T. "General Bennet Riley, Commandant at Fort Gibson and Governor of California." *Chronicles of Oklahoma* 19 (September 1941): 225–244.

Formisano, Ronald P. "Deferential-Participant Politics: The Early Republic's Political Culture, 1789–1840." *American Political Science Review* 68 (June 1974): 473–487.

"Forum: The Middle Ground Revisited." *William and Mary Quarterly,* 3rd ser., 63 (January 2006): 3–96.

"Forum on the American State." *Polity* 40 (July 2008).

Frank, Andrew K. *Creeks and Southerners: Biculturalism on the Early American Frontier.* Lincoln: University of Nebraska Press, 2005.

Franklin, John Hope. *The Militant South, 1800–1861.* Cambridge, Mass.: Harvard University Press, 1956.

Fredrikson, John C. *Shield of Republic, Sword of Empire: A Bibliography of United States Military Affairs, 1783–1846.* Westport, Conn.: Greenwood Press, 1990.

Galbraith, John S. "The 'Turbulent Frontier' as a Factor in British Expansion." *Comparative Studies in Society and History* 2 (January 1960): 150–168.

Gallant, Thomas W. "Brigandage, Piracy, Capitalism, and State Formation: Transnational Crime from a Historical World-Systems Perspective." In *States and Illegal Practices,* ed. Josiah McC. Heyman. Oxford: Berg, 1999.

Gardner, Charles K., comp. *A Dictionary of the Officers of the Army of the United States.* New York: G. P. Putnam, 1860.

Garrett, Julia K. *Green Flag over Texas.* Dallas: Cordova Press, 1939.

Garver, John B., Jr. "Practical Military Geographers and Mappers of the Trans-Missouri West, 1820–1860." In *Mapping the North American Plains: Essays in the History of Cartography,* ed. Frederick C. Luebke, Francis W. Kaye, and Gary Moulton. Norman: University of Oklahoma Press, 1987.

———. "The Role of the United States Army in the Colonization of the Trans-Missouri West: Kansas, 1804–1861." Ph.D. diss., Syracuse University, 1981.

Gates, David. *Warfare in the Nineteenth Century.* New York: Palgrave, 2001.

Gates, John M. "The Alleged Isolation of the U.S. Army Officers in the Late Nineteenth Century." *Parameters* 10 (Spring 1980): 32–45.

———. "Indians and Insurrectos: The U.S. Army's Experience with Insurgency." *Parameters* 13 (March 1983): 59–68.

Geison, Gerald L., ed. *Professions and the French State.* Philadelphia: University of Pennsylvania Press, 1984.

———. *Professions and Professional Ideologies in America.* Chapel Hill: University of North Carolina Press, 1983.

George, Alexander L., and William E. Simons, eds. *The Limits of Coercive Diplomacy*, 2nd ed. Boulder, Colo.: Westview Press, 1994.

Gerth, Hans, and C. Wright Mills. *Character and Social Structure: The Psychology of Social Institutions.* New York: Harcourt, Brace, 1953.

———, eds. *From Max Weber: Essays in Sociology.* New York: Oxford University Press, 1946.

Gibson, Arrell M. *The Kickapoos: Lords of the Middle Border.* Norman: University of Oklahoma Press, 1963.

Giddens, Anthony. *The Nation-State and Violence: Volume Two of a Contemporary Critique of Historical Materialism.* Berkeley: University of California Press, 1985.

Gilbert, Felix. *To the Farewell Address: Ideas of Early American Foreign Policy.* Princeton, N.J.: Princeton University Press, 1961.

Gitlin, Jay. "Private Diplomacy to Private Property: States, Tribes, and Nations in the Early National Period." *Diplomatic History* 22 (Winter 1998): 85–99.

Goldberg, David Theo. *The Racial State.* Oxford: Blackwell, 2002.

Gordon, William A., comp. *A Compilation of Registers of the Army of the United States, from 1815 to 1837.* Washington, D.C.: James C. Dunn, 1837.

Goss, Thomas J. *The War within the Union High Command: Politics and Generalship during the Civil War.* Lawrence: University Press of Kansas, 2003.

Gough, Terrence J. "Isolation and Professionalization of the Army Officer Corps: A Post-Revisionist View of the Soldier and the State." *Social Science Quarterly* 73 (June 1992): 420–436.

Gould, Eliga H. "The Making of an Atlantic State System: Britain and the United States, 1795–1825." In *Britain and America Go to War: The Impact of War and Warfare in Anglo-America, 1754–1815*, ed. Julie Flavell and Stephen Conway. Gainesville: University Press of Florida, 2004.

Grandstaff, Mark R. "Preserving the 'Habits and Usages of War': William Tecumseh Sherman, Professional Reform, and the U.S. Army Officer Corps, 1865–1881, Revisited." *Journal of Military History* 62 (July 1998): 521–545.

Grenier, John. *The First Way of War: American War Making on the Frontier, 1607–1814.* Cambridge: Cambridge University Press, 2005.

Griess, Thomas E. "Dennis Hart Mahan: West Point Professor and Advocate of Military Professionalism, 1830–1871." Ph.D. dissertation, Duke University, 1968.

Griffin, Charles C. *The United States and the Disruption of the Spanish Empire, 1810–1822.* New York: Columbia University Press, 1937.

Grippaldi, Richard N. "The Politics of Appointment in the Jacksonian Army: The (Non)Transfer of Ethan Allen Hitchcock to the Regiment of Dragoons, 1833." *Army History* 70 (Winter 2009): 26–35.

Gronet, Richard. "United States and the Invasion of Texas, 1810–1814." *Americas* 25 (January 1969): 281–306.

Guice, John D. W., and Thomas D. Clark. *Frontiers in Conflict: The Old Southwest, 1795–1830.* Albuquerque: University of New Mexico Press, 1989.

Gump, James O. *The Dust Rose Like Smoke: The Subjugation of the Zulu and the Sioux.* Lincoln: University of Nebraska Press, 1994.

Gunn, L. Ray. *The Decline of Authority: Public Economic Policy and Political Development in New York, 1800–1860.* Ithaca, N.Y.: Cornell University Press, 1988.

Gyarmati, Gabriel. "Ideologies, Roles, and Aspirations: The Doctrine of the Professions—The Basis of a Power Structure." *International Social Science Journal* 27 (November 1975): 629–654.

Haber, Samuel. *The Quest for Authority and Honor in the American Professions, 1750–1900.* Chicago: University of Chicago Press, 1991.

Hagan, Kenneth J., and William R. Roberts, eds. *Against All Enemies: Interpretations of American Military History from Colonial Times to the Present.* Westport, Conn.: Greenwood Press, 1986.

Hagan, William T. *The Sac and Fox Indians.* Norman: University of Oklahoma Press, 1958.

Hagerman, Edward L. *The American Civil War and the Origins of Modern Warfare: Ideas, Organization, and Field Command.* Bloomington: Indiana University Press, 1988.

Haggard, Villasana. "The Neutral Ground between Louisiana and Texas." *Louisiana Historical Quarterly* 28 (October 1945): 1001–1128.

Halbert, H. S., and T. H. Ball. *The Creek War of 1813 and 1814.* University: University of Alabama Press, 1969.

Hall, Peter Dobkin. *The Organization of American Culture, 1700–1900: Private Institutions, Elites, and the Origins of American Nationality.* New York: New York University Press, 1982.

Hall, Richard H. "Professionalization and Bureaucratization." *American Sociological Review* 22 (April 1957): 92–104.

Hamerow, Theodore S. *The Birth of a New Europe: State and Society in the Nineteenth Century.* Chapel Hill: University of North Carolina Press, 1983.

Hamersly, Thomas H. S., comp. *Complete Regular Army Register of the Unites States, for One Hundred Years (1779 to 1879).* Washington, D.C.: T. H. S. Hamersly, 1880.

Hannah, Matthew G. *Governmentality and the Mastery of Territory in Nineteenth-Century America.* Cambridge: Cambridge University Press, 2000.

Hansen, Marcus L. *Old Fort Snelling, 1819–1858.* Minneapolis: Ross and Haines, 1958.

Harries-Jenkins, Gwyn. *The Army in Victorian Society.* London: Routledge and Kegan Paul, 1977.

———. "The Development of Professionalism in the Victorian Army." *Armed Forces and Society* 1 (Summer 1975): 472–489.

Hartley, Janet. *Russia, 1762–1825: Military Power, the State, and the People.* Westport, Conn.: Praeger, 2008.

Harvey, Robert. *Liberators: Latin America's Struggle for Independence, 1810–1830.* Woodstock, N.Y.: Overlook Press, 2000.

Haskell, Thomas L. *The Emergence of Professional Social Science: The American Social Science Association and the Nineteenth-Century Crisis of Authority.* Urbana: University of Illinois Press, 1977.

Hatch, Nathan O., ed. *The Professions in American History.* Notre Dame, Ind.: University of Notre Dame Press, 1988.

Hatfield, Joseph T. *William Claiborne: Jeffersonian Centurion in the American Southwest.* Lafayette: University of Southwestern Louisiana, 1976.

Hauptman, Laurence M. *Tribes & Tribulations: Misconceptions about American Indians and Their Histories.* Albuquerque: University of New Mexico Press, 1995.

Haynes, Sam W. *Unfinished Revolution: The Early American Republic in a British World.* Charlottesville: University Press of Virginia, 2011.

Headrick, Daniel R. *The Tools of Empire: Technology and European Imperialism in the Nineteenth Century.* New York: Oxford University Press, 1981.

———. *When Information Came of Age: Technologies of Knowledge in the Age of Reason and Revolution, 1700–1850.* New York: Oxford University Press, 2000.

Hechter, Michael. *Internal Colonialism: The Celtic Fringe in British National Development, 1536–1966.* Berkeley: University of California Press, 1975.

Heidler, David S. "The Politics of National Aggression: Congress and the First Seminole War." *Journal of the Early Republic* 13 (Winter 1993): 501–530.

Heidler, David S., and Jeanne T. Heidler. "Between a Rock and a Hard Place: Allied Creeks and the United States, 1814–1818." *Alabama Review* 50 (October 1997): 267–289.

———. *Old Hickory's War: Andrew Jackson and the Quest for Empire.* Mechanicsburg, Pa.: Stackpole Books, 1996.

Heidler, Jeanne T. "The Military Career of David E. Twiggs." Ph.D. dissertation, Auburn University, 1988.

Heitman, Francis B., comp. *Historical Registry and Dictionary of the United States Army, from Its Organization, September 29, 1789 to March 2, 1903.* 2 vols. Washington, D.C.: Government Printing Office, 1903.

Henderson, Dwight F. *Congress, Courts, and Criminals: The Development of Federal Criminal Law, 1801–1829.* Westport, Conn.: Greenwood Press, 1985.

Henderson, Harry McCorry. "The Gutiérrez-Magee Expedition." *Southwestern Historical Quarterly* 55 (July 1951): 43–61.

Hendrickson, David C. *Union, Nation, or Empire: The American Debate over International Relations, 1789–1941.* Lawrence: University Press of Kansas, 2009.

Henri, Florette. *The Southern Indians and Benjamin Hawkins, 1796–1816.* Norman: University of Oklahoma Press, 1986.

Herman, Daniel J. "Romance on the Middle Ground." *Journal of the Early Republic* 19 (Summer 1999): 279–291.

Hernon, Ian. *Britain's Forgotten Wars: Colonial Campaigns of the 19th Century*. London: Sutton Publishing, 2003.

Herrera, Ricardo. "Self-Governance and the American Citizen as Soldier." *Journal of Military History* 65 (January 2001): 21–52.

Hickey, Donald R. *The War of 1812: A Forgotten Conflict*. Urbana: University of Illinois Press, 1989.

Higham, John. *From Boundlessness to Consolidation: The Transformation of American Culture, 1848–1860*. Ann Arbor, Mich.: William L. Clements Library, 1969.

Hill, Forest G. *Roads, Rails, and Waterways: The Army Engineers and Early Transportation*. Norman: University of Oklahoma Press, 1957.

Hinderaker, Eric. *Elusive Empires: Constructing Colonialism in the Ohio Valley, 1673–1800*. Cambridge: Cambridge University Press, 1997.

Hirst, Paul. *Space and Power: Politics, War, and Architecture*. Cambridge: Polity Press, 2005.

Hoffman, Paul E. *Florida's Frontiers*. Bloomington: Indiana University Press, 2002.

Hoig, Stanley W. *White Man's Paper Trail: Grand Councils and Treaty-Making on the Central Plains*. Boulder: University of Colorado Press, 2006.

Holden, Robert H. *Armies without Nations: Public Violence and State Formation in Central America, 1821–1960*. New York: Oxford University Press, 2004.

Holroyd, Richard. "The Bourbon Army, 1815–1830." *Historical Journal* 14 (September 1971): 529–552.

Horsman, Reginald. "The Dimensions of an 'Empire for Liberty': Expansion and Republicanism, 1775–1825." *Journal of the Early Republic* 9 (Spring 1989): 1–20.

———. *Expansion and American Indian Policy, 1783–1812*. East Lansing: Michigan State University Press, 1967.

———. *The Origins of Indian Removal, 1815–1824*. Lansing: Michigan State University Press, 1970.

———. *Race and Manifest Destiny: The Origins of American Racial Anglo-Saxonism*. Cambridge, Mass.: Harvard University Press, 1981.

Hoskin, Keith W., and Richard H. Macve. "The Genesis of Accountability: The West Point Connections." *Accounting, Organizations, and Society* 13, 1 (1988): 37–73.

Howard, Michael, ed. *Soldiers and Governments: Nine Studies in Civil-Military Relations*. Bloomington: Indiana University Press, 1959.

Howe, Daniel Walker. *Making the American Self: Jonathan Edwards to Abraham Lincoln*. Cambridge, Mass.: Harvard University Press, 1997.

———. *The Political Culture of the American Whigs*. Chicago: University of Chicago Press, 1979.

———. "Victorian Culture in America." In *Victorian America*, ed. Daniel Walker Howe. Philadelphia: University of Pennsylvania Press, 1976.

———. *What Hath God Wrought? The Transformation of America, 1815–1848*. New York: Oxford University Press, 2007.

Hoxie, Frederick E. *Parading through History: The Making of the Crow Nation in America, 1805–1935.* Cambridge: Cambridge University Press, 1995.

Hoxie, Frederick E., Ronald Hoffman, and Peter J. Albert, eds. *Native Americans and the Early Republic.* Charlottesville: University Press of Virginia, 1999.

Hruby, Dale E. "The Civilian Careers of West Point Graduates, Classes of 1802 through 1833." M.A. thesis, Columbia University, 1965.

Hsieh, Wayne Wei-siang. *West Pointers and the Civil War: The Old Army in War and Peace.* Chapel Hill: University of North Carolina Press, 2009.

Huntington, Samuel P. *Political Order in Changing Societies.* New Haven, Conn.: Yale University Press, 1968.

———. *The Soldier and the State: The Theory and Practice of Civil-Military Relations.* Cambridge, Mass.: Harvard University Press, 1957.

Hurt, R. Douglas. *The Indian Frontier, 1763–1846.* Albuquerque: University of New Mexico Press, 2002.

Huttenback, Robert A. *British Relations with the Sind, 1799–1843: An Anatomy of Imperialism.* Berkeley: University of California Press, 1962.

Hyam, Ronald. *Britain's Imperial Century, 1815–1914: A Study of Empire and Expansion.* New York: Palgrave Macmillan, 2002.

Ikegami, Eiko. *The Taming of the Samurai: Honorific Individualism and the Making of Modern Japan.* Cambridge, Mass.: Harvard University Press, 1995.

Jackson, Andrew. *The Papers of Andrew Jackson,* 7 vols. to date, ed. Harold D. Moser et al. Knoxville: University of Tennessee Press, 1980–.

Jackson, Robert H. *Quasi-States: Sovereignty, International Relations, and the Third World.* Cambridge: Cambridge University Press, 1990.

Jacobs, James Ripley. *The Beginning of the U.S. Army, 1783–1812.* Princeton, N.J.: Princeton University Press, 1947.

———. *Tarnished Warrior: Major-General James Wilkinson.* New York: Macmillan, 1938.

Janowitz, Morris. *The Professional Soldier: A Social and Political Portrait.* New York: Free Press, 1960.

Jasanoff, Maya. *Edge of Empire: Lives, Culture, and Conquest in the East, 1750–1850.* New York: Alfred A. Knopf, 2005.

John, Richard R. "Affairs of Office: The Executive Departments, the Election of 1828, and the Making of the Democratic Party." In *The Democratic Experiment: New Directions in American Political History,* ed. Meg Jacobs, William J. Novak, and Julian E. Zelizer. Princeton, N.J.: Princeton University Press, 2003.

———. "Governmental Institutions as Agents of Change: Rethinking American Political Development in the Early Republic, 1787–1835." *Studies in American Political Development* 11 (Fall 1997): 347–380.

———. *Spreading the News: The American Postal System from Franklin to Morse.* Cambridge, Mass.: Harvard University Press, 1995.

Johnson, John J. *A Hemisphere Apart: The Foundations of United States Policy toward Latin America.* Baltimore: Johns Hopkins University Press, 1990.

Johnson, Paul. *The Birth of the Modern: World Society, 1815–1830.* New York: Harper-Collins, 1991.

Johnson, Sally A. "The Sixth's Elysian Fields: Fort Atkinson on the Council Bluffs." *Nebraska History* 40 (March 1959): 1–38.

Johnson, Terence P. *Professions and Power.* London: Macmillan, 1972.

———. "The Professions in the Class Structure." In *Industrial Society: Class, Cleavage, and Control,* ed. R. Scase. London: Allen and Unwin, 1977.

Johnson, Timothy D. *A Gallant Little Army: The Mexico City Campaign.* Lawrence: University Press of Kansas, 2007.

———. *Winfield Scott: The Quest for Military Glory.* Lawrence: University Press of Kansas, 1998.

Kagan, Frederick W. *The Military Reforms of Nicholas I: The Origins of the Modern Russian Army.* New York: St. Martin's, 1999.

Kanya-Forstner, A. S. *The Conquest of the Western Sudan: A Study in French Military Imperialism.* Cambridge: Cambridge University Press, 1969.

Kappler, Charles J., ed. *Indian Affairs: Laws and Treaties.* 4 vols. Washington, D.C.: Government Printing Office, 1903–1929.

Karsten, Peter. "Armed Progressives: The Military Reorganizes for the American Century." In *Building the Organizational Society: Essays on Associational Activities in Modern America,* ed. Jerry Israel, with an introduction by Samuel P. Hays. New York: Free Press, 1972.

———. *The Naval Aristocracy: The Golden Age of Annapolis and the Emergence of Modern American Navalism.* New York: Free Press, 1972.

Kastor, Peter J. "'Motives of Peculiar Urgency': Local Diplomacy in Louisiana, 1803–1821." *William and Mary Quarterly,* 3rd ser., 58 (October 2001): 819–848.

———. *The Nation's Crucible: The Louisiana Purchase and the Creation of America.* New Haven, Conn.: Yale University Press, 2004.

Katznelson, Ira, and Martin Shefter, eds. *Shaped by War and Trade: International Influences in American Political Development.* Princeton, N.J.: Princeton University Press, 2002.

Kaufmann, William W. *British Policy and the Independence of Latin America, 1804–1828.* New Haven, Conn.: Yale University Press, 1951.

Kavanaugh, Thomas W. *The Comanches: A History, 1706–1875.* Lincoln: University of Nebraska Press, 1996.

Keep, John L. H. *Soldiers of the Tsar: Army and Society in Russia, 1462–1874.* Oxford: Clarendon Press, 1985.

Keller, Morton. *Affairs of State: Public Life in Late Nineteenth-Century America.* Cambridge, Mass.: Harvard University Press, 1977.

Kennedy, Charles S. *The American Consul: A History of the United States Consular Service, 1776–1914.* Westport, Conn.: Greenwood Press, 1990.

Kennedy, Roger G. *Burr, Hamilton, and Jefferson: A Study in Character.* New York: Oxford University Press, 2000.

———. *Mr. Jefferson's Lost Cause: Land, Farmers, Slavery, and the Louisiana Purchase.* New York: Oxford University Press, 2003.

———. *Orders from France: The Americans and the French in a Revolutionary World, 1780–1820.* Philadelphia: University of Pennsylvania Press, 1990.

Khodarkovsky, Michael. *Russia's Steppe Frontier: The Making of a Colonial Empire, 1500–1800.* Bloomington: Indiana University Press, 2002.

———. *Where Two Worlds Meet: The Russian State and the Kalmyk Nomads, 1600–1771.* Ithaca, N.Y.: Cornell University Press, 1992.

Khoury, Philip S., and Joseph Kostiner, eds. *Tribes and State Formation in the Middle East.* Berkeley: University of California Press, 1990.

Kieffer, Chester L. *Maligned General: The Biography of Thomas Sidney Jesup.* San Rafael, Calif.: Presidio Press, 1979.

Kiernan, V. G. *Colonial Empires and Armies, 1815–1960.* Phoenix Mill, U.K.: Sutton Publishing, 1998.

Killingray, David, and David Omissi, eds. *Guardians of Empire: The Armed Forces of the Colonial Powers, c. 1700–1964.* Manchester: Manchester University Press, 1999.

Kimball, Bruce A. *The "True Professional Ideal" in America: A History.* Oxford: Blackwell, 1992.

King, Desmond, and Robert C. Lieberman. "Finding the American State: Transcending the 'Statelessness' Account." *Polity* 40 (July 2008): 368–378.

Knetsch, Joe. *Florida's Seminole Wars, 1817–1858.* Charleston, S.C.: Arcadia Books, 2003.

Knupfer, Peter B. *The Union as It Is: Constitutional Unionism and Sectional Compromise, 1787–1861.* Chapel Hill: University of North Carolina Press, 1991.

Kohl, Lawrence Frederick. *The Politics of Individualism: Parties and the American Character in the Jacksonian Era.* New York: Oxford University Press, 1989.

Kohn, Richard H. "American Generals of the Revolution: Subordination and Restraint." In *Reconsiderations on the Revolutionary War: Selected Essays,* ed. Don Higginbotham. Westport, Conn.: Greenwood Press, 1978.

———. *Eagle and Sword: The Federalists and the Creation of the Military Establishment in America, 1783–1802.* New York: Free Press, 1975.

Krasner, Stephen D. "Approaches to the State: Alternative Conceptions and Historical Dynamics." *Comparative Politics* 16 (January 1984): 223–246.

Kruman, Marc W. "The Second American Party System and the Transformation of Revolutionary Republicanism." *Journal of the Early Republic* 12 (Winter 1992): 509–537.

Lamar, Howard, and Leonard Thompson, eds. *The Frontier in History: North America and Southern Africa Compared.* New Haven, Conn.: Yale University Press, 1981.

Lambrick, H. T. *Sir Charles Napier and Sind.* Oxford: Clarendon Press, 1982.

Lang, Daniel G. *Foreign Policy in the Early Republic: The Law of Nations and the Balance of Power.* Baton Rouge: Louisiana State University Press, 1985.

Langley, Lester D. *The Struggle for the American Mediterranean: United States—*

European Rivalry in the Gulf-Caribbean, 1776–1904. Athens: University of Geor gia Press, 1976.

Langston, Thomas S. *Uneasy Balance: Civil-Military Relations in Peacetime America since 1783.* Baltimore: Johns Hopkins University Press, 2003.

Larson, John L. *Internal Improvement: National Public Works and the Promise of Popular Government in the Early United States.* Chapel Hill: University of North Carolina Press, 2001.

———. *The Market Revolution: Liberty, Ambition, and the Eclipse of the Public Good.* Cambridge: Cambridge University Press, 2010.

Larson, John Lauritz. "'Bind the Republic Together': The National Union and the Struggle for a System of Internal Improvements." *Journal of American History* 74 (September 1987): 363–387.

———. "Liberty by Design: Freedom, Planning, and John Quincy Adams's American System." In *The State and Economic Knowledge: The American and British Experiences,* ed. Mary O. Furner and Barry Supple. Cambridge: Cambridge University Press, 1990.

Larson, Magali Sarfatti. *The Rise of Professionalism: A Sociological Inquiry.* Berkeley: University of California Press, 1977.

Layton, Susan. *Russian Literature and Empire: Conquest of the Caucasus from Pushkin to Tolstoy.* Cambridge: Cambridge University Press, 1994.

Le Donne, John P. *The Russian Empire and the World, 1700–1917: The Geopolitics of Expansion and Containment.* New York: Oxford University Press, 1997.

Lee, Wayne. "Peace Chiefs and Blood Revenge: Patterns of Restraint in Native American Warfare, 1500–1800." *Journal of Military History* 71 (July 2007): 701–741.

Leonard, Thomas C. *The Power of the Press: The Birth of American Political Reporting.* New York: Oxford University Press, 1986.

———. "Red, White, and Army Blue: Empathy and Anger in the American West." *American Quarterly* 26 (May 1974): 176–190.

Levy, Avigdor. "The Officer Corps in Sultan Mahmud II's New Ottoman Army, 1826–1839." *International Journal of Middle Eastern Studies* 2 (January 1971): 21–39.

Lewis, James E., Jr. *The American Union and the Problem of Neighborhood: The United States and the Collapse of the Spanish Empire, 1783–1829.* Chapel Hill: University of North Carolina Press, 1998.

———. *John Quincy Adams: Policymaker for the Union.* Wilmington, Del.: Scholarly Resources, 2001.

Lieven, Dominic. *Empire: The Russian Empire and Its Rivals, from the Sixteenth Century to the Present.* London: Pimlico, 2003.

Limerick, Patricia Nelson. *The Legacy of Conquest: The Unbroken Past of the American West.* New York: W. W. Norton, 1987.

———. "Turnerians All." *American Historical Review* 100 (June 1995): 697–716.

Lincoln, W. Bruce. *The Conquest of a Continent: Siberia and the Russians.* New York: Random House, 1994.

Linn, Brian M. *"The American Way of War Revisited." Journal of Military History* 66 (April 2002): 501–530.

———. *The Echo of Battle: The Army's Way of War.* Cambridge, Mass.: Harvard University Press, 2007.

———. *Guardians of Empire: The U.S. Army and the Pacific, 1902–1940.* Chapel Hill: University of North Carolina Press, 1997.

———. "The Long Twilight of the Frontier Army." *Western Historical Quarterly* 27 (Summer 1996): 141–167.

Lockey, Joseph B. "The Florida Intrigues of Jose Alvarez de Toledo." *Florida Historical Quarterly* 12 (Fall 1934): 145–178.

Long, David F. *Gold Braid and Foreign Relations: Diplomatic Activities of U.S. Naval Officers, 1798–1883.* Annapolis, Md.: Naval Institute Press, 1988.

López-Alves, Fernando. *State Formation and Democracy in Latin America, 1810–1900.* Durham, N.C.: Duke University Press, 2000.

Lynch, John. *The Spanish-American Revolutions, 1808–1826.* New York: W. W. Norton, 1973.

Mackenzie, David. "Russian Expansion in Central Asia: St. Petersburg versus the Turkestan Generals." *Canadian Slavic Studies* 3 (1969): 286–311.

Mahon, John K. "British Strategy and the Southern Indians." *Florida Historical Quarterly* 44 (April 1966): 285–305.

Mahoney, Timothy R. *Provincial Lives: Middle-Class Experience in the Antebellum Middle West.* Cambridge: Cambridge University Press, 1999.

Malone, Lawrence J. *Opening the West: Federal Internal Improvements before 1860.* Westport, Conn.: Greenwood Press, 1998.

Mamedov, Mikail. "'Going Native' in the Caucasus: Problems of Russian Identity, 1801–64." *Russian Review* 67 (April 2008): 275–295.

Mann, Michael. "The Autonomous Power of the State: Its Origins, Mechanisms, and Results." *European Journal of Sociology* 26 (1985): 185–213.

———. *The Sources of Social Power: The Rise of Classes and Nation-States, 1760–1914.* Cambridge: Cambridge University Press, 1993.

———. *States, War, and Capitalism: Studies in Political Sociology.* Oxford: Basil Blackwell, 1988.

Matthews, Jean V. *Toward a New Society: American Thought and Culture, 1800–1830.* Boston: Twayne, 1991.

Mattison, Ray H. "The Military Frontier on the Upper Missouri." *Nebraska History* 37 (September 1956): 159–182.

May, Ernest R. *The Making of the Monroe Doctrine,* 2nd ed. Cambridge, Mass.: Harvard University Press, 1992.

May, Robert E. *Manifest Destiny's Underworld: Filibustering in Antebellum America.* Chapel Hill: University of North Carolina Press, 2002.

McAlister, Lyle N. "Pensacola during the Second Spanish Period." *Florida Historical Quarterly* 37 (April 1959): 281–327.

McCormick, Richard L. *The Party Period and Public Policy: American Politics from the Age of Jackson to the Progressive Era.* New York: Oxford University Press, 1986.

McCormick, Richard P. *The Second American Party System: Party Formation in the Jacksonian Era.* Chapel Hill: University of North Carolina Press, 1966.

McCoy, Drew R. *The Elusive Republic: Political Economy in Jeffersonian America.* Chapel Hill: University of North Carolina Press, 1980.

McCrady, David G. *Living with Strangers: The Nineteenth-Century Sioux and the Canadian-American Borderlands.* Lincoln: University of Nebraska Press, 2006.

McElwee, William. *The Art of War: Waterloo to Mons.* Bloomington: Indiana University Press, 1974.

McKee, Christopher. *A Gentlemanly and Honorable Profession: The Creation of the U.S. Naval Officer Corps, 1794–1815.* Annapolis, Md.: Naval Institute Press, 1991.

Meinig, D. W. *The Shaping of America: A Geographical Perspective on 500 Years of History.* Vol. 2, *Continental America, 1800–1867.* New Haven, Conn.: Yale University Press, 1993.

Merk, Frederick, and Lois Bannister Merk. *Manifest Destiny and American Mission in American History: A Reinterpretation.* New York: Alfred A. Knopf, 1963.

Metcalf, P. Richard. "Who Should Rule at Home? Native American Politics and Indian-White Relations." *Journal of American History* (December 1974): 651–665.

Meyer, Jean. "States, Roads, Armies, and the Organization of Space." In *War and Competition between States,* ed. Philippe Contamine. Oxford: Clarendon Press, for the European Science Foundation, 2000.

Meyers, Marvin. *The Jacksonian Persuasion: Politics and Belief.* New York: Vintage, 1957.

Meyerson, Harvey. *Nature's Army: When Soldiers Fought for Yosemite.* Lawrence: University Press of Kansas, 2001.

Migdal, Joel S. *State in Society: Studying How States and Societies Transform and Constitute One Another.* Cambridge: Cambridge University Press, 2001.

———. *Strong Societies and Weak States: State-Society Relations and State Capability in the Third World.* Princeton, N.J.: Princeton University Press, 1988.

Migdal, Joel S., Atul Kohli, and Vivienne Shue, eds. *State Power and Social Forces: Domination and Transformation in the Third World.* Cambridge: Cambridge University Press, 1994.

Miller, Douglas T. *The Birth of Modern America, 1820–1850.* Indianapolis: Bobbs-Merrill, 1970.

———. *Jacksonian Aristocracy: Class and Democracy in New York, 1830–1860.* New York: Oxford University Press, 1967.

Miller, Perry. *The Life of the Mind in America: From the Revolution to the Civil War.* New York: Harcourt, Brace, and World, 1966.

Millett, Allan R. *Military Professionalism and Officership in America.* Columbus, Ohio: Mershon Center, 1977.

Millett, Nathaniel. "Britain's 1814 Occupation of Pensacola and America's Response: An Episode of the War of 1812 in the Southeastern Borderlands." *Florida Historical Quarterly* 84 (Fall 2005): 229–255.

———. "Defining Freedom in the Atlantic Borderlands of the Revolutionary Southeast." *Early American Studies* 5 (Fall 2007): 367–394.

———. "Slave Resistance during the Age of Revolution: The Maroon Community at Prospect Bluff, Spanish Florida." Ph.D. diss., Cambridge University, 2002.

Mills, C. Wright. *The Power Elite*. New York: Oxford University Press, 1958.

———. *White Collar*. New York: Oxford University Press, 1956.

Mitchell, Timothy. "The Limits of the State: Beyond Statist Approaches and Their Critics." *American Political Science Review* 85 (March 1991): 77–96.

Mkutu, Kennedy Agade. *Guns & Governance in the Rift Valley: Pastoralist Conflict & Small Arms*. Bloomington: Indiana University Press, 2008.

Morris, John D. *Sword of the Border: Major General Jacob Jennings Brown, 1775–1828*. Kent, Ohio: Kent State University Press, 2000.

Morrison, James L., Jr. *"The Best School in the World": West Point in the Pre–Civil War Years, 1833–1866*. Kent, Ohio: Kent State University Press, 1986.

———. "The Struggle between Sectionalism and Nationalism at Antebellum West Point." *Civil War History* 19 (June 1973): 138–148.

Moten, Matthew. *The Delafield Commission and the American Military Profession*. College Station: Texas A&M University Press, 2000.

Muir, William Ker, Jr. *Police: Streetcorner Politicians*. Chicago: University of Chicago Press, 1977.

Mullis, Tony R. *Peacekeeping on the Plains: Army Operations in Bleeding Kansas*. Columbia: University of Missouri Press, 2004.

Murphy, Lucy Eldersveld. *A Gathering of Rivers: Indians, Métis, and Mining in the Western Great Lakes, 1737–1832*. Lincoln: University of Nebraska Press, 2000.

Murrin, John. "The Jeffersonian Triumph and American Exceptionalism." *Journal of the Early Republic* 20 (Spring 2000): 1–25.

Myerly, Scott Hughes. *British Military Spectacle: From the Napoleonic Wars through the Crimea*. Cambridge, Mass.: Harvard University Press, 1996.

Narrett, David E. "José Bernardo Gutiérrez de Lara: Caudillo of the Mexican Republic in Texas." *Southwestern Historical Quarterly* 106 (October 2002): 195–228.

———. "Liberation and Conquest: John Hamilton Robinson and U.S. Adventurism toward Mexico, 1806–1819." *Western Historical Quarterly* 40 (Spring 2009): 23–50.

Nelson, Dana D. *National Manhood: Capitalist Citizenship and the Imagined Fraternity of White Men*. Durham, N.C.: Duke University Press, 1998.

Nelson, William E. *The Roots of American Bureaucracy, 1830–1900*. Cambridge, Mass.: Harvard University Press, 1982.

Nester, William R. *The Arikara War: The First Plains Indian War, 1823*. Missoula, Mont.: Mountain Press Publishing, 2001.

Nettl, J. P. "The State as a Conceptual Variable." *World Politics* 20 (July 1968): 559–592.

Newbury, Colin. *Patrons, Clients, and Empire: Chieftancy and Over-rule in Asia, Africa, and the Pacific.* Clarendon: Oxford University Press, 2003.

———. "Patrons, Clients, and Empire: The Subordination of Indigenous Hierarchies in Asia and Africa." *Journal of World History* 11 (Fall 2000): 227–263.

Ney, Virgil. *Fort on the Prairie: Fort Atkinson, on the Council Bluff, 1819–1827.* Washington, D.C.: Command Publications, 1978.

Nichols, David A. "Land, Republicanism, and Indians: Power and Policy in Early National Georgia, 1780–1825." *Georgia Historical Quarterly* 85 (Summer 2001): 199–226.

Nichols, David Andrew. *Red Gentlemen & White Savages: Indians, Federalists, and the Search for Order on the American Frontier.* Charlottesville: University Press of Virginia, 2008.

Nichols, Roger L. "The Army and Early Perceptions of the Plains." *Nebraska History* 56 (Spring 1975): 121–135.

———. "The Army and the Indians, 1800–1830—A Reappraisal: The Missouri Valley Example." *Pacific Historical Review* 41 (May 1972): 151–168.

———. "Backdrop for Disaster: Causes of the Arikara War of 1823." *South Dakota History* 14 (Summer 1984): 93–114.

———. *General Henry Atkinson: A Western Military Career.* Norman: University of Oklahoma Press, 1965.

———. "Martin Cantonment and American Expansion in the Missouri Valley." *Missouri Historical Review* 64 (October 1969): 1–17.

———, ed. *The Missouri Expedition, 1818–1820: The Journal of Surgeon John Gale with Related Documents.* Norman: University of Oklahoma Press, 1969.

Nordlinger, Eric A. *On the Autonomy of the Democratic State.* Cambridge, Mass.: Harvard University Press, 1981.

Novak, William J. "The Myth of the 'Weak' American State." *American Historical Review* 113 (June 2008): 752–772.

———. *The People's Welfare: Law and Regulation in Nineteenth-Century America.* Chapel Hill: University of North Carolina Press, 1996.

Noyes, Stanley. *Los Comanches: The Horse People, 1751–1845.* Albuquerque: University of New Mexico Press, 1993.

O'Connell, Charles F. "The U.S. Army and the Origins of Modern Management, 1818–1860." Ph.D. diss., Ohio State University, 1982.

Onuf, Peter S. *Jefferson's Empire: The Language of American Nationhood.* Charlottesville: University Press of Virginia, 2000.

———. "Liberty, Development, and Union: Visions of the West in the 1780s." *William and Mary Quarterly,* 3rd ser., 43 (April 1986): 179–213.

Onuf, Peter S., and Nicholas Onuf. *Federal Union, Modern World: The Law of Nations in an Age of Revolutions, 1776–1814.* Madison, Wisc.: Madison House, 1993.

Orren, Karen, and Stephen Skowronek. *The Search for American Political Development.* Cambridge: Cambridge University Press, 2004.

Ostler, Jeffrey. "Conquest and the State: Why the United States Employed Massive Military Force to Suppress the Lakota Ghost Dance." *Pacific Historical Review* 65 (May 1996): 217–248.

———. *The Plains Sioux and U.S. Colonialism from Lewis and Clark to Wounded Knee.* Cambridge: Cambridge University Press, 2004.

Owsley, Frank L., Jr. "Prophet of War: Josiah Francis and the Creek War." *American Indian Quarterly* 9 (Summer 1985): 273–293.

———. *The Struggle for the Gulf Borderlands: The Creek War and the Battle of New Orleans.* Gainesville: University Press of Florida, 1981.

Owsley, Frank L., Jr., and Gene A. Smith. *Filibusters and Expansionists: Jeffersonian Manifest Destiny, 1800–1821.* Tuscaloosa: University of Alabama Press, 1997.

Parker, Henry S. "Henry Leavenworth: Pioneer General." *Military Review* 50 (December 1970): 56–68.

Pasley, Jeffrey L. *"The Tyranny of Printers": Newspaper Politics in the Early American Republic.* Charlottesville: University Press of Virginia, 2001.

Patrick, Rembert W. *Aristocrat in Uniform: General Duncan L. Clinch.* Gainesville: University of Florida Press, 1963.

Pearce, Roy Harvey. *Savagism and Civilization: A Study of the Indian and the American Mind*, 2nd ed. Berkeley: University of California Press, 1988.

Peers, Douglas M. *Between Mars and Mammon: Colonial Armies and the Garrison State in India, 1819–1835.* London: I. B. Tauris, 1995.

Perkins, Bradford. *Castlereagh and Adams: England and the United States, 1812–1823.* Berkeley: University of California Press, 1964.

Perkins, Kenneth J. *Qaids, Captains, and Colons: French Military Administration in the Colonial Mahgrib, 1844–1934.* New York: Africana Publishing, 1981.

Perry, Lewis. *Boats against the Current: American Culture between Revolution and Modernity, 1820–1860.* New York: Oxford University Press, 1993.

Peskin, Allan. *Winfield Scott and the Profession of Arms.* Kent, Ohio: Kent State University Press, 2003.

Pessen, Edward. "The Egalitarian Myth and American Social Reality: Wealth, Mobility, and Opportunity in the 'Era of the Common Man.'" *American Historical Review* 76 (October 1971): 989–1034.

———. *Jacksonian America: Society, Personality, and Politics*, rev. ed. Homewood, Ill.: Dorsey Press, 1978.

———. *Riches, Class, and Power before the Civil War.* Lexington, Mass.: D. C. Heath, 1973.

Peters, Virginia B. *The Florida Wars.* Hamden, Conn.: Archon Books, 1979.

Polsky, Andrew J. "'Mr. Lincoln's Army' Revisited: Partisanship, Institutional Position, and Union Army Command, 1861–1865." *Studies in American Political Development* 16 (Fall 2002): 176–207.

Ponko, Vincent. "The Military Explorers of the American West, 1838–1860." In *North American Exploration*, vol. 3, *A Continent Comprehended*, ed. John Allen Logan. Lincoln: University of Nebraska Press, 1997.

Porch, Douglas. *Army and Revolution: France, 1815–1848*. London: Routledge and Kegan Paul, 1974.

———. *The Conquest of the Sahara*. New York: Alfred A. Knopf, 1984.

———. *Wars of Empire*. London: Cassell, 2000.

Porter, Andrew, ed. *Oxford History of the British Empire*. Vol. 3, *The Nineteenth Century*. London: Oxford University Press, 1999.

Porter, Kenneth Wiggins. *The Black Seminoles: History of a Freedom-Seeking People*, rev. and ed. Alcione M. Amos and Thomas P. Sutter. Gainesville: University Press of Florida, 1996.

———. "Negroes and the Seminole War, 1817–1818." *Journal of Negro History* 36 (July 1951): 249–280.

Porter, Valentine M., ed. "Journal of Stephen Watts Kearny, Part I: The Council Bluffs–St. Peter's Expedition, 1820." *Collections of the Missouri Historical Society* 3 (January 1908): 8–29.

Pouligny, Beatrice. *Peace Operations Seen from Below: UN Missions and Local People*. Bloomfield, Conn.: Kumarian Press, 2006.

Pound, Merritt B. *Benjamin Hawkins—Indian Agent*. Athens: University of Georgia Press, 1951.

Power, Daniel, and Naomi Standen, eds. *Frontiers in Question: Eurasian Borderlands, 700–1700*. London: Macmillan, 1999.

Price, Richard D. "The French Army and the Revolution of 1830." *European Studies Review* 3 (July 1973): 243–267.

Priest, Dana. *The Mission: Waging War and Keeping Peace with America's Military*. New York: W. W. Norton, 2003.

Prucha, Francis Paul. *American Indian Policy in the Formative Years: The Indian Trade and Intercourse Acts, 1790–1834*. Cambridge, Mass.: Harvard University Press, 1962.

———. *Broadax and Bayonet: The Role of the Army in the Development of the Northwest, 1815–1860*. Madison: State Historical Society of Wisconsin, 1953.

———. *The Great Father: The U.S. Government and the American Indians*. 2 vols. Lincoln: University of Nebraska Press, 1984.

———. *A Guide to the Military Posts of the United States, 1789–1895*. Madison: State Historical Society of Wisconsin, 1964.

———. *The Sword of the Republic: The United States Army on the Frontier, 1783–1846*. New York: Macmillan, 1969.

Pugh, David G. *Sons of Liberty: The Masculine Mind in Nineteenth-Century America*. Westport, Conn.: Greenwood Press, 1983.

Raelin, Joseph A. *The Clash of Cultures: Managers and Professionals*. Boston: Harvard Business School Press, 1986.

Rafuse, Ethan S. "'To Check . . . the Very Worst and Meanest of Our Passions': Common Sense, 'Cobbon Sense,' and the Socialization of Cadets at Antebellum West Point." *War in History* 16 (Fall 2009): 406–424.

Ralston, David B. *Importing the European Army: The Introduction of European Military Techniques and Institutions into the Extra-European World, 1600–1914.* Chicago: University of Chicago Press, 1990.

Ravenal, Earl C. "Ignorant Armies: The State, the Public, and the Making of Foreign Policy." *Critical Review* 14, 2–3 (2000): 327–374.

Razzell, P. E. "Social Origins of Officers in the Indian and British Home Army, 1758–1962." *British Journal of Sociology* 14 (September 1963): 248–260.

Reader, William J. *Professional Men: The Rise of the Professional Classes in Nineteenth-Century England.* New York: Basic Books, 1966.

Reese, Calvin. "The United States Army and the Indian: Low Plains Area, 1815–1854." Ph.D. diss., University of Southern California, 1963.

Reid, Russell, and Clell G. Gannon, eds. "Journal of the Atkinson-O'Fallon Expedition [1825]." *North Dakota Historical Quarterly* 4 (October 1929): 5–56.

Reinhard, Wolfgang, ed. *Power Elites and State Building.* Oxford: Clarendon Press, for the European Science Foundation, 1996.

Remini, Robert V. *Andrew Jackson and the Course of American Empire, 1767–1821.* New York: Harper and Row, 1977.

———. *Andrew Jackson and His Indian Wars.* New York: Viking, 2001.

Reséndez, Andrés. *Changing National Identities at the Frontier: Texas and New Mexico, 1800–1850.* Cambridge: Cambridge University Press, 2005.

Richter, William L. *The Army in Texas during Reconstruction, 1865–1870.* College Station: Texas A&M University Press, 1987.

Rippy, James F. *Rivalry of the United States and Great Britain over Latin America, 1808–1830.* Baltimore: Johns Hopkins University Press, 1929.

Ritter, Gerhard. *The Sword and the Scepter: The Problem of Militarism in Germany,* trans. Heinz Norden. 4 vols. Coral Gables, Fla.: University of Miami Press, 1969–1973.

Robbins, William G. *Colony and Empire: The Capitalist Transformation of the American West.* Lawrence: University Press of Kansas, 1994.

Robinson, Doane, ed. "Official Correspondence of the Leavenworth Expedition of 1823 into South Dakota for the Conquest of the Ree [Arikara] Indians." *South Dakota Historical Collections* 1 (1902): 179–256.

Robinson, R. E. "Non-European Foundations of European Imperialism: Sketch for a Theory of Collaboration." In *Studies in the Theory of Imperialism,* ed. R. Owen and B. Sutcliffe. Harlow, U.K.: Longman, 1972.

Robinson, R. E., and J. A. Gallagher. *Africa and the Victorians: The Official Mind of Imperialism.* London: Macmillan, 1961.

Rockwell, Stephen J. *Indian Affairs and the Administration State in the Nineteenth Century.* Cambridge: Cambridge University Press, 2010.

Rodriguez O., Jaime E. *The Independence of Spanish America*. Cambridge: Cambridge University Press, 1998.

Rogin, Michael Paul. *Fathers and Children: Andrew Jackson and the Subjugation of the American Indian*. New York: Alfred A. Knopf, 1975.

Rohrbough, Malcolm J. *The Land Office Business: The Settlement and Administration of American Public Lands, 1789–1837*. New York: Oxford University Press, 1968.

———. *The Trans-Appalachian Frontier: People, Societies, and Institutions, 1775–1850*. New York: Oxford University Press, 1978.

Rollings, Willard H. *The Osage: An Ethnohistorical Study of Hegemony on the Prairie-Plains*. Columbia: University of Missouri Press, 1992.

Rosen, Deborah A. *American Indians and State Law: Sovereignty, Race, and Citizenship, 1790–1880*. Lincoln: University of Nebraska Press, 2007.

———. "Wartime Prisoners and the Rule of Law: Andrew Jackson's Military Tribunals during the First Seminole War." *Journal of the Early Republic* 28 (Winter 2008): 559–595.

Rosen, Stephen Peter. "Alexander Hamilton and the Domestic Uses of International Law." *Diplomatic History* 5 (Summer 1981): 183–198.

Rothenberg, Gunther E. "The Austrian Army in the Age of Metternich." *Journal of Modern History* 40 (June 1968): 155–165.

Rotundo, E. Anthony. *American Manhood: Transformations in Masculinity from the Revolutionary Era to the Present*. New York: Basic Books, 1993.

"Roundtable on American Colonial, Postcolonial, and National Histories." *William and Mary Quarterly*, 3rd ser., 64 (April 2007): 235–286.

Royster, Charles. *A Revolutionary People at War: The Continental Army and American Character, 1775–1783*. Chapel Hill: University of North Carolina Press, 1979.

Rubinstein, Jonathan. *City Police*. New York: Farrar, Straus, and Giroux, 1973.

Rucker, Brian R. "In the Shadow of Jackson: Uriah Blue's Expedition into West Florida." *Florida Historical Quarterly* 73 (January 1995): 325–338.

Sadosky, Leonard J. *Revolutionary Negotiations: Indians, Empires, and Diplomats in the Founding of America*. Charlottesville: University Press of Virginia, 2009.

Sahlins, Peter. *Boundaries: The Making of France and Spain in the Pyrenees*. Berkeley: University of California Press, 1989.

Said, Edward W. *Orientalism*. New York: Pantheon Books, 1978.

Saunt, Claudio. *A New Order of Things: Property, Power, and the Transformation of the Creek Indians, 1733–1816*. Cambridge: Cambridge University Press, 1999.

Schelling, Thomas C. *Arms and Influence*. New Haven, Conn.: Yale University Press, 1966.

Schmidt, Hans. *Maverick Marine: Smedley Butler and the Contradictions of American Military History*. Lexington: University Press of Kentucky, 1987.

Schubert, Frank N. *Vanguard of Expansion: Army Engineers in the Trans-Mississippi West, 1819–1879*. Washington, D.C.: Office of the Chief of Engineers, Government Printing Office, 1980.

Schwarz, Ted. *Forgotten Battlefield of the First Texas Revolution: The Battle of Medina, August 18, 1813*. Austin, Tex.: Eakin Press, 1985.

Sefton, James E. *The United States Army and Reconstruction, 1865–1877*. Baton Rouge: Louisiana State University Press, 1967.

Sellers, Charles. *The Market Revolution: Jacksonian America, 1815–1846*. New York: Oxford University Press, 1991.

Shafer, Byron E., and Anthony Badger, eds. *Contesting Democracy: Substance and Structure in American Political History, 1775–2000*. Lawrence: University Press of Kansas, 2001.

Sheehan, Bernard W. *Seeds of Extinction: Jeffersonian Philanthropy and the American Indian*. New York: W. W. Norton, 1974.

Shefter, Martin. *Political Parties and the State: The American Historical Experience*. Princeton, N.J.: Princeton University Press, 1994.

Shoemaker, Nancy. *A Strange Likeness: Becoming Red and White in Eighteenth-Century North America*. New York: Oxford University Press, 2004.

Short, John Rennie. *Representing the Republic: Mapping the United States, 1600–1900*. London: Reaktion Books, 2001.

Showalter, Dennis. "Europe's Way of War, 1815–1864." In *European Warfare, 1815–2000*, ed. Jeremy Black. New York: Palgrave, 2002.

Shy, John. *Toward Lexington: The Role of the British Army in the Coming of the American Revolution*. Princeton, N.J.: Princeton University Press, 1965.

Silberman, Bernard S. *Cages of Reason: The Rise of the Rational State in France, Japan, the United States, and Great Britain*. Chicago: University of Chicago Press, 1993.

Silbey, Joel H. *The American Political Nation, 1838–1893*. Stanford, Calif.: Stanford University Press, 1991.

Silver, James W. *Edmund Pendleton Gaines: Frontier General*. Baton Rouge: Louisiana State University Press, 1949.

Sked, Alan. *The Survival of the Hapsburg Empire: Radetsky, the Imperial Army, and the Class War, 1848*. London: Longman, 1979.

Skeen, C. Edward. "Crawford, Calhoun and the Politics of Retrenchment." *South Carolina Historical Magazine* 73 (July 1972): 141–155.

Skelton, William B. *An American Profession of Arms: The Army Officer Corps, 1784–1861*. Lawrence: University Press of Kansas, 1992.

———. "The Army Officer as Organization Man." In *Soldiers and Civilians: The U.S. Army and the American People*, ed. Garry D. Ryan and Timothy K. Nenninger. Washington, D.C.: National Archives and Records Administration, 1987.

———. "The Commanding Generals and the Question of Civil Control in the Antebellum U.S. Army." *American Nineteenth-Century History* 7 (June 2006): 153–172.

———. "High Army Leadership in the Era of the War of 1812: The Making and Remaking of the Officer Corps." *William and Mary Quarterly*, 3rd ser., 51 (April 1994): 253–274.

———. "Officers and Politicians: The Origins of Army Politics in the United States before the Civil War." *Armed Forces and Society* 6 (Fall 1979): 22–48.

———. "Professionalization in the U.S. Army Officer Corps during the Age of Jackson." *Armed Forces and Society* 1 (Summer 1975): 443–471.

———. "Samuel P. Huntington and the American Military Tradition." *Journal of Military History* 60 (April 1996): 325–338.

———. "West Point and Officer Professionalism, 1817–1877." In *West Point: Two Centuries and Beyond*, ed. Lance A. Betros. Abilene, Tex.: McWhiney Foundation Press, 2004.

Skowronek, Stephen. *Building a New American State: The Expansion of National Administrative Capacities, 1877–1920*. Cambridge: Cambridge University Press, 1982.

Slezkine, Yuri. *Arctic Mirrors: Russia and the Small Peoples of the North*. Ithaca, N.Y.: Cornell University Press, 1994.

Slotkin, Richard. *Regeneration through Violence: The Mythology of the American Frontier, 1600–1860*. Middletown, Conn.: Wesleyan University Press, 1973.

Smith, Carlton B. "The American Search for a Harmless Army." *Annual Collection of Essays in History* (Corcoran Department of History, University of Virginia) 10 (1964–1965): 29–43.

———. "Congressional Attitudes toward Military Preparedness during the Monroe Administration." *Military Affairs* 40 (February 1976): 22–25.

———. "The United States War Department, 1815–1842." Ph.D. diss., University of Virginia, 1967.

Smith, Culver H. *The Press, Politics, and Patronage: The American Government's Use of Newspapers, 1789–1875*. Athens: University of Georgia Press, 1977.

Smith, F. Todd. *The Caddo Indians: Tribes at the Convergence of Empires, 1542–1854*. College Station: Texas A&M University Press, 1995.

———. *From Dominance to Disappearance: The Indians of Texas and the Near Southwest, 1786–1859*. Lincoln: University of Nebraska Press, 2005.

Smith, Gene A. "'Our Flag Was Display'd within Their Works': The Treaty of Ghent and the Conquest of Mobile." *Alabama Review* 52 (January 1999): 3–20.

Smith, Joshua M. *Borderlands Smuggling: Patriots, Loyalists, and Illicit Trade in the Northeast, 1783–1820*. Gainesville: University Press of Florida, 2006.

Smith, Mark A. *Engineering Security: The Corps of Engineers and Third System Defense Policy, 1815–1861*. Tuscaloosa: University of Alabama Press, 2009.

Smith, Merritt Roe. *Harpers Ferry Armory and the New Technology: The Challenge of Change*. Ithaca, N.Y.: Cornell University Press, 1977.

Smith, Sherry L. *The View from Officers' Row: Army Perceptions of Western Indians*. Tucson: University of Arizona Press, 1990.

Southerland, Harry DeLeon, Jr., and Jerry Elijah Brown. *The Federal Road through Georgia, the Creek Nation, and Alabama, 1806–1836*. Tuscaloosa: University of Alabama Press, 1989.

Spiers, Edward M. *The Army and Society, 1815–1914.* London: Longman, 1980.

Spiller, Roger J. "Calhoun's Expansible Army: The History of a Military Idea." *South Atlantic Quarterly* 79 (Spring 1980): 189–203.

———. "John C. Calhoun as Secretary of War, 1817–1825." Ph.D. diss., Louisiana State University, 1977.

Spurr, David. *The Rhetoric of Empire: Colonial Discourses in Journalism, Travel Writing, and Imperial Administration.* Durham, N.C.: Duke University Press, 1993.

Stagg, J. C. A. *Borderlines in Borderlands: James Madison and the Spanish-American Frontier, 1776–1821.* New Haven, Conn.: Yale University Press, 2009.

———. "The Madison Administration and Mexico: Reinterpreting the Gutiérrez-Magee Raid of 1812–1813." *William and Mary Quarterly,* 3rd ser., 59 (April 2002): 449–480.

———. *Mr. Madison's War: Politics, Diplomacy, and Warfare in the Early American Republic, 1783–1830.* Princeton, N.J.: Princeton University Press, 1983.

"State Autonomy." Special double issue. *Critical Review* 14 (Spring–Summer 2000).

Steinhauer, Dale R. "'Sogers': Enlisted Men in the U.S. Army, 1815–1860." Ph.D. diss., University of North Carolina, 1992.

Stephan, John J. *The Russian Far East: A History.* Stanford, Calif.: Stanford University Press, 1994.

Stephanson, Anders. *Manifest Destiny: American Expansion and the Empire of Right.* New York: Hill and Wang, 1995.

Stowe, Steven M. *Intimacy and Power in the Old South: Ritual in the Lives of the Planters.* Baltimore: Johns Hopkins University Press, 1987.

Strachan, Hew. "The Early Victorian Army and the Nineteenth-Century Revolution in Government." *English Historical Review* 95 (July 1980): 782–809.

———. *The Politics of the British Army.* Oxford: Clarendon Press, 1997.

———. *Wellington's Legacy: The Reform of the British Army, 1830–1854.* Manchester: Manchester University Press, 1984.

Stuart, Reginald C. *Civil-Military Relations during the War of 1812.* Santa Barbara, Calif.: Praeger Security International, 2009.

———. "Special Interests and National Authority in Foreign Policy: American-British Provincial Links during the Embargo and the War of 1812." *Diplomatic History* 8 (Fall 1984): 311–328.

———. *United States Expansionism and British North America, 1775–1871.* Chapel Hill: University of North Carolina Press, 1988.

———. *War and American Thought from the Revolution to the Monroe Doctrine.* Kent, Ohio: Kent State University Press, 1982.

Sugden, John. "The Southern Indians in the War of 1812: The Closing Phase." *Florida Historical Quarterly* 60 (January 1982): 273–312.

Sullivan, Anthony Thrall. *Thomas-Robert Bugeaud, France, and Algeria, 1784–1849: Politics, Power, and the Good Society.* Hamden, Conn.: Archon Books, 1983.

Sunderland, Willard. *Taming the Wild Field: Colonization and Empire on the Russian Steppe*. Ithaca, N.Y.: Cornell University Press, 2004.

Symonds, Craig L. *Navalists and Antinavalists: The Naval Policy Debate in the United States, 1785–1827*. Newark: University of Delaware Press, 1980.

Tagliacozzo, Eric. *Secret Trades, Porous Borders: Smuggling and States along a Southeast Asian Frontier, 1865–1915*. New Haven, Conn.: Yale University Press, 2005.

Takaki, Ronald T. *Iron Cages: Race and Culture in Nineteenth-Century America*. New York: Alfred A. Knopf, 1979.

Tate, Michael L. "The Multi-Purpose Army on the Frontier: A Call for Further Research." In *The American West: Essays in Honor of W. Eugene Hollon*, ed. Ronald Lora. Toledo, Ohio: University of Toledo Press, 1980.

Tatum, Edward H. *The United States and Europe, 1815–1823: A Study in the Background of the Monroe Doctrine*. Berkeley: University of California Press, 1936.

Taylor, Alan. *William Cooper's Town: Power and Persuasion on the Frontier of the Early American Republic*. New York: Alfred A. Knopf, 1995.

Taylor, Brian D. *Politics and the Russian Army: Civil-Military Relations, 1689–2000*. Cambridge: Cambridge University Press, 2003.

Teitler, Gerke. *The Genesis of the Professional Officer Corps*. Beverly Hills, Calif.: Sage, 1977.

Temperley, Harold W. *The Foreign Policy of Canning, 1822–1827: England, the Neo–Holy Alliance, and the New World*. London: G. Bell and Sons, 1925.

Thomas, Alfred B. "The Yellowstone River, James Long, and Spanish Reaction to American Intrusion into Spanish Dominions, 1818–1819." *New Mexico Historical Review* 4 (April 1929): 164–187.

Thomson, Janice E. *Mercenaries, Pirates, & Sovereigns: State-Building and Extraterritorial Violence in Early Modern Europe*. Princeton, N.J.: Princeton University Press, 1994.

Tilly, Charles. *Big Structures, Large Processes, Huge Comparisons*. New York: Russell Sage Foundation, 1984.

———. *Coercion, Capital, and European States, AD 990–1990*. Oxford: Basil Blackwell, 1990.

———, ed. *The Formation of National States in Western Europe*. Princeton, N.J.: Princeton University Press, 1975.

Tooker, Elisabeth, ed. *The Development of Political Organization in Native North America*. Washington, D.C.: American Ethnological Society, 1983.

Townshend, Charles. "Martial Law: Legal and Administrative Problems of Civil Emergency in Britain and the Empire, 1800–1940." *Historical Journal* 25 (March 1982): 167–195.

Tuveson, Ernest Lee. *Redeemer Nation: The Idea of America's Millennial Role*. Chicago: University of Chicago Press, 1968.

Unrau, William E. "The Civilian as Indian Agent: Villain or Victim?" *Western Historical Quarterly* 3 (October 1972): 405–420.

Van Alsytne, Richard W. *The Rising American Empire.* New York: Oxford University Press, 1960.

Vandervort, Bruce. *Indian Wars of Mexico, Canada, and the United States, 1812–1900.* London: Routledge, 2006.

———. *Wars of Imperial Conquest in Africa, 1830–1914.* Bloomington: Indiana University Press, 1998.

Vargas, Mark A. "The Military Justice System and the Use of Illegal Punishments as Causes of Desertion in the U.S. Army, 1821–1835." *Journal of Military History* 55 (January 1991): 1–19.

———. "The Progressive Agent of Mischief: The Whiskey Ration and Temperance in the United States Army." *Historian* 67 (Summer 2005): 199–216.

Vogel, Robert C. "Patterson and Ross' Raid on Barataria, Sept., 1814." *Louisiana History* 33 (Spring 1992): 157–170.

Wade, Arthur P. "Roads to the Top—An Analysis of General-Officer Selection in the United States Army, 1789–1898." *Military Affairs* 40 (December 1976): 157–163.

Wallerstein, Immanuel. *The Modern World-System III: The Second Era of Great Expansion of the Capitalist World-Economy, 1730s–1840s.* San Diego, Calif.: Academic Press, 1989.

Warren, Harris Gaylord. "The *Firebrand* Affair: A Forgotten Incident of the Mexican Revolution." *Louisiana Historical Quarterly* 21 (January 1938): 203–212.

———. "The Origin of General Mina's Invasion of Mexico." *Southwestern Historical Quarterly* 42 (July 1938): 1–20.

———. "Pensacola and the Filibusters, 1816–1817." *Louisiana Historical Quarterly* 21 (July 1938): 806–822.

———. *The Sword Was Their Passport: A History of American Filibustering in the Mexican Revolution.* Baton Rouge: Louisiana State University Press, 1943.

———. "Xavier Mina's Invasion of Mexico." *Hispanic American Historical Review* 23 (February 1943): 52–76.

Warshauer, Matthew. *Andrew Jackson and the Politics of Martial Law: Nationalism, Civil Liberties and Partisanship.* Knoxville: University of Tennessee Press, 2006.

Watson, Harry L. *Liberty and Power: The Politics of Jacksonian America.* New York: Hill and Wang, 1990.

Watson, Samuel J. "Developing 'Republican Machines': West Point and the Struggle to Render the Officer Corps Safe for America." In *Thomas Jefferson's Military Academy: Founding West Point,* ed. Robert M. S. McDonald. Charlottesville: University Press of Virginia, 2004.

———. "Flexible Gender Roles in the Era of the Market Revolution: Family, Friendship, Marriage, and Masculinity among U.S. Army Officers, 1815–1846." *Journal of Social History* 29 (Fall 1995): 81–106.

———. "The Growth of the Professional Army, 1815–1860." In *The Oxford Atlas of American Military History,* ed. James C. Bradford. New York: Oxford University Press, 2003.

————. "How the Army Became Accepted: West Point Socialization, Military Accountability, and the Nation-State during the Jacksonian Era." *American Nineteenth-Century History* 7 (June 2006): 217–249.

————. "Knowledge, Interest, and the Limits of Military Professionalism: The Discourse on American Coastal Defense, 1815–1860." *War in History* 5 (Fall 1998): 280–307.

————. "Professionalism, Social Attitudes, and Civil-Military Accountability in the U.S. Army Officer Corps, 1815–1846." 2 vols. Ph.D. diss., Rice University, 1996.

————. "Resisting Removal: Seminole Strategy, 1812–1842." In *America's Hundred Years' War: U.S. Expansion to the Gulf Coast and the Fate of the Seminole, 1763–1858, Essays in Honor of J. Leitch Wright, Jr.*, ed. William S. Belko. Gainesville: University Press of Florida, 2010.

————. "Soldier, Expansionist, Politician: Eleazer Wheelock Ripley and the Dance of Ambition in the Early American Republic." In *Nexus of Empire: Loyalty and National Identity in the Gulf Borderlands, 1763–1835*, ed. Gene A. Smith and Sylvia L. Hilton. Gainesville: University Press of Florida, 2009.

————. "Thomas Sidney Jesup: Soldier, Bureaucrat, Gentleman Democrat." In *The Human Tradition in the Early Republic*, ed. Michael A. Morrison. Wilmington, Del.: Scholarly Resources, 2000.

————. "The Uncertain Road to Manifest Destiny: Army Officers and the Course of American Territorial Expansionism, 1815–1846." In *Manifest Destiny and Empire: Essays on Antebellum American Expansionism*, ed. Christopher Morris and Sam W. Haynes. College Station: Texas A&M University Press, 1997.

————. "The U.S. Army to 1900." In *The Blackwell Companion to American Military History*, ed. James C. Bradford. Oxford: Wiley-Blackwell, 2009.

————. "What Do We Mean by Partisan? Army Officers and Politics during the Evolution of the Second Party System." Paper presented to the Southwestern Historical Association, 1999.

————, comp. *The International Library of Essays in Military History: Warfare in the USA, 1784–1861.* Burlington, Vt.: Ashgate Publishing, 2005.

Watts, Steven. *The Republic Reborn: War and the Making of Liberal America, 1790–1820.* Baltimore: Johns Hopkins University Press, 1987.

Wawro, Geoffrey. *Warfare and Society in Europe, 1792–1914.* London: Routledge, 2000.

Webb, Stephen Saunders. *The Governors-General: The English Army and the Definition of Empire, 1569–1681.* Chapel Hill: University of North Carolina Press, 1979.

Webster, Charles K. *The Foreign Policy of Castlereagh, 1815–1822.* London: G. Bell and Sons, 1925.

Weeks, William Earl. "American Nationalism, American Imperialism: An Interpretation of United States Political Economy, 1789–1861." *Journal of the Early Republic* 14 (Winter 1994): 485–495.

————. *Building the Continental Empire: American Expansionism from the Revolution to the Civil War.* Chicago: Ivan R. Dee, 1996.

————. *John Quincy Adams and American Global Empire.* Lexington: University Press of Kentucky, 1992.

————. "John Quincy Adams's 'Great Gun' and the Rhetoric of American Empire." *Diplomatic History* 14 (Winter 1990): 25–42.

————. "New Directions in the Study of Early American Foreign Relations." *Diplomatic History* 17 (Winter 1993): 73–95.

Weigley, Russell F. *History of the United States Army.* New York: Macmillan, 1967.

Weinberg, Albert K. *Manifest Destiny: A Study of Nationalist Expansionism in American History.* Baltimore: Johns Hopkins Press, 1935.

Welter, Rush. "The Frontier West as an Image of American Society: Conservative Attitudes before the Civil War." *Mississippi Valley Historical Review* 46 (March 1960): 593–614.

————. *The Mind of America, 1820–1860.* New York: Columbia University Press, 1975.

Wesley, Edgar B. *Guarding the Frontier: A Study of Frontier Defense from 1815 to 1825.* Minneapolis: University of Minnesota Press, 1925.

————. "A Still Larger View of the So-called Yellowstone Expedition." *North Dakota Historical Quarterly* 5 (July 1931): 219–238.

Wettemann, Robert P., Jr. "A Part or Apart? The Alleged Isolation of Antebellum U.S. Army Officers." *American Nineteenth-Century History* 7 (June 2006): 193–217.

————. *Privilege vs. Equality: Civil-Military Relations in the Jacksonian Era, 1815–1845.* Westport, Conn.: Praeger Security International, 2009.

————. "'To the Public Prosperity': The U.S. Army and the Market Revolution, 1815–1844." Ph.D. diss., Texas A&M University, 2001.

————. "West Point, the Jacksonians, and the Army's Controversial Role in National Improvements." In *West Point: Two Centuries and Beyond,* ed. Lance A. Betros. Abilene, Tex.: McWhiney Foundation Press, 2004.

White, Leonard D. *The Federalists: A Study in Administrative History, 1789–1801.* New York: Macmillan, 1948.

————. *The Jeffersonians: A Study in Administrative History, 1801–1829.* New York: Macmillan, 1959.

White, Lonnie J. *Politics on the Southwestern Frontier: Arkansas Territory, 1819–1836.* Memphis, Tenn.: Memphis State University Press, 1964.

White, Richard. *The Middle Ground: Indians, Empires, and Republics in the Great Lakes Region, 1650–1815.* Cambridge: Cambridge University Press, 1991.

Whittaker, William E., ed. *Frontier Forts of Iowa: Indians, Traders, and Soldiers, 1682–1862.* Iowa City: Iowa University Press, 2009.

Wiebe, Robert H. *The Opening of American Society: From the Adoption of the Constitution to the Eve of Disunion.* New York: Alfred A. Knopf, 1984.

————. *The Segmented Society: An Introduction to the Meaning of America.* New York: Oxford University Press, 1974.

Wilentz, Sean. *The Rise of American Democracy: Jefferson to Lincoln.* New York: Alfred A. Knopf, 2005.

Wilgus, Curtis A. "Some Notes on Spanish-American Patriot Activity along the Atlantic Seaboard, 1816–1822." *North Carolina Historical Review* 4 (April 1927): 172–181.

———. "Some Notes on Spanish American Patriot Activity along the Gulf Coast of the United States, 1811–1822." *Louisiana Historical Quarterly* 8 (April 1925): 193–215.

Wilkinson, Rupert. *Gentlemanly Power: British Leadership and the Public School Tradition.* London: Oxford University Press, 1964.

Williams, Robert A., Jr. *Linking Arms Together: American Indian Treaty Visions of Law and Peace, 1600–1800.* London: Routledge, 1999.

Williams, William Appleman. "The Age of Mercantilism: An Interpretation of the American Political Economy, 1763 to 1828." *William and Mary Quarterly,* 3rd ser., 15 (October 1958): 419–437.

———, ed. *From Colony to Empire: Essays in the History of American Foreign Relations.* New York: J. Wiley, 1972.

———. *The Roots of the Modern American Empire: A Study of the Growth and Shaping of Social Consciousness in a Marketplace Society.* New York: Vintage Books, 1969.

Willig, Timothy D. *Restoring the Chain of Friendship: British Policy and the Indians of the Great Lakes, 1783–1815.* Lincoln: University of Nebraska Press, 2008.

Wilson, James Q. *The Varieties of Police Behavior.* Cambridge, Mass.: Harvard University Press, 1968.

Wilson, Major L. "Republicanism and the Idea of Party in the Jacksonian Period." *Journal of the Early Republic* 8 (Winter 1988): 419–432.

Wilson, Mark R. *The Business of Civil War: Military Mobilization and the State, 1861–1865.* Baltimore: Johns Hopkins University Press, 2006.

———. "The Politics of Procurement: Military Origins of Bureaucratic Autonomy." *Journal of Policy History* 18 (January 2006): 44–73.

Wolf, Eric R. *Europe and the People without History.* Berkeley: University of California Press, 1982.

Wood, Gordon. *The Radicalism of the American Revolution.* New York: Alfred A. Knopf, 1992.

Woodward, Margaret L. "The Spanish Army and the Loss of America, 1810–1824." *Hispanic American Historical Review* 48 (November 1968): 586–607.

Wooster, Robert. *The American Military Frontiers: The United States Army in the West, 1783–1900.* Albuquerque: University of New Mexico Press, 2009.

———. "The Army and the Politics of Expansion: Texas and the Southwestern Borderlands, 1870–1886." *Southwestern Historical Quarterly* 93 (October 1989): 151–167.

———. *The Military and United States Indian Policy, 1865–1903.* New Haven, Conn.: Yale University Press, 1988.

———. "Military Strategy in the American West, 1815–1860." M.A. thesis, Lamar University, 1979.

Wright, J. Leitch, Jr. *Britain and the American Frontier, 1783–1815.* Athens: University of Georgia Press, 1975.

———. *Creeks and Seminoles: Destruction and Regeneration of the Muscogulge People.* Lincoln: University of Nebraska Press, 1986.

———. "A Note on the First Seminole War as Seen by the Indians, Negroes, and Their British Advisers." *Journal of Southern History* 34 (November 1968): 565–575.

Wyman, Mark. *The Wisconsin Frontier.* Bloomington: Indiana University Press, 1998.

Yapp, Malcolm. *Strategies of British India: Britain, Iran, and Afghanistan, 1798–1850.* Oxford: Clarendon Press, 1980.

Young, Tommy R., II. "The United States Army and the Institution of Slavery in Louisiana, 1803–1835." *Louisiana Studies* 13 (Fall 1974): 201–222.

———. "The United States Army in the South, 1789–1835." Ph.D. diss., Louisiana State University, 1973.

Zahendra, Peter. "Spanish West Florida, 1781–1821." Ph.D. diss., University of Michigan, 1976.

Zell, Carl J. "General Daniel Bissell." Ph.D. diss., St. Louis University, 1971.

INDEX

Adams, John Quincy
  and Amelia Island privateers, 131–134,
    137, 150
  and Argentines, 135
  and Britain, 41, 71, 77, 150
  and Florida, 167, 173, 174
  and French exiles, 109
  Graham and, 111
  and Indian removal, 233
  and Jackson, 150–151, 156–158, 174, 197
  Jacksonian opposition to, 204
  and Latin American rebels, 103
  Military Academy, support for, 247,
    382n28
  Neuville and, 151, 174
  and nonstate actors and alternative polities
    in Gulf, 135, 150
  and privateering, 104
  and Spain, 137, 150
  and Onís, 134, 137, 150, 174
  U.S. as future great power, 33
Adams-Onís Treaty (a.k.a. Transcontinental
    Treaty), 57, 160, 174–175, 184, 194
Aix-la-Chapelle, conference of European
    powers at, 150, 174
alternative polities, 2, 30, 35, 99, 103, 113,
    130, 136, 150, 192. See also Amelia
    Island; decentralization; entropy;
    filibusters; national cohesion; national
    sovereignty; "Patriots"; privateering
Ambrister, Robert, 152, 158, 166, 174
  death of, 149
  disavowed by Britain, 151
  and maroons, 149
  as nonstate actor/stateless adventurer, 149
Amelia Island, 131–137, 140, 171, 183, 238,
    349n15
  Adams and, 131–134, 137, 150
  Bankhead occupies, 132–136, 142, 184
  Britain and, 150
  Clinch's plantation on, 172

East Florida, base for offensive against,
    146, 170
  and Gaines, 137, 143
  Haitian privateers and, 130–132
  Monroe and, 131–134
  Navy and, 132, 142
  slave smuggling and, 132, 165
Amelung, Ferdinand, 331n35
American Fur Company, 210, 215, 219
Apalachicola River
  army operations along, 66, 78, 87, 90–91,
    100, 147, 165, 171–172, 338n46
  Spanish disclaim, 66, 360n
  U.S. seeks as supply route, 90, 100, 127,
    139, 146, 352n35
  See also Florida
Arbuckle, Matthew C., 143
  at Fort Scott, 145
  and Fowl Towns, 140
  plantation owner, 143
  and slave smuggling, 165
Arbuthnot, Alexander, 152, 158, 166, 174
  death of, 149
  disavowed by Britain, 151
  and Seminole resistance, 149
Arikara Indians, 203, 210, 212, 214
Arikara War, 210, 211–215, 219, 221, 226,
    233, 368n31. See also fur trade;
    Leavenworth, Henry; Missouri Fur
    Company
Arkansas River, 200–201, 367n16
"armed diplomacy" by army, 23, 227, 265
Armstrong, John, 66–67
Army, U.S. (a.k.a. Regular Army), 37, 232,
    233, 260, 375n13, 387n4
  administration, 232, 260, 264
  as agent of national cohesion, 271, 273,
    281
  Artillery School (Fortress Monroe), 244,
    259, 265
  augmentation of, 23, 24, 27–28, 234

437